Managing Financial Institutions

An Integrated Valuation Approach

World Scientific Series in Modern Finance: Advanced Topics in Finance for the Academician and Practitioner

Print ISSN: 2972-385X
Online ISSN: 2972-3868

Series Editor: Ivan E Brick (*Rutgers University, USA*)

Published:

Vol. 3   *Managing Financial Institutions: An Integrated Valuation Approach*
         by Michael Pagano & John Sedunow

Vol. 2   *Valuation and Financial Forecasting: A Handbook for Academics and Practitioners*
         by Ben Sopranzetti & Braun Kiess

Vol. 1   *Cases in Financial Management: Applications for Financial Analysis*
         edited by Ivan E Brick & Harvey Poniachek

World Scientific Series in Modern Finance:
Advanced Topics in Finance for the Academician and Practitioner
Volume 3

Managing Financial Institutions

An Integrated Valuation Approach

Michael Pagano • John Sedunov
Villanova University, USA

NEW JERSEY • LONDON • SINGAPORE • BEIJING • SHANGHAI • TAIPEI • CHENNAI

Published by

World Scientific Publishing Co. Pte. Ltd.
5 Toh Tuck Link, Singapore 596224
USA office: 27 Warren Street, Suite 401-402, Hackensack, NJ 07601
UK office: 57 Shelton Street, Covent Garden, London WC2H 9HE

British Library Cataloguing-in-Publication Data
A catalogue record for this book is available from the British Library.

World Scientific Series in Modern Finance: Advanced Topics in Finance for the Academician and Practitioner — Vol. 3
MANAGING FINANCIAL INSTITUTIONS
An Integrated Valuation Approach

Copyright © 2025 by World Scientific Publishing Co. Pte. Ltd.

All rights reserved. This book, or parts thereof, may not be reproduced in any form or by any means, electronic or mechanical, including photocopying, recording or any information storage and retrieval system now known or to be invented, without written permission from the publisher.

For photocopying of material in this volume, please pay a copying fee through the Copyright Clearance Center, Inc., 222 Rosewood Drive, Danvers, MA 01923, USA. In this case permission to photocopy is not required from the publisher.

ISBN 978-981-98-1378-0 (hardcover)
ISBN 978-981-98-1379-7 (ebook for institutions)
ISBN 978-981-98-1380-3 (ebook for individuals)

For any available supplementary material, please visit
https://www.worldscientific.com/worldscibooks/10.1142/14332#t=suppl

Desk Editors: Nambirajan Karuppiah/Nicole Ong

Typeset by Stallion Press
Email: enquiries@stallionpress.com

To my wife, Linda, and children, Nina and Mitch, for all their love and support.
— Mike

For my wife, Elizabeth, and children, Sam and Cecilia.
— John

Preface

Managing a financial institution such as a commercial bank has never been easy, and, in the 21st century, it has only become more complex due to increasingly rapid changes in technology, regulation, customer needs, and investor expectations. Managers at these organizations compete in a mostly commoditized business environment against not only traditional financial institutions like banks, brokers, insurers, and money managers but also newer entrants within the areas of financial technology ("fintech"), private credit, and digital asset management. In such a competitive landscape, it is of paramount importance to manage the financial institution's risks in an effective way that can maximize the firm's market value of equity.

This book takes a novel approach to solving the bank manager's problem by applying a *valuation focus* to the firm's risk management decisions. Rather than concentrating solely on defining and measuring a bank's risks, our approach goes a step further by explicitly considering how these risks can impact the value of the bank from a shareholder's perspective. We use an *integrated valuation framework* which quantifies the costs and benefits of how a bank should manage its main risks associated with key functions such as lending, investing, financing, and liquidity provision. To help students understand this framework, we provide two useful mnemonics to recognize the key drivers of firm value (**"MRT"** for Magnitude, Riskiness, and Timing of cash flows) as well as a firm's main risk management strategies (**"ART"** for Accept, Remove, or Transfer risk).

Based on fundamental principles from finance and microeconomics, our framework is built upon a classic dividend discount model of bank valuation, which we call the *Integrated Valuation Model*. By relying on this valuation method, we can use cost–benefit analysis to examine how factors such as credit risk, interest rate risk, and liquidity risk affect the bank's market value. The approach provides a new way of deciding what is the optimal mix of risks that can maximize a financial firm's stock price. These insights can be important to not only shareholders (both privately and publicly held banks) but also regulators and other participants in the financial services industry.

Audience

Managing Financial Institutions: An Integrated Valuation Approach is a concise and effective resource for advanced undergraduate and graduate courses in financial institutions and/or bank management. In addition, practitioners related to the financial services industry such as commercial bank managers, investment bankers, portfolio managers, regulators, and equity analysts could also benefit from this text (either by participating in executive education programs or by reading the book independently).

Key Features

The text contains several notable features to assist students with learning the material in a more efficient manner such as the following:

Modular structure for each chapter: Most chapters use *four key modules* that show how to (1) define the risk, (2) measure the risk, (3) manage the risk, and then (4) assess the impact of a risk management choice on the bank's market value. Instructors thus have the flexibility to focus on all these components within a chapter or a subset of them.

Within-chapter examples: Specific numerical examples are used in each chapter to apply key risk management concepts that allow students to check their understanding of the material as they read along.

Excel™ file for applying the integrated valuation model: This spreadsheet is available at the authors' website (*www.managingfinancial institutions.com*) and can help bring to life the concepts of quantifying and managing key financial risks to maximize a financial firm's market value. Each risk described in this book has specific examples in the spreadsheet and enables students to not only follow along with the numerical examples presented in the text but also enter data on real-world banks if they wish.

A "Managerial Implications" section in each chapter: To further assist students in understanding how to apply the text's concepts, we finish each chapter with a vignette based on two fictional bank managers, Nina and Sam, who must make a recommendation to a hypothetical bank's senior management team (i.e., "A Banking Company" or "ABC" for short). These mini stories challenge the student to use a chapter's risk management concepts to suggest a course of action related to managing the bank's risk in a way that will maximize shareholder value. Both quantitative and qualitative factors are considered in these sections.

End-of-chapter questions: To further reinforce their learning, students can work on conceptual, quantitative, and qualitative questions in each chapter.[1] Each of these chapters includes at least one Excel-based exercise as well as a *Managerial Implications* question which challenges the student to apply the chapter concepts in both a quantitative and qualitative way. Answers to the odd-numbered questions can be found at the end of this book.

Organization of the Text

This book is designed to be a concise treatment of a financial institution's main risks (rather than an exhaustive coverage of every possible risk). Although we discuss all four main types of financial institutions in **Chapter 1** (commercial banks, securities firms, insurance companies, and investment firms), we focus on commercial banks throughout most of this book. As we note in several chapters, the concepts presented in the text are applicable to all financial institutions even though our focus is on commercial banks. Also, Chapter 1 introduces the three main economic functions of financial institutions and how the form of a firm's balance

---

[1] It should be noted that generative AI tools were used to assist with the creation of some of the end-of-chapter questions that are in true-false, multiple choice, and short answer format and to suggest outlines for some topics to ensure completeness.

sheet and income statement follows these functions, a concept we refer to as *Form follows function*. **Chapter 2** introduces the student to the various methods we can use to value a financial firm. **Chapter 3** builds upon the prior chapter to explain why, despite its simplifying assumptions, the Constant Growth Dividend Discount Model can be a useful "engine of inquiry" for understanding the costs and benefits of different risk management strategies. This chapter also introduces the *Integrated Valuation Model (IVM)* and shows how it can be used by a bank manager to choose the optimal level of risk that maximizes shareholder value.

The second section of the text outlines the six primary risks that all financial institutions face (albeit to varying degrees depending on their form and function). It begins with **Chapter 4** which introduces the importance of managing *interest rate risk* to control the volatility of a bank's net interest income and maximize its stock price. **Chapter 5** extends the concept of interest rate risk to measure and manage *market risk* for the bank's entire investment portfolio (as well as trading assets, if applicable). We then turn to *credit risk* in **Chapter 6** and identify ways to measure and manage a bank's exposure to loan-related products and services. **Chapter 7** introduces the *risks of off-balance sheet activities* like offering lines of credit, loan commitments, and credit default swaps. **Chapter 8** then shows how the sudden demand for cash by borrowers or depositors/creditors can create *liquidity risk* which, in turn, can lead to a "bank run" and potentially a "banking panic" across multiple financial institutions. **Chapter 9** concludes this section of the text by showing how *operational risk* can affect a firm's market value.

The last section of this book begins with **Chapter 10** which provides a wider perspective on how the risk-taking and risk management choices of a financial institution are affected by regulators and their application of *financial regulations* such as those related to capital adequacy, safety and soundness, and fairness/integrity. **Chapter 11** builds upon the regulatory issues from the prior chapter to show how an increase in risk-taking at the bank level can aggregate across numerous firms to pose risks to the entire financial system, commonly referred to as *systemic risk*. In **Chapter 12**, we conclude with an analysis of how banks can perform *integrated risk management* by optimizing the firm's risk management choices over several risks in a simultaneous manner. In doing so, the bank has the potential to increase the firm's stock price by more than if it tries to optimize each risk individually (e.g., credit, interest rates, and liquidity). The Excel™ spreadsheet described above includes a final section that shows how such a multi-risk optimization can be done.

Preface xi

We are indebted to the following individuals who have helped either with the preparation of this book and/or provided invaluable feedback and encouragement. We thank you and greatly appreciate all your help to make this book a reality:

Ivan Brick	Isabella Patterson
Jin Cai	Phil Priolo
Diza Hasanaj	Elizabeth Sedunov
Jayneel Jadeja	Evan Silvia
Pranavi Katikali	Ben Sopranzetti
Avleen Kaur	Alvaro Taboada
Destan Kirimhan	Davies Edem Torgah
Christina Pagano	Linda Wu

We would like to especially thank Dr. Ivan E. Brick as well as the dedicated staff at World Scientific Publishing for their excellent guidance and assistance with preparing this text, including Nicole Ong Shi Min and Zvi Ruder.

Managing Financial Institutions

About the Authors

Michael S. Pagano is the Robert J. and Mary Ellen Darretta Endowed Chair in Finance at Villanova University where he has received several awards for both teaching excellence and academic scholarship, including the University-wide Outstanding Faculty Research Award. He currently serves as the Co-Editor of *The Financial Review* and has published over 50 articles in the areas of financial markets, financial institutions, risk management, and valuation. In addition to this book, Dr. Pagano has published *Liquidity, Markets, and Trading: An Interdisciplinary Approach*.

Beyond his academic work, Dr. Pagano is involved with various professional organizations such as the Board of Trustees of the ETF Architect Series Trust. He has also served as a member of the Board of Directors at Citadel Credit Union and Finra's Market Regulation Committee. In addition to media commentary and financial consulting work that he has performed in recent years, he holds the Chartered Financial Analyst (CFA®) designation. Further, he has prior professional experience in private banking, investment analysis, and general management.

John Sedunov is a Professor of Finance at Villanova University's School of Business. His research interests include financial institutions, financial crises, FinTech, and risk management. Professor Sedunov's work has been published in outlets such as *Management Science*, the *Journal of Financial Intermediation*, the *Journal of Financial Stability*, the *Journal of Banking and Finance*, and the *Journal of Financial Research*.

He currently serves as a banking subject editor for *Emerging Markets Review*, and an associate editor for *The Financial Review*, *The Journal of*

Financial Research, and the *Quarterly Journal of Finance.* Professor Sedunov's research and comments have been featured in a variety of media outlets, including *The Wall Street Journal, Financial Times, USA Today,* thestreet.com, CNBC.com, U.S. News & World Report, CNN, Kiplinger, *Washington Post, Los Angeles Times, Pittsburgh Post-Gazette, San Francisco Chronicle,* and Bankrate. In addition to research-oriented activities, Professor Sedunov teaches courses related to the risk management of financial institutions and alternative investments. Professor Sedunov has also been recognized by Villanova University with awards for excellence in Executive Education, research, and university service.

Contents

Preface		vii
About the Authors		xiii
Chapter 1	**Key Functions of Financial Institutions**	**1**
	1.1 The Concept of Financial Intermediation	1
	1.2 Problems Solved by the Core Functions of FIs	4
	1.3 Risks as a Result of FIs' Key Functions	13
	1.4 Regulation of FIs	17
	1.5 Types of Financial Intermediaries	19
	1.6 "Form Follows Function" in Financial Intermediaries	22
	1.7 Concluding Thoughts	24
	Chapter-End Questions	25
	References	26
Chapter 2	**Overview of Valuation Models**	**27**
	2.1 Introduction to Stock Valuation	27
	2.2 The Discounted Cash Flow Model	28
	2.3 An Extension of the DCF Model: Free Cash Flow to Equity (FCFE)	35
	2.4 The Dividend Discount Model	36
	2.5 The Ohlson Valuation Model	43
	2.6 Market Multiples	44
	2.7 Summary	46
	Chapter-End Questions	47
	References	48

xvi *Managing Financial Institutions: An Integrated Valuation Approach*

Chapter 3	**Introducing the Integrated Valuation Model**	**51**
	3.1 Introduction	51
	3.2 Basic Framework for the Integrated Valuation Model (IVM)	60
	3.3 A More Detailed Version of the Integrated Valuation Model and Its Components	64
	3.4 An Example of the Integrated Valuation Model (IVM)	68
	3.5 How to use the IVM to Explore the Impact of Risk on the Market Value of Equity	75
	3.6 Managerial Implications	82
	3.7 Summary and Concluding Thoughts about Applying the IVM	84
	A3.1 Appendix	85
	Chapter-End Questions	94
	References	97
Chapter 4	**Interest Rate Risk**	**99**
	4.1 What Is Interest Rate Risk?	99
	4.2 How to Measure Interest Rate Risk: Using the Repricing Gap (RGAP) to Understand the Short-term Impact of this Risk	100
	4.3 What is Asset–Liability Management (ALM)?	108
	4.4 How to Measure the Long-term Impact of Interest Rate Risk using the Modified Duration Gap (MDGAP)	115
	4.5 How to Use Both RGAP and MDGAP to Manage Interest Rate Risk?	124
	4.6 Using the Integrated Valuation Model (IVM) to Explore the Impact of Interest Rate Risk	126
	4.7 How can we Estimate the Impact of Interest Rate Risk on a Bank's Market Value of Equity?	129
	4.8 Managerial Implications	145
	4.9 Summary	145
	A4.1 Appendix — Foundations of Interest Rate Risk Management	146
	Chapter-End Questions	160
	References	164

Chapter 5 Market Risk — 165
- 5.1 Introduction — 165
- 5.2 How to Measure Market Risk? — 168
- 5.3 RiskMetrics Approach (or Variance–Covariance VaR method) — 171
- 5.4 Historic Simulation — 182
- 5.5 Monte Carlo Simulation — 185
- 5.6 Other Methods of Estimating Tail Risk: Expected Shortfall (ES) and Extreme Value Theory (EVT) — 189
- 5.7 Extreme Value Theory (EVT) — 191
- 5.8 Applications to Risk Management: Using VaR to Manage Market Risk and Stress-testing a Bank's Market Risk Exposure — 192
- 5.9 How Hedging Market Risk Can Affect the Distribution of Returns — 194
- 5.10 The Impact of Hedging Market Risk on a Financial Institution's Equity — 196
- 5.11 Managerial Implications — 206
- 5.12 Summary — 207
- Chapter-End Questions — 208
- References — 210

Chapter 6 Credit Risk — 211
- 6.1 Introduction — 211
- 6.2 Five Cs of Credit Analysis — 213
- 6.3 The Pricing of Risky Loans — 214
- 6.4 How to Measure Credit Risk? — 221
- 6.5 Altman's Z-score, Statistical Models, and Machine Learning Approaches — 221
- 6.6 Term Structure Approach — 224
- 6.7 The Merton/KMV Model Approach — 230
- 6.8 Credit Value at Risk and Credit RiskMetrics — 232
- 6.9 How to Use the Above Models to Make Informed Credit Decisions — 242
- 6.10 How to Manage Credit Risk? — 248
- 6.11 The Impact of Managing Credit Risk on a Financial Institution's Equity — 251
- 6.12 Managerial Implications — 262

6.13	Summary	262
A6.1	Appendix — Foundations of the Merton/KMV Model of Commercial Credit Risk	263
	Chapter-End Questions	268
	References	270

Chapter 7 Off-Balance Sheet (OBS) Risk — 273

7.1	Introduction	273
7.2	What Is OBS Risk?	275
7.3	How to Measure OBS Risk?	282
7.4	How to Manage OBS Risk?	294
7.5	The Impact of Managing OBS Risk on a Financial Institution's Equity	297
7.6	Managerial Implications	302
7.7	Summary	304
	Chapter-End Questions	304
	References	307

Chapter 8 Liquidity Risk — 309

8.1	Introduction	309
8.2	What is Liquidity Risk?	312
8.3	How to Measure Liquidity Risk?	317
8.4	Loan-to-Deposit Ratio (LN/Depo)	327
8.5	Liquidity Coverage Ratio (LCR) and Net Stable Funding Ratio (NSFR)	327
8.6	Liquidity Index (LI)	330
8.7	How to Manage Liquidity Risk?	331
8.8	The Impact of Managing Liquidity Risk on a Financial Institution's Equity	337
8.9	Numerical Example of Liquidity Coverage Ratio (LCR) Choices on ABC's Equity	341
8.10	Applying the IVM Method to Liquidity Risk	343
8.11	Managerial Implications	348
8.12	Summary	349
	Chapter-End Questions	350
	References	353

Chapter 9 Operational Risk — 355

9.1	What Is Operational Risk?	355
9.2	Types and Examples of Operational Risk	356
9.3	Managing Operational Risk: A Basic Qualitative Framework	360

	9.4	Managing Operational Risk: Quantitative Methods	364
	9.5	Operational Risk and the IVM	374
	9.6	Numerical Example of Operational Risk Management's Impact on Pretax Income	377
	9.7	Managerial Implications	383
	9.8	Summary	384
		Chapter-End Questions	384
		Reference	386
Chapter 10	**Regulatory Issues in Banking**		**387**
	10.1	Introduction	387
	10.2	Deposit Insurance	390
	10.3	Capital Requirements	393
	10.4	Ensuring the Banking System's Liquidity	398
	10.5	Other Regulatory Issues and Interventions	401
	10.6	Capital Adequacy and the IVM	405
	10.7	Managerial Implications	413
	10.8	Summary	414
		Chapter-End Questions	415
		References	416
Chapter 11	**Systemic Risk**		**419**
	11.1	Introduction	419
	11.2	Measuring Systemic Risk	420
	11.3	Sources of Systemic Risk	423
	11.4	Systemic Risk Arising from Bank Structure	423
	11.5	Sources of Systemic Risk Arising from the Bank's Decision-Making	425
	11.6	Mitigating or Preventing Systemic Risk and Crises	430
	11.7	Managerial Implications	434
	11.8	Summary	434
		Chapter-End Questions	435
		References	436
Chapter 12	**Integrated Risk Management: Putting It All Together**		**439**
	12.1	Introduction	439
	12.2	Market Risk Example of Stand-alone Risk Management (from Chapter 5)	443

	12.3	Liquidity Example of Stand-alone Risk Management (from Chapter 8)	446
	12.4	Example of Integrated Risk Management across All Bank Risks	451
	12.5	Summary	464
		Chapter-End Questions	465
		References	470

Solutions to Odd-Numbered Chapter-End Questions   473

Glossary   493

Index   517

Chapter 1

Key Functions of Financial Institutions

1.1 The Concept of Financial Intermediation

We start here with the basics of why banks are important to the economy. Unlike other types of firms, banks are special in that they facilitate economic growth and face their own unique set of risks. Primarily, banks (and other financial institutions) have the primary task of channeling funds from savers to borrowers. Throughout this book, we examine how this work creates challenges for financial institutions to overcome, and how overcoming those challenges matters for the institution's valuation.

As seen in Figure 1.1, a financial institution acts as an intermediary between those with a surplus of funds (savers) and those who face a shortfall of funds (borrowers). Note that in Figure 1.1, the intermediaries are not just the commercial banks that we primarily focus on in this book but also other kinds of financial intermediaries that we discuss in the following, including brokers, investment banks, money managers, and insurers. Borrowers, on the left side of the figure, are securing funding in exchange for debt or equity positions in their household or firm. The intermediaries, in turn, either deliver these debt and equity positions directly to savers or transform them into some other type of financial instrument. On the right side of the figure, we call the debt and equity contracts that the savers receive "securities" because these securities may not be exactly the same as the debt or equity delivered to the intermediary on the left side of the figure. Instead, the items on the right side of Figure 1.1 can be a claim against a pool of these securities (e.g., bank deposits).

Figure 1.1 The Basic Function of Financial Institutions.

By channeling funds from savers to borrowers, financial institutions provide "**liquidity insurance**" in ways that individuals and other firms cannot. Through taking advantage of economies of scale, financial institutions can create liquidity cheaply and efficiently, relative to others. There are many types of Financial Institutions (FIs) that behave as intermediaries and provide liquidity insurance, including commercial banks, securities firms, insurance companies, and investment management firms. In this book, though we mention other types of institutions from time to time, we focus primarily on depository institutions (that is, commercial banks). We describe these various types of FIs in more detail later in this chapter but, for now, we focus on the main economic functions of these firms which are generally called "**financial intermediation**."

1.1.1 *The key functions of FIs*

Financial Institutions provide liquidity insurance in three main ways: qualitative asset transformation, delegated monitoring, and brokerage (for a detailed discussion of an approach to estimating the *amount* of liquidity created by banks, see Berger and Bouwman, 2009). This service helps the bank to generate revenue via spreads or fees from these three main functions.

First, **qualitative asset transformation** (QAT) provides liquidity insurance to individuals by effectively converting low-liquidity instruments (like a small business loan) into high-liquidity instruments (like deposits) through a depository institution's (DI) management of a diversified loan portfolio, holdings of liquid assets, and the ability to borrow from other institutions.

A primary source of funding for DIs is deposits, and a primary asset is its portfolio of loans. These two items are at the core of QAT. The DI borrows through deposits, which it promises to pay out in full and on demand. Backing these deposits is the DI's pool of loans, which are generally (at least individually) illiquid. Without a DI, individuals would have a difficult time liquidating loans on demand to fund their own needs for cash due to asymmetric information costs (discussed in the following). The DI bears this risk on behalf of the depositor by managing liquidity as needed through its cash and Treasury reserve or by borrowing funds on a short-term basis. In turn, the DI earns a "**spread**" between the loan rate at which it lends and the financing rate it must pay to depositors and/or other creditors. Thus, the DI removes the need for a depositor to directly lend to a borrower, and instead acts as an intermediary in the process, bringing together savers and borrowers, and providing liquidity to the savers while reducing search costs for borrowers.

Next, intermediaries can function as **delegated monitors**. The academic finance literature has developed a theory to describe an intermediary's role as a delegated monitor (one seminal paper is Diamond, 1984). In the example above, the DI acts on behalf of the depositors to screen out weaker borrowers and to monitor the actions and behavior of borrowers to whom funds were already allocated. A depositor does not necessarily have the skill or resources to observe and evaluate the quality or actions of a borrower. A financial intermediary can step in on behalf of the depositor to monitor borrowers and ensure that borrowers are acting in the best interest of the lenders and paying their obligations in full if they are able. This process allows depositors to pool resources together and effectively split the cost of screening and monitoring while delegating the job to an institution that is skilled in doing so. By doing so, the delegated monitor earns a "**fee**" to manage this process (typically based on a percentage of the dollar value of the assets under management).

Delegated monitoring also has liquidity benefits for firms (borrowers), as it allows them to raise funds without incurring the need to sell equity (thus selling away a portion of ownership and control) and face the risk of monitoring from shareholders. The firm can avoid conflicts of interest that can arise when the shareholders also serve as monitors. Moreover, it can be costly for shareholders to monitor a firm, so delegated monitoring can provide cost savings to the firm in the form of lower borrowing costs.

Finally, **brokerage** services bring together savers and borrowers more directly in the sense that the institutions do *not* transform the assets that they are transacting with and simply transfer them to those savers who want to hold them. Thus, brokers do not hold the securities issued by borrowers (unlike what a DI might do with loans) but rather brokers pass these securities directly on to savers to hold. Instead of having a DI in the center of the process, a broker simply matches together savers and borrowers, allowing the saver to decide to what borrower, and in what quantity, they allocate their cash. Although DIs focus primarily on lending and deposit financing, they can also be brokers by actively trading foreign currencies, bonds, and derivatives in various financial markets. For their efforts, brokers either earn a fee (e.g., a commission) or a spread (e.g., receiving a sales price higher than the broker's purchase price) and can operate in both primary and secondary markets. In the *primary* market, a saver's funds would flow directly to the borrower, as the security offered (debt or equity) is being offered by the borrower for the first time. The borrower/issuing firm has increased transaction speed and some degree of price stability in their offering as their search costs for finding potential savers are greatly reduced by the broker functioning as a matchmaker.

In the *secondary* market, the broker is matching the saver (or buyer) up with another saver (a seller) who already holds the issued security. In this case, the seller has increased liquidity as the broker's function reduces search costs and (potentially) asymmetric information problems for the buyer. Also, the public dissemination of the prices and volume at which securities have traded is useful information for all market participants (even those who do not trade these securities). This "**positive externality**" benefits everyone and can make for a more efficient allocation of scarce financial resources. The result is a level of price stability in a transaction stemming from increased efficiency of the transaction, in which case gains and losses to the seller are more closely related to the fundamental value of the security rather than market frictions.

Moreover, the intermediaries at the core of brokerage services conduct research and provide information to savers to help resolve asymmetric information problems. The brokerage firm can provide information and advice to investors about what assets best suit their needs. This service may be especially important for small investors, who might have more difficulty finding good investments and making efficient transactions by themselves. This function assists investors in diversification of their portfolios, which can help them further reduce risk exposure.

1.2 Problems Solved by the Core Functions of FIs

As a result of the functions described above (QAT, delegated monitoring, and brokerage), financial intermediaries are important drivers of economic growth. Without intermediaries, savers would be on their own to lend funds and manage the resulting portfolio of assets. This creates several problems for an individual and would lead to an economy with no or low funds flowing from savers to borrowers and by extension a low level of economic growth. Thus, FIs are sometimes referred to as "special" institutions because they are at the heart of the economy and can influence a country's growth as well as have significant "knock-on" effects on the entire nation's well-being (a.k.a., bank-induced negative externalities).[1]

Well-developed financial systems are important for a country's economic growth. As access to financing improves, the likelihood of successful innovation and increased productivity grows (see King and Levine, 1993). Increased access to financing leads to more investment, which can lead to more and faster growth. On the other hand, the Global Financial Crisis (GFC) of 2008 is an example of how excessive and simultaneous risk-taking by large institutions can have an enormous impact not only on the U.S. but also on the world economy. In 2008–2009, one could say that the U.S. financial system had a "heart attack" and the rest of the economy suffered a sharp decline in income, jobs, and productivity. There were several large financial institution failures or emergency takeovers in the U.S., including banks (e.g., Wachovia), thrifts (e.g., IndyMac), securities firms (e.g., Lehman Brothers), and an insurance company (AIG).

Distress among financial institutions, however, was not limited to only the U.S. during the 2008–2009 GFC, for example: UBS and Credit Suisse in Switzerland, ABN AMRO and Fortis in the Netherlands, Northern Rock and the Royal Bank of Scotland in the United Kingdom, and Dexia in Germany. Many additional banks, other types of financial institutions, and non-financial firms, such as General Motors and Chrysler, received bailouts that may have prevented their failures. Globally, markets declined dramatically in value, and ripple effects from the crisis touched off the follow-on sovereign debt crisis in Europe. In all, the GFC was the most severe economic downturn in the U.S. since the Great Depression, and resolving it required unprecedented regulatory, fiscal, and monetary intervention. This type of system-wide breakdown is commonly referred to as "systemic risk" and is covered in more detail in Chapter 11. Consequently, many stakeholders (beyond the banks' shareholders) such as regulators and politicians pay close attention to the risk-taking behavior

---

[1] For example, see Chapter 1 of Saunders, Cornett, and Erhemjamts (2024) for more details on FI specialness.

of FIs. These negative externalities and systemic risk are also the main reason why banks are usually the most regulated sector of an economy.

Given the above, banks and other FIs clearly play an important role in the economy, given their specialness and the externalities they generate. To influence growth, FIs solve several problems that individual economic agents face. In the following, we discuss these problems and how financial institutions help solve them. Moreover, we show how the alleviation of these problems leads to increased fund flows, lower search costs, and improved economic outcomes.

First, lenders face a problem of asymmetric information, as they do not have a complete set of information about potential borrowers. This information is costly and difficult to obtain, and even with useful information, an individual who is lending money may not know how to effectively use it to evaluate the creditworthiness of a potential borrower. Thus, a lender may not be able to effectively screen out low-quality borrowers or may charge too little (or too much) interest relative to the true risk of a loan. This problem is more broadly known as **adverse selection**. One example that can illustrate the adverse selection problem is the market for used cars, as in Akerlof (1970). When buying a used car, there is asymmetric information — the seller knows more about the car's history and condition than does the buyer. In other words, the seller of the car knows whether the car is a "lemon," whereas the potential buyer does not. As a result, the buyer is likely only willing to pay an average price for the used car. This benefits the seller when the car is a lemon but disadvantages the seller when it is a high-quality car. This intuition can be extended to lending, where a potential borrower has more information about their own financial condition than does a potential lender. As banks have a relative advantage/competency in evaluating credit worthiness based on observable characteristics, they can better deal with this "lemons problem" than an individual trying to lend on their own directly to a potential borrower.[2] The bank can then better sort borrowers into more- or less-creditworthy groups and adjust prices (interest rates) accordingly.

The key to solving this asymmetric information problem is that the bank must identify *credible* "**signals**" of the borrower's quality just like the used car buyer must obtain a reliable indication of the car's quality

---

[2] When an individual lends directly to another borrower, it is referred to as "peer-to-peer" lending (a.k.a., "P2P" lending).

from the auto dealership. For example, the bank might require a larger down payment for obtaining a mortgage because only financially stronger borrowers can afford to put more money down on their home purchase. In the case of the used car dealer, they might offer a money-back guarantee or a multi-year warranty to signal to the prospective buyer that the car is of higher quality (i.e., the longer the warranty, the higher the car's quality). In both cases, a signal that is sufficiently costly is *credible* and thus can be trusted to resolve the asymmetric information problem.

An additional information cost comes *after* a loan is created. At that point, the borrower has the lender's funds in hand, and must decide how to deploy them. Without oversight, a borrower could misappropriate these funds by taking on excessively risky projects or investments, which is called the **moral hazard** problem. In an extreme example, a bank could lend money to a small business owner and the business owner could then choose to buy themselves a new car or go on an expensive vacation rather than invest in or expand their business. Thus, the loan may never be repaid, which creates a loss for the lender. In this situation, there is a need for strong oversight, or **monitoring**. Without monitoring, risk-averse lenders may be less likely to lend, or they may charge higher interest rates, which can impact economic growth.

So, in sum, a lender faces information problems both before (adverse selection) and after (moral hazard) a loan is made. By instead delegating their funds to financial institutions, the savers can allow these institutions to reduce these information problems in *six* important ways:

1. Taking advantage of economies of scale,
2. Delegated monitoring,
3. Managing liquidity risk,
4. Solving maturity mismatch issues,
5. Minimizing price risk, and
6. Reducing search and transaction costs.

The following paragraphs provide more details on these *six* challenges associated with financial intermediation:

First, intermediaries can leverage their **economies of scale** to more efficiently gather and process information about potential borrowers. Financial institutions have expertise in evaluating the creditworthiness of borrowers through the development of internal risk models as well as the use of data on the success or failure of past loans. Through these functions, financial institutions can help mitigate the adverse selection problem on behalf of their depositors.

Second, as discussed above, lenders face asymmetric information problems like the moral hazard problem. To solve this, financial institutions act as **delegated monitors**. It is often costly and inefficient for individuals who lend on their own to monitor borrowers. In fact, the high cost of monitoring creates a collective action problem, in which most (or all) lenders do not monitor, but rather wait for another lender to do so. In other words, this is a **free rider** problem. By instead pooling funds and delegating the monitoring function to a financial institution, lenders can spread out the cost of monitoring and allow a central party like a bank to handle this function, thus alleviating the moral hazard problem (see, e.g., Diamond, 1984, and Diamond, 1996).

The bank's function as delegated monitor requires that it maintains a diversified portfolio of loans. Though banks monitor borrowers on behalf of depositors, there is not necessarily a party who monitors the bank. Thus, functionally, deposits (and funds that the bank borrows) are a form of unmonitored debt (again, see Diamond, 1996). Without maintaining a diversified loan portfolio, a bank would be subject to a significant amount of borrower-specific credit risk. If a bank's credit risk is concentrated in this way, it will default on its depositors as often as other borrowers will. Thus, the bank diversifies its portfolio to avoid borrower-specific risk (leaving exposure only to "systematic" credit risk), and deposits act as a claim against a diversified pool of loans. This highlights an additional benefit provided by many types of intermediaries — low-cost access to diversification. In addition to the idea of diversified loan portfolios described above, other types of FIs provide access to diversification. For example, ETFs and mutual funds provide access to diversified pools or stocks or bonds. Further, insurance companies allow participants to pool resources and diversify the risk of providing auto, car, life, or health insurance.

Regulators and bond covenants can also play a role in dealing with information problems. Regulators act within the lending process by requiring certain types of firms to regularly disclose information, thus helping to reduce the adverse selection problem. Regulators (the Federal Reserve, Federal Deposit Insurance Corporation (FDIC), Office of the Comptroller of the Currency (OCC), and state banking regulators, among others) also act as monitors to financial institutions because deposits (and some other borrowed funds) are otherwise un-monitored. In the absence of a delegated monitor (or as a supplement to them), lenders can also impose covenants on borrowers, forcing them to regularly fulfill obligations (such as maintaining a given financial ratio or disclosing certain information) to maintain their loan, and thus reducing the moral hazard problem. Without strong monitoring, covenants may be necessary to force borrowers to make sound decisions with borrowed funds.

A third problem faced by individuals in the absence of intermediaries is the lack of liquidity. Due to the information costs discussed above, an individual would have a difficult time selling a loan they made independently. A potential purchaser would not have the same information about the borrower as the lender and would incur their own set of costs to re-evaluate the creditworthiness of the borrower to verify any information provided by the lender. As a result, it would make the loan difficult to sell, and likely, if a buyer was found, the loan would sell for a discounted price.

To solve this problem, FIs bear this **liquidity risk** on behalf of their depositors. This is the QAT function we described above. FIs, by holding loans in their portfolios that are funded by deposits, effectively convert illiquid assets into liquid assets. FIs can also pool the liquidity of several savers and use the funds to invest in a wide variety of assets. Thus, FIs must stand ready to fund withdrawals on demand. Figure 1.2 displays a simplified version of the balance sheet of a typical depository institution. The bulk of the bank's balance sheet is comprised of a (hopefully!) well-diversified portfolio of loans. These loans include loans to businesses (Commercial and Industrial, or "C&I" loans), personal loans (credit cards, auto loans, etc.), mortgages, and other types of specialized loans. Importantly, however, the bank also maintains a pool of cash and U.S. Treasury securities as assets to help with liquidity needs such as deposit withdrawals or loan drawdowns. This pool of liquid assets can be referred to as **stored liquidity**.

The right-hand side of the bank's balance sheet represents its sources of funding, some of which may also provide access to liquidity should the bank need it. As we know, depository institutions primarily rely on deposits for low-cost funding, for which they act as delegated monitors on behalf of the depositors. Again, we can think of deposits as a claim against the bank's diversified portfolio of loans. Banks also receive funding from other sources and can use these sources to "**purchase**" **liquidity** when it is needed. Banks typically lend to each other in the Federal Funds market via overnight loans. Moreover, banks can lend to each other in the market for repurchase agreements, which is another very short-term source of

Assets	Liabilities and Shareholder Equity
Cash	Deposits
Treasuries and Other Securities	Other Borrowed Money: Interbank Lending
Loans:	Repurchase Agreements
C&I Loans	Bonds
Personal Loans	
Mortgages	Preferred Equity
Other Loans	
	Equity
Net Fixed Assets	

Figure 1.2. A Simple Balance Sheet for a Depository Institution.

funding.[3] Both Federal Funds and repurchase agreements aid the bank in handling short-term liquidity needs if they prefer not to use cash or Treasuries to do so. We discuss more on the choice between stored liquidity management and purchased liquidity management in Chapter 8. Larger banks that have access to capital markets may also choose to issue bonds and preferred stock for longer-term funding. Finally, a bank has equity funding. The focus of this book is to understand how risk management decisions impact the valuation of the bank's equity. We discuss valuation methods, our integrated valuation model (IVM), and how each type of risk enters the model in subsequent chapters.

By extension, liquidity problems also cause difficulty for individual lenders in the form of **maturity mismatches**, which is a fourth problem that occurs in the absence of FIs. Without intermediaries, individuals who lend on their own would be faced with the challenge of aligning the maturities of their loans (or assets) with their need for repeated (e.g., utility bills and groceries) or unexpected (e.g., home or car repair) cash

---

[3] Also known as a "repo," repurchase agreements are short-term loans in which one participant sells an asset to the other participant (the "buyer") for a price P_0. The seller agrees to buy back the assets at a later date, usually for a higher price, P_1. Banks will typically buy and sell in the overnight repo markets, which means that the maturity is one day. One can calculate the repo rate as $\frac{P_1 - P_0}{P_0} \cdot \frac{365}{t_1 - t_0}$, where $t_1 - t_0$ is the length of the repurchase agreement (which, again, for a bank is typically one day).

outflows. In the event of an immediate need for cash, an individual would need to choose one of the following options: (a) use any cash or liquid asset reserves they have, (b) sell relatively illiquid assets (like investment securities or loans), or (c) borrow new money. These cases are all problematic for an individual. Option (a) forces the individual to hold more cash on hand than is optimal, thus forcing them to sacrifice potential higher returns from other investments. Option (b) can force the individual to sell securities or loans for potentially much less than their worth in what sometimes is called a "fire sale" (due to the asymmetric information problems we discussed earlier), leading to losses in value just to handle ordinary expenses. Option (c) forces the individual to pay interest on borrowed funds that would be used to pay ordinary expenses to avoid selling illiquid assets at a loss. This outcome again creates a potential loss for the individual if the interest they are earning on their illiquid assets is not greater than their cost of borrowed funds, and potentially leads to escalating costs of borrowing and limited credit availability if the individual continually needs to borrow.

A financial institution can solve this problem for individuals by bearing the maturity mismatch risk on behalf of the depositor. An individual lends to the bank (via a deposit), and the bank lends to others who face a funding shortfall. The deposit, as seen in the simple balance sheet above, becomes a short-term claim against the bank's pool of assets and is available to the depositor on demand and in full value. Instead of an individual worrying about selling illiquid assets or borrowing funds on their own, the bank handles liquidity needs in this way (which we discuss in more detail in Chapter 8), leaving the individual to treat their deposits as an asset that is highly liquid and that maintains a stable (or growing) value.

A fifth problem, related to the maturity mismatch problem described above, is **price risk**. An individual who holds their own portfolio of loans is subject to price fluctuations caused not only by liquidity (and asymmetric information) but also by market value fluctuations that can be related to interest rate shocks or to the credit quality of the borrowers. First, as interest rates rise (due to policy decisions or market-based fluctuations), the value of a simple fixed-income security, like a loan or a bond, will decrease in value. This outcome is driven by an increasing discount rate, which makes the current or "present value" of a security's cash flows worth less and therefore works to lower the instrument's price. More details about discount rates and the present value of cash flows will be discussed in our discussion of valuation models in Chapter 2.

Further, changes in a borrower's creditworthiness can impact the market interest rate on a loan or bond. This firm-specific interest rate shock (as opposed to the more systematic, market-wide shock from a regulatory policy decision) can also lead to decreases in the value of a loan or bond if a firm's credit quality drops, subsequently raising its cost of borrowing. People who lend in the absence of an intermediary are not likely to have access to the deep pool of funds that a financial institution would possess and thus have a more concentrated exposure to credit risk because their individual loan portfolios are not likely to be well-diversified. In this case, if a firm experiences a large shock, then an individual's loan portfolio would not be sufficiently diversified to weather the price impact, and the individual could experience large losses.

Banks and other institutions solve this price risk problem by pooling depositor funds together and managing a well-diversified portfolio of loans. By doing so, they reduce their exposure to firm-specific credit shocks and have a portfolio that is exposed mainly to systematic interest rate shocks that come from shifts across all interest rates (again, likely coming as the result of a policy shift). The remaining issue for the bank is to manage the relative shocks to the valuations of their assets and liabilities. Banks are better capable, relative to individuals, of matching the maturities or durations of their assets and liabilities or using derivatives to hedge this exposure. Duration measures the sensitivity of an asset's price to changes in interest rates. We discuss more about asset and liability management related to interest rate risk and price fluctuation in Chapter 4.

A sixth and final problem created in the absence of intermediaries is that **search and transaction costs** would be very high. Without access to a financial institution with a large source of funds available to lend, borrowers would need to source their funding from many lenders. If, for example, a firm wanted to borrow $1 million, and did not have access to financial intermediaries, it would, for example, potentially need to find 1,000 lenders who are each willing to lend $1,000. The firm would incur a tremendous amount of search costs to find these 1,000 lenders and then would need to draw up agreements with each lender, leading to a high level of transaction costs each time it wanted to borrow money. Institutions solve this transaction and search cost problem by pooling the resources of their depositors and lending cash in larger amounts. In this case, a borrowing firm would only need to contract with one institution to borrow the $1 million described above. This outcome then leads to a dramatic reduction in search and transaction costs for potential borrowers.

1.3 Risks as a Result of FIs' Key Functions

The functions we describe above create a unique set of risks for financial institutions. Importantly, when financial institutions operate, they do so with depositor funds, which are meant to be kept safe because they are the essential ingredients to provide bank customers with liquidity insurance. Moreover, institutions, to handle the issues we described above, also borrow and lend to each other and engage in derivative contracts with each other. These practices, while crucial, can also create the potential for widespread failure in the financial system, and the potential for the loss of depositor funds. In Diamond (1996), we see that loans made by individuals to DIs (deposits) are un-monitored debt (that is, depositors cannot directly observe how much and what type of risks the DI takes with their funds), as monitoring is costly for depositors. Institutions attempt to keep depositor funds safe by diversifying their pool of assets, but in an interconnected financial system where financial crises can occur, this practice may not be enough.

Here, we describe the *eight* key risks that financial institutions must manage. Though we provide much more detail in later chapters, these short descriptions serve as a preview for what comes in the subsequent chapters of this book. Along with each source of risk, we denote which of the following chapters provides a detailed discussion of that risk and how it fits in with our integrated valuation model. Also, keep in mind that even though we discuss these risks individually and in sequential order throughout this book, we know that, in reality, these risks are typically *inter-related* with each other. For example, when a bank establishes a line of credit or a loan commitment for a customer, it is not only exposing itself to credit risk but also to liquidity risk, interest rate risk, off-balance sheet risk, and possibly solvency risk. Another point to consider is that there are numerous other risks an FI faces, but we focus in this book on those that are considered most material by managers, investors, and regulators.[4]

---

[4]For example, foreign exchange risk might be very important for large international banks but not as important for smaller domestic banks. Thus, we have chosen to exclude an explicit chapter on foreign exchange risk (although we discuss this issue to some extent within the Market Risk chapter). For a more detailed treatment of a relatively large set of FI risks, see Saunders *et al.* (2024).

Interest Rate Risk (Chapter 4): Many financial institutions use short-term liabilities (like deposits) to fund long-term assets (like 30-year mortgages). This relates to the maturity mismatch problem we describe above, as banks take the burden of matching maturities away from households and firms. Further, this relates to the bank's QAT function, in which they transform illiquid assets into highly liquid liabilities. However, a side effect of solving these problems is that the banks are exposed to interest rate risk. While banks ideally borrow at one interest rate and lend at a higher interest rate, creating a **net interest margin**, it may be the case in a rising rate environment that banks must refinance their short-term liabilities at a higher interest rate before they can reinvest their long-term assets at these higher rates. This erodes the bank's net interest margin and potentially turns it negative. Banks can also view this interest rate risk through the lens of market values, as the market values of their liabilities and assets are sensitive to interest rates. The prices of loans, bonds, and other fixed-income instruments are inversely related to interest rates, and we can measure the sensitivity of this relation using the concept of **duration** noted earlier (which we describe further in Chapter 4). Thus, in addition to the maturity mismatch between assets and liabilities, banks must also monitor the duration mismatch between assets and liabilities. In all, this creates a risk that the bank must hedge either through managing these mismatches directly or by using derivative securities.

Market Risk (Chapter 5): Different types of financial institutions hold a wide variety of assets that include stocks, bonds, loans, sovereign debt, and foreign currency. While institutions hold these assets, market conditions can change, and can sometimes do so rapidly and unexpectedly. As market conditions fluctuate, so do the values of the assets held by these institutions. Market values can rise and fall for a variety of reasons, including firm-specific reasons (especially important if an FI has a highly concentrated exposure to a given entity), or systematic reasons (including shocks to the macroeconomy, political turmoil, or other instability around the world). Market conditions are difficult if not impossible to predict, which means that the risk of declining asset values relative to those market conditions must be carefully measured and managed.

Credit Risk (Chapter 6): Credit risk is the inability or unwillingness of a borrower to repay their obligations (e.g., on a loan or a bond). Banks encounter this risk through their QAT function, as they use depositor funds to make loans. Thus, it is important for banks to screen out weaker borrowers (solving the adverse selection problem) and act as delegated monitors (solving the moral hazard problem) to minimize their exposure to borrowers who are most likely to default. Even if banks effectively deal with these asymmetric information problems, there will still be loans that fail. In this case, it is important for banks to manage credit risk through diversification of their loan portfolio and/or hedging tools like derivative securities such as credit default swaps. Another version of credit risk is counterparty risk, which extends the definition of credit risk to other financial activities, like trading securities and derivatives.

Off-Balance Sheet Risk (Chapter 7): Banks also have assets and liabilities that do not immediately appear on their balance sheets. Loan commitments, lines of credit, derivatives, letters of credit, and loans sold can all be contingent on the occurrence of other events. We examine all these items in more detail in Chapter 7, but for this short discussion, we focus on loan commitments. A loan commitment is a *promise* to lend to a borrower at some future time, but it is not a loan until the borrower exercises its option to borrow. Therefore, the loan commitment remains "off-balance sheet" until the borrower decides to exercise this option, at which point the loan formally becomes an asset of the bank. The bank, in issuing this commitment to lend, faces uncertainty as to when the borrower will "draw down" their promised loan. This uncertainty brings along with it interest rate risk (e.g., if the loan commitment is made with a fixed rate, market rates may rise, meaning that the bank's cost of funding the loan will be higher than the interest it earns on the loan), credit risk (the borrower may draw down the commitment if their creditworthiness declines, as the loan commitment's terms may be more favorable than what they can find in the market), and liquidity risk (the bank needs cash to fund the loan when the commitment is drawn down). As a result, multiple risks that we have discussed above can manifest simultaneously for a financial institution in relation to off-balance sheet products.

Liquidity Risk (Chapter 8): Liquidity risk is the risk that a financial institution does not have enough cash to meet its obligations. This risk is associated with the QAT function and can occur when, for example, the bank faces sudden withdrawal requests from its depositors, or when it must fund a loan commitment drawdown. A lack of liquidity (or a perceived lack of liquidity) is associated with a "bank run," in which depositors quickly (and in large numbers) withdraw their deposits, leading the bank to scramble for cash by borrowing or selling assets. As a bank run deepens, the bank is forced to sell assets that are highly illiquid for fire sale prices. Over time, liquidity risk has been at the center of financial crises and panics (such as bank runs in the Great Depression; the Bear Stearns and Lehman Brothers meltdowns in the 2008 Global Financial Crisis; and the failure of crypto-finance institutions like Celsius and FTX in 2022).

Operational Risk (Chapter 9): Banks face risks associated with the day-to-day operations of the firm. These risks cover multiple areas of the firm but can include losses experienced from litigation, regulatory sanctions, data breaches, rogue traders, or natural disasters among others (a full list is provided in Chapter 9). Losses from operational events can be very large. One example of this comes from Société Générale, which lost $7.2 billion in 2008 from trades made by a single futures trader, Jérôme Kerviel. The implications of a large operational loss can be wide-ranging, including credit downgrades, stock sell-offs, reputational impacts, and potential solvency issues if the loss is large enough. As a result of these large potential impacts, banks are required to hold enough capital to compensate for extreme operational losses. The framework for calculating operational risk-based capital is changing over time. We outline the economic rationale for these changes in Chapter 9.

Solvency Risk (Chapter 10): Solvency risk is the risk that the market value of an FIs assets is less than that of its liabilities. If the bank does not have enough tangible assets to meet its obligations, then, like any other firm, it will be insolvent. A solvency issue is usually related to outcomes from other types of risk-taking, and in many cases is related to a combination of realized losses from multiple types of risk. Importantly, solvency issues can come from market perceptions or reputational issues. If a bank is rumored to be in a weak financial position (or illiquid), or if it suffers a reputational shock from an operational risk event, market participants could then put significant downward pressure on the bank's stock price (which can be compounded from short selling activity), endangering the bank's equity position and pushing it closer to a default. To counterbalance this risk, banks are required to hold sufficient levels of equity capital and regulators will monitor these levels via "capital adequacy" rules and regulations.

Systemic Risk (Chapter 11): A final type of risk faced by financial institutions is systemic risk. This is the risk that multiple institutions fail simultaneously or that one institution's failure brings about the failure of several other institutions (via a contagion, or "domino" effect). This type of risk is difficult for an individual institution to hedge against, as it involves system-wide risk and failure. Regulation is perhaps the best avenue to guard against systemic risk, as it forces financial institutions to be well-capitalized (to protect against individual failures in the first place) and manage interconnections between institutions that could contribute to contagion effects. We further discuss this type of risk, as well as sources of increased systemic risk and regulatory issues related to systemic risk, in Chapter 11.

1.4 Regulation of FIs

As a result of the risks described above, regulators are an important part of the financial system, as they monitor financial institutions to help ensure financial stability and the safety of financial institutions to avoid a financial system "heart attack" like the one that occurred in 2008. The regulation of financial institutions comes from several bodies in the United States, which we describe in the following.

The **Federal Reserve** is the central bank of the United States. It controls monetary policy through its open-market operations and inter-bank offering rate (thus influencing interest rates in the United States, which is associated with interest rate risk that we discussed above). Moreover, the Federal Reserve serves as a key banking regulator, leading annual stress-testing exercises and requiring frequent reporting from banks and other financial institutions (e.g., hedge funds). Through its supervisory role, the Federal Reserve can sanction individual banks (e.g., reducing or eliminating dividends or growth) if they fail the annual stress tests or otherwise conduct business improperly (see, e.g., Wells Fargo in 2020, which faced a cap on its total assets due to a "fake account" scandal). The Federal Reserve also is the country's lender of last resort (providing emergency loans to financial institutions that need access to liquidity) and sits at the center of the U.S. interbank lending market. It also operates the Fedwire system, which facilitates the transfer of funds between U.S. financial institutions. Around the world, other central banks (e.g., the Bank of England and the European Central Bank) serve in similar roles.

The **Federal Deposit Insurance Corporation (FDIC)** provides deposit insurance to commercial banks and savings banks in the United States. The agency was created because of the large number of bank failures that occurred at the outset of the Great Depression in the 1930s and was intended to increase trust in American financial institutions. Currently, the FDIC provides insurance on up to $250,000 in deposits at member banks. The FDIC's reserves are funded through insurance payments from member banks. When an institution fails, the FDIC is responsible for transferring insured funds and other healthy assets to a viable institution. The FDIC also developed the "CAMELS" rating system (Capital adequacy, Assets, Management Capability, Earnings, Liquidity, Sensitivity) to measure the overall health of a bank. This system is widely used by many types of banking regulators. Finally, the FDIC plays a role in examining banks for supervisory issues and safety and soundness.[5]

The **Office of the Comptroller of the Currency (OCC)** is a national regulator that adds another layer to bank supervision in the United States. The OCC charters, regulates, and supervises all national banks and thrift institutions (whereas the Federal Reserve regulates Bank Holding Companies). It also maintains safety and soundness, by monitoring bank asset quality, liquidity, and compliance, among other aspects of bank quality and management.

Additionally, **State Regulatory Authorities** play a role in the regulation and supervision of financial institutions. The U.S. operates under a dual charter system. Banks that are not national banks can be chartered at the state level. Each U.S. state has its own banking regulatory authority that oversees banks within the state and regulates them under the state's own set of banking rules and regulations.

The **Securities and Exchange Commission (SEC)** regulates financial markets and the financial institutions that provide brokerage or dealer functions within these markets. Equity and debt sold in public markets are not guaranteed by the U.S. government. Since losses from these investments can be large, it is important to decrease information asymmetries and ensure proper market function. The SEC requires firms seeking capital investments to disclose information on a regular basis, and to provide reliable information to those who invest in public markets (these disclosures are all available on the SEC's database, EDGAR).[6] The SEC's regulation and influence touch a variety of financial intermediaries, including banks, mutual funds, pension funds, and hedge funds.

The **Financial Industry Regulatory Authority (FINRA)** is a self-regulatory organization that oversees broker-dealers, securities exchanges, and over-the-counter financial markets operating in the U.S. This

---

[5] For more detail, see https://www.fdic.gov/resources/supervision-and-examinations/.
[6] See https://www.sec.gov/edgar.

organization is responsible for implementing and enforcing SEC rules through daily monitoring of these financial markets and the securities firms that trade in these areas. The body regulates trading in stocks, corporate bonds, options, and other derivatives.[7] FINRA's regulation is important for financial institutions that actively trade or provide brokerage services. The group regularly conducts exams of its regulated institutions. The goal of FINRA's oversight is to ensure a level playing field for all types of investors and to promote liquidity and smooth functioning within financial markets.

Finally, the **Commodity Futures Trading Commission (CFTC)** is a government agency that regulates U.S. derivatives markets (primarily futures and swaps contracts). This regulatory oversight is important for any institution that trades derivatives or acts as a dealer in these markets. As we discuss throughout this book, the use of derivatives is important for financial institutions to use as hedging instruments. Other large financial institutions serve as intermediaries (dealers) in these markets, facilitating the trading of derivatives between other financial institutions. The CFTC's role in this process is to ensure the integrity and functionality of derivatives markets.

1.5 Types of Financial Intermediaries

Finally, we take time in this chapter to discuss the various types of financial intermediaries that play a role in the financial system. Though we focus this book mostly on depository institutions, it is important to remember that all types of institutions face the risks that we present in this chapter and throughout this book. Moreover, through their various business lines and strategies, these institutions are not isolated by type but rather can be interconnected, weaving together the broader financial system.

The first type of intermediary is a lending institution. There are various types of lending institutions. First, **commercial banks** are institutions that are primarily focused on making loans, while funding this pool of loans with deposits. These are the depository institutions which we have

---

[7]One exception to FINRA's duties is the oversight and regulation of U.S. Treasury securities and foreign currencies, which are primarily conducted by the U.S. Treasury Department.

focused much of our discussion on in this chapter. Depository institutions can offer banking services to retail clients, providing services like online banking options, checking accounts, access to money market funds or other investments, and retirement planning, to name a few. Again, and importantly, depository institutions rely on collecting deposits for a large portion of their debt financing and, in general, earn a **"spread"** on the rates they charge for loans after paying the interest on customer deposits and other debt. For example, if a bank lends to a borrower at 5% and pays interest of 2% on its deposits, the firm earns a spread of 3% on this loan (5% − 2% = +3%). This practice contrasts with **finance companies**, which lend like a commercial bank would, but do *not* raise funding via deposits. Since finance companies do not rely on deposits (and thus are not an integral part of the nation's payments system), they are subject to much less stringent regulations, meaning that they can potentially lend to riskier borrowers than a traditional commercial bank would.

However, these finance companies do not benefit from the government's deposit insurance and so financing costs are typically higher than those that depository institutions face. As the financial system develops, some "**FinTech**" lenders entering this space do so as finance companies, rather than as depository institutions. Another type of lending institution is a **savings and loan** (or "**thrift**"), which focuses its lending portfolio on mortgages (by law, these institutions are restricted in what proportion of their loan portfolio is held in commercial loans and must meet a minimum threshold for how much of their loan portfolio is allocated to mortgage lending), but otherwise behave in the same way as a traditional commercial bank by taking in low-cost deposits. Finally, **credit unions** also provide the same services as a traditional commercial bank but are structured as a nonprofit institution that is owned by its members (depositors). Credit unions are tax-exempt entities that must focus on a specific "field of membership" and can typically offer lower fees and pay higher interest rates than other types of depository institutions.

Next, **investment banks** help those with funding shortfalls raise capital via underwriting new issuances of debt or equity, advise companies on mergers and acquisitions, and provide other services like asset management and securities research. In return for these services, these institutions typically earn a **fee** (as a percentage of the specific deal's size) although they can instead earn a **"spread"** depending on the type of financing arrangement. Investment banks can also engage in proprietary trading and tend to rely on high amounts of leverage. Stand-alone investment banks (that is, investment banks that did not merge with commercial banks following the repeal of the Glass-Steagall Act), like Lehman Brothers, Bear Stearns, Goldman Sachs, Morgan Stanley, and Merrill Lynch, were at the heart of the 2008–2009 Global Financial Crisis. These institutions experienced severe liquidity issues, related to market and credit risks, which were compounded by their lack of transparency and high degree of financial leverage.

Another type of financial intermediary consists of funds that pool together investor's resources to achieve diversification benefits and charge a **fee** for this type of service. Broadly, we can consider **mutual funds**, **exchange-traded funds (ETFs)**, and **hedge funds** to be a part of this group. These types of investment management firms do not raise capital by way of *deposits*; thus, investors are not protected as they would be with an FDIC-insured account. Instead, these intermediaries enable investors to take on more risk and hope to generate a higher return. Both mutual funds and ETFs allow investors to buy portfolios of securities without owning the underlying securities themselves. Most mutual funds are traded only at the market's close, where shares of the fund are created or redeemed. Alternatively, ETFs trade continuously throughout the financial markets' open hours. Evidence also suggests that when mutual funds and ETFs track the same underlying portfolios, ETFs are more tax efficient (see, e.g., Moussawi *et al.*, 2024). Hedge funds are similar in the sense that they pool investor funds, however, they face a lower level of regulation (as hedge funds have fewer investors, and investors are "accredited"), and thus can take more risk, deploy varying trading strategies, utilize leverage, and usually charge higher fees.

Insurance companies serve as financial intermediaries as well, allowing individuals to share risk by pooling funds. Insurance can take various forms, spanning various lines of business, such as property/casualty insurance, health insurance, and life insurance. Each of these forms of insurance presents unique challenges but the main risk of **expected losses** can be quantified by multiplying the **frequency** of loss by the **severity** of loss for the firm's insurance policies. For example, if a car insurance policy pays out a $10,000 claim at an average frequency of 10%, then the auto insurer would anticipate an expected loss of $1,000. A well-managed firm prices its insurance policy premiums to make sure they are large enough to handle this expected loss and cover the rest of the firm's costs to generate a profit.

Insurance companies, however, will also face the potential for liquidity risk (in the event of a large and unexpected need to pay out) and interest rate risk (given that they will need to commit to payments years in advance). Again, although we do not explicitly focus on insurance companies in this book, they are an important vehicle for individuals and companies to bring stability to their own balance sheets and manage risk.

Finally, **securities brokers**, as discussed above, perform a brokerage function, by bringing together buyers and sellers of securities for direct ownership and typically earn a commission for doing so. Brokers do not necessarily directly own the securities of those that they serve (although they usually act as custodians). In contrast to this, **dealers** work to make markets in certain securities (for example, in over-the-counter bond markets, or, importantly during the GFC, the mortgage-backed security markets), where they again serve to bring together buyers and sellers, but act as a principal intermediary between the two, buying from the seller and selling to the buyer. In return, a dealer will earn the bid-ask spread for making these transactions. In completing this function, dealers can face market risk as well as liquidity risk and must be careful not to be stuck holding securities in a market that is quickly falling in value.

1.6 "Form Follows Function" in Financial Intermediaries

As it relates to the types of intermediaries we discuss above, the concept that "form follows function" is especially relevant. For financial institutions, we mean that items that show up on the bank's financial statements (their "form") reflect the firm's primary activities (e.g., lending, investing, brokerage). Thus, the financial statements effectively capture the actions taken by the institution (the "function").

We can observe this idea via a high-level DuPont ratio analysis. First, the DuPont equation tells us that

$$ROE = ROA \cdot EM \qquad (1.1)$$

where ROE is the institution's return on equity, ROA is the institution's return on assets $\left(\frac{Net\ Income}{Total\ Assets}\right)$, and EM is an equity multiplier for the institution (defined as $\left(\frac{Total\ Assets}{Total\ Equity}\right)$. As a simple example, consider a bank with \$3 billion in Total Assets, \$30 million in Net Income, and \$250 million in Total Equity. We can estimate that the firm's ROE is then

$$ROE = ROA \cdot EM = \frac{\$30 \text{ million}}{\$3 \text{ billion}} \cdot \frac{\$3 \text{ billion}}{\$250 \text{ million}} = 12\% \quad (1.2)$$

The important point here is not the calculation of the bank's ROE, as we could more straightforwardly accomplish this by calculating it via $\frac{Net\ Income}{Total\ Equity}$. Rather, the point is that we can break down the components that *contribute* to the bank's *ROE*. Here, *ROE* is the product of the bank's *profitability* (captured with *ROA*) and its *financial leverage* (captured with the Equity Multiplier, EM). Thus, there are multiple ways for different firms to arrive at the same *ROE*, based on the variation in its underlying components. Though there are further ways to break down the bank's *ROE* than the method above, we rely on this simple calculation to illustrate the idea that for financial institutions, *form follows function*.

Given the above, we can hold a hypothetical value for *ROE* equal across the various institution types we discussed above. We would then likely observe the following, across broad classifications:

FI Type	ROA	EM	Primary Economic Function
Commercial Bank	Low	High	Qualitative Asset Transformation and Delegated Monitoring
Securities Firm	Lowest	Highest	Brokerage
Insurance Company	Moderate	Moderate	Qualitative Asset Transformation and Delegated Monitoring
Investment Managers	Highest	Lowest	Delegated Monitoring

The patterns we can observe above are reflective of the different risks and economic functions that each type of FI faces. A commercial bank may have a low *ROA* due to an overall lower net interest margin (or "spread") that it generates on its QAT function (taking deposits and making loans), as this industry can be very competitive. However, it makes up for the lower margins by using a large amount of financial leverage (e.g., deposits can be more than 70% of a bank's financing needs). This greater leverage leads to a higher equity multiplier and thus a much higher *ROE* relative to the *ROA* because the equity holders use the bank's debt to magnify their returns (which can also lead to larger losses if the bank has a net loss).[8]

---

[8] Keep in mind that a high Equity Multiplier (i.e., Assets much greater than Equity) implies that the firm is mostly financed by Debt, as described by the Accounting

Similarly, securities firms may have the lowest *ROA* due to their brokerage function and the large amount of investor cash and assets they manage. In addition, these firms typically buy and sell securities all day long but, at the end of the day, their *net* positions are usually near zero and thus they are *not* greatly exposed to much overall market risk. Due to the low-risk nature of these net positions, their ROA is quite low. Consequently, these firms will require a high degree of leverage to compensate for their relatively low ROA. Thus, their equity multiplier will likely be the largest of the group, and once again magnifying *ROA* to create a much larger *ROE*.

On the other hand, insurance companies and investment managers will have moderate-to-high values for *ROA*. Neither of these types of institutions rely on deposits or large amounts of other sources of leverage, meaning that neither will "need" a large equity multiplier to generate a satisfactory ROE. Instead, the larger contributor to their *ROE* will come from their *ROA* because of their delegated monitoring and (to a lesser extent) QAT functions of the Insurers (who can earn profits by investing the premiums they receive in the capital markets).

In total, we can see from the simple analysis above that although different types of institutions may generate similar performance (captured by *ROE*), they go about doing so in a variety of ways based on the economic functions that they provide to the economy.

1.7 Concluding Thoughts

Through this chapter, we have seen that banks play a unique, important, and active role in facilitating the transfer of funds from savers to borrowers, and how, through this role, banks provide several benefits for investors and firms to help promote economic growth and prosperity. But along with this role come unique risks that financial institutions must manage. In the remainder of this book, we walk through these risks that we described above and discuss how banks manage them. Importantly, we discuss in each chapter how these risks and the management of these risks affect the valuation of the bank. Managing risk creates trade-offs, and it is crucial to understand how these trade-offs can change the market value of the bank's equity.

Identity: Assets = Debt + Equity. So, when EM is high, it indicates that Equity is relatively low and therefore Debt must be very high to finance a given level of Assets.

Chapter-End Questions

Answers to odd-numbered questions can be found at the end of this book.

1. **True or False:** Lenders face a problem of asymmetric information, as they do not have a complete set of information about potential borrowers.
2. **True or False:** Many financial institutions use short-term liabilities (like deposits) to fund long-term assets (like 30-year mortgages).
3. **Multiple Choice:** What is the primary task of banks and other financial institutions?
   (A) Channeling funds from savers to borrowers
   (B) Investing in the stock market
   (C) Providing insurance
   (D) Manufacturing goods
4. **Multiple Choice:** Which type of institution is a nonprofit institution that is owned by its members?
   (A) Commercial bank
   (B) Finance company
   (C) Savings and loan institution
   (D) Credit union
5. **Multiple Choice:** What is the primary purpose of qualitative asset transformation (QAT)?
   (A) Converting high-liquidity instruments into low-liquidity instruments
   (B) Converting low-liquidity instruments into high-liquidity instruments
   (C) Transforming qualitative data into quantitative data
   (D) Transforming quantitative data into qualitative data
6. **Short Answer:** What is liquidity risk and how is it associated with the QAT function?
7. **Short Answer:** What does the concept that "Form Follows Function" mean in the context of financial institutions?
8. **Short Answer:** What is the simplest form of the DuPont equation?

9. **Short Answer:** A financial institution has a net income of $10 million, total equity of $150 million, and total assets of $2 billion. Using the DuPont equation, find the institution's *ROE*. What type of institution might we say this is?
10. **Comprehensive Question:** Nina and Sam are two entrepreneurs who are considering opening a commercial bank. What are the major risks the two will face if they decide to open the bank? What regulators will they be most likely to interact with?

References

Akerlof, G.A. (1970). The market for "Lemons": Quality uncertainty and the market mechanism. *The Quarterly Journal of Economics*, 84(3), 488–500.

Berger, A.N. and Bouwman, C.H.S. (2009). Bank liquidity creation. *Review of Financial Studies*, 22(9), 3779–3837.

Diamond, D.W. (1984). Financial intermediation and delegated monitoring. *Review of Economic Studies*, 51(3), 393–414.

Diamond, D.W. (1996). Financial intermediation as delegated monitoring, a simple example. *Economic Quarterly*, 82(3), 51–66.

King, R.G. and Levine, R. (1993). Finance, entrepreneurship, and growth: Theory and evidence. *Journal of Monetary Economics*, 32(3), 513–542.

Moussawi, R., Shen, K. and Velthuis, R. (2024). The role of taxes in the rise of ETFs. *Working Paper*.

Saunders, A., Cornett, M.M. and Erhemjamts, O. (2024). *Financial Institutions Management: A Risk Management Approach*, McGraw-Hill, New York.

Chapter 2

Overview of Valuation Models

2.1 Introduction to Stock Valuation

Valuing a firm is the process by which we determine the firm's economic value. In our case, we specifically consider how to estimate the value of the firm's common equity. In financial management, our goal, or "North Star," should be to make decisions that ultimately increase the market value of the firm's equity to its maximum potential level. Considering other goals (growing sales, pursuit of net income, etc.) can lead to unclear or inconsistent results that do not generate long-run value creation. Thus, our pursuit throughout this book is to best understand how to manage the risk of a financial institution while understanding the impact of those risk management choices on the value of the firm's equity. Importantly, a firm or bank's market value may fluctuate from time to time relative to its intrinsic value. Thus, modeling tools can help managers understand whether their firm is over- or undervalued by the market in the short run. However, we typically rely on the assumption that markets are efficient and that over the long run, and on average, market prices accurately reflect the firm's intrinsic value. Thus, maximizing the market value of a bank's equity should be the same as maximizing the intrinsic value of the bank as a whole. Accordingly, the models we present in this chapter and beyond focus on estimating *intrinsic* firm values.

There are multiple methods for estimating the intrinsic value of a firm. We will highlight a few here but note that most of these methods rely on using tools that require us to use discounting to determine present values.[1] Moreover, although we present multiple methods for valuing a firm, the Integrated Valuation Model (IVM) that is presented in Chapter 3 is derived from the Dividend Discount Model (DDM) we describe in the following. We present other models here, too, as (a) the DDM is a special case of one of the models (discounted cash flow model or DCF) and (b) it is important to have some versatility in understanding the basics of other methods of firm valuation, as these methods make different assumptions and can lead to different conclusions.

Overall, firm valuation is a valuable tool for the firm's stakeholders. Valuation can provide important insights into how a bank manager's decisions can impact an owner's return on investment. Moreover, valuation can help managers with benchmarks for assessing performance. Understanding and properly implementing valuation techniques can be a critical piece of the puzzle in the decision-making process, as managers can see how changes in the models' outputs are affected by changes to the models' inputs. In our case, we aim to focus on how the models will change relative to a bank's risk management decisions. Specifically, we include parameters like dividends, cash flows, growth rates, and required rates of return in our models. These variables are all influenced by the risks that the bank takes and how those risks are managed. Thus, these models, and the IVM that follows in Chapter 3, are important and useful tools to gauge the impact of these decisions on the overall value of the bank.

2.2 The Discounted Cash Flow Model

The Discounted Cash Flow (DCF) model is a widely used method for firm valuation. The central idea of the model is that the market value of the company's assets is equal to the *present value* of the future cash flows it is expected to generate over time. In this model, there are important assumptions that must be made. Some of these assumptions appear again as we discuss the Dividend Discount Model:

1. **Expected Future Cash Flows:** The financial analyst must estimate future cash flows for the firm by typically forecasting values of the firm's

---

[1] For a more detailed treatment of valuing non-financial companies, see Brigham and Ehrhardt (2020), Damodaran (2009), and Sopranzetti and Kiess (2024).

free cash flows (FCF) over time. FCF is the cash a company generates *after* it accounts for the cash needed to run its operations and maintain its fixed assets. In this book, for simplicity, we use *annual* free cash flows for a bank, however, those using the model may instead wish to change the periodicity to a shorter frequency, like quarterly. FCF are determined using accounting data, and here we present alternative but equivalent definitions. First,

$$FCF = \text{Cash Flow from Operations} + \text{Interest Exp.}$$
$$- \text{Tax Shield on Interest Exp.} - \text{CAPEX}$$

This definition uses Cash Flow from Operations and CAPEX, the level of the firm's investing activity during the year, which are obtained from the statement of cash flows, as well as Interest Expense and Tax Shield on Interest Expense (calculated by multiplying the bank's effective marginal tax rate by its income expense) from the income statement. Alternatively, one could estimate FCF from the income statement and the balance sheet:

$$FCF = EBIT(1-t) + \text{Depreciation \& Amortization}$$
$$- \Delta(\text{Curr. Assets} - \text{Curr. Liabilities}) - CAPEX \quad (2.1)$$

where $EBIT(1-t)$ and Depreciation & Amortization (D&A) come from the firm's income statement, while $\Delta(\textit{Curr. Assets} - \textit{Curr. Liabilities})$ come from the firm's balance sheet.[2] Finally, *CAPEX* is defined as above.

In the latter approach, D&A is added back into the firm's $EBIT(1-t)$ because D&A is a non-cash expense. D&A are expenses that have been paid in cash upfront by the firm but are expensed over the purchased asset's useful life. Further, $\Delta(\textit{Curr. Assets} - \textit{Curr. Liabilities})$ can also be referred to as the change in the firm's *Net Operating Working Capital*. These are subtracted from FCF because they are short-term assets and liabilities needed to run the firm. One example of this is *Accounts Receivable (A/R)*. An increase in *A/R* may be a net positive for a company because it represents more sales on credit. However, it is income that is

---

[2] EBIT stands for Earnings Before Interest and Taxes and, when added to D&A, is usually referred to as "EBITDA." In addition, t represents the marginal effective tax rate for the bank.

not yet realized as cash and therefore is not a positive cash flow for the firm. In short, a firm cannot spend A/R.

Given the approaches noted above, the user of the model must then project future values of the firm's FCF, making assumptions about the firm's rate of growth, the macroeconomy, and other important issues related to the firm's management. In the case of a bank, some assumptions would relate to the evolution of the bank's risk management practices and potential future regulatory changes that could impact how the bank manages risk and conducts its business.

Finally, we must also determine the length of time over which to estimate a firm's FCF on an individual year-by-year basis. Typically, a DCF model will range from three to ten years of annual FCF estimates and then all future FCFs are assumed to be summarized in the "horizon value," as described in the following in item 3. In building the DCF model, it is important to consider the potential length of an investment (time horizon) and how much uncertainty there is about future cash flows. If there is a substantial amount of uncertainty about the firm's future, it may make sense to project fewer cash flows.

2. **The Discount Rate:** Within the FCF model, an assumption of the discount rate is crucial. This is the interest rate at which all the estimated future cash flows will be discounted. This represents the required rate of return from a potential investor in the firm. Since the FCF model values the entirety of the firm's *assets*, a common assumption for the discount rate in an FCF model is the firm's Weighted Average Cost of Capital (WACC), which accounts for the cost each of a firm's capital sources (e.g., typically long-term debt, preferred stock, and common stock) and is a proxy for the expected rate of return required from all the firm's investors.[3] An alternative and commonly used discount factor is the risk-free rate of return, which is sometimes represented by the yield on ten-year Treasurys, plus some markup to reflect the riskiness of the firm.

---

[3] In equilibrium, the expected return on the firm's sources of capital will be equal to their *required* return, which can be estimated using various asset pricing models. However, the choice of the appropriate model(s) can be a complex (and controversial) process that is beyond the scope of our analysis in this book. See Brick (2017) and Brigham and Ehrhardt (2020) for more details on different ways to estimate a firm's WACC.

3. **The Firm's Horizon Value:** A firm does not have a defined end date. Thus, we expect when valuing a firm that it will last well beyond the final future FCF that we project. To handle this, we must calculate a *Horizon Value* for the cash flows that will occur beyond our projections (also referred to as a "Terminal Value"). A standard way of doing this is to use the following equation:

$$HV = \frac{FCF_T(1+g)}{(r-g)} \quad (2.2)$$

where FCF_T is the final projected free cash flow for the firm, g is the projected *constant* rate at which FCF will grow beyond the model's horizon, and r is the assumed discount rate we discussed above. This horizon value is then added to the present values of all other estimated FCF values to arrive at the *total* value of the firm (including debt, preferred stock, and common equity). The new and important assumption here is g. Within the model, different projections can be made using various growth assumptions, to better understand best- and worst-case scenarios. It is important that the growth rate is never larger than the discount rate. Although this can be true for a short length of time (commonly called a "supernormal" or "abnormal" growth period), it cannot be indefinitely true. If it were, then the case where it is assumed g will be indefinitely greater than r would generate a hypothetical infinite return, which is not reasonable.

Another possible approach is to use this horizon value approach upfront and not estimate yearly FCF but rather assume that FCF will grow at a constant rate in perpetuity, starting immediately, which we see in the following section.

2.2.1 *The DCF model with constant growth*

Once we have settled on appropriate assumptions for the model's inputs, we can move to implementing the model itself. A straightforward (but rather restrictive) way to approach the DCF model is to assume constant cash flow growth over time. In this case, the model relies only on using cash flows estimated *today* and then projecting that they will grow at a constant rate over time. Crucially, as it relates to the discussion of expected future cash flows above, this means that we do not need to project year-by-year cash flows nor do we need to project a time at which we implement a horizon value calculation. Instead, we assume that cash flows, as estimated with current data, will grow at a fixed rate in perpetuity (i.e., forever!), thus making today's free cash flow value equal to the company's horizon value. For this calculation, then, we can rely on the method for calculating the present value of a growing perpetuity:

$$V_{Op} = \frac{FCF_1}{r-g} = \frac{FCF_0(1+g)}{r-g} \qquad (2.3)$$

where FCF_0 is *today's* free cash flow, r is the appropriate discount rate (again, typically the firm's WACC), and g is the estimated constant rate at which free cash flow is projected to grow annually.[4,5]

It is important to note that whenever we discount FCF by WACC, whether we assume perpetual growth or not, we are determining the intrinsic value of the *total firm* from its operations (V_{Op}).[6] The intrinsic value of the firm includes all assets and does not isolate specifically the intrinsic value of the firm's equity (V_E). For this, we need a second step:

$$V_E = V_{Op} - \text{Debt} - \text{Preferred Stock} \qquad (2.4)$$

Here, because we know the foundational Accounting Identity (Assets = Liabilities + Equity, or $A = L + E$ for short), we can back out the implied value of the firm's equity, given that we have estimated the intrinsic value of the entire firm (V_{Op}) and that we can find the amount of the firm's liabilities (Debt) and Preferred Stock from the balance sheet.

---

[4] This constant growth rate, g, should also be less than the nominal GDP growth rate of the country in which the firm operates. For example, in the U.S., g should be less than or equal to 6% per year. The reason for this is that the firm's constant growth rate of cash flows must be less than GDP. Otherwise, the firm will ultimately become the entire economy (i.e., its size will essentially be equal to the nation's entire GDP!). Since this is not a reasonable possibility, we must set g to be less than or equal to 6% for U.S. firms.

[5] It may also be the case that free cash flow is not projected to grow at all but instead remain constant. In this case, we assume $g = 0\%$. This simplifies equation (2.3) to $V_{Op} = \frac{FCF_0}{r}$.

[6] The analyst should also add in the market value of any "non-operating" assets such as excess cash invested in marketable securities or unused assets like vacant real estate.

Example: Consider a bank that generated $100 million in free cash flow this year. Its WACC is 10%, and it projects that cash flows will increase annually at 2% in perpetuity. If the firm has $900 million in liabilities and $100 million in preferred stock, what is the intrinsic value of the firm's equity?

Solution: We first find the intrinsic value of the bank's operations using Equation (2.3) above:

$$V_{Op} = \frac{FCF_0(1+g)}{r-g} = \frac{\$100\text{ M}(1+0.02)}{0.10-0.02} = \$1,275\text{ M}$$

Thus, the implied value of the bank's operations is $1.275 billion (or $1,275 million). From this, we can use Equation (2.4) above to find the implied value of the bank's equity:

$$V_E = V_{Op} - \text{Liabilities} - \text{Preferred Stock}$$
$$= \$1,275\text{M} - \$900\text{M} - \$100\text{M} = \$275\text{M}$$

Given the above, we estimate that the intrinsic value of the bank's equity is $275 million. ∎

2.2.2 The DCF model with non-constant growth

Of course, it may not always be the case that free cash flow will grow at a constant rate in perpetuity from the outset. One possibility is that a bank may have an opportunity for supernormal growth (where $g > r$) in the short run, due to an outstanding business opportunity. Conversely, another possibility is that the bank may have a short period of negative free cash flow due to an increase in up-front investment.

In these cases, the assumptions we discussed above become much more important. Annual cash flows during the non-constant growth period must be modeled separately. The user must also determine for how many years it makes sense to forecast yearly cash flows before converting to cash flows growing at a perpetual, constant rate (and subsequently calculating the horizon value of cash flows).

Thus, in determining the intrinsic value of a firm when there is short-run non-constant growth, we can use Equation (2.2), which determines the firm's horizon value, along with year-by-year FCF estimates, to arrive at a method for discounting a firm's free cash flows:

$$V_{Op} = \frac{FCF_1}{(1+r)} + \frac{FCF_2}{(1+r)^2} + \cdots + \frac{FCF_T}{(1+r)^T} + \frac{HV_T}{(1+r)^T} \quad (2.5)$$

In this equation, we discount each annual estimated cash flow (FCF_t) individually by the firm's appropriate discount rate (r), until the point at which we project that the firm will shift to perpetual, constant growth (that is, in T years). At time T, we estimate the firm's horizon value (HV_T), which is the present value of the firm's future cash flows *as of time T*. The horizon value itself must then be discounted back to its present value as of today, which is reflected in Equation (2.5). Once again, this method estimates the intrinsic value of the *entire firm*, and we must again back out the intrinsic value of the firm's equity from the result of the above formula.

Example: The same bank as above generates $100 million in FCF today (that is, at time 0) as before. However, over the next five years, the bank projects that it will have the following FCF due to outstanding growth opportunities in the near term:

Year:	1	2	3	4	5
FCF:	$105	$110	$120	$125	$130

At the end of this five-year period, the bank projects that its FCF will settle into a growth rate of 2% in perpetuity. If its WACC is again 10%, what is the intrinsic value of the firm's equity? Recall that the bank has $900 million in liabilities and $100 million in preferred stock.

Solution: Using the DCF approach, we need to discount each of the bank's cash first five cash flows, using its 10% WACC:

$$PV(CF) = \frac{\$105}{(1.10)} + \frac{\$110}{(1.10)^2} + \frac{\$120}{(1.10)^3} + \frac{\$125}{(1.10)^4} + \frac{\$130}{(1.10)^5} = \$442.62$$

Following this, as we assume that the firm will continue in perpetuity, we must calculate the bank's horizon value:

$$HV_5 = \frac{FCF_5(1+g)}{r-g} = \frac{\$130(1.02)}{0.10-0.02} = \$1,657.50$$

Recall that the horizon value is the discounted value of the perpetual cash flows that the firm generates after its period of supernormal growth. What we calculate above is the intrinsic value of these combined cash flows *as of year 5*. We must then discount the horizon value back to time 0 so that it can be added to the $442.62 million present value of the first five cash flows that we calculated above. Thus,

$$HV_0 = \frac{HV_5}{(1+r)^5} = \frac{\$1,657.50}{(1.10)^5} = \$1,029.18$$

Given this, we can now combine the fully discounted horizon value with the sum of the discounted cash flows from years 1–5 to find the intrinsic value of the firm:

$$PV_{FCF} = V_{Op} = \$442.62 + \$1,029.18 = \$1,471.80$$

Note again that, as above, this calculation provides us with an estimate of the intrinsic value of the entirety of the firm. If we are concerned about the intrinsic value of the firm's *equity*, we again take the following step:

$$V_E = V_{Op} - \text{Liabilities} - \text{Preferred Stock}$$
$$= \$1,471.80\,M - \$900\,M - \$100\,M = \$471.80\,M$$

Given the above, we estimate that the intrinsic value of the bank's equity is $471.80 million. Note that this is higher than the intrinsic value we found in the first example, as the bank in this case has increased growth up-front, which increases the present value of the cash flows. ∎

2.3 An Extension of the DCF Model: Free Cash Flow to Equity (FCFE)

We may also wish to calculate the firm's free cash flow *to equity* directly, which can allow us to value the firm's equity without having to value the entire firm first. The model is very similar to the DCF model we present above, but we change our method of calculating FCF in Equation (2.1) to the following:

$$\text{FCFE} = \text{FCF} - \text{Interest Expense} + \text{Interest Tax Shield} \\ + \text{Net Change in Debt} \qquad (2.6)$$

The result from Equation (2.6) tells us how much cash is left for the equity holders of a firm after the company accounts for operating expenses, reinvestments, and debt repayments. Effectively, we can view FCFE as the amount of cash that the firm has available to pay dividends or conduct stock buybacks. FCFE is relevant for banks, especially for the Integrated Valuation Model (IVM) we developed in Chapter 3. There, we show that a bank's FCFE is equivalent to its dividend payments when the bank does not issue any new equity during the next year.

Functionally, we implement a discounted FCFE model in the same way we use FCF above. FCFE can be viewed as a growing perpetuity of the cash flows to equity investors that can have no growth, constant growth, or temporary non-normal growth rates, just like in the examples shown earlier. The main changes are that (a) we replace FCF with FCFE, (b) we use the required return on equity (R_E) rather than the WACC as the discount rate, and (c) we do not need to back out the implied value of equity because this model directly estimates V_E rather than V_{Op}.

2.4 The Dividend Discount Model

Instead of focusing on the total value of the firm via free cash flows, we may instead choose to concentrate on the intrinsic value of the firm's equity. It may be difficult to accurately estimate free cash flow for a bank, but dividends are much clearer. As we proceed in the textbook, we base our bank IVM on the Dividend Discount Model (DDM) presented here. We can view the DDM as a special case of the DCF model we present above.[7] Since nearly all banks pay dividends and it is usually quite

---

[7] It should be noted that for this DDM method to produce an accurate result, firms must pay dividends optimally. In practice, there is no way to guarantee that the firm's management can formulate this optimal stream of dividends, and even if they did do that, there is no way as an external shareholder to force them to pay those dividends because managers have a great deal of discretion over what they do with the bank's profits. However, the

difficult to define meaningful components of FCF such as the change in net working capital and operating cash flow for a bank, we focus on the DDM in Chapter 3 to develop our IVM. As mentioned above and discussed further in Chapter 3, a bank's FCFE is equivalent to its dividend payments when the bank does not issue any new equity during the next year.

We can establish a model of firm equity by considering the intrinsic value of the firm's stock via the DDM. Assume that you pay, P_0, for one share of a company's stock today. In one year, the firm will pay a dividend, D_1, and you will sell the stock, receiving the stock's future price P_1.[8] If you require a rate of return, r, to bear the risk of this firm's stock, what should you be willing to pay for it today? Like above, we can estimate this value by discounting the future cash flows that this transaction will generate:

$$P_0 = PV(CF) = \frac{D_1 + P_1}{1+r} \tag{2.7}$$

Of course, we may decide to hold the stock for more than one year. If we held the stock for two years, we would calculate

$$P_0 = PV(CF) = \frac{D_1}{1+r} + \frac{D_2 + P_2}{(1+r)^2} \tag{2.8}$$

And after three years, the equation becomes

$$P_0 = PV(CF) = \frac{D_1}{1+r} + \frac{D_2}{(1+r)^2} + \frac{D_3 + P_3}{(1+r)^3} \tag{2.9}$$

As the firm has an indefinite lifespan, this pattern would continue forever. Due to this, we continue expanding the equation above to infinity, which

---

DDM approach does provide a simple, clear way to understand how risk management choices affect a bank's market value.

[8] Note here that we are talking about the price of one share of stock. We can, and will, extend this to the value of the firm's total equity by multiplying the firm's stock price per share by the firm's total number of shares outstanding.

pushes off the problem of estimating the *future* market price of the stock (P_T) forever. In this case, we know that as time t approaches infinity,

$$\lim_{t \to \infty} \frac{P_t}{(1+r)^t} = 0 \qquad (2.10)$$

which means that the firm's future stock price never needs to enter the calculation (that is, we do not have to make any type of prediction of future stock prices — if we could do that, we would be better off trading stocks than reading this book!). Instead, we are left to be concerned only about how the firm's dividends evolve in the future:

$$P_0 = \frac{D_1}{(1+r)} + \frac{D_2}{(1+r)^2} + \frac{D_3}{(1+r)^3} + \frac{D_4}{(1+r)^4} + \cdots \qquad (2.11)$$

From this, we have multiple possibilities for how to approach valuing the firm's equity:

1. The firm pays no dividends. In this case, it is not possible to value a firm using a discounted dividend model, and instead, one must use an alternative like the DCF model we discussed above.
2. The firm pays a constant dividend, where over time, the dividend paid is not projected to change.
3. The firm pays a constantly growing dividend, where over time, the dividend is projected to grow at a constant rate, beginning immediately.
4. The firm pays a non-constant or non-traditional dividend in the short run, which after some time becomes a constantly growing dividend extending in perpetuity. In this circumstance, the short-run dividend could be $0, after which the firm initiates a dividend payment at some future time. Alternatively, the firm could pay a dividend which grows at a supernormal rate for a short time, after which the dividend settles to a constantly growing rate in perpetuity. Finally, the firm may even, in some circumstances, pay a dividend that is projected to decline over time — perpetually or temporarily.

In all the above cases, we can apply a similar methodology to what we developed with the DCF model. We walk through each, other than Case 1, in which the company does not pay dividends.

2.4.1 Constant dividends

Remember again that the idea with the Dividend Discount Model is that the intrinsic value of the firm's equity is the discounted value of the firm's future dividend payments. If dividends are constant over time, then $D_1 = D_2 = D_3 = D_4 = \cdots = D$. Thus, Equation (2.11) becomes

$$P_0 = \frac{D}{(1+r)} + \frac{D}{(1+r)^2} + \frac{D}{(1+r)^3} + \frac{D}{(1+r)^4} + \cdots \quad (2.12)$$

Finding the present value of this series of dividends is the same as finding the value of an ordinary, non-growing, perpetuity. That is,

$$P_0 = \frac{D}{r} \quad (2.13)$$

Like the DCF model above, one of the crucial assumptions underlying the model is the appropriate discount rate. In the case of the DDM, we are focusing on the intrinsic value of a firm's equity rather than the intrinsic value of the entirety of the firm. Thus, instead of using the WACC for our discount rate, it is more appropriate to use the required return on the firm's equity (what we refer to as R_E later in this chapter as well as in Chapter 3). This rate can be determined using asset pricing models like the Capital Asset Pricing Model (CAPM) or by other methods.[9]

Example: A bank pays a constant annual dividend of $5 *per share*. If investors *require* a 20% return on equity, then what is the intrinsic value of one share of the bank's stock? Further, if the bank has 4 million shares outstanding, what is the total value of the bank's equity?

Solution: To estimate the bank's intrinsic stock price, we plug in the information above to Equation (2.13):

$$P_0 = \frac{D}{r} = \frac{\$5}{0.20} = \$25$$

---

[9] The main concepts of asset pricing models go well beyond our book's focus. If you are not familiar with the basics of this asset pricing model, please refer to the relevant chapter on the CAPM as described in Brigham and Ehrhardt (2020) or other introductory finance textbooks.

Thus, the intrinsic price of *one share* of the bank's stock is estimated to be $25. If the bank has 4 million shares outstanding, then the *total* intrinsic value of the firm's equity (commonly referred to as its "market cap") is estimated to be

$$V_E = \$25 \cdot 4,000,000 = \$100,000,000 \qquad \blacksquare$$

2.4.2 Dividends with constant growth

Taking the above discussion one step further, we can estimate the intrinsic value of the firm's equity under the assumption that dividend payments begin growing in the next period (D_1) and continue to grow at the same rate in perpetuity. Thus, we can implement this model using the equation for a growing perpetuity as our basis:

$$P_0 = \frac{D_1}{r-g} = \frac{D_0(1+g)}{r-g} \qquad (2.14)$$

In the above equation, we see that there are three key drivers of firm value which we refer to here and in Chapter 3 by the acronym, "MRT." This stands for the Magnitude of the firm's cash flows (D_1), the Riskiness of those cash flows (r), and the Timing of those cash flows, which represents the growth (g) in those cash flows. We once again must come up with a reasonable estimate of the firm's required rate of return on equity (r). We also must include an estimate of the rate at which dividends will grow (g). Some possible methods for estimating the growth rate include estimating it from the growth rate of previous dividends paid, or, if previous stock prices, dividend payments, and the required rate of return are known, g can be estimated by backing it out of Equation (2.14).[10]

Regardless of how g is estimated, it is important to note that ultimately, management faces a trade-off when it comes to dividends and growth. If management decides to pay out 100% of its earnings as dividends, the growth rate will be zero, as there will be no growth in the firm's earnings. To achieve growth in dividends, there must be growth in earnings. Thus, if the firm wishes to achieve growth in dividends, it must reinvest some earnings, which means that the more earnings that are

---

[10] See, for example, Brick et al. (2016).

retained, the higher the potential growth rate. Both dividends and earnings are important factors that influence the value of a company.

Example: A bank *just paid* its annual dividend of $5 per share. This annual dividend is projected to grow at a rate of 2% per year in perpetuity. If investors *require* a 20% return on equity, then what is the intrinsic value of one share of the bank's stock? Further, if the bank has 4 million shares outstanding, what is the total value of the bank's equity?

Solution: To find the intrinsic value of the bank's stock price, we plug the information we have into Equation (2.14):

$$P_0 = \frac{D_0(1+g)}{r-g} = \frac{\$5(1.02)}{0.20-0.02} = \$28.33$$

Here, the intrinsic value of one share of the bank's stock is estimated to be $28.33. To find the total intrinsic value of the bank's equity, we calculate

$$V_E = \$28.33 \cdot 4,000,000 = \$113,333,333.33 \quad \blacksquare$$

2.4.3 Non-constant growth dividends

It may be the case where, as with the DCF model above, a firm has non-constant dividend growth in the short run (in which g may temporarily exceed r) that will eventually settle into a stream of constantly growing dividends that continues in perpetuity. Like before, we need to discount each of the early dividends one by one and then add to that the discounted horizon value of the growing perpetuity. Thus, we calculate

$$V_E = \frac{D_1}{(1+r)} + \frac{D_2}{(1+r)^2} + \cdots + \frac{D_T}{(1+r)^T} + \frac{HV_T}{(1+r)^T} \quad (2.15)$$

where the horizon value (HV_T) is calculated as

$$HV_T = \frac{D_T(1+g)}{(r-g)} \quad (2.16)$$

Otherwise, similar assumptions as noted earlier are required for r and g.

Example: A bank *just made* a dividend payment of $5/share. Over the next five years, the bank's dividends are projected to evolve in the following way:

Year	1	2	3	4	5
Dividend	$5.10	$5.25	$5.40	$5.55	$5.70

This annual dividend is projected to grow at a rate of 2% per year in perpetuity following this period. If investors require a 20% return on equity, what is the intrinsic value of one share of the bank's stock? Further, if the bank has 4 million share outstanding, what is the total value of the bank's equity?

Solution: In this case, we can first find the discounted value of the first five dividend payments:

$$PV = \frac{\$5.10}{(1.20)} + \frac{\$5.25}{(1.20)^2} + \frac{\$5.40}{(1.20)^3} + \frac{\$5.55}{(1.20)^4} + \frac{\$5.70}{(1.20)^5} = \$15.99$$

Next, we find the horizon value (HV) of the perpetuity that begins in year 6. The result of this formula is the horizon value *as of year 5*:

$$HV_5 = \frac{D_5(1+g)}{r-g} = \frac{\$5.70(1.02)}{0.20-0.02} = \$32.30$$

We then need to discount the horizon value we found above to its present value as of time 0:

$$HV_0 = \frac{\$32.30}{(1.20)^5} = \$12.98$$

Thus, the estimated intrinsic value of one share of the bank's stock is the sum of the discounted value of the first five dividend payments and the discounted horizon value:

$$P_0 = \$15.99 + \$12.98 = \$28.97$$

And the total intrinsic value of the bank's equity is estimated as

$$V_E = \$28.97 \cdot 4,000,000 = \$115,880,000$$ ∎

2.5 The Ohlson Valuation Model

Ohlson's (1995) model of valuation differs from the DCF model we present above. According to Ohlson (1995), the value of equity is equal to the sum of the current book value of equity and the present value of the excess profits the firm generates. The excess profits are known as the "residual income," which is the profit the firm generates beyond what it needs to pay back its shareholders (or after subtracting out the opportunity cost of retaining a portion of current earnings). The residual income valuation formula is analogous to a dividend discount model except for the substitution of future dividend payments with future residual earnings. The advantage of this model is that residual income can be obtained using data directly available from a firm's financial statements.

$$CF_E = (ROE - R_E) \cdot BV_E \qquad (2.17)$$

where R_E represents the rate of return required by the shareholders and ROE represents the firm's return on its book value of equity (BV_E). The difference between the two represents the net return to the firm, or *residual income*, left after the shareholders have achieved their required hurdle rate. Multiplying this difference by the bank's book value of equity yields the amount by which the bank's equity grows over the year, which we call here CF_E. We can then calculate the firm's value using a similar logic to the models above, by calculating the sum of the discounted future values of CF_E. We can add this to the firm's *current* book value of equity (BV_0), to then yield the estimated intrinsic value of the firm's equity:

$$V_E = \sum_{t=1}^{\infty} \frac{(ROE_t - R_E) \cdot BV_{E,t}}{(1+R_E)^t} + BV_0 = \sum_{t=1}^{\infty} \frac{CF_{E,t}}{(1+R_E)^t} + BV_0 \qquad (2.18)$$

Like our models above, we will at some point need to calculate a horizon value for CF_E, but if there is not a special case of supernormal growth, we can assume that CF_E will grow in perpetuity starting at $t = 0$. In this case, we have

$$V_E = \frac{CF_{E,t+1}}{R_E - g} + BV_0 \qquad (2.19)$$

Since we already have examples above of calculating values with supernormal growth, we, for the sake of conserving space, show only an example of a constant growth application of the Ohlson model.

Example: A bank currently has a book value of equity of \$100 million. It generates a return on equity (ROE) of 15% and must return 10% to its shareholders (R_E). Currently, the bank expects revenue to grow at a pace of 2% per year. What is the estimated intrinsic value of the bank's equity?

Solution: We first need to calculate $CF_{E,0}$ for the bank:

$$CF_{E,0} = (ROE - R_E) \cdot BV_E = (15\% - 10\%) \cdot \$100 \text{ million} = \$5 \text{ million}$$

This is the bank's CF_E as of time 0. Then, we plug into Equation (2.19) to find the model's estimate of the value of the bank's equity:

$$V_E = \frac{CF_{E,0}(1+g)}{R_E - g} + BV_0 = \frac{\$5 \text{ million } (1.02)}{10\% - 2\%} + \$100 \text{ million} = \$163.75 \text{ million}$$

■

Given that banks use a high amount of leverage and that banks must comply with capital adequacy rules, a method like this that focuses on ROE and the cost of equity can make sense for a financial institution. Though we do not utilize this model in the IVM, we develop in the following chapter, one can potentially alter it in such a way that it takes advantage of the ideas presented here.

2.6 Market Multiples

A final method of valuation we examine is based on peer comparisons. If a firm does not plan to ever pay dividends, then a dividend discount model cannot be used to value it. Moreover, estimating free cash flows and growth rates can be challenging and uncertain. Instead, a simple and common way to estimate the value of a bank is by comparing its value based on its value relative to the value of its peer institutions.

One straightforward market multiple method is to use the price-to-earnings (P/E) ratio. This ratio compares the *stock price* of a firm to its earnings-per-share (EPS). In calculating this for a peer (or set of peers), we can determine how the stock market values other, similar firms. Once we know how peer firms are currently valued at time t, we can apply the peer P/E ratio to our own firm, based on our time $t + 1$ EPS forecasts:

$$\frac{V_{E,t}}{\text{share}} = \frac{P}{E_{\text{comp},t}} \cdot \text{EPS}_{\text{firm},t+1} \qquad (2.20)$$

The above gives us a per-share estimate of the bank's value at time t. We can multiply this outcome by the bank's total shares outstanding to arrive at an estimated intrinsic market value of the bank's equity. Given this, we can work through a simple example.

Example: Suppose a bank forecasts EPS of $0.80 in the coming year. A single peer institution, with a similar size and business model, is currently trading at $5/share and has a current EPS of $0.50. What is the implied intrinsic value of the bank in question?

Solution: First, we calculate the P/E ratio for the peer institution:

$$\frac{P}{E_{\text{comp},t}} = \frac{\$5}{0.50} = 10$$

Following this, we simply apply the comparable firm's P/E ratio $\left(\frac{P}{E_{\text{comp},t}}\right)$ to our bank's forecasted EPS:

$$\frac{V_{E,t}}{\text{share}} = 10 \cdot \$0.80 = \$8.00$$

Thus, the implied per-share market value of the bank is $8 according to the Market Multiples approach. ∎

There are several considerations for banks to make when implementing a market multiple model. The selection of the peer institutions is very important. Peer institutions should be of a similar size, have a similar business model (e.g., having a similar loan portfolio composition and growth prospects), and face similar regulations. In fact, because no two institutions are exactly alike, it may be beneficial to calculate implied values across several comparable institutions, which yields a range of potential prices. This type of model is also helpful if a bank is privately held, as it can give a sense of what the market would be willing to pay for the bank's stock if it were publicly traded. Finally, the P/E ratio may not be the only choice. We can use other ratios, like $\frac{Price}{EBITDA}$ or $\frac{Price}{BV_E}$ as other choices upon which we can make a comparison. Ultimately, using a market multiple can provide a quick and simple idea of the valuation of a firm or bank, and this method can be especially useful in valuing an institution that is not publicly traded. It can also be used as a "sanity check" on valuation estimates generated by the DCF, DDM, and/or Ohlson models.

2.7 Summary

We present here several methods (among many) for estimating the value of a firm. As you can see, there are many assumptions and choices that need to be made to use any of these models. As you see in the coming chapters, we develop a model of bank valuation, the IVM, that has its foundations in the dividend discount model presented here.

The novel aspect of the IVM is that it directly builds on the impact of a bank's risk management decisions within the valuation model. As we discuss, like any of these models, the IVM does not provide a pinpoint estimate of the bank's value. Rather, it and other models like it should be used as a general guide to gauge the overall impacts of different choices the firm can make. In this sense, using the model is like the way ancient sailors used the North Star to get an approximate sense of their position when they navigated unfamiliar seas. Also, we should keep in mind that a model is only as good as its assumptions. Thus, the old acronym, "GIGO" (i.e., Garbage In, Garbage Out!), certainly applies to all the models discussed here. Nevertheless, the models can serve as a useful method for us to understand the overall direction and high-level magnitude of a bank's risk management decisions.

Chapter-End Questions

Answers to odd-numbered questions can be found at the end of this book.

1. **True or False:** The DCF model values only a part of the firm's assets.
2. **True or False:** The Ohlson valuation model calculates the value of equity as the sum of the current book value of equity and the present value of the excess profits the firm generates.
3. **Multiple Choice:** Which of the following is *not* explicitly considered to be a component of Free Cash Flow to the entire firm (FCF), based on the definition provided in Chapter 2?
   (A) Cash Flow from Operations
   (B) Operating Expense
   (C) Tax Shield on Interest Expense
   (D) Dividends
4. **Multiple Choice:** In the market multiples method of valuation, what does the *P/E* ratio represent?
   (A) The ratio of the stock price of a firm to its earnings-per-share
   (B) The ratio of the earnings-per-share of a firm to its stock price
   (C) The ratio of the stock price of a firm to its dividend
   (D) The ratio of the dividend of a firm to its stock price
5. **Multiple Choice:** In a valuation model, what does the horizon (or "terminal") value represent?
   (A) The discounted value of current dividends
   (B) The discounted value of all future cash flows beyond a certain point in time
   (C) The future value of all cash flows the firm is expected to generate
   (D) The future value of the firm's first three dividend payments

6. **Short Answer:** ABC bank decides to pay a perpetual dividend of $1.50/share today (that is, starting at $t = 0$). Investors currently require a 10% rate of return on ABC's stock. Estimate the value of one share of ABC's stock.
7. **Short Answer:** DEF bank decides to pay a dividend of $1.50/share today (that is, starting at $t = 0$). They expect this dividend to grow by 3% per year. Investors currently require a 10% rate of return on DEF's stock. Estimate the value of one share of DEF's stock.
8. **Short Answer:** GHI Bank is projected to have the following free cash flows to the entire firm:

Year	1	2	3	4
FCF	$10	$25	$30	$35

Following year four, the bank's FCF will grow at a 3% rate in perpetuity. GHI's WACC is 10%. What is the value of the firm's equity if GHI has $350 in liabilities and $35 in preferred stock?
9. **Short Answer:** Bank JKL does not currently pay a dividend. In three years (that is, at $t = 3$), the bank will begin paying a dividend of $0.50/share that it projects will grow by 5% per year in perpetuity. Bank JKL's investors require a 12% rate of return. What is the appropriate price for Bank JKL's stock today?
10. **Comprehensive Question:** Sam and Nina are managing bank ABC and would like to assess the value of the firm, as they are considering whether or not they should raise additional capital. Based on the information in this chapter, provide Nina and Sam with a discussion of which model (or models) might be best suited for valuing the bank.

References

Brick, I.E. (2017). *Lecture Notes in Introduction to Corporate Finance*, Vol. 1. World Scientific.

Brick, I.E., Chen, H.Y., Hsieh, C.H., and Lee, C.F. (2016). A comparison of alternative models for estimating a firm's growth rate. *Review of Quantitative Finance and Accounting*, 47, 369–393.

Brigham, E.F. and Ehrhardt, M. (2020). *Financial Management: Theory and Practice*, 16th edn. Cengage, pp. 821–822.

Damodaran, A. (2009). Valuing financial services firms. *NYU Working Paper*.

Ohlson, J.A. (1995). Earnings, book values, and dividends in security valuation. *Contemporary Accounting Research*, 11, 661–687.

Sopranzetti, B. and Kiess, B. (2024). *Valuation and Financial Forecasting: A Handbook for Academics and Practitioners*. World Scientific Series in Modern Finance: Advanced Topics in Finance for the Academician and Practitioner, Vol. 2.

Chapter 3

Introducing the Integrated Valuation Model

3.1 Introduction

As we learned earlier in Chapter 2 when we discussed the different types of valuation models, managers are entrusted with the assets of the financial institution (FI) and must generate revenue that will not only cover all funding and operational costs but also satisfy equity investors' expectations for an adequate return on their investment.[1] When managers fail in this task, investors will stop financing the FI and will instead invest their money elsewhere. Without a continuous and stable source of financing, a financial firm will be unable to remain in operation for very long.[2] This is true not only for financial firms but also for all firms: all firms must measure and manage profits to generate sufficient returns for investors and survive in the long run.

---

[1] For an excellent, detailed treatment of various financial valuation techniques, please see Sopranzetti and Kiess (2024). In addition, Dermine (2015) examined the valuation of banks based on a non-traditional approach while Egan *et al.* (2021) used a production function method to estimate the impact of lending and deposit-taking on a bank's market value.

[2] See the case of Lehman Brothers' failure on September 15, 2008, as an extreme example of how quickly investors can become skittish of lending to a financial firm that has growing risks and a high degree of financial leverage (i.e., a great deal of debt and very little equity to finance its operations).

In this chapter, we present a valuation model that is based on Net Income (NI) and Dividends (DIV) for analyzing the market value of an FI. As discussed in Chapter 2, Damodaran (2009), among others, notes that NI is much easier to define for a financial services firm compared to **Free Cash Flow to Equity (FCFE)** because of the difficulty in defining key cash flow items for a bank (e.g., net working capital and operating cash flow). In addition, unlike many non-financial firms, nearly all banks pay a dividend, thus a dividend-based valuation approach like the **Dividend Discount Model (DDM)** is directly applicable to the firms we wish to analyze.[3] Also, regulatory capital requirements focus on a firm's **Book Value of Equity (BVE)** and regulators can impose restrictions on dividend payments depending on the bank's level of NI and its financial leverage.[4] Thus, crafting a valuation model based on items that are easier to define (and observe) such as Net Income and Dividends will allow us to see more clearly the trade-offs between an FIs risks and expected returns.

Later, in this chapter, we provide a more detailed version of the valuation model which we call the **"Integrated Valuation Model"** (or **"IVM"** for short) because it attempts to integrate the main functions of a bank and its value drivers within one comprehensive system. But before discussing the IVM, we need to cover some of the fundamental sources of information about a bank, namely, those key items contained in its income statement and balance sheet. To do so, we start with a stylized Income Statement and then use this information to develop stylized versions of the FIs Balance Sheet and valuation model.

3.1.1 Stylized balance sheet

To begin our analysis, we present a basic, stylized balance sheet of a hypothetical financial institution, called **A Banking Company**, which we refer to as **"ABC"** in the following discussion.

---

[3] In the rare instance where a bank does not pay a dividend, we can still use the DDM but it will require the added step to forecast when in the future the bank would likely to start paying dividends. Once that is accomplished, we can then discount those dividends back to the present. For example, if the bank is expected to start paying dividends five years from now, we can value the firm at that point in time using the DDM and then discount this value back to the present to assess its current market value.

[4] For example, during the 2008–2009 Great Financial Crisis as well as the initial stages of the COVID-19 pandemic, regulators restricted dividends from several banks.

Assets	Value ($ mil.)	Liabilities & Equity	Value ($ mil.)
Cash & Reserves	$4	Deposits	$75
Investments	30	Other Borrowed Money	15
Net Loans	58		
Other Assets	8	Common Equity	10
Total Assets	$100	Total Liabilities & Equity	$100

As we had first noted in Chapter 1, an old saying that is quite appropriate for understanding a bank's financial statements is that "Form Follows Function." In our case, this means that the items appearing on a bank's Balance Sheet and Income Statement (i.e., the "Form") reflect the firm's primary lending, investing, and borrowing activities. As the above table shows, an FIs Balance Sheet captures the main features of a bank's actions (i.e., its "Function" as a Qualitative Asset Transformer).

The balance sheet is presented in an aggregated "T-account" format with ABC's assets on the left-hand side of the table and all the firm's liabilities and owner's equity reported on the right-hand side. The fundamental "Accounting Identity" requires that Assets = Liabilities + Equity. That is, a firm's Total Assets must equal Total Liabilities plus Owner's Equity because each dollar of a firm's Total Assets (TA) must be financed by creditors and equity investors.

Assets are listed in order based on their liquidity, with assets most easily converted to cash listed before less-liquid assets. Thus, *Cash & Reserves* are listed first, followed by *Investments* (which are typically marketable securities like U.S. Treasury notes and other fixed-income securities). *Net Loans* are less liquid than *Investments* and represent all loans and leases made by ABC. They are reported as *Net Loans* because the bank typically has some borrowers who do not repay their debts and thus ABC must set aside an estimate of possible future credit losses called the "Allowance for Loan Losses." Thus, *Net Loans* = *Total (or Gross) Loans* minus the bank's estimated *Allowance for Loan Losses (ALL)*. If the bank managers are doing a good job, the actual amount of credit losses will be a very small percentage of Gross Loans (usually 1% to 5%). In the above numerical example, we can assume ABC has granted $60 million in loans and has an ALL reserve of $2 million, thus leading to the $58 million in *Net Loans* reported on the balance sheet. The last item in the Assets column is *Other Assets* which represents all other assets, such as investments in buildings, equipment, intangibles, and goodwill. This last item is a catch-all category to ensure that the Accounting Identity holds. In terms of the concept of "Form follows Function," the FI can fulfill its role as a financial intermediary by investing in *Net Loans* (i.e., Gross Loans minus the Allowance for Loan Losses), marketable securities (Investments), as well as cash balances (Cash & Reserves) held in the central banking system.

The right-hand side of the above table is split into two parts: the amounts that creditors (Debt) and equity investors (Equity) have used to finance the firm's Total Assets. Since FIs are typically highly leveraged due to a heavy reliance on debt financing, we can divide the Debt category into several sub-categories. To keep it relatively simple, we break down the Debt item into two main sub-categories: Deposits and Other Borrowed Money (or OBM). In this case, OBM represents all other liabilities that are not defined as traditional bank deposits and includes "hot money" items that can be relatively quickly withdrawn from the balance sheet such as Fed Funds Purchased, Repurchase Agreements (repos), and Commercial Paper, as well as longer-term liabilities like Medium Term Notes and Long-Term Bonds.[5] Although Preferred Stock is a hybrid security that straddles both Debt and Equity, we can categorize it within the OBM bucket for ease of analysis for those FIs that use this financing instrument.[6]

Overall, the balance sheet is a great example of "Form follows Function" as we can see that our sample bank's assets are concentrated mostly in its lending and investing functions (via the *Net Loans* and *Investments* accounts) with nearly 90% of assets invested in these two categories. On the right-hand side of the balance sheet, we also see how most of the firm's financing reflects its function to provide stable sources of liquidity to customers via bank deposits (Deposits) and other short-term

---

[5] These "hot money" items are discussed in more detail when we examine Liquidity Risk in Chapter 8. Some of these items are also described in the introductory material of Chapter 1.

[6] Preferred stock is considered a hybrid security because it has no voting rights and usually has a fixed dividend rate (like bonds, but with quarterly rather than semi-annual payments). However, it is also lower in priority in terms of bankruptcy than other creditors (with only common stocks having lower priority). As we see in Chapter 11, preferred stock played an important role during the 2008–2009 U.S. financial crisis as a central component of the federal government's Troubled Assets Relief Program (TARP) of 2009 and ultimately helped mitigate risk throughout the global financial system, commonly referred to as "systemic risk."

debt instruments (OBM). This highlights the bank's role in providing "liquidity insurance," as first described in Chapter 1.

Another key characteristic of a bank's balance sheet is the relatively low amount of Common Equity used to finance the firm. As the above financial statement shows, ABC's *Total Assets* of $100 million are financed by only $10 million of *Common Equity*. This represents an Equity-to-Assets ratio (a.k.a. an "equity capital ratio") of 10% (i.e., $10/$100 = 0.10). A ratio of around 10% is common for a commercial bank and demonstrates the high degree of financial leverage that is needed for these firms to deliver their liquidity insurance services in an economically efficient manner.[7] As we discuss later in Chapter 10 on Capital Adequacy, this heavy reliance on debt to finance the bank's functions creates a potential concern with respect to the likelihood of bank insolvency (i.e., the possibility that assets are worth less than the bank's liabilities).

As an alternative to the T-account format presented above, the following formula, Equation (3.1), can also provide a concise way to describe a bank's balance sheet:

$$\begin{bmatrix} \text{Total Assets} = \text{Reserves} + (\text{Gross Loans} \\ \quad - \text{Allowance Loan Losses}) + \text{Investments} \\ \quad + \text{Other Assets} \\ = \text{Debt} + \text{Equity} \\ = \text{Deposits} + \text{Other Borrowed Money} + \text{Equity} \end{bmatrix} \quad (3.1)$$

As we show later in this chapter, we build upon Equation (3.1) and the income statement summarized in Equation (3.2) to help calculate a bank's market value of equity. So, having a good understanding of a bank's financial statements is essential to manage the firm's risks and maximize value for the bank's owners.

---

[7] Banks typically hold equity capital that exceeds the minimum regulatory requirements to serve as a "buffer" against unforeseen shocks to the economy and the banking industry. For example, Berger *et al.* (2008) show that total capital ratios in the U.S. are usually in the 12–14% range and Tier 1 capital ratios are frequently greater than 10%. However, banks cannot hold too much equity capital as this will cause the FIs return on equity to be too small if other banks can price their loans at similar loan rates (but do so when holding much less capital). That is, a bank that holds too much capital will not be economically efficient compared to its competitors and, in the end, the bank will lose its customers to other FIs that can afford to hold less capital while taking similar amounts of credit risk.

3.1.2 Stylized income statement

Like the balance sheet presented in the previous section, we can also develop an example of a stylized income statement for ABC, as shown in the following:

Income Statement	$ mil.	Calculations
Interest Income	$3.0	rL * Gross Loans = 0.05 * $60 = $3.0
Interest Expense	0.9	rD * (Deposits + OBM) = 0.01 * ($75 + $15) = $0.9
Net Interest Income (NII)	2.1	Interest Income − Interest Expense = $3.0 − $0.9 = $2.1
Loan Loss Provision (LLP)	0.1	ALL% * New Loans = 0.01 * $10 = $0.1
Non-Interest Income	1.0	Fee % * Total Assets = 0.01 * $100 = $1
Operating Expense	1.8	Operating Expense % * Total Assets = 0.018 * $100 = $1.8
Liquidity Risk Effects	0	Assumed to be zero for this example
Hedge Effects	0	Assumed to be zero for this example
Pretax Income	1.2	NII − LLP + Non-Int. Income − Oper. Exp. = $2.1 − 0.1 + 1.0 − 1.8 = $1.2
Taxes	0.3	Tax Rate (T) * Pretax Income = 0.25 * $1.2 = $0.3
Net Income (NI)	$0.9	Pretax Income − Taxes = $1.2 − $0.3 = $0.9

3.1.3 Overview of the main components of the stylized income statement

The bank generates fee income from providing services, for example, to small businesses and households (denoted here as *Non-Interest Income*) and earns *Interest Income* primarily from Loans, Leases, Investments in Marketable Securities, and bank Cash & Reserves. Larger financial firms can also have extensive trading, investment banking, and asset management operations, most of which generate fee income that would be included in the *Non-Interest Income* component of the above relationship. Bankers typically focus on the difference between the Interest Income they earn and the Interest Expense they pay, which is referred to as *Net Interest Income* (i.e., Net Interest Income = Interest Income − Interest Expense) as well as service-based fee income. All these items represent the "bread and butter" of banking and illustrate how banks can provide liquidity to customers by taking in deposits and making loans to earn an interest rate "spread" (the difference between the rate charged on loans and paid on deposits) and by collecting fees for asset management, brokerage, and other banking services.

In the above table, we have included a column labeled "Calculations" which provides some details on how we arrived at the various dollar values reported for ABC's income statement. For example, we make a simplifying assumption and assume *Interest Income* of $3 million is derived solely from the interest rate on loans ($rL = 5\% = 0.05$) and thus this rate is multiplied by the firm's Gross Loans ($60 million). In a more detailed example shown later in this chapter, we can relax this assumption so that Interest Income can also include interest earned on Investments as well as Cash & Reserves. Similarly, we can assume the average cost of *Deposits* and *OBM* (denoted as rD) is 1%. To find ABC's Interest Expense of $0.9 million, we can multiply rD by the firm's *Total Liabilities* (*Deposits* + *OBM*) of $75 million. This leads to ABC's Net Interest Income (NII) of $2.1 million, as shown in the above Income Statement. As we see, Net Interest Income is a key driver of a bank's cash flow and market value. Another potentially important source of cash flow is *Non-Interest Income*. Banks, especially larger firms, can generate a sizable share of their revenue via fees for various services such as arranging lines of credit, wire transfers, servicing mortgages, and possibly for non-banking activities such as brokerage, securities trading, and/or asset management.[8]

Due to FIs' essential "DNA" which requires them to take risks to provide the "special" services of liquidity creation and asset transformation for which banks are commonly known, the Income Statement also accounts for the effects of managing these risks.[9] For example, Loan Loss Provisions (LLP) represent a *non-cash* expense that takes account of the bank's best estimate about what will be the expected future *incremental* credit losses that are not already accounted for on the Balance Sheet via the Allowance for Loan Losses (ALL).[10] Thus, LLP appears on the

---

[8] Banks that provide a comprehensive set of both commercial banking and non-banking services are typically referred to as "universal banks."

[9] See Chapter 1 for a refresher on the "specialness" of FIs and why we wrote this book in the first place.

[10] More about the Balance Sheet's format is shown in the previous section of this chapter. Also, LLP is typically represented as a percentage of new loans.

income statement as the bank's best guess about *future* credit losses that are not already contained in the ALL portion of the prior period's balance sheet. In our example, we simply assume that ABC's LLP is based on the bank's existing ALL (expressed as a percentage of Gross Loans and denoted as "ALL%" in the above table). In our case, we assume 1% of the $10 million in new loans ABC made during the year might not be repaid and thus LLP is $0.1 million (0.01 · $10 million = $0.1 million).

The Income Statement also includes the costs of running the bank's day-to-day operations (denoted in the above equation as *Operating Expense*). ABC's income statement reports operating expenses of $1.8 million. To keep things simple, we assume that the ratio of Operating Expense-to-Total Assets equals 1.8% to capture the fact that a bank's expenses typically rise as the firm's assets grow.[11] Thus, we multiply this ratio by ABC's total assets of $100 million to obtain our estimated operating expense (0.018 · $100 million). Issues related to operating expenses and Operational Risk are covered later in Chapter 9.

In addition to the operational risk and credit risk noted above, Freixas and Rochet (2009) and Prisman *et al.* (1986) highlight the need to account for a bank's risk-taking and risk management choices that relate to handling customer demands for liquidity, either from borrowers demanding new loans or depositors and creditors suddenly withdrawing funds; these effects are sometimes called loan "takedown risk" and deposit "withdrawal risk," respectively. We capture the impact of these liquidity-related actions and denote them as *Liquidity Risk Effects*. For simplicity, we assume that the effects of liquidity risk are zero for ABC in the numerical example presented here in Chapter 3. More details on Off-Balance Sheet Risk and the related concept of Liquidity Risk are discussed in Chapters 7 and 8, respectively. For those familiar with accounting, one will note that it is *not* conventional according to Generally Accepted Accounting Principles (GAAP) to present a term such as *Liquidity Risk Effects* in an income statement. We include it here because it highlights the *economic* impact of the bank's risk management choices on Net Income. In most real-world financial statements, these effects would likely be embedded

---

[11] As we discuss later in this chapter, the bank's operating expenses can be deconstructed into two types: variable costs that vary with firm size and fixed costs such as investments in computer technology that might not vary with firm size. However, for the current example, we combine these costs into one operating expense ratio that varies with the bank's total assets.

within other main income statement variables or reported in some related footnotes to these statements.[12]

Another key area that FIs must contend with relates to fluctuations in interest rates and other financial market prices like those related to foreign currencies, commodities, and equities. To manage what we refer to as Interest Rate Risk (IR) and Market Risk, many FIs will use financial instruments called derivatives (e.g., forwards, futures, swaps, and options). These risk management choices can affect Net Income (NI), so we group these items together on our stylized Income Statement and call them *Hedging Effects*. The risk management actions related to derivatives and other mechanisms are discussed in greater detail later in Chapters 4 (Interest Rate Risk) and 5 (Market Risk). Like the treatment of *Liquidity Risk Effects*, the GAAP method typically does not include specific items on the income statement that explicitly refer to our concept of *Hedging Effects*.

For our purposes, it is better to construct a stylized income statement that explicitly shows a bank's true economic activities rather than try to follow GAAP methods that can obscure the bank's risk-taking and risk management decisions. However, for the numerical example in this chapter, we assume the effects of hedging activity are zero for ABC. Lastly, all for-profit firms must pay taxes on their profits and so we include *Taxes* to reflect the FIs' tax expense, which is also sometimes referred to as a tax provision. In this example, we assume ABC's effective tax rate is 25% and so we multiply this by ABC's *Pretax Income* of $1.2 million to obtain our $0.3 million estimate of the firm's *Taxes*.[13] Lastly, ABC's *Net Income* of $0.9 million can be found by subtracting *Taxes* from *Pretax Income* (i.e., $1.2 − $0.3 = $0.9 million). As we show in the following, ABC's net income is an important driver of the bank's market value of equity because it is an important source to pay a firm's dividends.

The income statement discussed here is summarized by the following formula, and we can label it as Equation (3.2):

---

[12] Some disclosure of liquidity-related risks can normally be found in the footnotes to a bank's financial statements but there is wide latitude in what a bank chooses to disclose publicly. So, in general, there is not a great deal of data available in these disclosures for an external bank analyst to use. In addition, banks must disclose more details about liquidity risk to regulators, but this information is kept confidential and thus an external analyst is not privy to these regulatory reports.

[13] Pretax Income can also be referred to as Earnings before Taxes (EBT) or Pretax Profit.

$$\begin{bmatrix} \text{NI} = \text{Interest Income} - \text{Interest Expense} - \text{Loan Loss Provision} \\ + \text{Non Interest Income} - \text{Oper. Exp.} + \text{Liquidity Risk} \\ \text{Effects} + \text{Hedge Effects} - \text{Taxes} \end{bmatrix} \quad (3.2)$$

This equation is an important component for estimating the bank's market value of equity, which is described in the following section.

3.2 Basic Framework for the Integrated Valuation Model (IVM)

As noted above, profits, dividends, and cash flows are all affected by trade-offs in a financial institution's risk-taking and risk management choices (e.g., due to the "specialness" of FIs as well as "organic" growth and unexpected market conditions, or "bumps in the road") which can lead to (semi)-random shocks to the market value of a firm's equity (V_E).

To create our "North Star" or "GPS" to help us navigate the sometimes confusing and counter-intuitive effects of various risk-taking choices, we need a valuation model that can integrate the main risks that a bank faces. Based on common textbook applications such as those found in Brigham and Ehrhardt (2020) and Brealey *et al.* (2020), we can construct a DCF-based valuation model that is mathematically equivalent to a Dividend Discount Model. As we had discussed in Chapter 2 regarding various valuation techniques, our approach shows how the firm's Free Cash Flow to Equity (FCFE) is equivalent (under the specific assumption that there is no new stock issuance) to the firm's Total Dividends (DIV). Since nearly all banks (both public and private) pay dividends, the dividend-focused approach is well suited for the financial services industry. For analytical convenience, we can also assume a constant growth (g) model so that we can create a tool that integrates all the FIs' main activities and risks within a manageable framework.[14,15]

---

[14] Technically speaking, we construct a stylized valuation model that integrates all the main FI risks but in a way that allows us to maximize a firm's equity without imposing an overwhelming number of constraints on the bank's optimization problem.

[15] It should also be noted that for this DDM method to produce an accurate result, firms must pay dividends optimally. In practice, there is no way to guarantee that the firm's management can formulate this optimal stream of dividends, and even if they did do that, there is no way as an external shareholder to force them to pay those dividends because managers have a great deal of discretion over what they do with the bank's profits.

3.2.1 An important concept to keep in mind: A model is an engine, not a camera

We must also remember that this valuation model is a simplification because we are distilling the key drivers of value into relatively few variables where, in practice, a financial institution faces numerous factors that can affect firm value. So, we use a simplified valuation model to test our "hypothesis" about what are the main drivers of firm value. As the Nobel Prize-winning economist Milton Friedman once said, "The only relevant test of the validity of a hypothesis is comparison of prediction with experience." MacKenzie (2006) uses this concept from Friedman in his book to suggest that financial models are an engine of inquiry rather than a camera, even if some of the model's assumptions seem unrealistic. That is, a good model is one that has enough factors to adequately (but not perfectly) describe reality and still allow the analyst to pose additional questions to the model and obtain useful answers. The approach presented in this chapter follows in this spirit and attempts to help us understand how different risk-taking and risk-management choices affect firm value in terms of *directional* changes or *trends* (rather than *exact* changes in value).

Stylized Valuation Model based on the Constant Growth Dividend Discount Model of an FIs equity (V_E):

$$V_E = \left[MVA - MVD = \frac{d \cdot NI}{(R_E - g)} \right] = \frac{0.4 \cdot \$0.9 \text{ million}}{(0.1024 - 0.0600)}$$

$$= \frac{\$0.36 \text{ million}}{(0.0424)} = \$8.491 \text{ million} \tag{3.3}$$

Equation (3.3) succinctly summarizes how the Market Value of Equity (V_E) is the difference between the firm's market values of Total Assets (MVA) and Debt (MVD). This, in turn, is determined by the firm's *Dividends* in the numerator ($DIV = d \cdot NI$), where d is the dividend payout ratio (i.e., $d = DIV/NI$) and NI is the bank's Net Income. To put some numbers in the formula, we have assumed a dividend payout ratio of 40% ($d = 0.40$) and used next year's NI estimate of $0.9 million shown earlier in ABC's stylized income statement, which results in an estimate of $0.36 million of total dividends. As we describe in more later in this section, we also assume the bank's expected cost of equity (R_E) is 10.24% and its constant growth rate is 6.00% which, in turn, leads to a market value of $8.491 million.

Keep in mind that regulators can also have an impact on the firm's dividend payout ratio by requiring the bank to maintain a minimum acceptable equity-to-asset capital ratio.[16] Thus, a firm might not be allowed to pay a dividend if the bank's ending common equity/asset ratio is below some recommended regulatory minimum that is considered "well capitalized." For example, if regulators would like to see a target equity/asset ratio of at least 8%, then the bank must first check whether the payment of a dividend would push the bank's equity/asset ratio *below* this threshold. If so, then the bank would have to suspend or cut its dividend and/or raise additional equity capital to bring this capital ratio back to 8%. Thus, the firm might have to sell additional stock to create an equity capital infusion that meets its 8% target capital ratio. In effect, such a capital infusion amounts to a "negative dividend."[17]

A bank manager can check how much of a dividend the firm can pay during the next period (DIV_1) by using the following relationship based on the current ($t = 0$) and expected ($t = 1$) levels of equity (E_0 and E_1), the target equity/asset ratio $(E/A)^*$, and the projected levels of Net Income (NI_1) and ending Total Assets (A_1):

$$DIV_1 = \{E_1 - \text{Target } E_1\} = (NI_1 + E_0) - \left[\left(\frac{E}{A}\right)^* \cdot A_1\right]$$

Based on the above relationship, we can create a numerical example based on our earlier assumptions of projected Net Income and Total Assets ($0.9 million and $100 million, respectively), a target equity/asset ratio (0.08), as well as the current level of common equity (assumed here to be $7.46 million). In this case, we can see that the bank has sufficient capital to pay the dividend of $0.36 million, which was originally estimated above with respect to the numerator of Equation (3.3). This can be seen from the following calculation:

---

[16] See Chapter 10 for more details and discussion of bank capital ratio requirements.

[17] Note that if the estimated dividend is negative, we *cannot* use the Constant Growth Dividend Discount Model (DDM) shown in Equation (3.3). Instead, we would need to use a multiple-period Discounted Cash Flow (DCF) model based on the bank's Free Cash Flow to Equity (FCFE). See Chapter 2 for more details on this DCF method, as well as other valuation approaches.

$$\mathrm{DIV}_1 = \{E_1 - \text{Target } E_1\} = (\mathrm{NI}_1 + E_0) - \left[\left(\frac{E}{A}\right)^* \cdot A_1\right]$$

DIV_1 = ($0.9 million + $7.46 million) − [0.08 · $100 million]
 = $8.36 million − $8.0 million
 = **$0.36 million**

For ease of presentation, we assume for all numerical valuation exercises in this book that our hypothetical bank, ABC, has sufficient equity capital to pay a dividend based on its desired payout ratio (d) and so we can use the constant growth version of the Dividend Discount Model for valuation purposes. We can think of this as the bank calculating the above DIV_1 estimate and then setting the payout ratio based on this dollar amount. However, in practice, senior management and board members at most banks try to set a dividend so that it grows at a relatively stable (if not exactly constant) growth rate that is in line with earnings growth. Thus, our assumption of using a constant payout ratio of d can be a reasonable approximation of real-world dividend payments for many financial institutions.

As mentioned earlier in terms of the denominator for Equation (3.3), we define the discount rate as the difference between the firm's Cost of Equity (R_E) of 10.24% and a constant, Sustainable Growth Rate (g) of 6.00% (or more precisely, 0.0600, in decimal format).[18] Plugging these three numbers into Equation (3.3) leads to an estimated market value of the bank (V_E) of $8.491 (with rounding). Since we are using millions of dollars as our measurement unit, this would mean that the bank's market value is $8.491 million (also known as its market capitalization, or "market cap," and defined as the stock price multiplied by the total number of equity shares outstanding). To find ABC's stock price, all we need to do is divide this market cap figure by the number of common shares outstanding. When doing this calculation, we need to make sure that we are using the *same measurement units*. For example, if the market cap is in millions of dollars, then we need to divide this number by the bank's shares outstanding (making sure that they are also expressed in millions

---

[18] In the Appendix to this chapter, we provide details on how to estimate a bank's expected equity return (R_E) based on the assumptions underlying the constant growth Dividend Discount Model that was introduced in Chapter 2.

64 *Managing Financial Institutions: An Integrated Valuation Approach*

of shares). If the bank has 1 million common shares outstanding, then the estimated stock price is $8.49 per share when rounded to the nearest penny (i.e., $8.491 million / 1 million shares).

In this format, the valuation model allows us to focus on the three key drivers of firm value: the **Magnitude** of cash flows (DIV), the **Riskiness** of the cash flows (R_E), and the **Timing** of cash flows, where *Timing* relates to *when* the dividends will occur in the future and is captured by the growth in dividends (*g*). Thus, the above model provides a concise analytical framework based on the acronym **MRT** and helps us understand how the level of expected dividends (*DIV*) can be converted into a present value of all future cash flows by using an appropriate discount rate (R_E) that is adjusted for risk and an assumed constant growth rate (*g*) in those dividends. Thus, we can analyze the effectiveness of bank decisions by focusing on these three main variables, which we refer to as "*value drivers*."

The above discussion of the stylized versions of a bank's financial statements and valuation model is useful to understand the basics of a firm's financial condition. However, a more detailed valuation model can help us **quantify the trade-offs between risk and return** that a bank faces in most real-world settings. So, we build on the stylized valuation model and extend it in some important ways in the following section.

3.3 A More Detailed Version of the Integrated Valuation Model and Its Components

The following two equations (3.4 and 3.5) include more details beyond the Stylized Income Statement and Valuation Model discussed in the previous section. After presenting the key NI and valuation equations here, we provide extensive explanations of each of the variables in Table 3.1 and the following text:

$$NI = \begin{bmatrix} \begin{pmatrix} (rL \cdot L) - (LLP) + (rS \cdot S) + (rRes \cdot R) - \\ (rD \cdot D) + (f \cdot A) - ((ovc + ofc) \cdot A) + \\ (\text{Liquidity Risk Effects}) + (\text{Hedge Effects}) \end{pmatrix} \cdot (1-t) \end{bmatrix} \quad (3.4)$$

When we substitute the more detailed description of Net Income into the stylized valuation model, we can use the following equation to create our more comprehensive valuation model, which we have referred to earlier as the *Integrated Valuation Model*, or IVM, in brief. This name is used to highlight the fact that the valuation model integrates both the FIs risk-taking and risk-management choices in an explicit way so that we can identify the primary positive and negative effects of management's decisions on firm value in a more direct manner:

$$V_E = \left[\frac{d \cdot \left[\left(\begin{array}{c} \text{Bank Operating Profit} + \\ \text{Liquidity Risk Effects} + \text{Hedge Effects} \end{array} \right) \cdot (1-t) \right]}{\text{Expected Dividend Yield}} \right]$$

$$= \left[\frac{d \cdot \left[\left(\begin{array}{c} (rL \cdot L) - (\text{LLP}) + (rS \cdot S) + (r\text{Res} \cdot R) \\ -(rD \cdot D) + (f \cdot A) - ((ovc + ofc) \cdot A) \\ + (\text{Liquidity Risk Effects}) + (\text{Hedge Effects}) \end{array} \right) \cdot (1-t) \right]}{(R_E - g)} \right] \quad (3.5)$$

where Bank Operating Profit = a summary variable for all items *not* directly included in the bank's risk management decisions $= ((rL \cdot L) - (\text{LLP}) + (rS \cdot S) + (r\text{Res} \cdot R) - (rD \cdot D) + (f \cdot A) - ((ovc + ofc) \cdot A)(1-t)$, Liquidity Risk Effects + Hedge Effects = the impact on cash flows from all bank risk management-related decisions, and Expected Dividend Yield = $(R_E - g)$.

3.3.1 Interest income

Recall from our stylized Income Statement shown earlier in Equation (3.2) that the first set of terms in this financial statement is Interest Income. In Equation (3.5), let rL be the average lending rate of the bank and L be the amount of gross loans. Hence, $(rL \cdot L)$ is the bank's lending income. Since the business of lending is risky, we need to adjust for the likelihood that some loans will not be repaid and so we include a non-cash deduction from Interest Income called Loan Loss Provision (LLP).[19] As we mentioned earlier when describing the stylized income statement, there are typically two other key components of Interest Income: income from securities investments as well as interest earned on reserves and cash balances held at the central bank. Thus, we include income earned on investments ($rS \cdot S$) in the numerator of Equation (3.5), where rS is the percentage return on the bank's securities portfolio and S is the dollar amount of assets invested in this portfolio. We also include interest income from reserves and cash balances ($rRes \cdot R$), where rRes is the percentage return on the bank's reserves and cash balances while R is the dollar amount of assets held at the central bank (such as the Federal Reserve in the U.S.).

3.3.2 Interest expense

We also include the **cost of the bank's debt funding**, ($rD \cdot D$), which represents the average interest rate the bank pays on all debt (including deposit and other borrowed money, or OBM), multiplied by the total amount of debt. The bank can also generate non-interest revenue which is usually referred to as Non-Interest Income. For example, fees and commissions generated from a bank's lending and deposit-taking activities as well as its brokerage unit and/or asset management business would be included in *Non-Interest Income* rather than in Net Interest Income. Larger firms might also have trading units that not only generate fees and commissions but can also capture "spreads" between the costs of buying and selling securities when serving as a dealer or market maker for derivatives and other financial instruments.[20] To account for this, we include the term ($f \cdot A$), which multiplies a non-interest revenue fraction, f, by the bank's total assets, A.

---

[19] These credit-related concepts, as well as other concepts related to the rest of this formula, are covered in greater detail in subsequent chapters. We briefly introduce these terms here to help understand the key components within the IVM; refer to later chapters for more details on these items (such as Chapter 6 on Credit Risk).

[20] These types of activities related to derivatives are discussed in greater detail in Chapter 7 (Off-Balance Sheet Risk).

3.3.3 Non-interest expenses

The bank can also incur non-interest expenses. We capture these in the form of operating expenses with the term, $((ovc + ofc) \cdot A)$. This term accounts for *variable* operating costs (ovc) and *fixed* operating costs (ofc) as a proportion of total assets, A. This is a simplifying assumption for the current numerical example, but, in reality, fixed costs such as investments in computer technology or offices might not vary with firm size dollar-for-dollar and instead could increase in a "lumpy" fashion (i.e., technology costs might remain fixed up until $10 billion in asset size and then will jump to a much higher level of fixed costs to handle additional capacity above $10 billion). Unless we are working within the bank itself as a manager or analyst, we will normally not have sufficiently detailed data to compute these two items separately and so we can focus here on the sum of the two ($ovc + ofc$) for modeling purposes.[21] As noted in Equation (3.5) all the above terms, including the corporate tax rate, t, can be categorized as the "Bank Operating Profit" that is generated by the firm when management does *not* choose to hedge any of its risks. We can think of this value as the profit the bank would earn from a "No Hedge" or "Do Nothing" **risk management policy**.

3.3.4 Liquidity risk effects

We also include a term that captures the *Liquidity Risk Effects*. For example, if a customer borrows from its line of credit or loan commitment, the bank may face a potentially large, unexpected demand to find cash to fund this loan, referred to as W in Table 3.1. Conversely, a depositor might decide to quickly withdraw a large sum of cash from its checking account, thus straining the bank's liquidity needs. In this situation, the bank addresses these needs by drawing on its cash and investment securities (denoted as S^*) and/or by using OBM. As we discuss in much greater detail in Chapter 8 on Liquidity Risk, there are many ways to model this effect and so we assume

---

[21] Note that many bank analysts also compute another ratio called the "Efficiency Ratio" where the bank's Non-Interest Expense (what we refer to as Operating Expenses) is divided by the sum of the bank's Net Interest Income and Non-Interest Expense (less the firm's Loan Loss Provisions). This is a useful ratio, but for our valuation model, the above usage of ovc and ofc is a more direct way to understand how operational risk can affect firm value (which is discussed in more detail in Chapter 9, Operational Risk).

here the following: rP · ($E[\max(0, W - S^*)]$). In this case, rP is a penalty rate (that is, a higher rate the bank pays as a tradeoff for obtaining immediate cash) that the bank must pay on any expected liquidity drains in excess of its reserve of cash and securities, S^*, as described by $E[\max(0, W - S^*)]$, where $E[\cdot]$ stands for an expected value. More details about this liquidity risk effect and other details related to the valuation model shown in Equation (3.5) can be found in Table A3.1, as well as Table A3.2 in the Appendix.

3.3.5 Hedge effects

Finally, we capture the effect of the bank's decision to hedge risk with the *Hedge Effects* by assuming there are explicit marginal costs related to managing this risk relative to its implicit marginal benefits. We model this effect by including the following term: Σ_j [$Reduction in market-related Risk Exposures — (Fixed Hedging Costs + Variable Hedging Costs)]. As discussed in more detail in Chapters 4 and 5, this term can capture the bank's hedging decision for each risk, j, and j can represent the risk reduction effects for various sources of risk related to interest rates, currencies, commodities, stocks, etc. In this set-up, we can include both fixed and variable costs of managing each of these various risks by using a derivative security such as a forward contract or an interest rate swap (where these instruments are discussed in Chapter 7, Off-Balance Sheet Risk).

Overall, Equation (3.5) identifies three key drivers of a bank's profitability: (1) "traditional" pretax operating profit, (2) the effects of liquidity risk management, and (3) all other hedging decisions. Despite the above discussion of each of the components of this equation, it is still a rather daunting formula. Thus, if we provide some more numerical details about the equation's key components, then its usefulness to quantify the trade-offs between risk and return will become clearer. So, let's plug some numbers into the above equation to get a sense of how the model works.

3.4 An Example of the Integrated Valuation Model (IVM)

Given the valuation model presented earlier, a useful next step is to learn how to apply this model to real-world financial institutions. However, before moving into real-world data, it is usually a good idea to construct a more detailed numerical example to gain some intuition about how different choices related to risk-taking and risk management can affect a bank's market value of equity (V_E). The numbers presented in Table 3.1 are purely hypothetical so that we can value the imaginary bank we have called "ABC." More detailed descriptions and definitions of the model's variables and how to obtain these estimates are presented after this numerical example. Also, for simplicity, we assume zero values for the *Liquidity Risk Effects* and *Hedging Effects* variables, since these effects can be quite complicated and are discussed in more detail in subsequent Chapters 4–9. The table below provides the numerical assumptions for each component in the valuation formula shown in Equation (3.5). In the Appendix, we provide an additional table (Table A3.2) which gives a more detailed description of these variables and how they relate to our IVM method.

Plugging the numbers from the above table into the IVM, ABC's value can be calculated as follows:

$$V_E = \left[\frac{0.40 \cdot \left[\begin{array}{c} (0.050 \cdot \$830) - (\$4) + (0.025 \cdot \$700) \\ + (0.015 \cdot \$25) - (0.0199 \cdot \$1400) \\ + (0.0136 \cdot \$1580) - ((0.0142) \cdot \$1580) \\ + (\$0) + (\$0) \end{array} \right] \cdot (1 - 0.20)}{(0.0859399 - 0.0505529)} \right] \quad (3.6)$$

V_E = \$6.066343 / 0.0353870 = **\$171.428**
Estimated Market Value of Equity (MVE_{t+1}) of ABC
= **\$171.428** million
Estimated SP_{t+1} = VE / Common Shares Outstanding
= \$171.428 million / 10.0 million = **\$17.14** *(rounded)*

As the above calculation shows, the expected market value of ABC's equity (MVE) is \$171.428 million. This is commonly referred to as a bank's market cap. Dividing this market cap by the number of common equity shares outstanding leads to an expected stock price per share of \$17.14. Remember that the numbers used for calculating these estimates must be on a *similar scale* in terms of unit size. For example, if the financial statement data are all reported in millions of dollars, then it is very important for the analyst to use a figure for common shares outstanding that is also in millions of shares. In this way, one can interpret the above numbers as a market cap of \$171.428 million, and then, by dividing by the bank's 10 million shares outstanding, we can find the stock price of \$17.14 per share.

Table 3.1. Detailed Numerical Assumptions for the IVM of a hypothetical bank ("ABC").

Description	Variable	Value
Total Assets	A = (Gross Assets − ALL)	\$1,580 = \$1,610 − \$30 (for ALL)
Total Liabilities	D	\$1,400
Other Assets	Net Fixed Assets + Goodwill	\$55
Lending Rate	rL	0.0500
Gross Loans	L	\$830
Allowance for Loan Losses	ALL	\$30
Loan Loss Provisions	LLP	\$4
Return on Securities	rS	0.0250
Securities Investments	S	\$700
Return on Cash & Reserves	$rRes$	0.0150
Cash Balances & Reserves	R	\$25
Cost of Funds	rD	0.0199
Non-Interest Income (% of A)	f	0.0136
Operating Expenses (% of A)	$ovc + ofc$	0.0142
Liquidity Risk Effects	$rP \cdot$ Unexpected shock = $rP \cdot (E[\max(0, W - S^*)])$	Set to zero for this example (see Chapter 8 for a more detailed discussion of Liquidity Risk)
Hedging Effects	$\sum_j$ [\$ Reduction in various bank-related Risk exposures − (fixed hedging costs + variable hedging costs)]	Set to zero for this example (see Chapters 4–7, and 9 for a more detailed discussion)
Tax Expense	$t = (1 - NI/EBT)$	0.20
Dividend Payout	$d = DIV / NI$	0.40
Sustainable Growth Rate	$g = (1 - d) \cdot ROE$	0.60 · 0.0838889 = **0.0505529**

Table 3.1. (Continued)

Description	Variable	Value
Expected Equity Return	$R_E = DY_t + \{[(1-d) + DY_t - (d \cdot DY_t)] \cdot ROE_{t+1}\}$	($5.12 / $152.00) + [(0.60 + 0.033684 − (0.40 · 0.033684)]· (0.0842548) = 0.033684 + (0.620210 · 0.0842548) = 0.033684 + 0.0522557 ≈ **0.0859399**
Prior Year's Dividend	$DIV_t = d \cdot NI$	$5.12 = 0.4 · $12.8
Prior Year's Net Income	NI_t	$12.8
Common Shares Outstanding	Shares O/S_t	10.0
Prior Year's MV of Equity (MVE_t)	$SP_t \cdot$ Shares O/S_t	$152.000
Prior Year's Stock Price	SP_t	$15.20
Estimated MV of Equity (MVE_{t+1})	$SP_{t+1} \cdot$ Shares O/S_t	$171.428
Estimated Stock Price	SP_{t+1}	$17.14

What we have done here is called "fundamental analysis" where the analyst develops forecasts for the key "MRT" factors that affect NI, DIV, R_E, and g in the valuation model. The resulting estimate of $17.14 is sometimes referred to as the "intrinsic value" of the firm's stock and this figure can then be compared to the current stock price ($15.20 in this example) to see if the firm is under-, over-, or fairly valued at this time. If, as is the case with our example, the intrinsic value estimate ($17.14) is greater than the current stock price ($15.20), then we would say the firm is "undervalued."[22] This finding could present a good opportunity to buy the stock

---

[22] Conversely, if our intrinsic value estimate was below $15.20 (e.g., $10), then the stock is "over-valued" and we should either avoid buying the stock at this time or, if we are bold enough to assume extra risk, we could "short" the stock today by borrowing shares in ABC and then selling them today at the (high) price of $15.20 with the hopes of buying them back at the lower $10 price in the future. In addition, most analysts consider a stock to be "fairly valued" if the estimated intrinsic value is within +/− 5% of the current stock price.

because it would represent a 12.8% increase in price (assuming our forecast is right and other investors eventually agree with us!). This type of analysis and investing, where one buys undervalued securities, is typically referred to as "value investing" and several successful investors like Warren Buffett have followed this type of investment approach.

Another point to consider in the above numerical example is the number of decimal places to use for the above calculations. As Table 3.1 shows, most of the numbers are reported with one to six decimals, whereas the final calculation of market cap contains NI and $(R_E - g)$ values that display seven decimals. The reason for the extra precision in the MVE calculation is that slight differences in either NI or $(R_E - g)$ can make for some relatively important changes in the result; this is especially true when R_E and g are relatively close in value. For example, if we were to use less granular estimates of NI and $(R_E - g)$ such as $6.0 and 0.036 (via 0.086 − 0.050 = 0.036), then the estimated MVE would be $166.667 million, which is nearly $4.8 million *less* than our earlier estimate (a difference of 2.9%). To the prospective sellers of ABC's stock, it pays to be more precise because a shareholder does not want to receive less than the bank's intrinsic value, especially by a total of around $4.8 million! However, we must always keep in mind that this estimate is based on a valuation model that contains *many* assumptions (such as constant growth rates) and so it is usually a good idea to round the stock price computation to at most two decimals or even less depending on the analyst's needs (such as whole dollars with no decimals, i.e., use $17 rather than $17.14).

To make it easier to apply the above IVM with real-world banking data, we make an Excel-based spreadsheet available in conjunction with this textbook. This spreadsheet can perform more complex calculations than those presented here and uses constrained optimization techniques within Excel's **Solver** function to compute a firm's maximum value subject to its resource and regulatory constraints.[23] For our purposes here, though, we focus on the key components of the above equation based on the previous paragraph's numerical example.

---

[23] See Chapter 12 (Integrated Risk Management: Putting it all together) for details on how to use this Excel™ spreadsheet to estimate the impact on a bank's market value of equity of the various risks described throughout this book.

3.4.1 *Main Drivers of Value: Dividend Payout Ratio, Sustainable Growth, and Expected Equity Return*

In Equations (3.5) and (3.6), we pulled together the three drivers of value that we discussed earlier in the context of **MRT** (Magnitude, Riskiness, and Timing of cash flows). First, in the numerator, we define the **Dividend Payout Ratio**, *d*, as the ratio of Dividends divided by Net Income (DIV / NI) so that d represents the portion of a bank's profit that is distributed to shareholders each year. We then multiply d by the firm's expected NI to formulate our estimate of next year's expected Total Dividend (DIV). As we can see from the Integrated Valuation Model presented in this chapter, DIV represents the **Magnitude** of cash flow and is an important driver of firm value.

Another key value driver is the bank's "Sustainable Growth Rate" (*g*) which provides us with an estimate of how fast the firm's earnings and dividends can grow without issuing new equity or changing the bank's profitability and capital structure. As shown in finance textbooks like Brigham and Ehrhardt (2020), the sustainable growth rate can be estimated by multiplying the firm's Return on Equity (ROE = NI / Common Equity) by its "Retention Ratio" (i.e., one minus the Dividend Payout ratio, or $1 - d$). Clearly, there are many other ways to estimate a firm's growth rate, but we use this definition for its relative simplicity and internal consistency with the rest of the constant growth DDM approach. Thus, we can use the following equation to estimate this growth rate: $g = (1 - d) \cdot ROE$.[24] This formula captures the **Timing** of cash flows within the "MRT" concept of firm value.

Lastly, we estimate the bank's "Expected Equity Return" (R_E). This variable is the most difficult variable to estimate because it must capture the analyst's best guess of what shareholders anticipate in terms of a satisfactory return on its stock investment. There are numerous ways to estimate R_E, including sophisticated asset pricing models, such as the Capital Asset Pricing Model (CAPM) first developed in Sharpe (1964), and multi-factor models, such as those found in Fama and French (1993, 2015) and Carhart (1997), among many others.[25] However, these

---

[24] For a comparison of alternative models of estimating a firm's growth rate, see Brick et al. (2016).

[25] A brief discussion of the CAPM is presented in the Appendix of this chapter in case an analyst would prefer to use this method to estimate the bank's cost of equity rather than one presented here.

approaches require a relatively large amount of data that is external to the bank's own financial statements. In addition, there is no clear consensus among academics and practitioners as to which asset pricing model is the correct one to use.

A simpler, internally consistent approach that does not require a formal asset pricing model is suggested in Brigham and Ehrhardt (2020) and other general finance textbooks. In this simpler approach, a stock's *expected* return can be decomposed into two components: (1) an expected **dividend yield** for the next period (where this is the income from dividends at time $t+1$ divided by the market value of the firm's equity at time t, $DY_{t+1} = \frac{DIV_{t+1}}{MVE_t}$) and (2) a **capital gain** (which equals the projected percentage change in the firm's stock price). When we assume the stock market is efficient, the firm's MVE will fully incorporate this *expected* return and, in equilibrium, this return will also be equal to the firm's *required* return. However, one benefit of our approach is that it does not require the financial markets to be in equilibrium. Thus, we use this expected return concept to estimate the return on equity (R_E) as the sum of the stock's expected dividend yield and its projected capital gain. In addition, we can use the bank's sustainable growth rate (g) as our estimate of the firm's capital gain.[26] The expected dividend yield is based on the dividend payout ratio and the projected net income for the next year ($d \cdot NI_{t+1}$) divided by the current market value of equity. This latter term can be referred to in abbreviated form as "MVE" or V_E and can be calculated as follows: MVE_t = current stock price, SP_t, multiplied by the current Common Shares Outstanding. So, we can define the bank's expected equity return (R_E) with the following equation[27]:

---

[26] Importantly, the capital gains rate is also related to the firm's dividend payments. The firm faces a choice as to how much profit to pay out in dividends relative to how much profit to reinvest. So, as long as the firm continues to allow dividends to grow at a constant rate and the firm's profitability and capital structure remains constant (as measured by ROE), then Net Income will also grow at this same rate. Thus, when the firm's discount rate (R_E) stays the same, the constant growth in net income and dividends will enable the market value of the firm's equity to grow at a constant capital gains rate that is equal to the sustainable growth rate, g.

[27] A detailed derivation of Equations (3.7)–(3.9) is provided in the Appendix to this chapter. Also, note these relationships indicate, via some basic algebra, that the expected dividend yield, DY_{t+1}, is equal to ($R_E - g$). Thus, the expected dividend yield is an important driver of the bank's market value because it captures both the expected return on the bank's equity, R_E, as well its constant growth rate estimate, g.

R_E = Expected Dividend Yield + Projected Capital Gain = $DY_{t+1} + g$
where

$$DY_{t+1} = \frac{(d \cdot NI_{t+1})}{V_E} = DY_t \cdot (1+g) \qquad (3.7)$$

$$g = (1-d) \cdot ROE_{t+1} \qquad (3.8)$$

We can then go one step further and substitute the above definitions of DY_{t+1} and g into the R_E formula and do some algebraic re-arranging to obtain the following expected equity return (R_E):

$$R_E = DY_t + \{[(1-d) + DY_t - (d \cdot DY_t)] \cdot ROE_{t+1}\} \qquad (3.9)$$

The above relationship shows that the shareholders' expected return is based on three key variables: (1) the bank's current dividend yield at time t (DY_t), (2) the dividend payout ratio (d), and (3) the expected return on the book value of equity (ROE_{t+1}). Estimates of these variables can be developed easily once we have collected the relevant data from the bank's financial statements as well as market-based data for its current dividend yield (all of which are available at low or no cost from popular finance websites, such as finance.yahoo.com). Equation (3.9) represents the **Riskiness** of cash flows within the "MRT" concept of firm value.

Further, we should also note that theoretical and empirical research by Gao and Martin (2021) supports our approach by showing that one can use a firm's current dividend yield to develop optimal estimates of a firm's cost of equity (R_E) and expected growth rate (g). The authors find that the **expected dividend yield** (equivalent to our $R_E - g$ term) and the classic constant growth Dividend Discount Model can be effective in describing real-world variation in stock prices. Thus, our method not only has the virtue of being straightforward to estimate but also is based on a solid theoretical and empirical foundation as described in Gao and Martin (2021).

3.5 How to use the IVM to Explore the Impact of Risk on the Market Value of Equity

Now that we have a better understanding of the IVM and its components, we can use the above data to see how ABC's lending decisions affect the firm's credit risk and market value of equity. Although Chapter 6 is devoted to Credit Risk, the current section provides a brief and early introduction to this key activity of all commercial banks. Most banks earn the largest portion of their revenue by lending to individuals, corporations, and other organizations. Bankers must price their loan rates to reflect the credit risk FIs face, i.e., the prospect that some borrowers will not pay them back.

In this example, we concentrate on the bank's allocation of assets to its loan portfolio, which can be expressed as the percentage of Total Gross Assets that are invested in loans. We define this percentage allocation to loans, C, where C = Gross Loans/Total Gross Assets.[28] As the bank changes its "credit allocation," (C) it might need to change its loan rate (denoted as rL in the IVM). For example, if the bank raises C by a large amount, it means the firm is making more loans than in the past. This could be driven by granting more credit within existing markets and/or lending to riskier clients. Thus, as the bank tries to raise its allocation of assets to loans, it will have to search harder for prospective clients and will ultimately be forced to lend to financially weaker borrowers. Thus, **the bank's credit risk is expected to rise as C is increased within our model's set-up**.[29]

As C rises, the bank will want to guard against higher default risk by increasing its **lending rate**, rL, assuming other "macro" factors remain constant (such as U.S. Treasury yields and inflation rates).[30] Likewise, the bank's creditors (both depositors and "OBM" lenders that are not protected by deposit insurance) may become nervous as C increases because it means that the bank's own credit risk is rising. In effect, the bank's choice to raise C sets off a chain reaction where the riskiness of the bank's

---

[28] Total Gross Assets adds back the bank's Allowance for Loan Losses to Total Assets that are normally reported on the balance sheet because Interest Income is generated on Gross Loans rather than Net Loans (i.e., Net Loans = Gross Loans – Allowance for Loan Losses).

[29] Keep in mind that there are many ways to quantify the bank's numerous choices and so the approach presented here is just one example of how credit risk can affect a bank's profitability and market value. Also, note that sensitivity and scenario analyses can help provide a more complete picture of the bank's risk-return trade-offs with respect to credit risk.

[30] Lending rates are usually based on some underlying interest rates that are relatively risk-free like U.S. Treasury securities, the Federal Funds rate, and Secured Overnight Financing Rate (SOFR). For example, fixed rate residential mortgages in the U.S. are typically based off the 10-year U.S. Treasury note's yield.

pool of loans increases. In turn, this translates into more uncertainty about the bank's ability to pay back its own creditors and leads to the unpleasant outcome that these creditors will then demand a higher rate on their uninsured deposits and OBM securities (referred to as **the interest rate on debt**, rD, in our model).

Although Chapter 6 goes into more detail on credit risk, we can show one possible way to quantify the chain reaction described above by allowing C to affect *both* the bank's lending rate (rL) and financing rate (rD), as follows:

$$rL = rL^* \cdot (1+C) \tag{3.10}$$

$$rD = rD^* \cdot (1+C)^C \tag{3.11}$$

where

rL^* = base lending rate that the bank would charge very low-risk customers and

rD^* = base financing rate that the creditors would charge a very low-risk bank.

Equations (3.10) and (3.11) allow both the lending and financing rates to increase as C is raised.[31] For simplicity, we assume the financing rate (rD) rises faster than the lending rate (rL) because the creditors of the bank are typically more sensitive to credit risk due to the highly leveraged nature of commercial banks. In reality, a bank manager would need to assess the riskiness and related rates for several different types of loan and deposit products based on internal bank pricing methods. We chose C as our key driver of these rates because it is easily observable by an external analyst.

---

[31] Theoretical justification for this functional form can be found in the seminal work on credit risk by Stiglitz and Weiss (1981). These authors showed that when borrowers know more about their ability to repay a loan than the lender (commonly referred to as an "asymmetric information" problem), the lender must guard against credit losses by charging a higher "promised" loan rate to achieve an acceptable "expected" net return on the loan. Thus, rL and rD are positively related to our proxy for credit risk, C, in the model. This relationship is driven by a "sorting" effect (a higher rL attracts riskier borrowers) and an "incentive" effect (where a higher rL emboldens borrows to engage in riskier behavior that leads to even greater credit risk). Both forces lead to a positive and potentially nonlinear relationship between credit risk (C) and the lending and financing rates shown in the above equations.

However, for an analyst within the bank, the FIs internal pricing models for lending and financing rates can be used instead of simply relying on C. The term, $(1 + C)^C$, in the rD equation captures the greater sensitivity of deposits by making the financing rate rise exponentially, especially as C is increased to very high levels.[32] In contrast, the bank itself will typically lend to relatively safe borrowers (those that have much less financial leverage) so that the bank's credit risk exposure is more manageable than the risk that other creditors might face. This effect is captured by the term $(1 + C)$ in the rL equation, which shows that the lending rate rises slower (and linearly) in comparison to the financing rate as C is increased.

We can now insert the above relationships for rL and rD into the IVM and start the analysis using the same interest rates that were used in the earlier numerical example (i.e., $rL = 0.050$ and $rD = 0.0199$). We also use ABC's level of loans and gross assets previously reported in Table 3.2 to compute C as follows: \$830 million / \$1,610 million = 0.5155. This reveals that the bank has a little more than 50% of its assets currently invested in loans. The level of C (0.5155) and the assumed starting values for rL (0.05) and rD (0.02) can then be used algebraically to find that the "base lending rate" (rL^*) and "base financing rate" (rD^*) are 0.0330 and 0.0161, respectively. These base rates can then be combined with different levels of C to see how the bank's lending and financing rates might respond to changes in credit risk. As we have previously noted several times, there are many ways to quantify the bank's numerous choices and so the approach presented here is just one example of how credit risk can affect a bank's profitability and market value.

Plugging the above numbers into the IVM leads to a stock price that is exactly the same as what we calculated earlier: \$17.14. This should not be that surprising because in this case we are using the same assumptions about lending and financing rates as in the earlier example and the level of C matches the bank's prior level of lending activity at 0.5155 (or 51.55% of Gross Assets). The interesting part of the analysis occurs when we vary the level of C from 0% to 100% to see how both rD and rL change. In effect, as C initially rises, the higher levels of rL outweigh the

---

[32] Although this relationship is chosen for its relative simplicity in capturing the possible nonlinear (and linear) dynamics of lending and financing rates, there is some empirical evidence that supports this assumption. Ozgur et al. (2021) employ a machine learning approach and report that the key drivers of bank lending exhibit nonlinearities related to both bank-related characteristics and macroeconomic factors.

Introducing the Integrated Valuation Model 79

gains in *rD* and so Net Interest Income starts to increase. However, at some point, as *C* continues to increase, *rD* will begin to rise faster than *rL* and can ultimately surpass the lending rate, thus causing Net Interest Income to eventually decline and even turn negative.[33] Given this effect, we expect that ABC's stock price will initially benefit as *C* increases but will fall if *C* is too high.

To build some intuition about what is driving the impact of credit risk on ABC's market value of equity, we first describe the results of a "what-if" simulation that quantifies the total costs and benefits of altering the bank's credit risk. Based on Equation (3.10), we can see that the benefits of a higher lending rate (*rL*) rise linearly with increased credit risk (i.e., due to the term, $1 + C$). In contrast, Equation (3.11) shows that the financing cost (*rD*) rises even faster at an exponential rate (i.e., via $(1 + C)^C$). This pattern is driven by the assumption that the bank will have to lend to riskier borrowers as C increases because there is only a limited number of "safe" borrowers within ABC's operating region. Thus, at low levels of credit risk (e.g., $C < 0.5$), the marginal benefits of lending to "safe" borrowers are greater than the marginal costs. Therefore, an increase in credit risk beyond 0.5 can maximize ABC's stock price. However, at very high levels of credit risk (e.g., $C > 0.7$), the marginal costs of taking on riskier borrowers outweigh the marginal benefits. This dynamic leads to an optimal level of credit risk, C^*, that lies somewhere between 0.5 and 0.7 (or, 50–70% of the bank's total assets). These patterns for lending, financing, and investor returns are shown in Figure 3.1.

As the above graph shows with the solid curved line, higher levels of *C* along the horizontal axis have *nonlinear effects* on the cost of debt (*rD*)

---

[33] The bank's expected cost of equity (R_E) will initially increase as the cost of debt rises because, as shown earlier in Equation (3.9), R_E is directly affected by changes in forecasted Net Income (NI) and ROE. So, in contrast to an equilibrium asset pricing model of *required* returns, our *expected* returns method allows NI to rise and fall dynamically depending on how *C* affects interest income and interest expense. For example, we show in Figure 3.1 that as *rD* begins to rise faster than *rL*, NI will fall, holding all else constant which, in turn, causes ROE and R_E to decrease at very high levels of credit issuance, *C*. This nonlinear pattern for R_E is consistent with a rational investor's expectations about future returns and, in our setup, allows the investor to earn a constant dividend yield (DY_{t+1}) across the entire credit risk spectrum (assuming there are no constraints on the bank's sustainable growth rate).

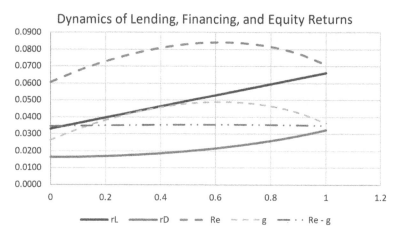

Figure 3.1. The Effect of Credit Risk on a Bank's Lending, Financing, and Equity Returns.

which, in turn, cause the dashed lines for both R_E and g to rise and then fall in tandem due to variations in the bank's Net Income (with a peak when C is around 0.6). Also, notice that this dynamic relationship between C and NI leads to a constant rate for the ($R_E - g$) term across all levels of C (at around 0.035, or 3.5%). Recall that $R_E - g$ is equal to the bank's expected dividend yield (DY_{t+1}). Figure 3.1 shows that an investor can earn a predictable return of around 3.5% on dividends in this numerical example. This outcome is due to our model's assumptions of constant growth (g) and expected equity return (R_E) that are both driven by changes in the firm's ROE, as well as a stable dividend payout ratio (d). The somewhat unrealistic assumption of a perpetually stable payout policy is a limitation of the model and reminds us that we cannot take the specific market value estimates too literally. However, it should also be noted that most bank managers strive to deliver stable, growing dividends that generate a predictable dividend yield which is attractive to income-oriented investors. Thus, our model's dividend assumptions do not strictly hold but might still serve as a reasonably good approximation of real-world dividend activity.

It should also be noted that the Constant Growth DDM imposes a *theoretical limit* on the sustainable growth rate, g, so that the bank's cash flows do *not* grow faster than the nominal growth rate of the overall macroeconomy. As noted in Chapter 2, the average nominal GDP growth rate in the U.S. is around 6% per year and so a bank's estimate of g should *not*

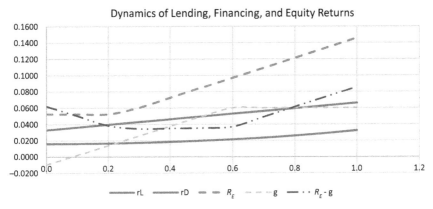

Figure 3.2. The Effect of Credit Risk when the Sustainable Growth Rate is Capped at 6%.

be greater than this amount.[34] We can model this by capping the growth rate, g, at 6% if the results of Equation (3.8) suggest a number greater than 6%. Our Excel™ spreadsheet has this constraint built into its sustainable growth rate estimates. Figure 3.2 presents an alternative numerical example where the expected dividend yield ($R_E - g$) can be *non-constant* when g is capped at 6%. Note that the expected dividend yield ($R_E - g$) now initially dips when C is below 0.2 and then begins to rise again when C is greater than 0.6. This nonlinear pattern will then have a different effect on the bank's market value as the credit allocation choice is varied.

Based on the above discussion, we can use the IVM relationship shown in Equation (3.6) to identify the level of C that maximizes the bank's market value of equity. Figure 3.3 displays the results of this type of simulation on the expected *level* of ABC's stock price. The graph shows how ABC's stock price reacts to varying levels of the bank's credit allocation decision, C.

We can now clearly see from Figure 3.3 that ABC's stock price is maximized by increasing C to around 0.6, or 60% of assets. In fact, the stock price reaches its maximum at $20.17 when $C = 0.5883$.[35] Interestingly, the

---

[34] We impose this limit because if the bank's cash flows were to grow faster than the overall economy *forever*, then the bank's revenue will ultimately become nearly 100% of the country's GDP! So, the growth limit is used to guard against this unrealistic outcome.

[35] In subsequent chapters and within our book's spreadsheet, we use this optimal stock price of $20.17 as our "base stock price" estimate to serve as a benchmark for all other risk management choices (such as hedging interest rate and market risks).

82 Managing Financial Institutions: An Integrated Valuation Approach

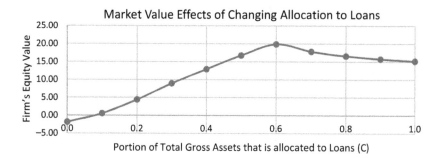

Figure 3.3.   The Effect of Credit Risk on ABC's Market Value.

incremental benefits of additional credit risk begin to diminish when the ratio approaches 0.6, as the graph shows that the stock prices of $16.84 at $C = 0.5$ and $17.81 at $C = 0.7$ are somewhat different than the peak value of $20.17. Based on this analysis, it appears that ABC's "sweet spot" in terms of credit allocation is somewhere between 50% and 70% of assets. Thus, levels of C at or below 50% suggest that the marginal benefits of an increased credit allocation are greater than the additional costs. As noted earlier, the bank should therefore increase its lending if its level of C is below 50% and, conversely, ABC's lending should be reduced if its C is greater than 70%. Figure 3.3 suggests that lending activity greater than 70% is value-destroying because the marginal costs of additional loans are much greater than the marginal benefits at these higher levels of C.

Another useful observation from Figure 3.3 is that ABC's current level of lending (at $C = 51.55\%$) is within the optimal range of 50–70%. For example, at ABC's current credit allocation level of 51.55%, its stock price is $17.14, which is approximately 15.0% lower than its potential peak value of $20.17 when C equals 58.83%. This finding indicates that ABC's management is managing its credit risk fairly well but could be doing a better job, as it is "leaving some money on the table" by not allocating more assets to lending. Thus, some additional increases in loan activity (up to around 59%) are likely to generate a substantially large gain in market value.

3.6 Managerial Implications

Based on all the quantitative analysis presented above, we must also consider the *qualitative* aspects of ABC's credit allocation choice. So, this section on managerial implications is included here, as well as in subsequent chapters, to help managers and analysts think about how different risk management choices can affect the bank's market value while also considering some of the behavioral aspects of these decisions. To help with this discussion, we introduce two mid-level managers who work within ABC bank, Nina and Sam, who are tasked with translating the quantitative analysis presented above into some meaningful questions and actions for the bank's senior management.[36] Both are "rising stars" within ABC and are well respected for their ability to focus on the key issues that underlie various risk management decisions.

The main credit allocation problem Sam and Nina must consider is as follows: **how much of the bank's assets should be devoted to lending?** As we see throughout this book, answers to questions like this depend largely on the bank's "risk appetite" which, in turn, is influenced by senior management's and investors' tolerance for risk. Nina and Sam must also think about the classic trade-off between the extra return and greater risk of loans relative to investing in safer but lower-yielding marketable securities like U.S. Treasury bonds and mortgage-backed securities. This choice can also be affected by macroeconomic conditions because loan demand becomes much weaker (and credit risk rises) during recessionary times. Thus, when the economy is doing poorly, it might be better for the bank to allocate a greater share of assets to safer fixed income securities and to curtail loan growth.

Given that Sam and Nina believe the economy is in a late expansionary mode with inflation and interest rates increasing, **what should ABC do in terms of allocating its investments in loans vs. securities?** Sam and Nina think **the best plan might be to increase the current credit allocation, 51%, but not go all the way up to the estimated optimal value of around 59% because of the growing possibility of an economic downturn**. Their reasoning is based on a concern that ABC should not be lending too aggressively at a time which might be viewed (in hindsight) as a peak in the business cycle. **Do you agree with Nina and Sam's recommendation? If not, then how would you handle it differently and what are your reasons for doing so?**

---

[36] Nina and Sam are also assisted by their trusted lieutenants, Mitchell and Cecilia, later on in Chapter 12 when all the bank's risks are assessed in a *simultaneous* manner because this integrated risk management approach requires a greater amount of communication and coordination across the bank's business units.

3.7 Summary and Concluding Thoughts about Applying the IVM

This chapter introduced our "North Star" model which can help guide us to make better risk management decisions and increase a financial institution's market value. We call this model the Integrated Valuation Model (IVM) because it incorporates not only the bank's operating profits but also the effects of managing the bank's liquidity risk and hedging choices. To keep the analysis as clear as possible, we make several simplifying assumptions by using a Constant Growth Dividend Discount Model. This method helps us focus on the three main drivers of market value, as described by the "MRT" acronym. That is, the bank's value will be affected by the Magnitude of its cash flows, the Riskiness of those cash flows, and the Timing (or growth) of cash flows. We then used a stylized income statement and balance sheet to develop a numerical example that helps illustrate the MRT concepts. This approach also enables us to provide an Excel™ spreadsheet with this book that you can use to perform various "what-if" analyses and solve for the optimal levels of risk that a bank should hold (such as what percentage of assets should be allocated to lending activities).

In sum, the analysis presented in this chapter can be an effective way to use the IVM to assess a bank's risk-taking and risk management choices. However, some caveats should be kept in mind for all the chapters contained within this book. For example, although the above analysis can be very helpful, we should remind ourselves that we are using a model with many strong underlying assumptions and that we should not take these valuation estimates too literally.

The model works best as an indicator of the *direction* a firm's stock price might follow by pursuing a particular action rather than a precise dollar amount. For example, we can conclude from the above analysis that ABC is likely to benefit from increasing its credit allocation from its current level of 51.55% because the stock price *trends lower* whenever the credit allocation percentage is reduced below 50% or raised above 70%. This is a better use of the integrated valuation model than to focus on a specific level of the firm's stock price because, as we learned from Milton Friedman earlier in this chapter, a useful model is best used as an "engine of inquiry" rather than as a camera that tries to exactly replicate the real world. Also keep in mind that the model's output is only as good as the quality of its main inputs, which are the manager's assumptions about key factors such as credit risk, financing choices, as well as the bank's cost of equity capital and expected growth rate. As we had noted in Chapter 2, we need to keep in mind the "GIGO" acronym when it comes to a model's assumptions **(Garbage In, Garbage Out)**.

It should also be noted that the above findings are specific to the assumptions used to measure the costs and benefits of ABC's credit allocation in this example. We cannot conclude that lending around 60% of assets is *always* optimal for the firm. In addition, the analysis presented here is "static" rather than "dynamic" because we are not changing other key drivers of value when we vary the level of credit risk. Thus, Figure 3.3 might not give us the complete picture if the credit allocation decision also affects other important factors like operating expenses and interest rate risk.

As we show in the following set of chapters, we can address this issue of dynamic analysis by using a spreadsheet-based valuation model that enables the analyst to optimize a bank's stock price while allowing multiple value drivers to vary simultaneously. However, the above numerical example is still helpful because it introduces our IVM approach and provides valuable insights into how trade-offs between risk-taking and risk management can directly affect firm value. This same principle can be applied to all the FIs main risks to get a sense, at least directionally, of how different choices affect firm value.

While we have already touched briefly on some of the concepts related to interest rate risk, the following chapter (Chapter 4) focuses even more deeply on this type of risk. In doing so, we can build off our knowledge of valuation methods to apply the "MRT" value drivers and the IVM to all the major types of FI-related risks in subsequent chapters.

A3.1 Appendix

A3.1.1 *Equivalence of dividends (DIV) and free cash flow to equity (FCFE)*

As noted earlier in this chapter, a bank's total dividend payments (DIV) are equivalent to the firm's free cash flow that is payable to equity investors (FCFE) when the bank does not issue any new common equity (net of stock repurchases) during the forecast period. We can see this equivalence by first starting with the definition of FCFE, as shown in Brigham and Ehrhardt (2020):

$$\text{FCFE} = \text{Net Income} - \text{Change in Net Operating Capital} + \text{Net Change in Debt}$$

where Net Operating Capital includes Net Working Capital plus Net Fixed Assets. We can also see that this Change in Net Operating Capital (ΔNOC) must be financed with Debt or Equity:

$$\Delta\text{NOC} = \Delta\text{Debt} + \Delta\text{Equity}$$

which can be re-arranged algebraically to isolate the firm's ΔEquity:

$$\Delta\text{Equity} = \Delta\text{NOC} - \Delta\text{Debt}$$

Note that the above relationship is equivalent to the last two terms in the FCFE formula, as follows:

$$\text{FCFE} = \text{Net Income} - \text{Change in Net Operating Capital} + \text{Net Change in Debt}$$

$$= \text{NI} - \Delta\text{NOC} + \Delta\text{Debt} = \text{NI} - \Delta\text{Equity}$$

So, we can see from the above equation that FCFE equals Net Income (NI) minus the Change in Equity (ΔEquity). We can also define this Change in Equity as made up of two parts: (1) the Change in Retained Earnings (ΔRE) and (2) the Issuance of New Equity (New Equity), as follows:

$$\Delta\text{Equity} = \Delta\text{RE} + \text{New Equity}$$

Now, if we assume the bank does not issue new common equity during the forecast period, then New Equity equals 0 and the above relationship becomes simply

$$\Delta\text{Equity} = \Delta\text{RE} + \text{New Equity} = \Delta\text{RE} + 0 = \Delta\text{RE}$$

Thus, we can see that, in this case (which is fairly typical because issuing new equity can be quite costly for the firm), the Change in Equity is equal to the dollar amount of NI that is retained by the bank during the forecast period. By substituting this final relationship into our definition of FCFE above, we find

$$FCFE = NI - \Delta NOC + \Delta Debt = NI - \Delta Equity = NI - \Delta RE$$

Next, we can see that FCFE is equivalent to DIV because total dividend payments are, by definition, equal to NI − ΔRE because Net Income can either be retained by the bank or paid out to shareholders as a dividend:

$$NI = \Delta RE + DIV$$

So,
$$DIV = NI - \Delta RE$$

Lastly, substituting the above formula for DIV into the FCFE thus shows the equivalence of these two variables:

$$FCFE = NI - \Delta RE = \Delta DIV$$

From the above derivation, we can see why we can use a Dividend Discount Model (DDM) approach in our discussions throughout this book. In effect, the DDM method is mathematically equivalent to using a Discounted Cash Flow (DCF) approach that was discussed earlier in Chapter 2. So, even though it appears that the DDM is somewhat specialized, it is equivalent to the more broadly defined DCF model when we assume there is no new net equity being issued during the forecast period. Since we are using a constant growth DDM that requires only next year's forecast, this assumption is not too restrictive because it means we just need to assume that no new equity will be issued over the next 12 months.

A3.1.2 Additional details of the valuation model and its components

Table A3.2 contains additional details beyond those shown in Table A3.1 and is meant to be a high-level summary and framework that we build upon in subsequent chapters. Table A3.2 contains the IVM's key variables, their formulas and definitions, as well as references to the relevant chapters in which these concepts are discussed in greater detail. Following Table A3.2, we provide some additional material that expands upon the rationale underlying the model's expected equity return (R_E).

Table A3.2. Components of the Integrated Valuation Model (IVM)

Concept	Variable	Formula/Relationship	Chapter	Definitions/Assumptions
Credit	Credit Risk-adjusted Interest Income	$(rL \cdot L) - LLP$	6	rL = lending rate based on a risk-free rate plus a risk premium (e.g., $R_f + YS$), where R_f = risk-free rate = U.S. Treasury (UST) yield of similar maturity, and YS = yield spread above the UST yield, L = Gross Loans (which includes Allow for Loan Losses), and LLP = Loan Loss Provisions (for expected credit losses)
Investments	Securities Return	$rS \cdot S$	8	rS = percentage return on Securities portfolio (e.g., UST yield), S = $ amount invested in Securities = $(EA - L - R)$, where EA = Reserves + Gross Loans – Investments
Reserves	Return on Cash plus Bank Reserves	$rRes \cdot R$	8	$rRes$ = percentage return on Cash & Reserves, Cash & Reserves = $R = EA - L - S$
Funding	Interest Expense	$rD \cdot D$	4	D = Deposits + OBM; rD = percentage return paid to depositors and other creditors based on their relative weights in financing the firm, rD = (wDepos · rDepos) + (wOBM · rOBM)
Fee-based Services	Non-Interest Income	$f \cdot A$	7, 9	f = Non-Interest Income / Total Assets; includes all non-interest activities (e.g., trading, investment banking, and asset management)
Operational Costs	Operating Expense	$(ovc + ofc) \cdot A$	9	ovc, ofc = Variable & Fixed Operating Expenses, each divided by Total Assets (A)

Introducing the Integrated Valuation Model   89

Liquidity Risk Effects	Expected Liquidity Risk Cost/ Penalty	$rP * E[\max(0, W - S^*)]$, where $E[\cdot]$ stands for an expected value	8	rP = penalty rate = opportunity cost of holding reserves instead of lending, W = unexpected drains on liquidity due to changes in loans, deposits, or other factors, and S^* = cash and securities held to meet sudden liquidity needs
Hedging Effects	Costs and Benefits of Hedging Choices	$\sum_j$ [\$ Reduction in market-related Risk Exposures − (fixed hedging costs + variable hedging costs)]	4, 5	\$Reduction in market-related Risk Exposures = the total benefit of hedging the jth Risk Exposure, where j can represent various sources of risk related to interest rates, currencies, commodities, stocks, etc., and the fixed and variable hedging costs represent the total cost of managing this risk
Tax Expense	Effective Tax Rate	$t = 1 - \left(\frac{NI}{EBT}\right)$	9	NI = Net Income, EBT = Earnings Before Tax (or Pretax Income)
Dividend Payout	Dividend Payout Ratio	$d = \frac{DIV}{NI}$ when Expected Equity$_1$ > Target Equity$_1$	2, 10	DIV = Total Dividends paid to Common Stockholders, NI = Net Income, Expected Equity$_1$ = ($NI_1 + E_0$), Target Equity$_1$ = $[(E/A)^* \cdot A_1]$, $(E/A)^*$ = target equity-to-asset ratio, and A_1 = projected Total Assets
Growth	Constant Sustainable Growth Rate	$g = (1 - d) \cdot ROE_t$	2, 10	d = Dividend Payout Ratio, Return on Equity = $ROE_t = \frac{NI_t}{EQ_t}$
Expected Equity Return	Expected Dividend Yield + Capital Gain	$R_E = DY_{t+1} + g =$ $= DY_t + \{[1 - d + DY_t$ $- (d \cdot DY_t)] \cdot$ $ROE_{t+1}\}$	2, 10	Based on the Constant Growth Dividend Discount Model which includes forecasts of the Dividend Yield (DY_{t+1}) and Sustainable Growth Rate (g), $DY_{t+1} = DIV_{t+1} / MVE_t$, where MVE_t = Market Value of Equity = Stock Price$_t$ · Common Shares Outstanding

A3.1.3 Derivation of expected dividend yield and expected cost of equity

As noted earlier in this chapter, an internally consistent approach to estimating a firm's expected cost of equity (R_E) that does not require a formal asset pricing model is suggested in Brigham and Ehrhardt (2020) and other general finance textbooks. In addition, building upon Campbell and Shiller (1988) and others, Gao and Martin (2021) developed a model that demonstrates both theoretically and empirically how the Constant Growth version of the Dividend Discount Model (also referred to as the Gordon Growth Model) and the current level of a stock's dividend yield can provide an internally consistent and reliable estimate of future expected equity returns. Thus, Brigham and Ehrhardt (2020), Gao and Martin (2021), and other authors show that a stock's expected return can be decomposed into two components: (1) an expected dividend yield (where this is the projected income from dividends divided by the current market value of the firm's equity, $DY_{t+1} = DIV_{t+1} / V_{E,t}$) and (2) an expected capital gain (which equals the projected percentage change in the firm's stock price). Thus, the expected return on equity (R_E) is the sum of the stock's expected dividend yield plus its projected capital gain. We can use the bank's sustainable growth rate (g) as our estimate of the firm's capital gain.[37]

The projected dividend yield is based on the dividend payout ratio and projected net income for the next year ($d \cdot NI_{t+1}$) divided by the current market value of equity ($V_{E,t}$).[38] The bank's equity market value can be

---

[37] As noted in the main text of this chapter, the capital gains rate is also related to the firm's dividend payments. The firm faces a choice as to how much profit to pay out in dividends relative to how much profit to reinvest. So long as the firm continues to allow dividends to grow at a constant rate and the firm's profitability is constant (as measured by ROE), then Net Income will grow at this same rate. Thus, when the firm's discount rate (R_E) remains the same, the constant growth in net income and dividends will enable the market value of the firm's equity to grow at a constant capital gains rate that is equal to the sustainable growth rate, g.

[38] The assumption of a constant dividend payout ratio (d) and a constant growth rate (g) leads to a constant expected dividend yield (DY_{t+1}) even when the bank chooses different levels of risk exposures. Thus, the bank's market value of equity will be driven by variations in expected Net Income (NI_{t+1}). This is a somewhat unrealistic set of assumptions because our earlier discussion of Equations (3.3) and (3.5) in the main text shows that regulatory capital requirements can affect how much of a dividend the bank can pay

referred to in abbreviated form as MVE or V_E and can be calculated as follows: MVE_t = current stock price, SP_t, multiplied by the current Common Shares Outstanding. So, in the context of our preferred valuation method, the Constant Growth Dividend Discount Model, we can define the expected return on equity (R_E) with the following equation:

$$R_E = \text{Expected Dividend Yield} + \text{Projected Capital Gain} = DY_{t+1} + g \qquad (A3.1)$$

where

$$\text{Expected Dividend Yield} = DY_{t+1} = \frac{(d \cdot NI_{t+1})}{V_E} = \frac{(d \cdot NI_t (1+g))}{V_E} = \frac{(d \cdot NI_t)}{V_E}(1+g)$$
$$= \text{Current Dividend Yield (}DY_t\text{) adjusted for growth} = DY_t \cdot (1+g) \qquad (A3.2)$$

and

$$\text{Projected Capital Gain} = g = \text{Retention Ratio}$$
$$\cdot \text{Expected ROE} = (1-d) \cdot ROE_{t+1} \qquad (A3.3)$$

Equation (A3.2) shows how the expected dividend yield (DY_{t+1}) is simply a function of the current dividend yield at time t (DY_t) and a constant growth factor $(1 + g)$. The Gao and Martin (2021) model supports this conclusion and illustrates how it is optimal to forecast a stock's future dividend yield based on a linear function of the current dividend yield.

In addition, Equation (A3.3) provides an estimate of a stock's projected capital gain that is equivalent to the firm's sustainable constant growth rate, g. The basic idea is that this growth rate is constant when we assume that several factors are held constant such as the firm's dividend payout ratio (d), profitability (ROE), and capital structure (e.g., the debt-to-assets ratio). When these factors are constant, then the firm's net income and dividends will grow at the same rate. In turn, if the firm's expected dividend yield ($R_E - g$) remains constant due to all these other factors remaining stable, then the market value of the equity has the

---

(DIV_{t+1}). However, bank managers and investors prefer predictable dividends that grow at a relatively stable rate. So, our assumption of a constant dividend yield might not be far from reality for most banks' dividend policies. In addition, as noted in the main text, when the sustainable growth rate, g, is capped at, say, 6%, then the expected dividend yield *can* vary over different risk management choices.

potential to grow at a constant rate equal to sustainable growth rate, g. Thus, our approach suggests that the growth rate will equal the firm's projected capital gain and this derivation further supports our claim that the firm's expected return on equity (R_E) can be described by Equation (A3.1). As noted in the main text, perpetually constant dividend yields and growth rates are unrealistic assumptions. However, there is ample real-world evidence that bank managers attempt to produce dividends that grow in a stable, predictable manner and that bank investors prefer firms that can deliver these types of income-oriented returns.

We can then go one step further and substitute the above definitions of DY_{t+1} and g from Equations (A3.2) and (A3.3) into the R_E formula of (A3.1) and do some algebraic re-arranging to obtain the expected cost of equity (R_E) as follows:

$$R_E = (1+g) \cdot DY_t + g$$

which, via factoring out g, results in

$$R_E = DY_t + \left((1+DY_t) \cdot g\right) \tag{A3.4}$$

And then substituting for g via Equation (A3.3) leads to

$$R_E = DY_t + \left\{(1+DY_t) \cdot (1-d) \cdot ROE_{t+1}\right\} \tag{A3.5}$$

Lastly, we can expand the above term in curly brackets to form the relationship within the square brackets shown as follows:

$$R_E = DY_t + \left\{\left[(1-d) + DY_t - (d \cdot DY_t)\right] \cdot ROE_{t+1}\right\} \tag{A3.6}$$

The above relationship shows that the shareholders' *expected* return is based on *three* key variables: (1) the bank's current dividend yield (DY_t), (2) the dividend payout ratio (d), and (3) the expected return on the book value of equity (ROE_{t+1}). Estimates of these variables can be developed easily once we have collected the relevant data from the bank's financial statements and its dividend yield (all of which are available at low or no cost from popular finance websites, such as finance.yahoo.com). In addition, the above relationship *does not* require us to create a *required* cost of equity and removes the need to choose a specific asset pricing model, such as the Capital Asset Pricing Model or some other multi-factor model. Given that there is no consensus among practitioners and academics as to what asset pricing model is most appropriate, the above equation enables us to avoid this contentious issue. In addition, we see from Gao and Martin (2021) that our approach can lead to optimal estimation of R_E based on the firm's current dividend yield. Thus, our method has the virtue of being relatively easy to estimate and is based on a solid theoretical and empirical foundation.

Although the R_E model presented above in (A3.6) can be useful as a *descriptive* model of *expected* returns, some analysts and bank managers might prefer a *prescriptive* model of *required* returns. Thus, we present in the following a summary of the Sharpe (1964) CAPM as an alternative way to estimate a bank's *required* cost of equity (R_E):

$$\text{Re} = R_f + \beta(R_m - R_f) \tag{A3.7}$$

where

R_f = Risk-free rate (usually based on a U.S. Treasury yield such as the 10-year Treasury note),

β = the bank's "beta" which measures the relative riskiness of the bank's equity returns versus the "market portfolio's" return (usually estimated by regressing past bank stock returns on the returns of a proxy for the portfolio of all risky assets such as the S&P 500 stock index, R_m), and $(R_m - R_f)$ = the "market risk premium" measures how much extra return is required for a risk-averse investor to invest in the market portfolio rather than hold a risk-free security such as a 10-year Treasury note.

To estimate (A3.7), the analyst needs data on the risk-free rate and the bank's beta, both of which are easily found on financial websites, such as finance.yahoo.com. In terms of the market risk premium, the analyst has quite a large amount of leeway to estimate this important component, although many analysts will use 6% for a firm that operates primarily in the U.S. because this has been close to the historical average market risk premium in this country since 1926.

So, if a bank manager or analyst wishes to apply the CAPM to estimate R_E, they must use (A3.7) in conjunction with current data on the key variables described above. This approach requires some additional input but enables the analyst to estimate R_E in a way that is not tied to our model's constant expected dividend yield assumption. Our Excel™ spreadsheet of the IVM uses the descriptive expected return of (A3.6) as its default method of estimating R_E. However, the spreadsheet can also be modified to use the CAPM method instead if you prefer to use this prescriptive model. If you choose to do so, keep in mind that you will need to *manually* adjust the bank's risk measure, beta, based on your professional judgment because there is no clear academic consensus as to how to alter a bank's beta as the firm chooses different hedge ratios.

Chapter-End Questions

Answers to odd-numbered questions can be found at the end of this book.

1. **True or False:** Managers of financial institutions (FIs) are responsible for generating revenue to cover funding and operational costs, as well as meeting equity investors' return expectations. If they fail in this task, investors may withdraw their financing, jeopardizing the FIs stability.
2. **True or False:** The balance sheet demonstrates the principle of "Form follows Function," where a sample bank's assets are primarily concentrated in its lending and investing functions (Net Loans and Investments accounts).
3. **Multiple Choice:** Which financial instruments are commonly used by financial institutions to manage Interest Rate Risk (IR) and Market Risk?
   (A) Stocks and bonds
   (B) Derivatives (e.g., forwards, futures, swaps, and options)
   (C) Real estate properties
   (D) Cash and equivalents
4. **Multiple Choice:** What is the primary purpose of a simplified valuation model, as mentioned in the text?
   (A) To precisely describe all factors affecting firm value
   (B) To predict exact changes in firm value
   (C) To mimic reality perfectly
   (D) To test hypotheses about the main drivers of firm value

5. **Multiple Choice:** What is the main concern that arises from heavy reliance on debt to finance a bank's functions?
   (A) Greater operating expenses
   (B) Increased profitability
   (C) Higher risk of insolvency
   (D) Enhanced capital adequacy
6. **Short Answer:** What is ABC Bank's expected equity return (R_E) if the firm's current dividends per share (DPS) is $1.20 and the current stock price (SP) is $24.00. In addition, ABC is projecting a dividend payout ratio of 40% and an ROE of 10% for next year.
7. **Short Answer:** Use the Constant Growth Dividend Discount Model (DDM) method to estimate ABC Bank's market value of equity based on the following questions and the data provided in the following:
   (A) Calculate the **expected total dividends** for ABC bank if its projected net income is $80 million and the dividend payout ratio is 60%.
   (B) Given an expected Return on Equity (ROE) of 12% and a dividend payout ratio of 40%, what is the **sustainable growth rate (g)** for the bank?
   (C) Using the Capital Asset Pricing Model (CAPM), estimate the **Expected Return on Equity (R_E)** for the bank if the risk-free rate is 4%, its beta is 0.8, and the market risk premium is 5%.
   (D) Use your answers to parts (A)–(C) and the Constant Growth Dividend Discount Model (DDM) to calculate ABC's market value of equity (i.e., its "market cap") and its stock price per share. You can assume ABC has 20 million shares outstanding.
8. **Short Answer:** Based on the following income statement data for ABC Bank, calculate the Net Income if the "base case" provision for loan losses (LLP) is 0.3% of the bank's $400.0 million in Total Gross Loans and the tax rate is 20%. Then, re-compute the bank's Net Income if credit risk is expected to increase and thus LLP would rise by an *additional* 0.5% of

loans. What is the percentage change in ABC's Net Income due to this increase in credit risk?

(in $ mil.)	Base case	Increased Credit Risk case
Interest Income	$36.0	$36.0
Interest Expense	$23.0	$23.0
Net Interest Income	$13.0	$13.0
Loan Loss Provision (LLP)	??	??
Non-Interest Income	$6.0	$6.0
Operating Expense	$14.0	$14.0
Pretax Income	??	??
Tax Expense	??	??
Net Income	??	??
% Change in Net Income:		??

9. **Excel-based Question:** What percentage of total assets should ABC allocate to loans and other credit products (C^*) if the Federal Reserve raises its Fed Funds rate target by 100 basis points? Use the **Integrated Valuation Model.xlsx** and the "Credit Allocation Choice – Ch 3" tab within that file to address this change in the Fed Funds rate. Try this by starting with the "base" scenario and then changing the values in the blue cells related to the *Base Lending Rate* (rL^*) and *Base Borrowing Rate* (rD^*). For example, raise both rates by 100 basis points (i.e., 1 percentage point) and then use the **Data…Solver…** function within Excel™ to re-estimate the Optimal Credit Allocation (C^*). What is the new level of credit allocation in this scenario and how does it compare to the previous value of C^* you initially saw in the spreadsheet? Then, try a second simulation where rL^* is increased by *another* 100 basis points but rD^* is *not* increased any further. What is the new level of C^* relative to your prior answer and why might C^* move in this direction? To help organize your response to this question, use the spreadsheet results to complete the following table:

	Base Scenario	ΔBase Rates by +1%	Δ only rL^* by +1% more
Base Lending Rate (rL^*)			
Base Borrowing Rate (rD^*)			
Lending Rate (rL)			
Borrowing Rate (rD)			
Rate Spread ($rL - rD$)			
Optimal Credit Alloc. (C^*)			

10. **Comprehensive Question:** Justify your recommended course of action related to ABC's credit allocation choice based on the following information. Given that Sam and Nina believe the economy is in a late expansionary mode with inflation and interest rates increasing, **what should ABC Bank do in terms of allocating its investments to loans vs. securities?** To answer this question, Nina and Sam must consider the classic trade-off between the extra return and greater risk of loans relative to investing in safer but lower-yielding marketable securities like U.S. Treasury bonds and mortgage-backed securities. This choice can also be affected by macroeconomic conditions because loan demand becomes much weaker (and credit risk rises) during recessionary times while interest rates typically fall and bond values rise.

References

Berger, A., DeYoung, R., Flannery, M., Lee, D.K. and Oztekin, O. (2008). How Do Large Banking Organizations Manage Their Capital Ratios? *Journal of Financial Services Research*, 34, 123–149.

Brealey, R., Myers, S. and Allen, F. (2020). *Principles of Corporate Finance*, 13th edition, McGraw-Hill.

Brick, I. E., Chen, H. Y., Hsieh, C. H. and Lee, C. F. (2016). A comparison of alternative models for estimating firm's growth rate. *Review of Quantitative Finance and Accounting*, 47, 369–393.

Brigham, E.F. and Ehrhardt, M. (2020). *Financial Management: Theory and Practice*, 16th edition, pp. 821–822, Cengage.

Carhart, M.M. (1997). On persistence in mutual fund performance, *Journal of Finance*, 52, 57–82.

Campbell, J. and Shiller, R. (1988). The dividend-price ratio and expectations of future dividends and discount factors, *Review of Financial Studies*, 1, 195–228.

Damodaran, A. (2009). *Valuing Financial Services Firms*, NYU Working Paper.

Dermine, Jean, (2015). *Bank Valuation and Value Based Management: Deposit and Loan Pricing, Performance Evaluation, and Risk*, 2nd edition, McGraw-Hill Education.

Egan, M., Lewellen, S. and Sunderam, A. (2022). The Cross-Section of Bank Value, *Review of Financial Studies*, 35, 2101–2143.

Fama, E. and French, K. (1993). Common risk factors in the returns on stocks and bonds, *Journal of Financial Economics*, 33, 3–56.

Fama, E. and French, K. (2015). A five-factor asset pricing model, *Journal of Financial Economics*, 116, 1–22.

Freixas, X., and Rochet, J-C. (2008). *Microeconomics of Banking*, 2nd edition, MIT Press: Cambridge, MA.

Gao, C. and Martin, I.W.R. (2021). Volatility, Valuation Ratios, and Bubbles: An Empirical Measure of Market Sentiment, *Journal of Finance*, 76, 3211–3254.

MacKenzie, D. (2006). *An Engine, Not a Camera: How Financial Models Shape Markets*, MIT Press: Cambridge, MA.

Ozgur, O., Karagol, E.T. and Ozbugday, F.C. (2021). Machine learning approach to drivers of bank lending: Evidence from an emerging economy, *Financial Innovation*, 7, 20–48.

Prisman, E., Slovin, M. and Sushka, M. (1986). A general model of the banking firm under conditions of monopoly, uncertainty and recourse, *Journal of Monetary Economics*, 17, 293–304.

Sharpe, W.F. (1964). Capital Asset Prices: A theory of market equilibrium under conditions of risk, *Journal of Finance*, 19, 425–442.

Sopranzetti, B., and Kiess, B. (2024). *Valuation and Financial Forecasting: A Handbook for Academics and Practitioners*, World Scientific Series in Modern Finance: Advanced Topics in Finance for the Academician and Practitioner, Vol. 2.

Stiglitz, J.E. and Weiss, A. (1981). Credit rationing in markets with imperfect information, *American Economic Review*, 71, 393–410.

Chapter 4

Interest Rate Risk

4.1 What Is Interest Rate Risk?

As we learned earlier in Chapter 1 about the different types of risks that a financial institution (FI) faces, a bank's managers must carefully consider the costs and benefits of their decisions. In the end, the FI must generate revenue that will cover not only all funding and operational costs but also satisfy equity investors' expectations for an adequate return on their investment. And, as discussed in Chapter 3 about the integrated valuation model, all firms must measure and manage profits and cash flows to generate sufficient returns to investors and survive in the long run.

In this chapter, we build upon the concepts of risk-taking and risk management first discussed in Chapters 1 and 3 and focus on a bank's interest rate risk exposure. This risk relates to how the bank's Net Interest Income (NII) and market value of equity (MVE) are affected by changes in interest rates. The key question is as follows: what is the main driver of interest rate risk and how does it affect a bank's NII and MVE? Interest rate risk is a natural by-product of a bank's provision of liquidity (also referred to in this book as "liquidity insurance"). One of the key functions of a bank that we discussed in Chapter 1 is Qualitative Asset Transformation (QAT). When a bank provides liquidity via QAT services, the FI transforms a liability (such as a bank deposit) into an asset that has distinctly different characteristics. For example, a bank will typically obtain financing via bank deposits that are shorter in maturity than the assets in which the bank invests in. Thus, a bank might take funds from a depositor in the form of a 1-year fixed rate certificate of deposit (CD) and then lend them out to a borrower in the form of a 2-year fixed rate loan.

This common QAT activity usually creates interest rate risk because the maturity of the asset (the 2-year loan) is different than the maturity of the liability (the 1-year CD). Even if the maturity of the assets and liabilities are exactly the same, interest rate risk can still exist when the bank chooses to, for example, borrow on a variable rate basis and invest in assets that earn a fixed rate of return. Thus, the bank's NII and MVE are exposed to fluctuations in interest rates and, depending on the direction of these changes, the FI stands to either benefit greatly in terms of gains in profits and stock price or suffer major losses in these all-important metrics of financial performance. More details about a bank's choices in terms of maturity and fixed vs. variable rates are presented later in this chapter when we discuss refinancing risk and reinvestment risk.

In what follows, we move directly into the various methods for measuring and managing exposure to interest rate risk. In the interest of conserving space, we do not include a discussion of interest rate drivers, duration, and convexity in the main body of the chapter but rather provide these details in an Appendix at the end of this chapter. We recommend reading through this Appendix first if you are not familiar with these topics or need to brush up on them.

4.2 How to Measure Interest Rate Risk: Using the Repricing Gap (RGAP) to Understand the Short-term Impact of this Risk

Based on the key drivers of interest rates such as inflation and liquidity described in the Appendix, we can see how changes in these rates affect the bank's short-term profitability. This is typically done by quantifying the impact of rate changes on a bank's annual level of Net Interest Income (NII). This is consistent with the old management saying, "You first need to measure it in order to manage it," where "it" in this case is interest rate risk. To measure this, the bank's managers must identify how the rates received on the bank's earning assets like loans and investment securities as well as the FIs rates paid on liabilities will vary over, say, one year.[1]

---

[1] Time horizons other than 1 year can be used for this analysis as well. For example, to see how interest rate risk varies over a longer horizon, banks typically measure RGAP for

Interest Rate Risk

As we can see from Equation (A4.5) in the Appendix, there are two main factors that can drive changes in interest rates: the risk-free rate ($R_{f,T}$) and the financial instrument's risk premium ($RP_{L,T}$). In turn, the risk-free rate is primarily affected by changes in the inflation premium ($IP_{L,T}$) and fluctuations in the perceived default risk premium ($DRP_{L,T}$). Thus, a risk manager should consider changes in both inflation and default risk when estimating the impact of interest rates on a bank's NII.

The bank's assets that "reprice" in a year are those that mature within 12 months or possess variable interest rate clauses. The dollar value of these assets represents "Rate Sensitive Assets" (RSA) because they will be affected by changes in interest rates over the next 12 months. Conversely, "Rate Sensitive Liabilities" (RSL) refer to the dollar amount of deposits and Other Borrowed Money (OBM) that will mature within the 1-year period or which have a variable interest rate. The difference between RSA and RSL is commonly referred to as the bank's "Repricing Gap" or **RGAP** for short. We can use RGAP as our measure of short-term interest rate risk by showing how this gap affects the bank's Net Interest Income (NII) as follows:

$$\Delta NII = RGA \cdot \Delta R \qquad (4.1)$$

where

ΔNII = change in annual Net Interest Income due to interest rate changes,

RGAP = Rate Sensitive Assets − Rate Sensitive Liabilities = RSA − RSL, and[2]

ΔR = assumed (instantaneous) change in interest rates (also referred to as an "interest rate shock").

In Equation (4.1), we can see that the expected change in NII can be found by multiplying the bank's 1-year RGAP by an assumed *instantaneous* change (or "shock") to interest rates that affects *both* RSA and RSL

---

several maturity "buckets" such as 0–3 months, 3–12 months, 0–12 months, 1–5 years, 5–10 years, and 10+ years. For our purposes, we focus on the 1-year RGAP because it is the most common metric to measure short-term interest rate risk.

[2] The RGAP can also be divided by the bank's Total Assets (TA) to obtain an RGAP *Ratio* which makes it easier to compare the firm's interest rate risk exposure over time and across different banks. That is, RGAP Ratio = RGAP / TA. For our purposes in this chapter, we can focus on the dollar value of RGAP rather than the RGAP Ratio.

simultaneously by the *same* amount. The rate change is assumed to be instantaneous because, by definition, it is assumed to be a sudden surprise (or shock) that bank managers did not expect during their planning/budgeting process. In addition, we typically assume a "parallel" shift in interest rates because (1) it simplifies the analysis and (2) both lending and financing rates typically rise and fall by roughly the same amount when there is a sudden shock to interest rates. Keep in mind that we could allow for non-parallel interest rate shocks by specifically forecasting different rate changes for RSA and RSL, respectively. For example, Equation (4.1) could be expanded to accommodate this extra level of detail as follows:

$$\Delta \text{NII} \equiv (\text{RSA} \cdot \Delta R_A) - (\text{RSL} \cdot \Delta R_L) \qquad (4.2)$$

where

ΔR_A = assumed (instantaneous) change in the interest rate for the bank's rate-sensitive assets and

ΔR_L = assumed (instantaneous) change in the interest rate for the bank's rate-sensitive liabilities.

For the rest of this chapter, we focus on the simpler version of short-term interest rate risk modeling described in Equation (4.1). In addition, we use the stylized financial statements from Chapter 3 to help illustrate a numerical example of interest rate risk. For convenience, we have reprinted in the following these financial statements for a hypothetical FI called "A Banking Company" (or "ABC" for short). Keep in mind we call them "stylized" financials because they do not contain all the items usually found on a real-world bank's accounting statements. Also, we are assuming these balance sheet items represent the true economic value of these assets and liabilities. That is, we are treating the following items as if they are *market values* of the bank's current operating assets and liabilities. In reality, we know that a bank's balance sheet (as reported to investors) is based mostly on book values and so we make the simplifying assumption of equating these book values to market values in order to focus on the true economic effects of managers' choices on the market value of equity (although, the practice of market-value accounting has gained traction).[3]

---

[3] In practice, this assumption is not overly strong because most bank assets and liabilities do not vary much from their book values and thus the market value of a bank's equity does not usually deviate far from its book value. For example, unlike technology companies where their market values are 10 or more times their book value, most publicly traded

4.2.1 Stylized balance sheet

Assets	Value ($ million)	Liabilities & Equity	Value ($ million)
Cash & Reserves	$4	Deposits	$75
Investments	30	Other Borrowed Money	15
Net Loans	58		
Other Assets	8	Common Equity	10
Total Assets	$100	Total Liabilities & Equity	$100

4.2.2 Stylized income statement

Like the balance sheet presented in the previous section, we can also develop an example of a stylized income statement for ABC, as shown in the following:

Income Statement	$ million	Calculations
Interest Income	$3.00	rL * Gross Loans = 0.05 * $60 = $3.0
Interest Expense	0.90	rD * (Deposits + OBM) = 0.01 * ($75 + $15) = $0.9
Net Interest Income (NII)	2.10	Interest Income – Interest Expense = $3.0 – $0.9 = $2.1
Loan Loss Provision (LLP)	0.10	ALL% * New Loans = 0.01 * $10 = $0.1
Non-Interest Income	1.00	Fee % * Total Assets = 0.01 * $100 = $1
Operating Expense	1.80	Operating Expense % * Total Assets = 0.018 * $100 = $1.8
Liquidity Risk Effects	0	Assumed to be zero for this example
Hedge Effects	0	Assumed to be zero for this example
Pretax Income	1.20	NII – LLP + Non-Int. Income – Oper. Exp. = $2.1 – 0.1 + 1.0 – 1.8 = $1.2
Taxes	0.24	Tax Rate (T) * Pretax Income = 0.20 * $1.2 = $0.24
Net Income (NI)	$0.96	Pretax Income – Taxes = $1.2 – $0.24 = $0.96

banks have market-to-book equity ratios between 1.0 and 2.0. Also, we should keep in mind that our stylized balance sheet represents the market value of *existing* operating assets and liabilities. Thus, we can interpret this as measuring the net market value of the bank's "assets in place." To the extent that the bank's growth rate is relatively low and stable, then our approach can still provide us with useful estimates of the *directional* impact of managers' choices on the market value of equity.

104   *Managing Financial Institutions: An Integrated Valuation Approach*

Based on the above financial statements, we can use the Integrated Valuation Model (IVM) from Chapter 3 to estimate ABC's current stock price. To do so, we can assume that ABC has a 40% Dividend Payout Ratio ($d = 0.4$), an expected Dividend Yield of 3.5% ($R_E - g = 0.035$), and 1 million common shares outstanding. Using this information and the IVM, we can see that ABC's stock price is $10.97, as follows:

$$V_E = \frac{\left[\frac{(d \cdot NI)}{(R_E - g)}\right]}{Sh.O/S} = \frac{\left[\frac{(0.4 \cdot \$0.96 \text{ million})}{(0.035)}\right]}{1.0 \text{ million shares}} = \frac{\frac{\$0.384 \text{ million}}{0.035}}{1.0 \text{ million shares}} = \$10.97 \text{ per share}$$

We can use the above stock price as a base case to compare the valuation effects of ABC's interest rate risk management choices that are presented later in this chapter.

4.2.3 *Estimating a bank's repricing gap*

From the above financials, we can see that ABC currently has an NII of $2.1 million and it has earning assets totaling $88 million (i.e., the sum of Investments and Net Loans) and total liabilities of $90 million (sum of Deposits and OBM).[4] Now, let's assume the following breakdown of assets and liabilities maturing or repricing before and after the 1-year horizon.

Table 4.1 shows that ABC has a *negative* $30 million 1-year repricing gap, which means it has $30 million *more* rate-sensitive *liabilities* ($50 million) than rate-sensitive *assets* ($20 million). We can now use Equation (4.1) to estimate the impact of this RGAP on ABC's NII when we assume an interest rate *increase* (ΔR) of 1 percentage point (also referred to as 100 *basis points*, where 1 basis point equals 0.01%):

$$\Delta NII = RGAP \cdot \Delta R = -\$30 \text{ million} \cdot (+0.01) = -\$0.3 \text{ million}$$

---

[4] We can assume that interest rate on the $4 million in Cash & Reserves is very low and does not vary over the annual forecast horizon. Thus, for simplicity, we do not include this amount in the RGAP calculations shown above.

Table 4.1. Repricing Gap Example.

In $ millions	Maturing 1 year or less	Maturing > 1 year	Totals
Investments	12	18	30
Net Loans	8	50	58
RSA	**20**	**68**	**88**
Deposits[a]	45	30	75
OBM	5	10	15
RSL	**50**	**40**	**90**
RGAP = RSA − RSL	**−30**	**+28**	**−2**

Notes: [a]Note that we include Deposits (including "core" demand deposits) in the RGAP calculations because even if these deposits pay no explicit interest rate, there is an implicit interest rate since banks do not normally charge full price for their checking services. For example, "no-fee checking" still has a cost that the bank must pay and is, in effect, an implicit interest rate paid to the depositor in the form of subsidized checking services.

The above calculation shows that ABC's NII will suffer a $0.3 million *decrease* if interest rates were to suddenly rise 1 percentage point. This is because the cost of the RSL will rise by $0.5 million (i.e., $50 million · 0.01) while the extra interest earned on the RSA will only increase by $0.2 million (i.e., $20 million · 0.01). Thus, the extra financing costs of the RSL swamp the additional earnings on the RSA and cause NII to decline. This is a classic example of *refinancing risk*, where liabilities reprice faster than the bank's assets (also referred to as being "liability-sensitive"). In this case, ABC is exposed to interest rate risks when rates *rise*.

Conversely, the bank's NII can *increase* when interest rates *fall* because in this case, the cost of the RSL declines more than the drop in interest earned on the RSA. This outcome can be seen when we assume interest rates fall by 100 basis points:

$$\Delta NII = RGAP \cdot \Delta R = -\$30 \text{ million} \times (-0.01) = +\$0.3 \text{ million}$$

As we can see from above, there is now a $0.3 million increase in ABC's NII because the cost of the RSL decreases by $0.5 million (i.e., $50 million $x - 0.01$) while the extra interest earned on the RSA will only fall by

$0.2 million (i.e., $20 million $x - 0.01$). In this case, the savings in terms of financing costs from the RSL more than offset the reduced earnings on the RSA and cause NII to *increase*. Note that ABC is exposed to interest rate risk when rates *rise* in the above example. However, the *reverse* is true if the firm's RGAP was *positive* rather than negative. Just for a moment let's assume the opposite sign for RGAP was used in our numerical example. That is, let's assume RGAP is a *positive* $30 million because RSA, in this case, is assumed to be $50 million and RSL is only $20 million. If this "alternate reality" were true, then ABC's NII would drop as interest rates *decrease*. To see this, we can repeat the same formula as before but now we use a +$30 million RGAP along with −100 basis point change in interest rates:

$$\Delta NII = RGAP \times \Delta R = + \$30 \text{ million} \times (-0.01) = -\$0.3 \text{ million}$$

In this alternative case, the interest earned on the RSA falls by $0.5 million (i.e., $50 million $x - 0.01$) while the interest paid on the RSL will only fall by $0.2 million (i.e., $20 million $x - 0.01$). Thus, the savings in terms of reduced financing costs from the RSL are too little to offset the reduced earnings on the RSA and so NII decreases in this case. This is a classic example of *reinvestment risk*, where assets reprice faster than the bank's liabilities. In this case, ABC is exposed to interest rate risks when rates *drop*. Conversely, the bank's NII can *increase* when interest rates *rise* because in this case the interest earned on the RSA rises faster than the increased cost of the RSL, as shown in the following:

$$\Delta NII = RGAP \times \Delta R = + \$30 \text{ million} \times (+0.01) = +\$0.3 \text{ million}$$

To give a better sense of how real-world financial institutions measure and report their repricing gaps for multiple time windows, reprinted in the following is a table from M&T Bank's annual report.

Table 4.2 breaks down the M&T's interest rate exposure into four different time windows or "maturity buckets" with the first two columns of data showing how much of a repricing gap exists for the bank's next 12 months. The second to last row of Table 4.2 shows the "Cumulative Gap" and reports an approximately +$17.89 billion mismatch between RSA and RSL over the next 12 months. Thus, this bank has nearly $18 billion more assets repricing within 1 year than its short-term liabilities, even after adjusting for the firm's choice to hedge some of this

Table 4.2. Sample Repricing Gap Report.

December 31, 2021	Contractual Repricing Data				
	Three Months or Less	Four to Twelve Months	One to Five Years (Dollars in thousands)	After Five Years	Total
Loans and leases, net	$47,499,655	$6,871,241	$19,866,684	$18,674,872	$92,912,452
Investment securities	212,554	92,732	737,854	6,112,720	7,155,860
Other earning assets	41,921,266	783	—	—	41,922,049
Total earning assets	89,633,475	6,964,756	20,604,538	24,787,592	141,990,361
Savings and interest-checking deposits	68,603,966	—	—	—	68,603,966
Time deposits	1,071,254	1,229,571	507.138	—	2,807,963
Total interest-bearing deposits	69,675,220	1,229,571	507.138	—	71,411,929
Short-term borrowings	47,046	—	—	—	47,046
Long-term borrowings	—	903,864	1,525,376	1,056,129	3,485,369
Total interest-bearing liabilities	69,722,266	2,133,435	2,032,514	1,056,129	74,944,344
Interest rate swap agreements	(15,000,000)	8,150,000	6,350,000	500,000	—
Periodic gap	$4,911,209	$12,981,321	$24,922,024	$24,231,463	
Cumulative gap	4,911,209	17,892,530	42,814,554	67,046,017	
Cumulative gap as a percentage of total earning assets	3.5%	12.6%	30.2%	47.2%	

Source: M&T FY 2021 10K

Table 4.3. The Effect of Interest Rate Risk Exposure on a Bank's Net Interest Income (NII).

Repricing Gap	Interest Rate Shock	
	Rising Rates ($\Delta R > 0$)	Falling Rates ($\Delta R < 0$)
Positive Gap (RSA > RSL)	$\Delta NII > 0$	$\Delta NII < 0$
Negative Gap (RSA < RSL)	$\Delta NII < 0$	$\Delta NII > 0$

exposure via interest rate swap agreements.[5] In this case, M&T is "asset-sensitive" because its RSA is greater than its RSL and thus is exposed to reinvestment risk (i.e., NII would drop if interest rates fell).

The above discussion about how a bank is exposed to interest rate risk can be summarized in the following table which shows how changes in interest rates (ΔR) can affect Net Interest Income (ΔNII):

Table 4.3 shows that interest rate risk is *highest* when the bank's RGAP and ΔR are of *opposite sign*. That is, bank managers should be most concerned with *rising* rates when RGAP is *negative* or when RGAP is *positive* and rates are expected to *fall*. As we show later in this chapter, this type of risk can affect both NII and the bank's MVE, thus prompting the firm to consider hedging this interest rate with some type of derivative security.

4.3 What is Asset–Liability Management (ALM)?

The prior section's numerical examples demonstrate the two key aspects of short-term interest rate risk: ***refinancing risk*** and ***reinvestment risk***. Bank managers typically refer to managing these risks as a form of **Asset–Liability Management (ALM)**. Managers use ALM methods such as interest rate hedging to quantify and control the risk of fluctuating interest rates by adjusting the dollar amount, as well as the level of rates as well as the mix of variable rate and fixed rate instruments used within the bank's assets and liabilities. We can think of this as the "ARM" of ALM, where the acronym stands for a manager's choices in terms of the dollar *Amount* (A), *Rates* (R), and *Mix* (M) of assets and liabilities on its balance sheet.

---

[5] Interest rate swaps and hedging are discussed not only later in this chapter but also in Chapter 7 which covers Off-Balance Sheet (OBS) risk.

Bank managers can therefore adjust the "ARM" of their *assets*:

1. the amount of funds they invest in assets (e.g., loans versus securities)[6];
2. the level(s) of interest rates they charge for their different loan products (e.g., mortgages vs. auto loans); and
3. the mix of variable vs. fixed rate loan products (e.g., adjustable rate vs. fixed rate mortgages).

Similarly, these managers can also adjust the "ARM" for their *liabilities*:

1. the amount of funds they borrow in relation to equity (e.g., deposits versus common equity);
2. the level(s) of interest rates they pay for their different liabilities (e.g., money market accounts vs. certificates of deposit); and
3. the mix of variable vs. fixed rate liabilities (e.g., money market accounts vs. medium-term notes).

The above points about the ARM approach can be summarized in Figure 4.1.

For example, we commonly see greater interest rate risk when a bank chooses to invest a large amount of funds in long-term, fixed rate loans and finances this investment with short-term, variable rate deposits and debt. In this case, the ARM choices for assets lead to fewer (or possibly no) assets repricing within a year while the ARM choices for liabilities are mostly (if not all) repricing within 1 year, thus causing a very large maturity mismatch and for RGAP to be *negative*. As noted in the previous section and Table 4.2, this means the bank's choices have left its NII vulnerable to interest *rate increases*. We should also keep in mind that it can be a slow process to adjust the bank's interest rate exposure via the ARM choices and thus it can take the firm away from its core business and ultimately lead to customer dissatisfaction.

---

[6] Keep in mind that the dollar amounts invested in loans versus securities will also change the bank's exposure to credit risk because loans typically have greater default risk than marketable securities.

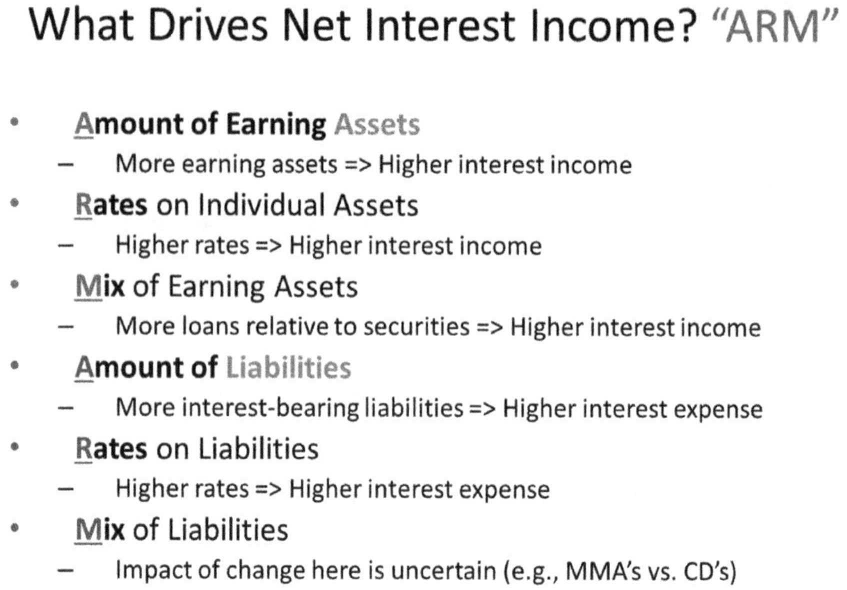

What Drives Net Interest Income? "ARM"

- **A**mount of Earning Assets
  - More earning assets => Higher interest income
- **R**ates on Individual Assets
  - Higher rates => Higher interest income
- **M**ix of Earning Assets
  - More loans relative to securities => Higher interest income
- **A**mount of Liabilities
  - More interest-bearing liabilities => Higher interest expense
- **R**ates on Liabilities
  - Higher rates => Higher interest expense
- **M**ix of Liabilities
  - Impact of change here is uncertain (e.g., MMA's vs. CD's)

Figure 4.1. The Two "ARMs" that Affect Net Interest Income.

4.3.1 Refinancing risk vs. reinvestment risk

To manage this interest rate risk, a good ALM risk manager must therefore consider both the asset's ARM and the liabilities' ARM, as well as their view on the most likely direction of future interest rates. The following two diagrams show one way to visualize the ALM manager's problem at ABC regarding refinancing risk and reinvestment risk. We start with refinancing risk because many banks typically have fewer short-term and variable rate assets than their liabilities and therefore have a negative RGAP.

Figures 4.2 and 4.3 show graphs of how a 2-year fixed rate asset earning a fixed rate of 6% per year (e.g., a business loan) could be financed with a shorter-term 1-year fixed rate bank deposit that pays 4% per year, thus creating **refinancing risk** for the bank. We can see this type of risk in Figure 4.2 by the dashed line in the lower right portion of the graph. Since ABC's loan rate is fixed at 6% for both years and the deposit financing rate is only "locked in" at 4% for the first year, the firm is exposed to uncertainty about what the 1-year deposit rate will be in the second year. Note that the "loan spread" in the first year is pre-determined

Interest Rate Risk   111

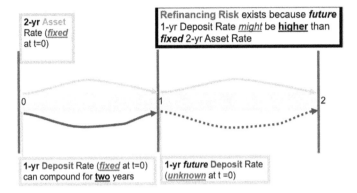

Figure 4.2.   Refinancing Risk Graph.

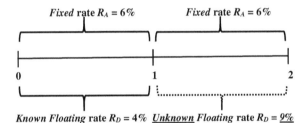

First Year's Loan Spread = 6% – 4% = +2%   *Second Year's Loan Spread = 6% – 9% = –3%*

Figure 4.3.   Refinancing Risk — Numerical Example.

at +2% (i.e., loan rate – deposit rate = loan spread = 6% – 4% = +2%) but the second year's loan spread is not known when the loan is first made at time = 0 in the timeline of Figure 4.2.

If inflation heats up and the deposit rate soars to, say, 9%, in the second year, then we can see that the loan spread quickly turns negative for this second period (i.e., 6% – 9% = –3%). In fact, the negative spread in the second year wipes out all the profit from the first year's +2% spread and leads to an overall *loss* on the loan over the full 2-year period. Note that this loss on the loan occurs even if the borrower pays back the loan (with interest) in full. So, we can see that interest rate risk, if unmanaged, can lead to bank losses even if there is no default. As we see throughout this book, there are many ways a bank can lose money and so risk management is extremely important to maximize firm value!

112   *Managing Financial Institutions: An Integrated Valuation Approach*

Clearly, the bank's managers would *not* be happy about the above turn of events and so they might choose to adjust their "ARM" for assets and liabilities in one or more of the following ways:

1. shortening the fixed rate loan's maturity,
2. lengthening the fixed rate deposit's maturity,
3. granting a variable rate loan rather than a fixed rate loan, or
4. offering variable rates for both the loan and the deposit.

If, for competitive reasons, changing the ARM of the asset and/or liability is not feasible or preferable, then the managers might decide to use some type of an interest rate derivative security such as a forward, future, option, or swap contract to hedge some portion of this interest rate risk. As noted earlier, the concept of interest hedging is introduced later in this chapter, but more details on these derivative securities are covered in Chapter 7 (OBS Risk).

Now let's examine the opposite situation where the fixed rate loan's maturity is shorter than the fixed rate deposit's maturity. This is a case of **reinvestment risk**, as shown in Figure 4.4.

As we can see from the graph below, the interest rate risk is now on the asset side because the proceeds of the 1-year fixed rate asset (assuming no borrower default) must be re-invested in the second year at an interest rate which is not known when the loan is first granted (i.e., at time $t = 0$ in the timeline of Figure 4.4). This can be a problem when the bank decides to finance this asset with a longer-term 2-year fixed rate deposit.

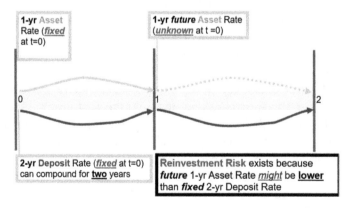

Figure 4.4.   Reinvestment Risk Graph.

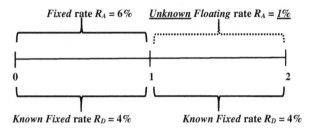

Figure 4.5. Reinvestment Risk — Numerical Example.

In this case, the risk is that interest rates will *fall* so far that the return on the asset in the second year is *less* than the fixed rate on the 2-year deposit.

The above refinancing risk can be quantified in the numerical example shown in Figure 4.5.

Once again, the bank's managers would not be happy about the above turn of events and so they might adjust their "ARM" for assets and liabilities in one or more of the following ways:

1. lengthening the fixed rate loan's maturity,
2. shortening the fixed rate deposit's maturity,
3. granting a variable rate deposit rather than a fixed rate liability, or
4. offering variable rates for both the loan and the deposit.

Like the case of refinancing risk, if, for competitive reasons, changing the ARM of the asset and/or liability is not feasible or preferable, then the managers might consider hedging at least a portion of the bank's interest rate risk exposure.

4.3.2 *Some challenges in using the repricing gap*

As we have seen from the above discussion, the repricing gap is an analytically convenient way to measure and manage short-term interest rate risk. However, it does have some limitations which can reduce its effectiveness as a risk management tool:

1. **Short-term focus:** RGAP, by definition, focuses on the bank's inflows and outflows from assets and liabilities over an arbitrary short-term

period (usually one year) and can ignore other inflows/outflows beyond this maturity. A more comprehensive approach would include all projected inflows and outflows rather than those occurring within, say, one year. As we show later in this chapter, a duration-based gap model called "MDGAP" considers all these flows and thus is able to see the impact of interest rates on the bank's market value of equity (rather than focusing solely on next year's NII).

2. **Instantaneous rate shocks:** We assume in this RGAP model that there is a sudden and instantaneous change in interest rates which might not be that realistic. Such a rapid change of, say, 100 or 300 basis points results in a much more severe impact on a bank's NII. If, for example, the rate change occurs more slowly over, say, 12 months, then the bank has time to adjust its RGAP in a way to minimize the impact of the rate change. So, a sudden, instantaneous rate shock could be viewed as a conservative test that provides a "worst case" scenario of its impact on NII. And, as was seen in 2022 when the U.S. Federal Reserve Board quickly raised short-term rates over 300 basis points, such sudden rate shocks do occur on occasion and thus are not entirely unrealistic.

3. **Runoffs:** The sudden withdrawal of longer-term deposits and/or the early repayment of long-term loans can lead to "runoff" that clouds the picture presented by RGAP. In our earlier example where ABC's 1-year RGAP is −$30 million, we saw that 1% interest rate increase can lower NII by $0.3 million. However, what if $60 million of long-term loans unexpectedly are repaid (i.e., "run off" the balance sheet) while $10 million of long-term deposits suddenly leave the bank? In this case, the new RGAP equals the old RGAP *plus* $60 million of newly created RSA and minus $10 million of "new" RSL. Thus, the new RGAP is +$20 million rather than −$30 million and so now a 1% rise in rates would lead to a $0.2 million *increase* in NII (rather than our original estimate of a $0.3 million *decrease* in NII). The key takeaway is that a bank manager must carefully estimate loan and deposit runoff to make sure the RGAP captures an accurate picture of short-term interest rate risk.

4. **Optionality:** Like sudden runoffs of loans and liabilities, the "optionality" of some bank products can also make it difficult to accurately estimate a rate change's impact on NII. For example, fixed rate mortgages typically can be repaid without penalty at the discretion of the borrower (especially when mortgage rates fall sharply). Or a

depositor with a long-term CD might decide to withdraw their money before maturity because they can earn a higher rate elsewhere (even after considering any early withdrawal fees). Thus, a borrower has an option to prepay the loan which, in turn, can quickly transform a long-term asset into a short-term RSA that then affects the RGAP calculation. So, a good bank manager needs to consider how many long-term assets and liabilities might take advantage of these refinancing and reinvestment options.

5. **Off-balance sheet items:** The RGAP model also uses RSA and RSL that are currently on the balance sheet and ignores possible off-balance sheet items such as lines of credit and loan guarantees that might be drawn upon during the year. If these "takedowns" are substantial and suddenly result in new variable rates or short-term loans, then the RGAP estimate will be off.

6. **Yield curve twists:** The estimated impact on NII will be affected if there are any "twists" in the yield curve where short-term and long-term rates do not move in tandem and short-term asset rates do not change by the same amount. In this case, using Equation (4.2) that accounts for different rate changes for RSA vs. RSL would be appropriate.

Despite the above points, RGAP is still a useful tool and one in which regulators and investors closely examine to see how sudden changes in interest rates can affect a bank's NII. However, another way to measure interest rate risk focuses on all the bank's cash flows related to its assets and liabilities rather than just, say, one year's worth of data. As the following section shows, this more comprehensive (and longer-term) view of interest rate risk can be quantified via estimating the "duration" of a bank's assets and its liabilities to come up with a "duration gap" or DGAP.

4.4 How to Measure the Long-term Impact of Interest Rate Risk using the Modified Duration Gap (MDGAP)

Although the RGAP is a helpful way to measure short-term interest rate risk, we can use the concept of "*duration*" to quantify and manage longer-term interest rate risk via a "duration gap" (referred to in this section as a modified duration gap, or "MDGAP" for short). This approach is more "holistic" than simply comparing maturities of different assets and liabilities because duration also considers the cash flows received over the entire lives of these fixed income instruments.

As we discuss later in this chapter, both RGAP and MDGAP can help inform a bank manager in two complementary ways. With its shorter-term focus, the RGAP approach shows how a sudden interest rate shock can affect next year's Net Interest Income (NII). In contrast, the MDGAP method takes a longer-term view to quantify the impact of interest rate shocks on the bank's market value of equity (V_E). Both RGAP and MDGAP are used because investors and regulators expect banks to manage the impact of interest rates on both their NII and V_E.

The prices of loans, bonds, and other fixed income instruments are *inversely* related to interest rates, and we can measure the sensitivity of this relation using the concept of **duration** (again, we cover the fundamentals of duration in this chapter's Appendix). Thus, in addition to the maturity mismatch between assets and liabilities, banks must also monitor the duration mismatch between assets and liabilities. Keep in mind that the *greater* the duration of an asset or liability, the *more* sensitive will be its market value to changes in interest rates. For example, a 10-year loan will have a much greater duration than a 1-year certificate of deposit (CD) and thus the longer-term loan's interest rate risk will be quite large relative to the shorter-term deposit. In all, this creates a risk exposure that the bank must hedge either through managing these asset–liability mismatches directly or by using derivatives.

We can apply the concept of duration to estimate the interest rate sensitivity of both a bank's assets and liabilities. This is possible because, for example, a bank's loans and deposits can be viewed as fixed income instruments that behave like a typical bond. So, we can estimate the modified duration of all the bank's assets (MD_A) as a weighted average of each specific asset's duration, as follows[7]:

$$MD_A = \sum\nolimits_i \left(W_{A,i} \cdot MD_{A,i} \right) \qquad (4.3)$$

---

[7] As described in the Appendix, modified duration uses a fixed income instrument's duration and divides it by $(1 + R)$, where R represents the instrument's current yield to maturity (YTM).

where

$w_{A,i}$ = percentage of Total Assets (TA) invested in the ith asset = (A_i / TA) and

A_i = dollar value invested in the ith asset.

Using the data from the Stylized Balance Sheet for ABC presented earlier in this chapter, let's assume the following about the modified durations of the bank's assets:

As shown in Table 4.4, ABC's modified duration of assets (MD_A) is 3.07 years due to the 58% weight placed on the relatively longer duration of the bank's Net Loans (at 4.00 years). Note that in the above calculation, we assume Cash & Reserves have a duration of zero and that Other Assets (such as Net Fixed Assets) do not have a duration associated with them. These assumptions could be relaxed to allow for non-zero durations for these assets but, in practice, they are usually set to zero.

Similarly, we can estimate the modified duration of a bank's liabilities (MD_L) as a weighted average of each liability's duration:

$$MD_L = \sum_j (W_j \cdot MD_{L,j}) \qquad (4.4)$$

where

$w_{L,j}$ = percentage of Total Liabilities (TL) borrowed in the form of the jth asset = (L_j / TL) and

L_j = dollar value borrowed in the form of the jth asset.

Like we did for ABC's assets, let's use the data from the Stylized Balance Sheet and assume the following about the modified durations of the bank's liabilities:

Table 4.4. Modified Duration of ABC's Assets.

Assets	Value ($ million)	Modified Duration (yrs)	Contribution to MD_A
Cash & Reserves	$4	0.00	(4 / 100) · 0.0 = 0.00 yrs.
Investments	30	2.50	(30 / 100) · 2.5 = 0.75 yrs.
Net Loans	58	4.00	(58 / 100) · 4.0 = 2.32 yrs.
Other Assets	8	N.A.	N.A.
Total Assets	$100	MD_A =	0.00 + 0.75 + 2.32 = **3.07 yrs.**

Table 4.5. Modified Duration of Liabilities.

Liabilities	Value ($ million)	Modified Dur. (yrs)	Contribution to MD_L
Deposits	$75	1.00	$(75 / 90) \cdot 1.0 = 0.83$ yrs.
Other Borrowed Money	15	3.24	$(15 / 90) \cdot 3.24 = 0.54$ yrs.
Total Liabilities	$90	$MD_L =$	$0.00 + 0.75 + 2.32 =$ **1.37 yrs.**

As shown in Table 4.5, the modified duration of liabilities (MD_L) is 1.37 years and is driven by the heavy reliance on shorter duration Deposits (83.33% of Total Liabilities). Note that Deposits of $75 million are a summary of different sub-components of ABC's short-term financing and typically include checking accounts/"core" deposits as well as longer-term money market accounts and certificates of deposit (CDs). There is an ongoing debate on how to estimate the duration of checking accounts and core deposits. In theory, these accounts allow for immediate withdrawal of funds and thus their durations would be zero. In practice, checking accounts and core deposits are "sticky" and are not immediately withdrawn even when interest rates change dramatically. Thus, their effective duration could be several years rather than zero! To be conservative, many bank managers will assign a zero duration to these core deposits to compute a larger interest rate risk exposure which, in turn, enables the bank to be cautious and hedge more of any possible risk.

To measure the impact of interest rate changes on the bank's market value of equity (V_E), we can simply subtract the modified duration of the bank's liabilities (MD_L) from the bank's assets (MD_A). This calculation is normally referred to as the bank's *Unadjusted Modified Duration Gap*[8]:

$$\text{Unadjusted MDGAP} = \text{UMDGAP} = MD_A - MD_L \quad (4.5)$$

Based on the numbers from Tables 4.4 and 4.5, we can compute the Unadjusted MDGAP as follow:

$$\text{Unadjusted MDGAP} = \text{UMDGAP} = MD_A - MD_L = 3.07 \text{ years} - 1.37 \text{ years} = +\mathbf{1.70 \text{ years}}$$

---

[8] This modified duration gap is called "unadjusted" because it does not adjust the calculation for the bank's degree of financial leverage. We describe the "leverage-adjusted MDGAP" later when we introduce Equation (4.8).

Note that the *sign* of the above calculation is important because it tells us whether ABC is *asset-sensitive* (UMDGAP is positive) or *liability-sensitive* (UMDGAP is negative). Given that ABC's UMDGAP is positive, we can see that the bank's assets will be affected more significantly to increases in interest rates. Thus, changes in the value of these assets will be the main driver of changes in ABC's market value of equity (V_E), as described in the following.

The reason we can use a modified duration gap to estimate the interest rate risk of the bank's equity is based on the Accounting Identity concept first discussed in Chapters 1 and 3: Total Assets (TA) equals Total Liabilities (TL) plus Shareholders Equity (or, in our notation here, TA = TL + E). If TA and TL are based on market values and not book values, then E in this identity is also equal to the bank's market value of equity (which we typically denote as V_E). If we re-arrange this identity, we can obtain the following:

$$V_E = E = \text{TA} - \text{TL} \qquad (4.6)$$

We can also take the dollar change of Equity (ΔE) of Equation (4.6):

$$\Delta E = \Delta \text{TA} - \text{TL} \qquad (4.7)$$

Thus, the change in the bank's market value of equity (ΔE) is positively related to changes in the bank's assets and negatively related to the bank's liabilities. We can then combine Equation (4.7) with our insights about modified duration and interest rate changes described in the Appendix by Equation (A4.10), as well as our definitions of MD_A and MD_L from Equations (4.3) and (4.4):

$$\Delta A = -\text{MD}_A \cdot \Delta R \cdot \text{TA}$$

$$\Delta L = -\text{MD}_L \cdot \Delta R \cdot \text{TL}$$

Inserting the above items into (4.7) yields[9]

$$\Delta E = [-\text{MD}_A \cdot \Delta R \cdot \text{TA}] - [-\text{MD}_L \cdot \Delta R \cdot \text{TL}]$$

---

[9] Note that both MD_A and MD_L have negative signs in front of them. This negative sign is included for both terms to account for the inverse relationship between interest rate changes and the market values of bank assets and liabilities.

which can then be re-arranged and re-defined as follows:

$$\Delta E = -\text{MDGAP} \cdot \Delta R \cdot \text{TA} \tag{4.8}$$

where

Leverage-adjusted Modified Duration Gap = MDGAP = $MD_A - \alpha \cdot MD_L$,

α = the bank's leverage ratio as measured by $\alpha = TL / TA$,

ΔR = estimated (instantaneous and parallel) change in interest rates, and

R = base level of interest rates just prior to the interest rate "shock".

Equation (4.8) provides a concise way to quantify the impact of a change in interest rates (ΔR) on the bank's assets and liabilities which, in turn, affects the market value of the bank's equity. Also, note that the term, α, is needed to adjust the bank's duration gap to account for the fact that the firm is not fully financed by liabilities (i.e., the bank also has equity in its capital structure). We call this alternate version of modified duration the *Leverage-Adjusted MDGAP*.

In this case, ABC's leverage-adjusted MDGAP is 1.837 years via the above formula, as follows:

$$\text{MDGAP} = MD_A - \alpha \cdot MD_L = 3.070 - [(90/100) \cdot (1.37)] = +3.070 - 1.233 = +1.837 \text{ years}$$

The *positive* MDGAP shown above means that the bank's assets have a longer duration than its liabilities and thus are vulnerable to *rising* interest rates because, in this rate scenario, the market value of the assets will decrease *more* than the drop in the liabilities' market value. So, shareholders, managers, analysts, and regulators all are interested in how much interest rate risk the bank can handle and how it affects the firm's market value.

To make things more concrete, we can use the following information to calculate the impact on market value of a 100-basis point increase in interest rates for our hypothetical bank, ABC, by plugging in the relevant numbers into Equation (4.8):

$$\Delta E = -\text{MDGAP} \cdot \Delta R \cdot \text{TA} = -(+1.837) \cdot (+0.01) \cdot (\$100 \text{ million})$$
$$= -0.01837 \cdot \$100 \text{ million} = -\$1.837 \text{ million}$$

As we had noted when we introduced ABC's stylized financial statements earlier in this chapter, we are focusing on the *market values* of the bank's operating assets and liabilities so that we can study the impact of interest rate risk on the market value of equity. Also, when performing the above calculation, make sure to use the *correct signs* and *decimal format* for each variable. For example, note that a 100-bps increase in interest rates (+0.01) causes a $1.837 million *decrease* in ABC's market value because the MDGAP of +1.837 years is multiplied by −1.0 due to the inverse relationship between asset values and interest rate changes. As interest rates rise, this drop in equity is driven by the decrease in the market value of longer-duration assets which, in this example, is a much bigger decline than the fall in the market value of ABC's shorter-duration liabilities. For example, as described earlier by Equation (4.7), we could decompose the change in market value of equity into the changes in the values of assets and liabilities to see how each component affects the result:

$$\Delta E = [-MD_A \cdot \Delta R \cdot TA] - [-MD_L \cdot DR \cdot TL]$$
$$= [(-3.07) \cdot (+0.01) \cdot (\$100)] - [(-1.37) \cdot (+0.01) \cdot (\$90)]$$
$$= -3.07 \text{ million} - (-1.233 \text{ million}) = -\$1.837 \text{ million}$$

The above calculation shows that the $1.837 million decline in ABC's equity is driven by a drop in the firm's assets of $3.07 million, which is partially offset by the $1.233 million decrease in the bank's liabilities. Since liabilities are *subtracted* from assets to obtain a firm's equity, any *decrease* in liabilities acts as a boost to equity (because arithmetic tells us that a negative of a negative number is a positive). We can also calculate the percentage change in ABC's equity by dividing ΔE by the bank's initial level of equity, E_0 (which can be found as $10 million in the Stylized Balance Sheet presented earlier in this chapter), as follows:

$$\%\Delta E = \frac{\Delta E}{E_0} = \frac{-\$1.837 \text{ million}}{\$10 \text{ million}} = -0.1837 \quad \text{or} \quad -18.37\% \quad (4.9)$$

Equation (4.9) shows us that the −18.37% loss to shareholders is quite large due to ABC's high degree of financial leverage. Thus, a relatively small drop in the bank's assets (−1.837%) leads to a much greater loss to shareholders because these investors have only financed 10% of the bank's total capital structure. Thus, the loss to shareholders is *10 times greater* than the loss in asset value (i.e., the firm's leverage affects the

Table 4.6. The Effect of Interest Rate Risk Exposure on a Bank's Market Value of Equity (V_E).

Modified Duration Gap	Interest Rate Shock	
	Rising Rates ($\Delta R > 0$)	Falling Rates ($\Delta R < 0$)
Positive MDGAP ($MD_A > MD_L$)	$\Delta V_E < 0$	$\Delta V_E > 0$
Negative MDGAP ($MD_A < MD_L$)	$\Delta V_E > 0$	$\Delta V_E < 0$

Equity Multiplier which is the reciprocal of the bank's equity-to-assets ratio = 1 / 0.10 = 10×). Due to the typical bank's high leverage, the bank's manager must manage interest rate risk (and all other risks) carefully because small losses in asset value can translate into very large losses for the bank's equity owners.

Table 4.6 summarizes the various interest rate shock scenarios and their impact on the bank's market value of equity (V_E) using a duration-based approach.

Table 4.6 reveals that interest rate risk is *highest* when the bank's MDGAP and ΔR are of the *same sign*. That is, bank managers should be most concerned with two scenarios: (1) rising rates when MDGAP is positive *and* rates are expected to rise or (2) when MDGAP is negative *and* rates are expected to fall. As we show later in this chapter, this type of risk can affect both NII and the bank's MVE, thus prompting the firm to consider hedging this interest rate with some type of derivative security.

Some Challenges in using the Modified Duration Gap
As we have discussed above, the modified duration gap is another analytically convenient way to measure and manage interest rate risk. However, it does have some limitations which can reduce its effectiveness as a risk management tool. Some of these points have already been mentioned in our discussion of RGAP but are included here because they also apply to the MDGAP method:

1. **Instantaneous rate shocks:** Like RGAP, we assume a sudden and instantaneous change in interest rates which might not be that realistic. Such a rapid change of, say, 100 or 300 basis points results in a much more severe impact on a bank's market value. If, for example, the rate change occurs more slowly over, say, 12 months, then the bank has time to adjust its MDGAP in a way to minimize the impact of the rate change. So, a sudden, instantaneous rate shock could be

viewed as a conservative test that provides a "worst case" scenario of its impact on market value. And, as was seen in 2022 when the U.S. Federal Reserve Board quickly raised short-term rates over 300 basis points, such sudden rate shocks do occur on occasion and thus are not entirely unrealistic.

2. **Runoffs:** The sudden withdrawal of longer-term deposits and/or the early repayment of long-term loans can lead to "runoff" that clouds the picture presented by MDGAP. These unexpected runoffs cause the duration of assets and liabilities to shorten. If, for example, the withdrawal of long-term deposits is much larger than any repayment of long-term loans, then the "true" MDGAP could be much more positive than originally projected. This could leave the bank exposed if interest rates suddenly rose after these deposit runoffs occurred. The main point is that a bank manager must carefully estimate loan and deposit runoff to make sure the MDGAP captures an accurate picture of long-term interest rate risk.

3. **Optionality:** Like sudden runoffs of loans and liabilities, the "optionality" of some bank products can also make it difficult to accurately estimate a rate change's impact on market value. For example, fixed rate mortgages typically can be repaid without penalty at the discretion of the borrower (especially when mortgage rates fall sharply). Or a depositor with a long-term CD might decide to withdraw their money before maturity because they can earn a higher rate elsewhere (even after considering any early withdrawal fees). Thus, the borrower has an option to prepay the loan which, in turn, can quickly transform a long-term asset into a short-term asset that then affects the MDGAP calculation. So, a good bank manager needs to consider how many long-term assets and liabilities might take advantage of any refinancing and reinvestment options.

4. **Off-balance sheet items:** The MDGAP model also uses assets and liabilities that are currently on the balance sheet and might ignore possible off-balance sheet items such as lines of credit and loan guarantees that can be drawn upon during the year. If these "takedowns" are substantial and result in more longer term loans, then the true MDGAP will be much greater than the bank's original estimate.

5. **Yield curve twists:** The estimated impact on market value will be affected if there are any "twists" in the yield curve where short-term and long-term rates do not move in tandem and long-term asset rates do not change by the same amount.

4.5 How to Use Both RGAP and MDGAP to Manage Interest Rate Risk?

Based on the above discussions of the RGAP and MDGAP models, we can see that they can help inform a bank manager in two complementary ways. With its shorter-term focus, the RGAP approach quantifies how a sudden interest rate shock can affect next year's Net Interest Income (NII). Although this information is focused on the short term, it is closely followed by investors because changes in NII can serve as an important signal about the strength of the bank's future earnings and cash flows. In contrast, the MDGAP method takes a longer-term view by factoring all future inflows and outflows from the bank's assets and liabilities. This latter approach allows us to directly estimate the impact of interest rate shocks on the bank's market value of equity (V_E). However, both RGAP and MDGAP are commonly used because investors and U.S. regulators expect banks to manage the impact of interest rates on both NII and V_E to maximize shareholder value as well as maintain a safe and sound financial system.

The numerical examples shown earlier in this chapter highlight the need to manage a bank's interest rate risk because, in the normal course of business, these firms typically borrow short term and lend long term, thus creating large mismatches in the maturities and durations of their assets and liabilities. In fact, it is possible for a bank to have positive values for *both* RGAP and MDGAP. That is, a bank like ABC might normally have more rate-sensitive assets than rate-sensitive liabilities (RSA > RSL) by granting many variable rate loans while also having interest-earning assets that are longer duration than those of ABC's deposits and other liabilities (MD_A > MD_L). In this case, ABC's positive RGAP would lead to higher NII when there is an *increase* in interest rates. In contrast, this same increase in rates could *decrease* ABC's market value of equity (V_E) due to the bank's positive MDGAP. Thus, if the bank's managers are more concerned about the firm's market value, then it might want to hedge some of this interest rate risk by (1) shortening the duration of assets, (2) lengthening the duration of liabilities, and/or (3) using derivatives to offset this MDGAP.[10]

---

[10] Keep in mind that U.S. regulators (and most investors) care about both *short-term* effects on Net Interest Income (due to a non-zero RGAP) as well as *long-term* effects on the bank's market value of equity. These two different risk metrics provide alternative and complementary ways to assess the bank's interest rate risk and so both are relevant for bank managers to quantify and manage.

Table 4.7. Maturity-based Interest Rate Risk Management.

RSA vs. RSL	Repricing Gap	IRR?	If rates rise	If rates fall
RSA > RSL	>0	**Falling** rates	Do nothing	**Pay Floating &** Receive Fixed
RSA < RSL	<0	**Rising** rates	Pay Fixed & Receive Floating	Do nothing

Table 4.8. Duration-based Interest Rate Risk Management.

DA vs. DL	Duration Gap	IRR?	If rates rise	If rates fall
$D_A > D_L$	>0	**Rising** rates	**Sell** Short	Do nothing
$D_A > D_L$	<0	**Falling** rates	Do nothing	**Go Long**

Tables 4.7 and 4.8 summarize the scenarios where RGAP and MDGAP can create interest rate risk (IRR) and provide possible actions by a bank manager to handle this risk. In Table 4.7, we can see that a bank with a positive RGAP is exposed to NII risk when rates are *falling*. In this declining rate situation, Table 4.7 suggests that a bank could use a "pay floating-receive fixed" interest rate swap to mitigate any negative impact on NII. We discuss derivatives such as interest rate swaps in more detail in Chapters 5 and 7 (Market Risk and Off-Balance Sheet Risk). For now, we can simply view such a swap instrument as one way to move RGAP closer to zero. The second row of Table 4.7 presents the opposite case where a bank has a negative RGAP and greater risk when interest rates are *rising*. In this alternative case, the bank manager can reduce its interest rate risk by, for example, entering a "pay fixed-receive floating" interest rate swap. In sum, the bank's interest rate risk occurs when RGAP and the projected change in interest rates (ΔR) are of *opposite* sign (e.g., positive RGAP and falling rates *or* negative RGAP and rising rates).

Table 4.8 repeats the analysis from above but with a focus on a bank's MDGAP. We can see that a bank with a positive MDGAP causes the bank's market value (V_E) to drop when rates are *increasing*. In this rising rate scenario, Table 4.8 suggests that a bank could "go short" via selling an interest rate futures and/or forward contract to reduce any potential negative impact on market value. At this point, we can view a futures or forward contract as two ways to move the bank's MDGAP closer to zero. The second row of Table 4.8 illustrates the opposite case where a bank has a negative MDGAP and greater interest rate risk when interest rates are *falling*. In this alternative situation, the bank manager can reduce its interest rate risk by, for example, "going long" a futures or forward contract. In sum, the bank's interest rate risk occurs when MDGAP and the projected change in interest rates (ΔR) are of the *same* sign (e.g., positive MDGAP and rising rates *or* negative MDGAP and falling rates).

4.6 Using the Integrated Valuation Model (IVM) to Explore the Impact of Interest Rate Risk

As we did in Chapter 3, we can use the IVM to analyze how changes in risk (in this case, interest rate risk) can affect a bank's market value of equity. After identifying the amount of interest rate risk the bank is exposed to, the bank's management team must weigh the incremental benefits of reducing this risk relative to the added costs of doing so (e.g., via hedging with derivatives or altering the bank's assets and liabilities). "On-balance sheet hedging" refers to the bank's choice to manage this interest rate risk by adjusting the maturity/duration of its assets relative to its liabilities. As noted earlier when we discussed the "ARMs" of Asset–Liability Management (ALM), this type of on-balance sheet hedging can be difficult to do because it can take considerable time to adjust the bank's loans, investments, and deposits and because it can disrupt or alienate the bank's customers.

So, in many cases, the bank's managers will find it faster, cheaper, and less disruptive to use "*Off-balance sheet hedging*" via derivative instruments, such as interest rate forwards, futures, options, and swaps. As we discuss in more detail in Chapter 7, off-balance sheet risk management can be an effective way to manage many types of risks, including interest rate risk. For now, we can focus on the incremental costs and benefits of hedging interest rate risk without getting into too much detail about the various types of derivative securities, as they are described more fully in Hull (2010) and Saunders *et al.* (2024).

Another point to keep in mind relates to the reason why a bank's managers would want to manage or adjust a bank's interest rate risk in the first place. In fact, we need to consider a fundamental concept in finance that was originally proposed in a Nobel Prize-winning research paper (Modigliani and Miller, 1958) and is commonly referred to as the "M-M Irrelevance Proposition." The basic idea is that a bank's financial decisions like hedging are *irrelevant* if financial markets are perfectly efficient. This occurs because any adjustments to the riskiness and cash flows of a firm's business operations can be costlessly replicated (or undone) by external investors and thus these hedging decisions do *not* affect the firm's market value. In effect, one implication of M-M Irrelevance Proposition is that anything investors can do themselves, there is no benefit for the firm to do. As mentioned above, this proposition hinges on a crucial (and unrealistic) assumption that financial markets are "perfect." That is, the authors assume a perfect-world scenario where "market frictions" such as taxes, financial distress/bankruptcy costs, agency problems, and asymmetric information do *not* exist.[11] In this perfect world, any investor in our hypothetical ABC bank can deal with ABC's interest rate risk just as easily as the bank's own manager.

According to this logic, if the investor wanted to remove ABC's interest rate risk exposure to their portfolio, then they could easily and costlessly use derivatives or adjust some on-balance sheet holdings. Thus, the investor does not need ABC's managers to make any adjustments to the bank's interest rate exposure, and therefore any changes made by the management team will *not* be valued by this investor (or any other investors). So, investors will *not* want to pay a premium over the market value of ABC's business operations for any hedging decisions the firm makes.

In practice, there *are* market frictions like taxes and bankruptcy costs and so ABC's managers *can* add value to the firm's equity by making hedging decisions on behalf of the investors because the management team can reduce the costs related to these market frictions more cheaply

---

[11]Asymmetric information problems occur when insiders (such as the bank's managers) know more than "non-insiders," such as external investors in the firm's stocks and bonds. In this case, the insiders could potentially exploit their informational advantage and harm the investments of the external investors.

Agency costs refer to conflicts between two or more parties, such as between the bank's managers and the bank's equity owners. When the managers and owners are not the same people, then the managers could take actions which benefit themselves but harm the equity investors. This is like the idea of how a real estate agent might be more focused on getting their commission rather than obtaining the highest sales price for the owner of the home. This type of agency conflict also exists between bondholders and shareholders in a firm. In this situation, the equity owners might want to take more risk than bondholders would like because the shareholders benefit if the extra risk pays off, but if it does not pay off, then the bondholders are left having to deal with losses and possible bankruptcy.

and effectively than an external investor. If the firm cannot hedge any better than other investors, then the management team should *not* spend any time or energy to mitigate or adjust the bank's interest rate risk (or any other financial risk, for that matter).

One other important point relates to *how* to manage the bank's risks. In this chapter, we focus on one way to manage risk based on using derivative instruments to hedge the bank's exposure. However, keep in mind that there are other ways to manage this risk and we can use the acronym, "ART," to think about this concept. The "ART" **of risk management** pertains to *three* different choices a firm can make when faced with a risk such as interest rate risk, as noted in the following:

1. **Accept the risk:** Keep in mind that the firm can always *do nothing*! That is, we do not need to hedge if the risk is relatively small and/or the risk is not "material" in its impact on the firms' cash flows and market value.
2. **Remove the risk:** If the risk is indeed large and material, then the firm could *diversify* by investing in other assets that are, ideally, negatively correlated with the bank's existing assets (thus removing the risk via the offsetting returns of this new investment). However, it is usually very hard to find assets that behave in this way.

    Alternatively, the managers can try to remove the risk by *divesting* themselves of the products or business units that are generating the risk. For example, if a company has operations in a foreign country and does not want to be exposed to currency risk, then the managers might decide to sell off this business unit. This type of risk management is sometimes referred to as "on-balance sheet hedging" and can clearly be costly, less flexible, and cumbersome to implement, as it could take a long time to find a buyer and finalize the divestiture of a foreign business unit. Also, some risks like a bank's interest rate and credit risks cannot be completely divested (unless the company does not want to be a bank anymore!).
3. **Transfer the risk:** This approach includes *hedging* with financial derivatives and traditional insurance products. By using these instruments, a bank can transfer the risk to a third party such as when the bank uses an interest rate forward contract to hedge against rising rates. In this case, the bank can quickly and cheaply transfer the risk of higher rates to someone else who is willing to bear this risk. This approach is also more flexible than the divestiture method because the

bank can always go back into the derivatives markets to reverse this initial forward contract. So, it is not surprising that banks are heavy users of derivative instruments that provide cheap, fast, and flexible protection against bank-related risks.

4.7 How can we Estimate the Impact of Interest Rate Risk on a Bank's Market Value of Equity?

Based on the "ART" of risk management discussed above and the fact that financial markets are imperfect, we have good reason to focus on a bank's decision to manage interest rate risk because these choices, if made well, can increase the firm's market value of equity. We can use a "hedge ratio" as a way to measure how much to reduce a bank's interest rate risk exposure. The hedge ratio (h) shows what percentage of the bank's total exposure is hedged by some type of interest rate derivative. This ratio varies in decimal form between 0.0 and 1.0 and typically represents a range from 0% to 100% of the bank's interest rate risk exposure. Note that the bank can choose any value along this range and thus the hedging choice is usually not an all (e.g., $h = 1.0$) or nothing choice ($h = 0.0$). In economic terms, the bank should choose an optimal level of hedging (h^*) where the marginal benefits and costs of hedging are equal. In effect, we are applying classical "cost-benefit analysis" to find the bank's optimal hedge ratio.

A key to a successful hedging strategy is to first identify the appropriate interest rate exposure to measure. As we have described earlier in this chapter, investors and regulators care about both short-term effects, as measured by RGAP's impact on NII, *and* long-term effects, as measured by MDGAP's influence on the bank's market value of equity (V_E). For example, we can use an interest rate swap to adjust the bank's RGAP to reduce the impact on NII of, say, a 100-basis point rate change. To quantify the potential impact of this hedging decision, we can estimate the hedge's *total costs* (e.g., the transaction costs and management time to put the hedge in place) and its *total benefits* (e.g., NII's reduced interest rate sensitivity due to an RGAP that is closer to zero).

Summarized in the following is one example of how we can model this trade-off. Clearly, there are numerous other ways to describe this hedging relationship and so bank managers have considerable leeway in identifying the key factors influencing the costs and benefits of interest rate risk management. For example, Hull (2010), among others, has suggested a "minimum variance hedge ratio" that can be estimated by performing a regression analysis of historical changes in the bank's risk exposure relative to past changes in a derivative security's value. Alternatively, Saunders *et al.* (2024) suggest a hedge ratio based on "immunizing" a bank's exposure so that there is no change in the firm's equity value. However, Hull's approach is best applied to "micro hedging" a specific sub-component of a bank's interest rate risk such as long-term bond holdings within its securities portfolio. Instead, throughout our book, we focus on "macro hedging" which looks holistically at the bank's specific risks (such as interest rate risk) across the entire balance sheet rather than focusing on sub-components of assets and liabilities. This approach is consistent with Saunders *et al.* (2024) and enables us to consider the trade-off between risk and return in terms of its overall effect on the bank's market value. However, in contrast to Saunders *et al.* (2024), our approach helps us find the hedge ratio that maximizes the bank's share price rather than restricting ourselves to a hedge ratio that results in a zero change in market value.[12] The following discussion is meant to be an initial attempt to examine the direct costs and benefits of this trade-off. As we discuss later in this chapter, using the IVM within an Excel™ spreadsheet allows us to consider a more detailed analysis that includes both direct and indirect effects of the bank's hedging decision.

First, we can approach this problem by spelling out the total benefits and total costs of hedging the bank's interest rate risk. In this way, we can see the change in the bank's market value of equity due to the hedging decision by comparing the value of the bank with hedging ($V_{E,\text{Hedged}}$) versus its value without hedging ($V_{E,\text{Unheded}}$) as follows:

$$\Delta V_E = V_{E,\text{Hedged}} - V_{E,\text{Unheded}} = \text{Total Benefit of Hedge} - \text{Total Cost of Hedge}$$

---

[12] Kim (2023) finds empirical evidence that is consistent with our notion that banks hedge to maximize firm value rather than minimize risk. For example, the author finds that banks actively manage their interest rate risk by increasing their hedging when faced with larger losses in their fixed income portfolios and then decreasing hedging when these securities generate gains. However, this hedging activity does not eliminate all risk and suggests that banks actively adjust their hedge ratios to maximize firm value.

ΔV_E = $ Reduction in RGAP · rate shock − (fixed heading cost + variable hedging cost)

$$\Delta V_E = [I \cdot (h \cdot \text{RGAP}) \cdot \Delta R] - [C + ((v \cdot h) \cdot (h \cdot \text{RGAP}))]$$
$$= [I \cdot (h \cdot \text{RGAP}) \cdot \Delta R] - [(c + (v \cdot h^2)) \cdot \text{RGAP})] \quad (4.10)$$

where

ΔV_E = change in the bank's market value due to hedging RGAP = $V_{E,\text{Hedged}} - V_{E,\text{Unhedged}}$,

I = indicator variable = −1 if (RGAP · ΔR) < 0 and 0 if (RGAP · ΔR) > 0,

h = hedge ratio = Dollar Amount Hedged / RGAP = $Hedged / RGAP,

C = fixed cost of hedging (in dollars) and can also be defined as $C = c \cdot \text{RGAP}$,
where c = the fixed dollar cost of hedging expressed as a percentage of the total risk exposure, RGAP,

v = variable cost of hedging as a percentage of RGAP (in decimal format),

$Reduction in RGAP = $amount of RGAP that is hedged = $h \cdot \text{RGAP}$, and

ΔR = interest rate shock = assumed instantaneous change in interest rates (in decimal format).

The first term in square brackets of Equation (4.10) identifies the incremental benefits of hedging all or a portion (h) of the bank's RGAP, while the second term in square brackets shows the costs of this hedge when a worst-case interest rate shock (ΔR) occurs. We define the hedging benefits as the dollar amount of losses *avoided* due to hedging a portion of the potential interest rate shock. We multiply this hedging benefit by an indicator variable (I) that is equal to −1 in Equation (4.10) when RGAP and ΔR are of *opposite* sign because our earlier discussion of RGAP showed that the bank faces interest rate risk in this situation (e.g., a negative RGAP and rising rates *or* positive RGAP and falling rates). Note that the indicator variable equals *zero* if RGAP and ΔR are of the *same* sign because, in this case, the bank is *not* facing interest rate risk and thus there is no benefit to hedging interest rate risk. Thus, when RGAP and ΔR have the *same* sign, then the optimal action is to *not* hedge at all. This observation is consistent with what we had summarized earlier about interest rate risk in Table 4.7 pertaining to the "Do Nothing" categories.

The second term in brackets of Equation (4.10) represents the total costs of implementing a hedging strategy and is broken down into the dollar amount of the hedge's **fixed costs** ($C = c \cdot$ RGAP) and **variable costs** (i.e., $(v \cdot h^2) \cdot$ RGAP)). Fixed costs include all **explicit, direct costs** to start up and maintain a risk management team even if they do not hedge any exposures. These costs usually include compensation for risk management and compliance personnel, as well as expenses for data, software, and any general overhead for the team. In addition, **implicit, indirect hedging costs** can play an important role such as time spent by senior management supervising the risk managers and the opportunity cost of using the direct hedging costs for other potentially more valuable purposes within the bank (like investing in new products or services). Depending on the complexity of the bank's exposures, these explicit and implicit fixed costs can be quite significant and run into the millions of dollars. The **variable costs** pertain to the actual expenses related to initiating and monitoring the bank's hedging positions, such as brokerage fees, bid-ask spreads, and margin/collateral requirements. These costs all increase directly with the size of the bank's hedging position and thus vary depending on the amount of hedging the risk management team decides to do.

The most important point to consider in this regard is that the bank should *not* hedge if the costs of hedging are greater than the maximum potential benefits from hedging. Thus, as a first step or "sanity check," the bank's senior management needs to decide if the fixed costs of hedging I are greater than the hedge's total benefits and, if so, then the FIs optimal hedge ratio is *zero*. For example, when the hedging program's fixed costs are $3 million and the maximum benefit of hedging is only $2 million, then the bank is clearly better off not incurring this fixed cost and, instead, should leave this interest rate risk unhedged.

So, a good "hedging rule of thumb" before embarking on a risk management program is to estimate the upfront fixed costs of such an initiative and compare this cost to the program's potential benefits. In terms of Equation (4.10), this means any decision to deviate from a "Do Nothing" strategy must ensure that (h · RGAP) · ΔR is at least *greater than C*.

If not, then it is not even worth moving to the next step to estimate a hedge's variable costs. **Remember, you can always do nothing when the costs do not justify the benefits!** This helps explain why many smaller banks do not hedge their interest rate risk (or other key risks). For these firms that lack economies of scale, the fixed costs of operating a risk management team can outweigh the relatively smaller benefits of hedging. However, for most larger commercial banks, hedging does make economic sense because the asset–liability mismatch normally creates a significant amount of interest rate risk. In this case, the potential benefits can be much greater than the fixed costs discussed above and so we see that large FIs typically employ a risk management team.

Based on the above discussion of RGAP and Equation (4.10), we can see how this interest rate risk management decision can impact the bank's market value of equity using the principles of the IVM. In fact, we can develop an estimate of the bank's hedging choice using the following extension of the IVM from Chapter 3 that explicitly quantifies the change in market value (denoted by the "delta" sign, Δ):

$$\Delta V_E = \left[\frac{\Delta(d \cdot NI)}{(R_E - g)} \right] = \left[\frac{d \cdot [(Hedge\ Benefit - Hedge\ Cost) \cdot (1-t)]}{(R_E - g)} \right]$$

$$= \left[\frac{d \cdot [(Hedge\ Benefit - Hedge\ Cost) \cdot (1-t)]}{Expected\ Dividend\ Yield} \right] \quad (4.11)$$

where

d = expected dividend payout ratio for next year (DIV_1 / NI_1),

Hedge Benefit = $(h \cdot RGAP) \cdot \Delta R$ (obtained from Equation 4.10),

Hedge Cost = $C + ((v \cdot h^2) \cdot RGAP)$ (obtained from Equation 4.10),

t = marginal corporate tax rate,

R_E = required return on the bank's equity,

g = constant growth rate of the bank's dividends, and

Expected Dividend Yield = $(DIV_1 / V_{E,0})$ and this term equals $(R_E - g)$ for the Constant Growth version of the IVM.

134 *Managing Financial Institutions: An Integrated Valuation Approach*

To keep the calculations somewhat manageable, Equation (4.11) makes some simplifying assumptions:

(1) The hedge ratio (h) does not impact other aspects of the bank's cash flows other than those shown in (4.11) and so the *after-tax net benefit of the hedge* (i.e., (Hedge Benefit – Hedge Cost) · $(1 - t)$ is the only factor affecting the bank's expected dividend. That is, ΔDIV = d · (after-tax net Hedge Benefit). Also, the sign of h tells us whether to use a *short* derivatives strategy such as selling an interest rate futures contract when $h < 0$ *or* to use a *long* derivatives strategy when $h > 0$.[13] **So, the *sign* of h is very important!**

(2) As noted earlier, the Hedge Cost has a fixed cost component (C) and a variable cost component that is a function of both an assumed variable cost factor, v, and the hedge ratio itself (h).[14] This interaction factor, ($v \cdot h$), when multiplied by the portion of RGAP that is hedged ($h \cdot$ RGAP), allows for a *nonlinear, exponential impact* of the hedge ratio on the cost of hedging via the term, ($v \cdot h^2$) · RGAP. Effectively, this is a scaling factor that reflects the rising cost of hedging when the bank decides to hedge a greater portion of its risk exposure. We can rewrite ($v \cdot h^2$) · RGAP as ($v \cdot$ Dollar Amount Hedged) · h to show more clearly that v is a variable cost that scales at an accelerating rate as the bank increases its level of hedging. This nonlinear effect is consistent with larger hedging costs when real-world financial markets exhibit *liquidity constraints* and *heightened volatility*.[15]

---

[13] A *short* derivatives strategy provides a *positive* payoff when the *price* of the underlying security (e.g., a bond in this example) *decreases*. Conversely, a *long* derivatives strategy provides a *positive* payoff when the *price* of the underlying security *increases*.

[14] As noted earlier in this chapter, the fixed cost (C) is independent of how much the bank chooses to hedge and can be viewed as the time and money spent by bank managers to decide how they want to manage their interest rate risk (e.g., costs for data terminals and software, hiring risk management professionals, compliance staff, and overhead).

[15] As Hull (2010) has noted, the cost of hedging also typically increases at a growing rate as the hedge ratio is increased. This is primarily due to *liquidity constraints* in the derivatives markets that the bank uses to initiate and liquidate a hedging position. For example, as the order size of the hedge grows in dollar terms, there might not be enough liquidity in the derivatives market to handle such a trade. This, in turn, causes bid-ask spreads and other transaction costs to rise. In addition, firms typically hedge *more* as *financial market volatility* grows and this causes hedging costs to rise even further because derivatives like

(3) The Expected Dividend Yield ($R_E - g$) remains constant even though the cash flow in the numerator of Equation (4.11) is changing. This is a simplifying assumption and is technically not true as the riskiness of the bank can change when the hedge ratio is adjusted. As discussed in Chapter 3, our IVM method assumes that any change in R_E or g directly offset each other and implies a constant expected dividend yield. This term therefore can be ignored for our calculation purposes.[16] For a more complete analysis of all potential effects of the hedging decision on firm value, we can use the Excel™ spreadsheet that is available on the authors' website and is discussed later in Chapter 12 (Integrated Risk Management: Putting it all together).

(4) The RGAP shown in Equation (4.11) is part of a constant growth IVM and thus, implicitly, we are assuming this repricing gap is permanent and will grow at a constant rate over time. Clearly, this is an oversimplification because RGAP can fluctuate widely over the long term. However, in practice, it is normally very difficult for bank managers and external analysts to forecast how RGAP will evolve beyond the next year. So, our approach addresses the problem in a simple way that most managers/analysts can use in a practical way. It also has the benefit that this assumption is consistent with logic and assumptions of the IVM first described in Chapter 3.

(5) The choice to hedge some portion of the bank's exposure depends on the management team's expectation of interest movements *and* the signs of the bank's RGAP and MDGAP. As shown earlier in Tables 4.7–4.8, the choice to hedge depends critically on the signs of RGAP and MDGAP *relative to* the expected interest rate shock. So, we assume that the bank will *selectively* hedge based on management's interest rate outlook and the bank's RGAP and MDGAP levels. For example, if rates are expected to rise, then the bank should hedge when RGAP is *negative* and MDGAP is *positive* but *not* hedge if the signs of these

---

options become more expensive in this situation. So, we have included here just one way we can model this nonlinear, exponential effect of hedging costs. Clearly, other forms of this hedging cost can lead to different conclusions about the optimal hedge ratio.

[16] This assumption can be a conservative estimate of the estimated change in market value (i.e., *lower* than what might occur) because hedging could, in theory, lower the bank's cost of equity (R_E) which would, in turn, raise the bank's valuation. So, assuming no net change in $R_E - g$ (as we do in our IVM method) might be a reasonably safe approach in this context.

gaps are *reversed* (i.e., RGAP is positive and MDGAP is negative). The reason is that, in the first case, the bank's NII and V_E would *decrease* as rates rise but in the latter case, the bank's NII and V_E would *increase* (and so the exposures should be left *unhedged* in this situation). So, we assume that the bank's managers rationally make their hedging choices based on both the bank's gaps and their interest rate outlook.

We can use the above variant of the IVM described in Equation (4.11) in a numerical example for our hypothetical bank, ABC, based on the initial data and assumptions presented earlier in this chapter as part of the Stylized Balance Sheet and Stylized Income Statement.

For simplicity, we do not consider a specific financial derivative instrument to hedge this risk as we can assume any one of the four major types of derivatives could be used to implement this hedge ratio (e.g., *shorting* this rate exposure via either interest rate forwards, futures, options, or swaps).

Table 4.9. Numerical Example of Hedging RGAP.

Rate Sensitive Asset (RSA)	$728.31
Rate Sensitive Liability (RSL)	$900.00
RGAP ($ million)	−171.69
Rate Shock	1.00%
Hedge FixedIst (c) % of RGAP	0.00%
Hedge Variable Cost (v) % of RGAP	2.00%
Dividend Payout	0.40
Tax Rate	0.20
Dividend Yield ($R_E - g$)	0.0357
Shares Outstanding (million)	1.00

Notes: Note that in this example ABC has a negative RGAP because it has $171.69 million more in rate-sensitive liabilities than rate-sensitive assets (RSL > RSA) and therefore its NII is vulnerable to increases in interest rates (i.e., positive rate shocks like the +100 basis points shown in Table 4.9). ABC's bank managers must decide whether this rate shock has a material effect and then choose the "optimal hedge ratio" (h^*) that maximizes the bank's stock price. In this example, we assume only variable costs are needed to implement the hedging program and are equal to 2% of the bank's RGAP exposure (i.e., no fixed costs are required here, but we relax this restriction shortly).

Interest Rate Risk 137

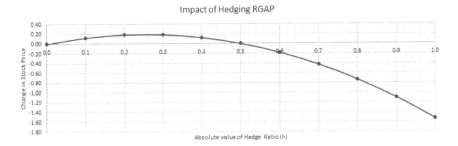

Figure 4.6. Impact of Hedging RGAP on ABC's Stock Price without any Fixed Costs.

We can find the answer to this important risk management decision by varying the absolute value of the hedge ratio from 0.0 (i.e., no hedging at all) to 1.0 (fully hedging 100% of the RGAP exposure). Figure 4.6 displays the results of this type of "what-if" simulation on the expected *change* in ABC's stock price. This graph is like the one presented in Chapter 3, but here we are looking at the impact of interest rate risk (rather than credit risk) on ABC's market value.

As we can see from Figure 4.6, ABC's stock price is boosted around $0.19 per share if it chooses an optimal hedge ratio, h^*, of 0.25 (or 25% of RGAP). In this case, ABC can maximize its market value by *shorting* 25% of its RGAP exposure. This specific hedge ratio is based on classical cost–benefit analysis and enables the marginal benefit of hedging to equal the marginal cost of this risk management strategy. It is at this specific point that we maximize the bank's stock price.[17] Any hedge ratio above or below 0.25 results in a *lower* change in ABC's stock price and therefore 0.25 is

---

[17]Technically, this optimal ratio is obtained by taking the mathematical derivative of Equation (4.10) with respect to the hedge ratio, h, and setting this derivative equal to zero. We can then solve algebraically for the optimal hedge ratio, h^*, using the data presented in Table 4.9. Based on these data and the model presented in Equation (4.10), the resulting **optimal hedge ratio**, h^*, is $h^* = I \cdot (\Delta R / (2 \cdot v)) = -1 \cdot (+0.01 / (2 \cdot 0.02)) = -1 \cdot (0.01 / 0.04) = -0.25 = -25\%$. This hedge ratio contains the benefits of hedging in the numerator ($I \cdot \Delta R$) and the related hedging *costs* in the denominator ($2 \cdot v$). Thus, $h^* = -0.25$ means the bank should *sell short* 25% of its RGAP to yield the maximum increase in the bank's stock price, which is confirmed by the graph displayed in Figure 4.6 (which, for convenience, displays the hedge ratio as an absolute value). Remember that shorting a fixed income derivative like a U.S. Treasury futures contract means that the bank will receive a *gain* on this short sale when interest rates *rise* (because bond prices fall as rates increase).

considered optimal because it increases market value the most. Another useful metric that can be derived from the optimal hedge ratio is the **optimal, or "target," RGAP*** that ABC should focus on to maximize the bank's market value. This target RGAP* can be found by using the absolute value of the optimal hedge ratio, $|h^*|$, in the following relationship:

$$\text{RGAP*} = (1 - |h^*|) \cdot \text{unhedged RGAP} \qquad (4.12)$$

In our numerical example, ABC's target RGAP* is –$128.768 million based on $h^* = 0.25$ and the unhedged RGAP is $171.690 million (i.e., (1–0.25) · (–$171.690 million) = –$128.7675). This figure is helpful to ABC's risk managers because they can use it as a benchmark to compare with the bank's actual RGAP over the course of the year.

However, even though it is helpful to have a target RGAP*, remember that in this numerical example the impact of interest rate risk is relatively small because RGAP only affects next year's NII and not any future profits beyond that one period. This change in stock price (+$0.19) is also relatively small in terms of a percentage change (+1.0%) when we compare it to the base stock price of $20.17 calculated earlier in Chapter 3. Keep in mind that even though the impact of hedging RGAP is modest, ABC's managers can choose to pursue this hedging strategy if the Hedge Benefits outweigh the Hedge Costs described by (4.11). Such a hedge can help ensure that the bank's NII is not too negatively impacted if rates do rise in the near future. This preservation of next year's NII can be important if ABC's management team is planning to use this inflow to help finance, for example, the bank's expansion of its target market or launching new products and services. It can also serve as a positive signal to investors about ABC's future earnings potential. In the long run, ABC's stock price could ultimately rise due to hedging in the short run to ensure the investment of next year's NII for future growth opportunities.

As mentioned earlier, a bank manager must also consider the fixed costs associated with setting up an interest rate risk management program (the C variable in Equation 4.10). We can now relax the assumption of

---

Also, the optimal hedge ratio formula shown here can be expanded to include "other costs" beyond the variable financial costs of the hedge itself, such as additional costs related to collateral/margin requirements, administrative expenses, operational constraints, and opportunity costs. This can be done by adjusting the above equation as follows: **h^* = 1 · (ΔR / (2 · (v + other costs))**. In general, the inclusion of these other costs (expressed as a percentage of RGAP) will push the optimal hedge ratio closer to zero.

Figure 4.7. Impact of Hedging RGAP on ABC's Stock Price with Fixed Costs.

zero fixed costs and assume that they are equal to 0.5% of the RGAP exposure for ABC. In this case, the addition of these fixed costs causes the total Hedge Costs to outweigh the total Hedge Benefits. This means that *no* hedge ratio can increase ABC's stock price, and, in fact, the optimal decision is to *not* implement an interest rate risk management program at all (i.e., $h^* = 0$ in this case). This can be seen in Figure 4.7, which shows that the 0.5% of fixed costs (or $858,450 in dollar terms) shifts the *entire* hedging curve down by a constant value of $0.77 per share. Thus, the *best* that ABC can do in this situation is to cause the firm's stock price to *fall* by around $0.58 when the hedge ratio is 0.25. This is certainly *not* a winning strategy! In this case, the best choice is to avoid the fixed cost in the first place and not hedge at all.

In addition to hedging RGAP, the bank also has the choice to manage its modified duration gap (MDGAP). We can explore this alternative way to manage interest rate risk by repeating the approach described earlier in Equation (4.10). Like with RGAP, we can consider the total benefits from the first term in Equation (4.13) and the total costs of hedging a bank's MDGAP in the second term as follows:

$$\Delta V_E = [I \cdot \text{MDGAP} \cdot \Delta R \cdot (h \cdot \text{TA})] - [C + ((v \cdot h) \cdot (h \cdot \text{TA}))]$$

$$= [I \cdot \text{MDGAP} \cdot \Delta R \cdot (h \cdot \text{TA})] - [(c + (v \cdot h^2)) \cdot \text{TA}] \quad (4.13)$$

where

ΔV_E = change in the bank's market value due to hedging MDGAP = $V_{E-\text{Hedged}} - V_{E,\text{Unhedged}}$,

I = indicator variable = -1 if MDGAP > 0 and +1 if MDGAP < 0 *and* 0 if (MDGAP · ΔR) < 0,

h = hedge ratio = Dollar Amount Hedged / Total Assets = \$Hedged / *TA*,

TA = total assets of the bank,

C = fixed cost of hedging (in dollars) and can also be defined as $C = (c \cdot$ Total Assets), where c = the fixed dollar cost of hedging expressed as a percentage of the bank's Total Assets (TA),

v = variable cost of hedging as percentage of \$Hedged (in decimal format),

\$Reduction in Interest Rate Risk = \$amount of Total Assets that is hedged = \$Hedged = $h \cdot TA$, and

ΔR = interest rate shock = assumed instantaneous change in interest rates (in decimal format).

Note that Equation (4.13) follows a similar structure to the model for RGAP shown in Equation (4.10). One key difference is that we are using the leverage-adjusted duration gap (MDGAP) rather than RGAP to quantify the bank's interest rate risk. Recall that MDGAP is a comprehensive measure of interest rate risk because it considers not only next year's NII but also all other future cash inflows and outflows from the bank's assets and liabilities. Thus, as Equation (4.8) showed earlier, any rate shock will typically have a different impact on bank value when we use this more "holistic" measure of interest rate risk because we are considering the impact of the rate shock on all interest-sensitive assets and liabilities.

To make sure the hedge ratio has the appropriate sign for shorting or going long the relevant derivative security, (4.13) includes an indicator variable, *I*, that equals -1 when MDGAP is positive, $+1$ when MDGAP is negative, and 0 when the product of MDGAP and DR is negative. Note that we multiply the hedging benefit by $+1$ or -1 in Equation (4.13) because our earlier discussion of MDGAP showed that the bank's interest rate risk occurs when MDGAP and DR are of the *same* sign (e.g., positive MDGAP and rising rates *or* negative MDGAP and falling rates). Thus, as shown earlier in Table 4.8, when MDGAP and the expected rate change are of *opposite* signs, the indicator variable is set to 0 because there are no negative effects of interest rate risk and thus there is no reason to hedge

Table 4.10. Numerical Example of Hedging MDGAP.

Total Assets ($ million)	1,580
Total Liabilities ($ million)	1,400
Mod. Duration of Assets (MD_A)	5.00
Mod. Duration of Liabilities (MD_L)	2.00
MDGAP (years)	3.23
Rate shock	1.00%
Hedge Fixed Cost, c (% of Tot. Assets)	0.00%
Hedge Variable Cost, v (% of Tot. Assets)	2.00%
Shares Outstanding (million)	10.00

in this situation. Once again, the "Do Nothing" strategy can be optimal depending on the bank's risk exposure and its outlook for interest rates.

Table 4.10 presents a numerical example of the key assumptions needed to estimate this impact. Many of these assumptions are like the ones used earlier for RGAP except for the first three rows. We now include Total Assets, Total Liabilities, and MDGAP because the model considers all assets rather than the RGAP's shorter term focus on next year's NII. Based on our example from earlier in this chapter, we assume that ABC has a leverage-adjusted duration gap of +1.837 years. This means ABC's assets are, on average, nearly two years longer in duration than its leverage-adjusted liabilities (i.e., $MD_A > \alpha \cdot MD_L$). As we have noted earlier, a bank that has a positive MDGAP is vulnerable to rising interest rates and so we assume a +100-basis point instantaneous rate shock in the following table.

We can also use the change in market value equity relationship described by Equation (4.8) to see the impact of the assumptions of Table 4.10 on ABC's stock price. Figure 4.8 displays the effect of various hedge ratios ranging from 0.0 (0%) to 1.0 (100%) in absolute value format.

As we can see from Figure 4.8, ABC's stock price rises around $2.05 per share if it chooses an optimal hedge ratio of *shorting* around 0.8 (or 80% of Total Assets). Any hedge ratio above or below 0.8 results in a lower change in ABC's stock price and therefore 0.8 is considered optimal because it increases market value the most. If we wanted to be more precise, we could solve for the level of h that equates the marginal benefits

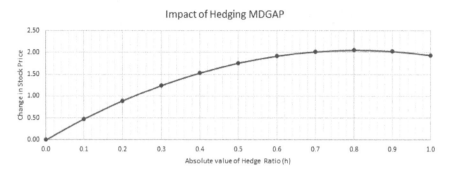

Figure 4.8. Impact of Hedging MDGAP on ABC's Stock Price.

and marginal costs of hedging. Given Equation (4.13) and the data in Table 4.10, we can see that the optimal hedge ratio, h^*, is nearly 0.807, or 80.7%.[18]

In contrast to our RGAP simulation which assumes the change in NII leads to a permanent increase in dividends, the impact on stock price based on MDGAP is much larger because it represents a one-time change in the bank's current market values of *both* assets and liabilities. For example, the impact based on MDGAP results in a percentage change of +10.2% (versus RGAP's + 1.0% estimate) when compared to the base stock price of $20.17. Given such a sizable impact on stock price, ABC's management has a stronger incentive to use some derivatives to hedge around 80% of the firm's assets.

As we described earlier for RGAP in Equation (4.12), we can use our duration-based optimal hedge ratio of 0.807 to estimate the **optimal, or**

---

[18]Like the solution to the optimal ratio for hedging the bank's RGAP discussed earlier, the optimal ratio for MDGAP is obtained by taking the mathematical derivative of Equation (4.13) with respect to the hedge ratio, h, and setting this derivative equal to zero. We can then solve algebraically for the optimal hedge ratio, h^*, using the data presented in Table 4.10. Based on these data and the model presented in Equation (4.12), the resulting **optimal hedge ratio**, h^*, is $h^* = (I \cdot (\text{MDGAP} \cdot \Delta R)) / (2 \cdot v) = -1 \cdot (+3.228 \cdot 0.01) / (2 \cdot 0.02) = -(0.03228 / 0.04) = -0.807 \approx -81\%$. Thus, $h = -0.807$ means the bank should sell short around 81% of its Total Assets (TA) to yield the maximum increase in the bank's stock price and is confirmed by the graph displayed in Figure 4.8 (which displays the hedge ratio as an absolute value). As we had mentioned in an earlier footnote related to RGAP, the optimal hedge ratio can be expanded to include other costs related to the hedging activity as follows: $h^* = (I \cdot (\textbf{MDGAP} \cdot \Delta R)) / (2 \cdot (v + \textbf{other costs}))$.

"target," **MDGAP*** that can maximize ABC's market value. This target MDGAP* can be found by using the absolute value of the optimal hedge ratio, $|h^*|$, in the following relationship:

$$\text{MDGAP}^* = (1 - |h^*|) \times \text{unhedged MDAP} \quad (4.14)$$

In our numerical example, ABC's target MDGAP* is around 0.62 years based on $h^* = 0.807$ and the unhedged MDGAP of 3.228 years (i.e., $(1 - 0.807) \cdot (3.228 \text{ years}) = 0.623$ years). This MDGAP* figure is useful to ABC's risk managers because they can use it as a benchmark to compare with the bank's actual MDGAP over the course of the year.

Also, as we showed earlier with RGAP, keep in mind that ABC must carefully manage the costs of hedging (i.e., the c and v factors within Equation 4.13) because increased hedging when variable costs are greater than the assumed 2% in Table 4.10 might actually *reduce* the firm's stock price. For example, if the variable cost factor, v, is 4% rather than the 2% assumed above, then ABC's stock price could decline at hedge ratios above 0.4 because the marginal costs of putting on such a large hedge outweigh the marginal benefits. In addition, if *fixed* costs represent 2% of Total Assets, then the optimal hedge ratio would be *zero* in this case because the potential Hedge Benefits are easily outweighed by these relatively large, fixed costs for *all* hedge ratios between 0.0 and 1.0. These points highlight the importance of performing **sensitivity and scenario analyses** to gain a more comprehensive understanding of the costs and benefits of hedging the bank's risks.

In this chapter, we have shown how to manage the short-term impact of interest rates on Net Interest Income (via RGAP) as well as the longer-term effect on stock price (via MDGAP). However, please keep in mind that ABC's management might want to focus *solely* on either RGAP *or* MDGAP rather than both risk measures. Within our valuation model, we can easily accommodate this approach by setting the hedge ratio for a specific gap measure to zero. For example, in the spreadsheet provided with this book, we could set h^* for RGAP to zero if we wish to manage only duration-based interest rate risk via MDGAP. Or, vice versa, we can set h^* for MDGAP to zero and focus on the short-term effects of RGAP on Net Interest Income. Most financial firms prefer to manage both RGAP and MDGAP, but you could certainly choose a different approach, as described here.

We should also remind ourselves of the discussion of the IVM's usefulness provided in Chapter 3 in identifying how market value can be impacted *directionally* by changes in the bank's risk-taking activities. Therefore, given all the assumptions we need to make to come up with a graph like Figure 4.8, we should not take the exact values plotted there too literally.[19] A better way to interpret Figure 4.8 is that ABC's stock price is likely to benefit the most from hedging its duration-based interest rate risk exposure within the range of 0.7–0.9. (i.e., 70–90% of assets). It is within this range that we see the biggest gain in ABC's stock price (between $2.02 and $2.06). However, this does not mean we should expect the price to move up by exactly this amount. Rather the analysis can be viewed as telling ABC's management that hedging *less than* 0.7 is probably *not* value-maximizing and thus a higher level of interest rate hedging could be more beneficial.

As noted earlier, we can address the issue of a more detailed dynamic analysis by using a spreadsheet-based valuation model that enables the analyst to optimize a bank's stock price while allowing multiple value drivers to vary simultaneously. We present more details about this type of dynamic analysis in Chapter 12 (Integrated Risk Management: Putting it all together). It is also important to remember that ABC's management team must consider the potential magnitude of the rate shock and the likelihood of its occurrence. For example, we are assuming that there is a reasonable chance of a 100-basis point shock. If the managers think the rate shock might be much larger than 100 bps and/or have a very high probability of occurring, then the above analysis must be re-estimated to see if a higher hedge ratio is warranted.

Conversely, if managers think a rate hike is very unlikely and/or is much lower than 100 bps, then a lower (or zero) hedge ratio might be more sensible. Nevertheless, the above numerical example is still helpful because it applies our IVM approach to identify key trade-offs between risk-taking and risk management that can affect firm value. This same principle can be applied to all the FIs main risks to get a sense, at least directionally, of how different risk management choices affect firm value.

---

[19] Recall our discussion of the North Star analogy and "GIGO" (Garbage In, Garbage Out) in Chapters 2 and 3.

4.8 Managerial Implications

The main interest rate risk problem Sam and Nina must consider is as follows: **how much interest rate risk is acceptable for ABC Bank if overall interest rates rise or fall a great deal (e.g., +/–100 bps or more) and they do so very quickly (e.g., in one year or less)?** The answer to the question depends largely on the bank's "risk appetite" which, in turn, is influenced by senior management's and investors' tolerance for risk. In addition, bank regulators can exert influence on this risk management decision by comparing the bank's exposure to its equity capital. Regulators have the power to recommend the bank issue more equity if the interest rate exposure is too high relative to the bank's current equity buffer. The concept of how much capital is sufficient to absorb any unexpected losses is commonly referred to as "capital adequacy" and is described in further detail in Chapter 10 (Regulatory Issues in Banking).

Nina and Sam must also think about the short-term impact of fluctuating interest rates on Net Interest Income due to mismatches between rate-sensitive assets and rate-sensitive liabilities and whether their sole focus should be on managing the bank's RGAP. **Or should they take a longer-term view of all the bank's cash flows and concentrate on the market value impact of the gap between the modified durations of assets vs. liabilities via MDGAP?** Sam and Nina **think the best plan might be to hedge MDGAP since this metric has a much larger impact on ABC's stock price, as shown in Figure 4.8.** However, they also realize that such a choice is likely to lead to higher short-term volatility in the bank's Net Interest Income. In terms of the "ART" of risk management, their approach is to Transfer some of the risk to other parties via various derivatives transactions and so the cost and liquidity of these derivatives markets will also play an important role. **Do you agree with Nina and Sam's recommendation? If not, then how would you handle it differently and what are your reasons for doing so?**

4.9 Summary

This chapter showed the importance of interest rate risk management and how metrics like Repricing Gap (RGAP = Rate Sensitive Assets minus Rate Sensitive Liabilities = RSA – RSL) can affect Net Interest Income and, ultimately, the bank's market value of equity. In addition, we discussed the leverage-adjusted Modified Duration Gap, or MDGAP for short. This metric measures the bank's sensitivity to interest rate changes by considering the entire set of future cash flows from assets and liabilities (rather than focusing on, say, one year's worth of cash flows). This more comprehensive measure is computed by subtracting the leverage-adjusted modified duration of liabilities from the modified duration of assets (i.e., MDGAP = ($MD_A - \alpha \cdot MD_L$)). These concepts help implement what is commonly called "Asset–Liability Management," or ALM for short. To do so, a risk manager must consider the "ART" of risk management (Accept, Remove, or Transfer the relevant risk). This ALM method explicitly considers refinancing and reinvestment risk by comparing the repricing of the interest rates on assets to the repricing of rates paid to creditors. We can think of this as the "ARM" of ALM, where the acronym stands for a manager's choices in terms of the dollar *amount* (*A*), *rates* (*R*), and *mix* (*M*) of assets and liabilities on its balance sheet. This chapter concluded with examples of how we can use cost–benefit analysis to identify optimal hedge ratios for interest rate risk which can maximize a bank's stock price. To complement these ideas and methods, the Appendix presents the key drivers of interest rates, the fundamentals of duration, and the bootstrapping technique for calculating forward interest rates.

A4.1 Appendix — Foundations of Interest Rate Risk Management

A4.1.1 *What drives interest rates?*

Before delving too deeply into the ways an FI can quantify and manage interest rate risk, it is a good idea to take a step back and examine what is an interest rate and what are the main drivers that affect the level and changes in interest rates. Many analysts consider an interest rate the "rental price of money" because it is the rate charged by a lender to provide them with an incentive to part with their money and hand it over to a borrower with hopes of getting their principal (and interest payments) repaid in a timely fashion.

So, we can start with what is usually called the "risk-free interest rate" and is typically associated with very short-term fixed-income securities issued by a stable national government (such as the U.S.). For example, a 1-month U.S. Treasury bill (or "T-bill") would normally have a low interest rate relative to other fixed-income securities because

1. it is easily traded (or "highly liquid"),
2. it matures relatively quickly (in one month),
3. it is assumed to be free of the risk of default (assuming the U.S. government remains financially strong over the next month), and
4. the high liquidity and low default risk both help make T-bill prices more stable.

In this case, the interest rate on a 1-month T-bill ($R_{f,1\text{-month}}$) is driven by two key factors: an Inflation Premium (IP) and a "real" interest rate (R^*) that provides a return above and beyond the inflation premium. The IP component provides an investor with protection against price increases in the goods and services that are commonly bought by consumers. This risk-free interest rate is often referred to as the yield to maturity (YTM) for the security and is summarized in Equation (A4.1):

$$R_{f,1\text{-month}} = R^* + IP \qquad (A4.1)$$

Based on the above relationship, we need an estimate of the real rate (R^*) and expected Inflation Premium (IP) over the forecast period. Keep in mind that these rates are normally quoted on an annual basis (i.e., the rate of inflation over a 1-year period). In the U.S., the real rate of return typically ranges between 0% and 1%, whereas the inflation premium has varied dramatically between deflation (e.g., –5%) and rapid inflation of 10+%. So, as a numerical example, let's assume the real rate is 1% and the expected rate of inflation is 4%. In this case, the 1-month T-bill rate ($R_{f,1\text{-month}}$) can be found by plugging these estimates into Equation (A4.1) as follows[20]:

---

[20] Although we focus on 1-month T-bill rate here, another important short-term interest rate for FIs in the U.S. is the Federal Funds rate (commonly referred to as "Fed Funds rate"). This rate represents the cost that banks and other financial institutions charge each other for short-term funds (usually overnight) to meet bank reserve requirements at the U.S. central bank. This rate is usually highly correlated with movements in short-term T-bill rates and so our discussion here also applies to Fed Funds rates.

$$R_{f,1\text{-month}} = R* + IP = 1\% + 4\% + 5\% \qquad (A4.2)$$

An investor in the 1-month T-bill would therefore earn enough total interest (5% on an annualized basis) to keep up with inflation (4%) and still earn a 1% return to compensate for tying up their money for that period.[21]

For most fixed income securities, they will have much longer maturities than a 1-month T-bill and so investors will want extra compensation for tying up their money for a longer period. This is referred to as a Maturity Risk Premium (MRP). In addition, for fixed income instruments other than U.S. Treasury securities and other low-risk country's government securities (e.g., Germany, Japan, and the U.K.), we will also need an even higher rate of interest to compensate for the possibility of default. This additional compensation for the potential loss of principal is called the Default Risk Premium (DRP). Lastly, many fixed income securities are not as easily traded and thus are less "liquid" than a 1-month T-bill. Investors will therefore demand a higher level of interest to compensate for any additional transaction costs incurred and discounts associated with selling a difficult-to-trade or "illiquid" security. This latter effect is commonly referred to as a Liquidity Risk Premium (LRP).

The following relation summarizes the above discussion by building on the original formula found in Equation (A4.1):

$$R_{L,T} = R* + IP_{L,T} + MRP_{L,T} + DRP_{L,T} + LRP_{L,T} \qquad (A4.3)$$

---

[21] In this example, given that the investor is only investing for one month the actual (*non*-annualized) return on the 1-month T-bill would be $\frac{1}{2}$th of 5.0% (or 0.4167%) because T-bills trade on a "discount basis" to their "par value" and do not explicitly make an interest payment. For most long-term fixed income securities that do make periodic interest payments, we can treat the interest rate described in this chapter as the annual "yield to maturity" (YTM). In addition, we should mention that the U.S. Treasury issues "TIPS" which are inflation-protected Treasury bonds that adjust their face value based on annual changes in U.S. inflation. For these bonds, the YTM is, in effect, a measure of the real rate (R*) because the IP for this type of bond is embedded in upward adjustments to its principal (or face value). In fact, some analysts subtract the YTM of a TIPS bond from the YTM of a conventional U.S. Treasury bond of similar maturity to estimate a "break-even" inflation premium, IP_{B-E} (i.e., $IP_{B-E} = YTM_{conventional} - YTM_{TIPS} \approx$ expected IP).

where

$R_{L,T}$ = interest rate (or yield to maturity) of a fixed income security, L, that has a maturity at time-T,

$IP_{L,T}$ = Inflation Premium over the T-period horizon,

$MRP_{L,T}$ = Maturity Risk Premium for security L over the T-period horizon,

$DRP_{L,T}$ = Default Risk Premium for security L over the T-period horizon, and

$LRP_{L,T}$ = Liquidity Risk Premium for security L over the T-period horizon.

If we use the earlier assumptions from Equation (A4.2) about the real rate and the inflation premium, we can compute the interest rate for, say, a 5-year fixed income security, L, by assuming risk premiums for maturity (e.g., MRP = 0.5%), default (e.g., DRP = 2.0%), and liquidity (e.g., LRP = 0.2%) as follows:

$$R_{L,5} = 1\% + 4\% + 0.5\% + 2\% + 0.2\% = 7.7\% \qquad (A4.4)$$

Note that the interest rate of 7.7% on this security can be viewed as the rate on a 1-month T-bill rate ($R_{f,1\text{-month}}$ = 5.0%) *plus* a set of risk premiums totaling 2.7%. In other words, the investor needs an extra 2.7% return (per year) to be enticed to choose the risky 5-year security over the "risk-free" 1-month U.S. T-bill. Although Equations (A4.3) and (A4.4) are quite precise in theory, it is in practice where things are a bit less clear. For example, it is very difficult to identify each of the individual components that make up the interest rate in the above formulas. In most cases, the best we can do is to split the interest rate into two pieces: (1) the risk-free rate for a U.S. Treasury that has the same maturity as the fixed income instrument we are analyzing (e.g., use $R_{f,\,5\text{-year}}$ if we want to find a 5-year loan's interest rate ($R_{L,5}$)) and (2) a risk premium that lumps together the remaining premiums associated with the loan's default risk and liquidity factors (DRP$_{L,T}$ and LRP$_{L,T}$). This can be expressed for a T-period loan rate as follows:

$$R_{L,T} = R_{f,T} + RP_{LT} \qquad (A4.5)$$

where

$$R_{f,T} = R^* + IP_{L,T} + MRP_{L,T}$$

$$RP_{L,T} = DRP_{L,T} + LRP_{L,T}$$

Equation (A4.5) shows that "risky" interest rates will fluctuate with U.S. Treasury rates and changes in the risk premium ($RP_{L,T}$). If we re-arrange Equation (A4.5) to put the risk premium on the left-hand side, we can obtain an estimate of this risk premium by simply subtracting the U.S. Treasury rate from the risky interest rate for an instrument of similar maturity. This difference is commonly referred to as the "yield spread" ($YS_{L,T}$) as it shows how much more a borrower must pay (or an investor can earn) above and beyond a U.S. Treasury security of similar maturity. For example, 30-year fixed rate residential mortgage rates in the U.S. are usually determined by adding a yield spread on top of 10-year U.S. Treasury note yields:

$$YS_{L,T} = R_{L,T} - R_{f,T} \quad (A4.6)$$

Based on the above discussion, we can see that there are several forces that affect the interest rates that banks charge for loans and pay for deposits. Equations (A4.3), (A4.5), and (A4.6) show that overall macroeconomic conditions and Federal Reserve Board actions can have a strong and direct impact on the level of interest rates through the R^* and $IP_{L,T}$ and terms. For example, as inflation heats up in the U.S. economy, interest rates rise in tandem with the increased inflation premium because the Fed's usual action is to raise interest rates so that inflationary pressures can eventually decline over time.[22]

In addition to macroeconomic factors and the Fed's actions, there are microeconomic forces that can affect a specific firm's or industry's interest rates. This can be seen by the remaining terms of Equation (A4.3): $DRP_{L,T}$, $MRP_{L,T}$, and $LRP_{L,T}$. Thus, as the creditworthiness of a firm changes, its default risk premium (DRP) will move accordingly. For example, greater default risk would cause the DRP to rise which, in turn, would increase the interest rate at which a firm can borrow. The firm's interest rate would also rise if the firm decided to issue longer-term notes

---

[22] To see timely updates on the Fed's monetary policy, you can go to websites such as https://www.federalreserve.gov/monetarypolicy.htm and https://www.newyorkfed.org/markets/data-hub.

and bonds because the maturity risk premium (MRP) increases as the maturity dates of these fixed income instruments are lengthened. In addition, the firm's liquidity risk premium can increase if it is not easy to buy and sell the firm's debt securities. It should also be noted that these last three terms (DRP, MRP, and LRP) can be inter-related because borrowers that have high default risk typically must pay a higher interest rate because an increase in DRP is usually positively related to LRP and MRP. Thus, when one of these interest rate factors is increased, it usually also leads to higher premiums for at least one of the other factors.

A4.1.2 *The fundamentals of duration*

We can think of the duration of an asset or liability as the weighted average time-to-maturity of these financial instruments. Macaulay (1938) proposed the initial concept of duration within the context of a bond with a fixed interest rate. For example, the duration of a fixed rate bond adjusts for the fact that some of the bond's cash flows come in the form of interest payments (or "coupons") that are received well before the principal is repaid at maturity. Thus, if we invested in such a bond, then we are recouping a portion of our investment earlier than the bond's stated maturity.[23]

The question is as follows: how do we adjust the bond's "effective maturity" for these interim cash flows? The answer is to compute the present values of each of the bond's cash flows and use them to estimate the relative weights of each of these payments. Thus, cash flows will have greater present values and weights when they are either (a) cash flows that arrive sooner (e.g., interest payments within the first few years) or (b) very large (e.g., the principal payment at maturity). The following is a diagram of a 2-year bond's annual cash flows as well as the calculations to compute the bond's duration when its yield to maturity (YTM) is equal to its coupon rate (CR) at 8.0%. The bond is assumed to have one principal payment of $1,000 at maturity (commonly referred to as its "face value," FV, or par value).

---

[23] For simplicity, we focus here on bonds that pay annual interest payments and where the full principal (or "face value") is received at maturity. We can adjust the above calculations for semi-annual payments by dividing the discount rate, YTM, in half and by doubling the number discounting periods (e.g., use YTM / 2 for the discount rate and 2 · t for the number of periods). In general, for a bond that pays interest m-times per year, we would use YTM / m and m x t for the discount rate and number of periods, respectively.

152 *Managing Financial Institutions: An Integrated Valuation Approach*

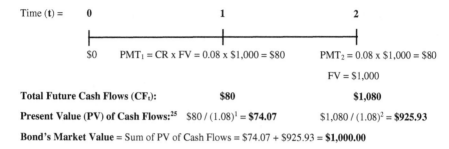

Figure A4.1. Two-year Bond's Cash Flows.

In general, the formula for calculating a fixed income instrument's value, BP_0, (including loans and deposits) is as follows:

$$BP_0 = \sum_t \frac{CF_t}{(1+YTM)^t} \qquad (A4.7)$$

If you are familiar with the concept of bond pricing, then you will recognize that the market value of any bond that has a YTM equal to its coupon rate (CR) will also be equal to its face value (FV). Calculating the bond's current value is important because it provides us with a benchmark to calculate the relative weights of the bond's two cash flows at years 1 and 2. That is, we can weigh the first year's time interval (i.e., $t = 1$) by the present value of this year's cash flows in relation to the bond's total market value. So, in Figure A4.1, the weight for the first interval would be $74.07/$1,000 = 0.07407, or about 7.4% of the bond's total market value. For the second interval, the weight would be the remainder, i.e., $925.93 / $1,000 = 0.92593, or around 92.6% of the total value. Now that we have these weights, we can compute the bond's duration according to the following formula:

$$\text{Duration} = D = \sum_t (wt \cdot t) \qquad (A4.8)$$

where

$w_t = $ (PV of CF_t) / BP_0 (discounted at the bond's YTM) and

---

[24]Note that these values are rounded to the second decimal for convenience and ease of presentation here. In practice, we would calculate this out to several more decimals.

t = time interval in which the cash flow (CF$_t$) occurred (expressed in years).

Plugging in the numbers for this numerical example, we can see that the bond's duration (D) is equal to 1.926 years as follows:

$$D = (0.07407 \cdot \text{1st year}) + (0.92593 \cdot \text{2nd year}) = 0.07407$$
$$+ 1.85186 = 1.92593 \approx \mathbf{1.926 \text{ years}}$$

Note that the bond's maturity is 2.0 years but its duration is slightly less than that (at 1.926 years) because some of the cash flows occur *before* the second year. Thus, some of the weight (7.407%) is placed on the first year's $80 cash flow and so the duration will be *less* than the maturity.[25]

This duration calculation is helpful because it allows us to quickly estimate the impact of a change in interest rates on the market value of the bond via the following formula:

$$\%\Delta BP_0 = -D \cdot \left(\frac{\Delta R}{1+R} \right) \qquad (A4.9)$$

where

$\%\Delta BP_0$ = percentage change in the bond's price,

$-D$ = duration of the bond (denoted as a *negative* value because bond prices and interest rates are *inversely* related),

ΔR = instantaneous change in the bond's YTM, and

R = the bond's current YTM (i.e., the yield to maturity immediately preceding the rate change).

In practice, a more convenient way to use Equation (A4.9) is to slightly re-arrange it to create a variable called "modified duration" or MD for short as follows:

---

[25] Note that the only case where a bond's duration is equal to its maturity is when all the cash flows occur at maturity. Bonds that pay all their cash flow at maturity are commonly referred to as "zero coupon bonds" because there are no interim payments or coupons received. On a related note, a variable rate loan's duration is equivalent to the time until the loan's interest rate is re-set. For example, if the loan has an interest rate that is re-set every 6 months, then the loan's duration is 0.5 years (6 months / 12 months = 0.5 years).

$$\%\Delta BP_0 = -MD \cdot \Delta R \qquad (A4.10)$$

where

$\%\Delta BP_0$ = percentage change in the bond's price,

$-MD$ = Modified Duration of the bond = $-D / (1 + R)$ and the *negative* value for D is used because bond prices and interest rates are *inversely* related,

ΔR = instantaneous change in the bond's YTM, and

R = the bond's current YTM (i.e., the yield to maturity immediately preceding the rate change).

Based on Equation (A4.10), we can continue with our numerical example of the **2-year 8% annual coupon bond**, to estimate the percentage change in the bond's price when we assume an instantaneous 100-basis point increase in interest rates by plugging in the appropriate numbers into Equation (A4.10):

$$\%\Delta BP_0 = -MD \cdot \Delta R = (-1.92593 / 1.08) \cdot (+0.01) = \\ -1.78327 \cdot 0.01 = -0.017833 \approx -1.78\%$$

Using Equation (A4.10) and the bond's MD of 1.78327 years with our numerical example shows that a 1-percentage point increase in interest rates leads to a decrease in bond value of -1.783% (and is nearly double the rate shock).

Table A4.1 builds upon the duration concept in Equation (A4.7) to show how a 5-year bond's modified duration differs from a 2-year bond

Table A4.1. Details for calculating a 5-year Bond's Market Value and Modified Duration.

t	CF_t	PV of CF_t	w_t	$t * w_t$	
1	$80.00	$74.074	0.07407	0.07407	
2	$80.00	$68.587	0.06859	0.13717	
3	$80.00	$63.507	0.06351	0.19052	
4	$80.00	$58.802	0.05880	0.23521	
5	$1,080.00	$735.030	0.73503	3.67515	
	Bond Price =>	$1,000.000	1.00000	4.31213	<= Duration
				3.99287	<= Mod. Dur.

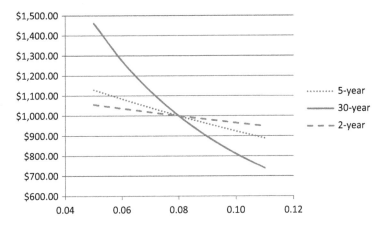

Figure A4.2. Interest Rate Risk and Duration for Three Different Bonds.

that has the same YTM and the same annual interest payment. As we can see from this table, the modified duration of the bond is now much longer (3.73 years vs. 1.78 years) and thus is much more sensitive to changes in interest rates.

So, for a **5-year 8% annual coupon bond**, the same 100-bps increase in interest rates leads to a much sharper drop in market value, as shown in the following:

$$\%\Delta BP_0 = -MD \cdot \Delta R = -3.99287 \cdot (+0.01) = -0.0399287 \approx \mathbf{-3.99\%}$$

In general, the longer the maturity, the longer will be the modified duration of a fixed income instrument/bond. Thus, the same change in interest rates leads to much bigger changes in the market value of the bond as the maturity is lengthened. This means interest rate risk *rises* greatly as the maturity of the bank's assets and liabilities are *lengthened*.[26] A graph of this interest rate sensitivity can help illustrate the interest rate risk by varying the level of interest rates (the YTM) and re-calculating the bond's value at each rate. Figure A4.2 shows the interest rate

---

[26] In the extreme, a bond could have no interim interest payments and will only make a payment at the time of the bond's maturity. This type of security is commonly referred to as a "zero coupon" bond and so its only payment is at the time of maturity. In this special case, the duration of the "zero coupon" bond is equal to its maturity. In all other cases, a coupon-paying bond will have a duration that is less than its maturity.

sensitivity of three bonds (the 2- and 5-year bonds discussed earlier as well as a 30-year bond).

The above graph plots the bond's price on the vertical axis and its YTM on the horizontal axis. The downward slope of each line in Figure A4.2 shows that all three bonds have a negative relationship with interest rates. In fact, the slope of these lines is equal to the bond's duration (D) at its current YTM. Note that the longer maturity bonds such as the 30-year have a much steeper angle. This means that longer-term bonds change in value much more dramatically than, say, the 2-year bond because a 30-year bond has many longer-term cash flows that will be more affected by changes in the bond's discount rate (a.k.a., the bond's discount rate). In contrast, the 2-year bond has cash flows spanning just the next two years and thus the present value of these two cash flows is not as greatly affected by changes in interest rates. In effect, the 2-year bond's value does not change that much even when rates vary a great deal and so the slope of the 2-year bond in Figure A4.2 is much *flatter*. In summary, the steepness of the slope for a bond indicates the interest rate risk of the security. That is, the *steeper* the slope, the *longer* the bond's duration, and this results in *greater* interest rate risk. In economic terms, the slope of a bond's price represents the sensitivity of the bond to interest changes and is sometimes referred to as the bond price's "elasticity" with respect to rate changes.

A4.1.3 Convexity: An extension of the duration approach

As shown in Figure A4.2, longer duration bonds have a steeper slope and thus possess greater interest rate risk, as measured by duration. Duration is a *linear* estimate of the bond's risk but, in reality, bond prices react to interest rates in a *nonlinear*, or curved, manner. Figure A4.3 shows this relationship with the curved line labeled the "Actual bond price." This curve shows the precise value for the bond at different levels of YTM (labeled as "Yield"). The straight line labeled "Duration-Based Estimate" represents the bond's duration because it touches the curved line at exactly the bond's current YTM (Y^* in the graph) and current price (P^*). The slope of the Tangent line at Y^* is exactly equal to ($-1 \cdot$ Duration) and can be used to estimate changes in the bond's price as the YTM rises and falls. For example, you can travel along the Tangent line upwards and downwards to see how the bond's current duration would forecast the bond's price as YTM falls and rises.

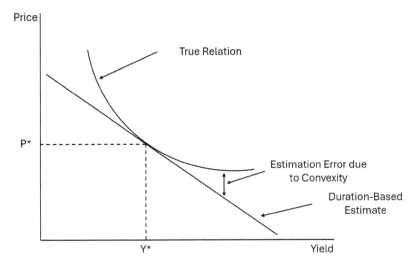

Figure A4.3. The Impact of Convexity on Fixed Income Instrument.

One interesting aspect of the Tangent line in Figure A4.3 is that its forecasts of bond prices are *"pessimistic"* because the duration's estimates of prices will nearly always predict a bond price that is *lower* than the "Actual bond price" (the only exception is when Y^* equals the bond's current YTM). Also, note that the "pessimism" gets worse as you move further to the left or right of Y^*. So, the prediction errors from the duration method (labeled as "Estimation Error due to Convexity" in the graph) rise as the change in interest rates increases. These growing errors are due to the bond's curvature, or what is commonly referred to as the bond's *"convexity."* To create a better estimate of the bond's price, a bank manager can estimate the bond's convexity and add this relatively small adjustment back to the duration-based forecast. Since most bonds have "positive convexity" as shown in Figure A4.3, the inclusion of convexity provides a more "optimistic" estimate of the bond's value that makes the manager's forecast closer to the actual bond price noted by the curved line in the graph.[27]

---

[27] Bonds or loans that can be prepaid can lead "negative convexity" because these instruments' duration might shorten dramatically as interest rates fall and borrowers exercise their prepayment option. A detailed treatment of these prepayment dynamics can be found in Fabozzi (2012).

158   *Managing Financial Institutions: An Integrated Valuation Approach*

The details of calculating a bond's convexity can be somewhat involved and are beyond what we need for our purposes.[28] We focus on duration rather than include the added complexity of convexity because the impact of convexity can be relatively small for most fixed income instruments, especially those that have shorter maturities. However, it is good to keep in mind that a duration-based estimate of bond value will be a *conservative* one in that the actual bond price will probably be slightly higher due to the convexity effects described above. As a bank risk manager, it is normally better to be conservative in one's estimates rather than too optimistic/aggressive. So, the focus on the duration method of estimating interest rate risk is appropriate for a bank's management team.

A4.1.4 *How to bootstrap forward interest rates*

An essential aspect of a bank's management of interest rate risk relates to how to properly price the cost of borrowing/investing in the future. *Forward interest rate contracts* enable banks and their clients to *set a price today* for funds that will be invested (or borrowed) *in the future*. This ability to lock in rates today for future periods is an essential building block for pricing not only forwards and futures contracts but also loans and various types of swaps.

As we can see from Figure A4.4, the bank and its clients would like to know what a "fair" price is for borrowing or investing for one year *but starting one year from now*. This is what we call a "forward interest rate" and is denoted by $R_{1,2}$ in Figure A4.4 because it represents the interest rate that would be fair to all parties if they wanted to borrow or invest for one year starting a year in the future. This contrasts with a "spot rate" which refers to the return from investing or borrowing *right now* (i.e., to borrow/lend "on the spot"). To "bootstrap" a forward rate, we therefore need data on at least two spot rates which are denoted in Figure A4.4 by $R_{0,1}$ for the 1-year spot rate and $R_{0,2}$ for the 2-year spot rate.

If we have information on the spot rates to borrow or invest for 1 and 2 years, we can then infer the forward rate ($R_{1,2}$) by equating the returns from a "Rollover" strategy to the returns from a "Buy and Hold" strategy. The rollover strategy is displayed in the upper half of Figure A4.4 and shows how an investor can invest in a fixed spot rate security at, say, 3%

---

[28] See Saunders *et al.* (2024) for a more detailed treatment of convexity.

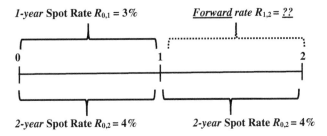

Figure A4.4. Bootstrapping Forward Rates: A Numerical Example.

for one year ($R_{0,1}$) and then *roll over* the proceeds of this investment to buy another 1-year security one year from now. This last portion of the rollover strategy is the 1-year forward interest rate ($R_{1,2}$) and is not known unless we compare the total return from this rollover strategy to the total return from a buy-and-hold strategy. The bottom half of Figure A4.4 shows the potential return to a buy-and-hold strategy where we *buy* a 2-year bond *today* at the 2-year spot rate of 4% ($R_{0,2}$) and *hold* this security for the full 2-year period.

When the securities that are bought using the above strategies have the *same* liquidity and credit risk (e.g., 1-year and 2-year U.S. Treasury notes), then it is reasonable to assume that the payoffs to both strategies should be the *same*.[29] In this situation, we can create an estimate of the future 1-year interest rate by using the following formula which equates the two strategies:

$$\text{Buy and Hold Return} = \text{Rollover Return} = (1 + R_{0,2})^2$$
$$= [(1 + R_{0,1})^1 \cdot (1 + R_{1,2})^1]$$

Re-arranging the above relationship leads to the following equation:

$$R_{1,2} = \left[\frac{(1 + R_{0,2})^2}{(1 + R_{0,1})^1} \right]^{\left(\frac{1}{(2-1)}\right)} - 1.0 \qquad (A4.11)$$

Plugging in the relevant spot rates shows the 1-year forward rate to be around 5.01%:

---

[29] Note that in this case we are assuming there is no maturity risk premium that is separate and distinct from the securities' liquidity and credit risk.

$$R_{1,2} = \left[\frac{(1.04)^2}{(1.03)^1}\right]^{(1)} - 1.0 = \left[\frac{1.0861}{1.0300}\right] - 1 = 0.050097 \approx 5.01\%$$

In *general form*, a forward rate that covers *(T − j)* years and starts *after* the *j*th year can be computed by the following equation:

$$R_{j,T} = \left[\frac{(1+R_{0,T})^T}{(1+R_{0,j})^j}\right]^{\left(\frac{1}{(T-j)}\right)} - 1.0 \qquad (A4.12)$$

Based on (A4.12), we can "bootstrap" any desired forward rate if we have the appropriate spot rate data. As noted earlier, these forward rates are useful for pricing many types of instruments that are of interest to both banks and their clients.

Chapter-End Questions

Answers to odd-numbered questions can be found at the end of this book.

1. **True or False:** Bank managers should not modify the "ARM" of their assets and liabilities, including factors like the level of interest rates and the mix of variable versus fixed-rate instruments.
2. **True or False: Interest rate risk** arises from a bank's provision of liquidity, and it relates to how the bank's Net Interest Income (NII) and market value of equity (MVE) are affected by changes in interest rates.
3. **Multiple Choice:** What is the primary concern of refinancing and reinvestment risks?
    (A) The possibility of changing the mix of assets and liabilities due to interest rate fluctuations.
    (B) The uncertainty about future interest rates.
    (C) The risk of not being able to find new assets and liabilities to replace existing assets and liabilities at profitable rates.
    (D) The exposure to inflation-related losses.

4. **Multiple Choice:** What is a limitation of the modified duration gap (MDGAP) approach?
   (A) It does not consider gradual changes in interest rates, which may not be realistic.
   (B) It does not consider the impact of sudden rate shocks.
   (C) It overestimates the impact of interest rate changes.
   (D) It only applies to short-term interest rate risk.

5. **Multiple Choice:** How can a bank transfer risk to a third party?
   (A) By diversifying its portfolio.
   (B) By using interest-rate forward contracts.
   (C) By accepting the risk.
   (D) By investing in negatively correlated assets.

6. **Short Answer:** What is modified duration and why is it a better metric to consider for quantifying the interest rate risk of loans and corporate bonds than their maturity? Also, how can a bank adjust its leverage-adjusted modified duration gap (MDGAP) to mitigate interest rate risk?

7. **Short Answer:** Answer the following questions using the data from the Stylized Balance Sheet for ABC shown in the following:

Modified Duration of ABC's Assets

Assets	Value ($ million)	Modified Duration (yrs)	Contribution to MD_A
Cash & Reserves	$5	0.00	
Investments	30	2.0	
Net Loans	60	5.00	
Other Assets	5	N.A.	
Total Assets	$100		$MD_A =$

Modified Duration of Liabilities

Liabilities	Value ($ million)	Modified Dur. (yrs)	Contribution to MD_L
Deposits	$60	1.50	
Other Borrowed Money	30	4.50	
Total Liabilities	$90		$MD_L =$

(A) Calculate the modified durations of assets and liabilities (MD_A and MD_L).
(B) Use the above calculations to estimate ABC's leverage-adjusted modified duration gap.
(C) What is the impact on ABC's market value of equity (as a percentage change from the current's current equity value of $10) if interest rates rise 200 basis points?
(D) Briefly describe at least one way the bank's managers can reduce this interest rate risk (no calculations necessary).

8. **Short Answer:** Answer the following questions about the leverage-adjusted modified duration gap (MDGAP) using the data shown in the following:

Total Assets ($ million)	1,000
Total Liabilities ($ million)	900
Mod. Duration of Assets (MD_A)	5.00
Mod. Duration of Liabilities (MD_L)	2.00
Leverage-adjusted MDGAP (years)	3.20
Interest Rate shock	1.00%
Hedge Fixed Cost, c (% of Tot. Assets)	0.00%
Hedge Variable Cost, v (% of Tot. Assets)	2.50%
Shares Outstanding (million)	10.00

(A) Calculate the optimal hedge ratio (h^*) to adjust the bank's modified durations of assets and liabilities to maximize the bank's value (*Hint*: review Equation (4.13) and footnote 16 in this chapter).
(B) How does h^* change if the variable hedging cost (v) rises to 4.0% of the interest rate risk exposure due to decreased liquidity and heightened volatility in the derivatives markets?
(C) As a second simulation, what happens to h^* if the increased variable cost for hedging also coincides with an increase in the expected rate shock to +200 basis points?
(D) What is the "target" MDGAP* based on Equation (4.14) and your answer to part A?

9. **Excel-based Question:** How much interest rate risk exposure, as measured by its repricing gap (RGAP), should ABC hedge (h^*) to maximize its stock price? Assume the bank's managers are concerned about a 200-basis point increase in both the RSA and RSL components of the balance sheet. To answer this question, use the RGAP model as shown in the "Interest Rate Risk – Ch 4" tab of the **Integrated Valuation Model.xlsx** file. Try this by starting with the "base" scenario where the variable costs (v) are 2% of the hedged exposure and then changing the values in the blue cells related to the Rate Sensitive Assets (RSA) and Rate Sensitive Liabilities (RSL) to $800 and $1,000 million, respectively.
   (A) What is the optimal hedge ratio (h^*) for the above interest rate shock?
   (B) Related to your answer in part A, what is the expected percentage change in ABC's stock price if management implemented this optimal hedge ratio?
   (C) What is the "target" RGAP* based on Equation (4.12) and your answer to part A of this question?
   (D) What if the bank expects a 300-basis point rate increase? Does this change your optimal hedge ratio? If so, what is the expected change in ABC's stock price? Also, can you find a pattern to h^* as you change the simulated interest rate shock from, say, +100 basis points to +200 basis points and then +300 basis points?

10. **Comprehensive Question:** Recommend and justify a recommended course of action for our protagonists in this chapter: Nina and Sam. Let's assume that they are concerned about interest rates rising +200 basis points because ABC has a negative RGAP of −$200 million and a positive MDGAP of +3.0 years. **Should they take a short-term view and focus on RGAP *or* should they take a longer-term view of all the bank's cash flows and concentrate on the market value impact of the leverage-adjusted gap between the modified durations of assets vs. liabilities?** This decision will be influenced by several factors such as the likelihood of the interest rate shock, the current level of Net Interest Income ($100 million), the volatility of Net Interest Income, the bank's risk appetite, and possibly by what the bank's main competitors are doing in terms of interest rate risk management. Briefly describe and justify your recommendation.

References

Fabbozzi, F. (2012). *Handbook of Fixed Income Securities*, McGraw-Hill Education, New York.

Hull, J.C. (2010). *Risk Management and Financial Institutions*, Prentice-Hall, Boston.

Kim, R. (2023). Do banks hedge the risk of fixed-income security holdings? *Working Paper*, www.ssrn.com.

Macaulay, F.R. (1938). *Some Theoretical Problems Suggested by the Movements of Interest Rates, Bond Yields, and Stock Prices in the United States since 1856*, Columbia University Press for the National Bureau of Economic Research, New York.

Modigliani, F. and Miller, M.H. (1958). The cost of capital, corporation finance, and the theory of investment, *American Economic Review*, 48, 261–297.

Saunders, A., Cornett, M.M. and Erhemjamts, O. (2024). *Financial Institutions Management: A Risk Management Approach*, McGraw-Hill, New York.

Chapter 5

Market Risk

5.1 Introduction

As we learned earlier in Chapter 1 about the different types of risks that a financial institution (FI) faces, a bank's managers must compare the risks and returns associated with the firm's numerous products and services. All three of a financial institution's main economic functions (qualitative asset transformation, brokerage, and delegated monitoring) can create **market risk**, which is the focus of this chapter. Market risk represents the possibility that the prices of a bank's main assets (e.g., loans, investments, and, for larger FIs, trading operations) can quickly decline in value due to changes in financial market conditions. Thus, changes in interest rates, exchange rates, commodity prices, and stock prices can all adversely affect the market value of a bank's assets. For example, if a bank has a $100 million exposure to the U.S. Dollar–Euro exchange rate (EUR) because it holds this amount of euros on its balance sheet, then a 10% decline in the euro will decrease this holding to only $90 million, thus resulting in a very sudden $10 million drop in assets. Given that banks are highly levered with little equity as a "cushion" against various economic shocks, sudden shifts in financial prices like this can cause the market value of the bank's equity to plummet and, in extreme cases, lead to bank insolvency. So, bank managers, investors, and regulators are all keenly interested in seeing how the FI manages its exposure to market risk.

A typical commercial bank must decide how much of its assets to invest in two primary areas: loans or marketable securities (also referred to as investments). In general, banks prefer to invest in their loan portfolio because they can generate higher returns than investing in relatively safe fixed income securities, such as U.S. Treasury notes (UST) and mortgage-backed securities (MBS). However, if the economy is weak and loan demand is low (or deemed too risky from the bank's perspective), then the banks will typically invest a larger percentage of their assets in a lower-yielding investment portfolio. This also provides the bank with added liquidity because the securities held in an investment portfolio are much more liquid than the loans in their lending portfolio. From an economic perspective, the bank is acting as a delegated monitor when it manages this investment portfolio and therefore must balance the risk–return trade-off of selecting securities with varying degrees of risk (although banks mostly hold different types of bonds).

Larger banks also have the choice to invest in a "trading account" to assist clients who are interested in buying and selling assets, such as bonds, currencies, commodities, and equities. Thus, the bank's decision to hold marketable securities in its investment portfolio and/or trading account creates exposure to market risk. In contrast to the bank's investment portfolio, a trading operation can hold a much more diverse set of financial instruments depending on senior management's risk appetite and client needs. For example, large banks will typically serve as brokers for bonds, currencies, commodities, derivatives, and, to a lesser extent, equities. As we have discussed throughout this book, a good manager will weigh the risks versus the returns of these choices to maximize the value of the shareholders' investment in the bank.

Based on our discussion in Chapter 1 related to the key functions of a financial institution, we know that banks provide "liquidity insurance" to their clients in numerous ways. In turn, the banks themselves must manage their own liquidity needs and frequently rely on the financial markets to help. A bank is normally a heavy user of the fixed income markets to buy and sell UST and MBS instruments depending on whether the firm has an influx of extra deposits that need to be invested or if it must sell some of these securities to meet a sudden surge in loan demand.

In some of these situations, the bank might not be able to hold fixed income securities until they mature and thus the price the bank obtains in the financial market can vary significantly from the bank's original price. For example, if the bank buys a bond when its yield is 4% and then interest rates on similar bonds rise to 6%, the market value of the bank's bond decreases and, if sold at that point, can lead to a large capital loss. Conversely, if yields on the bond fall to 2%, the bank could realize a large capital gain if it sold them before maturity. However, if the bond is held to maturity, then the bank will receive the bond's face value and no capital gain or loss will be realized. Consequently, management's decision to trade the bond before maturity can affect the amount of market risk exposure the bank faces in terms of interest rates.

The above discussion is the reason why banks must categorize their fixed income securities as "Available For Sale" (AFS) or "Held To Maturity" (HTM). Thus, we would expect more volatility and more market risk when the bank holds most of its bonds in the AFS bucket vs. the HTM category.

Similarly, the bank can serve as a broker and market maker in various currencies, commodities, derivatives, and equities which results in short-term exposure to market risk. To the extent that the bank can immediately match a buyer of, say, a specific currency like the euro with a seller of this currency, the "bid-ask spread" between these buying and selling prices can be captured by the financial institution, and the bank's foreign currency market risk exposure is negligible. However, if the bank buys the euro from one customer but cannot sell it right away, then the firm is exposed to market risk (in this case, the risk to the bank is that the euro declines in value versus the U.S. dollar).

Thus, the **net exposure** to these marketable securities is critical in determining the amount of market risk to which the bank is exposed. This net exposure is measured by subtracting the amount of, say, euros the bank has sold (also referred to as a "short euro" position) from the amount of euros the bank currently owns (also referred to as a "long euro" position). For example, if a bank has sold $80 million worth of euros to clients today and bought $100 million worth of euros, then the bank's net exposure is +$20 million (+100 million − 80 million). Note that the sign matters! Long positions are treated as positive values and short positions are denoted as negative values, as shown in Equation (5.1)[1]:

---

[1] As detailed in Chambers et al. (2023), a "short position" means that the bank has first borrowed a security from another person/entity to sell it at, say, today's price in the hope that this instrument will decline in value in the future. Then, when the bank, as "short seller," decides it is time to unwind the position in the future, it hopes to buy back the security at a lower price. In doing so, the short seller profits by selling high (today) and buying low (in the future). To initiate such a short position, the seller typical posts a good faith deposit (or "margin") and is obligated to pay interest on the value of the security lent to the bank. This type of transaction is the reverse of a long position which occurs when the bank first buys the security with the hope that the price will go up and then sells it for a profit at a higher price in the future.

$$\text{Net Market Exposure in a Marketable Security} = \text{Long Position} - \text{Short Position} \tag{5.1}$$

The sign matters because it tells us what type of market risk will negatively affect the bank's stock price. As noted in the above example, a net *long* position of $20 million in euros means that a *weakening* euro (or, conversely, the flip side of that coin is a *strengthening* U.S. dollar) will *decrease* the value of the bank's assets and will lead to a drop in the firm's stock price (holding all other factors constant). In contrast, a strengthening euro would help the bank's stock price in this scenario. So, we can see that market risk is a double-edged sword that needs to be managed to find the optimal level of exposure to not only euros but also to all currencies, commodities, bonds, and equities that the bank holds in its investment portfolio and trading account.

5.2 How to Measure Market Risk?

To manage a bank's market risk, we must first find a way to measure this risk. There are multiple methods to do this, so we first focus on the one that is most commonly used, Value-at-Risk (VaR), but we also briefly consider other metrics based on "Expected Shortfall" (ES) and "Extreme Value Theory" (EVT) later in this chapter. In addition, we must choose a time horizon for measuring market risk and so we use *one day* for this purpose because the prices of marketable securities fluctuate on a daily basis.[2] Thus, we focus on *1-day VaR* in this chapter, also known as "Daily Earnings at Risk" (or "DEAR" for short). In subsequent chapters, we focus on assets with longer horizons, like loans, which fluctuate on a less-frequent basis. There, we expand the VaR calculations to horizons, such as one year.

The VaR method helps us see how much exposure to "tail risk" a bank's investment portfolio and/or trading operation possesses.[3] In effect, we are assuming that a "high impact" but "low frequency" event is

---

[2] Due to advances in technology and data access, many firms now measure their market risk in real time during the entire trading day, especially for fast-moving markets where the banks have extensive trading operations.

[3] For most of this chapter, we focus on a bank's investment portfolio because all commercial banks have investments in marketable securities. However, larger banks can also have extensive trading operations to meet client needs and thus the market risk metrics

what we are most concerned about in terms of a bank's market risk. That is, we are more worried about the impact of a large drop in the value of the bank's investments, which might occur very infrequently. Usually, the concern is focused on the amount of investment loss that can occur 1% of the time over short time intervals (usually 1 or 10 days). This 1% threshold can change based on the application (for instance, we might be concerned about very extreme events, and look to the 0.01% threshold).

These events can have a large negative impact on the bank's market value of equity (V_E) because, as the "Accounting Identity" described earlier in Chapter 3 showed us, a *change* in a firm's Equity equals the *change* in Assets minus the *change* in Liabilities. So, in this chapter, we are focused on changes in the bank's investment portfolio which directly affect the market value of the bank's equity. If we assume the change in bank liabilities is zero, then we can see that a decrease in the bank's investment portfolio will lead directly to a drop in the firm's equity.[4]

As noted earlier, a sudden large loss can wipe out a sizable chunk of the bank's equity and so managers, investors, and regulators are all focused on those market-related events that are relatively low frequency but can have a big impact on the firm's value (e.g., events that normally occur 2–3 days per year because 1% of 250 trading days represents 2–3 days). Note that our focus here is on "high impact-low frequency" **events**, whereas in other cases, the FI might be more concerned with low impact-high frequency events such as when an automobile insurance company manages its financial exposure to car accidents (which, sadly, occur quite frequently but each individual accident has relatively low monetary impact for the insurer). We revisit this trade-off between impact and frequency in more detail when we discuss Operational Risk in Chapter 9.

Figure 5.1 shows a graph of the probability distribution of the expected return on a bank's investment portfolio. The probability of each possible return is shown on the *y*-axis, while the estimated percentage change in the portfolio is displayed on the *x*-axis. This distribution is

---

discussed in this chapter can be directly applied to both a bank's investment portfolio and trading services.

[4] We could easily relax this assumption of "no change in bank liabilities" due to market risk factors. In this case, we would then consider the impact on equity by examining the change in assets *net* of any market-induced change in liabilities. For simplicity and clarity of the discussion, we maintain the zero-liability-change assumption throughout this chapter.

Table 5.1. Key Assumptions from the Detailed Numerical Example for ABC Bank in Chapter 3.

Variable	Value
Total Assets ($ million)	1,580
Investment in Securities ($ million)	700
Common Equity ($ million)	180
Total Shares Outstanding (million)	10.0
Daily Average Return on Investment Portfolio	0.000320
Daily Standard Deviation of Investments	0.003173

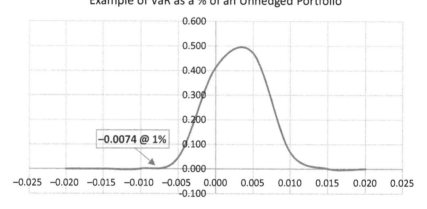

Figure 5.1. Daily Value at Risk (VaR) Expressed as a Percentage of a Bank's Investment Portfolio.

based on some of the data used earlier in Table 3.1 of Chapter 3 where we assume the following key numbers for our hypothetical bank, ABC.

Note that we are using *daily* estimates of the bank's tail risk exposure to fluctuations in market prices, such as currency, interest rate, and commodity price movements. We focus on the *left-side tail* of the distribution because this is where the bank can lose money (whereas the right tail shows the largest "upside" return for the portfolio). Most banks focus on daily or 10-day horizons because this is the typical timeframe that it takes to liquidate some marketable securities at reasonable prices and avoid incurring larger losses by selling too quickly at low "fire sale" prices.

Figure 5.1 tells us that there is a 1% chance that the portfolio will lose 0.74% (or more) of its value on any given day (i.e., −0.0074 in decimal format), as a 74-basis point loss is located at the 1st percentile of the distribution. In risk management jargon, this market exposure can also be expressed as a dollar value based on multiplying this estimated loss by the bank's total investment portfolio value at the beginning of the period (in this case, −0.0074 · $700 million = −$5.180 million). Another industry convention is to express this "Value at Risk" as a *positive* value of $5.180 million. Just keep in mind that it is a projected loss and therefore is technically a negative value that reduces the investment portfolio. This VaR estimate is commonly used because it is relatively straightforward for bank managers, investors, and regulators to understand as a measure of extreme tail risk due to financial market fluctuations.

Now, you must be wondering how we came up with such a precise estimate of this tail risk. As we show in the following sections, there are multiple ways to estimate this VaR measure of market risk such as the RiskMetrics method, Historic Simulation, and Monte Carlo Simulation. As noted earlier, we could also use other methods such as Expected Shortfall (ES) and Extreme Value Theory (EVT). We start with the RiskMetrics VaR approach and then discuss in subsequent sections these other market risk measurement methods.

5.3 RiskMetrics Approach (or Variance–Covariance VaR method)

The RiskMetrics approach was pioneered by J.P. Morgan in the early 1990s and ultimately was spun off from the financial firm. This method gained widespread acceptance because it is one of the more intuitive and computationally easier ways to estimate a bank's market risk. Its underlying assumption is that the returns to an investment portfolio are normally distributed (which, as we can see, can be a questionable assumption). In this case, all we need are estimates of the average and standard deviation of the portfolio's returns to estimate VaR. Note that we included these statistics in the last two rows of Table 5.1 as 0.000320 (0.032%) for the daily average return and 0.003173 (0.3173%) for the portfolio's **standard deviation**. To find the 1% tail on the left side of Figure 5.1, we can rely on the fact that this point on the normal distribution occurs at 2.33 standard deviations below the mean (we know this from looking up the appropriate z-score in a normal distribution table). Thus, we can use the following formula to estimate the 1% daily VaR for any portfolio (or individual security):

1% daily VaR = Critical Value · Daily Standard Deviation (S.D.) of Returns
· Invested Assets = 2.33 · 0.003173 · $700 million
= 0.007393 · $700 million = **$5.175 million**   (5.2)

where

Critical Value = the number of standard deviations below the mean where the 1% tail event occurs (this equals 2.33 for a normal distribution). The term, "critical value" is a reference to the statistical property of the normal distribution where 2.33 standard deviations represent the location of the lower 1% tail.[5]

Note the above calculation is slightly different than the $5.180 million reported earlier due to our rounding up to 0.0074 rather than using the more precise estimate of the adverse percentage daily return of 0.007393 that is shown with Equation (5.2). In effect, we expect the portfolio to fall by 0.74% (or more) during 1% of the trading days within a given year. Since there are typically around 250 trading days in a year, this means that the bank's managers should *not* be surprised if this investment portfolio has 2 or 3 days during the year in which it loses 74 or more basis points (i.e., derived from 0.01 · 250 days = 2.5 days or between 2 and 3 full days). The bottom line is as follows: please do *not* fire your risk managers if the portfolio loses 0.74% or more 2 or 3 days during the year, as that is what should be expected if returns follow a normal distribution! Instead, if this level of risk makes you uncomfortable, you need to adjust the portfolio's holding and/or engage in some hedging strategies to manage this risk. We discuss this later in this chapter.

---

[5] Since we are using VaR to estimate a portfolio's tail risk, we are most concerned with the lower 1% portion of the normal distribution. It is in this lower tail where the portfolio losses can be quite large. The VaR estimate produced by Equation (5.2) represents the expected dollar value of portfolio loss (or more) that can occur 1% of the time. Note that losses *beyond* the VaR estimate are certainly possible as the normal distribution allows, technically, for an *infinite* loss! As we discuss later in this chapter, these problems associated with the normal distribution have led to more recent attempts to use Expected Shortfall and Extreme Value Theory to gauge a portfolio's tail risk more accurately.

The above calculation is useful information as it prepares the management team (as well as investors and regulators) for what to expect in terms of the market risk associated with the bank's investments. Another benefit of this approach is that it is easy to estimate the VaR for time horizons longer than 1 day by simply multiplying the 1-day VaR by the square root of the number of days you wish to consider (i.e., 10-day VaR = 1-day VaR · $\sqrt{10}$). However, keep in mind that this extension ignores the effect of inter-relationships between, say, today's returns and yesterday's returns, commonly referred to as the "autocorrelation" in returns.[6] The method also allows ABC's managers to decide whether this is an acceptable amount of risk in relation to the firm's equity capital and profitability targets, such as return on equity (ROE) and risk-adjusted return on capital (RAROC). However, we wait until Chapter 6 (Credit Risk) to discuss how to apply VaR in this manner. Regulators also want to know about market risk because Basel III regulations require banks to hold sufficient capital to protect against these potential investment losses. We go into more detail in Chapter 10 (Regulatory Issues in Banking) about the role regulators play in helping banks manage their risks to maintain a safe, fair, and sound financial system.

Another point to keep in mind is that the above calculation assumes that returns are normally distributed which, in practice, does *not* appear to be the case for most real-world securities. Also, note that this VaR

---

[6]Like the concept of correlation described later in this chapter, autocorrelation is a statistical measure of the pattern of changes in returns over several time periods, from today (time-t) to many periods in the past (e.g., 30 days ago, which is denoted as time-t-30). This measure can range between +1.0 (today's returns move in exactly the same direction as yesterday's returns) and −1.0 (where today's returns move in a zig-zag pattern in the opposite direction of yesterday's returns). To account for autocorrelation in our VaR estimate, as Hull (2010) shows, we should multiply it by $\sqrt{T + 2(T-1)\rho + 2(T-2)\rho^2 + 2(T-3)\rho^3 + \cdots + 2\rho^{T-1}}$, where ρ is the estimate of daily autocorrelation and T is the number of days. Ignoring the effect of autocorrelation can lead to under-estimating the true level of risk present in the portfolio. Hull (2010) shows the VaR for T greater than 1 day can be several times larger than the 1-day VaR · $\sqrt{T}$ estimate when there is autocorrelation. For example, when $T = 250$ and autocorrelation is +0.20, then the "true" VaR estimate is over 19 times greater than a simple VaR · $\sqrt{T}$ estimate. Thus, we should consider the method described in the text above as a "back of the envelope" calculation to help provide a quick estimate of the longer-range VaR.

estimate simply estimates the 1% chance of losses that are *at least* of this magnitude but, in reality, the actual portfolio loss could be *much more* than that amount! In fact, many empirical studies find that most securities have a "fat-tailed" or "leptokurtic" distribution, which means that the average return and the two extreme tails of the distribution are more likely to occur when compared to a normally distributed set of investment returns (and this is especially true when considering assets that are less liquid, for example). One quick "fix" is to use a larger "Critical value" to account for fat-tailed, non-normal distributions. Saunders *et al.* (2024) suggest using an adjustment factor of 2.65 rather than 2.33 as one way to adjust for this non-normality, but analysts can use other methods to explicitly account for this phenomenon by using Historic Simulation or other approaches (as we describe later, this simulation method uses the *actual* return distribution rather than forcing the data to conform to the normal distribution). Using this larger adjustment factor would lead to a $5.886 million VaR estimate and represents a 13.7% increase over the VaR estimate based on normality.

Although Equation (5.2) is general in nature and therefore applicable across many portfolios, it is sometimes helpful to modify this formula to account for specific types of investments, such as bonds, currencies/commodities, and equities, as shown in the following.

5.3.1 *VaR for a bond*

Bond VaR = Critical value · Daily Standard Deviation (S.D.) of Interest Rates · Modified Duration · Invested Assets (5.3)

Note that in (5.3) we build upon our discussion from Chapter 4 about the interest rate risk associated with fixed income securities. To estimate Bond VaR, we first need to use daily fluctuations in an overall measure of interest rates to compute the Daily S.D. of Interest Rates. We then must convert that generalized interest *rate* volatility measure into a variability of bond *prices* and so we use the specific bond portfolio's average modified duration for this purpose. Thus, multiplying the S.D. of Interest Rates by the Modified Duration gives us an idea of the *typical* daily percentage change in the market value of the bond portfolio.

Since we want to derive a tail risk estimate, we must also use a Critical value to find the potential loss that would occur 1% of the time. For a normal distribution, this factor is equal to 2.33, as noted earlier. The last step is to then multiply this extreme bond price change by the dollar amount of Invested Assets within the bond portfolio. Thus, Bond VaR will be greater when either price volatility or the dollar investment (or both) is relatively high.

5.3.2 VaR for an equity

$$\text{Equity VaR} = \text{Critical value} \cdot \text{Daily Standard Deviation (S.D.) of Market Porfolio's Returns} \cdot \text{Market Beta of the Portfolio (or individual stock)} \cdot \text{Invested Assets} \quad (5.4)$$

Note that in (5.4) the format is like the Bond VaR in Equation (5.3) except we now must factor in the volatility of market-wide stock returns (e.g., based on the standard deviation of returns for a broad stock market index) and the equity portfolio's sensitivity to these market-wide returns (commonly measured by the equities' "market beta" based on the Capital Asset Pricing Model). To find the Equity VaR, we multiply these two key inputs with the Critical Value to account for the extreme tail event as well as the dollar amount invested in the bank's equities portfolio.

5.3.3 VaR for a foreign currency or commodity

$$\text{Currency or Commodity VaR} = \text{Critical value} \cdot \text{Daily Standard Deviation (S.D.) of Currency or Commodity Price Changes (in \%)} \cdot \text{Invested Assets} \quad (5.5)$$

Like Equations (5.3) and (5.4), the format for Currency or Commodity VaR estimates needs to account for the extreme tail event and the dollar amount invested in the bank's equities portfolio. However, the estimate of volatility is a bit simpler than that for bonds and equities because we can use the standard deviation of returns for each specific exchange rate or commodity price rather than rely on some broad, generalized measure of returns.

Based on Equations (5.2)–(5.5), we present in Table 5.2 some numerical examples to estimate VaR for each of these types of investments as well as for the total investment portfolio.

Table 5.2. Numerical Examples for ABC Bank's VaR estimates based on various securities in the Investment Portfolio.

Variable	Extreme Factor	Total Return	Volatility	$Invested	VaR
		Int. Rate S.D.	Modified Duration		
Bonds	2.33	0.0002	3.0	$350	$0.489
		Market S.D.	Beta		
Equities	2.33	0.011	1.2	$140	$4.306
		Price Change S.D.			
Currencies or Commodities	2.33	0.0025	N.A.	$210	$1.223
		Return S.D.			
Total Portfolio	2.33	0.0074	N.A.	$700	$5.175

Table 5.2 illustrates how VaR can be computed differently depending on the key drivers of Total Portfolio Return Volatility (as defined by the standard deviation and noted in the table by the "S.D." terms). For example, the VaR for the Bond portion of the investment portfolio takes into account the variability in interest rates as well as the average modified duration of the bank's bond investments. The overall dollar value invested in Bonds ($350 million) will also affect its VaR. Thus, the overall size of the Investment portfolio and the Bonds' relative weight in the portfolio (i.e., $350 / $700 = 50% in this case) will affect this VaR estimate. In addition, the Equities portfolio is affected by its relative weight (20%) while also considering the overall volatility of the stock market (σ_M) and the average beta of the stocks held by the bank (e.g., 1.2). The VaR estimate for foreign currencies and commodities (based on 30% of the portfolio) is the simplest to compute because all that is needed is the standard deviation of the daily percentage changes in these instruments' prices. In all cases, these total return volatility estimates are multiplied by Critical value (i.e., 2.33) and the dollar amount invested in each of the various types of investments. For completeness, we also report in the last row of Table 5.2 the VaR estimate of the Total Portfolio that we had shown earlier (i.e., $5.175 million).

Keep in mind the simplest way to figure out the VaR of the total portfolio is to first use the portfolio weights for each asset class (bonds, equities, and currencies/commodities) and each asset's daily returns to compute the daily portfolio returns. We can then take the standard deviation of these portfolio returns (0.0074) and use Equation (5.2) to estimate the portfolio's VaR of $5.175 million.

However, sometimes we would prefer to decompose the impact of individual asset classes on the total portfolio. For example, we can use the following relationship to identify the individual effect of, say, the bond portfolio's VaR (denoted for the ith sub-component of the portfolio by VaR_i) and its correlations with other asset classes (denoted by $\rho_{i,j}$):

$$1\text{-}day\ \text{VaR}_P = \sqrt{\sum_i \text{VaR}_i^2 + \sum_{i \neq j} 2 \cdot \rho_{i,j} \cdot \text{VaR}_i \cdot \text{VaR}_j} \qquad (5.6)$$

where

$\rho_{i,j}$ = **correlation** between the VaR estimates for security-i and security-j for all securities held within the bank's portfolio.[7]

What is especially interesting is that the Total Portfolio's daily VaR ($5.175 million) is *much less than the simple sum of the VaRs* of the various sub-components ($6.018 million). This is driven by the fact that the portfolio benefits from a "diversification effect" because the daily movements in bonds, stocks, currencies, and commodities are *not* perfectly (and positively) correlated with each other. Thus, by not putting the bank's money all in one "basket" of securities, the total portfolio's risk is

---

[7] Correlation is a statistical term which quantifies the amount that two variables (e.g., bond and stock returns) move in tandem with each other. For example, if these returns move in a perfect, lock-step manner where gains (losses) in bonds coincide with gains (losses) in stocks, then the correlation between the two types of securities is +1.0 and represents perfect positive correlation. Conversely, if bonds and stocks move in the exact opposite manner each day (i.e., a "zig-zag" pattern of daily returns), the correlation statistic would be −1.0 and indicates a perfect negative pattern. In addition, if there is no pattern between stocks and bonds, then the correlation would be 0.0 and would represent a random pattern with no correlation. Typically, most securities exhibit less-than-perfect positive correlation with other securities and thus we normally observe correlations between +0.2 and +0.8. This level of correlation suggests that diversification can help reduce a portfolio's overall risk.

Table 5.3. Correlation Matrix for the Components of ABC's Investment Portfolio.

	Bonds	Equities	Currencies/ Commod.
Bonds	1.00	0.60	−0.20
Equities	0.60	1.00	0.40
Currencies/ Commodities	−0.20	0.40	1.00

substantially reduced because declines in, say, bonds, could be offset by gains in stocks and currencies.

We can quantify this as a "Diversification Benefit" (also sometimes referred to as a "Covariance Adjustment") whenever we have estimates of the **correlations** ($\rho_{i,j}$) between the returns of each of the portfolio's individual holdings. Let us continue with the assumptions for ABC in Table 5.2 and consider the possible return correlations between the bond, equities, and currencies/commodities' sub-components of the bank's investment portfolio, as shown in Table 5.3.

Using the data from Tables 5.2 and 5.3, we can decompose the total portfolio's daily VaR with the help of Equation (5.6) as follows.

In the first four rows of Table 5.4, we report for ABC the various parts that make up the bank's Total Portfolio VaR of $5.175 million. These values correspond to the components of Equation (5.6) and capture the effects of each asset's VaR, as well as the effects of the covariation in the returns on ABC's investments in bonds, equities, and currencies/commodities. The last three rows of Table 5.4 highlight the $0.844 million diversification benefit of owning assets that are not perfectly, positively correlated with each other. As we saw earlier in Table 5.3, the three asset classes have correlations between −0.2 and +0.6, which are all much less than +1.0. This reduces the overall risk of the total investment portfolio. This diversification benefit of nearly 1 million dollars represents a 14.0% reduction from the simple sum of each of the three asset's VaRs. In effect, adding up the individual VaRs for the three assets implicitly assumes that these investments have a perfect +1.0 correlation with each other.[8]

---

[8] Note that you can prove this to yourself by replacing all the correlations in Table 5.3 ($\rho_{i,j}$) with +1.0 and then re-calculating the VaR of the portfolio using Equation (5.6). If so, you

Market Risk 179

Table 5.4. ABC's VaR Estimates and Its Portfolio Diversification Benefit.

	VaR_i^2	Bond Covariance	Equities Covariance
Bonds	0.239		
Equities	18.540	2.528	
Currencies/Commodities	1.496	−0.239	4.214
Total Portfolio VaR	**5.175**		
	$ millions		
Sum of VaRs	6.018	% Reduction	
Diversification Benefit	***0.844***	14.0%	
Total Portfolio VaR	**5.175**		

Presented in the following is an example from Citigroup's financial statements on how it discloses its VaR estimates (found in Citigroup's annual report, 2021). As we can see from Table 5.5, the firm's diversification benefit (denoted as the "Covariance Adjustment") is quite substantial. For example, the first column reports a total Covariance Adjustment of $88 million and represents a 53% reduction from the simple sum of $167 million based on Citigroup's VaR estimates for each of its major asset holdings within its trading portfolio. Clearly, Citigroup's trading activity in these various asset classes was not very highly correlated!

In sum, we can use the RiskMetrics method to analyze the impact of various sub-components of the portfolio by, say, varying our assumptions about the standard deviations and correlations of these investments. This can be very useful for a bank manager to conduct "what-if" analyses as well as perform "stress tests" for extreme scenarios. After the Great Financial Crisis of 2008–2009, regulators in the U.S. elsewhere require large financial institutions to conduct such stress tests to see if these firms can withstand large, sudden adverse movements in the financial markets and the macroeconomy.

Overall, the RiskMetrics method is analytically convenient and can help us see how changes in assumptions about volatility and correlation

---

will find that the VaR equals the $6.018 million figure reported in the "Sum of VaRs" row of Table 5.4. In this case, the Diversification Benefit would be zero.

Table 5.5. Example of Citigroup's VaR Disclosures.

Year-end and Average Trading VAR and Trading and Credit Portfolio VAR

In millions of dollars	December 31, 2021	2021 Average	December 31, 2020	2020 Average
Interest rate	$50	$65	$72	$66
Credit spread	59	71	70	86
Covariance adjustment	(35)	(42)	(51)	(48)
Fully diversified interest rate and credit spread	$74	$94	$91	$104
Foreign exchange	36	42	40	26
Equity	29	33	31	36
Commodity	28	34	17	22
Covariance adjustment	(88)	(102)	(85)	(82)
Total trading VAR — all market risk factors, including general and specific risk (excluding credit portfolio)	$79	$101	$94	$106
Specific risk-only component	$3	$1	$(1)	$(2)
Total trading VAR — all market risk factors only (excluding credit portfolios)	$76	$100	$95	$108
Incremental impact of the credit portfolio	$45	$30	$29	$49
Total trading and credit portfolio VAR	$124	$131	$123	$155

alter our VaR estimate. However, the method is not perfect and so we present in the following some of the pros and cons of using this technique:

Pros:

1. The formula for this method is straightforward and transparent, so a manager can quickly see what is driving changes in the VaR estimate. Moreover, the normal distribution is well understood and easy to work with.
2. Easy to do "what-if" analyses to see the impact on market risk due to changes in volatility and the amount invested in the portfolio and its sub-components. This also makes it very clear how market risk changes under "stress test" scenarios.

Cons:

1. The main drawback is the assumption of normally distributed asset returns. Numerous empirical studies have shown that financial asset returns are usually leptokurtic, or fat-tailed, and potentially skewed. This means that the normal distribution assumption will lead to *under*-estimates of the true levels of VaR and market risk. Altering the Critical Value to be 2.65 standard deviations (vs. 2.33) can help but does not fully alleviate the problem, especially if the portfolio's returns are skewed by nonlinear payoffs from options or other instruments that have options embedded within them such as callable bonds and mortgages with prepayment options.
2. Typically relies on historical data to develop the model's key inputs related to standard deviations and correlations, which can lead to "backward-looking" market risk estimates. Ideally, we prefer to have "forward-looking" VaR estimates because that can lead to more effective risk management decisions.

Later in this chapter, we discuss some of the regulatory implications of a bank's market risk and its capital requirements. For now, we turn to other ways to estimate VaR such as the Historic Simulation approach which allow us to relax the assumption of normally distributed returns.

5.4 Historic Simulation

The Historic Simulation method (sometimes referred to as a Historical or Back Simulation) is conceptually and computationally a much simpler way to estimate a bank's Value at Risk (VaR). Thus, we can derive a VaR estimate from historical data about the portfolio's returns rather than rely on an assumed probability distribution like the normal distribution. All that is needed is a time series of past returns for each asset class within the bank's portfolio as well as the dollar amounts invested in each of these sub-components (e.g., bonds, stocks, currencies, and commodities). In other words, we will rely on the *actual* distribution of returns rather than making an explicit assumption about the underlying return distribution. For example, two years' worth of daily returns are typically used for this type of analysis, resulting in around 500 data points for each asset class. Once we have collected the relevant return and portfolio data, there are essentially *five steps* to estimate VaR via historic simulation:

1. Compute the daily dollar changes for each asset class based on the historical data by multiplying the daily percentage change by the dollar amount invested in each of these assets. For example, if ABC has $140 million in equities and they fall by 2.0% on a specific day, then the dollar change is –$2.8 million (i.e., –0.02 · $140 million) for that component of ABC's portfolio.
2. Sum these dollar changes for each day across all the asset classes so that we can see the daily change in the dollar value of ABC's *Total Portfolio*.
3. We can then rank the daily dollar changes in the bank's Total Portfolio returns from highest to lowest over all 500 observations.
4. Identify the *lowest 1%* of these dollar changes in the Total Portfolio returns for each asset class. For example, we can identify the *fifth-worst* return for each asset if we are using 500 days because 1% of 500 is 5. This tail risk value can easily be found via either the Excel™ =SMALL(..) or =PERCENTILE(..) commands to locate the day that represents the lowest 1% portfolio return.
5. The value obtained in Step 4 can be viewed as our estimate of the bank's Value at Risk based on the Historic Simulation method because it represents the lowest 1% tail of the historical distribution of

portfolio returns and explicitly considers the correlations between assets as well as the possible non-normality of these returns.

Table 5.6 illustrates the results of the five steps noted above for a hypothetical set of returns for ABC's portfolio that invests in stocks, bonds, currencies, and commodities. In this case, we can see that the 1% VaR estimate is $6.426 million because on its fifth-worst day over the past 2 years, ABC's total portfolio lost 0.92% (see the second-to-last row of Table 5.6). Note that this VaR estimate is 24% higher than what we estimated using the RiskMetrics method ($6.426 vs. $5.175 million). This type of pattern is typically found when returns are not normally distributed and "fat-tailed."

As a bank manager, we must recognize that risk management is both an art and a science, and thus we need to use judgment when faced with different tail risk assessments. As we see in the following, the Monte Carlo simulation method can produce a third VaR estimate which is different than the two reported here. So, a good bank manager should incorporate information for all these methods and decide whether to focus on one estimate or to combine the various VaR estimates into a consolidated figure. Unfortunately, there is no formula or clear guidance on how to best do this and so sound judgment is still required to effectively manage a bank's market risk.

As we mentioned earlier for the RiskMetrics method, there are pros and cons to using the Historic Simulation technique, as shown in the following:

Pros:

1. The method is simple to compute (e.g., the Excel = SMALL(..) or = PERCENTILE(..) commands can be used to locate the day that represents the lowest 1% portfolio return).
2. No need for correlation and volatility estimates.
3. Allows for returns to follow a *non*-normal distribution, which is a more realistic assumption in practice.
4. Provides us with a specific worst-case estimate based on the lowest return during the sample period (whereas the RiskMetrics approach does not provide this because a normal distribution implies an infinitely large loss is possible). For example, in Table 5.6, we can see that the worst-case scenario represents the lowest portfolio return within the 2-year sample (−4.21% or −$29.441 million).

Table 5.6. Sample Data to Estimate ABC's VaR using Historic Simulation Method.

	$Invested			$350	$140	$210		$700
	Bonds	Equities	FX / Comm.	Bonds	Equities	FX / Comm.	Total Portfolio	
Highest Day	0.0083	0.0906	0.0485	2.908	12.684	10.191	**0.0368**	25.784
	0.0102	0.0550	0.0137	3.571	7.696	2.875	0.0202	14.142
	0.0155	0.0084	0.0148	5.439	1.175	3.113	0.0139	9.726
	0.0057	0.0298	0.0165	2.008	4.170	3.457	0.0138	9.635
	0.0063	0.0276	0.0044	2.197	3.859	0.924	0.0100	6.980
⋮								
1% Rank	0.0119	−0.0279	−0.0319	4.169	−3.906	−6.689	**−0.0092**	**−6.426**
⋮								
Lowest Day	−0.0274	−0.0750	−0.0446	−9.583	−10.500	−9.358	−0.0421	−29.441

Cons:

1. Relies on past historical data and thus implicitly assumes history will repeat itself. Thus, by construction, the VaR estimates will be "backward-looking" which can be problematic for future decision-making.
2. The number of observations is relatively small in a statistical sense if we use the latest 2 years' worth of daily data (i.e., only about 500 data points). We could use a longer time series but the relevance of using data from, say, 10 years ago might be questionable. One solution is to use a longer time series but weigh the more recent data more heavily, but this still does not overcome the backward-looking nature of this approach.

One way to overcome some of the drawbacks of both the Historic and RiskMetrics methods is to create a *forward-looking* estimate of VaR based on Monte Carlo simulation. This approach can use the historical return data, along with summary statistics of the components of the portfolio's time series (e.g., the means, standard deviations, and correlations of the bond, stock, currency, and commodity investments) to create hypothetical returns for the portfolio that might occur in the future. The following section provides some more details on this third way to estimate VaR.

5.5 Monte Carlo Simulation

As noted in the prior section, one way to overcome the drawbacks of the backward-looking nature of the Historic and RiskMetrics methods is to create a forward-looking estimate of VaR based on Monte Carlo simulation. This approach enables the analyst to use historical return data, along with summary statistics of the components of the portfolio's time series to create hypothetical returns for the portfolio that might occur in the future. The following section briefly summarizes this third way to estimate VaR.[9]

The Monte Carlo (MC) method holds the potential for generating more useful, forward-looking estimates of market risk, but, as with any approach, it makes certain assumptions. In this method, the key assumption is that the analyst can construct a model which will replicate the possible future volatilities and correlations between *all* the assets held in the

---

[9] For more technical details on applying Monte Carlo techniques for estimating market risk within a financial institution, consult Jorion (2007) and Saunders *et al.* (2024).

bank's investment portfolio. For example, the analyst must specify the specific relationships between how bond returns on a given day in the future will behave when, say, commodities returns rise and stocks fall.

To do this, we use volatilities and correlations from the past as a starting point but then create hypothetical daily returns for each asset that, if done successfully, will capture the overall portfolio's distribution of future returns. We can create this set of simulated daily returns for the bank's marketable assets and store them to estimate the portfolio's return for that hypothetical day. The MC algorithm can then repeat this simulated set of asset returns for a very large number of possible portfolio outcomes and store them in rank order from worst to best returns (e.g., 100,000 simulations are commonly created). We can also multiply these simulated returns by the initial dollar amount invested in each asset so that we can see the simulated dollar value of these estimates.

We can summarize the MC method process with *five steps*:

1. Estimate the standard deviations and correlations of each asset within the portfolio.[10]
2. Generate X-thousand hypothetical return scenarios that conform to the volatilities and correlations specified in Step 1 (where X is usually 100,000).
3. Compute the impact of these simulated returns on the dollar values of each asset holding and sum across all assets to formulate a hypothetical total portfolio value for each of the X-thousand scenarios.
4. Rank the scenarios from lowest portfolio value to highest value and then locate the 1% lower tail of this simulated distribution (e.g., the 1,000th-worst if there are 100,000 scenarios).
5. Compute the VaR by subtracting the 1% portfolio value from the current market value of the portfolio.

---

[10] Note for portfolios that have many individual securities within the total portfolio, the number of correlations between assets grows exponentially and can be difficult to manage computationally. So, in practice, most risk managers will use "factor models" which estimate the returns and volatilities for each individual asset based on a smaller set of "factors," such as broad, market-wide variables like a U.S. stock market index, U.S. Treasury rates, and a subset of "major" currencies and commodities. This reduces the computational complexity considerably.

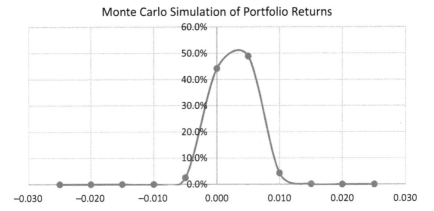

Figure 5.2. Example of a Monte Carlo Simulation of Portfolio Returns.

From the simulation process described above, we can then form a picture of the probability distribution of hypothetical future values of ABC's total portfolio like the graph shown in Figure 5.2. In this graph, we used the standard deviations for each asset from Table 5.2 and chose to create 1,000 simulated daily portfolio returns (to save on the number of calculations for this specific example).

From a distribution such as the one shown in Figure 5.2, we can then identify the point on the graph where the 1% lower tail is located. Since we have done 1,000 simulations in our example, we can use the return that is the 10th-worst value of the portfolio (i.e., $0.01 \cdot 1{,}000 = 10$). In Figure 5.2, this 1% value is −0.65% in daily returns or $4.581 million in terms of VaR (based on ABC's $700 million investment portfolio) Note this VaR estimate is different than those obtained by the RiskMetrics method ($5.175 million) and the Historic Simulation technique ($6.426 million). This finding should not be that surprising given that each method is based on different assumptions. However, a key drawback of the MC approach is the lack of clarity in understanding what are the main drivers that underly this alternative VaR forecast. This is due to many of the inter-relationships between asset returns being obscured by the MC simulation process. Thus, many analysts perceive the MC's estimates to be developed within a "black box" that cannot be easily interpreted by external users of VaR forecasts, such as senior management, public investors, and regulators.

So, this is where the art (as opposed to the science) of risk management comes into play and requires human judgment by the bank's managers to decide which VaR estimate to use. In practice, risk managers will typically focus on the MC method for risk management purposes, but many will also check these MC estimates against the other two methods' VaR estimates as a "sanity check." Depending on the results, the manager might then formulate a final VaR estimate that is a blend of estimates from all three methods.

Like the other VaR methods discussed earlier, the MC approach also has its strengths and weaknesses, as outlined in the following:

Pros:

1. As noted earlier, its most attractive feature is that it can produce a forward-looking VaR estimate by simulating numerous future scenarios for the portfolio's performance. However, as we have noted earlier in this book on more than one occasion, we must be careful of the "GIGO" critique because poor inputs can provide misleading VaR forecasts.
2. Provides us with a specific worst-case estimate based on the lowest return during the sample period.
3. Allows for returns to follow a *non*-normal distribution, which is a more realistic assumption in practice.

Cons:

1. Many of the inter-relationships between assets that determine the portfolio VaR results are hidden within the MC method and thus represent a "black box." Thus, it is difficult for many people to understand the model's complexity and how to explain the key drivers of the VaR estimate to senior management, regulators, and investors.
2. Although the method provides forward-looking estimates, it typically still relies on past historical data and thus implicitly assumes history will repeat itself (or at least "rhyme" with past relationships).

5.6 Other Methods of Estimating Tail Risk: Expected Shortfall (ES) and Extreme Value Theory (EVT)

Beyond the methods outlined above, there are two other ways that a risk manager can estimate a portfolio's tail risk, Expected Shortfall and Extreme Value Theory, and we describe them briefly in the following:

5.6.1 *Expected Shortfall Approach (ES)*

$$\text{ES} = -E(\Delta V_p | \Delta V_p < -\text{VaR}_p) \qquad (5.7)$$

One way to view Expected Shortfall is that it represents the expected change in the bank's investment portfolio when it experiences an "extreme event" such as when the portfolio's loss exceeds its 1-day VaR. Another way to think about this concept is to define the ES as the average portfolio return *conditional* on a loss *greater than* the VaR threshold. ES essentially answers the following question: when market conditions are very bad, what is the expected loss on this portfolio?

Accordingly, Equation (5.7) describes how the market value of an investment portfolio is expected to change (ΔV_p) when this portfolio's value drops below its VaR estimate (i.e., when $\Delta V_p < -\text{VaR}_p$ occurs). Since this, by definition, examines what happens to the portfolio once it surpasses its VaR, it enables us to provide a more coherent risk measure that allows for non-normal behavior in this lower 1% tail of the distribution.

We can compute ES in many ways and where one of the simpler methods is to use the distribution of past returns from the Historic Simulation approach and take an equally weighted average of all historical returns *below* the 1% tail. So, if the average of all past daily returns in the 1% tail was, say, −1.50%, then the ES for ABC's $700 million portfolio would be $10.5 million (i.e., 0.015 · $700 million). Note that this estimate is much larger than the VaR estimates of $5–$6 million presented earlier in this chapter. This is typically the case because we are now trying to estimate the expected decline once we are in the lower tail. The ES must be at least as large of a loss as the VaR and is usually much larger if the distribution behaves non-normally when losses exceed the 1% VaR threshold. The same approach as described here could be used with simulated worst-case returns based on a Monte Carlo technique.

Table 5.7. Numerical Example of Expected Shortfall Calculation.

Probability	Change in Portfolio (DVP)		
99.0%	+$0.350 million		
0.4%	−$5.175 million	VaR occurs here @ 1%	
0.6%	−15.000 million		ES includes this possible change in value as well
		Value at Risk (VaR)	**Expected Shortfall (ES)**
		$5.175 million	**$11.070 million** [0.4% / (0.6% + 0.4%) · $5.175] + [0.6% / (0.6% + 0.4%) · $15.000]

Yet another way to compute ES is to explicitly assign probabilities to different possible market values once the portfolio crosses the 1% VaR threshold. This can be accomplished by computing a probability-weighted average change in the portfolio, as noted in Table 5.7.

As we can see from Table 5.7, the ES estimate is more than double the RiskMetrics VaR estimate for ABC's investment portfolio because ES explicitly quantifies a potentially very large $15 million loss when it crosses over the 1% VaR threshold. From a regulatory perspective, global regulators have developed risk management rules (referred to as the Basel regulations) that are encouraging banks to use ES as a more accurate and coherent method of market risk[11]:

Pros:

1. The method is simple to compute if the Historic or Monte Carlo methods are used to estimate the VaR threshold because ES can use these portfolio distributions to directly estimate the expected loss when the portfolio exceeds this VaR estimate.

---

[11] By "coherent" we mean that ES estimates of various units within a bank can be aggregated in a logical, consistent manner. In contrast, VaR estimates across different business units might not always lead to consistent firm-wide tail risk estimates due to a "subadditivity" problem when some assets have nonlinear payoffs, as described in Hull (2010).

2. As noted earlier, ES is a coherent risk measure that avoids some of the issues of VaR when aggregating market risk across multiple business units at the bank.
3. Allows for returns to follow a *non*-normal distribution, which is a more realistic assumption in practice.

Cons:

1. Typically relies on past historical data and thus implicitly assumes history will repeat itself. Thus, by construction, the VaR estimates will be "backward-looking" which can be problematic for future decision-making.
2. It can be somewhat less intuitive to understand compared to VaR because it requires an understanding of conditional probability as well as non-normal probability distributions.

5.7 Extreme Value Theory (EVT)

Another way to account for the dynamics of what happens to a portfolio when it crosses into the 1% tail is based on Extreme Value Theory. As Haan and Ferreira (2006) and others have suggested, ES can be a more informative tail risk metric than VaR, but it is also even more sensitive to outliers when using information that is far below the 1% threshold. EVT attempts to address this issue by borrowing from existing statistical techniques used in the physical sciences to help quantify rare events that represent large outliers. For example, one EVT method is called the Peak-Over-Threshold (POT) method and was first developed by hydrologists to estimate how high the water level behind a dam could rise during, say, a massive flood of historic proportions. This is indeed very important to know when building a dam and so various approaches have been explored over the past 100 years with POT usually providing superior estimates. Examining the properties of such an approach is very technical and thus we do not provide a numerical example of this technique. We refer the interested reader to Haan and Ferreira (2006) for more details. However, we should keep in mind that for larger, more complex financial institutions, the additional expertise and effort needed to use EVT might be worthwhile.

5.8 Applications to Risk Management: Using VaR to Manage Market Risk and Stress-testing a Bank's Market Risk Exposure

Despite the drawbacks of VaR discussed above, it is still a popular and intuitive way to quantify and manage market risk. For example, we can show in Figure 5.3 an example of Citigroup's daily VaR measure over the course of one year to see how many times the bank's trading losses are beyond the bank's VaR estimates, as shown in the following[12]:

In Figure 5.3, the jagged solid line below zero represents the firm's daily VaR estimates which fluctuated with market conditions and the bank's level of trading activity. The vertical bars represent the actual daily gains and losses incurred during 250 or so trading days that make up the year. A well-managed trading operation should expect to have losses, or "exceptions," that fall below the solid line 2–3 times during the year. However, as we can see from Figure 5.3, there is only one exception, occurring in November of the year. One could argue that this means the risk manager did *not* do that good of a job because they were too conservative in their VaR estimates (meaning that the VaR numbers were too far below zero compared to the actual trading behavior).

Although it might sound counter-intuitive that one exception is not considered a good performance, it is sensible when we consider that a *higher* VaR estimate means the bank is required to hold *more* equity capital to protect against large losses. The risk manager is being *too conservative* in this case. Conversely, if the actual number of exceptions exceeded the firm's solid line more than three times, then we can consider this result to be another example of weak risk management performance. In this case, the VaR estimate is *too aggressive* and leads to holding *less* capital than what is required and can *increase* the bank's chances of insolvency. Ideally, we would like the risk manager to set a VaR estimate that is like a "Goldilocks" solution (where the bank estimates a *just-right* level of VaR that results in 2–3 exceptions each year). However, this is easier said than done and so senior management should understand that any given year might look like the pattern shown in Figure 5.3 but that, over several years, the number of days exceeding the bank's VaR estimates should average around 2–3 days per year.

---

[12] This graph is taken from Citigroup's 2021 Annual Report and 10-K filing (Citigroup, 2021).

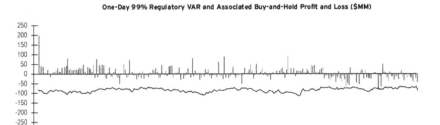

Figure 5.3. Example of Citigroup's Usage of VaR to Measure Market Risk for its Trading Portfolio.

VaR can also be a useful tool for "stress-testing" a bank's investment portfolio. Basel guidelines and various regulators like the Federal Reserve require large banks to conduct stress tests of many aspects of the bank's risk exposures, including market risk. For example, rather than relying on "normal" market conditions to estimate the portfolio's standard deviation via the RiskMetrics method, the risk manager could use an "abnormal" standard deviation based on, say, the highest level of volatility over the past 25 years. For example, if a typical standard deviation for ABC's portfolio return is 0.3173% as shown earlier, then the "normal" VaR estimate is around 0.74% per day.[13]

We can stress-test this portfolio by using the highest standard deviation of a similar portfolio that is comprised of 50% bonds, 20% equities, and 30% currencies/commodities. Let's assume that the highest standard deviation of such a portfolio occurred in 2008 at a level of 1.00% per day. In this case, our "stressed VaR" based on the RiskMetrics method would be 2.33% because we would multiply the stressed standard deviation of 1.00% by the

---

[13] Recall that we obtained this estimate from the data in Table 5.1 which showed ABC's portfolio had a daily standard deviation of 0.3173%. Thus, based on a normal distribution, there is a 1% chance that the portfolio will lose 0.74% (or more) of its value on any given day (i.e., −0.0074 in decimal format) because a 74-basis point loss is located at the 1st percentile of the distribution.

normal distribution's critical value of 2.33. In this case, our stressed VaR estimate for ABC's $700 million portfolio is $16.310 million, which is *more than triple* the "un-stressed" or "normal" VaR of $5.175 million we had calculated earlier.

Given the numerous ways to estimate a bank's market risk, we can see that many different elements need to be considered by ABC's senior managers to decide which methods and numbers are most useful for risk management purposes. The above discussion suggests once again that current risk management techniques represent both an art and a science that must be blended with sound human judgment. We now turn to how market risk, once measured properly, might be managed through bank actions, such as hedging.

5.9 How Hedging Market Risk Can Affect the Distribution of Returns

The earlier discussion in this chapter has focused on various ways to model the distribution of a bank's portfolio returns using VaR and ES methods. For example, the RiskMetrics VaR approach assumes returns are normally distributed and thus the standard deviations and correlations for the portfolio's assets have a direct impact on the ultimate shape of return distribution. Another point to consider is how hedging some portion of this market risk can affect the overall distribution of returns. In theory, if an "ideal" or "perfect" hedging instrument could be found, then a bank's entire amount of market risk could be eliminated and thus the portfolio's return distribution becomes a single vertical line with no dispersion around its expected (or average) value!

However, before delving into the details of hedging, we should keep in mind that the bank can also manage its market risk in other ways by (1) imposing **position (or risk) limits** on specific assets and/or trading units and (2) altering the mix of assets in its investment portfolio. For example, the bank's managers commonly place limits on how much dollar exposure can be invested or traded in a specific security as well as at the individual trader level. These limits act as "guard rails" to ensure the dollar amount of exposure is not too large relative to senior management's appetite for risk and the bank's ability to absorb losses. In addition to dollar limits, the percentage of the portfolio allocated to a particular asset class can be capped to make sure that more volatile assets like stocks are not more than, say, 10%

of the portfolio. In fact, regulators will also mandate such investment **portfolio allocation caps** to reduce a bank's incentive to invest a large portion of its portfolio in the riskiest types of securities.

As we show in the following, it is usually *not* optimal to hedge 100% of a bank's market risk because of not only the explicit costs of implementing and maintaining such a hedge but also the indirect costs in terms of managerial focus and the opportunity cost of investing this time and money for other more productive uses (e.g., launching a new product or entering a new geographic region).

One can see the impact of hedging on a portfolio by showing a picture of a hypothetical investment portfolio with and without a hedge in place. For example, Figure 5.4 compares the distribution of daily returns of a portfolio of securities that is unhedged and therefore has a hedge ratio, h, equal to zero ($h = 0$) to one that is partially hedged by, say, a derivative security for half of its market risk exposure ($h = 0.5$). The graph shows the classic trade-off between risk and return where the unhedged portfolio is normally distributed with a mean of 0.40% (0.004 on the graph) and a standard deviation of 0.60%. In contrast, the other distribution shows the same portfolio but now with 50% of the risk hedged so that the resulting mean is 0.025% and its standard deviation is 0.300%. Note that the hedged portfolio considers both the explicit and indirect costs of hedging and so its return is much lower than the unhedged portfolio (0.025% vs. +0.40%), but the reduction in volatility is also quite large (0.30% vs. 0.60%).

So, it is the bank manager's choice as to which distribution they prefer (i.e., the high risk-high return of the unhedged portfolio or the low risk-low return of the hedged portfolio). To some extent, the choice depends on management's tolerance for risk, but it should also (primarily) consider what shareholders prefer. We show in this section how the IVM manages this trade-off between risk and return.

To estimate the impact of hedging on an investment portfolio as shown in Figure 5.4, we need to make some assumptions about the distribution of daily returns and its dispersion around the mean, or expected, return for these investments. For clarity and simplicity, we can assume the portfolio's returns are normally distributed and that the hedging instrument can perfectly hedge the bank's market risk. In effect, we can think of this hedging instrument (e.g., a swap or futures contract) as converting the portion of the portfolio that is hedged, h, into a *cash position with no return variability* and no correlation with the other assets in the portfolio.

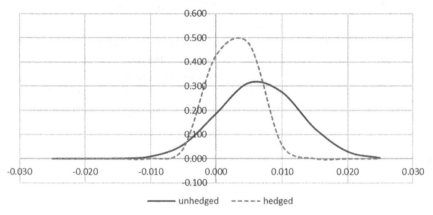

Figure 5.4. Return Distributions for an Unhedged and Hedged Portfolio.

Admittedly, this is a strong assumption but one that is feasible if we were to sell off a percentage of the portfolio equal to h and put the proceeds into a cash account earning no interest. Economically, a perfect hedge of h-percentage of the portfolio is equivalent to converting that portion of the bank's investments into an interest-free cash account.[14] This approach allows us to simplify the calculation of the impact of hedging on an investment portfolio's market risk, as measured by the investment's standard deviation and VaR, as described in the following.

5.10 The Impact of Hedging Market Risk on a Financial Institution's Equity

In this section, we use the definition of portfolio variance (σ_p^2), the RiskMetrics Variance–Covariance approach, and the IVM method from Chapter 3 to estimate the impact of hedging on the portfolio's risk and the

---

[14] Note that if we cannot find a perfect hedge, then there will be what is called "basis risk." In this case, the imperfect hedge will mean that not all the risk for the percentage of the investment hedged, h, will be eliminated and thus the risk of this hedged portion of the portfolio possesses a positive standard deviation and some "residual" correlation with the unhedged portion of the portfolio.

market value of the bank's equity.[15] The variance for a portfolio that holds *two* assets can be defined in the following equation:

Variance of a Portfolio with 2 Assets:

$$\sigma_P^2 = \left(w_1^2 \cdot \sigma_1^2\right) + \left(w_2^2 \cdot \sigma_2^2\right) + \left(2 \cdot \rho_{1,2} \cdot w_1 \cdot w_2 \cdot \sigma_1 \cdot \sigma_2\right) \quad (5.8)$$

where

w_1, w_2 = the percentage of the total portfolio invested in assets 1 and 2, respectively,

σ_1^2, σ_2^2 = **the variances of the daily returns for assets 1 and 2, respectively, and**

$\rho_{1,2}$ = **the correlation between the daily returns of assets 1 and 2.**

Equation (5.8) shows us that the portfolio's variance depends not only on the volatility of each asset (σ_1^2, σ_2^2) but also on the correlation between the two assets ($\rho_{1,2}$).

Based on the concepts from the previous section and Chambers et al.'s (2023) discussion of the properties of the standard deviation within a portfolio, we can think of the bank's investment portfolio as a combination of two distinct "assets" with one being the unhedged portion of the portfolio $(1 - h)$ that is comprised of bonds, currencies, etc. and the other asset being the hedged portion (denoted by the **hedge ratio, *h*)** that behaves as a "perfect hedge" and, in effect, acts like a ***zero-risk*** **cash account**.[16] Taking this concept and applying it to Equation (5.8) yields the following variance relationship for a hedged investment portfolio:

---

[15] Note that the portfolio variance is a statistical term that equals the square of the portfolio's standard deviation (i.e., $\sigma_P^2 = \sigma_P \cdot \sigma_P$).

[16] We can think of this as putting some money in a checking account with zero interest and no credit risk. In this case, there is no variance in the value of the cash account and thus it is conceptually the same as using a *"perfect" hedging instrument* which moves exactly in tandem with the market value of bank's investment portfolio. As we show later in this section, the standard deviation of a portfolio that hedges a portion, *h*, of the market risk via some type of zero-risk vehicle is equal to *Hedged* $\sigma_p = (1 - h) \cdot \sigma_{p,\text{unhedged}} + (h \cdot 0) = (1 - h) \cdot \sigma_{p,\text{unhedged}}$.

$$\sigma_P^2 = \left[(1-h)^2 \cdot \sigma_{UH}^2\right] + \left[h^2 \cdot \sigma_H^2\right] + \left[2 \cdot \rho_{UH,H} \cdot (1-h) \cdot h \cdot \sigma_{UH} \cdot \sigma_H\right] \quad (5.9)$$

where

$(1 - h)$, h = the percentage of the total portfolio invested in the unhedged (*UH*) and hedged (*H*) portfolios, respectively,

σ_{UH}^2, σ_H^2 = the variances of the daily returns for the unhedged and hedged portfolios, respectively, and

$\rho_{UH,H}$ = the correlation between the daily returns of the unhedged and hedged portfolios.

The first term in brackets on the right side of Equation (5.9) shows the portion of the portfolio's variance that is attributable to the *unhedged* component of the bank's investments. The remaining two terms in brackets on the right side of Equation (5.9) represent the volatility associated with the *hedged* portfolio and its correlation with the unhedged component. Now, recall that we assume that there is no variance associated with the hedged portion because it uses an instrument that perfectly hedges the market risk of the bank's investments. In this case, one can view h as the "weight" of the total portfolio that is invested in a zero-risk cash account and $(1 - h)$ as the weight that is invested in assets that are exposed to market risk. A perfect hedge also implies that both the hedged portfolio's variance and its correlation with the unhedged component is *zero*. Thus, the portfolio variance of (5.9) simplifies to the following equation[17]:

---

[17] Recall from an earlier footnote that "basis risk" exists when the hedging instrument is *imperfect*. Technically, we must use Equation (5.9) and *cannot* use the simplified version shown in (5.10) in this case. As Hull (2010), Saunders *et al.* (2024), and many others have noted, one can estimate a "minimum variance" hedge ratio by regressing the unhedged portfolio's returns on the relevant hedging instrument's returns. However, a minimum variance hedge ratio is rarely value-maximizing for a firm. Thus, we must acknowledge that, in the presence of basis risk, our model in Equation (5.10), as well as a minimum variance hedge ratio approach, will provide only an approximation of the "true" optimal hedge ratio. Thus, when basis risk is relatively small, our model should work well in terms of maximizing the bank's market value. However, like all types of hedging models, our model's hedge ratio will be less reliable when there is a large degree of basis risk.

Hedged $\sigma_p^2 = \left[(1-h)^2 \cdot \sigma_{UH}^2\right]$ (5.10)

Equation (5.10) is therefore a very useful way to directly quantify the impact of the bank's hedging choice (h) on the investment portfolio because σP² will vary as the $(1 - h)^2$ term changes. This occurs because the unhedged portfolio volatility (σ_{UH}^2) is, by construction, *independent* of the bank's hedge ratio, h. Based on the above equation, we can also easily find the standard deviation of the hedged portfolio (σ_p) by taking the square root of (5.10) because the hedged portfolio is defined by the following formula:

$$\sigma_p = \sigma_H = \sqrt{\sigma_p^2} = \sqrt{(1-h)^2 \cdot \sigma_{UH}^2} = (1-h) \cdot \sigma_{UH}.$$

We then use this standard deviation relationship to help construct the probability distributions for hedged and unhedged portfolios such as the ones shown earlier in Figure 5.4.

Now that we have a convenient way to quantify the impact of hedging on a portfolio's risk, we can then use the RiskMetrics method to translate these hedging decisions into changes in the bank's market value. To do this, we can first estimate the VaR for the portfolio using Equations (5.2) and (5.10):

$$\text{VaR}_P = 2.33 \cdot \text{Hedged}\,\sigma_P \cdot \$\text{Invested} = 2.33 \cdot \left[(1-h) \cdot \sigma_{UH}\right] \cdot \$\text{Invested}$$
(5.11)

When there is no hedging, $h = 0$ and (5.11) simplifies to our original Equation (5.2) from the beginning of this chapter. However, the portfolio's VaR will be *less* than this amount whenever h is *greater* than zero. In fact, when $h = 1$, Equation (5.11) indicates that VaR will be *zero* because hedging 100% with a *perfect* hedge will, by our definition, eliminate all market risk from the portfolio. However, there are clearly costs associated with placing a hedge in terms of **explicit, direct hedging costs**, such as those associated with bid-ask spreads, commissions, computer equipment, data services, and risk management personnel expenses. In addition, **implicit, indirect hedging costs** also can play an important role such as time spent by senior management supervising the risk managers and the opportunity cost of using the direct hedging costs for other potentially more valuable purposes within the bank.

What is needed is a way to balance the total costs and total benefits of hedging a bank's market risk. Fortunately, we have seen in Chapter 4 an analytical framework that can help us conduct this type of cost–benefit analysis. In that chapter, the focus was interest rate risk, but we can apply the same logic here in Chapter 5 for market risk, as discussed in the following.

We approach this problem by identifying the total benefits and total costs of hedging the bank's market risk. In this way, we can see the change in the bank's market value of equity due to the hedging decision by comparing the value of the bank with hedging ($V_{E,\text{Hedged}}$) versus its value without hedging ($V_{E,\text{Unhedged}}$) as follows:

$\Delta V_E = V_{E,\text{Hedged}} - V_{E,\text{Unhedged}} =$ Total Benefit of Hedge − Total Cost of Hedge

$\Delta V_E =$ \$Reduction in Portfolio VaR − (fixed hedging cost + variable hedging cost)

$$\Delta V_E = [2.33 \cdot (\sigma_{UH} - \text{Hedged } \sigma_p) \cdot \text{Invested Assets}] - [C + ((v \cdot h) \cdot (h \cdot \text{Invested Assets}))]$$

$$= [2.33 \cdot (\sigma_{UH} - \sigma_H) \cdot \text{Invested Assets}] - [C + ((v \cdot h^2) \cdot \text{Invested Assets})]$$

$$= [2.33 \cdot (h \cdot \sigma_{UH}) \cdot \text{Invested Assets}] - [(c + (v \cdot h^2)) \cdot \text{Invested Assets}]$$

(5.12)

where

$\Delta V_E =$ change in market value due to hedging some portion of the Invested Assets $= V_{E,\text{Hedged}} - V_{E,\text{Unhedged}}$,

$h =$ hedge ratio = Dollar Amount Hedged/Invested Assets = \$Hedged/Invested Assets,

$C =$ fixed cost of hedging (paid upfront, in dollars; and can also be expressed as a percentage of the bank's Invested Assets, where $C = c \cdot$ Invested Assets),

$v =$ variable cost of hedging as a percentage of \$Hedged, where \$Hedged $= h \cdot$ Invested Assets,

$\sigma_{UH} =$ unhedged portfolio's standard deviation,

Hedged $\sigma_p = \sigma_H = (1 - h) \cdot \sigma_{UH} =$ hedged portfolio's standard deviation,

Critical value = 2.33 (based on the normal distribution assumption), and

$Reduction in Portfolio VaR = $value of extreme volatility that is reduced by hedging = 2.33 · $(\sigma'_{UH} - \sigma'_H)$ · Invested Assets, which simplifies to: 2.33 · $(h \cdot \sigma'_{UH})$ · Invested Assets.

The first term in square brackets of Equation (5.12) identifies the incremental benefits of hedging all or a portion (h) of the bank's market risk while the second term in square brackets shows the costs of this hedge when a worst-case 1% tail event (2.33 · σ'_p) occurs. We define these hedging benefits as the dollar amount of losses *avoided* due to hedging a portion of the potential price shock to the portfolio from market risk. Using the notation from above, we show that this "Total Benefit of Hedge" equals 2.33 · $(h \cdot \sigma'_{UH})$ · Invested Assets. So, as the hedge ratio (h) rises, this benefit also increases. However, the second term in (5.12) illustrates the exponentially rising "Total Cost of Hedge" due to its variable cost component: $((v \cdot h^2)$ · Invested Assets. Thus, there is a classic trade-off between the costs and benefits of hedging.

Based on the above discussion of Portfolio VaR and Equation (5.12), we can see how this market risk management decision can impact the bank's equity value using the principles of the IVM by varying the hedge ratio, h, between 0 (no hedging) and 1.0 (hedging the entire risk exposure).

As we did in Chapter 4, we make some simplifying assumptions with Equation (5.12) to estimate the change in the bank's market value because we are:

1. The hedge ratio (h) does not impact other aspects of the bank's cash flows other than those shown in (5.12) and so the *net benefit of the hedge* (i.e., (Hedge Benefit – Hedge Cost)) is the only factor affecting the bank's market value.
2. The Hedge Cost has a fixed cost component (C) as well as a variable cost component that is a function of both an assumed variable cost parameter, v, and the hedge ratio itself (h). This interaction factor, $(v \cdot h)$, when multiplied by the portion of market risk that is hedged (h · Invested Assets), allows for a nonlinear, exponential impact of the hedge ratio on the cost of hedging via the term, $(v \cdot h^2)$ · Invested Assets. This is a scaling factor that reflects the rising cost of hedging

when the bank decides to hedge a greater portion of its risk exposure.[18]

3. The Expected Dividend Yield ($DY_{t+1} = R_E - g$) remains constant even though the cash flows in Eq. (5.12) are changing. As originally noted in Chapter 4, this is a simplifying assumption and is technically not true as the riskiness of the bank can change when the hedge ratio is adjusted. However, we are assuming that bank investors desire a constant expected dividend yield so that the changes in R_E and g move in tandem and thus offset each other and result in no net change in ($R_E - g$). So, in this case, the hedging choice's effect on ($R_E - g$) can be ignored.[19]

We can use the above variant of the IVM described in Equation (5.12) with a numerical example for our hypothetical bank, ABC, based on its $700 million investment portfolio and the expected return (0.01%) and standard deviation (0.25%) assumptions from Figure 5.4.

As shown earlier in this chapter, the RiskMetrics method predicts that there is a 1% chance of losing 0.5825% or more during one trading day. Therefore, ABC is vulnerable to *increases* in volatility that might emanate from various markets in which it invests (i.e., bonds, stocks, currencies, and commodities). ABC's bank managers must decide whether this

---

[18] The fixed cost (*C*) is independent of how much the bank chooses to hedge and can be viewed as the time and money spent by bank managers to decide how they want to manage their market risk (e.g., costs for data terminals, hiring risk management professionals, and compliance staff). As Hull (2010) has noted, the cost of hedging also typically increases at a growing rate as the hedge ratio is increased. This is primarily due to liquidity constraints and fluctuations in volatility within the derivatives markets that the bank relies upon to initiate and liquidate a hedging position. So, we have included here the term, ($v \cdot h^2$), to show just one way we can model this nonlinear, exponential effect of hedging costs. Clearly, other forms of this hedging cost can lead to different conclusions about the optimal hedge ratio. Thus, sensitivity and scenario analyses can be used to develop a more comprehensive understanding of this market-related risk-return trade-off.

[19] This assumption can be a *conservative* estimate of the estimated change in market value (i.e., *lower* than what might occur) because hedging could, in theory, lower the bank's cost of equity (R_E) which would, in turn, raise the bank's valuation. So, assuming no change in $R_E - g$ might be a reasonably safe approach in this context. Also, as noted earlier in Chapter 3, when the growth rate, g, is capped at some fixed rate such as 6%, then ($R_E - g$) can vary as the hedge ratio is changed.

Table 5.8. Numerical Example of Hedging Market Risk using VaR.

Invested Assets ($ million)	700
Expected Daily Average Return	0.01%
Unhedged Daily Standard Deviation	0.25%
Hedge Fixed Cost, as % of Portfolio (c)	0.0%
Hedge Variable Cost, as % of Portfolio (v)	0.5%
Dividend Payout	0.40
Tax Rate	0.20
Dividend Yield ($R_E - g$)	0.0357
Shares Outstanding (million)	10.00

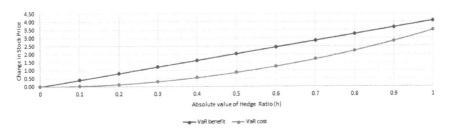

Figure 5.5. The Costs and Benefits of Hedging a Bank's Market Risk.

market risk exposure on its $700 million investment portfolio has a material effect and then choose the "optimal hedge ratio" that maximizes the bank's stock price. For simplicity, we do not consider a specific financial derivative instrument to hedge this risk as we can assume any one of the four major types of derivatives could be used to implement this hedge ratio (e.g., *shorting* this market exposure via either forwards, futures, options, or swaps). We can find the answer to this important risk management decision by varying the absolute value of the hedge ratio from 0.0 (i.e., no hedging at all) to 1.0 (fully hedging 100% of the investment portfolio).

To build some intuition about what is driving the impact of hedging on ABC's market value of equity, we first show in Figure 5.5 the results of a "what-if" simulation that quantifies the Total Costs and Benefits of hedging the bank's market risk. The graph shows that the benefits of

204 *Managing Financial Institutions: An Integrated Valuation Approach*

hedging rise linearly based on the first component described earlier in square brackets for Equation (5.12) while the hedging-related costs are rising exponentially. This dynamic leads to an optimal hedge ratio, h^*, that lies somewhere between 0.0 and 1.0 (or, 0% to 100% of the bank's investment portfolio).

Based on the above cost–benefit analysis, we can use the IVM relationship shown in Equation (5.12) to identify the level of h that maximizes the bank's market value of equity. Figure 5.6 displays the results of this type of what-if simulation on the expected *change* in ABC's stock price.

As we can see from Figure 5.6, ABC's stock price is boosted to around $0.12 per share if it chooses an optimal hedge ratio, h^*, of around 0.6 (or 60% of the portfolio). In this case, ABC can maximize its market value by *shorting* about 60% of its long exposure to bonds, stocks, etc. More precisely, we can identify a specific hedge ratio of 0.5825 that enables the marginal benefit of hedging to exactly equal the marginal cost of this risk management strategy and thus maximizes the bank's stock price.[20,21]

---

[20] Technically, this optimal ratio is obtained by taking the mathematical derivative of Equation (5.12) with respect to the hedge ratio, h, and setting this derivative equal to zero. We can then solve algebraically for the optimal hedge ratio, h^*, using the data presented in Table 5.8. Based on these data and the model presented in Equation (5.12), the **optimal hedge ratio,** h^***, is** $h^* = -1 \cdot (2.33 \cdot \sigma_{UH}) / (2 \cdot v)) = -(2.33 \cdot .0025) / (2 \cdot 0.005)) = -(0.005825 / 0.01000) = -0.5825 = -58.25\%$. Thus, $h = -0.5825$ means the bank should *short* around 58% of its investment portfolio to yield the maximum increase in the bank's stock price, which is confirmed by the graph displayed in Figure 5.6 (which, for convenience, shows the hedge ratio as an absolute value). Also, note that the optimal hedge ratio uses a -1 as a multiplier because it is assumed that the bank normally owns (or has "gone long") the securities in its portfolio. In the very unusual situation where the bank is "net short" its total investment portfolio, then the optimal hedge ratio should use a $+1$ multiplier to indicate that the bank should buy (or "go long") with some derivatives to offset the portfolio's short position.

[21] Additional "other costs" beyond the hedging-specific variable costs, v, such as collateral/margin requirements, administrative expenses, and opportunity costs can also be included in the denominator of the optimal hedge ratio (expressed as a percentage of Invested Assets) as follows: $h^* = -1 \cdot (2.33 \cdot \sigma_{UH}) / (2 \cdot (v + \textbf{other costs}))$. Further, some other factors can affect the numerator of this optimal hedge ratio formula. One common example would be a "capital charge" that the bank might apply to its VaR exposure to account for any additional capital that the bank needs to support this level of market risk (expressed as a percentage of the VaR exposure). In this case, the optimal hedge formula can be expanded further as $h^* = -1 \cdot (2.33 \cdot \sigma_{UH} \cdot \textbf{capital charge}) / (2 \cdot (v + \textbf{other costs}))$.

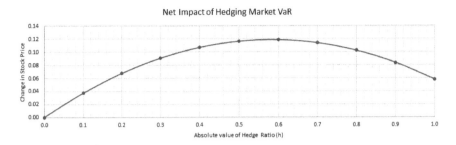

Figure 5.6. The Net Effect of Hedging Market Risk on the Bank's Equity.

Any hedge ratio above or below this value results in a lower change in ABC's stock price and therefore 0.5825 is considered optimal because it increases market value the most. This impact on stock price is relatively small because the overall daily return volatility of the investment portfolio is only 25.0 bps. In addition, we are focusing solely on a 1-day tail event.

However, this market risk exposure would be more than three times greater if we were to examine a 10-day tail event (because $\sqrt{10} = 3.162$). This $0.12 change based on 1-day VaR is also relatively small in terms of a percentage change (+0.6%) when we compare it to the base stock price of $20.17 we had calculated back in Chapter 3. However, if we use a 10-day horizon, the impact on market value would be a bit larger (at around $0.38 per share, or +1.9%). Overall, our cost–benefit analysis suggests that hedging this relatively low-volatility investment portfolio does not provide a significant boost to ABC's stock price and thus the bank managers might choose not to hedge this market risk.

As we had first introduced in Chapter 4 related to Interest Rate Risk, another useful metric that can be derived from our optimal hedge ratio is the **optimal**, or "Target VaR*" that ABC should focus on to maximize the bank's stock value. This target VaR* can be found by using the absolute value of the optimal hedge ratio, $|h^*|$, in the following relationship:

$$\text{VaR}^* = (1 - |h^*|) \cdot \text{unhedged VaR} \tag{5.13}$$

Assuming ABC's managers wish to hedge the bank's market risk, the above equation suggests that ABC's target VaR* would be $1.702 million based on $h^* = -0.5825$ and an unhedged VaR of $4.078 million (i.e., $(1 - |-0.5825|) \cdot (\$4.078 \text{ million}) = \$1.702 \text{ million}$). This figure is helpful to ABC's risk managers because they can use it as a benchmark to compare with the bank's actual VaR over the course of the year.

We should also remind ourselves of the discussion of the IVM's relevance in Chapter 3 in identifying how market value could be impacted *directionally* by changes in the bank's risk-taking activities. Therefore, given all the assumptions we need to make to come up with a graph like Figure 5.6, we should not take the exact values plotted there too literally. A better way to interpret Figure 5.6 is that ABC's stock price is likely to benefit the most from hedging its interest rate risk exposure within the range of 0.5–0.7. (i.e., 50–70% of the portfolio's assets). It is within this range that we see the biggest gain in ABC's stock price. However, this does not mean we should expect the price to move up by exactly this amount. Rather, the analysis can be more reliably viewed as telling ABC's management that hedging *less than* 0.5 or *more than* 0.7 is probably *not* value-maximizing. We should also remember that our results will be affected by our assumptions about hedging-related costs and, as we have noted in previous chapters, the analyst might want to perform some sensitivity analysis on these key inputs to the model.

Overall, there appears to be a positive, albeit small, net change in ABC's stock price, but it seems the exponentially rising hedging costs are limiting the benefits of hedging the bank's investment portfolio. Although we have set the fixed hedging costs to zero in the above example, keep in mind that the market risk management program's fixed costs will also affect the bank's final hedging decision. As noted in Chapter 4 related to managing interest rate risk, we must first verify that the maximum potential benefits outweigh any fixed costs. Otherwise, the optimal decision is to set the hedge ratio to *zero* to avoid these fixed costs and preserve the bank's market value. This is very useful information because it suggests that other aspects of the bank's operations (e.g., credit and interest rate risks) might be more likely to increase ABC's stock price. The bank's managers can then use this analysis to help focus on those risks and possibly consider market risk management only after first addressing the bank's credit and interest rate risks. This reminds us of the "ART" of risk management and that, in some cases, the "A" (for *accept* the risk and *not* manage it) is the optimal decision.

5.11 Managerial Implications

The primary market risk problem Nina and Sam must consider is as follows: **how much market risk is acceptable for ABC based on the current risk and return of its investment portfolio?** As discussed in prior chapters, this answer once again depends on the bank's "risk appetite," which is based on senior management's and investors' risk tolerance. Sam and Nina must also think about the fixed and variable costs of hedging this market risk relative to the associated benefits. **When comparing these hedging costs and benefits, they are confronted with the old saying:** "is the juice worth the squeeze"? That is, are the benefits large enough to justify the extra time, money, and effort required to set up a market risk management program? These hedging costs can be quite significant in terms of additional personnel (with specialized skills), financial/accounting software, data services, etc. Also, they must consider that there is an opportunity cost of using these funds for risk management rather than for other business purposes. Nina and Sam **think the best plan might be to follow a** "Do Nothing" **strategy because the benefits are relatively small when compared to the anticipated hedging costs, as shown in Figure 5.6.** In terms of the "ART" of risk management, their approach is to Accept this market risk rather than try to transfer this risk to other parties. **Do you agree with Nina and Sam's recommendation? If not, then how would you handle it differently and what are your reasons for doing so?**

5.12 Summary

This chapter showed the importance of market risk management and how metrics like Value at Risk (VaR) and Expected Shortfall (ES) can be used to quantify this risk. In addition, three different methods of estimating VaR were presented because there is no perfect way to estimate market risk (e.g., via the RiskMetrics Variance–Covariance, Historic, and Monte Carlo simulation methods). The pros and cons of each method were also discussed to help understand which technique might be best for your specific bank's needs. Consideration was also given to how VaR can be estimated differently for stocks, bonds, currencies, and commodities. Further, the effects of diversification on the VaR of a portfolio of various investments were shown to present a more complete picture of the financial institution's true exposure to multiple sources of market risk. This diversification benefit (or covariance adjustment) can be quite large when the assets held in the bank's investment portfolio are not highly correlated with each other. Lastly, we developed an explicit model of the costs and benefits of hedging and used a numerical example to illustrate how a bank can use VaR to manage its market risk to maximize its stock price.

Chapter-End Questions

Answers to odd-numbered questions can be found at the end of this book.

1. **True or False:** The Expected Shortfall (ES) estimate is typically smaller than the RiskMetrics Value-at-Risk (VaR) estimate for a portfolio of securities.
2. **True or False:** The total portfolio's daily VaR is greater than the simple sum of the VaRs of the various sub-components.
3. **Multiple Choice:** What risks can adversely affect the market value of a bank's assets?

    (A) Changes in interest rates
    (B) Changes in exchange rates
    (C) Changes in commodity prices
    (D) All the above

4. **Multiple Choice:** Which VaR method has the most potential to anticipate large changes in future levels of market risk?

    (A) RiskMetrics method (Variance–Covariance technique)
    (B) Historic Simulation method
    (C) Monte Carlo Simulation method
    (D) None of the above

5. **Multiple Choice:** Using the RiskMetrics approach, calculate the 1% daily VaR for a portfolio with a daily standard deviation of returns of 0.004 and invested assets of $800 million.

    (A) $7.464 million
    (B) $32.000 million
    (C) $8.000 million
    (D) $7.456 million

6. **Short Answer:** How does the Historic Simulation method overcome some of the drawbacks of the RiskMetrics method?
7. **Short Answer:** What is the diversification benefit of a portfolio if its VaR = $5.175 million and the sum of the components' VaR = $6.018 million? Also, what is the percentage reduction in VaR due to the diversification benefit?
8. **Short Answer:** If the FIs hedge ratio, h, is 0.50, the standard deviation of the unhedged portfolio, σ_{UH}, is 0.30, the fixed cost

of hedging, C, is $50,000, the variable cost of hedging, v, is 0.02, and the amount invested is $1,000,000, then:

(A) What is the FIs *unhedged* VaR?
(B) What is the FIs "target" VaR?
(C) What is the change in market value of equity due to hedging using the model, as described by Equation (5.12)?

9. **Excel-based Question:** How much market risk exposure on its $700 million securities portfolio, as measured by its RiskMetrics' Value-at-Risk (VaR), should ABC hedge ($h*$) to maximize its stock price? Assume the bank's managers are concerned about an increase in the "Unhedged Portfolio's" **standard deviation** from the base scenario of 0.25–0.40%, as shown in the "Market Risk – Ch 5" tab of the **Integrated Valuation Model.xlsx** file. Try this by starting with the "base" scenario where the variable costs (v) are 0.5% of the hedged exposure and then changing the values in the blue cell related to the *Unhedged Portfolio std. dev. in %* from 0.25% to 0.40%.

(A) What is the optimal hedge ratio ($h*$) for the above volatility shock and how does it compare to the base scenario's $h*$?
(B) Related to your answer in part A, what is the expected percentage change in ABC's stock price if management implemented this optimal hedge ratio?
(C) What is the "target" VaR* based on Equation (5.12) and your answer to part A of this question?
(D) How do your answers to parts A–C change if the bank expects the variable costs of hedging to increase (due to increased market-wide volatility) to 2.0%? Briefly explain the results you observe from this sensitivity analysis.

10. **Comprehensive Question:** Please recommend and justify a recommended course of action related to managing the bank's market risk for our protagonists in this chapter: Sam and Nina. **What is the primary market risk problem that Nina and Sam must address for ABC Bank?** Also, how does this problem relate to the bank's "risk appetite" as well as the costs of hedging some of the portfolio's market risk? Are there any other factors that are likely to influence the decision?

References

Chambers, D.R., Anson, M.J.P., Black, K.H. and Kazemi, H.B. (2023). *CAIA Curriculum Level I Volume I*, J. Wiley & Sons, Hoboken, NJ.

Citigroup. (2021). *Annual Report and 10-K*, SEC filing.

Haan, L. and Ferreira, A. (2006). *Extreme Value Theory: An Introduction*, Springer, New York.

Hull, J.C. (2010). *Risk Management and Financial Institutions*, Prentice-Hall, Boston.

Jorion, P. (2007). *Value at Risk*, McGraw-Hill, New York.

Saunders, A., Cornett, M.M. and Erhemjamts, O. (2024). *Financial Institutions Management: A Risk Management Approach*, McGraw-Hill, New York.

Chapter 6

Credit Risk

6.1 Introduction

All three of a financial institution's main economic functions (Qualitative Asset Transformation, Brokerage, and Delegated Monitoring) can create **credit risk**, although qualitative asset transformation (QAT) is usually the main driver of this risk. Recall from Chapter 1 that QAT refers to the process of obtaining financing via one type of financial instrument (e.g., a short-term bank deposit) and then "transforming" it by investing the proceeds in a different type of financial instrument (e.g., a long-term loan such as a mortgage).

Credit risk represents the possibility that the bank's borrowers do not fully repay the principal and interest they owe on their loans to the financial institution. This can occur for one of many reasons including credit downgrades, bankruptcy, default, mergers/corporate restructuring, and government actions such as changes in regulation or increased enforcement of current regulations. In fact, the word "credit" comes from the Latin word *credere,* which means **to believe or to trust**. Thus, when a bank extends credit to a customer, it is explicitly trusting that the borrower will be able to fully repay the loan.

A bank's credit risk is also affected by the **mix** of investments and loans it grants to its customers. For example, a bank or thrift institution that focuses almost exclusively on making long-term fixed rate residential mortgages to financially strong borrowers can have a much lower credit risk exposure than another bank that makes unsecured loans to small and

Table 6.1. Typical Bank Loans and Investments.

Consumer-Focused	Business-Focused	Fixed Income Securities
Credit Cards	Lines of Credit	U.S. Treasury Bills, Notes, Bonds
Automobile Loans	Term Loans	Mortgage-backed Securities
Unsecured Personal Loans	Asset-backed Loans	Municipal Bonds
Residential Mortgages	Loan Commitments	Foreign Government Bonds
Home Equity Lines of Credit	Letters of Credit	Corporate Bonds

medium-sized business entities (also referred to as "SMEs").[1] In addition, when economic conditions are weak and loan demand is lackluster, a bank might choose to invest a large percentage of its assets in safer, more liquid mortgage-backed securities and corporate bonds that are publicly traded. These fixed income securities still have credit risk, but it can be less than the riskiness of a typical bank loan portfolio. The most common types of loans and securities that FIs hold are listed in Table 6.1.

The bank's choices related to their specific mix of loans and investments will depend on management's risk appetite as well as the preferences and needs of the people and firms that are within the bank's operating region. Regulators can also play a role by establishing guidelines for how much of a bank's assets can be invested in different categories. For example, regulators and/or senior management itself might impose **concentration limits** so that, for example, no more than 10% of its assets can be invested in foreign government bonds or lent to a single borrower. These limits ensure that the bank's assets are well diversified and not highly concentrated within a specific asset type (or within an industry sector or individual borrower). This is just one of many ways that a bank can manage its credit risk and we discuss these risk management issues later in this chapter.

Before delving into ways to quantify and manage credit risk, it is helpful to begin with an understanding of the *qualitative* aspects of credit

---

[1]The industry typically uses the term "thrift" institution to refer to an FI that makes most of its loans in the form of residential mortgages and finances them primarily with traditional deposits. To receive this designation, the firm must commit to making the vast majority of its loans in the residential mortgage market.

risk. This qualitative approach is an essential component of effective credit decision-making and should not be overlooked by focusing exclusively on quantitative measures. These qualitative components can be summarized by the "Five Cs of Credit Analysis" shown in the following. Note that some banks can gain a competitive advantage by being better at evaluating these qualitative aspects of lending, commonly referred to as "soft information" (e.g., as opposed to "hard information" such as financial statements and other quantitative data).

6.2 Five Cs of Credit Analysis

A sound credit analysis should incorporate the 5 Cs to ensure that the banker is making loan decisions that are likely to result in full repayment of both interest and principal.

Capacity: This refers to the capacity to repay the loan and is normally the most important aspect of the 5 Cs. It represents the borrower's ability to repay the bank from internal sources such as their cash flow and cash (or "near-cash") balances. Bankers are typically taught to make sure there are at least two "ways out" of a loan and so cash flow and cash balances are normally the primary ways to receive repayment.

Capital: This refers to how much equity is invested in the business (or, for an individual, how much net worth they possess). Lenders want to know if the borrower has "skin in the game" in case they run into financial difficulties that diminish the firm's or person's capacity to repay. By having more capital on hand, the borrower is also less likely to engage in moral hazard activities, such as taking on very risky ventures/activities. Higher capital levels reduce these excessive risk-taking incentives because the second way out of a loan could be to force the borrower into bankruptcy which, in turn, can cause the borrower to lose all, or most, of their equity capital.

Collateral: This represents additional security to provide the lender with extra protection if capacity and capital are insufficient to cover full repayment. Collateral means that the borrower pledges some asset (such as a fixed income instrument or a tangible asset such as a house/building) that can be taken by the bank if principal and interest are not fully repaid.

Given this extra protection, lenders will typically charge a lower loan rate although it limits the borrower's flexibility in terms of managing their assets.[2]

Conditions: This includes both (1) the loan-specific conditions (e.g., the purpose of the loan and any restrictions/covenants related to the loan) and (2) the local economic and/or industry-specific conditions in which the borrower operates. For example, weak economic conditions and/or lax loan covenants can result in greater credit risk for the bank.

Character: This is the most qualitative aspect of the 5 Cs and represents the lender's overall assessment of the borrower's trustworthiness and willingness to repay the loan. However, it can also be the most important deciding factor in the bank's credit decision because, quite simply, the lender should not make loans to borrowers who they do not trust (even when the first four Cs suggest the borrower is very creditworthy). Here are a couple of quotes from the famous financier, John Pierpont Morgan (and the namesake of the financial firm, J.P. Morgan Chase & Co.), that summarize nicely the importance of character in the lending business:

> The first thing (in credit) is character ... before money or anything else. Money cannot buy it.
>
> A man I do not trust could not get money from me on all the bonds in Christendom. I think that is the fundamental basis of business.

6.3 The Pricing of Risky Loans

Bankers are expected to make loans at an interest rate that is fair to the borrower (in terms of ability to repay) *and* provides the FI with an adequate return for its investors. Thus, we must move beyond the concept of the 5 Cs to quantify what is the right loan rate (rL) that delivers that "sweet spot" which balances risk and return for both the bank and the borrower.

---

[2]One example of a study that examines the economic relationship between collateral and interest rates is Brick and Palia (2007). The authors find a positive, jointly determined lending relationship which implies that collateral is required for more risky borrowers.

Finding the right "price" for a loan is essential because the bank's market value can decline quickly when the FI significantly underestimates the **likelihood** of a borrower's default and/or the **severity** of the credit loss when the client cannot repay its debts. Thus, banks must be very careful when estimating **expected credit losses** by making accurate forecasts of a client's **probability of default** (i.e., the loan's **frequency** of default) and the amount of principal and interest lost due to the default (i.e., the **severity** of credit losses). Before digging into the concept of loan pricing, it can be helpful to first consider the problem that insurance companies face when pricing, say, an automobile insurance policy. In this context, we refer to the firm's exposure to the property/casualty risk of an insured driver getting into an accident that "totals" the car, as its **expected loss** on the insurance policy. These insurance firms usually estimate this expected loss by multiplying the **frequency** of the loss by its **severity**.

For example, if the likelihood of a good driver totaling their car within the next year is 1% and they have a $50,000 car insurance policy, then the insurance company's expected loss (or "payout") on the policy equals the frequency of the loss times its severity or **Expected Loss = Frequency · Severity** = 0.01 * $50,000 = $500. So, a car insurer must charge the driver at least $500 per year for insurance. However, the insurer also has operating costs and is expected to earn a profit for its equity investors/owners. Let us assume the operating costs related to processing claims, salaries, rent, etc. are $1,500 per year for this policy. In addition, the firm would like to generate a $300 annual profit from this policy. In this case, the total annual premium should be $2,300 because it accounts for the expected loss *plus* the **expected** "net return" (i.e., the $E(R_N)$ in our following notation) that covers operating costs and yields an appropriate profit. Now we can see why car insurance can be so expensive! We can summarize this with the following basic equation for pricing insurance premiums:

$$\begin{aligned}
\text{Expected Insurance Premium} &= \text{Expected Loss} + \text{Expected Net Return} \\
&= (\text{Frequency} \cdot \text{Severity}) + E(R_N) \\
&= (0.01 \cdot \$50{,}000) + \$1{,}500 + \$300 = \$500 \\
&\quad + \$1{,}500 + \$300 = \$2{,}300 \qquad (6.1)
\end{aligned}$$

The above example explains why an accurate estimate of expected losses is critical for the success of a car insurer. If, for example, the firm is wrong and the true likelihood of an accident by this driver is 10%, then the actual potential loss is $5,000 (i.e., 0.10 · $50,000 = $5,000). However, the firm only charged the driver $2,300 for this insurance and thus the expected payoff of this policy to the insurer is a *loss* of $2,700 (i.e., $2,300 premium collected minus the $5,000 expected loss = –$2,700 net loss on the policy). If the insurance company makes this mistake for several thousand drivers, it is likely to go bankrupt very quickly!

The above example demonstrates the need for all financial firms to accurately estimate and manage any expected losses and these losses should be "priced into" the quoted cost of the firm's products and services. We can see a direct analogy between the insurance pricing example and the pricing of a loan, by using the same "Frequency · Severity" logic of Equation (6.1). However, the jargon for a loan's expected loss is slightly different than for an insurance policy. For example, a bank's **expected credit loss** could be $4 million if a bank makes a $100 million loan to a large industrial firm and there is a 10% **Probability of Default** (commonly referred to as "PD" for short, rather than "frequency") and, when in default, the bank loses 40% of its principal (normally described as the "Loss Given Default" or "LGD" for short, rather than "severity"). In this example, the $4 million is obtained by first multiplying the PD by the loan's LGD (0.10 · 0.40 = 0.04) and then applying this **expected loss rate** of 4% to the $100 million loan principal (i.e., 0.04 · $100 million = $4 million). This discussion leads us to our first way to think about a bank's credit risk, as shown in the following:

$$\text{Expected Credit Loss Rate} = \text{Probability of Default} \cdot \text{Loss Given Default} = PD \cdot LGD \qquad (6.2)$$

where

PD = likelihood of *not* getting repaid and ranges between 0% and 100% (0.00 to 1.00 in decimal format) and

LGD = percentage of principal lost due to the default. Note that *LGD* can be also defined as (1 – RR) where RR = the "Recovery Rate," or the percentage of the loan that *is* repaid (and both are expressed from 0.00 to 1.00 in decimal format).

Given that banks are highly levered with little equity capital as a "cushion" against various economic shocks, any sudden shift in expected credit losses can cause the market value of the bank's equity to plummet and, in extreme cases, lead to insolvency. Thus, bank managers, investors, and regulators are all very interested in seeing how well the FI is managing its exposure to credit risk.

A typical commercial bank is faced with the important decision of how much of its assets to invest in various types of loans. In general, banks prefer to invest in their loan portfolio because it can generate higher returns than investing in relatively safe fixed income securities such as U.S. Treasury notes (UST) and mortgage-backed securities (MBS). Banks are willing to face the additional risk of making loans because higher lending rates can lead to greater profits and higher returns for shareholders. If, on the other hand, investors only want a riskless investment then they could invest in Treasuries themselves and avoid the added cost of paying bank managers to do this. Thus, both investors and bank managers want the FI to invest in risky loans rather than very low-risk securities.

From an economic perspective, the bank is acting as a qualitative asset transformer (QAT) when it manages this loan portfolio and therefore must balance the risk-return trade-off of selecting various types of loans to make (e.g., corporate or consumer loans, and secured or unsecured). Thus, a bank's QAT function is inherently risky and so the firm must price its primary product (i.e., loans) to guard against expected credit losses, as defined earlier in Equation (6.2). We can use the logic of the insurance example and the relationship in Equation (6.1) to help us find a simple way to set a loan rate (rL) to charge a customer as follows:

$$rL = E(R_N) + \text{PD} \cdot \text{LGD} \tag{6.3}$$

where

$E(R_N)$ is the sum of the dollar amount of the loan-related operating costs, costs of financing the loan, and the net profit of the loan (all expressed as a percentage of the loan's principal, L). This expected net return covers the bank's operating and financing costs, as well as provides an appropriate profit on the loan (expressed as a percentage of the loan's principal),

PD is the probability of default, and

LGD is the loss given default (also expressed as a percentage of the loan's principal, L).

In Equation (6.3), we can see that the "promised" loan rate (rL) is what the bank must charge to cover operating costs, financing costs, and an expected net profit, $E(R_N)$, that go above and beyond the compensation needed to protect against expected credit losses in case there is a default, (PD · LGD). Equation (6.3) shows how a well-managed bank can create a profitable loan portfolio by

1. controlling **operating costs** (e.g., by reducing the bank's **efficiency ratio**),[3]
2. lowering **financing costs** from depositors and other creditors (but not offering rates that are uncompetitively low),
3. accurately estimating **expected credit losses** based on good forecasts of PD and LGD, and
4. pricing in an **acceptable profit** (by embedding a target ROA that reflects the loan portfolio's overall risk which, for most banks, is around 1%).

Note that a loan rate based on (6.3) estimates what the borrower promises to pay and, if the PD and LGD are estimated correctly, this will indeed be the gross return the bank receives. But this is the best-case scenario for the bank. Otherwise, like in our insurance example, the bank must carefully estimate the frequency (PD) and severity (LGD) of credit losses to price the loan properly. If the bank makes a mistake in this area, we can see from the following numerical example that the firm can lose a great deal of money quickly. Like other financial assets, greater risk on a loan should mean that it yields a greater return.

6.3.1 *Numerical example of mispricing a loan*

Let's assume ABC's expected net return, $E(R_N)$, is 5% so that it covers the firm's operating costs and financing costs and delivers a sufficient profit. The likelihood of default by this borrower is 10% and the loss given default is assumed to be 20%. Using Equation (6.3), we can see that ABC should charge 7% for the loan:

$$rL = E(R_N) + PD \cdot LGD = 0.05 + (0.10 \cdot 0.20) = 0.05 + 0.02 = 0.07 = 7\%$$

---

[3] The Efficiency Ratio is used as a measure of how well a bank is managing its operating costs and is normally calculated by dividing Total Operating Expenses by the bank's Total Net Revenue (i.e., net interest revenue plus non-interest income). Thus, the lower this ratio, the bank is viewed as more efficient.

However, if ABC *underestimates* PD and/or LGD, then the bank will charge the borrower a rate that is *lower* than what it should be to fairly compensate for the extra credit risk. For example, what if the loan's PD = 0.20 and LGD = 0.40? If so, then ABC has a big credit risk problem because they *should have* charged 13% (i.e., 0.05 + (0.20 * 0.40) = 0.05 + 0.08 = 0.13) but, instead, only charged the borrower 7%. In this case, ABC is likely to *lose* 6% of the loan principal on average (7% − 13% = −6%). This is a large loss because most banks like ABC have a target ROA of 1% and usually hold only around 10% in equity capital. Thus, if these credit losses were repeated across all of ABC's investments, then losing 6% on each loan and bond would wipe out most of the bank's equity capital and could cause a "run" on the bank's deposits and ultimately lead to insolvency.

We can see from the above example that credit risk is an important component of a bank's overall risk and must be managed well to maximize the FIs market value of equity. Before moving further in this chapter, we also should make one refinement to the loan pricing model described by Equation (6.3) to account for the reality that a bank typically does not receive interest on the full amount of a loan when the borrower defaults. Technically, Equation (6.3) implies that interest is received on *all* principal even when the borrower defaults on its principal payments.

A more realistic assumption is that interest is received only on the portion of principal that is not expected to be lost during a default. That is, when in default, the bank can still receive interest on the assets that are recovered (i.e., the recovery rate = RR = (1 − LGD)). So, in default, the bank expects to receive interest based on $(1 - LGD) \cdot rL$. Using this more realistic assumption rather than assuming the bank receives the full *rL* when in default (i.e., as if LGD equals zero) leads to a modified version of Equation (6.3) as follows[4]:

---

[4] The model described by (6.4) here is obtained by solving algebraically for the loan rate, *rL*, using the following equation: $E(R_N) = [(1 - PD) \cdot (rL - 0)] + \{PD \cdot [((1 - LGD) \cdot rL) - LGD]\}$. This equation breaks out the expected interest payments when *not* in default (1 − PD) and those interest payments that are received *during* default (PD). Solving for *rL* in this formula results in the model shown by Equation (6.4). If you wish, try solving for *rL* to prove it to yourself! Also, keep in mind that other factors can affect the return on a loan, such as origination fees and compensating balances. For competitive reasons, such origination fees and balance requirements are not as frequently used in more recent times for many types of loans but, if used, can increase the loan's return beyond what we estimate here as *rL*. See Saunders *et al.* (2024) for more details on this aspect of loan pricing.

$$rL = \frac{E(R_N) + (\text{PD} \cdot \text{LGD})}{(1 - (\text{PD} \cdot \text{LGD}))} \qquad (6.4)$$

Note that (6.4) is very similar to Equation (6.3) but now has in the denominator a term $(1 - (\text{PD} \cdot \text{LGD}))$ that "grosses up" the lending rate, rL, to a *higher* interest rate based on the probability of default and loss given default. Thus, higher levels of PD and/or LGD lead to increases in the loan rate above and beyond those implied earlier by Equation (6.3). This occurs because the bank will have to charge a higher rate of interest when some portion of interest is lost during default. For our purposes, we use (6.4) for loan pricing but keep in mind that different assumptions of how much interest is lost during default, as well as the possible presence of collateral, can affect the specific lending rate formula. Interestingly, Equation (6.4) describes credit risk's *nonlinear, exponential effect* on the loan rate as PD and/or LGD are increased. That is, rL will rise at an exponential pace as expected credit losses are perceived to be greater. We examine this nonlinear effect in more detail later in this chapter when exploring the impact of credit risk management on a bank's market value of equity.

6.3.2 *The role of asymmetric information in loan pricing*

The problem of asymmetric information described in Chapter 1 will affect a bank's loan rates due to **adverse selection** (unobservable quality *before* the loan is made) and **moral hazard** (unobservable action *after* the loan is made). Since the banker cannot perfectly identify the borrower's quality in terms of creditworthiness, the loan rate might be mispriced due to errors in estimating the "true" PD and LGD for the loan. For a *safe* borrower, the risk is that the bank charges too *high* a rate and thus loses the loan business to a competing bank. Conversely, the bank might charge too *low* a rate for a *risky* borrower and thus lead to unusually large credit losses that could lead to insolvency and, in the extreme, a run on the bank by its depositors.

The moral hazard problem makes this situation even worse because once the loan is granted, the borrower has the incentive to take on more risk because these funds are considered "Other People's Money" (or, "OPM") and, like a car rental, are typically not treated as carefully as if it were the borrower's own asset. PD and LGD are higher when the borrower has an incentive to take more risk due to the distortionary impact of OPM. Thus, the borrower benefits if things go well and the extra risk pays off, but the borrower's losses are not as large when the gamble does not pay off (e.g., due to the limited liability nature of a firm's common equity).

To reduce the impact of adverse selection on loan pricing, banks can "ration" credit by restricting loans to only high-quality borrowers with, for example, relatively strong credit scores or who can put down relatively large down payments/deposits for the purchase of an asset. These are positive and credible "signals" of the high creditworthiness of the borrower. Background checks and/or credit history reviews are another way to reduce the adverse selection problem faced by the bank. To mitigate the moral hazard incentive and excessive risk-taking, the lender can require collateral and/or impose loan covenants which restrict what the borrower can do with the loan proceeds and its future activities. Although these common lending practices can be useful in reducing credit risk, they are not perfect and thus it is still important for a bank to be able to properly quantify its credit risk.

6.4 How to Measure Credit Risk?

Based on the above discussion of loan pricing, we can see that it is essential that a bank can properly estimate its expected credit losses and so a quantitative approach to modeling credit risk has grown up over the past 50–60 years. We first start with some of the earliest statistical models which originated with Altman's (1968) Z-score during the 1960s. This approach, generally referred to as a "credit scoring" model, looks at past data to predict future outcomes such as the likelihood of default (i.e., PD). We then discuss some forward-looking credit risk models based on data gleaned from the bond and stock markets (e.g., the Term Structure and Merton/KMV models, respectively). Lastly, we explore an extension of the RiskMetrics model from Chapter 5 that can be applied to credit risk called Credit RiskMetrics.

6.5 Altman's *Z*-score, Statistical Models, and Machine Learning Approaches

Edward Altman (1968) collected key financial ratios of individual firms (i.e., leverage, the availability of cash, market value, and profitability) and related these to corporate default risk. He used a technique called "discriminant analysis" that essentially allows you to separate the "wheat from the chaff" in a systematic way. The idea is to create a credit score based on a weighted average of five financial variables related to being either "chaff" or "wheat" (i.e., defaulting or not defaulting). Borrowers with a *high* score are *unlikely* to default and those with a low score are more likely to do so. The basic Z-score model is presented in the following and, somewhat amazingly, is still a relatively accurate predictor of financial distress for businesses even when used with coefficients that were first estimated in 1968!

$$Z = 1.2 \cdot X_1 + 1.4 \cdot X_2 + 3.3 \cdot X_3 + 0.6 \cdot X_4 + 1.0 \cdot X_5 \qquad (6.5)$$

- X_1 = Working capital / total assets.
- X_2 = Retained earnings / total assets.
- X_3 = EBIT / total assets.
- X_4 = Market value equity / book value of Long-term debt.
- X_5 = Sales / total assets.

The **critical value** of the model's Z-score is **1.81**. Thus, borrowers with a *larger* score than Z =1.81 are **unlikely** to default and borrowers with a *lower* score than Z = 1.81 are *likely* to default in the near future. For example, a Z-score of 3.00 or higher would suggest a very low likelihood of default. Presented in the following is a numerical example of how to use Altman's Z-score for a potential business borrower.

Numerical Example: Suppose a firm has the following values for $X_1 - X_5$:

$X_1 = 0.3$ (more current assets than current liabilities)

$X_2 = 0.0$ (negative earnings and therefore no increase in the firm's retained earnings)

$X_3 = -0.25$ (negative earnings)

$X_4 = 0.2$ (somewhat leveraged firm)

$X_5 = 1.5$ (maintaining sales volume and using assets efficiently)

$$\mathbf{Z} = 1.2 \cdot (0.3) + 1.4 \cdot (0.0) + 3.3 \cdot (-0.25) + 0.6 \cdot (0.2) \\ + 1.0 \cdot (1.5) = \mathbf{1.155}$$

Our Z-value is *less* than the Critical Value of 1.81, so there is a *high* likelihood of default within the next 1–2 years and thus the bank ***should not*** lend to this borrower.

The key **strength** of Altman's is its simplicity and transparency, as it is easy for a lender to see what factors are driving the Z-score and there is a cutoff point (1.81) that gives a clear recommendation. Given that the model and its coefficients have not changed substantially for over 50 years also shows the model is stable and reliable.[5] Thus, Altman's Z-score is still widely used as an initial way to estimate a firm's credit risk even though more advanced/complicated models have been developed, as described later in this chapter.

In terms of the **weaknesses** of Altman's Z, we can summarize them as follows:

- The model only considers two extreme cases (i.e., default or no default),
- the weights may not be constant over time, and
- the model ignores hard-to-quantify factors including the reputation of the borrower, business cycle effects, etc. that we had described earlier by the 5 Cs of credit.

Alternatives to Altman's Z-score model include regression-based linear or nonlinear credit scoring models. Altman (1989) himself also developed a "mortality model" approach which used historical data and principles from actuarial science to estimate a corporate bond's probability of default. These alternative models address some of the weaknesses noted above and enable bankers to also apply a statistical approach to modeling credit risk for consumer loans like credit cards, auto loans, and mortgages. This quantitative approach has automated the credit approval process and thus made it more efficient for banks and "fintech" firms to grant consumer loans.

As a consequence, consumers have generally benefited from greater access to credit and lower lending rates (when compared to a more labor-intensive qualitative approach to credit analysis). Due to recent advances in data analysis, banks and other financial firms have continued to improve upon earlier statistical models by developing credit decision-making

---

[5] See Altman (1985) and others for more details on refinements to the original Altman Z-score method.

models based on machine learning (ML) techniques. These models rely on "big data" analytical techniques and are usually applied to consumer credit products given the abundance of consumer data that are available to many banks.

Although ML models have the potential to make credit decisions even more accurate and efficient, a weakness of this approach is that the method is not as transparent and simple as Altman's Z-score. For example, ML models have been criticized for being a "black box" that makes it difficult (or nearly impossible) to understand why an ML model generated a specific credit decision. Another weakness is that the reliance on large datasets of prior credit decisions can lead to unintended bias against some borrowers if the past data include decisions based on prior (and illegal) discriminatory lending practices.[6] Thus, the bank's data analysts must be careful to use datasets that are free from such biases and, if possible, construct ML models where the decision process is more transparent to external parties, such as bank regulators.

6.6 Term Structure Approach

Although credit scoring models such as Altman's Z-score can be quite useful, they are best applied to less complicated credit decisions where past data can be a reliable predictor of future behavior (such as consumer lending and small business loans). However, bank lending to larger corporations and other organizations for commercial purposes such as working capital, capital expenditures, and specialized buildings/structures typically requires detailed financial analysis by a trained lending officer. To assist in these more complex situations, it can be helpful to use insights from fixed income markets that tabulate bond yields for both risk-free securities, such as U.S. Treasury notes and corporate bonds.

This "Term Structure" approach uses the current yield to maturity of government and corporate bonds for varying maturities (e.g., 1- and 2-year yields) to infer the likelihood of default for a company that has a

---

[6]For example, fair lending laws in the U.S. prohibit discrimination along several dimensions and thus the "black box" nature of some ML scoring models makes it difficult to develop bias-free and transparent algorithms (e.g., see the discussion in Brotcke, 2022). In a survey of fintech lending, Berg *et al.* (2021) indicate that the evidence is "mixed" at best in terms of ML's ability to reduce bias and enhance outcomes in consumer lending.

Table 6.2. Example of Spot and Forward Rates to Estimate the Probability of Default (PD).

2-year Term Structure	1	2
Government Spot Rates ($RF_{0,1}$)	3.00%	4.00%
Government Forward Rates ($RF_{1,2}$)		5.0097%
"A" Spot Rates ($RC_{0,1}$)	4.50%	6.00%
"A" Forward Rates ($RC_{1,2}$)		7.5215%
Implied Repayment Probabilities	0.985646	0.976639
Cumulative Prob. of Default (2 years)		**0.037380**

similar bond rating.[7] Thus, the method provides an objective estimate of a firm's PD based on the collective judgment and trading of bond market participants. In effect, it provides the bond market's *forward-looking* opinion of what the firm's PD might be over a loan's life. This estimate can then be used by a banker or other creditors to form their own opinion about the firm's creditworthiness.

Table 6.2 provides a numerical example of the Term Structure methodology based on data for 1- and 2-year bonds. To keep things simple, we focus on the first two years of the bond market's term structure of interest rates, but this example can easily be extended to 3 or more years by repeating the process outlined here for additional yields of longer-term bonds. The shaded values in Table 6.2 show the yields that are available in the bond market to buy risk-free government securities ($RF_{0,1}$) and A-rated corporate bonds ($RC_{0,1}$) right now.[8] This is typically referred to as the "spot" market because it means you can buy the bond "on the spot" and get control of the bonds usually within 1–2 days after the bonds are

---

[7] Technically, we should use zero coupon bond yields to implement the Term Structure method outlined here, so we can view the rates used in the following numerical example to be obtained from a zero-coupon bond term structure (also referred to as a "yield curve"). See Saunders *et al.* (2024) for more details on the term structure approach to estimating credit risk.

[8] The subscripts represent the points on the timeline for which that rate pertains. So, spot rates always start at time-0 and then continue to time-1 or beyond, depending on the spot bond's maturity. In our case here, we use "0,1" in the subscript to signify that these are 1-year spot rates starting at time-0 and ending at time-1.

Figure 6.1. Graph of Spot and Forward Rates.

cleared and settled within the financial market system. As we had shown earlier in the appendix of Chapter 4, we can use these spot rates to infer "forward" interest rates that, for example, inform us about what the current term structure (also commonly referred to as the "yield curve") is implying about *future* short-term interest rates. You might recall from Chapter 4 that we called this the "bootstrapping" approach to finding forward rates. Figure 6.1 displays a graph of these rates based on the data in Table 6.2.

We can see in Table 6.1 that the 1-year implied forward rates for the government ($RF_{1,2}$) and corporate securities ($RC_{1,2}$) are 5.0097% and 7.5215%, respectively.[9] These are also shown as two dots in year 2 in Figure 6.1. That is, these rates represent the cost of borrowing funds for 1-year *starting 1 year from now and continuing until the beginning of the second year*. These 1-year forward rates, along with the current 1-year spot rates, enable us to infer what the bond market is thinking about the future probability of *repayment* in each year (i.e., the probability of *not*

---

[9] Note that these forward rates have "1,2" in the subscript to represent that these rates are 1-year interest rates that will be paid starting 1-year from now and ending right before the beginning of the second year. Similarly, if we had more data for a third year of spot rates, then we could bootstrap a 1-year forward rate that starts 2 years from now. This type of forward rate would include the subscript of "2,3" to represent a 1-year forward rate that is paid between time-2 and time-3. This process can then be repeated for the fourth and subsequent years, if necessary.

defaulting each year). These implied repayment probabilities are shown in the next-to-last row of Table 6.1 and are computed based on the following relationship:

1. For the *first* year, you can use the 1-year spot rates for both the U.S. Treasury note ($RF_{0,1}$) and corporate bond ($RC_{0,1}$) to equate the future value of dollar invested in the government security to the expected future value of dollar invested in the risky corporate bond as follows:

$$(1 + RF_{0,1}) = p_1 \cdot (1 + RC_{0,1})$$

where p_1 = probability of repayment in the first year by the corporate borrower.[10]

Solving algebraically for p_1 results in a handy way of estimating this probability from the two 1-year spot rates:

$$p_1 = \frac{(1 + RF_{0,1})}{(1 + RC_{0,1})} \tag{6.6}$$

2. For the *second* year (and subsequent years if we had spot rate data for the third year and beyond), we use the 1-year forward rates implied via the bootstrapping approach for each particular year. In our case, we can use the 1-year forward rates that start 1 year from now to compute the repayment probability in the second year (p_2) as follows:

$$p_2 = \frac{(1 + RF_{1,2})}{(1 + RC_{1,2})} \tag{6.7}$$

---

[10] Note that this probability equates the risk-free return to the *expected* return on a risky security and thus is called the "risk-neutral" probability because this equation strictly holds for investors that are *not* averse to risk. Thus, the probability shown here represents an estimate of a *lower* chance for repayment than if an investor *is* risk averse (i.e., p_1 < "true" risk-averse probability). Conversely, this implies that the risk-neutral probability leads to a *higher* estimate of default (i.e., $1 - p_1$) than a risk averse investor would require. Thus, this risk-neutral probability leads to a *conservative* estimate of PD and means that the *actual* PD is likely to be *less than* the probability computed above. So, we can view this equation's PD estimate as an *upper bound* on the default probability.

3. Once the various annual repayment probabilities are obtained from the government and corporate yield curve data, we find the *cumulative* probability of default (PD) by subtracting the product of each of these probabilities from 1.0:

$$PD = 1 - (p_1 \cdot p_2)$$

which can be expressed more generally for a T-maturity corporate bond as follows:

$$PD_{O,T} = 1 - \prod_t^T \cdot p_t \qquad (6.8)$$

Based on the three-step process described above and Equations (6.6)–(6.8), we can see how we derived the two annual repayment probabilities and the cumulative probability of default (PD) as follows:

$$p_1 = \frac{(1+RF_{0,1})}{(1+RC_{0,1})} = \frac{(1.030)}{(1.045)} = \cdot 0.985646$$

$$p_2 = \frac{(1+RF_{1,2})}{(1+RC_{1,2})} = \frac{(1.050097)}{(1.075215)} = \cdot 0.976639$$

$$PD_{0,2} = 1 - (p_1 \cdot p_2) = 1 - (0.985646 \cdot 0.976639) = \mathbf{0.037380}$$

The above calculations show that there is around a 98.6% chance the corporate bond will *not* default in the first year. In addition, there's a 97.7% chance of no default during the second year. This pattern of decreasing repayment probabilities as we extend beyond the first year is not that surprising because more "bad" things can occur to the firm or the economy as the bond's time horizon is lengthened. The above approach is helpful because it gives us year-by-year information about the evolution of the firm's credit risk over the bond's life. Overall, this results in a probability of default of about 3.74% during the bond's 2-year life ($PD_{0,2}$).

We should also mention that there's a shortcut way to estimate this cumulative PD if we are *not* interested in seeing how the probability of repayment varies from year to year. In this case, we can simply take the government and corporate *spot rates* for the relevant time horizon from the current yield curves and enter them into the following formula:

$$p_{0,2} = \frac{(1+RF_{0,2})^2}{(1+RC_{0,2})^2} = \frac{(1.040)^2}{(1.060)^2} = 0.962620$$

and

$$PD_{0,2} = 1 - p_{0,2} = 1 - 0.962620 = \mathbf{0.037380}$$

Note that this method is mathematically equivalent to the more detailed approach shown earlier when the assumption of "no arbitrage" holds. In the case where no arbitrage opportunities exist, the "buy and hold" return to, say, a 2-year spot bond should be equal to the return of a "rollover" strategy that first invests in a 1-year spot bond of similar risk and then re-invests in a 1-year forward rate (starting one year from now). Thus, if the analyst is most concerned about the borrower's probability of default over the full 2-year horizon, then the two 2-year spot rates can be used to quickly find this 2-year default rate ($PD_{0,2}$). This approach can be applied to any time horizon if you have reliable spot rate data for the risk-free bond and relevant corporate bond. For example, 10-year spot rates for both securities can be used to solve for the 10-year cumulative probability of default using $T = 10$ in the following generalized formula:

$$p_{0,T} = \frac{(1+RF_{0,2})^T}{(1+RC_{0,2})^T} \tag{6.9}$$

and

$$PD_{0,T} = 1 - p_{0,T}$$

This discussion demonstrates a *transparent* and *forward-looking* way to estimate credit risk for a company based on bond market data. Keep in mind that this presumes the bond market is informationally efficient and sufficiently liquid so that the observed bond yields are reliable indicators of the current credit risk of companies that have the same bond rating. Also, note that this method might be difficult to use if the company you wish to analyze does not have publicly traded bonds or a bond rating.

6.7 The Merton/KMV Model Approach

Like we saw with the Term Structure method for analyzing more complex commercial loans, it can be helpful to use insights that are forward-looking and based on objective information from financial markets to estimate credit risk. Rather than using bond market information, the **Merton/KMV credit model** relies on data from the *equity* markets and option pricing concepts.[11] This method provides an objective estimate of a firm's PD based on the collective judgment and trading of stock market participants. In effect, it provides the stock market's forward-looking opinion of what the firm's PD could be over a loan's life. This estimate can then be used by a banker or other creditor to form their own opinion about the firm's creditworthiness.

Continuing with the example of a 2-year corporate bond, Table 6.3 provides a numerical example for the Merton credit risk model based on data like that used in our Term Structure example (e.g., a 2-year risk-free rate of 4% and an A-rated corporate bond). The shaded values in Table 6.3 show the market data available in the financial markets that can

Table 6.3. Numerical Example of Merton/KMV Credit Risk Model.

Data for analyzing a 2-year risky bond	
Market Value of Bond (Face Value · e^{-it})	92.312
Face Value of Bond or Loan (K)	100
Total Assets of the Firm (A_t)	200
Time to Maturity (t, in years)	2
Risk-Free Rate ($RF_{0,2}$)	0.04
Annualized Return Volatility (S.D.) of Assets (s_A)	0.275
Financial Leverage = d = MV of Debt / Tot. Assets (A_t)	0.461558
PD = −1 − N(d)	**0.036444**
Implied Credit Spread (over Risk-Free Rate)	**0.0025**

---

[11] A Nobel Laureate in economics, Robert C. Merton, first developed the concept of using option pricing models to estimate corporate credit risk (see Merton, 1974). The firm, KMV, then applied the insights from Merton's model to provide credit analysis on a commercial basis. KMV stands for Kealhofer, McQuown, and Vasicek, who were the founders of the firm. Ultimately, the firm was sold to Moody's in 2002 and became a subsidiary of the Moody's Analytics unit of this credit ratings agency.

be used to estimate the extra yield needed to convince an investor to buy a risky 2-year A-rated corporate bond ($RC_{0,2}$) rather than invest in a risk-free government security ($RF_{0,2}$). This extra yield is typically called a "credit spread" (s) and, in this case, is defined as $s_{A,2}$:

$$\text{Credit Spread for an A-rated 2-year bond} = s_{A,2} = RC_{0,2} - RF_{0,2}$$

Based on the bond yield data in Table 6.3 and the option pricing model, the credit spread for this A-rated 2-year bond is 0.25% when the risk-free rate is 4.00% and the riskiness of the borrower's assets is 27.5% (as measured by the standard deviation of the firm's annual return on assets). In this case, we can see that the estimated corporate bond yield is 4.25% (i.e., $RC_{0,2}$ = the risk-free rate of 4.00% plus the 0.25% credit spread). Another interesting aspect of the Merton model which is described in more detail in the Appendix of this chapter is that it also provides us with an estimate of the bond's probability of default (PD) which, for this bond, is around 3.64%. Note that this PD estimate is close but not the same as the 3.74% PD figure we found with the Term Structure method. So, in theory, Merton/KMV and Term Structure models address the problem from two very different perspectives (e.g., stock option pricing vs. bond market yield curves) but can provide potentially similar estimates of credit risk.

6.7.1 A brief discussion of the Merton model's logic

Table 6.3 includes the key variables that are needed to convert an estimate of the firm's equity risk (as measured by the standard deviation of annual *stock* returns) into an estimate of the firm's *asset* risk (noted earlier as σ_A and shown as 0.275 or 27.5% per year). In turn, to compute the value of the equity investor's option to default on the debt, we can use this asset volatility, along with other key inputs, to estimate the credit spread. Thus, we also need to know the following information: the bond's market value ($92.312) and face value ($100) in relation to the firm's total asset value ($200). This information, along with the bond's time to maturity (2 years) and the current risk-free rate for a U.S. Treasury security of similar maturity (0.04 or 4.00%), can be used with Merton's option pricing model to estimate the credit spread of 0.25%, as shown in Table 6.3. Although it sounds quite complicated, his model can be programmed in an Excel™ spreadsheet fairly easily.

Since the model essentially translates a volatility estimate into a probability distribution, we can also find the probability of default (PD) by looking at the chance within this distribution that the firm's asset value might trigger a default by falling *below* the face value of debt at the time of the bond's maturity. As noted earlier, Table 6.3 displays this PD estimate at around 3.64%. Thus, the Merton/KMV method provides another theoretically sound way to estimate the credit risk of a portion of the bank's bond and loan portfolios. However, we should keep in mind that this method can only be used for borrowers that have publicly traded equity and thus it would not be applicable for private companies of smaller and midsize businesses (which are usually the primary target markets for a bank's commercial lending activities).

6.8 Credit Value at Risk and Credit RiskMetrics

In contrast to the approaches described in the prior sections which focus on individual loans or bonds, the Credit RiskMetrics method is a generalized approach that can be used not only for specific assets but also for the bank's entire credit portfolio of bonds and loans. This method builds upon the concept of Value-at-Risk (VaR) that was first introduced in Chapter 5 related to Market Risk. Since we have already presented a detailed discussion of the VaR methodology in Chapter 5, we focus here on how VaR can be modified for use with credit risk (commonly referred to as the Credit RiskMetrics' estimate of "Credit VaR" or "CVaR" for short). Like with VaR, Credit VaR requires a choice of time horizon and so 1 year is a typical value, although the credit analyst can choose a longer or shorter horizon depending on their needs.

The CVaR method helps us see how much "tail risk" exposure exists within a bank's loans and risky bond investments. In effect, we are assuming that a "high impact" but "low frequency" event is what we are most concerned about in terms of a bank's credit risk. That is, we are more worried about the impact of a large drop in the value of the bank's loans and bonds due to changing *credit* conditions which might occur infrequently (as opposed to changing *interest rate* conditions like those discussed in Chapter 4). Usually, the concern is focused on the amount of loss that can occur 1% of the time *over a 1-year period*. This 1% threshold can change based on the application (for instance, we might be concerned

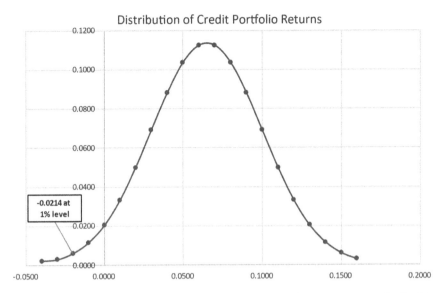

Figure 6.2. Annual Credit Value at Risk (CVaR) expressed as a percentage of a Bank's Total Credit Portfolio.

about very extreme events and thus focus on the 0.01% threshold in the case of a possible severe recession/depression).

Figure 6.2 shows a graph of the probability distribution of the expected return on a bank's portfolio of loans and bonds, which we refer to more generally as the bank's total "credit portfolio." The probability of each possible return is shown on the y-axis while the estimated percentage change in the portfolio's market value is displayed on the x-axis.

This distribution is based on some of the data used earlier in Table 3.1 of Chapter 3 where we assume the following key numbers for our hypothetical bank, ABC.

Note that we are using *annual* estimates of the bank's tail risk exposure to fluctuations in the value of the credit portfolio due to changes in the creditworthiness of one or more borrowers. We focus on the left tail of the distribution because this is where the bank can lose money (whereas the right tail shows the largest "upside return" for the portfolio). The tail risk value will be affected by the portfolio's average return (6.00%) and its variability, as measured by the return's standard deviation (3.50%). For our

Table 6.4. Key Assumptions from the Detailed Numerical Example for ABC Bank in Chapter 3.

Variable	Value
Total Assets ($ mil.)	1,580
Investment in Securities ($ mil.)	700
Loans	830
Common Equity ($ mil.)	180
Total Shares Outstanding (mil.)	10.0
Annual Average Return on the Credit Portfolio	0.0600
Annual Standard Dev. of Credit Portfolio Returns	0.0350

purposes, we can assume that a bank analyst was able to compute these statistics from historical data on the bank's credit portfolio returns.

Figure 6.2 tells us that there is a 1% chance that the total credit portfolio will lose 2.14% (or more) of its value during a given year due to weakening credit conditions (i.e., −0.0214 in decimal format) because a 214-basis point loss is located at the 1st percentile of the distribution. In risk management jargon, this credit exposure can also be expressed as a dollar value (CVaR) based on multiplying this estimated loss by the bank's total credit portfolio value at the beginning of the period (in this case, CVaR = −0.0214 · ($700 million + $830 million) = −$32.776 million). Another industry convention is to express this "Credit Value at Risk" as a *positive* value of $32.776 million. Just keep in mind that this figure is a projected *loss* and therefore is technically a negative value that reduces the credit portfolio. This CVaR estimate is commonly used because it is relatively straightforward for bank managers, investors, and regulators to understand as a measure of extreme risk due to deteriorating credit conditions.

Like we discussed in the previous chapter on market risk, we need to understand how to come up with such a precise estimate of this tail risk described above. The discussion of VaR in Chapter 5 demonstrated that there are multiple ways to estimate a VaR measure of *market* risk using the RiskMetrics method, such as Historic (or "Back") Simulation and Monte Carlo Simulation. We do not reiterate most of the details for these three methods and, instead, focus on the differences in their application to *credit* risk. The interested reader should review Chapter 5 on Market Risk if they are not familiar with these VaR methods.

6.8.1 Credit RiskMetrics approach (or variance–covariance CVaR method)

As we discussed in Chapter 5, the RiskMetrics approach was pioneered by J.P. Morgan Inc. in the early 1990s and this method gained widespread acceptance because it is one of the more intuitive and computationally easier ways to estimate a bank's market risk. The concept was then extended to model credit risk in 1997 and dubbed "Credit RiskMetrics." Its most basic underlying assumption is that the returns to a credit portfolio are normally distributed (which can be a questionable assumption for a fixed income investment). The method also allows ABC's managers to decide whether the tail risk associated with the bank's credit portfolio represents an acceptable amount of risk in relation to its equity capital. This can be done by comparing the credit portfolio's return to its risk via the firm's profitability targets, such as return on equity (ROE) and risk-adjusted return on capital (RAROC). We discuss how to apply Credit VaR in this manner later in the chapter. The firm can also use Credit VaR to manage this credit risk exposure by adjusting the credit portfolio's holdings and/or hedging a portion of this risk with derivative securities. Regulators also want to know about credit risk because Basel III regulations require banks to hold sufficient capital against any potential credit losses.

6.8.2 Credit VaR (CVaR) for a portfolio of loans and bonds

Credit VaR = Critical Value · Annual Standard Deviation (S.D.) of Interest Rates · Modified Duration · Invested Assets in loans and bonds (6.10)

Note that in (6.10) we build upon our discussion of interest rate risk associated with bonds from Chapter 4. To estimate Credit VaR, we first need to use *annual* fluctuations in an overall measure of interest rates to compute the Annual S.D. of Interest Rates.[12] Note that, depending on the application, this interest rate volatility estimate could be due to changes in

---

[12] This approach is slightly different than the statistical total return approach presented earlier with Table 6.1, as sometimes it is easier for the analyst to obtain historical data on interest rates rather than credit portfolio returns.

the credit conditions of a particular bond/loan or the entire credit portfolio. For example, if a bond is downgraded from, say, an A credit rating to a BBB rating, then the key question is as follows: what is the likely change in the bond's yield due to this change in credit status? Since BBB represents higher risk, we expect the yield on the bond to rise and therefore its price will fall once the downgrade is announced.

Also, keep in mind that this same process can be applied to a bank's loans even though they do not have formal, publicly available credit ratings. Nearly all banks have some form of internal loan rating system that categorizes bank loans by creditworthiness from high quality to low quality and essentially serves the same purpose as a bond rating. So, even though our examples focus on a bond's rating change, the same logic applies to bank loans and their private, internal ratings. That is, we assume that a downgrade of a loan within the bank's internal rating system will have the same effect as a bond downgrade and will lead to a similar decline in the loan's "true" value (as if it were a publicly traded bond).

For our bond example, we can use past instances of rating downgrades to quantify the movement in interest rates and bond prices associated with such a change in credit conditions. Usually, the data that are collected will be based on interest rate changes rather than price changes. We then must convert that generalized interest *rate* volatility measure into a variability of bond *prices* and so we use the specific bond's modified duration for this purpose.[13] Thus, multiplying the S.D. of Interest Rates by the Modified Duration gives us an idea of the *typical* percentage change in the market value of the bond portfolio.

Since we want to derive a tail risk estimate, we must use a Critical Value to find the potential loss that would occur 1% of the time. For a normal distribution, this factor is equal to 2.33, as noted previously in Chapter 5. The last step is to then multiply this extreme price change by the dollar amount in Invested Assets within the specific loan, bond, or

---

[13] We can use a similar approach for an individual loan or a portfolio of bonds and loans by first estimating their modified durations. We can view a fixed rate loan as very similar to a fixed rate bond in terms of its cash flows and thus both instrument's durations can be estimated in the way described in the Appendix of Chapter 4 on interest rate risk. Note also that the duration of a floating rate loan or bond can be estimated by using the time period within which the instrument's rate will be re-set. For example, a six-month adjustable rate mortgage would have a duration of 6 months (even though its maturity might not be for another 30 years).

Table 6.5. Numerical Example for ABC Bank's Credit RiskMetrics' VaR estimate based on investments in Loans and Bonds within the Credit Portfolio.

Variable	Extreme Critical Value	Total Return Int. Rate S.D.	Volatility Modified Duration	$Invested	Credit VaR
Bonds & Loans	2.33	0.0050	5.0	$1,530	$89.1225

credit portfolio. Thus, Credit VaR will be greater when either price volatility or the dollar investment (or both) are relatively high.

Based on Equation (6.10), we present in Table 6.5 a numerical example to estimate CVaR for the bank's total investments in bonds and loans.

Table 6.5 illustrates how Credit VaR can be computed based on the key drivers of the credit portfolio's Return Volatility (as defined by its annual standard deviation and denoted in the table by "Interest Rate S.D."). For example, the CVaR for ABC's Bond & Loans portfolio considers the variability in interest rates as well as the modified durations of the bank's bond investments (assumed to be 3.0 years) and the loans (assumed to be 6.68 years). The relative value invested in Bonds ($700 million, or 45.7% of the total dollar amount invested) and Loans ($830 million, or 54.3% of the total) will also affect the *asset-weighted average* Modified Duration of the total credit portfolio (shown as 5.0 years in Table 6.5). Thus, the total portfolio's MD of 5.0 years is obtained by multiplying the modified durations of each of the portfolio's sub-components by their respective weights (i.e., $MD_{portfolio}$ = 5.0 years = (0.457 · 3.0 years) + (0.543 · 6.68 years)). In addition, the total dollar invested in the credit portfolio of $1,530 million (shown in the "$Invested" column of Table 6.5) also affects the Credit VaR estimate. Consequently, to find the tail risk of this credit portfolio, the total return volatility estimates are multiplied by the relevant Critical Value (i.e., 2.33) and the dollar amount invested in each of the various types of investments.[14]

---

[14] Note that we could have broken out the loan and bond portfolios and estimated their Credit VaR's separately and then created a total credit portfolio Credit VaR based on the correlations in loan and bond returns. Like we had shown in Chapter 5, we could then use that chapter's techniques to help identify the diversification benefits of a portfolio of bank assets. However, to help focus our discussion on credit risk, we concentrate on the entire credit portfolio rather than the diversification aspects of different bank investments.

To arrive at the CVaR estimate of $89.1225 million noted above in Table 6.5, the analyst usually relies on historical data about the distribution of credit rating changes for the bank's bonds and loan portfolios. Rather than focus on an entire credit portfolio, it can also be useful for us to examine specific holdings, such as a large, individual bond investment. Presented in Table 6.6 is a numerical example of the probability distribution for a $100 million *A*-rated 3-year corporate bond with a 5% annual coupon and a current yield to maturity (YTM) of 4% (with a current market value of $102.775 million). In practice, these data would be based on past experience of credit rating changes for bonds with the same credit rating and maturity.

Figure 6.3 shows a graph of the probability distribution for this bond based on the data reported in Table 6.6. Note that there is a very high chance the bond will remain an *A*-rated bond (84%) but the distribution is negatively skewed, as there is a greater chance of the bond being downgraded to BBB or lower when compared to a rating upgrade to AA or higher. This "negative skewness" of bond values is common because a fixed income security usually has limited upside potential but large downside risk (e.g., if the bond defaults).

Table 6.6 shows us how to calculate the expected value of the bond (referred to as the "Mean Value" of $101.57 million in the fifth column) as well as its standard deviation (denoted by "Estimated S.D." of $1.9059 million). These estimates are based on the historical probabilities of the bond either staying at an A rating (84%), experiencing a downgrade to BBB (6.7%) or lower, or getting upgraded to AA (4.2%) or higher. The other key input is the expected YTM for each of the possible bond ratings which are shown in the third column of Table 6.6.

To get a forward-looking estimate of the annual CVaR, these YTMs should be based on the *current* yields in the corporate bond market. The other nuance to this calculation is that it provides an estimate of the bond's value *12 months from today*. Thus, when computing the bond's market value (denoted as the "Ending Value" in the fourth column), we must remember that a 3-year bond becomes a *2-year* bond after 12 months have elapsed. Accordingly, the ending values shown in Table 6.6 are for a 2-year annual bond. These values show us what the 3-year bond would be worth at the beginning of the bond's second year because, at that time, the bond has effectively become a 2-year bond.

Table 6.6 also reports estimates of the CVaR for a 5% normal probability of $3.14 million using a Critical Value of 1.65 standard deviations.

Credit Risk   239

Table 6.6. Numerical Example of Calculating CVaR for a Corporate Bond.

Principal ($M)	Coupon (%)	Term (Yrs.)	current YTM
100	5.00%	3	4.00%

Credit RiskMetrics Approach

Year-End Rating	Probability	YTM	Ending Value (beg. of Yr. 2)	Weighted Value	Diff. from Mean	Weighted Squared Difference
AAA = 1	0.10%	3.00%	103.83	0.10	2.26	0.0051
AA = 2	4.20%	3.50%	102.85	4.32	1.28	0.0690
A = 3	**84.00%**	**4.00%**	**101.89**	85.58	0.32	0.0849
BBB = 4	6.70%	4.50%	100.94	6.76	−0.63	0.0267
BB = 5	4.00%	6.00%	98.17	3.93	−3.40	0.4628
B = 6	0.70%	9.00%	92.96	0.65	−8.60	0.5183
CCC = 7	0.20%	20.00%	77.08	0.15	−24.48	1.1990
Default = 8	0.10%	30.00%	65.98	0.07	−35.59	1.2668
	100.00%		Mean Value	101.57	Variance	3.6326

Credit Value-at-Risk (CVaR) Estimates

	Critical Value	Estimated S.D.			CVaR
5% CVaR with Normality	1.65	1.9059			3.14
1% CVaR with Normality	2.33	1.9059			4.44

Historic Simulation CVaR Estimates

	Mean	95%-ile	99%-ile		CvaR
5% CVaR — Actual Dist.	101.57	98.17			3.40
1% CVaR — Actual Dist.	101.57		92.96		8.60

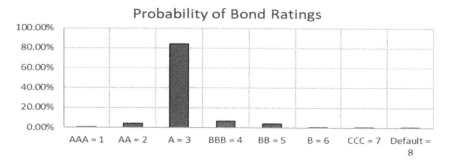

Figure 6.3. Probability Distribution of Ratings for an A-rated corporate bond.

This tail risk is lower than the $4.44 million CVaR estimate based on a 1% probability because the tail probability of 5% will, by definition, occur more frequently and thus will be closer to the bond's mean value. Some bank analysts prefer to focus on this 5% level rather than the more extreme 1% tail.

In addition, the last two rows of Table 6.6 use the *historical* probability distribution data rather than the *normal* distribution assumption to locate the 5% and 1% tail estimates of the bond's value. To do this, we find in Table 6.6 the bond values that correspond to the cumulative probabilities at the 95th and 99th percentiles (which relate to the 5% and 1% lower tails of the distribution). Based on the data in Table 6.6, the 5% tail occurs when the bond's value is $98.17 million and the 1% tail corresponds to a $92.96 million valuation. We can then easily find the estimates of CVaR by subtracting these lower tail bond values from the bond's expected value (denoted as "Mean" in the lower portion of Table 6.6). For example, the 1% CVaR estimate of $8.60 million is obtained by subtracting the value of the bond at the first percentile ($92.96 million) from the bond's mean value of $101.57 million (i.e., $101.57 − $92.96 = $8.60 million, with rounding).

This latter approach of estimating CVaR is based on the **Historic Simulation** method we had described in Chapter 5, where we use past data to find the 1% tail of the actual distribution rather than relying on the assumption of normally distributed values. As shown in Figure 6.3, the negatively skewed distribution of the bond's value leads to *higher* CVaR estimates when the Historic Simulation method is compared to CVaR estimates based on a normal distribution. In the above numerical example, the $8.60 million CVaR using Historic Simulation is nearly double the normally distributed CVaR estimate of $4.44 million. Thus, negative skewness in bond values is an important factor to consider when estimating the tail risk of a credit portfolio.

Also, keep in mind that we can convert these dollar-based CVaR values into percentages by simply dividing these figures by the 3-year bond's initial value of $102.775 million. In this case, the Historic Simulation's 1% CVaR is equivalent to 8.37% of the bond's value and the normal distribution's 1% CVaR is 4.32%. So, the bond's expected loss in the case of a 1% tail event (i.e., a downgrade to a B rating) is between 4% and 9% of its current market value. This is a substantial amount of potential loss due to credit risk because most banks hold only around 10% of equity capital as a buffer against unexpected losses. Later, in this chapter, we discuss some of the ways to manage a bank's credit risk and its impact on the market value of equity.

6.8.3 *Historic and Monte Carlo simulation of CVaR*

As discussed in detail in Chapter 5, the **Historic Simulation** method (sometimes referred to as a "Back" Simulation) is conceptually and computationally a much simpler way to estimate a bank's Credit Value at Risk. All that is needed is a reliable distribution of past bond values and returns for each credit-related asset within the bank's credit portfolio as well as the dollar amounts invested in each of these sub-components (e.g., bonds, loans, and leases, etc.), in other words, we can rely on the *actual historical* distribution of returns rather than making an explicit assumption about the return distribution like we did above. However, several years' worth of annual returns related to changes in credit quality are typically needed for this type of analysis.

Once we have collected the relevant return and portfolio data, we can use the process for Historic Simulation described in Chapter 5 to create a table like the bottom portion of Table 6.6 shown earlier. Since the 1% cumulative probability in Table 6.6 occurs at a B rating, we can use the bond value of $92.96 million to help compute our tail risk estimate. Note that this 1% tail is found by summing the probabilities starting with the lowest rating (Default) and adding up all relevant probabilities until we find the 1% cumulative probability distribution. In Table 6.6, this occurs at the B rating level because the sum of the probabilities for ratings of Default (0.1%), CCC (0.2%), and B (0.7%) add up to a cumulative probability of 1.0%. This same process can be used to find the 5% cumulative probability level of the bond's value which occurs at the BB rating. As detailed in the prior section, Table 6.6 displays the data used to calculate the $8.60 million estimate of our 1% CvaR threshold based on the Historic Simulation approach.

Consistent with our discussion in Chapter 5 about the **Monte Carlo Simulation** method, we can also apply the process explained there to a credit portfolio. Thus, instead of relying on a historical distribution, we can use past data to help us form estimates of future possible scenarios of the bond's credit conditions and then simulate these scenarios thousands of times. What results from this process is a *forward-looking*, hypothetical probability distribution of the bond's market value. This approach has the benefit of potentially more accurate outcomes when compared to relying on past data or assuming a normal distribution. But, as noted in earlier chapters, the results of the Monte Carlo approach are typically hard to understand as it is usually viewed as a "black box" model. In addition, the GIGO problem of "Garbage In, Garbage Out" also applies to this technique.

As a bank manager, we must remember that risk management is both an art and a science and thus we need to use judgment when faced with different tail risk assessments. So, a good bank manager should incorporate information from all these methods and decide whether to focus on one estimate or to combine the various CvaR estimates into a consolidated figure. Unfortunately, there is no simple formula or clear guidance on how to best do this and so sound judgment is still required to effectively manage a bank's credit risk.

6.9 How to Use the Above Models to Make Informed Credit Decisions

6.9.1 *The RAROC model*

The discussion of credit models in the previous section can be used by bank managers to make more informed credit decisions and to assess the impact on the bank's financial condition. First, we can use the "RAROC"

(*Risk Adjusted Return on Capital*) method to decide whether a loan, bond, or entire credit portfolio is delivering an acceptable return for the level of risk the bank is facing. This RAROC metric can be computed as follows:

$$RAROC = \frac{\text{Net Income on Credit Instrument}}{\text{Extreme Credit Loss Estimate}}$$

$$= \frac{(rL - RF)\text{Principal Value}}{\text{CVaR}} \quad (6.11)$$

where

rL = promised rate on the loan or bond,

RF = the risk-free rate for a U.S. Treasury of comparable maturity (this is a proxy for the bank's financing costs but other proxies can be used such as the bank's cost of deposits or some inter-bank borrowing rate), and

$CVaR$ = the Credit RiskMetrics estimate for the bond or loan portfolio based on the discussion from the prior section and represents our "Extreme Credit Loss Estimate."

In Equation (6.11), we are comparing the profitability of the credit investment (net of its financing costs) to the tail risk associated with this investment. Note that in this example we have used the CVaR method to estimate the Extreme Credit Loss Estimate, but other tail risk methods can be used depending on the bank managers' preferences and data availability.

For example, if we use the data in Table 6.6 for a $100 million, 3-year 5% coupon corporate bond with a YTM of 4%, we can see from our prior analysis that its 1% CVaR is $4.44 million based on the Credit RiskMetric's Variance–Covariance method. If we assume that the relevant risk-free rate is 3% in this example, then we can estimate this bond's RAROC as follows:

$$RAROC = \frac{(rL - RF)\text{Face Value}}{\text{CVaR}} = \frac{(0.04 - 0.03)\$100\,\text{million}}{\$4.44\,\text{million}}$$

$$= \frac{\$1\,\text{million}}{\$4.44\,\text{million}} = 0.2252 = 22.52\% \quad (6.12)$$

This RAROC estimate should then be compared with the bank's required, or "target," **return on equity** (i.e., a target ROE). So, if ABC's target ROE is 15%, then we would say *yes* to investing in the above bond because its RAROC of 22.52% is *greater than* the bank's required return. So, the basic credit decision rule using RAROC is as follows:

Accept the bond/loan *if* RAROC ≥ the bank's target ROE

Reject the bond/loan *if* RAROC < the bank's target ROE

As we can see from the above example, the RAROC rule provides a clear-cut decision that helps managers decide which bonds and loans provide acceptable returns relative to their respective credit risk. In theory, we compare RAROC to a target ROE because the CVaR in the denominator of (6.12) should be equal to the *extra equity capital* that the bank needs to support the incremental investment in the relevant bond or loan. In this way, we can think of RAROC as measuring the investment's *marginal* return (the numerator) relative to the *marginal* capital at risk (the denominator). This is why we call it the *Risk Adjusted Return on Capital*.

Note that ABC's managers might want to compute more than one RAROC metric given our earlier discussion about the variability in tail risk estimates across credit risk models. So, some **sensitivity analysis** might be useful in this situation. For example, as we saw in Table 6.6, the CVaR for this bond could be as high as $8.60 million if we rely on a Historic Simulation approach. In this case, we can use Equation (6.12) to re-compute the bond's RAROC as follows:

$$\begin{aligned} \text{RAROC} &= \frac{(rL - RF)\text{Face Value}}{\text{CVaR}} \\ &= \frac{(0.04 - 0.03)\$100 \text{ million}}{\$8.60 \text{ million}} \\ &= \frac{\$1 \text{ million}}{\$8.60 \text{ million}} = 0.1163 = 11.63\% \end{aligned} \quad (6.13)$$

Note that ABC's managers now have a dilemma because the RAROC of 11.63% is *lower* than the bank's 15% target return and thus indicates that we should *reject* this bond investment from the credit portfolio. So, we have a "mixed signal" in that the Credit RiskMetrics method (which assumes normally distributed bond returns) tells us to accept this investment while the Historic Simulation approach indicates rejection. Once again, this is where the bank managers must use their judgment because, ideally, you would like the RAROC to be above the target return regardless of which credit risk model is used. However, this is not the case in this situation and thus the bank must decide whether one method is preferred over another (or if a mixed set of credit risk signals is acceptable).

Remember that bond prices are typically negatively skewed and so the assumption of a normal distribution in the Variance–Covariance method might be problematic, especially in this example. So, if ABC's management believes this, then it should focus on the *Historic Simulation* approach and *reject* an investment in this bond. On the other hand, ABC's managers might think that all credit risk models are flawed to some extent and thus using *both* model's CVaR estimates is better than picking just one method. For example, the Historic Simulation method suffers from a backward-looking focus which might not reflect future credit conditions. In this case, ABC's managers might be willing to *accept* an investment in this bond because at least one of the two methods shows a positive credit recommendation.

Before moving on from this RAROC topic, we should also note an "alternative method" that banks use to estimate a credit instrument's tail risk in a more general way based on the instrument's modified duration[15]:

$$\text{Alternative Extreme Credit Loss Estimate} = MD_{\text{loan or bond}} \cdot \text{Face Value} \cdot \Delta R_{1\% \text{ tail}} \quad (6.14)$$

where

$MD_{\text{loan or bond}}$ = the modified duration of the bond or loan,[16]

Face Value = the face value of a bond or the principal amount of loan, and

---

[15] This approach can be quite useful especially for small or midsize banks where estimating CVaR might be difficult to implement for smaller commercial loans. In the above alternative model, the analyst only needs an estimate of the loan's or bond's modified duration and an expected change in the instrument's credit spread over similar maturity U.S. Treasury yields.

[16] Note that a bank must calculate these modified durations (MDs) from both external sources (such as the bond markets) and their own internal sources (like an internal loan rating and pricing system). Depending on the size of the bank's credit portfolio, these calculations can be quite complex and might require extensive analysis of the bank's cash flows from all its loans and bonds.

246 *Managing Financial Institutions: An Integrated Valuation Approach*

$\Delta R_{1\% \text{ tail}}$ = expected change in "yield spread" due to a credit downgrade at the 1% level of the distribution.

For example, the modified duration is 2.707 years for the $100 million 3-year 5% coupon bond with a 4% YTM that we have been analyzing. To compute the $\Delta R_{1\% \text{ tail}}$ variable, we can refer to the YTM values for the bond in Table 6.6 based on its current YTM as an *A*-rated bond (4.00%) and its potential YTM if it was downgraded to a *B*-rated bond (9.00%). The *B*-rating YTM is chosen because this corresponds to the lowest 1% tail of the probability distribution. Thus, the change in YTM due to a 1% tail downgrade is 5.00% (i.e., 9.00% − 4.00% = 5.00%). Putting all this together using Equation (6.14) results in

$$\text{Alternative Extreme Credit Loss Estimate} = \text{MD}_{\text{loan or bond}} \cdot \text{Face Value} \cdot \Delta R_{1\% \text{ tail}} = 2.707 \cdot \$100 \text{ million} \cdot (+0.05) = \$13.535 \text{ million} \quad (6.15)$$

Note that if we used this value in the denominator of the RAROC equation, then the resulting RAROC is 7.39% ($1 million / $13.535 million = 0.0739), which is much lower than the two prior estimates and well below the target ROE of 15%. Thus, if we were to use all three RAROC estimates, it suggests that ABC should *not* invest in the bond because two out of the three metrics do not meet the target ROE. Once again, despite all the quantitative analysis we can do, good judgment is still needed to make sound credit decisions.

6.9.2 *The impact of credit risk on bank financial statements*

Bank managers must also consider how credit decisions impact the FIs income statement and balance sheet. We briefly outline some of the basics in this section. First, we focus on the balance sheet by showing a stylized statement we have used in previous chapters:

Table 6.7 shows the primary impact of credit risk in rows 3–6 of the balance sheet by reporting the Gross Loans, the Allowance for Loans (ALL), and the difference between these two values, Net Loans.[17] The ALL of $2 million is a "contra" account in accounting terms and is the bank's best estimate of credit losses on the loan portfolio over the lives of

---

[17] The Investments account on the balance sheet can also be impacted by changes in credit risk when the bonds held by the bank suffer credit downgrades. This is reflected by marking these bonds down to their fair market value based on their lower credit rating levels.

Table 6.7. Stylized Balance Sheet.

Assets	Value ($ million)	Liabilities & Equity	Value ($ million)
Cash & Reserves	$4	Deposits	$75
Investments	30	Other Borrowed Money	15
Gross Loans	60		
Allowance for Loans (ALL)	(2)		
Net Loans	58		
Other Assets	8	Common Equity	10
Total Assets	$100	Tot. Liabilities & Equity	$100

these loans. This figure will be adjusted over time depending on changing credit conditions and the addition of new loans.[18] Clearly, higher expected credit losses lead to a larger ALL, and, holding Gross Loans constant, the Net Loans will decrease, thus depressing the bank's Total Assets.

Given that a bank's debt is a more senior claim in the capital structure, a credit loss-induced decrease in Assets leads initially to a drop in the bank's Common Equity. In severe cases like during the 2008–2009 Great Financial Crisis, a bank's entire equity can be wiped out, as well as a portion of the bank's debt. Thus, both the equity investors and creditors of the bank must pay careful attention to the FIs credit risk.

Regarding the bank's income statement (shown in Table 6.8), we can see the impact of credit risk in the Loan Loss Provisions (LLP) line item.

Table 6.8 shows that the expected credit losses need to be increased by $0.1 million. This LLP estimate is a *non-cash* charge (like depreciation expense) and is based on management's judgment about future credit losses. This is an important figure to estimate because a higher level of LLP, holding all else constant, decreases Net Income and ROE while also increasing the ALL on the balance sheet. In addition, regulators pay attention to the bank's LLP choice because they want to see that the bank is properly accounting for future credit losses so that the FI can withstand any deterioration in future credit conditions.

---

[18] In the U.S., commercial banks must estimate the credit losses for each loan over the entire anticipated life of the loan using the Current Expected Credit Losses (CECL) method. This approach blends historical credit data, current information, and forecasts of future conditions.

Table 6.8. Stylized Income Statement.

Income Statement	$ million
Interest Income	$3.0
Interest Expense	0.9
Net Interest Income (NII)	2.1
Loan Loss Provision (LLP)	0.1
Non-Interest Income	1.0
Operating Expense	1.8
Liquidity Risk Effects	0
Hedge Effects	0
Pretax Income	1.2
Taxes	0.3
Net Income (NI)	$0.9

At times, the regulators can require the bank to increase their LLP estimates if they feel that the bank is not being as realistic as it should be about future losses. Given that credit risk can affect a bank's financial statements, it will also affect key financial ratios, such as the Net Interest Margin, ROA, ROE, and financial leverage (e.g., the Equity Multiplier = Assets / Equity). This is important to keep in mind because external analysts, investors, and regulators rely on these statements and ratios to assess the FIs performance and overall financial health.

6.10 How to Manage Credit Risk?

Now that we understand how to quantify a bank's credit risk, make credit decisions, and understand the impact on its financial statements, we can examine ways in which this risk should be managed. There are essentially two ways to do this: (1) on-balance sheet and (2) off-balance sheet risk management.

6.10.1 On-balance sheet ways to manage credit risk

The most direct way to manage a bank's credit risk is to control its impact on financial statements by what we refer to as "on-balance sheet risk management." In this case, the bank makes careful and conscious decisions to hold a *well-diversified portfolio* of bonds and loans (see, e.g., Diamond, 1984). This usually means maintaining "concentration limits" so that the bank does not make too many loans to a single industry, a specific geographic region, and/or a small set of customers. For example, senior management can impose concentration limits so that all loans to a single customer should not be larger than, say, 5% of the FIs total common equity and/or that no single industry sector should comprise more than 10% of the loan portfolio. The "loan and bond portfolio mix" is another important way for management to control credit risk. For example, if ABC's managers are worried about a possible recession next year, they could decide to change the credit portfolio mix to increase the percentage of the portfolio that is invested in safe, liquid marketable securities like government bonds and reduce the exposure to certain types of riskier loans, such as commercial loans and consumer credit cards.

Conversely, if the economy is expanding swiftly, then the percentage allocated to loans can be increased and financed by selling some of the bonds from the bank's Investments account. For those banks that have extensive trading operations, **margin accounts** and **trading limits** can be used to make sure the credit risk related to a bank's trading counterparties does not grow too large as market conditions change. Margin accounts make sure that counterparties have sufficient cash on hand to cope with daily fluctuations in their trading positions. Trading limits ensure the total dollar exposure to counterparties does not exceed acceptable debt levels.

At the *individual loan* level, the bank can also manage credit risk by running **credit checks** and obtaining **credit scores** on the prospective borrower, as well as by requiring **collateral** (remember, this is one of the 5 Cs), and imposing restrictions on the borrower called **loan covenants**. An example of a loan covenant could be to maintain a maximum debt-to-assets ratio of no more than, say, 35%. In this way, the bank makes sure the borrowing firm is not too highly leveraged and thus this covenant increases the chances that the borrower will repay the bank's loan exposure.

6.10.2 *Off-balance sheet ways to manage credit risk*

Although on-balance sheet management of credit risk at both the individual loan and portfolio levels can be a direct control mechanism, it can also be costly and cumbersome if a bank such as ABC faces a very strong set of competing banks. In this case, prospective customers can decide to bank with these competitors if these other FIs offer less demanding loan requirements (e.g., no collateral required and few or no covenants). Also, if ABC decides to not offer, say, commercial real estate loans because of rising economic risks, then existing customers might decide to take their business elsewhere. Thus, "off-balance sheet risk management" can be a cheaper and more flexible way to control credit risk that does not disrupt the bank's existing customer relationships. This can be a "win-win" situation where the bank controls its credit exposure while also satisfying what the customers want even when facing a very competitive banking market.

We use the term, "off-balance sheet" as a shorthand way to refer to any derivative securities that might be used to control the bank's credit risk. Typically, these derivative securities have been accounted for off the balance sheet in various footnotes. However, accounting changes over time now require some estimates of the market values of these derivative securities which are included on the balance sheet. However, the "off-balance sheet" term is still used to refer to these securities.

In Chapters 4 and 5 related to interest rate and market risks, we showed how derivatives such as forwards, futures, options, and swaps can be used to manage these risks. In the case of credit risk, the primary off-balance sheet tool is the credit default swap (CDS). A CDS is essentially a credit insurance product where a bank can pay an upfront fee as well as annual premiums to another FI to insure against a default by the bank's borrower(s). The annual premiums on a CDS function in a manner like property-casualty insurance. The riskier the underlying entity, the higher the CDS premium (e.g., if you get a speeding ticket, your car insurance can cost more). During the 2023 banking crisis, five-year CDS premiums on Credit Suisse jumped before it was acquired by UBS, to over 10% of face value after previously trading around 4%.[19] So, for our example bank, ABC, it could choose to purchase a CDS on a pool of auto loans if it is concerned about its exposure to auto loans.[20]

---

[19] See https://www.ft.com/content/6cef2f2d-5f92-4cc3-8522-41976da75a50.

[20] You might be wondering why a bank would pay such a high CDS premium to protect against another firm's default because this additional cost will negatively affect the net return on this bond and ultimately make it an unprofitable investment. However, if the credit risk exposure is very large, it still might make sense for the bank to pay a very high CDS premium to avoid major credit losses which, in turn, could cause a run on the bank. Thus, the bank's high credit insurance costs might still be worthwhile if it enables the bank to avoid a potentially disastrous bank run.

Or, if ABC is concerned about its investment in a specific company's bonds, then ABC can purchase a CDS to protect against these bonds defaulting. In the event of default, the *seller* of the CDS (usually an investment bank or securities firm) must pay the CDS owner (i.e., ABC in this case) to cover any decline in the bond's value. This CDS payment offsets the loss on the bond due to the default and thus protects ABC from any credit losses associated with its original bond investment. CDS contracts can also be purchased for general credit indexes to protect against market-wide declines in credit conditions rather than specific borrowers. In the following section, we discuss the impact of hedging a bank's credit risk but do not delve into the details of CDS pricing and other credit-related derivatives. See Hull (2010) and Chambers *et al.* (2023) for more details on these instruments.

6.11 The Impact of Managing Credit Risk on a Financial Institution's Equity

6.11.1 *How hedging market risk can affect the distribution of returns*

Our earlier discussion in this chapter focused on various ways to model the distribution of a bank's portfolio returns using CVaR and other methods. For example, the Credit RiskMetrics CVaR approach typically assumes returns are normally distributed and thus the standard deviations and correlations for the portfolio's assets have a direct impact on the ultimate shape of the return distribution. As we had discussed in Chapter 5 regarding market risk, another point to consider is how hedging some portion of the bank's credit risk can affect the overall distribution of returns. In theory, if an "ideal" or "perfect" hedging instrument could be found, then a bank's entire credit risk could be eliminated and thus the credit portfolio's return distribution becomes a single vertical line with no dispersion around its expected value! In this case, the FIs credit portfolio would not be taking any credit risk and therefore it would be expected to earn only the risk-free rate, which is not very attractive to equity investors.

As we show in the following, it is usually *not* optimal to hedge 100% of a bank's credit risk due to not only the explicit costs of implementing and maintaining such a hedge but also the indirect costs in terms of managerial focus and the *opportunity cost* of investing this time and money for other more productive uses (e.g., launching a new product or entering a new geographic region).

One can analyze the impact of hedging on a credit portfolio (or a specific bond or loan in the portfolio) by seeing how the portfolio's distribution is altered with a hedge in place. Since we have already discussed hedging's impact on portfolio distributions in the prior chapter on market risk, we refer the interested reader to review that section of Chapter 5. In addition, to estimate the impact of hedging on a credit portfolio, we need to make some assumptions about the distribution of annual returns and its dispersion around the mean value of these credit investments. For clarity and simplicity, we can assume the credit portfolio's returns are normally distributed and that the hedging instrument can perfectly hedge the bank's credit risk. In effect, we can think of this hedging instrument (e.g., a credit default swap) as converting the portion of the portfolio that is hedged, h, into a zero-risk cash position with no return variability and no correlation with the other assets in the portfolio. In the following set of numerical examples, we first estimate the CVaR for a specific bond investment and then present a CvaR estimate for ABC's entire credit risk exposure to its portfolio of loans and investments.

As noted in Chapter 5, this assumption of converting a portion of the portfolio to cash is a strong one but, in practice, it is feasible if we were to sell off a percentage of the credit portfolio equal to h and put the proceeds into a cash account earning little or no interest. Economically, a **perfect hedge** of h-percentage of the portfolio is equivalent to converting that portion of the bank's investments into an interest-free (and risk-free) cash account.[21] This approach allows us to simplify the calculation of the impact of hedging on a credit investment portfolio's credit risk, as measured by the portfolio's standard deviation and VaR, as described in the following. Like the logic presented in Chapter 5, these assumptions lead to the following relationship for quantifying the impact of hedging on the credit portfolio's standard deviation (σ'_p):

---

[21] Note that if we cannot find a perfect hedge, then there will be what is called "basis risk." In this case, the imperfect hedge will mean that not all the risk for the percentage of the investment hedged, h, will be eliminated. Thus, as discussed in Chapters 4 and 5, the risk of this hedged portion of the portfolio will possess a positive standard deviation and some additional "residual" correlation with the unhedged portion of the portfolio.

$$\text{Hedged } \sigma'_P = \sqrt{(1-h)^2 \cdot \sigma'^2_{UH}} = (1-h) \cdot \sigma_{UH} \quad (6.16)$$

Equation (6.16) is therefore a useful way to directly quantify the impact of the bank's hedging choice (h) on the credit portfolio's risk because Hedged σ_P will vary as the $(1-h)^2$ term changes and the unhedged portfolio variance (σ_{UH}^2) is, by construction, independent of the bank's hedge ratio, h.

Now that we have a convenient way to quantify the impact of hedging on a portfolio's risk, we can use the Credit RiskMetrics method to translate these hedging decisions into effects on the bank's market value. To do this, we can first estimate the CVaR for the credit portfolio using the model's variables from Table 6.6 and Equation (6.16):

$$\text{CVaR} = 2.33 \cdot \text{Hedged } \sigma_P \cdot \$\text{Invested} = 2.33 \cdot [(1-h) \cdot \sigma_{UH}] \cdot \$\text{Invested} \quad (6.17)$$

Like the discussion in Chapter 5, when $h = 1$, Equation (6.17) indicates that CVaR will be zero because hedging 100% with a perfect credit hedge will, by our definition, eliminate all credit risk from the portfolio. However, there are clearly costs associated with placing a hedge in terms of **explicit, direct hedging costs**, such as those associated with bid-ask spreads, commissions, computer equipment, data services, and risk management personnel expenses. In addition, **implicit, indirect hedging costs** can play an important role such as time spent by senior management supervising the risk managers and the opportunity cost of using the direct hedging costs for other potentially more valuable purposes within the bank.

We can approach this problem by identifying the total benefits and total costs of hedging the bank's credit risk. As in Chapters 4–5, we can see the change in the bank's market value of equity due to the hedging decision by comparing the value of the bank with hedging ($V_{E,\text{Hedged}}$) versus its value without hedging ($V_{E,\text{Unhedged}}$) as follows:

$\Delta V_E = V_{E,\text{Hedged}} - V_{E,\text{Unhedged}} = $ Total Benefit of Hedge – Total Cost of Hedge

$\Delta V_E = $ \$Reduction in CVaR – (fixed hedging cost + variable hedging cost)

$\Delta V_E = [2.33 \cdot (\sigma_{UH} - \text{Hedged } \sigma_P) \cdot \text{Invested Assets}] - [C + ((v \cdot h) \cdot (h \cdot \text{Invested Assets}))]$

254 *Managing Financial Institutions: An Integrated Valuation Approach*

$$= [2.33 \cdot (h \cdot \sigma_{UH}) \cdot \text{Invested Assets}] - [C + ((v \cdot h^2) \cdot \text{Invested Assets})]$$

$$= [2.33 \cdot (h \cdot \sigma_{UH}) \cdot \text{Invested Assets}] - [c + ((v \cdot h^2) \cdot \text{Invested Assets})] \quad (6.18)$$

where

ΔV_E = change in the bank's market value due to hedging a portion of Invested Assets (i.e., the total amount invested in credit-sensitive assets such as bonds and loans) = $V_{E,\text{Hedged}} - V_{E,\text{Unhedged}}$,

h = hedge ratio = Dollar Amount Hedged / Invested Assets = $Hedged / Invested Assets,

C = fixed cost of hedging (upfront, in dollars), and can also be defined as $C = (c \cdot$ Invested Assets), where c = fixed costs are expressed as a percentage of Invested Assets,

v = variable cost of hedging as a percentage of $Hedged, where $Hedged = ($h \cdot$ Invested Assets),

σ_{UH} = unhedged portfolio's standard deviation,

Hedged $\sigma_p = (1 - h) \cdot \sigma_{UH}$ = hedged portfolio's standard deviation,

Critical Value = 2.33 (based on the normal distribution assumption), and

$Reduction in CVaR = $value of extreme volatility that is reduced by hedging = $2.33 \cdot (\sigma_{UH} -$ **Hedged** $\sigma_p) \cdot$ Invested Assets, which simplifies to: $2.33 \cdot [h \cdot \sigma_{UH}] \cdot$ Invested Assets.

The first term in square brackets of Equation (6.18) identifies the total benefits of hedging all or a portion (h) of the bank's credit risk while the second term in square brackets shows the total costs of this hedge when a worst-case 1% tail event ($2.33 \cdot \sigma_p$) occurs. We define these hedging benefits as the dollar amount of losses *avoided* due to hedging a portion of the potential credit shock to the portfolio. Using the notation from above, we show that this "Total Benefit of Hedge" equals $2.33 \cdot (h \cdot \sigma_{UH}) \cdot$ Invested Assets. So, as the hedge ratio (h) rises, this benefit also increases. However, the second term in (6.18) illustrates the exponentially rising "Total Cost of Hedge" due to its variable cost component: $((v \cdot h^2) \cdot$ Invested Assets. Like prior chapters, there is a classic trade-off between the costs and benefits of hedging.

Based on the above discussion of CVaR and Equation (6.18), we can see how this credit risk management decision can impact the bank's equity value using the principles of the IVM by varying the hedge ratio, h, between 0 (no hedging) and 1.0 (hedging the entire risk exposure). Like we did in Chapters 4 and 5, we can use the Integrated Valuation Model shown in Equation (6.18) to estimate the change in the bank's market value because we are making some simplifying assumptions such as (1) the hedge ratio's impact is focused on the change in Dividends, (2) the hedging costs rise exponentially with the hedge ratio due to liquidity constraints, and (3) the Expected Dividend Yield ($R_E - g$) remains constant even though the cash flow in the numerator of the IVM is changing.[22]

We can use the above variant of the IVM described by Equation (6.18) in a numerical example for our hypothetical bank, ABC, based on the initial data and assumptions presented in Table 6.6 for a $100 million 3-year A-rated corporate bond with a YTM of 4.00% and a 3.00% financing cost.

As before, we can assume that ABC has an A-rated bond with a face value of $100 million and a current market value of $102.775 million. It also has an expected annual net income and standard deviation of $1.0 million and $1.9059 million, respectively. As shown earlier in this chapter, the Credit RiskMetrics method predicts that this bond has a 1% chance of losing $4.44 million or more during the next year due to an extreme credit downgrade (i.e., from an A to a B rating). Therefore, ABC is vulnerable to *increases* in volatility that might emanate from weakening credit market conditions. ABC's bank managers must decide whether the credit risk exposure on this corporate bond has a material effect and then choose the "optimal hedge ratio" that maximizes the bank's stock price. For simplicity, we do not consider a specific financial derivative instrument to hedge this risk, although a CDS contract on this specific corporate borrower would be the most likely choice in this situation. We can find the answer to this important risk management decision by varying the absolute value of the hedge ratio from 0.0 (i.e., no hedging at all) to 1.0 (fully hedging 100% of the investment portfolio).

---

[22] As noted in previous chapters, this assumption can be a *conservative* estimate of the estimated change in market value (i.e., *lower* than what might occur) because hedging could, in theory, lower the bank's cost of equity (R_E) which would, in turn, raise the bank's valuation. So, assuming no change in $R_E - g$ might be a reasonably safe approach in this context (and can be relaxed when we cap the bank's growth rate, g, at a fixed rate, such as 6%).

Table 6.9. Numerical Example of Hedging Credit Risk for a Corporate Bond Using CVaR.

Invested Assets – $100 mil. Face Value	100.000
Market value of $100 mil. 3-year Bond	102.775
Expected Annual Bond Income ($ million)	1.0000
Unhedged Standard Deviation ($ million)	1.9059
Hedge Fixed Cost, % of Investment (c)	0.973%
Hedge Variable Cost, % of Investment (v)	5.0%
Dividend Payout	0.40
Tax Rate	0.20
Dividend Yield ($R_E - g$)	0.0357
Shares Outstanding (million)	10.00

To build some intuition about what is driving the impact of hedging on ABC's market value of equity, we first show in Figure 6.4 the results of a "what-if" simulation that quantifies the Total Costs and Benefits of hedging the bank's credit risk. The graph shows the benefits of hedging rising linearly based on the first component shown earlier in square brackets for Equation (6.18) while hedging-related costs are rising exponentially. Based on the data in Table 6.9, there is *no* level of hedging (e.g., 0.0 through 1.0), where the marginal benefits of hedging outweigh the marginal costs of hedging. This is driven by the relatively high upfront fixed costs (C) of $1.0 million (0.973% of the bond's value) and the large variable cost (v) of hedging that represents another 5% of the bond's market value. These fixed and variable costs create a cost–benefit imbalance at *all* levels of hedging, although the imbalance nearly disappears around hedge ratios between 40% and 50%. In contrast to Chapters 4 and 5, this cost–benefit analysis leads to an optimal hedge ratio, h^*, of *zero* for this $100 million bond because the benefits never outweigh the hedge-related costs. In this case, the optimal decision is *not* to "micro hedge" this bond at all.[23]

---

[23] A "micro hedge" means that the firm is hedging a specific sub-component of the credit portfolio (in this case, a $100 million corporate bond). As we discuss later in this chapter, a "macro hedge" is a way to manage the credit risk of an entire portfolio of loans and/or bonds.

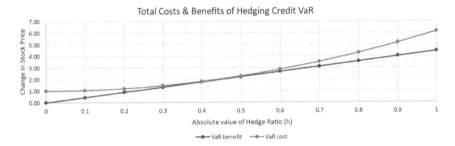

Figure 6.4. The Costs and Benefits of "Micro Hedging" a Bank's Credit Risk.

Based on the above cost–benefit analysis, we can use the IVM relationship shown in Equation (6.18) to identify how different levels of h affect the bank's market value of equity. Figure 6.5 displays the results of this type of what-if simulation on the expected *change* in ABC's stock price.

As we can see from Figure 6.5, ABC's stock price *decreases* at *all* levels of h, although the smallest drop occurs when h ranges between 40% and 50%. For example, the stock price falls less than 1 penny per share in this range (i.e., $h = 0.4$ to 0.5). However, these hedge ratios still represent a price decline and so ABC can maximize its market value by simply *doing nothing* to hedge this bond's credit risk![24] The high fixed costs of this hedge simply outweigh the relatively low benefits and so ABC's stock price is maximized by *not* engaging in any credit risk hedging at this time.[25] This is an important point to keep in mind: managers *always* have

---

[24] Note that if ABC does not engage in a credit risk management program at all, then it saves the $1 million fixed cost, as well as any variable costs, and so the change in stock price is zero. In contrast, Figure 6.5 shows a stock price decline of $0.10 per share when $h = 0$, but this estimate assumes that ABC *does* decide to engage in a credit risk management program and thus must pay the $1 million fixed cost even though it does *not* do any hedging. So, the optimal thing to do in this case is to avoid incurring this $1 million fixed cost and simply "do nothing" in terms of credit risk management.

[25] On the other hand, if the total hedging benefits were larger than the fixed costs, then we can use the relationship described in Chapter 5 to find the optimal ratio for hedging the bank's CVaR. This can be obtained by taking the mathematical derivative of Equation (6.18) with respect to the hedge ratio, h, and setting this derivative equal to zero. Based on the model presented in Equation (6.18), the resulting **optimal hedge ratio**, h^*, is $h^* = -1 \cdot (2.33 \cdot \sigma_{UH}) / (2 \cdot v)$, when the benefits of hedging outweigh the fixed costs of the risk management program. In addition, the denominator of the optimal hedge ratio can be expanded to include other costs related to the hedging activity, such as collateral/margin requirements,

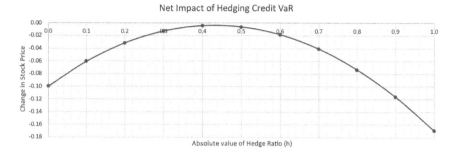

Figure 6.5. The Net Effect of "Micro Hedging" Credit Risk on the Bank's Equity.

the choice to pursue a "Do Nothing" **strategy** in terms of hedging, especially when hedging costs are very high and the underlying position's volatility is very low. In this case, the cost of hedging can often outweigh the benefits of hedging and so $h^* = 0$ is the optimal strategy. As you might recall, this was one of the outcomes we saw in Chapter 4 when we increased the fixed costs of hedging interest rate risk. That is, the first step is always to make sure that the potential hedging benefits are above the fixed costs of implementing a risk management program.

Like we had discussed in Chapters 4–5, another useful metric that can be derived from our optimal hedge ratio is the **optimal, or** "Target CVaR*" for this specific corporate bond investment. By maintaining this target CVaR*, ABC's managers can maximize the bank's stock value. This CVaR* estimate can be found by using the absolute value of the optimal hedge ratio, $|h^*|$, in the following relationship:

$$\text{CVaR}^* = (1 - |h^*|) \cdot \text{unhedged CVaR} \qquad (6.19)$$

In our numerical example, ABC's target CVaR* is $4.441 million based on $h^* = 0.0$ and thus it also equals the unhedged CVaR of $4.441 million in this situation (i.e., $(1 - 0.0) \cdot (\$4.441 \text{ million}) = \$4.441$ million). This

---

additional administrative expenses, and opportunity costs, as follows: $h^* = -1 \cdot (2.33 \cdot \sigma_{UH}) / (2 \cdot (v + \text{other costs})$. Further, additional factors can also affect the numerator of this optimal hedge ratio formula. One common example is a "capital charge" that the bank might apply to its VaR exposure to account for any additional capital that the bank needs to support this level of market risk (expressed as a percentage of the VaR exposure). In this case, the optimal hedge formula can be expanded further as $h^* = -1 \cdot (2.33 \cdot \sigma_{UH} \cdot \textbf{capital charge}) / (2 \cdot (v + \textbf{other costs}))$.

figure is helpful to ABC's risk managers because they can use it as a benchmark to compare with the bank's actual CVaR observed over the course of the year.

We should also remind ourselves of Chapter 3's discussion of the IVM's relevance in identifying how market value could be impacted *directionally* by changes in the bank's risk-taking activities. Recall that in Chapter 3 we examine the impact of credit risk on the bank's market value without hedging. In that chapter, we analyzed how changes in the percentage of assets invested in loans (C) could affect the firm's equity by altering the interest rates associated with ABC's loans and deposits. In that chapter, variations in C led to changes in Net Interest Income that ultimately affected firm value in a positive manner. That analysis showed ABC's credit portfolio was within the optimal range of 50% of 70% of assets and thus, from a directional standpoint, the bank did *not* need to change its credit exposure.

Like what we saw in previous chapters, we should not take the exact values plotted in Figure 6.5 too literally. A better way to interpret this graph is that ABC's stock price change is likely to be slightly negative when hedging around 40%–50% of the bond's credit risk exposure. It is within this range that we see the smallest decrease in ABC's stock price. However, this does *not* mean we should expect the price to move down by exactly this amount. Rather, the analysis can be viewed as telling ABC's management that hedging this bond's credit risk is probably *not* value-maximizing. We should also remember that our results will be affected by our assumptions about hedging-related costs and thus the analyst should perform some sensitivity analysis on these key inputs to the model.

Given that we have considered above how ABC's market value is affected by the CVaR for a *specific* $100 million bond, we can now analyze the CVaR of the bank's *entire* portfolio of loans and investments. Table 6.10 presents the relevant data.

Like the formulas and methods described above for the CVaR of a specific bond, we can use the Credit RiskMetrics approach to develop an annual estimate of tail risk associated with ABC's *total* credit portfolio of $1,530 million (or $1.53 billion). One wrinkle we need to consider in a portfolio context is the degree of correlation between the returns on the bank's lending and securities portfolios. For simplicity, we assume that these investments are perfectly and positively correlated (i.e., +100%). The Integrated Valuation Model spreadsheet provided in this book enables us to relax this assumption, but the main insights will remain the same even though we are using +100% correlation in the current example.

Table 6.10. Numerical Example of Hedging ABC's Total Portfolio Exposure to Credit Risk.

Securities Portfolio ($ million)	700.0
Gross Loan Portfolio ($ million)	830.0
Total Credit Portfolio ($ million)	1,530.0
Unhedged Securities Portfolio Std. Dev. (ann.)	3.50%
Unhedged Loan Portfolio Std. Dev. (ann.)	3.50%
Correlation between Securities & Loans	100%
Annual std. dev. of Total Credit Portfolio	3.50%
Integrated Valuation effects for CVaR hedging	
Unhedged Portfolio Std. Dev. ($ million)	53.6
Extreme Shock Assumption (S.D.)	2.33
Hedged Portfolio Std. Dev. ($)	24.437
Hedge Fixed Cost as % of Invested Assets (c)	0.973%
Hedge Variable Cost as % of Invested Assets (v)	7.50%
Dividend Payout	0.40
Tax Rate	0.20
Div. Yield ($R_E - g$)	0.0357
Sh. Outstanding	10.00

Applying the Credit RiskMetrics method to the data in Table 6.10 yields the following results for a "macro hedge" of ABC's total credit portfolio:

Unhedged CVaR ($ mil.)	124.772
Optimal hedge ratio (h^*)	−0.5437
Target CVaR* ($ mil.)	56.937
Stock Price ($ / share)	$22.07
% Change in Stock Price	9.4%

We can also see these "macro hedge" results in graphical form via Figure 6.6.

Figure 6.6 shows that ABC's stock price is maximized when senior management decides to hedge around 54% of ABC's credit risk exposure. As the numbers above Figure 6.6 suggest, such a hedge ratio reduces CVaR from $124.772 million to a target level of $56.937 million. By hedging some of this credit risk, ABC's stock price can rise to $22.07,

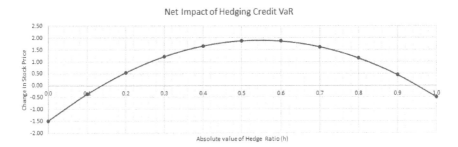

Figure 6.6. The Net Effect of "Macro Hedging" Credit Risk on the Bank's Equity.

which represents a +9.4% change versus the base price of $20.17. Clearly, this finding rests critically on the bank's estimates of the fixed and variable costs of hedging this credit risk. In addition, this analysis should include in these costs any potential liquidity constraints related to hedging nearly $832 million of loans and bonds in the credit derivatives market (or via some other risk management techniques).[26]

Overall, when considering a specific $100 million corporate bond, there appears to be a negative, albeit small, net change in ABC's stock price due to a "micro hedge" of this bond's credit risk. As noted earlier, this occurs because the fixed costs and exponentially rising variable hedging costs limit the benefits of hedging this bond investment. In contrast, a more holistic view of the bank's entire credit portfolio of $1.53 billion illustrates a much different insight. In this case, a "macro hedge" of total portfolio could boost ABC's stock price by 9.4% (assuming there is sufficient liquidity in the credit derivatives market to obtain this level of credit protection). These examples provide very useful information because they suggest that a macro hedging approach might be more beneficial than micro hedging specific sub-components of ABC's credit exposure.

---

[26] This figure can be found by multiplying the absolute value of the optimal hedge ratio by the bank's total credit risk exposure (i.e., 0.5437 · $1,530 million = $831.861 million ≈ $832 million). The negative sign related to the hedge ratio shown above in the main text (−0.5437) indicates that the bank would, in effect, "sell short" that percentage of the credit portfolio by, for example, buying CDS protection. In this case, if ABC's credit portfolio weakens, any defaults on these loans and bonds could be offset by payouts on the CDS derivatives purchased from the bank's CDS counterparties.

6.12 Managerial Implications

The main credit risk problem Sam and Nina must consider is as follows: **how much credit risk is acceptable for ABC Bank based on its current investment in loans and fixed income securities?** Once again, this answer is driven by the bank's risk appetite, as well as senior management's and investors' risk tolerance levels. Nina and Sam must also carefully estimate the fixed and variable costs of hedging this credit risk relative to the associated benefits. This requires an analysis of the liquidity of the relevant credit derivatives markets to ensure any recommended hedges can realistically be put in place. The opportunity cost of using these hedging-related resources for other, more valuable business initiatives must also be considered. Sam and Nina have already examined both the micro hedge of a $100 million corporate bond as well as a macro hedge of ABC's entire $1.53 billion credit portfolio. **Based on this analysis, they feel that the macro hedge can be more value-enhancing than a micro hedge, as shown in Figures 6.5 and 6.6.**

However, **are the benefits of either type of hedge large enough to justify the extra time, money, and effort required to set up a credit risk management program?** These hedging costs, along with possible liquidity constraints noted above, can be quite significant in terms of additional personnel, financial/accounting software, data services, etc. Nina and Sam must also consider current macroeconomic conditions as well as what ABC's major competitors might be doing in terms of credit risk management. For example, if Sam and Nina think the economy is going to weaken, then buying credit risk protection can be worthwhile, especially if competitors decide to remain unhedged to this risk. However, if Nina and Sam are wrong and the economy remains strong, then they will incur unnecessary extra hedging costs and are likely to lag ABC's competitors in terms of ROA, ROE, and stock performance. In terms of the "ART" of risk management, their approach is to Transfer some credit risk rather than Accept all this risk. **Do you agree with Sam and Nina's recommendation? If not, then how would you handle it differently and what are your reasons for doing so?**

6.13 Summary

This chapter showed the importance of credit risk management and how the Term Structure, KMV/Merton Option Pricing, and Credit Value at Risk

(CVaR) methods can be used to calculate this risk. In addition, the key drivers of loan pricing and other statistical models of credit risk like Altman's Z-score were introduced because there is no single, commonly accepted way to quantify a bank's credit exposure. The classic 5 Cs of credit analysis highlighted the importance of "soft information" that can complement one's quantitative analysis. To help gauge whether a specific loan or bond is worth investing in, we discussed the RAROC measure to explicitly relate an investment's return to its credit risk. This can present a clear-cut decision rule where loans and bonds can be accepted into the portfolio whenever their RAROC values are at or above the bank's required return target (which is usually some pre-determined ROE benchmark). After quantifying the bank's level of credit risk, the next important step is to decide how to best manage this risk. To do so, both on-balance sheet management tools like concentration limits and loan covenants as well as off-balance sheet tools like credit default swaps (CDS) can be used. Lastly, we developed explicit models of the costs and benefits for both "micro" and "macro" hedges of credit risk. We then showed via two numerical examples the impact of these hedges on a bank's market value of equity.

A6.1 Appendix — Foundations of the Merton/KMV Model of Commercial Credit Risk

This section builds on the earlier (brief) discussion of the Merton/KMV credit risk model and the results shown in Table 6.3. To gain more insight into how option pricing techniques and equity market data can provide insight into a firm's credit risk, we can briefly summarize the logic of Merton's (1974) model.

First, we know that the basic capital structure of a firm is based on the accounting identity of assets (A_t) equal debt (D_t) plus equity (E_t):

$$A_t = D_t + E_t$$

Next, we can assume default happens at the maturity of debt if the asset's value falls below the face value of the debt. We define debt as a face value of K so that the firm's equity (E_T) at the bond's maturity at time-T equals:

$$E_T = \max[A_T - K, 0]$$

And the payoff (D_T) to bondholders at maturity (time T) is

$$D_T = K - \max[K - A_T, 0]$$

In this set-up, the firm's equity payoff looks and behaves like the payoff of a European "call" option, which Black and Scholes (1973) showed how to calculate (also called the "Black–Scholes" model).[27]

The bondholders get the face value of the debt *unless* the face value is *less than* the value of the assets. Merton (1974) showed that this process of possible default is like a "put" option where the borrower has the right but not the obligation to default on the bond. The put price (P_t) from the Black–Scholes option pricing model is

$$P_t = Ke^{-r\tau} * N\left(-d + \sigma_A \sqrt{\tau}\right) - A_t * N(-d)$$

Merton's model showed that, in this case, the **credit spread** (S_t) is priced as

$$S_t = -\frac{1}{\tau} * \ln\left[N\left(d - \sigma_A \sqrt{\tau}\right) + \frac{A_t}{K} e^{r\tau} * N(-d)\right] \qquad (A6.1)$$

where

$N(d)$ = the probability for the value of d based on the normal probability distribution,

$$d = \frac{\ln\left(\frac{AT}{K}\right) + \left(r + 0.5\sigma_A^2\right) * \tau}{\sigma_A \sqrt{\tau}}$$

r = the risk-free rate for a T-year government bond,

τ = the bond's maturity (in years, and equals T in our discussion), and

σ_A^2 = variance of the return on the borrower's assets (and measures the riskiness of the borrower's assets).

Although the above model in Equation (A6.1) looks technically daunting, the good news is that all these components can be programmed into a spreadsheet like Excel™. The analyst can then just enter the key

---

[27] The details of option pricing go well beyond the scope of our book. Consult Hull (2010) or other finance textbooks that focus on derivatives securities and their pricing.

inputs, as shown earlier in Table 6.3, to obtain the estimated credit spread for a bond or loan. In addition, one other important outcome of the model is that we can easily find the borrower's probability of default (PD) via the following relationship:

$$PD_{0,T} = \Pr[A_t \leq K] = 1 - N(d) \qquad (A6.2)$$

Equation (A6.2) indicates that the PD for a T-year bond is equal to 1 minus the probability of repayment which, in this model, is based on the normal probability of the borrower's value for d (as defined earlier). We can see that (A6.2) is very similar in format to our earlier discussion of the Term Structure method. However, in this case, we are using stock market data rather than bond market data to estimate the PD.

A6.1.1 Some limitations of the Merton model

Although the Merton model provides useful insights about a borrower's credit risk based on forward-looking data, it can be difficult to implement in practice because

- debt has varying types of coupons (rather than assuming one common coupon for all debt),
- interest rates are random and can vary over the specific time horizon (T), and
- parameters for the market value of assets (A_t) and the asset return volatility (σ_A^2) are not easily observable.

A6.1.2 Strengths of the Merton model

Despite its limitations, the Merton model can be beneficial in several ways because it

- is an objective, market-based, and forward-looking estimate of credit risk,
- is a useful complement to other market-based methods such as the Term Structure approach, and
- provides insights into the key drivers of PD such as the bonds or loans:

Sensitivity to *Maturity (T)*
- Probability of default increases as time to maturity increases.
- Increasing at a decreasing rate as maturity increases.

Sensitivity to *Asset Volatility (σA)*
- Probability of default and credit spread increase as volatility of the asset increases.

Sensitivity to *Financial Leverage (d)*
- Probability of default and credit spread increase as leverage increases.

Sensitivity to the *Risk-Free Rate (r)*
- Dependent on how the rate of return on the asset is assumed to react to changes in the risk-free rate.

A6.1.3 *KMV model*

Given some of the limitations noted above, KMV extended Merton's model to estimate the volatility and total value of the firm's underlying assets by relying on information directly from the stock market and the riskiness of the firm's equity (E_t). Since we cannot easily and directly estimate the market value and riskiness of the firm's total assets (A_t or σ_A), we instead back them out of the model based on what we know about the borrower's credit spread and market value of the debt. The model cleverly exploits the relation between the riskiness of the market values of equity (E_t) and total assets (A_t):

$$\sigma_E = \frac{A_t}{E_t} \Delta \sigma_A \quad (A6.3)$$

where Δ is the change (or "delta") in the equity with respect to changes in the market value of the firm's assets. Under the Merton model, this is equal to the normal distribution's repayment probability, $N(d)$. The KMV model solves Equation (A6.3) simultaneously to back out the estimate of the riskiness of the firm's assets (σ_A) by using the following relationship:

$$E_t = A_t * N(d) - K * e^{-r\tau} * N\left(d - \sigma_A \sqrt{\tau}\right)$$

One of the main outputs of the model is an estimate of the borrower's "Distance to Default" (DD). This represents the percentage difference between a firm's assets and its default "trigger" relative to the volatility of its assets, as defined in the following:

$$DD_t = \frac{A_t - K}{A_t \cdot \sigma_A} \qquad (A6.4)$$

where K is the default trigger of the firm. In the KMV model, this is the weighted average of future values of the borrower's short- and long-term debt.[28]

A6.1.4 Numerical example of measuring the distance to default (DD)

Let us assume the following:

- Firm assets = $1,000
- $K = \$900$
- Let us also assume that the firm's assets must decline 10% to trigger default.
- In this case, (A6.4) would indicate the following relationship: $DD = \frac{(1000-900)}{1000\sigma_A} = \frac{0.1}{\sigma_A}$
- The **DD** is the *number of standard deviations* that the assets must *decline* in value to reach the default trigger, K.

Thus, if $\sigma_A = 0.04$, then, according to (A6.4) and the above assumptions, **DD = 2.5 standard deviations** (i.e., 0.10 / 0.04 = 2.5).

Another important output of the KMV model is the "Expected Default Frequency" (EDF). EDF measures the probability that loans that possess certain characteristics could default. For example, we can use our estimate of DD to ask the following: what is the *probability* that the value of a firm's assets could drop by N standard deviations over the next T-periods? So, if we have a large historical database of firm defaults and loan repayments, as well as a market-based estimate of the firm's DD for T-period debt, we can ask the following:

---

[28] In the Merton model, this default trigger is the future value of total debt.

- What percentage of firms in the database defaulted within one year when their asset values placed them N-standard deviations away from default?
- How does that figure compare to the total population of firms that were N-standard deviations from default?

Numerical Example of Expected Default Frequency (EDF): Suppose there are 5,000 firms with DD = 2.5 at the beginning of the year. Of these 5,000 firms, let's assume 40 defaulted by the end of the year. What is the expected default frequency (EDF)?

$$\text{EDF} = \frac{40 \text{ defaults}}{5000 \text{ borrowers}} = \mathbf{0.8\%} \text{ (for firms with DD} = 2.5)$$

We realize that the above discussion of the Merton / KMV approach can be somewhat technical in detail and requires some familiarity with statistics and probability distributions.

Overall, the Merton/KMV credit model provides an important alternative way to examine complex commercial credit decisions that can be a useful complement to Altman's Z-score statistical models and the bond market-based Term Structure approach.

Chapter-End Questions

Answers to odd-numbered questions can be found at the end of this book.

1. **True or False:** A bank's credit risk is not affected by the mix of investments and loans it grants to its customers.
2. **True or False:** Hedging 100% of a bank's credit risk is usually optimal.
3. **Multiple Choice:** What is the most qualitative aspect of the "5 C's of Credit" and represents the lender's overall assessment of the borrower's trustworthiness and willingness to repay the loan?
   (A) Capacity
   (B) Capital
   (C) Collateral
   (D) Character

4. **Multiple Choice:** What is the effect of higher levels of PD and/or LGD on the loan rate?

    (A) They decrease the loan rate
    (B) They increase the loan rate
    (C) They have no effect on the loan rate
    (D) They make the loan rate negative

5. **Multiple Choice:** What is one way that banks can effectively reduce the impact of adverse selection on loan pricing?

    (A) By increasing the loan rate
    (B) By granting loans to all borrowers regardless of their creditworthiness
    (C) By using screening to restrict loans to only high-quality borrowers
    (D) By ignoring the borrower's credit score

6. **Short Answer:** What is the impact of the moral hazard problem on PD and LGD?

7. **Short Answer:** If 1-year spot rate for a risk-free government security ($RF_{0,1}$) is 2.00% and a corporate bond ($RC_{0,1}$) is 3.00%, then what is the probability of repayment in the *first year* by the corporate borrower (p_1)? Also, what is the probability of default in the first year (PD_1)?

8. **Short Answer:** Use the following information to calculate the various RAROC measures for a $200 million, 5-year 6% coupon corporate bond with a YTM of 5%.

    (A) What is the bond's RAROC if its 1% CVaR is $8.88 million and the relevant risk-free rate is 4%?
    (B) If the bank's target ROE is 20%, should the bank invest in the bond from part A?
    (C) Re-calculate the RAROC from part A if the CVaR for the bond is as high as $17.76 million.
    (D) If the bank's target ROE is still 20%, should the bank invest in the bond from part C?

9. **Excel-based Question:** As measured by its Credit RiskMetrics' Value-at-Risk (CVaR), how much market risk exposure on its $1,530 million total credit portfolio (which includes total loans and securities) should ABC hedge (h^*) to maximize its stock price? Assume the bank's managers are concerned about an

increase in credit risk due to weakening macroeconomic conditions. To do so, change the estimated annual **standard deviations** for *both* the **"Unhedged Security Portfolio"** and **"Unhedged Loan Portfolio" to 5.00%** from the base scenario of 3.5%, as shown in the "Credit Risk – Ch 6" tab of the **Integrated Valuation Model.xlsx** file. Try this by starting with the "base" scenario where the variable costs (v) are 7.5% of the hedged exposure and then changing the values in the blue cells related to the *Unhedged Sec. Port. std. dev.* and the *Unhedged Loan Port. std. dev.* from 3.50% to 5.00%:

(A) What is the optimal hedge ratio (h^*) for the above credit shock and how does it compare to the base scenario's h^*?

(B) Related to your answer in part A, what is the expected percentage change in ABC's stock price if management implemented this optimal hedge ratio?

(C) What is the "target" CVaR* based on Equation (6.19) and your answer to part A of this question?

(D) How do your answers to parts A–C change if the bank's credit risk does *not* rise (i.e., the standard deviations remain at 3.5% rather than 5.0%) but the *fixed cost* of hedging increases from 0.973% of the total credit portfolio's value to 3.0% (i.e., from $14.9 million to $45.9 million)? Briefly explain the results you observe from this sensitivity analysis.

10. **Comprehensive Question:** Briefly explain what are the key factors that Sam and Nina must consider when deciding how **much credit risk is acceptable for ABC Bank**. Also, what are the potential implications of a "micro hedge" or a "macro hedge" on the bank's stock performance?

References

Altman, E. (1968). Financial ratios, discriminant analysis and the prediction of corporate bankruptcy, *Journal of Finance*, 23, 589–609.

Altman, E. (1985). Managing the commercial lending process, in *Handbook of Banking Strategy*, (ed.), R.C. Aspinwall and R.A. Eisenbeis (Wiley, New York), pp. 473–510.

Altman, E. (1989). Default risk, mortality rates, and the performance of corporate bonds, *Journal of Finance*, 44, 909–912.

Berg, T., Fuster, A. and Puri, M. (2021). Fintech Lending, *NBER Working Paper*, No. 29421, http://www.nber.org/papers/w29421.

Black, F. and Scholes, M. (1973). The pricing of options and corporate liabilities, *Journal of Political Economy*, 81, 637–659.

Brick, I. E. and Palia, D. (2007). Evidence of jointness in the terms of relationship lending. *Journal of Financial Intermediation*, 16, 452–476.

Brotcke, L. (2022). Time to Assess Bias in Machine Learning Models for Credit Decisions, *Journal of Risk and Financial Management*, 15, 165–174. https://doi.org/10.3390/jrfm15040165.

Chambers, D.R., Anson, M.J.P., Black, K.H. and Kazemi, H.B. (2023). *CAIA Curriculum Level I Volume I*, John Wiley & Sons, Hoboken, NJ.

Diamond, D. (1984). Financial intermediation and delegated monitoring, *Review of Economic Studies*, 51, 393–514.

Hull, J.C. (2010). *Risk Management and Financial Institutions*, Prentice-Hall, Boston.

Merton, R.C. (1974). On the pricing of corporate debt: The risk structure of interest rates, *Journal of Finance*, 29, 449–470.

Saunders, A., Cornett, M.M. and Erhemjamts, O. (2024). *Financial Institutions Management: A Risk Management Approach*, McGraw-Hill, New York.

Chapter 7
Off-Balance Sheet (OBS) Risk

7.1 Introduction

A depository financial institution's primary economic function (Qualitative Asset Transformation) can create **off-balance sheet risk**. This risk (referred to here as "OBS risk" for short) pertains to the impact on the FIs performance when a bank's future obligations quickly turn into actual outflows to its customers or other counterparties. Recall from Chapter 1 that QAT refers to the usual process of obtaining financing via one type of financial instrument (e.g., a short-term bank deposit) and then "transforming" it by investing the proceeds in a different type of financial instrument (e.g., a long-term mortgage). In addition, the role of QAT in providing "liquidity insurance" also applies to helping bank customers manage the *frequency* and/or *severity* of future demands for cash, i.e., **contingent financing needs**.

For example, a corporate borrower might need some financing *in the future* if it plans to purchase some expensive equipment or open a new office or factory. In this case, obtaining a loan commitment from the bank today will ensure that the firm will have sufficient liquidity to make a large purchase/investment in the future. Beyond investment needs, a corporation may also want to use a line of credit as a way of managing its own liquidity risk and guard against unforeseen cash shortfalls. Similarly, a retail customer might be planning a vacation for later in the year and needs funds now to secure hotel and airline reservations. Thus, this customer can use a credit card (which is essentially a personal line of credit) to make these reservations even though they do not currently have the cash on hand.

The main types of **asset-based contingent financing** needs are as follows:

1. lines of credit,
2. loan commitments,
3. letters of credit,
4. loan guarantees, and
5. derivative securities transactions.

In addition, OBS risk exists if the bank engages in **asset securitization** activities like selling off some of its mortgages or other loans such as credit cards and/or auto loans. By combining many such loans of a similar type and riskiness into a common pool, the bank can sell off these assets as a new security which helps the FI manage its credit risk and frees up some of the bank's cash and equity capital for investment in new loans and investments.

Further, the FIs customers might want to buy and sell **derivative securities** from the bank. Thus, trading in instruments such as forward and futures contracts, as well as options and swaps, can also lead to **contingent assets** (CA) or **contingent liabilities** (CL). Lastly, *liability-based* OBS activities can lead to contingent liabilities. For example, the FI might sell corporate credit risk protection to some customers by "writing" **Credit Default Swap** (or **CDS** for short) contracts which can lead to large liabilities for the bank if the borrower that underlies the CDS defaults. Other examples of contingent liabilities are lawsuits and fines against the FI, as well as taking back onto the FIs balance sheet any assets that were previously securitized and sold with recourse.

In all the above instances, the FI faces OBS risk. In effect, the bank must be aware that these contingent assets and liabilities might "hop on" the balance sheet at any moment and, in many cases, it can occur at an inopportune time, thus causing additional stress on the FIs financial condition. That is, the provision of "liquidity insurance" on a contingency basis can expose the FI to credit risk, interest rate risk, market risk, and/or liquidity risk all at once. The bank must therefore charge sufficiently high fees to compensate for this OBS risk. In turn, the trade-off between the risk and return of OBS activities can affect the bank's profitability, stability, solvency, and market value of equity. So, both investors and regulators are interested in how well the FI can manage this OBS risk.

7.2 What Is OBS Risk?

7.2.1 *Asset-based contingent liquidity*

As noted above, a bank can provide contingent financing services to help insure borrowers against the frequency and severity of both expected and unexpected cash shortfalls. An FI helps in this way by offering contingent financing alternatives that, when exercised, lead to an *asset* being added to the bank's balance sheet.[1] Presented in the following is a brief description of the most common types of asset-based contingent financing.

Lines of credit: This is a common way for a bank to provide contingent liquidity to a borrower. In this case, the bank pre-approves a dollar amount limit based on how much the bank is willing to lend to a customer on an "on-demand" basis. Typically, these lines of credit are short-term extensions of credit that are reviewed and approved annually. In this way, the bank protects itself from having to commit funds to the borrower for a term longer than one year. In turn, the bank can charge a lower (and variable) rate of interest because the line will typically need to be repaid in full over the short term. Depending on the client's relationship with the bank, a small annual fee of 0.1–2.0% of the maximum limit of the line of credit might be charged to compensate the FI for having to hold in reserve enough liquidity to finance future drawdowns on the line (also referred to as "takedowns").

For example, a commercial line of credit is usually extended for one year and the total amount of borrowings must be fully repaid (or "cleaned up" in banking jargon) for at least one month during that period. These commercial lines of credit are very useful for firms with seasonal cash needs to help pay, for example, inventory, payroll, or rent at times during the year when revenues are typically low. Consumer lines of credit like a home equity loan normally have a longer clean up period in the sense that

---

[1] We refer to these OBS items as "contingent assets" even though the U.S. FDIC "call reports" for each federally insured bank refer to these items as "contingent liabilities." We call them contingent assets because, in practice, these OBS items become bank *assets* when they jump on the balance sheet.

they usually need to be fully repaid in 5 or fewer years but, nonetheless, they are not allowed to be extended indefinitely unless the consumer can fully repay the principal outstanding for at least one month.

Loan commitments: These are different from lines of credit and are usually used by commercial borrowers who are planning to need a relatively large amount of financing sometime in the next 1–2 years. For example, a company might be planning on building a new plant or purchasing some expensive equipment in the future but does not know exactly when the funds will be needed. In this case, the firm can ask its bank for a loan commitment, usually at a fixed interest rate, for the expected dollar amount of these expenses. Typically, the bank charges an annual "commitment fee" of 2.0% or less to compensate for the fact that the FI will need to make sure it has the necessary funds available on short notice to honor its fixed rate commitment to the borrower.[2] However, if the borrower does not decide to borrow within the time horizon of the commitment, then the bank keeps the commitment fee but is no longer obligated to lend the funds to the borrower. Consumers can also obtain loan commitments in terms of "pre-approved" loans which are commonly used for residential mortgages when people are beginning their home-buying searches.

Letters of credit: An "L/C" as they are frequently called, is essentially a "backstop" form of credit support for a commercial client. Typically, these contingent credit instruments are used to facilitate international trade between buyers and sellers who do not know much about the counterparty's creditworthiness. For example, if a U.S. company wants to import some goods or equipment from, say, a British firm, then the U.K. business takes on credit risk if they ship the goods to the U.S. without first receiving payment. Similarly, the U.S. firm is reluctant to pay cash upfront to the British seller prior to receiving the goods. To resolve this stalemate, the U.S. importing firm can go to a large FI that is willing to issue an L/C on behalf of the U.S. firm. In effect, the large FI is committing to pay the U.K. exporter if the U.S. importing firm reneges and does not pay for the

---

[2]Note that by pre-committing to a fixed interest rate, the bank can also be exposed to interest rate risk if rates move up sharply after the borrower has agreed to the loan commitment's terms. That is, the borrower essentially has the option, and financial incentive, to borrow at the lower pre-committed fixed rate if market interest rates rise quickly after signing the loan commitment documents.

imported goods. If, indeed, the L/C is activated, then the large FI pays the British seller and then must turn around and ask the U.S. firm to pay the bank back (along with relevant interest) because the L/C has now been effectively converted into a commercial loan that the U.S. firm must repay.

Typically, an annual fee of 2% or less is charged by the large FI to the U.S. importer to compensate for setting aside funds for a possible drawdown on this L/C. In the end, if all goes well, everyone is better off because the British seller makes a sale with less credit risk, the U.S. company gets the goods it needs at relatively low cost, and the large FI earns some fees and interest for taking on this credit risk and facilitating global trade. Another common use of L/Cs is for maintaining margin-based trading accounts with other financial institutions. Rather than post a form of collateral in margin trading accounts such as cash or Treasury securities, it can be more cost-effective for the trading firm to provide an L/C to the counterparty because the L/C fee is normally much lower than the interest the trader could lose by posting cash or securities.

Loan guarantees: Like Letters of Credit, loan guarantees can act as a credit backstop to facilitate business and consumer transactions. In this case, the bank normally charges an annual fee of 2% or less to compensate for the possibility that the bank's client does not make its promised payment(s) to another creditor. For example, in the municipal bond market, some municipalities will ask a large FI to provide a loan guarantee on these municipalities' future bond offerings. In this way, a municipality can obtain a lower coupon rate and/or borrow a larger amount of money because the municipal bond investors know that the large FIs stronger creditworthiness can protect them in case the municipality defaults. In addition, when lending to a subsidiary of a larger corporation, a bank will typically ask for a guarantee from the parent company because the parent entity usually has greater financial resources at its disposal than the subsidiary. Similarly, a consumer with weak creditworthiness can ask another individual to personally guarantee a loan to convince the bank to make the loan and/or charge a lower interest rate.

Derivatives transactions: At times, both commercial and retail customers might want to use derivative securities such as forward and futures contracts, as well as options and swaps, to manage risk and/or speculate on price movements in financial markets. Typically, large and midsize FIs are willing to accommodate trading in these derivative securities by engaging in the "Brokerage" economic function first discussed in Chapter 1. These FIs earn fees, commissions, and bid-ask spreads in exchange for facilitating trading in these derivative instruments. This trading will also usually expose the bank to credit risk with its trading partners because nearly all these instruments have embedded financial leverage where the customer needs to only put down cash that is a small fraction of the underlying derivatives position. For example, a customer purchasing a futures contract might only have to put down less than 10% of the contract's total value (also referred to as a "margin deposit" on the "notional amount" of the contract).

7.2.2 Asset securitization and loan sales

Many FIs, especially large and midsize banks, can package up collections of relatively homogeneous assets such as auto loans, credit card receivables, and mortgages to sell to other investors as "Asset-Backed Securities," or **ABS** for short. The securitization and sale of ABS has grown tremendously over the past few decades because it provides banks with a way to earn additional fees as well as manage their balance sheets and equity capital more efficiently. This securitization activity also provides other investors like investment managers with liquid, relatively safe investments that provide a higher return than U.S. Treasuries.

Presented in Figure 7.1 is a diagram that displays in Panel A the traditional "make and hold" **model** of financial intermediation for residential mortgages. In both panels of Figure 7.1, the arrows represent the flow of funds and securities within the two types of financial systems. Flows to the left represent cash being transferred from one party to another while flows to the right indicate the types of securities/financial contracts that are exchanged. Note that the bank originates the mortgages by sending cash to borrowers and the FI then holds these loan contracts on its balance sheet while financing these assets with bank deposits. This is essentially the set-up we had described in Chapter 1 in terms of the classic theory of qualitative asset transformation.

In contrast, Panel B shows the "elongated originate and distribute" **model** where commercial banks (denoted as "CBs") still make the mortgage loans to borrowers but now package them up into homogeneous pools that are then bought by investment banks who restructure these

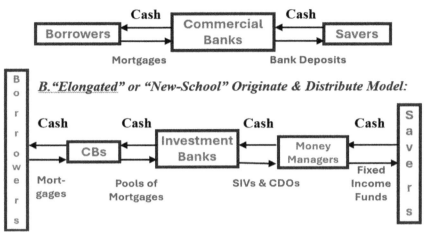

Figure 7.1. Diagram of Traditional and Securitized Models of Financial Intermediation.

mortgages into ABS instruments, such as structured investment vehicles (SIV) and collateralized debt obligations (CDO). In turn, the investment banks sell these securitized assets to professional money managers who then hold these securities in portfolios for other investors (denoted as "savers" in the diagram) such as mutual funds, exchange-traded funds, and hedge funds. This elongated process in Panel B is usually referred to as the "shadow banking" **system** because it is not as transparent to investors and regulators as the more traditional make-and-hold model.[3] In theory, the elongated model can disperse risk to those entities best suited to holding this risk rather than forcing the bank to hold all these assets on its balance sheet (and thus shadow banking can require less bank capital to support the mortgage lending process). Consequently, shadow banking in the U.S. has grown quite large and represents tens of trillions of dollars in annual financing.

In the end, the bank can earn upfront fees for making these loans and selling them off while freeing up costly equity capital, all of which can increase the bank's ROE. However, as we saw during the 2008–2009 Great Financial Crisis (GFC), the bank's incentive to monitor the quality of these loans can be distorted and lead to excessive risk-taking and

---

[3] See Pozsar *et al.* (2013) for more details on this elongated distribution network.

unsustainably high levels of financial leverage. Thus, there can be a significant trade-off in risk vs. return when we compare the traditional banking model in Panel A with the shadow banking model in Panel B. So, both regulators and investors must be vigilant in assessing and monitoring the securitization process.

7.2.3 Liability-based contingencies

A bank can also provide other contingency-based services to its customers that, when exercised, lead to a *liability* being added to the bank's balance sheet. Presented in the following is a brief description of the common types of liability-based contingencies.

Credit default swaps: The most common liability-based contingency service is the Credit Default Swap (CDS). Normally, only the largest and most creditworthy FIs can offer this service to their clients because the FI acts as an insurer of another borrower's credit risk. As we had described in Chapter 6 on credit risk, a *buyer* of a CDS will usually do so on a specific borrower's bonds to protect against a decline in these bonds if there is a default. The CDS buyer pays an upfront fee as well as annual fees (called "premiums") to be insured against some creditor's risk of default. In effect, the CDS buyer is purchasing "credit insurance" from a large, financially strong FI. In turn, the FI is the *seller* of the CDS and is thus exposed to credit risk if the underlying bond goes into default.

So, we can see that this is a contingent *liability* for the FI because it will have to make a payment to the insured party (the CDS buyer) to make up any difference between the defaulted bond's value and its par value. Thus, the large FI owes money to the CDS buyer but *only if* the bond defaults. In this case, the FI essentially takes possession of the defaulted bond which has a current market value of, say, $60 million, but the FI will have to pay the CDS buyer the full par value of the bond (e.g., $100 million). In this case, the FI loses $40 million (by paying out $100 million in cash but receiving a bond worth only $60 million). This loss is cushioned somewhat by the CDS premiums the FI would have collected prior to the default, and in aggregate across the entire portfolio of CDS contracts they have written, which ideally will be well diversified. For example, if the FI collected an upfront fee of 5% on the par value of the bond and the default occurred prior to collecting the next year's premium, then the FIs overall loss is $35 million in this example (the $60 million bond value *plus* $5 million premium received *minus* the $100 million payment to the CDS buyer).

If there is no default, then the FI keeps the $5 million premium and does not have any corresponding liability. Consequently, the large FIs incentive to sell CDS contracts is like when an automobile insurance company provides car insurance policies and hopes that no driver gets into an accident. However, as we saw in the 2008–2009 GFC, some FIs might have too strong of an incentive to sell this credit insurance which, in the case of the large FI called AIG, led to a "near-death" experience for the firm and required well over $100 billion of support from the U.S. government to help the firm honor its CDS liabilities.[4] As we had noted in Chapter 6, an FI can hedge some of its own credit risk by *purchasing* CDS contracts from another FI. So, in the case of AIG, many large FIs hedged their subprime mortgage credit risk by buying CDS contracts from AIG and, in the end, the firm was dangerously exposed to these other institutions' credit risk.

Other contingent liabilities: Banks are also exposed to other contingent liabilities due to their normal activities as an FI such as lawsuits, regulatory fines, and potentially buying back securitized assets that were sold to investors "with recourse." For example, loans sold with recourse provide the securitized asset buyer with the right to sell the loans back to the bank at a price higher than the current market value when the assets under-perform due to greater-than-expected credit losses. During the 2008–2009 GFC, many of the large FIs faced billions of dollars in other contingent liabilities due to sub-prime mortgage-backed securities that performed poorly. These largest FIs were hit simultaneously with all the contingent liabilities described here: payouts on CDS contracts, lawsuits, and fines, as well as buying back securitized assets due to either explicit or implicit recourse obligations. In turn, this led to the forced sale of Bear

---

[4] To find out more about the U.S. GFC and the problems at AIG, start with these sources: https://pubs.aeaweb.org/doi/pdf/10.1257%2Fjep.29.2.81 and https://www.investopedia.com/articles/economics/09/financial-crisis-review.asp as well as https://www.investopedia.com/articles/economics/09/american-investment-group-aig-bailout.asp#:~:text=High%2DFlying%20AIG&text=The%20epicenter%20of%20the%20crisis,sold%20insurance%20against%20investment%20losses.

Stearns, the failure of Lehman Brothers, the gigantic bailout of AIG, as well as expedited mergers of other FIs like Merrill Lynch (to Bank of America) and Wachovia (to Wells Fargo). In addition, the economic and financial losses to the overall economy were staggering and long-lasting. Thus, a good bank manager must always be mindful of these contingent liabilities because they can have far-reaching effects not only on the manager's specific bank but also on the overall financial system and macroeconomy.

7.3 How to Measure OBS Risk?

Based on the above discussion of these OBS activities as a way to provide liquidity insurance, we need to understand the mechanism by which these services can create various forms of risk for the bank.

7.3.1 *A numerical example of a typical OBS activity: Offering a commercial line of credit*

To begin our analysis, we present in Table 7.1 the stylized balance sheet of our hypothetical financial institution, called A Banking Company (ABC), which was first described in Chapter 3.

Now, let's assume that ABC has granted a line of credit (also referred to simply as "a line") of $5 million to a corporate borrower. We can also assume there is no annual fee associated with the line and, for simplicity,

Table 7.1. ABC's Stylized Balance Sheet *Before* a "Takedown" on a Line of Credit.

Assets	Value ($ million)	Liabilities & Equity	Value ($ million)
Cash & Reserves	$4	Deposits	$75
Investments	30	Other Borrowed Money	15
Gross Loans	60		
Allowance for Loan Losses	(2)		
Net Loans	58		
Other Assets	8	Common Equity	10
Total Assets	$100	Total Liabilities & Equity	$100

Table 7.2. ABC's Stylized Balance Sheet *Immediately After* a "Takedown" on a Line of Credit.

Assets	Value ($ million)	Liabilities & Equity	Value ($ million)
Cash & Reserves	$4	Deposits	$75
Investments	25	Other Borrowed Money	15
Gross Loans	65		
Allowance for Loan Losses	(3)		
Net Loans	62		
Other Assets	8	Common Equity	9
Total Assets	**$99**	Total Liabilities & Equity	$99

all interest (at 4%) and principal are due in one lump sum in 12 months. At the time the line is established, the balance sheet looks the same as the one shown in Table 7.1.

We can then assume that the next day the borrower "takes down" the full $5 million and does not repay the loan until it needs to be "cleaned up" in 12 months. This takedown leads to both credit risk and liquidity risk for ABC as it now has a $5 million loan to the borrower which the bank needs to fund via "stored" or "purchased" liquidity.[5] In this example, we assume that ABC will sell some of its *Investments* to fund the loan. As we had discussed in Chapter 6 on credit risk, according to regulatory requirements, ABC must establish a loan loss provision (LLP) on the income statement based on the expected credit losses over the life of the loan. Let's assume that the LLP should be $1 million (this is an admittedly large LLP but represents a nice, round number). This provision then results in a $1 million increase in ABC's Allowance for Loan Losses (ALL) on its balance sheet. In Table 7.2, we show the new balance sheet after the above actions have taken place. All balance sheet items that are affected by these actions are highlighted in italics and boldface.

---

[5] The liquidity risk management concepts of stored and purchased liquidity are discussed in more detail in Chapter 8 (Liquidity Risk). For our purposes here, we simply note that the bank must either sell some assets (stored liquidity) or borrow from other creditors (purchased liquidity).

Table 7.3. ABC's Stylized Balance Sheet *After Repayment* of the "Takedown" on a Line of Credit.

Assets	Value ($ million)	Liabilities & Equity:	Value ($ million)
Cash & Reserves	$9.2	Deposits	$75
Investments	25	Other Borrowed Money	15
Gross Loans	60		
Allowance for Loan Losses	(2)		
Net Loans	58		
Other Assets	8	Common Equity	10.2
Total Assets	**$100.2**	Total Liabilities & Equity	**$100.2**

Note that in Table 7.2 ABC's Total Assets *decreased* by $1 million because the bank must fully fund the takedown by selling $5 million of Investments but it replaces this decline in assets with only a $4 million increase in Net Loans. We can also see that the $1 million LLP causes the ALL to rise by this same dollar amount. In effect, the credit risk associated with this new loan causes Total Assets to fall from $100 million to $99 million. To balance the statement, we must then reduce Common Equity by this $1 million because shareholders are the residual claimant on the bank's assets and so they are first in line to absorb any expected credit losses. We can see from this numerical example how OBS risk can negatively affect a bank's market value because Common Equity falls by 10% (i.e., from $10 million to $9 million) even though an *actual* credit loss has not even occurred!

Now, let's assume the borrower repays the line of credit in full (with 4% interest) at the end of the 12-month period. In this case, ABC's balance sheet would look like the following statement in Table 7.3.

Note that in Table 7.3 the bank's Total Assets rebound to $100.2 million because the $5 million loan principal and $0.2 million in interest income (i.e., 0.04 x $5 million) are placed in ABC's Cash & Reserves for a new total of $9.2 million (i.e., $9.2 million = $4 million original balance + $5 million principal repayment + $0.2 million interest payment). Also, note that Common Equity rose by $1.2 million due to the full repayment of principal (which results in gross loans falling to $60 million and a $1 million reduction in Allowance for loan losses) and collection of the extra interest income. This increase likely overstates the true change in market value of equity because it assumes there are no incremental operating costs associated with collecting this interest payment but, for simplicity in the calculations, we make this strong assumption. Overall, the numerical example displayed in Tables 7.1–7.3 shows how ABC's OBS activities can create credit and liquidity risks. However, if managed properly, these OBS risks can provide another source of profitability for the bank while serving the customer's liquidity insurance needs.

7.3.2 The "optionality" of contingent assets

The numerical analysis described in the prior section can be generalized by considering a bank's contingent assets as "call" **options** that are "sold" to ABC's customers.[6] For example, a commercial line of credit can be viewed as a corporate borrower's right (but not obligation) to "call away" funds from the bank. The borrowing firm will "exercise" this call option when it has cash needs that *exceed* the firm's internal liquidity resources. The bank is therefore obligated to provide these funds whenever the corporate borrower needs them.

This "optionality" of a bank's contingent assets can be summarized with the diagram shown in Figure 7.2.

Figure 7.2 plots on the y-axis the total dollar amount a corporate borrower is expected to take down from the bank in the form of credit lines, loan commitments, and/or L/Cs. The x-axis represents the firm's anticipated dollar amount of financing needs. This financing need is general in nature and could be related to the firm's plans for new investment, operating costs, or other cash needs. The solid kinked line depicts the firm's takedowns from ABC and shows that there are *no* bank borrowings for the area *below* the point labeled "$ Amount of 'Excess' Cash & Mkt. Securities" like the point denoted as "A."[7] In this area, the firm's cash holdings and marketable

---

[6] We are relating these OBS activities to options in this section, but the specific details and nuances of option pricing are beyond the scope of our text. See Hull (2010) or other textbooks that focus on derivative securities for more details.
[7] We refer to this balance as "excess" because these cash holdings and marketable securities are more than the company's "near-cash" balances that are needed to maintain daily

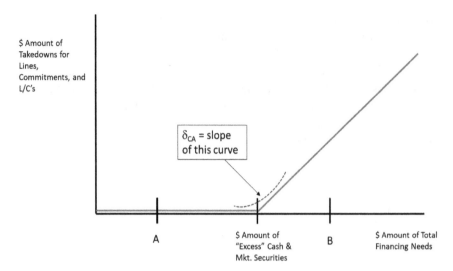

Figure 7.2. Diagram of the "Call Option" of Contingent Assets like Lines, Commitments, and L/C's.

securities are more than sufficient to meet their financing needs. For example, if point A represents the firm's expected financing needs of $3 million and the firm has, say $5 million of "excess" near-cash balances, then it is cheaper and more efficient for the firm to use this excess cash rather than borrow from the bank. In contrast, if point B represents a firm financing need of $7 million, then the company will need to first use its $5 million of excess cash and then take down from the bank an additional $2 million to fully meet its $7 million in financing needs.

Figure 7.2 shows a call option where the "strike" price is equal to the borrower's excess cash and marketable securities. For any financing needs above this strike price, the borrower will "exercise" this call option by taking down funds from the lines, commitments, and L/Cs that it has

---

operations. We could also include the firm's expected operating cash flow and treat it as part of this excess cash estimate if it is earned early enough in the year to pay for future expenditures. For simplicity, we assume in this example that there is no operating cash flow available to help cover the expected financing needs. Also, a financial manager might decide to start borrowing *before* excess cash goes to zero if they want to have additional financial flexibility because they are concerned that access to the external financing market might dry up (as it did after the Lehman Brothers failure in September 2008).

pre-arranged with the bank.[8] One can imagine a call option's strike price as a bar that a pole vaulter must jump over to earn a track and field medal. In a similar way, the borrower can "win" by accessing bank financing whenever the firm's spending plans clear the "bar" of the firm's excess cash balances.

In effect, the same principles that affect a stock option first noted in the Black and Scholes (1973) model also apply here to this "OBS option." Thus, we can estimate the sensitivity of this option by identifying the option's "delta" (denoted as δ_{CA} in Figure 7.2), which quantifies the dollar change in the contingent assets *relative to* the dollar change in the firm's financing needs. This delta ranges between 0 and 1.0.

In practice, it is difficult to use the Black–Scholes option pricing model to estimate these deltas for most OBS items. Instead, banks normally estimate these deltas by looking at past data with respect to their OBS activities. To do so, the bank can check how much money has been taken down during a given year on lines, loans, L/Cs, etc., as a percentage of these OBS items at the beginning of the year. For example, if the bank had $200 million of lines of credit at the *beginning* of the year and then customers took down on average $20 million *during* the year, then we would estimate the bank's delta to be 0.10, or 10% of the total amount of these credit lines.

In options parlance, a call option like the one shown in Figure 7.2 is "in-the-money" (ITM) if the firm's financing needs are *greater than* its excess cash. It is at a point like B in this graph that the call option will be exercised, and the bank will need to provide funds to the borrower. Conversely, at a point like A in the graph, the OBS option is "out-of-the-money" (OTM), and the borrower will *not* exercise this option (i.e., no funds will be taken down). In general, this dynamic of ITM vs. OTM is called the "moneyness" of the option (with *greater* moneyness existing when the option is *more* ITM).

The delta (δ_{CA}) is, in effect, the slope of the curved and dashed line in Figure 7.2. Thus, the delta for the contingent asset will be low (i.e., close to zero) when the option is out of the money and high (close to 1.00) when

---

[8] In this example, we assume the firm relies solely on one FI (e.g., ABC bank) for these financing arrangements. In practice, larger borrowers will typically have credit relationships with multiple FIs and might also have access to financing from the capital markets via stock and bond offerings. However, the kinked line in Figure 7.2 still applies even when the borrower relies on more than one FI for financing.

it is far into the money.[9] So, when delta is *high*, OBS risk will be commensurately *greater* because it means *more* lines, commitments, and L/Cs are likely to be taken down by the bank's customers. Thus, point *B* in Figure 7.2 has much more moneyness than point *A* and so *B*'s delta will be closer to 1.0 while *A*'s delta will be nearly zero. In this case, point *B* will lead to higher OBS risk for the bank than point *A*.

Now, that we understand contingent assets as acting like a call option on the bank's liquidity, we can use the concept of delta to quantify the likely impact of OBS activities on the bank's risk exposure. Once we have an estimate of the bank's δ_{CA}, then the only other item we need is the bank's total dollar amount of lines, commitments, L/Cs, and derivative positions it has offered to its customers. This total dollar amount is commonly referred to as the "notional value" of the OBS item. For example, if the bank has issued a $5 million line of credit, then this dollar amount represents its notional value even if no funds have been taken down on this line. The same logic applies to derivatives like a $100 million interest rate swap contract. In this case, the notional value of the swap is $100 million, but the actual amount of money exchanged between the swap's parties can be much less than this amount. In fact, the largest banks typically have notional values of their OBS items in the *trillions* of dollars even though their actual dollar outlays are likely to be "only" in the billions.

Given the above discussion, we can formulate Equation (7.1) to succinctly summarize a bank's estimate of its possible dollar outlay for these contingent assets:

$$\textit{Contingent assets "exercised" in each period} = CA = \delta_{CA} \cdot N_{CA} \quad (7.1)$$

where

δ_{CA} = the average "delta" of the bank's OBS Assets (based on the overall "moneyness" of these various assets) and

N_{CA} = Notional Value of OBS Assets = total dollar amount of potential takedowns and payments on the bank's lines, commitments, L/Cs, and derivative positions.

---

[9] As shown in Hull (2010), other factors beyond the strike price that affect an option's price and delta are the current value of the underlying asset, the asset's return volatility, the time to expiration, and the risk-free rate.

The notional value of OBS Assets in Equation (7.1) is relatively easy for an external investor to obtain from a bank's footnote disclosures or, for an internal bank manager, from internal sources. Therefore, the real challenge in estimating CA is how to develop a reliable estimate of the delta variable (δ_{CA}). Admittedly, this is a difficult task for external analysts because they cannot directly observe the bank's actual takedowns on items like lines of credit and loan commitments. As mentioned earlier, for internal bank managers, they can examine past levels of, say, lines of credit and what percentage of those lines are utilized over a specific year. In effect, this percentage can be used as a reasonable estimate of delta if the bank expects recent historical experience to be a good indicator of future takedown behavior. Depending on economic conditions, this delta estimate can also be adjusted based on how OBS-related takedowns behaved in past periods of macroeconomic expansions and contractions. For an external analyst, one rather rough and crude delta estimate could be obtained by studying the relative growth trends in N_{CA} and Total Assets (A) because Contingent Assets should increase somewhat in line with changes in notional OBS assets and Total Assets.

Table 7.4 presents a numerical example of how to use Equation (7.1) to quantify the dollar amount of ABC's Contingent Assets (CA) that are likely to move onto the balance sheet over the next 12 months.

Table 7.4 reports the bank's overall delta (δ_{CA}) is 0.175 and represents a weighted average of the individual deltas for each of the OBS items (where the weights are based on the notional values of these items). This estimate indicates that, on average, ABC is expecting 17.5% of the bank's notional values will appear as assets on the balance sheet over the next 12 months. Thus, ABC's managers should ensure that they have sufficient

Table 7.4. Numerical Example of how to estimate ABC's Contingent Assets.

OBS Item	Delta (δ_{CA} for each item)	Notional Value ($ million)	Contingent Asset ($ million)
Lines of Credit	0.30	30	9
Loan Commitments	0.20	10	2
Letters of Credit/ Guarantees	0.20	20	4
Derivative Positions	0.10	60	6
Totals	**0.175**	**120**	**21**

290 *Managing Financial Institutions: An Integrated Valuation Approach*

liquidity to meet an expected $21 million worth of takedowns and derivative payouts by its customers (i.e., $0.175 \cdot \$120$ million = $21 million). Keep in mind that this is the bank's best guess of how many contingent assets might suddenly appear on the balance sheet, but the delta estimates will vary depending on business conditions, fluctuations in customers' financing needs, and historical trends. So, ABC's managers should be continuously updating the bank's estimates of Contingent Assets, as well as Contingent Liabilities. In this way, senior management can monitor the impact of OBS activities on the bank's market value of equity.

7.3.3 The "optionality" of contingent liabilities

The above discussion for a bank's contingent assets (CA) has a close parallel to a bank's contingent liabilities (CL), such as Credit Default Swap (CDS) contracts sold to customers, lawsuits, fines, and assets sold with recourse. However, in contrast to a bank's contingent assets' **call optionality**, the bank's CL can be viewed as a "put" option. For example, the bank's *sale* of a CDS contract provides credit risk protection to a customer but creates a contingent liability for the bank if the underlying borrower defaults on their loan or bond. The customer that purchased the CDS will "exercise" this put option when the borrower of the underlying bond or loan defaults on its payments. The bank is therefore obligated to pay out funds to eliminate the decline in the customer's bond or loan value due to the default.

This "optionality" of a bank's contingent liabilities can be summarized with the diagram shown in Figure 7.3.

Figure 7.3 plots on the *y*-axis the total dollar amount owed to a bank customer if the value of the underlying asset falls below some critical value (denoted as the "Strike" Value in the graph). For example, ABC might have sold a CDS contract to a customer who wants protection against a default on the bonds of a prominent automobile manufacturer. In this case, a bond default will cause the bond's value to fall *below* the strike value (e.g., the par value of the bond) to a point, such as A in the diagram. In this case, we say that the put option is ITM because the CDS buyer is likely to exercise the option to receive a payout from ABC which offsets the loss in the bond's value due to its default. In this case, the CDS's delta will be close to 1.0. Conversely, if the bond is *not* in default, then the bond's value will be at a point like B and the put option is "Out-of-the-Money" (OTM). In this

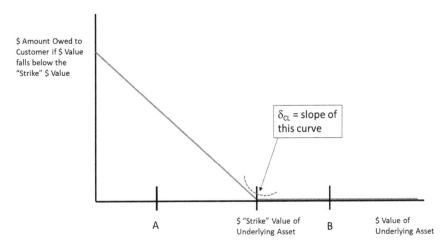

Figure 7.3. Diagram of the "Put Option" of Contingent Liabilities like CDS sales, fines, and lawsuits.

situation, the CDS buyer will not exercise the option because the bond's market value at point B is higher than the strike value the customer would receive (and the CDS's delta will be near zero). If, at the end of the CDS contract, the bond is not in default, then the bank, ABC in this case, gets to keep the premiums it received from the CDS buyer but does not have to make any payouts. Like the pole vaulter analogy for a call option, we can think of a limbo dancer as an example of a put option. In this case, the limbo dancer strives to go *below* the bar. This limbo dancer is like the CDS *buyer* in Figure 7.3 who gains when a CDS-protected bond defaults and thus the bond's market value drops below the CDS's strike price.

Although the above example and Figure 7.3 focus on a bank that sells CDS contracts, this put option-style diagram applies to all sorts of contingent liabilities. For example, one can view regulatory fines and lawsuits as a put option where regulators and investors can "exercise" it whenever regulations and laws are violated. In this case, the "strike" value is a regulatory or legal requirement that is not met by the bank. In this case, the bank falls *below* the regulatory "bar" or legal "benchmark" and creates a liability that jumps on the balance sheet. For example, a U.S. bank might not meet the federal fair lending laws for consumer loans and thus be penalized by regulators for $100 million. This dollar amount shows up on the bank's balance sheet as a liability which will then have to be paid by selling assets and/or obtaining additional financing. Clearly, it is in everyone's best interest for bank managers to act in an ethical manner and comply with all relevant laws and regulations. Not only is it good for the bank's customers and society in general, but it can also help improve the bank's financial condition by reducing OBS risk.

Like we saw with contingent assets, the slope of the kinked solid line in Figure 7.3 represents the slope of this curve and is denoted as the "delta" for the contingent liabilities (δ_{CL}). Note that the contingent liabilities' delta can be computed in a similar manner as shown earlier in Table 7.4 for contingent assets (i.e., by using a notional-value-weighted average of each contingent liabilities' deltas).

Given the above discussion, we can formulate Equation (7.2) to summarize our estimate of the possible dollar outlay for a bank's contingent liabilities:

$$\text{Contingent liabilities exercised in each period} = CL = \delta_{CL} \cdot N_{CL} \quad (7.2)$$

where

δ_{CL} = the average "delta" of the bank's OBS liabilities and

N_{CL} = Notional value of OBS liabilities = total dollar amount of potential payments to bank customers due to CDS contracts, fines, lawsuits, loans sold with recourse, derivative positions, etc.

To conserve space, we simply assume an average for ABC's δ_{CL} of 0.22 and that the bank has $100 million in contingent liabilities (CL) for our numerical example.

7.3.4 *The net effect of OBS risk on a bank's equity*

The above discussion of the balance sheet effects of OBS risk is helpful. However, throughout this book, we have focused on the impact of a manager's choices on the bank's market value of equity (MVE), and so we now turn our attention to this topic. As we can see from Figure 7.3, a bank's CL represents a put option and can be viewed as a mirror image of the bank's contingent assets (CA). However, the *net* impact of CA and *CL* on a bank's common equity (EQ) depends on the dollar amount of both these exposures and their respective deltas. This net effect of OBS risk on a bank's equity can be seen by using the "Accounting Identity" concept first discussed in Chapter 1. This concept can be expanded to include CA and CL as follows:

$$\text{Bank Common Equity} = EQ = A - L + (CA - CL) \quad (7.3)$$

where

EQ = the bank's common equity = market value of equity (MVE) *if* all the other components of (7.3) are based on their respective market values,

A = on-balance sheet Total Assets,

L = on-balance sheet Total Liabilities,

CA = contingent assets = potential off-balance sheet assets, and

CL = contingent liabilities = estimated off-balance sheet liabilities.

Equation (7.3) concisely describes the immediate impact of OBS activities on the bank's equity via the term in parentheses: $(CA - CL)$. That is, if we can estimate the market values of each component on the right-hand side of (7.3), then the difference between the estimates of contingent assets and contingent liabilities will tell us how OBS risk is affecting the bank's equity.

We can extend our earlier numerical example of ABC to see the net impact of CA and CL as follows:

$$EQ = A - L + (CA - CL)$$

$$= \$100 \text{ million} - \$90 \text{ million} + ([0.175 \cdot \$120 \text{ million}] + [0.22 \cdot \$100 \text{ million}])$$

$$= \$10 \text{ million} + (\$21 \text{ million} - \$22 \text{ million})$$

$$EQ = \$10 \text{ million} - \$1 \text{ million} = \textbf{\$9 million}$$

The above calculations reveal that ABC's equity is worth *less* when we account for the bank's OBS activities. That is, the conventional definition of the Accounting Identity indicates that the bank's equity should be worth $10 million based on the assumed market values of *on-balance* sheet assets and liabilities ($A - L$ = $100 million − $90 million = $10 million). However, when we include the immediate impact of off-balance sheet items of $21 million in CA and $22 million in CL, we can see that this *reduces* ABC's equity by $1 million (e.g., $21 million − $22 million = −$1 million) and represents a relatively large drop of 10% in market value. So, even though ABC has a larger *notional* value of contingent assets than contingent liabilities ($120 million vs. $100 million), our estimate of the dollar value of CA is lower than CL because the contingent liabilities' delta (δ_{CL}) is higher than CA's delta (0.220 vs. 0.175).

In addition, regulators and investors are interested in seeing how OBS risk affects the bank's equity capital ratio. In the above example, we can compute this impact by adjusting both the Common Equity and Total Assets to include the contingent assets and liabilities that are estimated to immediately "hop on" the balance sheet. In this case, we see that $21 million worth of contingent assets and $22 million in contingent liabilities jump on the balance sheet and, in turn, this causes Common Equity to fall to $9 million. Thus, in economic terms, the new equity capital ratio is 9.09% (i.e., $9 million/($100 million + $21 million − $22 million) = $9 million/$99 million = 0.0909).[10] This is a significant drop from the equity capital ratio of 10% based on the bank's traditional balance sheet that only includes on-balance sheet items (e.g., $10 million / $100 million = 0.1000). Both regulators and equity investors would be concerned about such a sudden decline, and they would expect the bank to remediate the situation by adding more capital or reducing its OBS exposure.

The numerical example shown above illustrates the importance of quantifying the OBS risks the bank faces both on the asset and liability sides of the balance sheet. Clearly, the negative impact of OBS activity on bank equity and the equity capital ratio shown here is dependent on several assumptions and so a good analyst would also do some sensitivity analysis and stress testing to create a more complete picture of this risk. We return to this issue later in this chapter but now turn to ways we can manage OBS risk.

7.4 How to Manage OBS Risk?

The discussion and numerical example from the previous section demonstrate the importance of managing a bank's OBS risk, as it can have

---

[10] In bank regulatory jargon, this type of capital ratio calculation that incorporates estimates of OBS items is usually called a "Supplementary Leverage Ratio" because it provides a broader view of how much equity the FI holds to cover unexpected losses from *both* its on- and off-balance sheet activities.

serious consequences for the FIs equity value and capital ratios. In most cases, a bank does not have an easy way to manage or hedge this risk. Thus, we have four main ways to control OBS risk:

(1) hedge with offsetting derivatives transactions,
(2) impose limits on OBS activities,
(3) adjust the FIs on-balance sheet items, and
(4) develop robust regulatory compliance and ethics programs.

7.4.1 *Hedging with derivative securities*

One area where the bank can manage OBS risk in a direct and cost-efficient manner is the bank's derivatives positions related to facilitating customers' trading needs. This OBS risk could be hedged with **offsetting derivatives securities**. For example, if the bank has sold a CDS contract and is worried about a default on the bond underlying this contract, it can then *buy* a CDS to offset some or all this risk. For insurance firms, this way of offsetting risk is typically called "reinsurance." Similarly, if the bank has *sold* a futures or forward contract, it can enter a *long* futures or forward contract to mitigate this risk. However, bank managers must keep in mind that if they hedge away all derivatives-related risk, the profitability of this trading activity can be reduced considerably. As we have discussed throughout this book, a good bank manager must weigh the costs and benefits (both explicit and implicit) of hedging an FI's risks.

7.4.2 *Rule-based limits to OBS risk*

Other than derivatives positions, it can be difficult for a bank to hedge most OBS risks. For example, once a line of credit or loan commitment is made, the bank is obligated to provide funds whenever the customer needs them (and many times this occurs on very short notice to the banker). Also, if the bank engages in customer-focused trading activities related to foreign currencies, fixed income securities, and other marketable securities, then the FI is exposed to counterparty credit risk. To manage these risks, the bank will normally use **concentration limits, position limits, margin accounts,** and **collateral**. Many of these items have already been discussed in Chapter 6 (Credit Risk) because OBS activities typically lead to some sort of credit risk exposure.

Accordingly, the bank will guard against this credit risk by setting up pre-established rules before engaging in many OBS activities. For example, the bank can use concentration limits to make sure that no single borrower or industry sector makes up more than, say, 10% of the bank's OBS exposure to lines, commitments, and L/Cs. If a bank is actively trading with its customers and other FIs, then the FI can establish position limits so that each counterparty has sufficient funds to cover its maximum long or short exposure to the bank. As an example, a large counterparty might be granted a $100 million position limit whereas a smaller, financially weaker counterparty's limit might be only $5 million. Margin accounts and collateral requirements are additional mechanisms to control credit risk, especially for OBS-related trading activities. Although these rule-based limits are not perfect, they can help bank managers monitor the overall magnitude of the firm's OBS risk and help them mitigate a substantial portion of this risk.

7.4.3 On-Balance sheet adjustments to manage OBS risk

The two main techniques of managing OBS risk noted above are the more cost-effective ways to handle the bank's exposure to these activities. However, another way to handle OBS risk pertains to direct adjustments of **on-balance sheet items** that can, at least partially, offset some of this risk. For example, a bank like ABC could hold a larger amount of equity capital to guard against unexpected losses associated with rapid loan takedowns from customers who are experiencing a sudden deterioration in their financial condition. As we discuss in more detail in Chapter 8 about liquidity risk, ABC might also hold a greater amount of its assets in low-yielding (but highly liquid) fixed income securities to meet any sharp increase in takedowns on its lines, commitments, and L/Cs. ABC could also borrow from more costly sources of credit (compared to relatively cheap financing from insured depositors) in order to meet any unexpectedly high customer demand for funds. Clearly, holding extra equity capital as well as investing in low-yielding securities and/or borrowing from uninsured creditors are more costly for the bank and will typically reduce ABC's profitability. So, once again, ABC's managers must balance costs versus benefits of this form of OBS risk management.

7.4.4 *Regulatory compliance and ethics programs*

Given all the fines and lawsuits associated with a bank's potential mismanagement and misbehavior within the heavily regulated financial services industry, it is essential that the FI has a robust regulatory compliance program and that its employees act in an ethical manner. If not, then the bank is vulnerable to investigations by various regulatory authorities as well as investor- and client-driven lawsuits. The subprime mortgage crisis during 2007–2009 is a classic example of Contingent Liabilities suddenly jumping onto the balance sheet. In addition to large credit losses, billions of dollars in liabilities quickly appeared in many of the large U.S. banks due to regulatory fines and lawsuits. These additional liabilities were a direct result of many banks' inadequate disclosures and improper management of the subprime mortgage origination and securitization processes. This, in turn, led to the 2008–2009 Great Financial Crisis and subsequent increase in U.S. bank regulation via the 2010 Dodd–Frank Act. From this experience, we can see why it is imperative for banks to have not only strong compliance programs but also effective employee training programs to promote ethical behavior and cultivate a healthy corporate culture.[11]

7.5 The Impact of Managing OBS Risk on a Financial Institution's Equity

In this section, we build on the earlier exploration of the net effect of OBS risk on a bank's market value of equity. In a previous example, we showed how a mismatch in the amounts of ABC's contingent assets and liabilities (i.e., $21 million vs. $22 million) can lead to a decrease in its common equity (–$1 million) as well as its capital ratio (from 10.0% to 9.1%). However, this example is only one of many possible outcomes based on ABC's OBS risk and is driven by our assumptions about the "deltas" for the contingent assets (δ_{CA}) and contingent liabilities (δ_{CL}).

Given this uncertainty about the actual levels of contingent assets and contingent liabilities, it is customary to perform some sensitivity analysis and stress testing to account for possible alternative scenarios. This type

---

[11] These compliance and ethics programs are also a way to manage "Operating Risk," which we discuss in more detail in Chapter 9.

Table 7.5. Matrix of OBS Risk's Impact on ABC's *Total Common Equity* (in $ million).

Delta for Contingent Liabilities (δ_{CL})	Delta for Contingent Assets (δ_{CA})				
	0.05	0.10	0.15	0.20	0.25
0.05	11	17	23	29	*35*
0.10	6	12	18	24	30
0.15	1	7	13	19	25
0.20	−4	2	8	14	20
0.25	−9	−3	3	9	15

of analysis can be done via a "Matrix Approach" where the bank analyst can vary both delta estimates to create a range of possible effects on the bank's common equity and capital ratio.[12] Since the deltas for most OBS items are, on average, usually between 5% and 25% of their notional values, we can develop a matrix that allows both deltas to vary from 0.05 to 0.25, as shown in Table 7.5.

Columns 2–6 in Table 7.5 represent different levels of ABC's total common equity based on contingent asset deltas that vary from 5% to 25% of CA's notional value of $120 million. Likewise, rows 3–7 in Table 7.5 show ABC's common equity when the bank's contingent liability delta varies between 5% and 25% of CL's notional value of $100 million.[13] As we read from left to right in Table 7.5, we can see that ABC's equity value rises in tandem with increases in the contingent asset delta (δ_{CA}). So, we can see that when more CA hops on the balance sheet, the bank's equity increases (while holding the contingent liabilities delta, δ_{CL}, constant).

For example, in the upper right corner of Table 7.5, we show (in boldface and italics) ABC's common equity is worth $35 million when ABC's δ_{CA} represents 25% of CA's notional value and δ_{CL} is only 5% of CL's notional amount. This is the "best case" scenario for ABC because

---

[12] Saunders *et al.* (2024) uses a similar approach to model the impact of OBS risk on a bank's equity. See this text if you are interested in finding out more about this method.

[13] Note that in this numerical example we vary both deltas but hold the notional dollar amounts of CA and CL constant at $120 million and $100 million, respectively. We do this for simplicity but, in practice, the FI can allow both the deltas and notional values to vary simultaneously.

it suggests that the firm's common equity will rise from $10 million to $35 million due to a $30 million increase in CA (0.25 × $120 million) while the firm's CL only rises by $5 million (0.05 × $100 million). Thus, the *net* increase in ABC's common equity equals $25 million (i.e., the change in equity equals the difference between the CA of $30 million and the CL of $5 million). This represents a 250% increase in ABC's equity if this scenario is realized (i.e., ($35 million − $10 million) / $10 million = 2.50 or 250%). Note that when we perform the matrix analysis in Table 7.5, we are assuming that these changes in CA are net of any increases in credit risk. That is, the changes in CA and their impact on the bank's equity shown in Table 7.5 are net of any related increases in the Allowance for Loan Losses (ALL) for these new loans.

In contrast to the upper right corner of Table 7.5, the lower left corner shows (again in boldface and italics) the "worst case" scenario for ABC where its common equity turns *negative* at −$9 million. Since the market value of equity cannot go below zero (due to limited liability), such a result means the bank is insolvent and the equity investors' stake is wiped out. Unless there is an immediate injection of capital by new equity investors, regulators will be forced to either put the bank into receivership or find another bank that would want to assume ABC's assets and liabilities. This dramatic and painful turn of events for ABC is due to 25% of its $100 million in CL ($25 million) jumping onto the balance sheet and is offset by only 5% of the bank's $120 million in CA ($6 million). In this case, the *net* decrease in common equity is −$19 million (i.e., $6 million *minus* $25 million) and thus wipes out ABC's original $10 million of equity value. In turn, this leads to the −$9 million of total common equity estimate shown in Table 7.5 (i.e., $10 million minus $19 million equals −$9 million). Clearly, this is a scenario that ABC's management wants to avoid. Alternatively, the matrix shows that if these OBS risks are managed well, then the bank's common equity is likely to increase, as reported in the last two columns of Table 7.5. We can summarize the dollar change in a bank's market value of equity due to OBS risk via the following equation:

$$\$\Delta \text{ Equity due to OBS risk} = CA - CL = (\delta_{CA} \cdot N_{CA}) - (\delta_{CL} \cdot N_{CL}) \quad (7.4)$$

The above analysis is of particular interest to ABC's shareholders. Regulators are also concerned about how OBS affects ABC's equity. However, they are usually more focused on the bank's equity capital ratio because this figure indicates how much of a "buffer" the FIs equity can provide in case of unexpected losses. Since we are concerned with OBS risk in this chapter, we can use the broader definition of the equity capital ratio which is commonly referred to as the "Supplementary Leverage Ratio" (SLR). As we described earlier in this chapter, a stylized version of the SLR can be computed as follows and SLR is covered in more detail in Chapter 10 related to capital adequacy:

$$\text{Supplementary Leverage Ratio} = \text{SLR} = \frac{[\text{Common Equity} + (\text{CA} - L)]}{[A + (\text{CA} - \text{CL})]}$$

(7.5)

The SLR is a more comprehensive measure of capital adequacy because it explicitly accounts for OBS risk. Table 7.6 presents ABC's SLR for various combinations of deltas.

The results of Table 7.6 mirror those of Table 7.5 in that the best-case scenario is shown in the upper right corner with a 28.0% SLR while the worst-case scenario is located in the lower left at −11.1%. Once again, shareholders and regulators would be concerned with this wide range of capital ratios and might require ABC's managers to mitigate this OBS risk by using one or more of the mechanisms described in the prior section, "How to Manage OBS Risk."

Table 7.6. Matrix of OBS Risk's Impact on ABC's *Supplementary Leverage Ratio* (in decimal format).

Delta for Contingent Liabilities (δ_{CL})	Delta for Contingent Assets (δ_{CA})				
	0.05	0.10	0.15	0.20	0.25
0.05	0.109	0.159	0.204	0.244	*0.280*
0.10	0.063	0.118	0.167	0.211	0.250
0.15	0.011	0.072	0.126	0.174	0.217
0.20	−0.047	0.022	0.082	0.135	0.182
0.25	*−0.111*	−0.034	0.032	0.091	0.143

Overall, there appear to be several scenarios in Tables 7.5–7.6 where ABC's equity could drop dramatically and possibly be completely wiped out. For example, of the 25 possible scenarios outlined in these tables, three of them report negative values and another 5 scenarios show an SLR below 8%. Thus, 8 of the 25 scenarios (32%) suggest there is a chance that OBS risk can cause ABC to become seriously under-capitalized. This is useful information because it suggests that ABC's managers might need to reduce its OBS risk from its current level. As we have shown all along in this book, there is truly an "ART" to risk management and that, in this case, the "*R*" (for *remove* some of the OBS risk) might be the better choice for ABC's shareholders.

The above numerical example and discussion were based on hypothetical values for ABC drawn from an earlier example drawn from Chapter 3. However, to be consistent with the integrated stock valuation model contained in the Excel™ spreadsheet we have provided with this book, we also present in Table 7.7 some assumed values for ABC based on total assets of $1,580 million (or $1.58 billion) and common equity of $180 million ($0.18 billion), as well as notional values of $1,000 million ($1 billion) and $400 million ($0.4 billion) for ABC's Contingent Assets and Contingent Liabilities.

Table 7.7. ABC's Spreadsheet Example of the Impact of OBS Risk.

Initial Total Assets ($million)	$1,580.0	Initial Equity	$180.0
Shares Outstanding (million)	10.00	Initial E/A Ratio	11.4%
Initial Equity / Sh.	$18.00		
Ending Equity / Sh.	$20.00	Ending E/A Ratio	12.5%
% Chg. In Equity / Sh.	11.1%		
Contingent Assets	$1,000.0	Contingent Liabilities	$400.0
Delta Cont. Assets (δ_{CA})	0.100	Delta Cont. Liab, (δ_{CL})	0.200
Tot. Assets + CA − CL	$1,600.00	Equity = EQ + CA − CL	$200.00

Table 7.8. Matrix of OBS Risk's Impact on ABC's SLR (using the IVM's spreadsheet data).

Delta for Contingent Liabilities (δ_{CL})	Delta for Contingent Assets (δ_{CA})				
	0.05	0.10	0.15	0.20	0.25
0.05	0.130	0.157	0.181	0.205	0.227
0.10	0.119	0.146	0.172	0.195	0.218
0.15	0.108	0.136	0.162	0.186	0.209
0.20	0.097	**0.125**	0.152	0.176	0.200
0.25	0.085	0.114	0.141	0.167	0.191

Using the values shown in Table 7.7, we can formulate a matrix of OBS Risk's effect on ABC's Supplementary Leverage Ratio (SLR) like we did in our earlier example and shown in Table 7.8.

Table 7.8 shows how ABC's initial equity capital ratio of 11.4% varies depending on different combinations of delta values for CA and CL. In the spreadsheet, we assume the most likely scenario is that 10% of CA and 20% of CL "hop on" the balance sheet. As we can see from Table 7.8 in boldface, this leads to an *increase* in the bank's SLR to 0.125 which is shown (or 12.5% of the firm's OBS-adjusted total assets). This occurs because 10% of $1.0 billion in CA is actually larger than 20% of $0.4 billion of CL (i.e., $100 million vs. $80 million) and thus increases equity by $20 million. If this were to translate directly into an effect on ABC's stock price, it would increase the share price by $2.00/share (i.e., +$20 million/10 million shares = +$2.00/share). As shown in Table 7.7, based on an assumed starting price of $18 per share, this represents an +11.1% gain in ABC's stock price. So, the bank could benefit if it manages its OBS risk well enough to achieve this most likely scenario. However, this can be a big "if" depending on the competition the bank currently faces as well as prevailing macroeconomic conditions.

7.6 Managerial Implications

The dilemma facing Nina and Sam is quite stark: **how aggressively should ABC Bank market its line of credit products to business and** consumer customers as interest rates continue to climb if macroeconomic conditions are expected to weaken? Given that these lines are tied to variable rate benchmarks, their floating rates can help reduce interest rate risk by matching variable rate debt with floating rate assets (thus locking in a stable net interest margin). However, as the economy weakens, the credit risk associated with takedowns on these lines will grow and, at some point, the costs of this extra credit risk could outweigh the benefits of reduced interest rate risk. Nina and Sam need to formulate a plan for senior management that addresses this OBS problem. Beyond the quantitative matrix analysis shown in Tables 7.5–7.8, the two colleagues have also considered some *qualitative* aspects of this OBS risk management decision. Nina and Sam realize that although the quantitative analysis of these tables shows there is a chance of negatively impacting ABC's equity, there are several qualitative factors to consider such as the importance of maintaining good relationships with its customers, especially with small businesses that depend heavily on lines of credit and loan commitments to finance their operations and growth plans. For example, a sudden pullback by ABC in providing these lines (or reducing their credit limits) can alienate customers and cause them to take their business to a competitor, thus eroding ABC's market share and reputation.

Based on the strong level of competition in ABC's market and the bank's reliance on small businesses for a large amount of its Net Interest Income, **Nina and Sam believe the prudent path is to continue growing OBS-type assets with its more creditworthy customers but to decelerate growth in such lines and commitments to its financially weaker customers or, where appropriate, offer such products to these less creditworthy borrowers with a larger credit risk premium.** Thus, even though there is some elevated risk to ABC's equity from such an approach, both Sam and Nina are more concerned with tarnishing ABC's reputation within its operating community if the bank were to rapidly reduce its availability of lines, commitments, and letters of credit to its existing customers. And, if the underwriting of new OBS assets is done carefully for the bank's stronger customers, then the additional revenue can more than offset the increased risk to equity. So, even though the quantitative analysis in the prior section suggests employing the "R" from the ART of risk management (for "Remove" the risk), ABC's managers must also weigh the important qualitative aspects of competition, reputation, and community involvement. **Do you agree with Nina and Sam's recommendation? If not, how would you handle it differently and what are your reasons for doing so?**

7.7 Summary

Overall, this chapter showed us how to view contingent assets (CA) and CL as conceptually similar to call and put options on the bank's liquidity, respectively. Contingent assets like lines of credit, loan commitments, and letters of credit can be an important way for banks to provide liquidity to their clients while boosting the bank's fee and interest income. Contingent liabilities like payouts for lawsuits or credit default swaps are a bit more difficult to quantify but can be quite significant and, as we saw in the case of AIG during the 2008–2009 GFC, these items can quickly wipe out an FIs equity. Another challenge for a bank manager is to estimate the "deltas" for both CA and CL so that the bank can quantify how much of bank's notional OBS values will "hop on" the balance sheet and cause common equity to decline in value. To answer these quantitative questions, historical data and experience related to utilization rates of credit lines, loan commitments, etc. can be used. However, as noted above in our story with Nina and Sam, qualitative factors such as competition, macroeconomic conditions, long-standing customer relationships, and reputation within the community can play a large role in a bank's OBS risk management decision. As we have said several times in this book, effective risk-related decision-making therefore requires good judgment from a bank's managers.

Chapter-End Questions

Answers to odd-numbered questions can be found at the end of this book.

1. **True or False:** The main types of asset-based contingent financing needs are lines of credit, loan commitments, letters of credit, loan guarantees, and derivative securities transactions.
2. **True or False:** The bank's sale of a CDS contract provides credit risk protection to a customer and creates a contingent asset for the bank if the underlying borrower defaults on their loan or bond.

3. **Multiple Choice:** Which of the following is a liability-based OBS activity that can lead to contingent liabilities?
   (A) Lines of credit
   (B) Loan commitments
   (C) Asset securitization
   (D) Selling corporate credit risk protection via Credit Default Swap (CDS) contracts
4. **Multiple Choice:** Which of the following is *not* a way to manage OBS risk?
   (A) Hedge with offsetting derivatives transactions
   (B) Raise the bank's dividend payout ratio
   (C) Impose limits on OBS activities
   (D) Adjust the FIs on-balance sheet items
5. **Multiple Choice:** What is the impact of OBS risk on a bank's market value of equity?
   (A) It increases the market value of equity
   (B) It decreases the market value of equity
   (C) It has no impact on the market value of equity
   (D) It depends on several factors
6. **Short Answer:** What is a Credit Default Swap (CDS) and how can it lead to contingent liabilities?
7. **Short Answer:** If a bank's on-balance sheet Total Assets (A) are $300 million and on-balance sheet Total Liabilities (L) are $250 million and it has contingent assets (CA) of $80 million and contingent liabilities (CL) of $90 million, then what is the impact on the bank's common equity (EQ)?
8. **Short Answer:** If a bank's on-balance sheet Total Assets (A) are $500 million and on-balance sheet Total Liabilities (L) are $450 million, with contingent assets (CA) of $120 million and contingent liabilities (CL) of $130 million, then how does off-balance sheet risk affect the bank's Supplementary Leverage Ratio (SLR), as described by Equation (7.5)? How does this figure compare to the bank's conventional on-balance sheet equity/assets ratio (EQ/A)?
9. **Excel-based Question:** How much does the bank's OBS risk exposure on its $1,580 million in total assets affect ABC's *market value of equity* (i.e., its market capitalization or "market

cap")? Assume the bank's managers are concerned about how changes in contingent assets (CA) and contingent liabilities (CL) affect the bank's market value due to weakening macroeconomic conditions. To do so, change the dollar amounts of CA and CL, as well as their OBS "Delta" sensitivities (δ_{CA} and δ_{CL}) based on the following parts A–D. To answer these questions, use the "OBS Risk – Ch 7" tab of the **Integrated Valuation Model.xlsx** file. For example, try this by starting with the current values in the blue cells related to the *Loan Commitments, Lines of Credit, and Total Contingent Liabilities*, as well as those related to the OBS "Delta" sensitivities (δ_{CA} and δ_{CL}):

(A) As a starting point, use $\delta_{CA} = 0.10$ and $\delta_{CL} = 0.20$ to compute the Supplementary Leverage Ratio (SLR) based on Equation (7.5) if the *notional values* of Loan Commitments and Lines of Credit both increase by 10% while Total Contingent Liabilities grow by 25%.

(B) Related to your answer in part A, compute ABC's conventional "on-balance sheet" EQ/A ratio (also referred to as the "E/A ratio") and compare it to your SLR estimate. Briefly explain any differences between the E/A and SLR results.

(C) In addition to your assumptions from part A, calculate the *dollar change* in ABC's market cap and stock price if δ_{CA} drops to 0.05 while δ_{CL} rises to 0.25 when compared to ABC's initial "base" market cap of $180 million and stock price of $18.00 per share.

(D) How does your answer to part C change if δ_{CA} rises back to 0.10 while δ_{CL} declines to 0.10? Briefly explain any pattern you observe between your answers to parts C and D.

10. **Comprehensive Question:** Considering the dilemma faced by Nina and Sam at ABC Bank described in this chapter, **how would you evaluate the balance between maintaining customer relationships and managing credit risk in a weakening economy?** If you were in their position, would you follow the same strategy of growing off-balance sheet (OBS) assets with more creditworthy customers while decelerating growth with financially weaker customers, *or* would you propose a different approach? Provide your reasoning and a brief explanation of your proposed strategy.

References

Black, F. and Scholes, M. (1973). The pricing of options and corporate liabilities, *Journal of Political Economy*, 81, 637–659.

Hull, J.C. (2010). *Risk Management and Financial Institutions*, Prentice-Hall, Boston.

McDonald, R. and Paulson. A. (2015). AIG in Hindsight, *Journal of Economic Perspectives*, 29(2), 81–106.

Pozsar, Z., Adrian, T., Ashcraft, A.B. and Boesky, H. (2013). Shadow Banking, *Federal Reserve Bank of New York Economic Policy Review*, 19(2).

Saunders, A., Cornett, M.M. and Erhemjamts, O. (2024). *Financial Institutions Management: A Risk Management Approach*, McGraw-Hill, New York.

Chapter 8

Liquidity Risk

8.1 Introduction

All three of a financial institution's primary economic functions (Qualitative Asset Transformation, Brokerage, and Delegated Monitoring activities) can create **liquidity risk**. We define liquidity risk as the FIs exposure to sudden demands for cash from its customers who need to borrow and/or withdraw funds. Thus, when a bank provides liquidity insurance to its customers, the FI is exposed to liquidity risk because the frequency and severity of these demands for cash can vary widely and unexpectedly.

We should also define what we mean by "liquidity." Broadly speaking, we can define liquidity as the ability to *quickly* convert a financial instrument into cash *at, or close to, its fair market value*.[1] For example, if we have a U.S. Treasury security that has a "fair" value of $1,000, then we would say this is a *highly liquid* security if we can swiftly sell it and receive a sum that is very close to its fair value of $1,000. In contrast, if we have invested $1,000 in a corporate bond issued by a relatively small and obscure company in a foreign country, then we would say it is a *very illiquid* security if it took a long time to sell it and, when we did, the price we received was far below its $1,000 fair value. Note that the terms *"quickly"*

---

[1] For a more in-depth discussion of liquidity as it relates to FIs and financial markets, see Foucault *et al.* (2013) and Ozenbas *et al.* (2022).

and "*at, or close to, its fair market value*" are somewhat vague terms and will mean different things to different people because there are no specific quantitative values that are accepted by all market participants.

Despite the relatively vague definition of liquidity, most people "know it when they see it," which means highly liquid securities typically **trade very fast** (e.g., in milliseconds), in **large dollar volume** each day (millions of dollars), and with **minimal transaction costs** (e.g., well below 1% of the asset's value). However, depository FIs specialize in making longer-term, illiquid loans that are typically financed by highly liquid shorter-term deposits because they can be withdrawn (i.e., converted into cash) at a moment's notice.[2] Thus, a typical commercial bank has a very large "maturity mismatch" between its longer-term assets and shorter-term liabilities (as we introduced in Chapter 1). This situation can lead to a funding crisis if many customers want to rapidly draw down on their lines of credit (a.k.a. *asset-based* liquidity risk) and/or depositors suddenly withdraw their funds from the bank (a.k.a. *liability-based* liquidity risk). Both forms of liquidity risk can affect a bank's Net Interest Margin, Return on Assets, Return on Equity, and capital ratios. Consequently, bank executives must carefully consider the costs and benefits of managing this liquidity risk to maximize the FI's market value of equity.

One stark example of how liquidity risk can lead to "bank runs" as well as cause a possible "banking panic" occurred in the first half of 2023 in the U.S. when Silicon Valley Bank (SVB) was forced into receivership on March 10, 2023, after sustaining a very sudden withdrawal of $42 billion worth of deposits in one day (March 9, 2023). This event was driven by the bank's decisions about how much interest rate risk to take in their securities portfolio and miscalculations in managing the liquidity risk of this exposure in relation to their short-term (and mostly uninsured) deposit financing. A **bank run** occurs when many depositors and other creditors "run" to withdraw their funds simultaneously from a bank. In modern banking, a run like this can be accelerated by bank technology like mobile apps. As depositors now have virtually instant access to their

---

[2] In fact, checking accounts are commonly referred to as "Demand Deposit Accounts" (or DDAs) because the owner of such an account can demand to withdraw all or some of the account's balance without any prior notice. Also, Brunnermeier and Pedersen (2009) demonstrate the importance of managing an FI's short-term liquidity position relative to its market-based liquidity needs, especially during stressful market conditions.

accounts, they do not need to literally wait in line at a bank's office to withdraw funds, as they would have in previous bank runs (e.g., the Great Depression and the 2008–2009 Great Financial Crisis). Thus, withdrawal requests can now happen in larger sums at more frequent intervals, thus making the bank run snowball even faster.

In turn, a **banking panic** occurs when the run on one bank causes creditors of other banks to suddenly withdraw their funds from these other FIs, causing stress across the entire banking system. For example, by March 26, 2023, it was announced that the bulk of the remaining assets in SVB were sold to First Citizens BancShares, along with the FDIC injecting funds into SVB, while also assuming a portion of SVB's securities portfolio. This was a stunning collapse of a bank that had over $200 billion of assets just three months earlier![3] During that same month of March 2023, two other smaller U.S. banks, Signature Bank and Silvergate Bank, also failed as bank runs on these FIs left them with insufficient financing to continue as independent entities.[4] In all these cases, the market value of the banks' equity quickly fell to zero (or very near-zero)! It should also be noted that regulators and political leaders also become involved when bank runs and panics occur because these FI-specific disruptions can have a major impact on the broader economy.

Even though the initial reasons for the runs on these three banks were quite different (e.g., interest rate risk related to long-term fixed income securities at SVB and credit risk related to cryptocurrency loans and other activities at Silvergate and Signature), they all suffered the same fate because of a surge in liquidity risk that could not be overcome. Outside the U.S., the impact of SVB's failure also led to the forced sale of Credit Suisse (CS) to its Swiss banking rival, UBS, in March 2023. Once again, large and relatively sudden deposit outflows occurred, although the reasons for CS's problems were primarily attributed to long-standing concerns about senior management and past scandals that tarnished the Swiss firm's reputation. However, as we have noted in Chapter 1, an FI's most important asset is the *trust* of its customers and creditors. In all the cases

---

[3] For a detailed timeline of the collapse of SVB and resulting turmoil in the U.S. banking sector, see the *Wall Street Journal* article on May 11, 2023 (https://www.wsj.com/articles/bank-collapse-crisis-timeline-724f6458?mod=saved_content).

[4] For example, see details about these bank failures (Signature Bank and Silvergate Bank), as reported by Lauren Hirsch in a *New York Times* article on March 27, 2023 (https://www.nytimes.com/2023/03/27/business/silicon-valley-bank-first-citizens.html).

briefly noted here, there was a rapid erosion of trust in these FIs. It should also be noted that most governments have implemented deposit insurance programs to protect depositors from the liquidity risk problems described here. However, as the failure of SVB and other depository FIs has shown, these deposit insurance programs are no guarantee that liquidity risk can avoid systemic problems like a banking panic. We discuss deposit insurance's role in the banking industry later in Chapter 10 when we examine regulatory issues related to managing an FIs various risks.

8.2 What is Liquidity Risk?

8.2.1 *Asset-based liquidity risk*

As noted above, a bank can provide liquidity insurance services to its customers such as lines of credit and checking accounts. **Asset-based liquidity risk** typically refers to sudden customer demands for bank funds to finance items, such as pre-approved lines of credit, loan commitments, and letters of credit. As we had discussed in Chapter 7 about OBS risk, these credit services are off-balance sheet items that can quickly hop on the *asset* side of the bank's balance sheet and affect the bank's market value equity either positively or negatively. In this chapter, we concentrate on how a bank can raise cash to finance "takedowns" on these popular credit services either by selling other assets or holding cash outright (referred to as "Stored Liquidity") or by obtaining additional borrowing (via "Purchased Liquidity"). Later in this chapter, we discuss the pros and cons of these two different ways to manage liquidity risk. For now, we focus on an example that demonstrates how a takedown on a line of credit creates liquidity risk for the bank.

8.2.2 *A numerical example of asset-based liquidity risk: Offering a commercial line of credit*

To begin our analysis, we present in Table 8.1 the stylized balance sheet of our hypothetical financial institution, called A Banking Company (ABC), which was first described in Chapter 3. Note that a similar example was used in Chapter 7 to demonstrate the concept of OBS risk.

Let's assume that ABC has granted a line of credit (also known as "a line") of $5 million to a corporate borrower. We can also assume there is no annual fee associated with the line and, for simplicity, we abstract away

Table 8.1. ABC's Stylized Balance Sheet *Before* a "Takedown" on a Line of Credit.

Assets:	Value ($ million)	Liabilities & Equity:	Value ($ million)
Cash & Reserves	$4	Deposits	$75
Investments	30	Other Borrowed Money	15
Gross Loans	60		
Allowance for Loan Losses	(2)		
Net Loans	58		
Other Assets	8	Common Equity	10
Total Assets	$100	Total Liabilities & Equity	$100

from any credit risk or repayment terms. At the time the line is established, the balance sheet looks exactly the same as the one shown in Table 8.1.

We can then assume that the next day the borrower "takes down" the full $5 million and does not repay the loan until some unspecified time in the future. This takedown leads to liquidity risk for ABC because it now has a $5 million loan to the borrower which the bank needs to fund via **Stored** or **Purchased** liquidity. We assume that ABC will sell $5 million of its investments to fund the loan and thus will be using a stored liquidity risk management approach in this example. Since we are focusing on liquidity risk in this chapter, we can assume the line's takedown has *no* credit risk and thus it does *not* need to increase its Allowance for Loan Losses (ALL).[5] In Table 8.2, we show the new balance sheet after the above action has taken place. All balance sheet items that are affected by these actions are highlighted in italics and bold face.

Note that in Table 8.2, ABC's Total Assets are *unchanged* because the $5 million increase in Net Loans (from $58 million to $63 million) is exactly offset by a $5 million *decrease* in Investments. This occurs because the bank has chosen to use its Investments portfolio as a way to "store liquidity" in case of sudden asset-based liquidity needs. We can see from this numerical example how a well-designed stored liquidity

---

[5] This is admittedly a strong assumption about ALL, but, like our zero-fee assumption, we do so to simplify the numerical example to highlight the main points of liquidity risk. Allowing for a non-zero line of credit fee and/or change in ALL would not alter these main points.

Table 8.2. ABC's Stylized Balance Sheet *Immediately After* a "Takedown" on a Line of Credit.

Assets	Value ($ million)	Liabilities & Equity	Value ($ million)
Cash & Reserves	$4	Deposits	$75
Investments	25	Other Borrowed Money	15
Gross Loans	65		
Allowance for Loan Losses	(2)		
Net Loans	63		
Other Assets	8	Common Equity	10
Total Assets	$100	Total Liabilities & Equity	$100

strategy can help meet customers' needs *without* negatively affecting a bank's market value.

8.2.3 Liability-based liquidity risk

Liability-based liquidity risk normally refers to sudden demands for bank funds to finance deposit withdrawals or make payments to other parties, such as creditors, Credit Default Swap (CDS) owners, regulators (for fines), and plaintiffs (for lawsuits). These payments to depositors or other external parties alter the liability side of the bank's balance sheet and thus can also affect the firm's market value of equity. We show in the following an example of this liability-based liquidity risk.

8.2.4 A numerical example of liability-based liquidity risk: Financing a large deposit outflow

To continue our analysis, we once again display in Table 8.3 the stylized balance sheet of our hypothetical financial institution before any deposit has occurred. In this case, the balance sheet looks exactly like the one shown earlier in Table 8.1.

Table 8.3. ABC's Stylized Balance Sheet *Before* a Large Deposit Outflow.

Assets	Value ($ million)	Liabilities & Equity	Value ($ million)
Cash & Reserves	$4	Deposits	$75
Investments	30	Other Borrowed Money	15
Gross Loans	60		
Allowance for Loan Losses	(2)		
Net Loans	58		
Other Assets	8	Common Equity	10
Total Assets	$100	Total Liabilities & Equity	$100

Let's assume that a large depositor then decides to withdraw $5 million from its checking account and there are no incoming deposits that can offset this withdrawal. This sudden outflow of deposits creates liquidity risk for ABC because it now has a $5 million withdrawal that the bank needs to fund via stored or purchased liquidity. In this example, we employ a purchased liquidity strategy and assume that ABC can borrow $5 million of "Other Borrowed Money" (OBM) from the Federal Funds market. This is an interbank lending market where banks can borrow from each other on an unsecured, short-term basis (typically for a term of 1–2 days). ABC will have to pay interest on this short-term unsecured loan (commonly referred to as the "Fed Funds Rate"), but, for our purposes, we can abstract away from this interest payment by assuming its rate is 0% and focus on how this "purchase" of liquidity in the Fed Funds market directly impacts ABC's balance sheet. In Table 8.4, we show the new balance sheet after the above action has taken place. All balance sheet items that are affected by these actions are highlighted in italics and bold face.

Note that in Table 8.4, ABC's Total Assets are *unchanged* because the $5 million decrease in Deposits (from $75 million to $70 million) is exactly offset by a $5 million *increase* in Other Borrowed Money ($15 million to $20 million). This occurs because the bank has chosen to use its borrowing capabilities in the Fed Funds market to purchase liquidity in case of sudden liability-based liquidity needs. We can see from this

Table 8.4. ABC's Stylized Balance Sheet *Immediately After* a "Takedown" on a Line of Credit.

Assets	Value ($ million)	Liabilities & Equity	Value ($ million)
Cash & Reserves	$4	**Deposits**	*$70*
Investments	30	**Other Borrowed Money**	*20*
Gross Loans	60		
Allowance for Loan Losses	(2)		
Net Loans	58		
Other Assets	8	Common Equity	10
Total Assets	$100	Total Liabilities & Equity	$100

numerical example how a well-designed purchased liquidity strategy can help meet customers' needs *without* negatively affecting a bank's market value.[6]

Although the two examples presented above focus either on the asset or liability sides of the balance sheet, keep in mind that most banks will use a combination of *both* stored and purchased liquidity risk management strategies. For example, a bank manager might choose to fund an increase in loan demand or sudden deposit withdrawal by selling some securities *and* borrowing in the Fed funds market, depending on market conditions. A bank's choices related to these two strategies will depend on management's evaluation of the pros and cons of each strategy, which are discussed later in this chapter. However, before delving into these issues, we first want to consider the most common ways to measure liquidity risk.

---

[6] Technically, the above statement is only true in an exact sense when the amounts reported in the balance sheet of Table 8.4 are based on accounting *book values* of assets, liabilities, and equity. In contrast, the market values of these items could be affected by the change in the bank's financing structure because it, in turn, could alter the FIs cost of capital and market value of equity (due to the shift toward potentially higher-cost OBM rather than cheaper Deposit financing). However, in this example, the shift in the composition of liabilities is relatively small, and thus the impact on the FIs cost of capital is assumed to be negligible. Accordingly, the results described in Table 8.4 are generally valid.

8.3 How to Measure Liquidity Risk?

8.3.1 *Financing pyramids and financing diamonds*

Based on the above discussion, it is important to quantify the degree of liquidity risk the bank faces. We can start by considering the basics in which a bank's "Financing Needs" can be funded either by stored or purchased liquidity. So, we can use the "Liquid Assets" component of a bank's balance sheet if we want to rely on stored liquidity and we can use purchased liquidity by obtaining external financing in the form of "Other Borrowed Money" (OBM). This relationship can be defined as follows:

$$\text{Financing Needs} = \text{Liquid Assets} + \text{Other Borrowed Money} \quad (8.1)$$

where

Financing Needs = bank's total needs to cover incremental expenses, withdrawals, and investments,

Liquid Assets = "Excess" bank reserves + Fed Funds sold + Reverse Repurchase Agreements ("reverse repos") + Investments in marketable securities available for sale, and

Other Borrowed Money (or OBM) = uninsured deposits + Fed Funds purchased + Repurchase Agreements ("repos") + other non-depository borrowings like short- or medium-term notes.

As noted in Chapter 1, the Liquid Assets and OBM components of (8.1) include some important short-term financing markets. For example, many banks and other financial institutions lend to each other through the Federal Funds market via overnight loans. If a bank lends money in the Federal Funds market, it is called "Fed Funds sold" because it is a short-term unsecured investment in another bank. In contrast, if a bank borrows in the Federal Funds market, then it is called "Fed Funds purchased" and represents an unsecured short-term liability. Moreover, banks can lend to each other in the market for Repurchase Agreements, which is another very short-term source of funding.[7] Both Federal Funds and Repurchase

---

[7] Also known as a "repo," repurchase agreements are short-term collateralized loans in which one participant sells an asset to the other participant (the "buyer") for a price P_0. The seller agrees to buy back the assets later, usually for a higher price, P_1. Banks will typically

Agreements aid the bank in handling short-term liquidity needs if they prefer not to use cash or Treasurys to do so.

Although Equation (8.1) provides a good number of instruments that banks can use for liquidity risk management, it is not meant to be an exhaustive list and many banks, especially smaller ones, will not rely on some of them.[8] Rather, (8.1) provides a broad, stylized picture of some of the more common vehicles used to manage this risk. Also, if the bank prefers to use liquid assets first to meet its financing needs, then we can re-arrange Equation (8.1) to identify how much external OBM (also referred to as "hot money") the bank needs to borrow[9]:

$$\text{Other Borrowed Money} = \text{Financing Needs} - \text{Liquid Assets} \qquad (8.2)$$

Equation (8.2) shows that any financing needs that are greater than the FIs unrestricted or "unencumbered" liquid assets will lead the bank to

---

buy and sell in the overnight repo markets, which means that the maturity is one day. One can calculate the repo rate as $\frac{P_1 - P_0}{P_0} \times \frac{365}{t_1 - t_0}$, where $t_1 - t_0$ is the length of the repurchase agreement (which, again, for a bank is typically one day). Where a "repo" is used by a bank to obtain short-term financing on a secured basis, a "reverse repo" represents a bank's decision to lend to another FI on short-term secured basis. Thus, a repo is a liability for the bank, whereas a reverse repo is considered a short-term bank asset.

[8] Larger banks will typically rely on most if not all these items as well as additional ones, such as issuing "commercial paper" (i.e., unsecured short-term marketable securities with maturities of 270 days or less). Also, an FI must be part of the Federal Reserve System to access the market to purchase or sell Federal Funds (which are, in effect, unsecured short-term loans between banks). In addition, the U.S. government has created Federal Home Loan Banks (FHLBs) to provide short- and medium-term loans to banks (and credit unions) of any size that might need additional liquidity. To access these loans, a bank must be an investor in the FHLB and, in addition to obtaining liquidity on favorable terms, the bank can receive dividends from the FHLB.

[9] The term, "hot money," refers to the lack of stability in this source of external financing. For example, uninsured depositors or short-term creditors in the Fed Funds and repo markets are not obligated to finance the bank's liquidity needs on a long-term basis. Thus, if these depositors and creditors become nervous about the bank's asset quality, they can then quickly choose to withdraw deposits and not roll over any short-term loans. The bank might then have to scramble to find other sources of external financing on short notice, thus heightening the firm's liquidity risk. This ability to suddenly leave the FI with a gap in its financing is why it is called "hot money." This contrasts with financing the bank's needs with "core insured deposits" which are unlikely to suddenly leave the bank because they are protected by FDIC insurance.

seek external financing from "hot money" sources whenever traditional insured depositors (i.e., "core deposits") cannot meet all the firm's liquidity needs.

In most cases, safer and more reliable core deposits are the preferred way to finance a bank's operations. This gives rise to the concept of the "Financing Pyramid" where there is a pecking order to a bank's sources of financing. The basic logic is that the bank should rely first and foremost on low-cost and stable sources of financing such as insured deposits and then, if that is not sufficient to meet all financing needs, to then rely on higher-cost and more volatile financing such as OBM and, ultimately, Common Equity. This type of financing pyramid can be depicted graphically as shown in Figure 8.1.

Note that the base of the pyramid in Figure 8.1 is larger than the other rows within the diagram. That is intended to reinforce the idea that the largest percentage of financing should come from stable, low-cost insured deposits. This not only helps reduce liquidity risk but can also help improve the bank's Net Interest Margin (NIM) by lowering the firm's overall financing costs. Only after gathering the maximum amount of core deposits should the bank move up the pyramid to use OBM to finance its assets. As noted earlier, this segment is viewed as less desirable because it is hot money which typically leads to higher financing costs and less reliability in accessing these funds. Lastly, regulators and shareholders would also require some (smaller) percentage of assets to be financed by the relatively high cost of equity financing. As we discuss in more detail in Chapter 10 regarding capital adequacy and regulatory requirements, equity capital acts as a buffer against unexpected losses in bank asset values. It also serves to reduce some moral hazard incentives of the bank's owners by requiring them to have more "skin in the game" (i.e., the shareholders can lose all their investments if asset losses are sufficiently large).

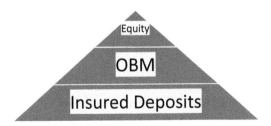

Figure 8.1. A stable Financing Pyramid structure.

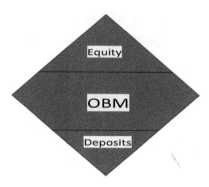

Figure 8.2. Less stable Financing Diamond structure.

However, equity capital is very costly in terms of the required return that investors demand and thus this form of capital is used sparingly.

We should also note that not all FIs follow the classic stable financing pyramid shown in Figure 8.1. For example, some banks choose to rely more heavily on OBM rather than insured deposits. In addition, *non-depository* FIs such as insurers, brokers, and asset managers are not legally allowed to take in insured deposits and thus are forced to deviate from the classic structure shown in the previous diagram. In addition, specialty finance companies like those that focus on residential mortgages rely solely on OBM and common equity to fund their operations. The amount of liquidity risk these non-depository FIs face depends on how much of their OBM is short term (less than 1 year) versus long term. Non-depository firms with a large amount of short-term OBM will typically face greater liquidity risk than competitors that rely more on long-term OBM. One can think of this alternative financing choice (where core deposits are minimal or non-existent) as a "Financing Diamond" like the one shown in Figure 8.2.

As Figure 8.2 illustrates, the OBM portion is the largest component of financing the FIs operations. As we discuss in more detail in a later section, there are strengths and weaknesses when an FI relies heavily on OBM as it can provide more flexibility and also increase liquidity risk, especially when the firm uses short-term OBM. For example, Lehman Brothers (with no deposits) in 2008 and Silicon Valley Bank in 2023 (with a lack of insured deposits) both relied on a financing diamond structure rather than a financing pyramid format. These two FIs, along with several others over time, successfully used the diamond approach for many years, but, in times of crisis, the inherent instability of using hot money can create huge liquidity risk and ultimately lead to catastrophic results for the firm and, in some cases, the entire financial system.[10] Thus, it is standard practice that most commercial banks, especially smaller and midsize firms, can substantially reduce liquidity risk by using the financing pyramid structure of Figure 8.1 rather than the financing diamond approach shown in Figure 8.2. As one can see from Figure 8.2, the structure is inherently more fragile and "wobblier" than Figure 8.1 and is therefore more likely to "tip over" (i.e., lead to bank failure) if economic conditions become severely stressed.

8.3.2 The "optionality" of liquidity risk management

Building on the financing pyramid concept, we can generalize this notion by considering a bank's financing needs as a "call" **option** on the FIs liquid assets and sources of OBM.[11] For example, a bank's liquid assets and sources of OBM can be viewed as the firm's right (but not obligation) to "call away" funds to finance sudden financing needs. The bank will usually "exercise" this call option when it has financing needs that *exceed* the firm's "excess" liquid assets.[12] However, one key conceptual difference in this call option analogy is that although the bank has the right to, say, call away funds (i.e., borrow) from a short-term creditor, it *cannot* force the creditor to do so. That is, the OBM creditor *is not* obligated to honor this credit request, whereas with a conventional call option, the seller of the option *is* obligated to act. Thus, using hot money via purchased liquidity can be a *much riskier strategy* than using a stored liquidity approach that relies instead on selling liquid assets from the bank's balance sheet. However, keep in mind that a bank manager has considerable flexibility in how they fund a liquidity need. Depending on market conditions, the manager might actually prefer to use OBM rather than

---

[10] See Demirgüç-Kunt and Huizinga (2010) for an examination of the impact of bank funding choices on the riskiness of individual firms and the broader financial system. They conclude that "a sizable proportion of banks, however, attract most of their short-term funding in the form of non-deposits at a cost of enhanced bank fragility."

[11] We are relating these liquidity risk management activities to options in this section. However, the details and nuances of option pricing are beyond the scope of our text. See Hull (2010) or other textbooks that focus on derivative securities for more details.

[12] Excess liquid assets are typically cash or fixed income securities that are not restricted from being liquidated on short notice to meet the bank's liquidity needs.

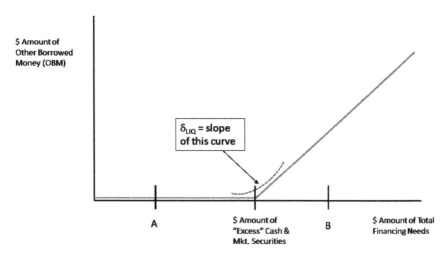

Figure 8.3. Diagram of the "Call Option" Related to Using Liquid Assets and OBM to Manage a Bank's Liquidity Risk.

liquid assets despite the higher risks of purchased liquidity (e.g., if the market for the bank's liquid assets is severely stressed but the Fed funds rate is very low).

As we discuss later in this chapter, the strengths and weaknesses of purchased vs. stored liquidity can lead to a preference for one method over another, although, in practice, most banks use a combination of both purchased and stored liquidity strategies. However, for smaller and mid-size banks during normal market conditions, it is usually safer and more reliable to *first* meet any financing needs by selling liquid assets such as U.S. Treasury bills and, after exhausting this liquidity source, *then* using OBM to fund any additional financing needs.

This "optionality" of this approach to managing a bank's financing needs and liquidity risk can be summarized with the diagram shown in Figure 8.3.

Figure 8.3 plots on the y-axis the total dollar amount of financing an FI is expected to obtain from hot money/OBM sources. The x-axis represents the FIs anticipated dollar amount of financing needs. This financing need is general in nature but, in this context, we can imagine this need might be due to a sudden surge in liquidity risk (due to rapid loan take-downs and/or depositor withdrawals). The solid kinked line depicts the FIs approach to managing this liquidity risk and shows that there are *no* changes in OBM for the area *below* the point labeled "$Amount of 'Excess' Cash & Mkt. Securities" such as the point denoted as "A."[13] In this area, the FIs cash holdings and marketable securities are more than sufficient to meet their financing needs. For example, if point A represents the FIs expected financing needs of $30 million and the firm has, say, $50 million of "excess" near-cash balances, then it is usually cheaper and more efficient for the firm to use this excess cash rather than borrow from OBM creditors. In contrast, if point "B" represents an FIs financing need of $70 million, then the company will typically first use its $50 million of excess cash and then rely on OBM sources for an additional $20 million to fully meet its $70 million in financing needs.

Figure 8.3 shows a call option where the "strike" price is equal to the borrower's excess cash and marketable securities. For any financing needs above this strike price, a bank like ABC will "exercise" this call option by borrowing funds via uninsured deposits, Fed Funds, short-term Federal Home Loan Bank (FHLB) loans, and/or repos. However, as we noted earlier, this is not a strict, enforceable strike price because these OBM lenders are not obligated to provide this financing, especially if economic conditions are stressful or there is serious concern about ABC's creditworthiness.

As we had discussed in Chapter 7 about OBS risk, the same principles that affect a stock option first noted in the Black–Scholes (1973) pricing model also apply here to this "Liquidity Risk option." Thus, we can estimate the sensitivity of this option by identifying the option's "delta" (denoted as δ_{LIQ} in Figure 8.3), which quantifies the dollar change in OBM *relative to* the dollar change in the bank's financing needs. This delta ranges between 0 and 1.0.

In practice, it is very challenging to use the Black–Scholes option pricing model to estimate this delta. Instead, banks normally estimate the liquidity delta by looking at past data with respect to their cash outflows, liquid asset sales, and OBM activities. In addition, a well-managed bank will also project its expected cash outflows over, say, the next 30 days due to sudden liquidity demands. One (rough) way to estimate a δ_{LIQ} is to

---

[13] Note that we could also include the firm's expected operating cash flow and treat it as part of this excess cash estimate if it is earned early enough in the year to meet future liquidity demand. For simplicity, we assume in this example that there is no operating cash flow available to help cover these expected financing needs.

compute the bank's expected short-term cash outflows as a percentage of a bank's total assets.[14]

By doing so, the bank can forecast how much of its total assets might be affected by loan takedowns and/or deposit withdrawals during the next 30 days. For example, if the bank had $100 million in total assets and the expected short-term cash outflow is $20 million, then we would estimate the bank's delta to be 0.20, or 20% of total assets. Note that this sudden $20 million liquidity demand could be due to new loans and/or deposit withdrawals. Either way, the bank must use stored liquidity (selling liquid assets) and/or purchased liquidity (borrowing hot money) to fund these liquidity-related needs.

We call this a rough estimate of δ_{LIQ} because this approach assumes that all the bank's expected cash outflows will be financed by either liquid assets, OBM, or some combination of the two but does not distinguish between these sources. That is, this delta estimate does not differentiate between the bank's preference to use stored or purchased liquidity. To the extent that the bank relies *more* on liquid assets (i.e., stored liquidity), then the actual liquidity delta will be *lower*.[15] For simplicity, we can use a bank's Total Assets as the basis for this calculation as follows[16]:

---

[14] As we discuss later in this section, larger banks are required to estimate and report their expected cash outflows over the next 30 days to compute a measure of liquidity risk called the Liquidity Coverage Ratio. Thus, for larger banks, one can use the required disclosures in their financial statements to estimate Equation (8.3). We are relating the expected cash flow to the dollar value of total assets because, in theory, liquidity demands can come from either side of the balance sheet (e.g., loan takedowns and/or deposit withdrawals). Thus, the total financing need shown in Figure 8.3 is, in effect, related to total assets.

[15] We can view δ_{LIQ} and Equation (8.3) as a *comprehensive* metric of liquidity risk which measures the *total* amount of liquidity that might be suddenly demanded and thus needs to be financed by some combination of *both* liquid assets and OBM.

[16] One could try to be more precise in terms of the denominator of this equation by excluding those items like longer-term liabilities (medium term notes and long-term bonds) and common equity which cannot be called/retired within the next 12 months. However, for simplicity, we use total assets in this example because the data are easy to obtain and require less subjective judgment on the part of the analyst. Alternatively, one could try to estimate this delta by looking at past changes in OBM versus prior changes in total assets. It is up to the bank's managers to decide which of these approaches can best capture the optionality of liquidity risk management strategies.

$$\delta_{LIQ} = \frac{\text{Expected Cash Outflows over next 30 days}}{\text{Total Assets}} \quad (8.3)$$

where

δ_{LIQ} = the average liquidity "delta" = the percentage of the bank's Total Assets that might be needed for meeting sudden liquidity demands.

For example, if we use Equation (8.3) with data from Citigroup's 2022 10-K annual report, we can see that this large FI had $489.0 billion in expected short-term cash outflows and $2,416.7 billion in Total Assets. Thus, a rough estimate of the bank's liquidity delta is 0.202, or 20.2% of its total assets (i.e., $489.0 billion/$2,416.7 billion = 0.202).

As we had described in Chapter 7 about OBS risk, a call option like the one shown in Figure 8.3 is "in-the-money" (ITM) if ABC's financing needs are *greater than* its excess cash. It is at point B in this graph that the call option will be exercised, and the bank will need to obtain OBM financing from short-term creditors. Conversely, at point A in the graph, the OBS option is "out-of-the-money" (OTM) and ABC will *not* exercise this option (i.e., no OBM funds will be obtained). In general, this dynamic of ITM vs. OTM is called the "moneyness" of the option (with *greater* moneyness when the option is *more* in-the-money).

The delta (δ_{LIQ}) is, in effect, the slope of the dashed curve in Figure 8.3. Thus, the delta for OBM financing will be low (i.e., close to zero) when the option is out of the money and high (closer to 1.00) when it is far into the money.[17] So, when delta is *high*, both the need for OBM financing and liquidity risk will be commensurately *greater* because it means more external financing is needed on short notice by the bank. Thus, point B in Figure 8.3 has much more moneyness than point A and so B's delta will be closer to 1.0 while A's delta will be nearly zero. In this case, point B will typically have a *higher* liquidity risk than point A.

8.3.3 *Alternative measures of liquidity risk*

Now that we understand liquidity risk and the optionality of choosing purchased vs. stored liquidity, we can explore several of the liquidity risk

---

[17] As shown in Hull (2010), other factors beyond the strike price that affect an option's price and delta are the current value of the underlying asset, the asset's return volatility, the time to expiration, and the risk-free rate.

metrics that are commonly used for commercial banks. These measures include the following:

- Percentage of assets financed by OBM (% OBM),
- Loan-to-deposit ratio (LN/Depo),
- Liquidity coverage ratio (LCR),
- Net stable funding ratio (NSFR), and
- Liquidity index (LI).

First, we can consider a simple measure that builds on the discussion related to OBM and the liquidity delta described by Equation (8.3).

8.3.4 *Percentage of assets financed by OBM (% OBM)*

One way to measure liquidity risk is by seeing what percentage of total assets are financed with hot money such as the items usually included in OBM (e.g., Federal Funds Purchased, Repos, Uninsured Deposits, and Commercial Paper). Like the liquidity delta of Equation (8.3), we can see that a bank's liquidity risk is greater when more of the FIs assets are financed with OBM (compared to, say, financing the FI with more stable insured deposits). The following relationship also builds on the Financing Pyramid and Financing Diamond concepts discussed earlier with Figures 8.1 and 8.2:

$$\%OBM = \frac{Other\,Borrowed\,Money}{Total\,Assets} \qquad (8.4)$$

Thus, a bank with a *low* %OBM ratio typically has *low* liquidity risk because this would indicate the FI has a stable financing "pyramid" shape like the one shown in Figure 8.1. It also means that a large percentage of the bank's deposits are likely to be very reliable and thus are not usually withdrawn even in stressful conditions. These are called "core deposits" because the bank can rely on them as a stable source of financing. Conversely, a *high* %OBM suggests *high* liquidity risk because the bank is likely to have few core deposits and an unstable financing "diamond" shape like the one displayed in Figure 8.2.

8.4 Loan-to-Deposit Ratio (LN/Depo)

Another way to measure liquidity risk is by comparing most banks' primary sources (Deposits) and uses (Loans) of funds. A simple ratio of the average levels of Total Gross Loans to Total Deposits can quantify this approach to liquidity risk[18]:

$$\frac{LN}{Depo} = \frac{\text{Average Gross Loans}}{\text{Average Total Deposits}} \qquad (8.5)$$

Liquidity risk will be *higher* when the **LN/Depo** ratio is *higher* because it means more deposits are needed to fund the bank's lending activity. Since lending is usually a bank's primary activity, a higher LN/Depo ratio means there is greater demand for funds and thus can lead to an elevated risk of not having enough cash on hand to meet sudden spikes in withdrawals and/or loan requests. For example, it is possible for this ratio to be above 100%. Such a high ratio implies that the bank needs to rely on OBM or some other sources of funds to finance the bank's relatively high loan demand. A bank with such a high LN/Depo ratio is therefore more susceptible to being caught shorthanded if an unexpected surge in liquidity arises from its customers. In contrast, a *lower* **LN/Depo** ratio below 100% would suggest the bank has *lower* liquidity risk because it means the FI has a larger "cushion" of "excess" deposits that are readily available to be able to meet any rapid increases in loan demand or deposit withdrawals.

8.5 Liquidity Coverage Ratio (LCR) and Net Stable Funding Ratio (NSFR)

Although the liquidity risk metrics mentioned above are easy to calculate from a bank's balance sheet, the Great Financial Crisis of 2008–2009 demonstrated the need for a more *forward-looking measure*. Consequently, the Bank for International Settlements (BIS) Basel Committee on Banking

---

[18] One can take an average of quarterly data within a given year. Or, if working with annual data, one can take a simple average of the beginning and ending yearly values for both loans and deposits.

Supervision recommended in 2014 the calculation of two such measures: the **Liquidity Coverage Ratio** (LCR) and the **Net Stable Funding Ratio** (NSFR).[19] Both have the advantage of requiring the bank to make estimates of future liquidity needs and then relating them to sources of "high-quality liquid assets" (HQLA) and "stable funding sources." The LCR is computed as follows:

$$LCR = \frac{\text{High Quality Liquidity Assets}}{\text{Expected 30-day Net Cash Outflows}} \qquad (8.6)$$

where

High Quality Liquid Assets = HQLA = Level 1 assets + Level 2A assets + Level 2B assets,

Level 1 assets = Cash + Reserves at the Central Bank + Sovereign government debt,

Level 2A assets = Government-guaranteed mortgage-backed securities (MBS) + conventional corporate bonds with minimum of an AA-bond rating, and

Level 2B assets = Non-guaranteed residential MBS + lower-rated conventional corporate bonds + "blue chip" common stock,

Expected 30-day Net Cash Outflows = bank-specific estimate of cash outflows over the next 30 days due to a severely stressed economic scenario (net of any expected inflows in this scenario, although these inflows are capped at a maximum of 75% of outflows).

To accurately compute LCR via Equation (8.6), "haircuts" of 15% and 50% must be applied to Level 2A and 2B securities and all Level 2 assets must not be more than 40% of the bank's total HQLA.[20] In addition, there are several assumptions about "drawdown factors" for various funding sources, such as retail deposits, collateralized funding, and unsecured wholesale funding. Details about these assumptions can be found at the BIS website (www.bis.org) and in Saunders *et al.* (2024). For our

---

[19] See Saunders *et al.* (2024) for a more detailed description of the LCR and NSFR calculations.

[20] Also, Level 2B assets cannot be more than 15% of HQLA.

purposes, we can provide a simplified numerical example of the LCR for our hypothetical bank, ABC, as follows:

Numerical Example of LCR for ABC bank:
Level 1 assets = $100 million
Level 2A assets = $200 million
Level 2B assets = $300 million

Expected 30-day Net Cash Outflows = $150 million

We can use some basic algebra to solve for the bank's HQLA and how much can be funded with Level 2 assets as follows:

HQLA = Level 1 assets + capped amount of Level 2 assets = Level 1 + (0.40 · HQLA) = ($100 million + 0.40 · HQLA) = [Level 1 assets/(1 − 0.4)] = [$100 million / 0.6] = **$166.7 million**, where $100 million is held in Level 1 assets (60% of $166.7 million) and $66.7 million (or 40% of HQLA) is held in Level 2 assets.

LCR = HQLA / Net Outflows = $166.7 million / $150 million = 1.113 or **111.3%** of Expected 30-day Net Cash Outflows.

Note that the above LCR calculation only includes $66.7 million of Level 2 assets even though ABC has $500 million in these less-liquid asset categories. Thus, the LCR is designed to be a *conservative* (or worst-case) estimate of the bank's ability to cover sudden cash outflows. According to the BIS, **a bank should have an LCR of 100% or greater** to be considered adequately protected in terms of liquidity risk. Thus, the above example indicates ABC has sufficient liquid assets to cover a sudden outflow of $150 million over the next 30 days. Thus, *higher* levels of LCR suggest *lower* liquidity risk for a bank. In addition, analysts can examine the trend in the bank's LCR over time and across its main competitors to get a more complete picture of the FIs liquidity risk.

In addition to the LCR, the BIS has required large banks to compute another liquidity risk metric called the Net Stable Funding Ratio (NSFR) which compares the available amount of stable funding (ASF) to the bank's required amount of stable fund (RSF) needed over a 1-year period as follows:

$$\text{NSFR} = \frac{\text{Available Stable Funding}}{\text{Required Stable Funding}} = \frac{\text{ASF}}{\text{RSF}} \quad (8.7)$$

where

ASF = bank equity capital + preferred stock maturing in more than 1 year + long-term liabilities with maturities greater than 1 year + dollar value of retail and uninsured deposits that are not expected to be withdrawn during stressful economic conditions (like "core" deposits) and

RSF = sum of the dollar value of the bank's on-balance sheet items weighted by specific RSF factors (ranging from 0% to 100%) plus the dollar value sum of the bank's off-balance sheet items (OBS) weighted by their respective RSF factors. These RSF factors are determined by the BIS and country-level regulators and assume a severe liquidity event will occur within the 1-year evaluation period.

Numerical Example of NSFR for ABC bank:
Bank Equity Capital = $100 million
Long-term Preferred Stock = $50 million
Long-term Liabilities = $450 million
"Core" Deposits = $200 million
ASF = sum of the above items = $100 million + $50 million + $450 million + $200 million = **$800 million**
Let us also assume **RSF** is comprised of a weighted sum of $500 million in on-balance sheet items and $200 million in OBS items for a total of $700 million (i.e., RSF = $500 million + $200 million = **$700 million**).
NSFR = ASF / RSF = $800 million / $700 million = 1.143 or **114.3%** of required stable funding.

Like the case of LCR, **the BIS regulators want to see an NSFR of 100% or greater** to consider the bank adequately protected against liquidity risk. The above example for ABC shows it meets the regulator's requirement because its ASF is 114.3% of the bank's required stable funding. Thus, *higher* NSFR levels signify *lower* levels of liquidity risk. As noted for LCR, it is also beneficial to examine trends in NSFR over time and across the bank's peers to gain a more complete perspective on the bank's liquidity risk.

8.6 Liquidity Index (LI)

This measure attempts to quantify the potential losses on a bank's assets if some of them must be sold quickly at "fire sale" prices to meet a rapid surge in liquidity needs. The losses are measured as the relative difference in "fire sale" (P_n) and "fair market" prices (FP_n) for each asset that needs to be sold to meet sudden liquidity demands as follows:

$$LI = \sum_{n=1}^{N} w_n \cdot \left(\frac{P_n}{FP_n} \right) \qquad (8.8)$$

where
P_n = fire sale price of the nth asset if sold in the market under stressful conditions,
FP_n = fair market price of the nth asset if sold in the market under normal (non-stressful) conditions, and
w_n = the percentage of bank assets invested in the nth financial instrument.

Typically, the **LI** is calculated for the bank's investment portfolio and the fire sale prices are estimated by bank managers talking with securities dealers and brokers, as well as observing actual transaction prices for the relevant securities. However, in theory, the LI can also include less-liquid assets such as the bank's loan portfolio. The LI will range between zero and 1.00, with *lower* LI values indicating *higher* liquidity risk. In addition, LI will vary over time depending on the bank's mix of assets as well as the overall liquidity of the financial markets. Like the other metrics, it is important to calculate LI over time and across peers to get a good sense of the bank's liquidity risk.

8.7 How to Manage Liquidity Risk?

The discussion and numerical examples from the previous section demonstrate the importance of managing a bank's liquidity risk, as it can have serious consequences for the FIs equity value, as well as the broader economy if this risk creates a bank run and a banking panic. In most cases, a bank does not have an easy way to control or hedge this risk. Thus, we have three main ways to manage liquidity risk: (1) impose rules and policy limits on lending and financing activities, (2) adjust the FIs on-balance sheet items, and (3) develop a robust contingency funding plan.

8.7.1 *Rule-based limits to manage liquidity risk*

It can be difficult for a bank to hedge most liquidity risks. For example, once a line of credit or loan commitment is made, the bank is obligated to provide funds when the customer needs them (and many times this occurs on very short notice to the banker). Similarly, depositors who hold checking and money market accounts expect the bank to provide immediate access to their funds, thus creating liquidity risk for the bank. To manage these risks, the bank will normally use **policy limits**, which are set by the bank's board of directors and senior management. For example, these individuals, as well as members of the bank's Asset Liability Management (ALM) committee, will establish benchmarks for key ratios that can affect liquidity risk such as maximum and/or minimum values for:

- Loans-to-Deposits (the LN/Depo ratio discussed earlier),
- Investments/Deposits,
- Liquid Assets/Total Assets,
- Fixed Rate Loans/Total Assets,
- Wholesale Short-term Funding/Total Assets (e.g., the %OBM ratio),
- Uninsured Deposits/Total Deposits, and
- Available Lines of Credit to the FI/Total Liabilities.

These ratios are complementary to the LCR and NSFR metrics that large banks are required to compute in accordance with BIS regulations. Accordingly, the bank's leaders can guard against liquidity risk by setting up pre-established limits to help bank managers in their daily investing and financing decisions. For example, the bank can use an LN/Depo ratio limit to make sure that this metric never goes above, say, 100% so that the bank always has some financial "slack" in terms of "excess deposits" which can then be invested in safe, liquid fixed income securities. This policy limit can reduce liquidity risk and also diminish the bank's profitability because loans typically earn more interest than liquid securities like U.S. Treasury bills. Another point to keep in mind is that these board-approved liquidity risk management policies should be part of an **iterative process** where bank managers and board members continuously monitor market conditions and make policy adjustments on an as-needed basis. Although rule-based limits and policies are not perfect, they can help bank managers better understand the trade-offs between risk and return related to liquidity risk management decisions.

8.7.2 On-Balance sheet adjustments to manage OBS risk

As we had discussed in Chapter 4 about Interest Rate risk, senior leaders and the ALM committee must consider how the bank's investing and financing choices affect refinancing risk and reinvestment risk. Managers can manage not only interest rate risk but also liquidity risk by adjusting the dollar amount, the level of interest rates, as well as the mix of variable rate and fixed rate instruments used within the bank's assets and liabilities. As discussed in Chapter 4, we can think of this as the "ARM" of ALM, where the acronym stands for a manager's choices in terms of the dollar *amount* (A), *rates* (R), and *mix* (M) of assets and liabilities on its balance sheet.

Bank managers can therefore adjust the "ARM" of their assets:

(1) the amount of funds they invest in different types of assets (e.g., loans versus securities);
(2) the level(s) of interest rates they charge for their different loan products (e.g., mortgage rates vs. auto loan rates); and
(3) the mix of variable vs. fixed rate loan products (e.g., adjustable rate vs. fixed rate mortgages).

These managers can also adjust the "ARM" for their liabilities:

(1) the amount of funds they borrow in relation to equity (e.g., deposits and OBM versus common equity);
(2) the level(s) of interest rates they pay for their different liabilities (e.g., money market accounts vs. certificates of deposit); and
(3) the mix of variable vs. fixed rate liabilities (e.g., money market accounts vs. medium term notes).

For example, we commonly see greater liquidity risk when a bank chooses to invest a large amount of funds in long-term, fixed rate loans and to finance this investment with short-term, variable rate deposits. As noted at the beginning of this chapter, this creates a large "maturity mismatch" between assets and liabilities. In this case, the ARM choices for assets lead to fewer (or possibly no) assets maturing within a year while the ARM choices for liabilities are mostly (if not all) maturing within 1 year, thus causing the bank to search for additional funds to repay these short-term liabilities. To remedy this, the bank could, for example, stop issuing long-term fixed rate loans and replace them with short-term variable rate loans. We should also keep in mind that it can be a slow process to adjust the bank's liquidity risk exposure via these ARM choices and thus it can take the firm away from its core business and might also lead to customer dissatisfaction (e.g., because clients might strongly prefer fixed rate loans rather than variable rate loans).

8.7.3 *Contingency funding plans*

A well-managed bank should also have a plan in case there is an abnormally high degree of loan takedowns and/or deposit withdrawals. This plan should be an extension of policy limits discussed above by creating a specific **action plan** to

- address increasing levels of liquidity stress based on an assessment of possible stress events,[21]
- designate responsibilities, communication protocols, required reporting/disclosures, and
- identify a detailed (and updated) list of contingent sources of liquidity.

By assessing the severity and timing of a liquidity stress event in conjunction with the contingency funding plan, the bank's managers can be prepared to mitigate the impact of liquidity risk on the FIs financial condition. We can think of a well-designed contingency funding plan as an ideal set of "wish list" liquidity sources, such as:

- Strong core deposit base;
- Stable financing pyramid (large % of insured deposits and small % of OBM);
- Sufficient cash balances and short-term, liquid Securities;
- Extra borrowing capacity at the Federal Home Loan Bank (or other governmental sources);

---

[21] Liquidity stress events can come from several sources such as disruptions to (1) economic growth, (2) payments systems, (3) credit markets, (4) geopolitical relationships, and (5) bank-specific business model choices (e.g., a concentrated customer base financed with uninsured deposits).

- Ready access to Lines of Credit and Wholesale Funding (Repurchase Agreements, Fed Funds purchased, Negotiable CD's, and/or Brokered CD's); and
- Federal Reserve's discount window access or other stress-induced funding vehicles.

Note that if a bank like our hypothetical bank, ABC, has all the attributes identified in the above wish list, then its managers should be able to handle even some of the most stressful liquidity events such as the 2008–2009 Great Financial Crisis and 2020–2022 COVID-19 pandemic. By doing so, the negative impact of such events on ABC's market value of equity can be reduced even if they cannot be fully eliminated.

8.7.4 *Pros and cons of stored vs. purchased liquidity risk management strategies*

As noted earlier in this chapter, the two main liquidity risk management strategies are based on holding lower-yielding liquid securities (Stored) or borrowing in the wholesale funding market via OBM (Purchased). The contingency funding plan described in the previous sub-section includes elements of both stored and purchased liquidity. Thus, it is up to the bank's managers to decide what is the optimal mix of these two strategies because they both have their advantages and disadvantages, as noted in the following.

8.7.5 *Liquidity risk at non-depository financial institutions*

Although the primary focus of this chapter has been on depository financial institutions like commercial banks, we should also keep in mind that *all* FIs are subject to liquidity risk, albeit to varying degrees. For example, a life insurance company can experience a "run" if many policyholders become concerned about the creditworthiness of the FI and decide to cancel their policies and cash in any "surrender value" of their policies (i.e., the cash value that has built up in various types of policies, such as "whole life" insurance).[22] This surrender value of life insurance policies is a

---

[22] A whole life insurance policy combines a traditional term life insurance policy with an investment account which can grow in value over time and is a valuable benefit to the

Table 8.5. Pros and Cons of Stored vs. Purchased Liquidity.

Stored Liquidity	
Pros	**Cons**
Safer (due to more liquid assets and lower financial leverage)	**Lower ROA** (due to reduced yield on securities vs. loans)
Reduced financing costs (because deposit rates are usually lower than wholesale financing rates)	**Lower ROE** (due to lower financial leverage)
Lower refinancing risk (due to reliance on typically shorter-term securities)	**Reduced flexibility** (by tying up funds in low-yielding securities even when there are no large liquidity needs)
	Possible smaller balance sheet size (if securities are used to pay for sudden deposit withdrawals)

Purchased Liquidity	
Pros	**Cons**
Higher ROA (due to greater yield on loans vs. securities)	**Riskier** (due to fewer liquid assets and higher financial leverage)
Higher ROE (due to higher financial leverage)	**Higher financing costs** (because deposit rates are usually lower than wholesale financing rates)
Greater flexibility (by borrowing funds only when there are large liquidity needs)	**Higher refinancing risk** (due to reliance on typically longer-term assets and shorter-term uninsured funds)
Possible larger balance sheet size (if purchased wholesale funds are used to finance more loans)	

liability for the insurer and thus can trigger serious liquidity problems if many customers rush to cancel their policies at once. Similarly, property-casualty insurers can experience liquidity risk if there is a sudden surge in insurance claims due to, for example, a hurricane hitting a heavily populated area. Hedge funds and other money managers can experience a "run on a fund" if investors become very nervous about the true value of the

---

customer. The surrender value of the policy is directly related to the accumulated value in this investment account.

assets held in the funds that are managed by these delegated monitors. Thus, liquidity risk is a pervasive problem for all FIs.

8.8 The Impact of Managing Liquidity Risk on a Financial Institution's Equity

In this section, we build on our prior discussion of the net effect of liquidity risk on a commercial bank's common equity. However, rather than focusing on the accounting relationships described earlier in Tables 8.2–8.4, we now approach this issue from a financial economics perspective. Academic research by Freixas and Rochet (2008) and Prisman *et al.* (1986) shows that liquidity's impact on bank profitability and market value is based on the opportunity cost of stored liquidity and the explicit cost of purchased liquidity. As these authors note, one way to incorporate liquidity risk in a bank valuation model is to allow for some randomness or uncertainty about the funds received or paid out over a short time (driven primarily by the demand for loans and the supply of deposits). We can quantify the opportunity cost of stored liquidity as lost income due to earning a lower return on the bank's securities portfolio (rS) vs. the higher return from making a loan (rL). Further, the explicit cost of purchased liquidity can be estimated by comparing the "penalty" rate (rP) for borrowing hot money vs. paying a lower deposit rate (rD) when insured deposits are used to finance customers' demand for liquidity.

Freixas and Rochet (2008) developed a highly stylized model of the factors affecting a bank's net income. Their basic model, presented in Equation (8.9), is even simpler than our integrated valuation model (IVM), first presented in Chapter 3. However, their model captures the essential trade-offs between higher profits from lending versus the greater liquidity risk associated with holding fewer securities and/or relying on hot money. So, we use this model of net income (NI) as a starting point and then apply it to our IVM approach:

$$\text{NI} = (rL \cdot L) + (rS \cdot S) - (rD \cdot D) - (rP \cdot E[\max(0, W - S^*)]) \qquad (8.9)$$

where

rL = loan rate the bank can charge its customers for its total dollar amount of loans (L) and where $L = D - S$ (i.e., loans are funded by deposits after deducting the bank's investment in securities),

rS = return on the bank's total dollar investments from both "operational" liquid asset balances (S') and "excess" balances held in securities, cash, and reserves, S^* (i.e., total liquid assets = $S = S' + S^*$),[23]

rD = interest rate the bank pays its insured depositors for its total dollar amount of deposit financing (D),

rP = the "penalty" interest rate the bank must pay to uninsured creditors for any funds needed to meet the bank's immediate liquidity demands by its customers (e.g., over the next 30 days), and

W = the dollar amount of cash needed to meet customers' immediate demand for liquidity.

The first two items on the right-hand side of (8.9) represent the interest income earned from the bank's lending and securities portfolios, while the third term is the interest expense paid to its insured depositors. Note that we are assuming deposits (D) can only fund loans (L) or investments in securities (S) and this relationship shows how increases in stored liquidity (by increasing S) will directly cause decreases in lending because every dollar increase in S reduces loans by the same amount via the relationship, $L = D - S$. The last term on the right side of (8.9) captures the "Liquidity Risk Effect" we had first introduced in Chapter 3 when describing the IVM method of valuing a bank's market value of equity. This portion of (8.9) is reprinted below as follows so that we can focus on its contents:

$$\text{Liquidity Risk Effect} = (rP \cdot E[\max(0, W - S^*)]) \quad (8.10)$$

where

$E[\max(0, W - S^*)] = \text{Prob}(W > S^*) \cdot (W - S^*)$ = Expected Liquidity Demand Net of Excess Liquid Assets and

---

[23] We assume that there is some dollar amount of the FIs total securities and cash (S) that are needed for normal operational purposes (S') such as reserve requirements, daily wire transfers, expected deposit withdrawals/loan takedowns, and trading accounts. Thus, the amount of the FIs liquid assets *not* used for daily operations can be viewed as "excess" balances which act as "emergency cash on hand" in case of a large, sudden liquidity risk event. In effect, $S^* = \%$ of S is not needed for daily operations ($x \, S$).

Prob$(W > S^*)$ = Probability of experiencing a cash shortfall and occurs whenever the demand for liquidity (W) is greater than the excess liquid assets available to meet this demand (S^*).

The above formula includes the variable, W, which quantifies the total dollar amount of a liquidity risk event, such as a sudden withdrawal of depositor funds and/or an increased need for funds to finance an unexpected surge in loan demand. The term, $E[\max(0, W-S^*)]$, represents the *expected* dollar amount of funds that are needed above and beyond the "excess" securities the FI has on hand for this type of liquidity risk event. This represents the dollar amount that needs to be borrowed via OBM/hot money (i.e., the E stands for an "expected" value). This expectation term includes S^* because these additional liquid assets can help offset some (or all) of the total liquidity demand, W. The expected value is also affected by the probability that W exceeds the bank's emergency cash on hand (Prob$(W > S^*)$). Note that this term equals *zero* if the bank already has sufficient liquid assets to cover the liquidity need (i.e., when $S^* > W$).

Alternatively, this term can be a positive dollar value equal to the amount of cash needed that is greater than the bank's emergency cash on hand (i.e., $W > S^*$). Lastly, this expected dollar amount is multiplied by the bank's *penalty rate* (rP), which is a relatively high interest rate that is demanded by OBM creditors and/or a "lender of last resort" entity, such as the discount window rate charged by the Federal Reserve. The rate is higher because the bank's need to borrow on such short notice provides a negative signal of the FIs ability to manage its credit and liquidity risks. In sum, Equation (8.10) tells us that the cost of a liquidity risk event is either zero (if the bank has sufficient liquid assets, $S^* > W$) or some positive value equal to $rP \cdot (W - S^*)$ if the bank does not have enough cash on hand (because $W > S^*$).

As the above discussion suggests, the crux of the problem is the expectation of a possible cash shortfall which, in turn, is affected by the *probability distribution* of such an event occurring. The probability of a cash shortfall will be affected by several factors including the bank manager's choices, customers' choices in terms of loans and deposits, as well as conditions in financial markets and the overall macroeconomy. However, Freixas and Rochet (2008) do not provide a specific recommendation regarding how to model this probability distribution. So, what is needed is a metric which captures all these influences. Luckily, we have already described such a metric: the **Liquidity Coverage Ratio** (LCR). This is an ideal measure for us to use because, as you can see in the following from the reiteration of the LCR formula from Equation (8.6), it includes the bank's stored liquidity choices in the numerator (*High Quality Liquid Assets*) and is equivalent to S in our model, as well as customers' liquidity demands in the denominator (i.e., *Expected 30-day Net Cash Outflows*). Also, both the numerator and denominator will be affected by conditions in the financial markets and macroeconomy:

$$LCR = \frac{\text{High Quality Liquidity Assets}}{\text{Expected 30-day Net Cash Outflow}} \quad (8.11)$$

To incorporate the LCR into the Liquidity Risk Effect formula of (8.10), we make a simplifying assumption that the probability of a cash shortfall beyond the bank's emergency cash ($W > S^*$) is driven by the bank's LCR and that this metric can be reasonably approximated by the normal distribution.[24] As we know from a basic understanding of the normal distribution that we had introduced in an earlier chapter on market risk (Chapter 5), only two things are needed to describe the entire distribution: the mean and standard deviation of the relevant variable. In our case, we need estimates of the mean and standard deviation of the bank's LCR. This can be obtained by looking at the prior history of changes in LCR or by bank managers using judgment about their views of the bank's future values of LCR's average and standard deviation. Figure 8.4 depicts the *cumulative* probability of *avoiding* a cash shortfall when the bank's average LCR is 1.10 and its standard deviation is 0.05.[25]

---

[24] Note there are many other ways to model this liquidity risk. For example, we could assume the expected net cash outflows will follow a specific non-normal probability distribution and then use it to estimate the costs of stored vs. purchased liquidity. However, for external analysts (and even for internal bank managers), it might be more difficult to estimate this distribution of cash outflows than the more observable and less volatile LCR metric. So, we focus on LCR in this chapter but please keep in mind that are several other ways to model the underlying distribution(s) that drive a bank's liquidity risk.

[25] A cumulative probability is a simple sum of all probabilities up to a specific point within the range of possible values for LCR. So, for values far below the average value of LCR, the cumulative probability will be near zero while values well above the average have a cumulative probability close to 1.00 (or 100%), as shown in Figure 8.4.

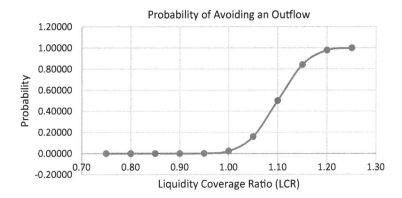

Figure 8.4. Probability Distribution of Avoiding a Potential Liquidity Risk-related Outflow.

8.9 Numerical Example of Liquidity Coverage Ratio (LCR) Choices on ABC's Equity

To make our discussion of the Liquidity Risk Effect a bit more concrete, we begin with the IVM valuation approach of Chapter 3 and the detailed numerical example presented there. As Figure 8.4 shows, a cumulative normal distribution has an S-shape because extreme values for LCR above and below the average LCR value of 1.10 have a very low probability of occurring. The above graph is based on the values presented in Table 8.6, which summarizes key information for a numerical example of ABC bank based on Chapter 3's data and contained within the "*Liquidity Risk – Ch 8*" tab of the **Integrated Valuation Model.xlsx** file. In this example, we assume LCR is normally distributed with a mean of 1.10 (i.e., HQLA is 110% of the bank's expected cash outflow, on average) and a standard deviation of 0.05, or 5% of the outflow.

Based on the figures described in Table 8.6 and the IVM method, ABC's estimated stock price *prior to* any adjustments for liquidity risk is $20.17 per share (i.e., [0.40 · $18.0 million / 0.0357] / 10.0 million shares = $20.17 per share).

Since we are focusing on liquidity risk in this chapter, the table also includes data in the last set of rows that are relevant to help us quantify liquidity risk's impact on ABC's market value of equity. Accordingly, numerical values are required for all the variables contained in Equation (8.9) to adjust ABC's Net Income (NI) to account for sudden

Table 8.6. Assumptions for the Numerical Example of Liquidity Coverage Ratio (LCR) choices on ABC's Equity.

Total Assets ($ million)	1,580
Cash & Sec. ($ million)	725
Net Loans ($ million)	800
Total Deposits ($ million)	1,400
Projected Net Income ($ million)	18.0
Initial Stock Price ($ per share)	20.17
Dividend Payout	0.40
Tax Rate	0.20
Dividend Yield ($R_E - g$)	0.0357
Shares Outstanding	10.00
Loan rate (rL)	0.0524
Securities Return (rS)	0.0250
Deposit rate (rD)	0.0211
Penalty rate (rP)	0.0600
LCR Average	1.10
LCR Standard Deviation	0.05
Excess Cash & Sec. (%)	50.0%
S^* = Excess Cash & Sec. ($ million)	362.5
Expected Cash Outflows ($ million)	700
Initial LCR	1.036

liquidity demands. So, Table 8.6 shows that we are assuming ABC can lend at 5.24% (rL) or invest in marketable securities and earn a lower rate of 2.50% (rS). Thus, any funds the bank chooses to invest in securities will result in an *opportunity cost* based on the difference in these two rates (i.e., the opportunity cost in this example is 2.74% because 5.24% minus 2.50% equals 2.74%). ABC also must pay its depositors an interest rate of 2.11% (rD).

The next set of numbers shown below ABC's deposit rate of 2.11% pertain to the bank's expected Liquidity Risk Effect, as described by Equation (8.10). For example, the cost of borrowing funds due to a liquidity risk is called a *"penalty" rate* (rP) and, at 6.00%, is much more costly than deposit rate financing. Due to a need for emergency borrowings, ABC will have to pay a relatively high punitive rate of 6.00% to compensate creditors who are concerned about the bank's viability. Clearly, ABC would prefer to avoid this explicit cost, if possible, but to do so, the bank will have to hold more excess cash which, as noted above, has its own opportunity cost due to the lower return on securities vs. loans. Thus, there is a classic trade-off between paying a higher borrowing cost associated with purchased liquidity versus foregoing higher interest income on loans due to investments in stored liquidity. The key is for ABC's managers to carefully weigh both sides of this trade-off to find an optimal dollar amount of excess securities, S^*, that can maximize the bank's value.

To accomplish this task, the bank's managers must choose a mechanism that measures and manages this liquidity risk and its impact on market value. As noted earlier, we suggest the Liquidity Coverage Ratio (LCR) is an analytically convenient way to explore this trade-off. As shown in Table 8.6 and Figure 8.4, we assume that ABC's LCR is normally distributed with a mean of 1.10 and a standard deviation of 0.05. We also require an estimate of the amount of ABC's "excess" liquid assets (S^*) which, in our case, we assume this figure equals 50% of the total portfolio of cash and securities ($362.5 million = 0.50 · $725 million). In addition, ABC's management will need to use historical data, statistical analysis, and good judgment to estimate the bank's Expected Net Cash Outflow in case there is a sudden liquidity event (assumed to be $700 million in Table 8.6). For reference, the table also reports ABC's current LCR prior to any liquidity risk event at a level of 1.036 (i.e., current LCR = current HQLA / E(Net Cash Outflows = $725 million/$700 million = 1.036)). Note that we are making another simplifying assumption by treating all of ABC's cash and securities as HQLA items (High Quality Liquid Assets). So, as we can see from ABC's current level of securities holdings, the bank is potentially facing a greater degree of liquidity risk due to its LCR of 1.036 being only slightly higher than Basel III's benchmark of 1.00.

8.10 Applying the IVM Method to Liquidity Risk

Summarized in the following is one example of how we can model the liquidity risk trade-off. As we have stated in earlier chapters, there are several other ways to describe a bank's numerous risk-return choices and so bank managers have considerable flexibility in identifying the key factors influencing the costs and benefits of stored and purchased liquidity. The following discussion is meant to be an initial attempt to examine these direct costs and benefits of this trade-off. In addition, using the IVM within an Excel™ spreadsheet allows us to consider a more detailed analysis that includes both direct and indirect effects of the bank's liquidity risk management decision.

First, we can approach this problem by spelling out the total benefits and total costs of managing the bank's liquidity risk. In this way, we can see the change in the bank's market value of equity by comparing the value of the bank using stored "excess" liquidity with the value associated with purchased liquidity, as described by the net profit formula of Equation (8.9), which is reprinted in the following for convenience as follows:

$$\text{NI} = (rL \cdot L) + (rS \cdot S) - (rD \cdot D) - (rP \cdot E[\max(0, W - S^*)]) \quad (8.12)$$

Based on the above drivers of a bank's net profit, we see how liquidity risk management decisions can impact the bank's market value using the principles of the IVM. In fact, we can estimate the bank's risk management choice by using the following extension of the IVM from Chapter 3 that explicitly quantifies the change in market value due to liquidity risk (denoted by the "delta" sign, Δ):

$$\Delta V_E = \left[\frac{\Delta(d \cdot NI)}{(R_E - g)}\right]$$

$$= \left[\frac{d \cdot [(\text{Liquidity Risk Benefit} - \text{Liquidity Risk Cost}) \cdot (1 - t)]}{(R_E - g)}\right]$$

$$= \left[\frac{d \cdot [(\text{Liquidity Risk Benefit} - \text{Liquidity Risk Cost}) \cdot (1 - t)]}{\text{Expected Dividend Yield}}\right] \quad (8.13)$$

where

d = expected dividend payout ratio for next year ($\text{DIV}_1 / \text{NI}_1$),

Liquidity Risk Benefit = the total cost of *purchased* liquidity that can be *avoided* by holding excess cash on hand = $rP \cdot (1 - \text{Prob}(W > S^*)) \cdot \max[0, W - S^*]$,

Probability of avoiding a cash shortfall = $(1 - \text{Prob}(W > S^*))$, and where $\text{Prob}(W > S^*)$ is the probability of a cash shortfall whenever the demand for liquidity (W) is greater than the supply of liquid assets available to meet this demand (S^*),

Simulated excess liquid assets = S^* = Excess Liquid Assets as a % of Total Securities · LCR · E[Net Cash Outflow], so that S^* can vary with the bank's choice of LCR,[26]

Liquidity Risk Cost = the opportunity cost of *stored* liquidity *incurred* by holding excess cash on the balance sheet = $(rL - rS) \cdot S^*$, and where S^* is defined as shown above and in the footnote below (i.e., S^* = Excess Liquid Assets as % of Total Securities · LCR · E[Net Cash Outflow]) so that it can vary with the bank's choice of LCR,

t = marginal corporate tax rate,

R_E = expected return on the bank's equity,

g = constant growth rate of the bank's dividends, and

Expected Dividend Yield = $(DIV_1/V_{E,0})$ and, as shown earlier in Chapter 3, equals $(R_E - g)$ from the Constant Growth version of the IVM.

With Equation (8.13), we are making a couple of simplifying assumptions like the ones described in prior chapters:

1. The Liquidity Coverage Ratio (LCR) does not impact other aspects of the bank's cash flows other than those shown in the net profit formula of (8.12) and so the *after-tax net benefit of the risk management strategy* (i.e., (Liquidity Risk Benefit – Liquidity Risk Cost) · (1–t)) is the only factor affecting the bank's expected dividend. That is, Δ DIV = d · (after-tax *net* Liquidity Risk Benefit).
2. The Expected Dividend Yield $(R_E - g)$ remains constant even though the cash flow in the numerator of Equation (8.13) is changing. This is a simplifying assumption and is technically not true as the riskiness of the bank can change when the level of LCR is adjusted. We are

---

[26] Recall from Equation (8.11) that LCR = HQLA / E(Net Cash Outflows). Re-arranging this equation algebraically shows that HQLA = LCR · E(Net Cash Outflows) and this can be used as a proxy for S (if we assume all securities, S, are considered High Quality Liquid Assets). Thus, S^* can be estimated by multiplying S by the percentage of securities that are *not* needed for daily operations (i.e., S^* = Excess Liquid Assets as % of Total Securities · Total Securities). We can then use this relationship, along with HQLA = S = LCR · E(Net Cash Outflows), to allow S^* to vary as the bank changes its LCR via S^* = Excess Liquid Assets as % of Total Securities · LCR · E(Net Cash Outflows).

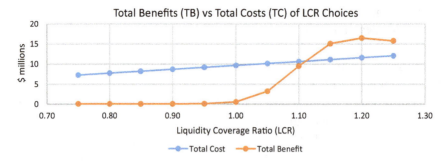

Figure 8.5. The Costs and Benefits of Various Liquidity Coverage Ratios.

assuming that any changes in R_E or g are relatively small and can cancel each out and thus be ignored in this example.[27] For a more complete analysis of all potential effects of the hedging decision on firm value, we can use the Excel™ spreadsheet.

We can now use the above variant of the IVM described in Equation (8.13) in a numerical example for our hypothetical bank, ABC, based on the initial data and assumptions shown in Table 8.6. The results of this analysis are presented in graphical forms as Figures 8.5 and 8.6.

Figure 8.5 illustrates the total costs and benefits of managing the firm's liquidity risk (expressed in millions of dollars on an annual basis). As we vary the bank's LCR from 0.75 to 1.25, a clear pattern emerges where, at first, the opportunity costs of stored liquidity outweigh any benefits of avoiding the penalty rate of purchased liquidity. This makes sense because when the LCR is very low, there is not much excess cash on hand to cover any liquidity shortfalls. Thus, on the left side of Figure 8.5, there is a very high chance that the bank must use purchased liquidity and pay the relatively high penalty rate (rP) of 6.00%. In contrast, the right-hand side of the graph shows a large jump in the benefits of holding excess cash. This occurs because LCR levels around 1.10 indicate that the benefits of avoiding the cash shortfall begin to outweigh the opportunity cost of reduced

---

[27] As described in previous chapters, this assumption can be a *conservative* estimate of the estimated change in market value (i.e., *lower* than what might occur) because liquidity risk management could, in theory, lower the bank's cost of equity (R_E) which would, in turn, raise the bank's valuation. So, assuming no change in $R_E - g$ might be a reasonably safe approach in this context.

interest income due to ABC's investment in lower-yielding securities (*rS*). Figure 8.5 shows the *net* benefit of holding stored liquidity is maximized when the LCR is around 1.20.[28]

We can use the above analysis, along with the IVM model of Equation (8.13), to quantify the impact of the bank's liquidity risk management decisions on ABC's market value of equity. Figure 8.6 shows how changes in LCR affect ABC's stock price. As the graph demonstrates, *low* levels of LCR (i.e., *less* usage of stored liquidity) lead to *decreases* in stock price, with a very large decline of $8.17 per share (−40.5%) occurring at an LCR of 1.00. In contrast, the graph shows that an LCR of 1.20 leads to a big increase of $4.39 per share from the base price of $20.17 (+21.8%). Since ABC's original LCR was 1.036 before performing this analysis, we can see that the bank's stock price can be maximized by building up more stored liquidity. It appears that LCR levels between 1.15 and 1.25 lead to the best trade-off between the costs and benefits of stored vs. purchased liquidity. We should also note that levels further above 1.20–1.25 can *reduce* the change in ABC's stock price. This occurs even though a very high level of LCR leads to lower purchased liquidity costs because interest income from lending declines even more. Consequently, the costs of stored liquidity once again outweigh the strategy's benefits at LCR levels above 1.20. So, an LCR around 1.20 appears to be the "Goldilocks" solution which represents the optimal trade-off between stored and purchased liquidity strategies.

The above discussion presents us with some useful, actionable information because it suggests that ABC's managers have room to increase their use of stored liquidity, which can reduce the bank's liquidity risk and maximize its stock price. As we have shown all along in this book, there is truly an "ART" to risk management and that, in this case, the "R" (for *remove* some of the liquidity risk) might be the preferred choice by holding more liquid assets. And, as we have also suggested in prior chapters, the IVM's estimates of stock price changes are best used as indications of the general direction of liquidity risk's impact on firm value rather than exact estimates.

---

[28] The precise LCR that maximizes ABC's value is 1.187, which can be found via an optimization algorithm like the *Solver* feature within Excel™. When the LCR is set to 1.187, ABC's stock price increases by $4.46 per share for a +22.2% gain over the original value of $20.17.

Figure 8.6. Impact on a Bank's Market Value of Equity of Liquidity Risk Management Choices.

8.11 Managerial Implications

The liquidity risk problem Nina and Sam must contemplate is as follows: **how much liquidity risk is tolerable for ABC Bank if a competing bank, XYZ, recently failed due to a sudden run on its deposits?** Given that any bank failure is unsettling to the entire banking industry, the two colleagues must quickly come up with a liquidity risk management recommendation for ABC's CEO and board of directors. It is clear to Sam and Nina from the quantitative analysis shown in Table 8.6 and Figures 8.5–8.6 that ABC must move rapidly to raise its Liquidity Coverage Ratio to not only maximize shareholder value but also to avoid a run on the bank. However, given the bank's total Cash and Securities balance is $725 million and its expected cash outflow is $700 million, ABC will need to find a way to obtain an additional $115 million in liquid assets (i.e., Desired liquid assets − Actual liquid assets = (1.20 · $700 million) − $725 million = $840 million − $725 million = $115 million). Nina and Sam realize that to raise these funds, it can either sell off some of its loans (currently totaling $800 million) and/or borrow in the short-term market via OBM (Other Borrowed Money). Since ABC's loans are relatively illiquid and the bank has no existing OBM (i.e., all $1,400 million of liabilities are from insured depositors), Sam and Nina **think the best plan is to use a Purchased Liquidity strategy and borrow $115 million in the form of short-term OBM (via either Fed Funds purchased or Repos) and then invest the proceeds in high quality liquid assets (HQLA)**. In this way, ABC can achieve an LCR of 1.20 in a relatively quick manner.

However, both colleagues realize that relying on short-term "hot money" to finance the increase in liquid assets can be a risky strategy over the longer term because these creditors might decide to not renew their short-term loans to ABC. In addition, the increase in liabilities reduces the bank's capital buffer relative to its assets, as the equity-to-assets ratio will decline once the additional OBM is obtained. **So, Nina and Sam would also recommend that, over time, the short-term OBM be replaced with some form of more stable, longer-term debt financing such as a 5-year medium term note or by borrowing on a 2- or 3-year fixed rate term loan basis from the Federal Home Loan Bank Board to remove the risk of losing the support of short-term, uninsured creditors.**

From a qualitative perspective, the two colleagues felt that by acting quickly and decisively to raise the LCR from 1.036 to 1.20, both investors and regulators will view this as a *positive signal* about ABC's overall liquidity position. In addition, the increase in financial leverage can also be viewed favorably by external parties if the bank can succeed in eventually replacing the short-term OBM with some longer-term debt financing (possibly also from an increase in insured deposits). This approach will allow the loan portfolio to remain intact and can continue to earn a higher return. Whenever there is heightened uncertainty in the industry due to a bank failure, Nina and Sam think that generating positive "signals" of financial strength is essential to calm potentially nervous investors and/or regulators. In this case, both the quantitative and qualitative aspects of the problem are consistent with each other, and both suggest employing the "R" from the ART of risk management (for "Remove" the liquidity risk as much as possible). **Do you agree with Nina and Sam's recommendation? If not, then how would you handle it differently and what are your reasons for doing so?**

8.12 Summary

Overall, this chapter demonstrated the importance of liquidity risk management and how various metrics from basic ones (like the loan-to-deposit ratio) to more sophisticated ones (e.g., the LCR) can be used to measure a bank's vulnerability to a bank run due to sudden demands on the asset and liability sides of its balance sheet. This rapid need for funds by the bank's customers can be viewed as a call option on the FIs liquid resources where the sensitivity of the bank to this need can be measured by a "delta" (δ_{LIQ}). In addition, we learned how a bank can use Stored Liquidity and Purchased Liquidity strategies to manage this liquidity risk. There are pros and cons to the two strategies and so many banks use both methods. Banks can also set liquidity-related limits on various types of assets and liabilities, as well as develop contingency funding plans to meet sudden liquidity demands. These methods, along with the "ARM" approach to asset–liability management, enable senior management to control liquidity risk by altering the dollar *amount* (*A*), *rates* (*R*), and *mix* (*M*) of assets and liabilities on its balance sheet. In the end, senior management must consider both quantitative and qualitative factors when deciding how much liquidity risk to incur and how best to manage this risk so that the bank's market value of equity can be maximized.

Chapter-End Questions

Answers to odd-numbered questions can be found at the end of this book.

1. **True or False:** The "Financing Pyramid" suggests that the largest percentage of bank financing should come from stable, low-cost insured deposits.
2. **True or False:** Stored liquidity strategy is riskier due to fewer liquid assets and higher financial leverage.
3. **Multiple Choice:** What is asset-based liquidity risk typically referred to?
   (A) Sudden customer demands for bank funds to finance deposit withdrawals
   (B) Sudden customer demands for bank funds to finance items such as pre-approved lines of credit, loan commitments, and letters of credit
   (C) Sudden demands for bank funds to make payments to other parties such as creditors, Credit Default Swap (CDS) owners, regulators (for fines), and plaintiffs (for lawsuits)
   (D) None of the above

4. **Multiple Choice:** A bank with a high loan-to-deposit ratio (LN/Depo) is
   (A) More susceptible to being caught shorthanded if an unexpected surge in liquidity demand arises from its customers.
   (B) Less susceptible to being caught shorthanded if an unexpected surge in liquidity demand arises from its customers.
   (C) Not affected by liquidity risk.
   (D) None of the above.
5. **Multiple Choice:** In the "Financing Pyramid," which of the following is considered the least desirable source of financing?
   (A) Insured Deposits
   (B) Common Equity
   (C) Other Borrowed Money (OBM)
   (D) Preferred Stock
6. **Short Answer:** If a bank has Level 1 assets of $200 million, Level 2A assets of $300 million, Level 2B assets of $400 million, and Expected 30-day Net Cash Outflows of $250 million, then what is the bank's Liquidity Coverage Ratio (LCR)?
7. **Short Answer:** If a bank's total assets are $100 million, cash and securities are $34 million, net loans are $58 million, total deposits are $90 million, and the projected net income is $2.288 million, then what is the bank's stock price if the dividend payout is 0.40, the tax rate is 0.20, the dividend yield ($R_E - g$) is 0.0357, and there are 1.00 million shares outstanding? Also, what is the bank's loan-to-deposit ratio (LN/Depo) and expected ROE?
8. **Short Answer:** If the expected dividend payout ratio (d) for next year is 0.4 (or 40%), the *Liquidity Risk Benefit* is $1.2 million per year, the *Liquidity Risk Cost* is $0.5 million per year, the marginal corporate tax rate (t) is 0.2 (or 20%), and the expected dividend yield is 0.0357 (or 3.57%), then what is the expected dollar change in the bank's market value due to managing the bank's liquidity risk?

9. **Excel-based Question:** How much does the bank's liquidity risk exposure on its $1,580 million in total assets affect ABC's *market value of equity* (i.e., its market capitalization or "market cap")? Assume the bank's managers are concerned about how changes in sudden demand for cash from borrowers and/or creditors can affect the bank's market value due to investor concerns about the stability of the financial system. To do so, change the levels of expected cash outflows and "excess" liquid assets, as well as the "penalty rate" for short-term uninsured borrowing based on the following parts A–D. To answer these questions, use the "OBS Risk – Ch 8" tab of the **Integrated Valuation Model.xlsx** file. For example, try this by starting with the current values in the blue cells related to the *Expected Outflows, Penalty Rate (rP), and Excess Cash & Securities*.
   (A) As a starting point, what happens to the bank's stock price and optimal Liquidity Coverage Ratio (LCR*) if the bank's expected "emergency" cash outflows (i.e., the *E(Outflows)* variable) rise from $700 million to $900 million *and* the bank responds by increasing its "excess" liquid assets from 50% to 60% of ABC's total cash and securities? *Note: You will need to use the spreadsheet's **Solver function** to find this optimal solution because the model presented in this chapter does not have a closed-form, analytical solution. Follow the directions in the spreadsheet to operate this Solver function.*
   (B) In addition to your assumptions from part A, compute ABC's new stock price and LCR* if the "penalty rate" (rP) also rises from 6.0% to 8.0% due to an increase in system-wide liquidity risk.

10. **Comprehensive Question:** Given the scenario presented in the text with Nina and Sam, **how would you evaluate the potential risks and benefits of ABC Bank's proposed strategy** to increase its Liquidity Coverage Ratio (LCR) from 0.85 to 1.10 by using *purchased liquidity*? Consider the implications of this strategy on the bank's liquidity risk, financial leverage, and overall market perception. Additionally, discuss the potential impact of this strategy on the bank's equity-to-assets ratio and the possible consequences of relying on short-term "hot money".

References

Black, F. and Scholes, M. (1973). The pricing of options and corporate liabilities, *Journal of Political Economy*, 81, 637–659.

Brunnermeier, M.K. and Pedersen, L.H. (2009). Market liquidity and funding liquidity, *Review of Financial Studies*, 22, 2201–2238.

Demirgüç-Kunt, A. and Huizinga, H. (2010). Bank activity and funding strategies: The impact on risk and returns, *Journal of Financial Economics*, 98, 626–650.

Freixas, X. and Rochet, J-C. (2008). *Microeconomics of Banking*, MIT, Cambridge, MA.

Foucault, T., Pagano, M. and Roell, A. (2013). *Market Liquidity: Theory, Evidence, and Policy*, Oxford, Oxford.

Hull, J.C. (2010). *Risk Management and Financial Institutions*, Prentice-Hall, Boston.

Ozenbas, D., Pagano, M.S., Schwartz, R.A. and Weber, B. (2022). *Liquidity, Markets and Trading in Action: An Interdisciplinary Perspective*, Springer, New York. Available via Open Access at: https://link.springer.com/book/10.1007/978-3-030-74817-3.

Prisman, E., Slovin, M. and Sushka, M. (1986). A general model of the banking firm under conditions of monopoly, uncertainty and recourse, *Journal of Monetary Economics*, 17, 293–304.

Saunders, A., Cornett, M.M. and Erhemjamts, O. (2024). *Financial Institutions Management: A Risk Management Approach*, McGraw Hill, New York.

Chapter 9

Operational Risk

9.1 What Is Operational Risk?

Broadly speaking, operational risk is the risk related to people and processes at financial institutions. The Basel Committee defines operational risk as the "risk of loss resulting from inadequate or failed internal processes, people, and systems or from external events."[1] Furthermore, the Basel Committee notes that operational risk is "inherent in all banking products, activities, processes, and systems, and the effective management of operational risk has always been a fundamental element of a bank's risk management program." In other words, operational risk is pervasive and something that is important for a financial institution to monitor in all its business activities.

In addition to its pervasiveness, operational risk can be costly, especially in extreme circumstances. For example, Société Générale and JPMorgan Chase lost over $7 billion and $5 billion in trading-related events. Banks and other financial institutions lost billions of dollars in Bernard Madoff's Ponzi scheme during the 2008–2009 Global Financial Crisis. Wells Fargo faced a $1 billion fine along with additional regulatory penalties after a series of operational issues.[2] Moreover, operational risk losses and events are not limited to only large financial institutions. Also,

---

[1] See Basel Committee on Banking Supervision "Revisions to Principles for the Sound Management of Operational Risk" (https://www.bis.org/bcbs/publ/d515.htm).

[2] See (i) *New York Times*: "French Bank Says Rogue Trader Lost $7 Billion" (N. Clark and D. Jolly, January. 25, 2008), (ii) *New York Times*: "New Fraud Inquiry as JPMorgan's Loss Mounts" (J. Silver-Greenberg, July 13, 2012), (iii) *Wall Street Journal*: "Top Broker Accused of $50 Billion Fraud" (A. Efrati, T. Lauricella and D. Searcey, December 12, 2008), and (iv)

former Federal Reserve Bank of St. Louis President James Bullard noted that "operational risk will someday equal or exceed credit risk for many community banks."[3]

Despite the potential for extraordinary loss, it is difficult to manage operational risk. In general, a bank cannot simply buy, say, a futures contract or a swap to protect itself against the potential activity of a rogue trader (although there are some sources of operational risk, e.g., an employee injuring themselves on the job, that a bank could potentially buy an insurance policy to cover). Rather, the bank must be vigilant about observing and scrutinizing its business practices and placing safeguards along the way to prevent operational risk failures. This becomes especially true in a banking system that is increasingly digital and in an economy where new innovations (and newly emerging risks) in FinTech occur seemingly by the day. On top of this, financial institutions must maintain an appropriate equity capital buffer to protect against these losses, should they occur. Without enough capital to offset a "black swan" operational risk event (that is, an event with a very low probability that creates a dramatic loss), a financial institution can easily turn the operational risk event into an insolvency problem.

In this chapter, we discuss operational risk by first examining its sources: event types and examples from throughout the bank. Following this, we discuss ways that a bank can potentially mitigate its exposure to operational risk events, both from a qualitative and a quantitative perspective. Within that discussion, we provide a brief overview of the Basel capital standards for operational risk-based capital. Finally, we look at how the costs of operational risk management fit into the IVM model we have developed throughout this book.

9.2 Types and Examples of Operational Risk

The Bank for Institutional Settlements (BIS) Basel II framework outlines seven different categories for operational risk events.[4] We briefly define

---

CNN: "Wells Fargo's 20-Month Nightmare" (J. Wattles, B. Geier, M. Egan and D. Wiener-Bronner, April 24, 2018).

[3] See *Federal Reserve Bank of St. Louis*: "Welcoming Remarks" at the Sixth Annual Community Banking in the 21st Century Research and Policy Conference by J. Bullard (October 3, 2018).

[4] See, for example, the 2004 document, "Basel II: International Convergence of Capital Measurement and Capital Standards: A Revised Framework" (https://www.bis.org/publ/bcbs107.htm).

and provide simple examples of each in this section. Further, we include a discussion of some risks related to cybersecurity issues.

9.2.1 *Execution delivery and process management (EDPM)*

EDPM events are defined by the BIS in the Basel II documentation as "losses from failed transaction processing or process management, from relations with trade counterparties and vendors." This category is somewhat wide-ranging, as it can result from sources that are internal or external to the bank. Internally, the bank could have a problem with data entry, missed deadlines, or other accounting errors. Further, the bank could maintain incorrect client records, negligently lose client assets, or have problems with missing client permissions. Alternatively, the bank's external risk sources also include disputes with vendors or the underperformance of counterparties.

9.2.2 *Clients, products, and business practices (CPBP)*

CPBP events are defined by the BIS in 2004 as "losses arising from an unintentional or negligent failure to meet a professional obligation to specific clients (including fiduciary and suitability requirements), or from the nature or design of a product." As it relates to the bank's customers, these events include breaches of privacy, disclosure issues (e.g., Know Your Client, or "KYC," rules), the misuse of confidential information, or account churning (in which a broker trades client assets repeatedly to generate excessive commissions). Moreover, business practice issues such as antitrust violations, market manipulation, insider trading (on the firm's account), or money laundering are events included within this category.

9.2.3 *Internal fraud (IF)*

The BIS defines IF events as "losses due to acts of a type intended to defraud, misappropriate property, or circumvent regulations, the law, or company policy, excluding diversity/discrimination events, which involves at least one internal party." These events can include unauthorized activity in which transactions are not reported or traders' positions are intentionally misrepresented, or other forms of theft or fraud like forgery, check kiting, or tax evasion.

9.2.4 External fraud (*EF*)

EF events are defined by the BIS as "losses due to acts intended to defraud, misappropriate property, or circumvent the law, by a third party." These issues relate to external actors committing crimes against the bank, including theft, forgery, or hacking. We discuss issues related to cybersecurity further in the following.

9.2.5 Employment practices and workplace safety (*EPWS*)

The BIS defines EPWS events as "losses arising from acts inconsistent with employment, health, or safety laws or agreements, from payment of personal injury claims, or from diversity, discrimination, or harassment events." In this category, loss events can include discrimination, liability concerns (e.g., slip and fall), employee health and safety concerns, and issues related to compensation.

9.2.6 Business disruption and system failures (*BDSF*)

BDSF events are defined by the BIS as "losses arising from the disruption of business or system failures." This category includes issues mostly related to the bank's systems, including failure of hardware and software, telecommunications, and other utility outages and disruptions.

9.2.7 Damage to physical assets (*DPA*)

The BIS defines DPA events as "losses arising from loss or damage to physical assets from natural disaster or other events." This category includes losses resulting from natural disasters or external actors (e.g., terrorism or vandalism).

9.2.8 Cybersecurity risk

Cybersecurity risk is a wide-ranging category of operational risk events. These events, though not given their own designation, can be a part of many of the categories listed above. Accordingly, it is important to give this risk some special treatment in this chapter, considering the increasing level of digitization in banking and consistent innovation in the FinTech space. Here, we list some examples of cybersecurity risk that are important for financial institutions to be aware of and defend against. Cybersecurity becomes more and more important as financial assets are increasingly held online and with the advent of products related to cryptocurrencies that require sensitive information (e.g., private keys for "digital wallets") and that provide some degree of anonymity for users. In all, the following discussion highlights the importance of operational risk management, especially as it relates to cybersecurity risk and the widespread impact that cyberattacks can have.

Attacks against payment systems: Events in this category include attacks against international payment systems like SWIFT.[5] Here, attackers can gain access to bank systems and attempt to send messages across SWIFT (or other systems) to direct funds to their own accounts. One notable example of this is the 2016 attack on the Bank of Bangladesh that saw hackers attempt to steal and launder $950 million via SWIFT transfers. The hackers were successful in stealing $81 million after some of the transactions were held at the Federal Reserve Bank of New York (where the Bank of Bangladesh had a U.S. Dollar account).[6]

Phishing: Phishing attacks are attempts by attackers to gain data (e.g., passwords, usernames, and credit card numbers) or install malware on the bank's computers by sending fraudulent e-mails (or other communications) that appear to be coming from a reputable source. These attacks can lead to issues related to ransomware (which encrypts the user's data, with the attacker demanding a ransom to decrypt, or unlock, the data) or Advanced Persistent Threats (APT), where an attacker can access the institution's computers and network and remain undetected for a long period of time. In the case of the Bank of Bangladesh event mentioned above, the attackers had access to the Bank's network for several months before executing their theft. During that time, they became intimately

---

[5] It is important to note that SWIFT is not a *settlement* system in which funds are directly transferred from bank to bank, but rather it is a *messaging* system for transfer instructions. FIs still must find other means by which to transfer funds after receiving a SWIFT message.

[6] For much more detail, see https://www.bbc.com/news/stories-57520169 and the associated podcast "The Lazarus Heist."

familiar with risk management protocols at the institution and worked on ways to defeat them.

Credential Stuffing: These attacks see the attacker using stolen credentials (e.g., usernames and passwords) to attempt to access accounts on other systems via a (very) large number of automated login requests. Typically, the attacker will use credentials from a data breach at one website or service and use the stolen credentials to log in at a different website, taking advantage of individuals who may use the same password for multiple accounts. This is like a "brute force" attack, in which the attacker does not know the passwords associated with various usernames but attempts to guess at passwords multiple times until they eventually guess correctly. One example of this form of attack was at HSBC in 2018, although the bank noted that less than 1% of all U.S. accounts were affected.[7]

Denial of Service: In this attack, the attacker attempts to make an institution's website unavailable to users. This can be accomplished by flooding the bank's systems with numerous requests in an attempt to overload them. At banks, these attacks have the potential to make services unavailable for long periods of time, which can lead to losses in revenue or disruptions to customer payments.

Data Breaches: Data breaches occur when sensitive information is stolen, transmitted, or copied without authorization. For financial institutions, this can occur on a large scale and can create a serious risk to the bank's reputation. One significant example of this was a 2019 data breach at Capital One that impacted approximately 100 million individuals in the United States.[8]

9.3 Managing Operational Risk: A Basic Qualitative Framework

Managing operational risk is not necessarily the same as managing other types of risks that a financial institution faces. As we have noted earlier, to manage the risk that someone injures themselves at work, a rogue

---

[7] See https://www.bbc.com/news/technology-46117963.
[8] See https://www.capitalone.com/digital/facts2019/.

trader costs the bank billions of dollars, a natural disaster destroys critical infrastructure, or a cyber attacker compromises the data of the bank's customers, it is not as simple as buying a derivative that pays off when the event happens. Although insurance can be valuable in these times, it will not necessarily help the bank recover its reputation and potentially lose future business. Insurance also may not cover all sources of operational risk (e.g., if the bank faces regulatory action due to poor operational risk management practices). Thus, the best defense against operational risk is to make sure that these events do not happen (or are greatly limited) in the first place. As the saying goes, "an ounce of prevention is worth a pound of cure."

Although operational risk management can provide great benefits to a bank (that many times go unseen), it can also carry significant costs. For example, there are costs associated with operational risk's best practices, both in terms of the framework we discuss next (e.g., hiring additional employees, developing resources to manage the risk, and the use of other employees' time) and from holding additional operational risk-based equity capital (which can increase the bank's overall cost of capital) that we discuss after that. We discuss these options and then describe how the bank manager can view the costs and benefits of operational risk management through the lens of the IVM.

9.3.1 *Elements of managing operational risk*

We start here with a discussion of a framework for banks to understand and manage their operational risk exposure. Starting from a baseline of data collection, an institution can then use this data to assess risks, monitor risks, and finally manage them. We briefly discuss each of these points in the following.

9.3.1.1 *Data collection*

The process starts with identifying areas of potential operational risk and collecting relevant data. These data include internal and external operational risk loss data that can be used to develop key risk indicators (KRIs). KRIs can help monitor risk factors within the bank and provide early warning signals for areas of increasing risk to help avoid incurring future losses, as the bank can set baseline levels for KRIs that are used as thresholds to indicate emerging problems. KRIs in operational risk can include items like employee turnover, the number of transaction processing errors, or response times to resolve customer complaints, and high call volume to customer help centers. It is helpful for KRIs to be objective, easy to measure, timely, and reliable. Moreover, the bank can collect data and information on operational risk "near misses" that can help guide the focus of management. In all, it is important for data collection to be a consistent process, as it is the bedrock of managing an institution's exposure to operational risk.

9.3.1.2 *Assessment*

The second area of operational risk management is assessing risk based on the data and information collected above. Assessment can include statistical methods that we discuss in the following section (e.g., using the Power Law function) or other methods like stress testing and scenario analysis. In scenario analysis, the bank identifies potential operational risk scenarios (developed from loss data and/or expert opinion) and assesses the likely impact on the bank of these scenarios. For example, the bank might model the impact of a cyberattack on the bank. Through this modeling exercise, the bank works through potential weaknesses in existing controls, models potential losses, and develops strategies to mitigate risk.

Through continuous assessment, the bank can understand the **frequency** and **severity** of operational risk events and act to prevent them, as well as develop a plan for limiting damage from them if they should occur. This is especially true for helping the bank prepare for and mitigate the impact of low-frequency, high-severity events.

9.3.1.3 *Monitoring*

After data collection and the assessment/analysis of the data, a bank must then continuously review its operational risk profile. As part of this process, the bank regularly assesses its KRIs, controls, and the effectiveness of its risk management process. In its monitoring, the bank can regularly conduct risk control self-assessments (RCSA), which is a systematic process by which the firm reviews its operational risk controls. From this assessment, the bank can prioritize remediation efforts for shortfalls (note that management always has the option to simply "Accept" the risk, according to the "ART" of risk management).

The bank, through this process, should also regularly assess its compliance with regulations, like the operational risk-based capital rules we outline in the following. Moreover, the monitoring process may lead to reassessment and the development of new scenarios or updated stress tests. Regular monitoring keeps the bank up to date with the most recent data on loss events and ensures that the bank's risk mitigation strategies are reflecting its most recent and important operational risk threats.

9.3.1.4 *Management*

Finally, the bank must manage its operational risk, which is the culmination and combination of the three previous steps outlined above. Part of the management process also includes the development of the bank's risk tolerance and how the bank's business goals and strategy relate to, and inform, the bank's "risk appetite." Importantly, risk managers, as well as senior management, can view these four parts of the framework as circular and ongoing. Over time, these steps should be continuously repeated and sharpened, with the bank aiming for consistency in its process.

9.3.1.5 *Lines of defense*

Once an institution has developed the routines above for understanding and assessing its exposure to operational risk and controls to mitigate it, the bank should seek independent risk management procedures across multiple lines of defense. Allowing independence across the various levels of the bank provides multiple layers of review that are not influenced by each other. We outline here *three* key "lines of defense" for a bank:

- *Business line level*: This is the bank's first line of defense. It supports the management of the business line, and control functions that can be used to keep operational risk within defined thresholds. As this group is on the "front line," it should be regularly assessing operational risk and identifying and capturing data on operational risk events. At this level, some examples of operational risk management include the consideration of how different business lines directly interact with customers (and the data and asset security needs of those customers, while mitigating issues as they arise), vigilance for cybersecurity breaches and technology malfunctions, or direct workplace safety considerations at the business line level. The data collected at this level (e.g., KRIs,

realized operational risk losses) can be aggregated at the next level to construct firm-wide estimates of the likelihood and severity of operational risk events.
- *Enterprise level*: Here, the bank receives independent risk management based on bank-wide risk management policies and frameworks. This group recommends risk tolerance, defines policy, measures, monitors risk, and develops tools for managing operational risk across the entire bank. For example, at the Enterprise Level, decisions related to firm-wide cybersecurity products and policies; legal, regulatory compliance, and human resources policies; or employee health and safety considerations can be made and passed throughout the firm. Broadly, at this level, the bank can also oversee operational risk decisions made at the business line level, as well as aggregate and summarize data collected to better model the sources of operational risk.
- *Internal audit*: This group provides independent testing of risk management processes from the first and second lines of defense. Independent internal audit provides another layer of review that can help the bank catch anything overlooked at the business line or enterprise levels.

A consideration to add here is the importance of communication and accountability *across* these lines of defense. An institution's operational risk management teams work in conjunction with each other, communicating via risk committees, meetings with multiple risk managers, and working alongside business managers in other parts of the firm. This collaborative approach allows for data to be shared easily, creates open lines of communication, and provides a more comprehensive and holistic approach to managing operational risk.

9.4 Managing Operational Risk: Quantitative Methods

Given that we know what operational risk is and how we may try to defend against it in a qualitative way, we can also think about how to manage operational risk with some quantitative methods. It is very difficult to predict the precise type of operational event that can occur within the institution. However, we can attempt to predict the **frequency** of operational events and the **severity** of the operational events that our bank will face over a given period. Note this concept is like the approach described earlier in Chapter 6 about quantifying credit risk for investments in bonds and loans. Insurance companies also use the "Frequency times Severity" approach to estimate "Expected Losses" on insurance policies. This estimate can then inform the bank's decision when it comes to how much operational risk-based equity capital to hold. In particular, the bank may be specifically concerned with events that are low in frequency but high in severity (for example, the $7 billion trading loss to Société Générale or the $1 billion fine to Wells Fargo we mentioned earlier). The following is a simple example of a matrix approach used by many organizations to classify operational risk events by frequency and severity. Within the matrix, we list some simple examples of operational risk events that might commonly fall into each category[9]:

	Low Frequency	High Frequency
Low Severity	Employee trips and falls in the office, leading to personal injury	Small losses due to simple clerical errors
High Severity	Loss due to cybersecurity breach, employee fraud, or trading error	Natural disasters that destroy homes and businesses

Though there are minimum amounts of required capital for operational risk, a bank's managers might want to set aside more than the minimum, especially if they believe that its exposure to an operational risk event is relatively high, or if it is particularly concerned about a low frequency but high severity event. While it is true that holding additional equity can increase the bank's overall cost of capital and lower its profitability for shareholders, these increased costs may not be nearly as high as the increased risk premiums that can be associated with an institution that poorly manages its operational risk (or, really, any other type of risk).

---

[9] Ideally, the bank should *not* have any items in the lower right portion of the matrix (High Frequency and High Severity) because these risks can be very costly and could even threaten the FIs survival. Given the rising frequency of wildfires, hurricanes, tornadoes, and other natural disasters in certain areas round the globe, an FI might classify the effects of these on consumer and business lending as a high frequency–high severity operational risk. We can also see this in the reduction of property-casualty insurance coverage in certain geographic regions and/or a large increase in the cost of this coverage.

9.4.1 Operational risk-based capital

A direct method of preparing for an operational risk event is to set aside equity capital to serve as a buffer for the bank against a potential unexpected large loss. We first start by examining the regulatory requirements set forth by the Basel Committee. These regulations define the minimum amounts of capital that an institution should hold to protect against an operational risk event. These regulations have changed over time and will likely continue to evolve going forward. However, their main goal remains unchanged. In all, the aim of capital requirements is to insulate the bank's debtholders (e.g., depositors and bondholders) against a large, unexpected loss. By building up the bank's capital, the bank effectively has a greater "distance to default," which means that it can absorb larger shocks without the serious risk of insolvency or bankruptcy (see Chapter 6 which talks about this distance to default in a credit risk context). We discuss more about capital requirements and other regulatory issues in Chapter 10. However, because operational risk-based capital (RBC) is a key component for managing exposure to this type of risk, we discuss the framework here.

9.4.2 Basel guidelines and formulas for the standardized measurement approach

As guidelines from the Basel Committee on Banking Supervision (BCBS) have evolved, the recommended method for estimating the *amount* of capital to be set aside to account for operational risk events has changed. In 2017, the BCBS introduced a standardized approach to estimating operational RBC that replaces all other approaches for operational RBC calculations from the Basel II guidelines.[10] Whereas in the past institutions could rely on internal modeling to estimate their required operational RBC, the new guidelines require all institutions to follow the same method for calculating their amount of RBC.

The baseline equation for operational RBC under this approach is given as

$$\begin{aligned}\text{Operational RBC} &= \text{Business Indicator Component} \\ &\quad \cdot \text{Internal Loss Multiplier} \\ &= \text{BIC} \cdot \text{ILM} \end{aligned} \quad (9.1)$$

---

[10] See https://www.bis.org/basel_framework/chapter/OPE/25.htm.

Here, the *Business Indicator Component* (BIC) is a measure of income that grows with the bank's size, whereas the *Internal Loss Multiplier* (ILM) is related to the bank's operational risk losses over the previous ten years. The basic idea of Equation (9.1) is to find a measure of bank size and then scale it by a measure of operational losses over time. We can break each of these components down further.

The *BIC* requires first the calculation of the **Business Indicator** (BI):

$$BI = ILDC + SC + FC \qquad (9.2)$$

The Business Indicator is a way of assessing the bank's size, and the BIS refers to it as "a financial-statement-based proxy for operational risk." First, ILDC is the *interest, leases, and dividend component*. Within this variable, the bank will include interest income, interest expenses, interest earning assets, and dividend income. Its general aim is to capture the bank's net interest margin across all sources of interest revenue and expense. SC is the *services component*, which includes fee income and expenses, other operating income (e.g., rental income from investment properties or gains from non-current assets), and expenses (e.g., losses from non-current assets and losses from operational loss events). Finally, FC is the *financial component* which captures the bank's net profit on the changes in the values of the assets and liabilities in both the banking and trading books. This is distinct from the bank's interest margin (in ILDC) as it relates to the market values of the assets and not the gain or loss related to borrowing and lending.[11]

Following this calculation, the bank must then calculate the *BIC*, which is the BI multiplied by the following marginal coefficients, which increase with the size of the *BI*. Table 9.1 presents the BIS guidelines related to BI and the BI's marginal coefficient (α_i).

---

[11] Formally, $ILDC = \min(Abs(\overline{\text{interest income} - \text{interest expense}}), 2.25 \cdot \overline{\text{interest earning assets}}) + \overline{\text{dividend income}}$.

$SC = \max\left(\overline{\text{other operating income}}, \overline{\text{other operating expense}}\right) + \max\left(\overline{\text{fee income}}, \overline{\text{fee expense}}\right)$

$FC = Abs(\overline{\text{Net P\&L Trading Book}}) + Abs(\overline{\text{Net P\&L Banking Book}})$

More details about each of these equations are found at https://www.bis.org/basel_framework/chapter/OPE/10.htm?inforce=20230101&published=20200327. Note that here, the bar over a given term indicates that it is the average over three years.

Table 9.1. BIS guidelines related to the Business Indicator (BI).

Bucket	BI Range (€ billions)	BI marginal coefficients (α_i)
1	≤1	12%
2	1 < BI ≤ 30	15%
3	>30	18%

The BIC is then the bank's BI multiplied by the marginal α_i as it increases. Thus, a bank with BI = €20 billion will have BIC = (1 · 12%) + (20 − 1) · 15% = €2.97 *billion*.[12]

The bank's ILM is based on the idea that banks that have experienced large operational risk losses in the past will continue to do so. The ILM is given as

$$\text{ILM} = \ln\left(e^1 - 1 + \left(\frac{\text{LC}}{\text{BIC}}\right)^{0.8}\right) \tag{9.3}$$

Here, LC is the bank's operational *loss component*, which is equal to 15 times the average annual operational risk losses the bank has incurred over the previous 10 years. Moreover, included again here is the bank's BIC that we calculated before. This helps scale the bank's operational risk losses by the bank's size. Thus, banks with high losses relative to the BIC will be required to hold more equity capital. The ILM grows exponentially as LC grows larger relative to the *BIC* factor:

Returning to our example from before, let's say that our bank with BIC = €2.97 billion has had total operational risk losses of €500 million over the past 10 years. In this case, the bank's ILM would be

$$\text{ILM} = \ln\left(e^1 - 1 + \left(\frac{\text{€500 million}}{\text{€2.97 billion}}\right)^{0.8}\right) = 0.67 \tag{9.4}$$

---

[12] Note that we use Euros here, as it follows the thresholds and examples from the BIS documents that define the approach. Also, note further that the values presented (e.g., α_i) in Table 9.1 and Equation (9.3) are the result of negotiations among bankers, regulators, and researchers and are not necessarily a result stemming directly from finance theory.

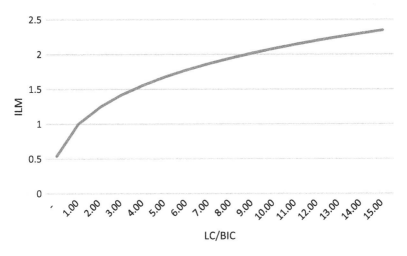

Figure 9.1. Graph of ILM Estimates.

The above analysis suggests that the bank's required minimum operational RBC is

Operational RBC = BIC · ILM = €2.97 billion · 0.67 = €1.99 billion (9.5)

If the bank had instead, say, operational risk losses of €4 billion over the past 10 years, ILM would become 1.35, and its minimum operational RBC would then be a much higher value of €3.25 billion (+63%).

9.4.3 *Internal modeling*

Financial institutions may also want to model operational risk events separately from calculating their required minimum RBC. Internal modeling might be helpful to understand the frequency and severity of events that the institution experiences. Data sharing via ORX[13] or other repositories can also give banks guidance about events that have happened throughout the industry and allow them to better gauge the probability and severity of a far left-tail event (that is, an event that is a rare and extreme negative outcome). Estimating operational risk using industry-wide data

---

[13] Operational Riskdata eXchange Association (ORX), https://managingrisktogether.orx.org/.

can be insightful, as looking internally at *only* your own bank's operational loss data can limit your understanding of what a true extreme event might be if your institution has not faced one. Given all of this, the result of internally modeling operational risk may push an institution to hold more operational RBC than prescribed by regulation. Here, we introduce some statistical methods that can help guide these calculations. We stress that the following discussion reflects some basic statistical modeling techniques that would allow a bank to model the probability and/or severity of operational losses. It is then up to the institution to decide how to use this information, whether it be holding additional capital above regulatory minimums, buying insurance contracts, or taking other actions to mitigate potential catastrophic events from occurring in the first place. Regardless, there is no one-size-fits-all approach to hedging or protecting operational risk, as the sources of this type of risk are highly dependent on the type of institution, the institution's business model, and other choices the bank makes (e.g., related to technological investment and organizational structure).

9.4.4 *Probability of a large loss*

One possibility for estimating the probability that the institution faces an extreme loss is to implement the power-law function, which is an alternative to the normal distribution and allows for a probability distribution to be fat-tailed[14,15]:

$$\text{Prob}(L > x) = kx^{-\alpha} \qquad (9.6)$$

where x represents a minimum loss threshold and L is a potential operational loss that is greater than x. Further, k and α are parameters that help us define the distribution: k is a scaling factor,[16] while α, which is typically

---

[14] Power-law distributions are quite common in natural and sociological settings. For example, the distributions of the magnitudes of earthquakes and the size of city populations conform to a power-law function.

[15] For more details and examples of the Power Law and the Poisson Distribution (that we discuss next), see Hull (2012).

[16] Note that the Power Law does not necessarily create a probability distribution. To achieve this, the scaling factor is used to make sure that the total area under the curve is equal to 1.

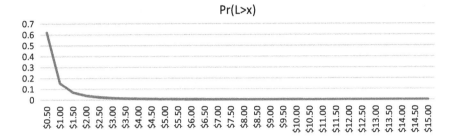

Figure 9.2. A Sample Power Law Function.

greater than 1, defines the fatness of the tail of the distribution (remember in these calculations, we consider that losses run along the *x*-axis, while the *y*-axis represents the probability of incurring such a loss, so the fatter the tail, the larger the probability of an extreme loss). There is not necessarily a one-size-fits-all approach to α, and a bank will typically estimate it from its own internal operational loss data. However, values for α typically will range between 1.5 and 3.5. Higher values of α relate to a thinner tail, and thus a lower probability of extreme outcomes. The power-law function with $\alpha = 2$ and $k = 0.155$ (that is, $\Pr(L > x) = 0.155x^{-2}$) will appear as follows:

In this figure, the *x*-axis can represent potential loss thresholds (in dollars, euros, or some other currency), and the *y*-axis represents the probability that a loss incurred is greater than the respective loss thresholds. So, given this approach, we can also see in this case, the probability of a loss larger than, say, $5 million would be

$$\Pr(L > \$5) = 0.155(5)^{-2} = 0.62\% \tag{9.7}$$

Again, we can adjust the power-law formula's α parameter to influence the fatness of the tails and, by extension, change the estimated probability of larger losses.

We can also reverse the above process. If we know k and α, we can infer the minimum loss we can expect at a pre-specified probability level by taking natural logarithms and reorganizing Equation (9.7) as follows:

$$\ln[\Pr(L > x)] = \ln(k) - \alpha \ln(x) \rightarrow \frac{\ln[\Pr(L > x)] - \ln(k)}{\alpha} = \ln(x) \tag{9.8}$$

Returning to our previous example, we can now ask the following: what is the minimum loss our bank should expect at a probability of 5%? We find this by solving Equation (9.8):

$$\frac{\ln[\Pr(L>x)]-\ln(k)}{\alpha} = \frac{\ln(5\%)-\ln(0.155)}{2} = \ln(x)$$

$$-0.5657 = \ln(x) \rightarrow e^{-0.5657} = x \rightarrow \mathbf{0.567} = x \qquad (9.9)$$

So, in this example, the bank will make a loss of $0.567 million *or more* 5% of the time.

9.4.5 *How frequent are losses? The Poisson distribution*

We can also estimate the frequency of events using a discrete probability distribution. A discrete probability distribution gives us the probability of different exact outcomes. For example, we might want to model the probability of a coin toss, which has two discrete outcomes: heads or tails. Here, there are no half-outcomes and there is no need for estimating fractional events. In operational risk, we could use a distribution like this to model the number of operational loss events that we might experience. Like with a coin toss, there are no "half-events," so we want the probability of exactly 1, 2, 3, etc. events and nothing in between.

A common and well-known discrete distribution is the Poisson distribution. We can use it to determine the probability of a specific number of operational risk events that occur during a fixed length of time. Probabilities in this distribution are given as

$$\Pr(X=n) = e^{-\lambda T}\frac{(\lambda T)^n}{n!} \qquad (9.10)$$

where
n represents the number of events that might occur,
T is the length of time we are studying,
λ is the average number of events that occur during this length of time, and
$n!$ represents the *factorial* of n.[17]

---

[17] If you are not familiar with it, the factorial function means that you multiply all numbers together from 1 to n. As an example, $4! = 1 \cdot 2 \cdot 3 \cdot 4 = 24$.

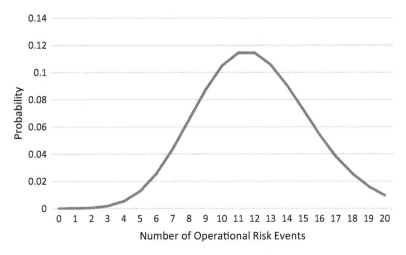

Figure 9.3. The Poisson Distribution for λ = 12 and $t = 1$.

As an example, consider a bank that experiences 12 operational risk events per year (that is, λ = 12). We can then use the Poisson distribution to calculate the probability that the bank would experience a higher-than-usual number of events in the next year. Let's say we are interested in knowing the probability of incurring 15 events. Then,

$$\Pr(X=15) = e^{-12 \cdot 1} \frac{(12 \cdot 1)^{15}}{15!} = 7.24\% \qquad (9.11)$$

We can graph the distribution in Figure 9.3 to gauge the probabilities of the possible number of operational events over the next year.

We can also extend this approach to consider the probability that the bank experiences 15 operational risk events over the next *two* years:

$$\Pr(X=15) = e^{-12 \cdot 2} \frac{(12 \cdot 2)^{15}}{15!} = 1.46\% \qquad (9.12)$$

The bank can use this method to evaluate the likelihood that it faces any number of operational risk events, or it can restrict the calculation to evaluate the likelihood that it would experience several operational risk events of a certain magnitude or larger (e.g., by adjusting the λ parameter to be the average number of large losses).

Again, using a discrete distribution like this, or the power law noted earlier, can complement the bank's qualitative aspects of its operational risk management program. By modeling the frequency, severity, and expected value of large operational losses, the bank may discover that it should enhance its risk management protocols or increase the amount of operational RBC it sets aside.

9.5 Operational Risk and the IVM

Based on the "ART" of risk management we have discussed throughout this book, we can see that operational risk is yet another key area that can affect the bank's market value of equity. However, as we have mentioned, we cannot simply use a derivative security to hedge this type of non-loan-related risk. Instead, bank managers must decide how much money to spend on people, processes, and systems that can reduce the costs of operational problems like fraud and administrative errors described earlier in this chapter. For example, by spending money on "GRC" **methods** (i.e., systems to manage **Governance, Risk, and Control**), the bank should be able to decrease the expected cost of operational risk problems because these tools can reduce both the frequency and severity of fraud, administrative errors, etc.

As noted earlier in Equation (9.6), the likelihood of incurring operational losses that are greater than a specified amount can be estimated via a power-law function. To use such a function, the bank must project the average operational losses (usually expressed as a percentage of revenue) based on historical experience or internal forecasts. We can then use this average operational loss figure as a benchmark for comparing the impact of different spending levels for "Operational Risk Management" (ORM) tools on the bank's expected level of operational losses. By doing so, we can answer the all-important question: if we spend OC-percentage of revenue on ORM tools, then by how much can we reduce our operational losses, L (also expressed as a percentage of revenue)?

Summarized in the following is one example of how we can model this trade-off. Clearly, there are numerous other ways to describe this relationship and so bank managers have considerable discretion in identifying the key factors influencing the costs and benefits of operational risk management. The following discussion is meant to be an initial attempt to examine the direct costs and benefits of actively managing this risk. As we show later in this chapter, using the IVM within an Excel™ spreadsheet allows us to consider a more detailed numerical analysis that includes both direct and indirect effects of the bank's risk management decision.

First, we can approach this problem by identifying the total benefits and total costs of managing the bank's operational risk. In this way, we can see the change in the bank's market value of equity due to different levels of spending on operational risk management techniques. This enables us to compare the value of the bank with, say, more GRC risk management tools ($V_{E,ORM}$) versus its value without these additional tools ($V_{E,No\ ORM}$) as follows:

$$\Delta V_E = V_{E,\ ORM} - V_{E,\ No\ ORM}$$

= Total Benefit of Operational Risk Management (ORM)

− Total Cost of Operational Risk Management (ORM)

= After-tax Present Value of:

[{1 − $Prob(L > x)$} · (Average Operational Loss) · Total Revenue]
− [OC · Total Revenue]   (9.13)

where

- ΔV_E = change in the bank's market value due to spending OC-percentage of revenue on operational risk tools = $V_{E,ORM} - V_{E,No\ ORM}$,
- $Reduction in Expected Operational Losses (Pre-tax) = [{1 − $Prob(L > x)$} · (Average Operating Loss) · Total Revenue],
- $Operational Fixed Costs of ORM tools (Pre-tax) = [OC · Total Revenue],
- {1 − $Prob(L > x)$} = probability of *avoiding* an operational loss as a percentage to total revenue, L, that is greater than x and can be expressed via the power law function of Equation (9.6) = 1 − $Prob(L > x)$ = 1 − $(kx^{-\alpha})$,
- Average Operational Loss = the bank's average (or typical) amount of operational risk-related losses, expressed as a percentage of total revenue,

- OC = the bank's operational risk management expenditures (these are usually operational fixed costs but we express them here as a percentage of total revenue for consistency in units with L),[18] and
- **Total Revenue** = the bank's total revenue in dollar terms.

The first term in square brackets of Equation (9.13) shows the *annual* benefits of operational risk management while the second term in square brackets shows the annual dollar costs of this risk management strategy. The difference between these two values represents the change in the bank's pre-tax income during the first year of the operational risk management program. We define these benefits as the expected dollar amount of operational losses *avoided* due to spending a specific amount on ORM tools, personnel, and processes. Note that these expected benefits will vary as the bank chooses different levels of spending. In effect, the bank's operational risk spending rate (OC) is equivalent to varying the term, x, in the power law's probability function shown earlier in Equation (9.6). As the bank spends *more* on ORM, we assume the probability of operational losses exceeding this level *decreases* exponentially based on the power-law relationship. Thus, we assume an *inverse* relationship between the bank's ORM spending and the power-law function's probability of incurring a large operational loss. For example, we assume that if the bank spends $x\%$ of revenue on ORM, then this will *reduce* the probability that operational losses (L) will be *greater* than this $x\%$ level.

To find the bank's *expected* operational loss, we multiply the probability of avoiding an operational loss by the bank's estimate of an **Average Operational Loss**. As noted above in Equation (9.13), this item represents the bank's average (or typical) amount of operational risk-related losses, expressed as a percentage of total revenue. This figure could be determined from historical data or forecasted by internal bank staff. For analytical convenience, this estimate is assumed to be determined *independently* from the loss probability function. In this way, we can multiply

---

[18] In Chapter 3, we referred to these and other operating fixed costs as *ofc* and expressed them as a percentage of total assets. Here, we express the operational risk-related costs as a percentage of *revenue* because these expenses directly affect Net Income and the bank's cash flows. However, as we do in our IVM spreadsheet, we could also express these costs as a percentage of *assets* and the basic logic described here would remain the same.

[{1 − Prob$(L > x)$}] with the Average Operational Loss to generate an expected percentage loss due to operational risk.[19]

Clearly, there are other ways to estimate the impact of ORM spending on operational risk, but this approach here makes the problem easier to solve analytically and is also consistent with the typical real-world relationship between ORM spending and risk reduction. That is, the initial amounts spent on ORM can normally lead to large reductions in operational risk, but, beyond a certain level, the benefits of additional spending are greatly diminished and can drop below the incremental expense of OC · Total Revenue. The power-law function, multiplied by the bank's Average Operational Loss, neatly captures this economic reality.

9.6 Numerical Example of Operational Risk Management's Impact on Pretax Income

For example, if a bank has $100 million in annual revenue, a typical average operating loss of 3% of revenue, and spends 1% of revenue on ORM controls, then the net pre-tax benefit of this additional spending is $1.7 million per year. This can be seen by plugging the numbers into Equation (9.13) to determine the first year's change in pre-tax income, along with assuming a constant, k, of 0.00001 as follows:

ΔPre-tax Income = [{1 − Prob$(L > x)$} · (Average Operational
Loss) · Total Revenue] − [OC · Total Revenue]
= [{1 − Prob$(L > 0.01)$} · (0.03) · $100 million] −
[0.01 · $100 million]

= [{1 − (0.00001 · 0.01^{-2})} · $3 million] −
[$1 million] = [{0.90} · $3 million] − [$1 million]

= $2.7 million − $1 million = +$1.7 million per year.

---

[19] We could relax this assumption to allow for changes in the firm's spending (x) to affect the *Average Operational Loss* estimate, but this type of interaction effect would lead to a much more complex calculation that goes beyond the scope of our book. Also, it is not likely to alter the main insights shown here based on our assumption of independence between these two variables and so we focus on the simpler case described above.

378 *Managing Financial Institutions: An Integrated Valuation Approach*

This ORM choice is value-enhancing for the bank because it shows that pre-tax income can be increased by $1.7 million on an annual basis. In effect, it is worthwhile for the bank to spend $1 million per year so that it can increase its chances to 90% of avoiding operational losses of *more than* $1 million per year.[20] This numerical example, as well as Equation (9.13), illustrates how operational risk management choices affect a bank's cash flows which, in turn, can impact the bank's market value of equity using the principles of the IVM. In fact, we can develop an estimate of the bank's risk management choice using the following extension of the IVM from Chapter 3 that explicitly quantifies the change in market value (denoted by the "delta" sign, Δ):

$$\Delta V_E = \left[\frac{\Delta(d \cdot NI)}{(R_E - g)}\right] = \left[\frac{d \cdot [(ORM\,Benefit - ORM\,Cost) \cdot (1-t)]}{(R_E - g)}\right]$$

$$= \left[\frac{d \cdot [(ORM\,Benefit - ORM\,Cost) \cdot (1-t)]}{Expected\,Dividend\,Yield}\right] \qquad (9.14)$$

where

- **d** = expected dividend payout ratio for next year (DIV_1 / NI_1),
- **ORM Benefit** = $\{1 - Prob(L > x)\}$ · (Average Operational Loss) · Total Revenue (obtained from Equation (9.13)),
- **ORM Cost** = OC · Total Revenue (obtained from Equation (9.13)),
- **t** = marginal corporate tax rate,
- **R_E** = expected return on the bank's equity,
- **g** = constant growth rate of the bank's dividends, and

---

[20] The ORM spending affects the probability (in this case, the 90%) of having losses larger than x (i.e., $1 million in the above example). So, as ORM spending goes up (x is larger than $1 million), the probability of avoiding a loss greater than x also increases (e.g., let's assume from 90% to 99%). However, as you spend more, the incremental, or marginal, benefit in terms of a higher probability of avoiding the loss *diminishes* so that, at some optimal point, the benefit is maximized relative to the firm's ORM spending rate of x. To quantify this, we take the loss probability (driven by x) and multiply it by the independently derived *Average Operational Loss*. Thus, the total expected benefit will eventually be offset by the increased spending of x and help us determine the amount of ORM spending that maximizes the bank's market value of equity.

- **Expected Dividend Yield** = $(DIV_1 / V_{E,0})$ and this term equals $(R_E - g)$ for the Constant Growth version of the IVM.

To keep the calculations manageable, Equation (9.14) makes some of the same simplifying assumptions that we have discussed in prior chapters:

1. The **ORM spending** (OC · Total Revenue) does not impact other aspects of the bank's cash flows other than those shown in (9.13) and so the *after-tax net benefit of this spending per year* (i.e., (ORM Benefit − ORM Cost) · (1−t)) is the only factor affecting the bank's expected dividend. That is, $\Delta DIV = d \cdot$ (after-tax Net ORM Benefit).
2. The **Expected Dividend Yield** $(R_E - g)$ remains constant even though the cash flow in the numerator of Equation (9.14) is changing. This is a simplifying assumption and is technically not true as the riskiness of the bank can change when the ORM spending rate is adjusted. As discussed in Chapter 3, our IVM method assumes that any change in R_E or g can directly offset each other and implies a constant expected dividend yield. This term therefore can be ignored for our calculation purposes.[21] For a more complete analysis of all potential effects of the hedging decision on firm value, we can use the Excel spreadsheet that is available on the authors' website and is discussed later in Chapter 12 (Integrated Risk Management: Putting it all together).
3. The **Pre-tax Income effect** shown in Equation (9.13) is part of a constant growth IVM and thus, implicitly, we are assuming this ORM spending choice is permanent and will grow at a constant rate over time. Clearly, this is an over-simplification because ORM expenses can change over the long term. However, in practice, it is normally very difficult for bank managers and external analysts to forecast how ORM spending will evolve beyond the next year. So, our approach addresses the problem in a simple way that most managers/analysts can apply in a practical manner. It also has the benefit that this assumption is consistent with logic and assumptions of the IVM first described in Chapter 3.

---

[21] This assumption can be a *conservative* estimate of the estimated change in market value (i.e., *lower* than what might occur) because operational risk management could, in theory, lower the bank's cost of equity (R_E) which would, in turn, raise the bank's valuation. So, assuming no net change in $R_E - g$ (as we do in our IVM method) might be a reasonably safe approach in this context.

4. The **Probability of Operational Losses** greater than x is capped at 100%. As discussed above, the power law does not create a full probability distribution unless scaled properly. Thus, there can be points in the distribution where the probability of a given outcome is greater than 100%. Since probabilities cannot be greater than 100%, we follow the rule that $\{1 - \text{Prob}(L > x)\} = \min\{1 - \text{Prob}(L > x), 100\%\}$ to ensure that $\text{Prob}(L > x)$ ranges between 0% and 100%.

We can use the above variant of the IVM described in Equation (9.14) in a numerical example for our hypothetical bank, ABC, based on some of the data we have been using in previous chapters related to ABC's Stylized Balance Sheet and Stylized Income Statement.

Note that in this example ABC has an expected Average Operating Loss of 1.85% of the bank's $86.092 million in annual revenue (or about $1.6 million in dollar terms). ABC's bank managers must decide how much they should spend on ORM tools this year to mitigate some or all this operational risk. To do so, the FI's staff must estimate how much spending on operating expenses like an ORM software system will affect the probability of operational losses exceeding this level of expenditure. As noted before, we can assume that as ABC spends a larger percentage of revenue on ORM methods, the probability of a loss exceeding that amount will decrease exponentially according to a power-law function. Intuitively, it does not make economic sense to spend, say, 1% of revenue to save operating losses of less than 1%.

The power law function helps us translate different levels of spending into an estimate of the probability of an operating loss. Table 9.2 includes ABC's choices for the two key inputs of power-law function: k and α. Based on those inputs, there is a 2.9% chance that ABC's annual operating losses would be greater than the Average Operational Loss of 1.85% of revenue. Senior management will then have to decide if that is an acceptable level of operational risk and, if not, they will need to spend a larger amount to further reduce this probability of loss.

We can find the answer to this important risk management decision by varying the percentage of revenue spent on ORM tools from some minimum level of, say, 0.05% to over 2%.[22] These values are assumed to

---

[22] With the power-law function in our set-up, we must have at least some small positive amount of ORM spending because a zero percentage will cause the function to be undefined. So, in this chapter, we assume the bank spends at least 0.05% of total revenue on

Table 9.2. Numerical Example of Operational Risk Management.

Total Revenue ($ million)	$86.092
Initial Net Income ($ million)	$18.000
Initial Dividend / sh.	$0.72
Initial Stock Price / sh.	$20.17
Average Oper. Losses / year (% of Tot. Rev.)	1.85%
Sensitivity of Spending on Op. Risk (k)	0.000010
Distribution's Power Law parameter (α)	2.0
Prob. of Projected Losses exceeding: 1.85%	2.9%
Minimum Operating Cost (% of Tot. Rev.)	0.05%
Optimal Operational Cost ratio (OC*)	0.72%
Dividend Payout	0.40
Tax Rate	0.20
Dividend Yield ($R_E - g$)	0.0357
Shares Outstanding (million)	10.00
Estimated Change in Stock Price / sh.	+$0.60

represent the x in the power-law function. This assumption makes it straightforward for ABC to estimate the impact of increased ORM spending on the bank's expected operating losses. As we have noted several times in this book, this is just one of several ways to examine such a trade-off, but for our purposes, this approach provides a direct and measurable way to do so. Figure 9.4 displays the results of this type of "what-if" simulation on the expected *change* in ABC's stock price.

As we can see from Figure 9.4 and the data in Table 9.2, ABC's stock price is boosted around $0.60 per share (+3%) if it chooses an **optimal cost ratio, OC***, of around 0.7% of total revenue.[23] This specific OC*

ORM tools (i.e., 5 basis points of revenue). In addition, it is best practice to also have an upper bound on this percentage to avoid very large or very small effects on the FIs market value of equity. In the spreadsheet that accompanies this book, we allow the user to enter these minimum and maximum values, although we recommend values of 0.05% and 2.50%, respectively.

[23] More precisely, our model suggests that spending 0.72% of total revenue is expected to increase the stock price by $0.597 per share, or +2.96%.

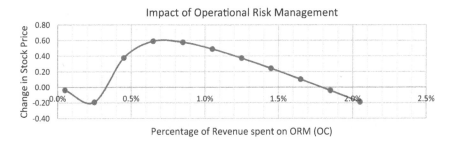

Figure 9.4. Impact of Managing Operational Risk on ABC's Stock Price.

ratio equates the marginal benefit to the marginal cost of this operational risk management strategy and thus maximizes the bank's stock price.[24] Any OC ratio above or below 0.72% results in a lower change in ABC's stock price. The trade-off between the total costs and benefits of the bank's ORM strategy can be seen in Figure 9.5. As this graph shows, the benefits outweigh the costs when ABC spends around 0.7% of its revenue on ORM systems and staff. It is at around this point on the graph that ABC's stock price is maximized.

Figure 9.5 shows that operational risk management's costs rise linearly while the ORM benefits grow in a nonlinear manner because ABC's increased spending ultimately reduces the probability of large operational losses. Eventually, at spending levels beyond 0.72% of revenue, we can see from the graph that reductions in this probability do not keep pace with these increased operational expenses and thus lead to lower stock prices. Although it is useful to conduct this type of quantitative analysis, it is also important to consider the qualitative aspects of operational risk management which are considered in the following.

---

[24] Technically, this optimal expense ratio is obtained by taking the mathematical derivative of Equation (9.13) with respect to the OC ratio and setting this derivative equal to zero. We can then solve algebraically for the optimal OC ratio, OC*, using the data presented in Table 9.2. Based on these data and the model shown in Equation (9.13), the resulting **optimal OC ratio is OC*** $= (\alpha \cdot k \cdot \text{Average Operating Loss})^{(1/\alpha+1)} = (2 \cdot 0.00001 \cdot 0.0185)^{(1/2+1)} = \sqrt[3]{2 \cdot 0.00001 \cdot 0.0185} = 0.0072 = 0.72\%$ Thus, OC* = 0.0072 means the bank should spend 0.72% of its revenue to reduce the likelihood of incurring operational losses of 1.85% or greater. It is at this level of spending that maximizes the total benefit versus the total cost of the bank's ORM strategy.

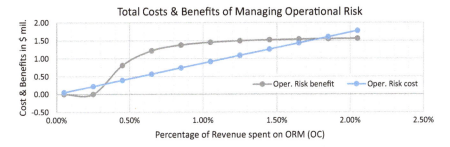

Figure 9.5. Impact of Managing Operational Risk on ABC's Stock Price.

9.7 Managerial Implications

Sam and Nina are considering the acceptable level of operational risk exposure for ABC Bank. Although they can use the IVM model described above to work out an appropriate level of spending on operational risk management, it is important for them to consider the sources of operational risk that are present at ABC. From this analysis, they can get a better idea of the sources of the 1.85% of annual revenue that the bank loses to operational risk events. Nina and Sam first focus on fraud-related risk associated with "Know-Your-Customer" (KYC) and "Anti-Money Laundering" (AML) regulations but realize there can be several other operational risks to consider. **Given ABC bank's status as a commercial bank, what are some other important sources of operational risk that Sam and Nina need to consider?**

Moreover, while it is important for Sam and Nina to consider day-to-day sources of operational risk, they must also consider the potential for low-probability, high-severity outcomes. The bank may need to take special action to mitigate these risks. **What types of high-severity events should Sam and Nina consider for ABC bank?** Moreover, Sam and Nina should consider ABC's exposure to other financial institutions. Given that operational risk events can come with reputational risk (e.g., both to the troubled bank as well as to the banking system in general), **how should Sam and Nina view ABC's potential exposure to an operational risk event at a peer institution? In what ways could such an event spill over to ABC, or are there any ways that ABC bank would benefit from such an event at a competing bank?**

9.8 Summary

In this chapter, we discuss the importance of operational risk management. This process is not a wholly quantitative one, and it relies on a careful consideration of the bank's sources of operational risk, of which there are many. Moreover, we discuss the regulatory view of operational risk here and highlight the capital requirements associated with this form of risk. We also show the impact on a bank's market value by using the IVM to quantify the trade-off between spending on operational risk management tools and the expected reduction in operational losses. Operational risk, especially in high-severity cases, can have dramatic effects on the financial health of a bank, both in terms of direct costs and in terms of reputational risk and the loss of future business. This source of risk is easy to overlook but immensely important to a comprehensive risk management program for any financial institution.

Chapter-End Questions

Answers to odd-numbered questions can be found at the end of this book.

1. **True or False:** Operational risk is the risk related to people and processes at financial institutions.
2. **True or False:** Managing operational risk is the same as managing other types of risks that a financial institution faces.
3. **Multiple Choice:** What is the first step in managing operational Risk?
   (A) Data Collection
   (B) Assessment
   (C) Monitoring
   (D) Management
4. **Multiple Choice:** What is the role of the Internal Audit group in managing operational risk?
   (A) It supports the management of the business line
   (B) It receives independent risk management based on bank-wide risk management policies and frameworks

(C) It defines policy, measures, monitors risk, and develops tools for managing operational risk

(D) It provides independent testing of risk management from the first and second lines of defense

5. **Multiple Choice:** What is the purpose of setting aside equity capital for an operational risk event?

   (A) To increase the bank's profits
   (B) To decrease the bank's operational risk
   (C) To serve as a buffer for the bank against a potential unexpected large loss
   (D) To increase the bank's operational risk

6. **Short Answer:** What is the purpose of the Business Indicator Component (BIC) and the Internal Loss Multiplier (ILM) in the calculation of operational RBC?

7. **Short Answer:** Use the Power Law to estimate the probability that a bank faces a loss of $10 million, given parameters of $a = 1.5$ and $k = 0.4$.

8. **Short Answer:** A bank experiences an average of 15 operational risk events per year. What is the probability that the bank would experience 20 events in a particular year?

9. **Excel-based Question:** How sensitive is ABC's stock price to changes in the bank's Power-Law function? To answer these questions, use the "Operational Risk – Ch 9" tab of the **Integrated Valuation Model.xlsx** file. Start from the base case provided, in which the average operational losses are 1.85%, $k = 0.00001$, and $\alpha = 2.0$.

   (A) Assess the impact on ABC's operational risk management should the sensitivity of spending on operational risk (k) double. What happens to the bank's optimal operational risk-related costs?
   (B) What is the impact of this increased sensitivity level on the bank's stock price?
   (C) What is the new probability that the bank's operational losses exceed their average of 1.85% of annual revenues?
   (D) Return to the original assumption of $k = 0.00001$. What is the impact on ABC's stock price should average operational

losses per year increase to 2% of total revenue if the bank continues to hedge its operational risk at optimal levels?

10. **Comprehensive Question:** Sam and Nina are concerned about managing operational risk at their bank. Provide them with a recommendation for how they may structure qualitative operational risk management protocols to assess, monitor, and manage potential operational risks in the bank.

Reference

Hull, J. C. (2012). *Risk Management and Financial Institutions, Third Edition.* John Wiley & Sons, Hoboken, NJ.

Chapter 10
Regulatory Issues in Banking

10.1 Introduction

Banking regulation has continually evolved over time. The ever-changing nature of the rules that govern banking operations, bank risk management, and financial system stability means that it is paramount for bank managers to always keep an eye on forthcoming changes to the environment, and to proactively address them. Like all the sources of risk we discussed earlier in this book, changing bank regulation (and the bank's subsequent response to it) can impact the value of the institution.

Evolving bank regulation (and deregulation) has led to, in some cases, increased competition and greater risk-taking in financial services (e.g., the Garn–St. Germain Act of 1982, which removed caps on interest rates that banks paid depositors so that banks could compete with money market funds[1]). In other cases, regulatory changes have led to increased consolidation in the industry (e.g., the Riegle–Neal Act of 1994, which lifted most remaining interstate bank branching limitations at the time).

Bank consolidation creates increasing challenges for regulators because it directly affects banking services and financial system stability. As banks become fewer in number but larger in size, there are some important implications. First, access to credit, especially for smaller borrowers, can become more limited (see, e.g., Berger *et al.*, 2005, who show that smaller borrowers tend to match with smaller banks, while larger

---

[1] For more, see Garcia (2013): https://www.federalreservehistory.org/essays/garn-st-germain-act.

borrowers tend to match with bigger banks). This effect is largely due to the idea that small banks can handle "soft" qualitative information better while large banks handle "hard" quantitative information better.

Further, banks can benefit from economies of scale, which create incentives for institutions to grow larger and for the financial system to subsequently become more concentrated. As banks become more concentrated, the largest institutions become "Too Big to Fail" (or **TBTF**). As regulators show their willingness (or the necessity) to rescue or bail out the largest financial institutions in the event of a potential bank failure, the incentive for a bank to grow (to access government bailouts) increases.

We should also keep in mind that sometimes regulators fail to act in a timely manner, whether by choice or by circumstance. When regulators make a choice to *not* intervene with a troubled bank or set of banks, we refer to it as "regulatory forbearance." Regulators remaining fully or partially "on the sidelines" contributed to both the U.S. Savings & Loan (S&L) crisis of the 1980s and the regional banking crisis related to the run on Silicon Valley Bank and other financial institutions that unfolded in 2023.[2] Sometimes this practice can happen because of regulators wanting to allow institutions to try to save themselves (although this can lead to a **moral hazard problem** where banks are "gambling for resurrection," by taking on excessive amounts of risk in the hopes of a "jackpot" payout that will save them). This forbearance activity could also occur because

---

[2]During the 1980s, the U.S. savings and loan (S&L) industry experienced a severe financial crisis, with many of these institutions either folding or merging with healthier firms. A significant and sustained rise in inflation and interest rates during the 1970s and early 1980s created two major problems. First, the interest rates they paid on deposits were capped by federal banking laws and were lower than what could be earned elsewhere, causing savers to withdraw their funds and move them to higher-yielding assets like money market mutual funds. This process has been referred to as "disintermediation" because the S&Ls were no longer the primary financial intermediary in many communities. Second, S&Ls held a vast majority of its assets in long-term fixed-rate mortgages, which lost value when interest rates rose, thus eroding the industry's aggregate net worth. Efforts to deregulate the industry were implemented in the early 1980s in the hope that these institutions would grow out of their problems. Instead, the situation worsened and, ultimately, U.S. taxpayers had to bail out the industry, leading to additional reform legislation by the end of the 1980s that tried to limit the problems of "regulatory forbearance" noted above in the main text. See the following link for more details about this crisis on the Federal Reserve History website (https://www.federalreservehistory.org/essays/savings-and-loan-crisis).

it is possibly too difficult for regulators to fully assess the risk of a given institution (which, as noted in Chapter 1, can be an **adverse selection problem**). Throughout this chapter, we discuss regulatory issues and policies with the assumption that regulators will remain focused and follow through on their policy guidance in full, despite our need to be mindful of the possible failure of regulators to act.

In this chapter, we discuss some main areas of banking regulation, some of which we have already discussed in earlier chapters, such as deposit insurance, liquidity, capital requirements, and other areas related to financial stability. In total, the areas of regulation we discuss in this chapter, while largely prescribing bank-level requirements, are also focused on maintaining financial system stability relative to the industry's overall profitability. In fact, the trade-off between profitability and stability is an important motivator for why we consider regulatory issues in the first place. As regulation increases, it is more difficult and expensive for banks to take risks, which has the potential to impact profitability, as displayed in Figure 10.1. Over time, the banking industry has oscillated between periods of higher profit (e.g., the 1920s and 2000s) and higher safety (e.g., the 1930s and the 2010s), as the "regulatory pendulum" swings back and forth between deregulation and re-regulation.

As we progress in this chapter, we introduce and discuss various types of regulation that are central to the banking system, including deposit insurance, capital regulation, liquidity regulation, and stress testing. As the regulatory pendulum continues to swing, these regulations may be modified or take on different forms, but the core ideas behind them should remain intact. Moreover, these regulations are tied to most of the topics we have discussed earlier in this book. For example, deposit insurance and

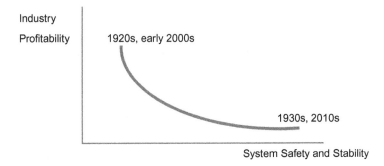

Figure 10.1. A Stylized Version of the Trade-off between Profitability and Stability.

liquidity regulations are related to the liquidity risks we have mentioned earlier; capital regulations relate to market, credit, and operational risk, in addition to impacting the bank's funding mix; and stress testing relates to nearly all forms of risk, depending on the stress scenarios put forth by regulators.

10.2 Deposit Insurance

The aim of deposit insurance is to establish and maintain confidence in a country's banking system. As mentioned in Chapter 8 related to Liquidity Risk, deposit insurance is run by a governmental entity and protects deposits (although not all deposits, as some can be uninsured) against the failure of a depository institution. Without deposit insurance, banks would be more prone to runs. Since deposit withdrawals are first come, first served, it is fully rational for any uninsured depositor to quickly withdraw their funds if there is even a *rumor* of distress at their bank. When depositors line up to withdraw in large numbers, it will create a liquidity problem for the bank (e.g., see Chapter 8). As banks attempt to fulfill withdrawal requests, they will draw down their own cash and sell liquid assets (stored liquidity) while borrowing from other institutions and capital markets (purchased liquidity) to the extent that they are able. At some point, however, the bank runs out of cash and liquid assets, while lenders are unwilling to lend to the institution, and the bank's liquidity problem becomes an insolvency problem (i.e., its assets might be worth less than its liabilities, either on a temporary or permanent basis).

Deposit insurance is aimed at mitigating these bank runs. If depositors know that they will be "made whole" in the event of a bank's failure (i.e., they are fully repaid), their incentive to run the bank is eliminated. However, depositors' incentive to monitor the bank is also eliminated, as they no longer need to worry about the health of their financial institution. In turn, this creates a **moral hazard problem** and an increase in bank risk-taking, as the level of monitoring of the institution is now reduced. This increase in system-wide risk-taking can then raise the chances of not only a bank run but also a banking panic, where multiple FIs experience a run on their deposits.

Many countries around the world have deposit insurance schemes (see, e.g., Demirgüç-Kunt *et al.*, 2015). Deposit insurance has existed in the United States since the Great Depression in 1933, when the Federal

Deposit Insurance Corporation (FDIC) was created amidst the banking panic that occurred at the time. At its inception, the FDIC guaranteed bank deposits up to $2,500. Today, the FDIC's deposit guarantee extends to $250,000 per account, per bank.[3]

Note again that deposits beyond the FDIC's $250,000 cap are *uninsured*. Deposits of amounts beyond the limit (which can include companies who use deposit accounts for working capital needs) are subject to loss if the bank fails. This does incentivize large, uninsured depositors to monitor the bank. Uninsured depositors played a pivotal role in the banking crisis of 2023, when they launched a bank run on Silicon Valley Bank after it was apparent that the bank was facing extremely large unrealized losses on its bond portfolio due to interest rate risk.

Indeed, as we mentioned above, deposit insurance can create moral hazard problems, because insured depositors no longer have an incentive to monitor the bank. If the bank knows that the depositors do not care how their money is utilized (given that they are backstopped by the FDIC in the U.S.), then the bank is incentivized to take on additional, and possibly excessive, risk. In any firm, there is always a conflict of interest between debtholders and equity holders. Since debtholders have a fixed payoff with the value of their investment decreasing as the value of the firm's assets drops below the book value of the firm's liabilities, they prefer the firm to use their money to take on lower-risk projects with safe, predicable cash flows. However, equity holders have a theoretically unlimited upside payoff, as they are the firm's residual claimants, and are entitled to anything that is left over after the debtholders are paid.

Figure 10.2 illustrates the relationship we described above. In this figure, the dashed line is vertical to the point on the *x*-axis that represents the value of the firm's assets that is worth exactly the amount of debt that the firm owes (for a bank, this may include a large dollar amount of deposits). Beyond this point to the right, the line representing the debtholder's payoff flattens, as the payoff to debtholders is fixed, and cannot increase even if the firm performs well above expectations. To the left of the dashed line, the debtholders' payoff is decreasing, as the firm's assets

---

[3] This limit was increased from $100,000 to $250,000 because of the 2008–2009 Global Financial Crisis, as legislators and regulators worked to stabilize the banking system. In some cases, like the Silicon Valley Bank (SVB) failure in 2023, the limit was temporarily removed so that all deposits were, in effect, insured to reduce the chances of the run on SVB turning into a full-blown banking panic.

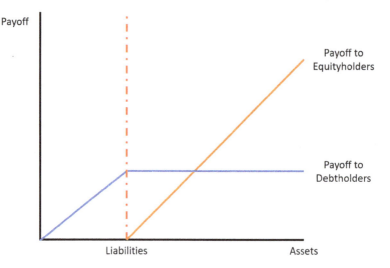

Figure 10.2. The Debtholder–Equity Holder Conflict.

become worth progressively less, and debtholders' recovery in default shrinks. Moreover, the equity holders receive *nothing* until the value of the firm's assets is worth *more* than its liabilities (which, again, is the dashed red line). At this point and to its right, the debtholders will have been paid in full, and the equity holders, as the *residual* claimants, keep whatever is left over. Thus, their payoff, as mentioned above, is unlimited in theory. This figure, in total, helps us visualize the conflict that exists between the debtholders and equity holders in a firm, as we can clearly see the limited upside for debtholders versus the unlimited upside that equity holders have an incentive to chase.

For a commercial bank, the insured depositors, who are generally the primary debtholders of the FI, no longer have an incentive to monitor, as their downside (that is, the region when the value of the bank's assets falls below the value of the bank's liabilities) is non-existent, as their credit exposure is fully insured by the FDIC. Thus, the insured debtholders do *not* need to encourage the bank to take on safe and reliable projects. The incentive to monitor then lies with larger, uninsured depositors and other creditors with claims that are subordinated to the insured depositors. To mitigate this problem, regulators like the FDIC play a supervisory role in requiring quarterly disclosures from the bank and for the bank to undergo regular examinations.

When the FDIC views an institution as no longer viable, it can and will take action to close the bank. A common misconception is that the FDIC simply writes a check to make all the depositors whole, however, this is not the case. The FDIC will instead find another, healthy institution to take on the insured deposits and any viable assets of the failing bank. To the extent that the failing bank's viable assets are worth more than its insured deposits, then some or most of the uninsured deposits might also be transferred to the healthy institution. However, if the failing bank's assets are worth less than the value of insured deposits, then uninsured depositors are not guaranteed to be made whole (although there are notable exceptions to this rule, including Silicon Valley Bank, as noted earlier), and the FDIC will then contribute a cash payment from its Deposit Insurance Fund (DIF). Additionally, any insured institution must submit a resolution plan to the FDIC to help regulators resolve the bank in the event of its failure.

The FDIC further mitigates moral hazard concerns by assessing insurance premiums to member banks based on the banks' risk profiles. These insurance premiums contribute to the DIF. In some cases (e.g., after the 2008–2009 GFC), the FDIC may also charge special assessments to banks to replenish the fund. Like property-casualty insurance, higher deposit insurance premiums are charged to riskier banks. For example, if you cause a car accident or accrue speeding tickets (or other traffic violations), your car insurance company will increase your annual premiums. Similarly, the FDIC will examine a bank's CAMELS ratings, among other risk metrics, to assess the riskiness of a given institution, and to subsequently calculate appropriate insurance premium charges.[4]

10.3 Capital Requirements

In addition to deposit insurance, and its associated disclosure and supervision requirements, banks must also adhere to capital adequacy requirements. We have mentioned these requirements in some of our book's

---

[4]CAMELS is an acronym that stands for each component of the rating system: Capital Adequacy, Asset Quality, Management, Earnings, Liquidity, and Sensitivity to market risk. Banks are assessed along each criterion and assigned a composite score. Each rating, as well as the composite score, ranges on a scale from one to five. CAMELS ratings are typically not publicly disclosed. Though we do not describe in detail the risk-based premium schedule here, these details are available in numerous other sources, including Saunders et al. (2024).

chapters already (e.g., Chapter 6 mentions the use of capital to serve as a buffer against credit losses; and Chapter 9 explains the calculation of risk-based capital to mitigate operational risk). Here, we take a closer look at capital requirements related to credit risk, as these are most closely related to the bank's core business of creating liquidity for its borrowers via qualitative asset transformation.

Capital requirements set rules for the portion of a bank's funding that must come from equity. The aim is to create a buffer to protect the bank's depositors and other liabilities holders from a large decrease in the value of the bank's assets. Since equity holders are residual claimants, as we discussed above, their payout is not fixed, and although they reap the lion's share of the rewards from the bank's risk-taking, they are the primary party to take initial losses related to that risk. The larger the portion of the bank's assets that are funded by equity, the larger the dollar amount of losses that can be absorbed by that equity. Conversely, if a bank relies on an exceptionally small amount of equity for its funding (thus being highly leveraged), then the possibility of a default is much higher, and the bank has less "wiggle room" for losses on its portfolio of assets. The primary economic function of this equity is to act as a "buffer," or final, line of defense against large, *unexpected* losses that might come from all the major sources of risk already described in this book (e.g., interest rate, market, credit, off-balance sheet, liquidity, and operational risks).[5]

Given the above, regulators have agreed upon a set of rules to govern the maximum levels of financial leverage a bank can use. In other words, these regulations set a standard for the minimum amount of capital the bank may use for funding. These requirements help guard against unexpected or extreme losses and thus protect the bank's solvency. Moreover, these rules help reduce moral hazard incentives. Consequently, banks must fund themselves with more equity capital when they take on more risk. Thus, even though depositors are not incentivized to monitor (because of deposit insurance), the bank must "pay" for the risk they take via the higher cost of capital that comes with relying on equity for funding. This higher cost of capital then has follow-on effects related to the set of

---

[5] Remember from our discussion of loan pricing in Chapter 6 that *expected* losses should be embedded in the loan rate that the bank charges its customers. So, equity is a "shock absorber" to protect against unusually large, *unexpected* losses. In this way, the bank can continue to remain viable even in the face of severely stressful conditions.

projects the bank can undertake (given its required return on investment, or "hurdle rate") and the market value of the bank's assets.

Regulatory capital minimums have been defined in the Bank for International Settlements' (BIS) Basel Accords since the 1980s and have evolved over time with new iterations of the Accords. The Basel Accords are an international standard for banking. We do not provide exhaustive details of the BIS capital requirements and their calculations because (1) they can be quite complex, (2) are not universally applied around the world, and (3) are continuously changing. Instead, we will give a conceptual framework for how capital requirements work and discuss some of the key ratios that regulators check. It is important to keep in mind that these regulations will continue to change over time — the spirit of the rules and methods of calculation might remain consistent, but key ratios and minimum levels may differ.[6]

Importantly, when calculating capital adequacy ratios, not all equity is treated equally. Banks must differentiate between Tier 1 and Tier 2 capital. The Basel III guidelines note that Tier 1 capital is related to the bank as a "going concern" and Tier 2 capital is related to the bank as a "gone concern." Tier 2 capital items are generally items that absorb the bank's losses before depositors and other creditors (e.g., loan loss provisions) when a bank fails. Tier 1 capital is the bank's capital that absorbs losses on an ongoing basis, and within this category, banks must also differentiate between *Common Equity Tier 1* **(CET1)** and *Additional Tier 1* **(AT1)**.[7] Basel III defines CET1 as the "sum of common shares (equivalent for non-joint stock companies) and stock surplus, retained earnings, other comprehensive income, qualifying minority interest, and regulatory adjustments." CET1 is regarded as the highest-quality capital the bank has — it can absorb losses the instant they occur. Further, AT1 includes items that are not part of the bank's common equity but can behave like equity and absorb losses when needed, like hybrid securities such as preferred stock.

A second consideration for the bank is the calculation of its risk-weighted assets. In many of the bank's capital requirements, they will balance measures of equity against the value of their assets calculated on

---

[6] For much more details on these ratios, visit https://www.bis.org/fsi/fsisummaries/defcap_b3.pdf.

[7] An even stricter measure of equity capital that many investors prefer to monitor removes intangible assets like Goodwill from CET1 to show the bank's **"Tangible Common Equity,"** (or "TCE").

a risk-adjusted basis. Here, the Basel rules classify all possible assets a bank may hold into risk categories. Some assets (like cash) have a risk weighting of 0%. Other assets have risk weights of well over 100%, based on the creditworthiness of the borrower.[8] Once all assets have been classified into different categories, the bank will multiply the book value of each of these assets by its risk weight, to get the asset's risk-weighted value. Finally, the total *Risk-Weighted Assets* (RWA) is the sum of all the bank's risk-weighted assets. Measuring assets in this way allows the bank and regulators to properly view the bank's size in the context of the riskiness of its assets. A bank with a high level of low-risk assets thus could worry less about large and unexpected losses and thus might need a smaller capital buffer to protect itself.[9]

We now list *five* key capital ratios that banks must monitor and for which they must meet minimum thresholds:

1. **CET1 Risk-Based Capital Ratio:** $CET1/RWA \geq 4.5\%$. Banks must maintain a 4.5% ratio of their *Common Equity Tier 1 capital* (CET1) to their *Risk-Weighted Assets* (RWA). Some banks denoted as **Globally Systemically Important Banks** (G-SIBs) face an additional *surcharge* on this ratio that varies between 1.0 and 3.5%. The BIS developed its own methodology to classify banks as G-SIBs, based on variables like the bank's size, complexity, and level of interconnection with other institutions. This surcharge is added to institutions viewed as potentially too big to fail, as their failure would bring about negative impacts to other institutions, likely causing more failures within

---

[8] For more details on risk weights, visit https://www.bis.org/basel_framework/chapter/CRE/20.htm.

[9] However, this approach can sometimes lead to a large under-estimate of the FIs true risk because some assets can possess much higher levels of risk when compared to their BIS-mandated risk weights. A good example of this issue occurred during the 2011–2012 Eurozone debt crisis where Greek and Italian government bonds had a 0% risk weight despite these nation's weak macroeconomic conditions at that time. Thus, many bank analysts will also look at simpler capital ratios that do not adjust for risk such as a "Core Equity Ratio" (that is, CET1 / Total Assets) or the "Supplementary Leverage Ratio" which accounts for OBS items. By not weighting the assets by risk, this alternative set of ratios gives a more conservative, worst-case, estimate of the amount of the FIs equity buffer holds against unexpected shocks.

the banking system. This type of risk is called *systemic risk*, and we discuss it further in Chapter 11.

2. **Tier 1 Risk-Based Capital Ratio:** $Tier\,1\,Capital/RWA \geq 6\%$. Banks must maintain a 6% ratio of their total Tier 1 Capital to their *RWA*.
3. **Total Risk-Based Capital Ratio:** $Tier\,1\,Capital + Tier\,2\,Capital/RWA \geq 8\%$. Banks' total capital must be larger than 8% of its *RWA*.
4. **Tier 1 Leverage Ratio:** $Tier\,1\,Capital/Total\,Assets \geq 4\%$. Banks must maintain Tier 1 Capital at a level above 4% of *Total Assets*. It is important to note that the leverage ratios described here and in #5 below are the only ratios of the group that use total assets and not risk-weighted assets. Here, the Tier 1 Leverage Ratio helps prevent banks from "gaming the system" by loading up on an exceptionally large amount of lower-risk assets to allow it to have excessive leverage.
5. **Supplementary Leverage Ratio (SLR):** $CET1\,/Total\,Assets + off$-$alance\,Sheet\,Items \geq 3\%$. Since the standard Tier 1 Leverage Ratio does not capture off-balance sheet exposures, the SLR can be utilized to better capture the full extent of exposure that a given institution might have, especially if it has a large amount of derivatives or loan commitments.

In all, the capital ratios above are meant to help institutions survive a large and unexpected shock to their balance sheet. By extension, if bank failures are prevented (especially for large and "systemically important financial institutions," or "SIFIs"), then these capital ratios go a long way toward maintaining safety and soundness in the banking system. To further this idea, the Basel III regulations also introduce the idea of capital conservation buffers and countercyclical capital buffers.[10]

The *capital conservation buffer* is meant to make sure that banks have an additional layer of capital that can be used to absorb losses. This buffer is set to 2.5% of RWA, and only CET1 capital may be used. This 2.5% buffer is more than the regulatory minimum for CET1 established above (i.e., 2.5% above and beyond the required 4.5% minimum for an effective minimum of 7.0%). When this buffer falls below 2.5%, constraints on dividends and other capital distributions are automatically implemented, with the constraints becoming more severe as the bank's shortfall increases.

---

[10] For more on the capital conservation buffer and the countercyclical capital buffer, visit https://www.bis.org/fsi/fsisummaries/b3_capital.htm.

The *countercyclical capital buffer* (**CCyB**) is meant to "protect the banking sector from periods of excess aggregate credit growth." Times of excessive credit growth have been shown empirically to precede financial crises (e.g., Berger and Bouwman, 2017), so it can be beneficial for banks to recognize this and prepare ahead of time. The CCyB is not in force all the time, but rather can be activated by authorities when they believe that credit growth is increasing at a rapid rate. The CCyB ranges from 0.0 to 2.5% of RWA, and, like the capital conservation buffer, can only be fulfilled with CET1 capital.

In sum, capital requirements work to maintain stability in the banking system by capping the amount of financial leverage that can be utilized by a bank. By using a capital buffer, banks can absorb unexpected losses without calling into question their ability to repay their obligations to debtholders (primarily depositors). Capital buffers also serve to supplement deposit insurance, as they reduce the likelihood that an FDIC-led unwinding of an institution will be necessary. Further, through the risk-weighting process, banks will be forced to "pay" a higher amount for riskier assets, via their funding sources, which helps mitigate the moral hazard problem that is created by deposit insurance.

10.4 Ensuring the Banking System's Liquidity

As a further supplement to capital adequacy and deposit insurance, banks are also required to meet certain criteria related to liquidity. Two important liquidity-specific regulations are related to liquidity ratios and reserve requirements. In both cases, regulators focus on the ability of banks to fund sudden deposit withdrawals and meet other liquidity needs, especially in times of crisis.

The 2008–2009 Global Financial Crisis (GFC) highlighted the need for institutions to enhance their liquidity management. Two regulatory liquidity requirements that large banks must meet are as follows:

1. $Net\ Stable\ Funding\ Ratio = \dfrac{Available\ Stable\ Funding}{Required\ Stable\ Funding} \geq 100\%$ \hfill (10.1)

2. $Liquidity\ Coverage\ Ratio = \dfrac{High\ Quality\ Liquid\ Assets}{Expected\ 30\text{-}day\ Net\ Cash\ Outflows} \geq 100\%$ \hfill (10.2)

These ratios shown above by Equations (10.1) and (10.2) are a product of the Basel III accords that followed the GFC. The **Net Stable**

Funding Ratio is designed to ensure that banks have stable sources of funding to guide them through a difficult period, as shorter-term, uninsured funding (also referred to as "hot money") can be a source of instability (see, e.g., Demirgüç-Kunt and Huizinga, 2010). Moreover, the **Liquidity Coverage Ratio** ensures that banks have enough stored liquidity to withstand 30 days of typical cash outflows. Chapter 8 provides an in-depth discussion of liquidity risk, and a detailed overview of these liquidity ratios, so we will not devote more attention to them here.

A second set of liquidity-based regulations is related to reserve requirements. In the United States, commercial banks and other Depository Institutions (along with U.S. branches of foreign DIs) must set aside cash relative to the amount of deposits that they have on their balance sheet. This represents the portion of deposits that banks take in but are not allowed to lend. This regulation is meant to ensure that banks have enough liquidity to fund withdrawal requests as needed.

Reserve requirement levels were updated by the Federal Reserve in 2020 and are based on the bank's net transaction accounts. In prior years, smaller institutions faced a reserve requirement of 3%, while larger institutions faced a reserve requirement of 10%. Reserve requirements, however, were all set to 0% on March 26, 2020, with the onset of the COVID-19 pandemic. The aim was to free up as much liquidity as possible to allow banks to increase their funds available for lending, and to, by extension, further stimulate the economy. At the time of this writing, reserve requirements remain at 0%. It is not clear if or when the Federal Reserve will raise reserve requirements again. Other countries do not use reserve requirements (e.g., Canada and the United Kingdom), so it would not be out of the ordinary, on a global basis, for the U.S. to leave the requirement permanently at 0%.

It is also useful to note that reserve requirements are another tool that can be used by the Federal Reserve (or other central bank) to implement its "contractionary" or "expansionary" **monetary policy**. For example, a contractionary policy could include increasing reserve requirements. By doing so, the central bank is restricting the amount of cash available to be lent in the financial system, thus making it scarcer, and raising its rental price (that is, interest rates). Alternatively, an expansionary policy could include reducing reserve requirements so that banks can lend more. This action can increase the supply of available money, and thus lower interest rates.

10.4.1 Stress testing

Stress testing is a simulation exercise in which bankers and regulators test how the bank would perform under severely adverse conditions. Currently, the United States requires banks with $100 billion or more in assets to participate in the Federal Reserve Board's supervisory stress test and capital planning requirements. In part, for these institutions, capital requirements are determined by the results of these stress tests.[11] For stress-tested banks, this additional capital buffer (a minimum of 2.5%), called the "Stress Capital Buffer," replaces the capital conservation buffer we had described earlier.

Following the GFC, bank stress tests have been a routine procedure in the U.S. banking system. The sweeping post-crisis regulatory change from the 2010 Dodd–Frank Wall Street Reform and Consumer Protection Act mandated stress testing. Since then, stress testing has evolved over time, with the first iteration of tests coming in 2009 (known as the *Supervisory Capital Assessment Program*, "SCAP"). Following this, in 2011, the stress testing process moved to a combination of the *Comprehensive Capital Analysis and Review* (or "CCAR") and the *Dodd–Frank Act Stress Tests* (or "DFAST").[12] CCAR was originally a qualitative and quantitative assessment, of which the results were publicly reported. This assessment checked whether institutions had enough capital to withstand times of severe economic and financial stress. The qualitative portion examined whether banks had a forward-looking capital planning process that could account for the unique risks faced by each bank. In 2019, the qualitative assessment became a confidential, supervisory process, and in 2020, the quantitative process was replaced with the Stress Capital Buffer mentioned above. Another change came in 2018 when the Economic Growth, Regulatory Relief, and Consumer Protection Act was signed into law. This act reduced both the frequency of stress testing and the number of stress scenarios required for banks below $250 billion in total assets.

The DFAST component remains a stress test in which banks simulate the impact of worst-case scenarios on their business. Each year, the Federal Reserve presents at least two different stress scenarios for banks

---

[11] Annual capital requirements for large banks can be found at https://www.federalreserve.gov/supervisionreg/large-bank-capital-requirements.htm.

[12] For more details, see https://www.federalreserve.gov/supervisionreg/stress-tests-capital-planning.htm.

to consider. For example, in 2023, stress tests simulated a severe global recession with stress in commercial and residential real estate markets, as well as corporate debt markets.[13] Moreover, within this scenario, the unemployment rate was expected to rise by a simulated 6.5%, peaking at 10%. In addition to this hypothetical test, banks with large trading operations were tested against a global shock to financial markets that stressed their primary trading positions.

Overall, stress testing has become an important tool for regulators in achieving their goal of financial stability. Through simulated stress scenarios, banks and regulators can have a better understanding of how a bank would perform in a critically severe scenario and plan accordingly. Of course, it is important to recognize that in addition to bank managers accurately simulating outcomes related to the stress events, it is imperative for regulators to pick plausible and realistic scenarios that are reflective of severe events that could potentially occur given the current economic climate. If executed properly, stress testing can reveal potential weaknesses in the banking system before they become apparent during times of actual stress.

10.5 Other Regulatory Issues and Interventions

10.5.1 *Dodd–Frank Act*

We noted in the previous section that the current bank stress testing framework was brought about by the **2010 Dodd–Frank Wall Street Reform and Consumer Protection Act** (henceforth, "Dodd–Frank"). However, Dodd–Frank was responsible for many additional significant changes to banking's regulatory landscape. As the legislation followed the GFC, Dodd–Frank brought a focus on systemic risk (that is, the risk of financial system failure, which we discuss further in Chapter 11) to the forefront. The law created both the Financial Stability Oversight Council (FSOC) and the Office of Financial Research (OFR) to identify and monitor threats to financial stability. FSOC's primary roles include monitoring threats to financial stability, facilitating coordination and information sharing among regulatory agencies, designating nonbank institutions for regulatory oversight from the Federal Reserve, and recommending heightened standards

---

[13] https://www.federalreserve.gov/newsevents/pressreleases/bcreg20230209a.htm.

for large financial institutions with the goal of mitigating threats to financial stability.[14] The OFR supports FSOC's mission through research and data/information collection. Voting members of FSOC include, among others, the U.S. Treasury Secretary (also chair of the council), Chair of the Federal Reserve, and heads of the FDIC and SEC.

Dodd–Frank also established the Orderly Liquidation Authority (OLA) to organize the process by which the liquidation of large financial institutions can occur and expand these rules to cover non-bank financial institutions and insurance companies. The Act also creates the Orderly Liquidation Fund, which is overseen by the FDIC, and is used to unwind an institution that is not insured by the FDIC or the Securities Investor Protection Corporation (SIPC).

Moreover, Dodd–Frank also included the Volcker Rule (named after former Federal Reserve Chair Paul Volcker) that aims to limit the ability of commercial banks to engage in proprietary trading, a practice in which a bank would use depositors' funds to trade (or make potentially speculative investments) on behalf of the bank itself. Though Dodd–Frank was enacted in 2010, the implementation of the Volcker Rule took several more years, ranging until 2015 when the rule finally took effect. Despite this, exceptions for some illiquid securities and other investments extended past the 2015 implementation of the rule.

Dodd–Frank had numerous other provisions — too many to list here — that changed how banks and nonbank financial institutions are regulated. In the interest of brevity, we will list here a few additional and noteworthy (in our view) changes set forth by Dodd–Frank, with the caveat that we are leaving many out. These additional changes include the following:

- increased disclosure requirements for hedge funds,
- the requirement that hedge fund and private equity fund managers register as investment advisers,
- reforms to the insurance industry,
- the requirement that over-the-counter swaps be cleared through a clearinghouse or exchange,
- changes to how credit rating agencies are regulated (and aimed at reducing conflicts of interest and inaccuracies), and
- substantial reforms to mortgage lending.

---

[14] See https://home.treasury.gov/policy-issues/financial-markets-financial-institutions-and-fiscal-service/financial-stability-oversight-council/council-work.

10.5.2 *Interventions in times of crisis*

During the GFC and the COVID-19 crises, regulators took dramatic action to restore and maintain stability in the banking system and other financial markets. Here, we provide a short overview of some of these activities. It is important to note that the "playbook" developed during the GFC was enacted quickly at the onset of the COVID-19 crisis. Many actions taken by regulators in 2020 mirrored those (or were identical to) actions taken in 2008–2009. The rapidity with which regulators acted during the heart of the 2020 crisis was likely critical to ensuring that financial markets and institutions were able to function. As we discussed in Chapter 1, financial markets and institutions play a very important role in the economy, by making sure funds find their way from savers to borrowers. In fulfilling this role, these institutions absorb and manage important risks (e.g., maturity mismatch and information asymmetries) on behalf of participants. It is essential for regulators to act to preserve the efficient functioning of markets and institutions, without which economic activity would grind to a halt, forcing firms to stop operations (or close) and creating uncertainty about asset valuations across markets.

One major intervention during these times of stress was a variety of special lending facilities organized by the Federal Reserve. It is important to note that the structure of these facilities is such that the Federal Reserve does not take credit risk — the facilities are created as separate corporations in which the U.S. Treasury is the equity holder, and the Federal Reserve is the debtholder. If the equity in the facility is depleted, Treasury would need to recapitalize the facility to prevent the Federal Reserve from being exposed to credit losses. During the COVID-19 crisis, these lending facilities were created to provide liquidity and backstop activities in the municipal bond, commercial paper, and money markets while also supporting small- and medium-sized business lending, as well as primary dealers in government bond markets. Moreover, during the 2023 regional bank crisis, the Federal Reserve created the *Bank Term Funding Program* (or "BTFP"), which allowed banks to borrow against their U.S. Treasury and agency debt/MBS holdings *at par value*. Given the fast pace of interest rate increases following the COVID-19 crisis, many banks had large unrealized losses on their held-to-maturity portfolios.[15] These institutions

---

[15] See Chapter 5 (Market Risk) for a brief discussion of "Held-to-Maturity" and "Available-for-Sale" securities.

could benefit from the liquidity provided from this BTFP program, and the program generally was helpful in stemming the tide of a few bank runs that occurred at the time.

Moreover, the Federal Reserve implemented dollar swap lines (from the GFC era) to support central banks and dollar-denominated businesses around the world. The Federal Reserve also, as mentioned before, reduced reserve requirements to 0%. Finally, the Federal Reserve (and other central banks around the world) implemented accommodative monetary policy, pushing the Federal Funds rate to 0% nearly overnight. During the GFC, the Federal Reserve began **Quantitative Easing** (or "QE"), which expanded its balance sheet by trillions of dollars, and saw the central bank purchase a large amount of Treasuries and, for the first time, mortgage-backed securities.

Finally, the government can intervene through fiscal policy and legislative action. The COVID-19 crisis saw the U.S. Congress approve trillions of dollars in spending to stimulate the economy and support individuals who were out of work due to the pandemic. Though this was not necessarily direct support of banks and the financial system, this aid package helped maintain stability in financial markets and institutions as it likely prevented individuals and businesses from quickly liquidating securities and drawing down deposits. Another noteworthy government action during the GFC was the *Troubled Asset Relief Program* (or "TARP"), which saw the U.S. Treasury buy troubled mortgage-backed securities (the Federal Reserve bought only "high quality" agency-backed MBS through its open market operations) to help recapitalize the financial system and increase its liquidity. Academic studies have shown TARP to be effective at reducing systemic risk during a crisis (see, e.g., Berger, Roman, and Sedunov, 2020).[16] As noted earlier, during the 2023 regional bank crisis, regulators also intervened to stop the emerging banking panic from spreading further, by insuring Silicon Valley Bank's uninsured depositors. Though there were some conflicting statements surrounding this action from government officials, this step was a positive signal for the uninsured depositors at other institutions and was meant to prevent them from starting runs on other institutions.

---

[16] Two additional, excellent references are Berger *et al.* (2023) who provide an overview of COVID-19 relief efforts and the broader impact of the crisis and Berger and Roman (2020) who provide a thorough overview of TARP and other bank bailout programs.

10.5.3 Fairness: Going beyond safety and soundness

Regulators are also concerned about issues beyond safety and soundness in the banking system. Importantly, regulators have enacted rules to ensure that everyone has fair access to banking services. One hallmark regulation in this space is the **Community Reinvestment Act** (or "CRA"), which was enacted in 1977. The CRA requires the Federal Reserve and other regulators (namely the FDIC and the Office of the Comptroller of the Currency, OCC) to ensure that commercial banks are meeting the credit needs of the communities within which they operate.[17] Importantly, this means that banks should be working to meet the needs of low- and moderate-income neighborhoods. The Act is meant to reduce discrimination against low-income neighborhoods, a practice known as "redlining." It is important to note that the Act does not require banks to fulfill the law by making risky loans but requires banks to make loans in their operating regions that are safe and sound.

Another regulatory change from the Dodd–Frank Act was the creation of the **Consumer Financial Protection Bureau** (or "CFPB"). The CFPB is an independent bureau that exists within the Federal Reserve. According to the CFPB, the bureau protects "consumers from unfair, deceptive, or abusive practices and take action against companies that break the law." The CFPB allows consumers to file complaints against many types of financial institutions for what the consumer may feel are unfair practices. The bureau's purview extends beyond traditional commercial banks and includes other entities like payday lenders, credit unions, and debt collection agencies. Beyond handling consumer complaints, the bureau also has the power to enforce rules, and monitor and examine financial institutions. Some of the bureau's power was limited in a push for deregulation in 2018, including from the **Economic Growth, Regulatory Relief, and Consumer Protection Act**.

10.6 Capital Adequacy and the IVM

Based on the "ART" of risk management we have discussed throughout this book, we can see that the choice of equity capital ratio (denoted here as "E/A") is yet another key factor that can affect the bank's market value

---

[17] For more information about the Federal Reserve's role in the CRA, see https://www.federalreserve.gov/consumerscommunities/cra_about.htm.

of equity.[18] This E/A ratio can be viewed as a safety "buffer" to protect the bank from becoming insolvent if the bank experiences large, unexpected losses. However, we cannot simply use a derivative security to hedge this type of insolvency risk. Instead, bank managers must decide how much equity capital to hold that balances this risk against the added cost of additional equity. Recall from our discussion earlier in this chapter, as well as Chapters 2 and 3 on bank valuation techniques, that equity investors are the residual claimants on the firm's assets and thus are exposed to the greatest financial risk and require a much higher return than bank depositors and other creditors. Bank managers must decide what level of E/A ratio is large enough to minimize insolvency risk while also not holding too much of this very costly form of capital (in terms of an expected return to equity investors, R_E). In effect, the bank must find the "Goldilocks" level of the E/A ratio that maximizes the bank's market value of equity (V_E), while also remaining in compliance with capital regulations.

Presented below is one example of how we can model this trade-off. Clearly, there are many other ways to describe this relationship and so bank managers have considerable leeway in identifying the key factors influencing the costs and benefits of choosing an acceptable level for the E/A ratio, which is commonly referred to as "Capital Adequacy." The following discussion is meant to be an initial attempt to examine the direct costs and benefits of the bank's capital adequacy choice. As we show later in this chapter, using the IVM within an Excel™ spreadsheet allows us to consider a more detailed analysis that includes both direct and indirect effects of the bank's decisions about equity capital.

We approach this problem by first identifying the total benefits and total costs of a bank's E/A choice. Total Benefits are estimated by quantifying the impact of E/A on the bank's cost of debt (i.e., the interest rate paid to depositors and other creditors, denoted here as rD). The bank's Total Costs are estimated by calculating the effect of E/A on the bank's expected

---

[18] As noted earlier in this chapter, there are many different capital ratios used in the banking industry. Here, we focus on a simple ratio of Tangible Common Equity (E) divided by Total Assets (A). One could use alternative measures that adjust Total Assets by the relative riskiness of the bank's specific assets (e.g., the CET1 Risk-Based Capital Ratio) or we could add in an estimate of off-balance sheet items (e.g., the Supplementary Leverage ratio). The basic trade-offs between the cost and benefits of bank capital will remain the same regardless of the chosen capital ratio, so we focus on the simplest measure: Tangible Common Equity / Total Assets.

return and long-term growth rate (denoted in Chapter 3 as R_E and g in our IVM method). In this way, we can see the change in the bank's market value of equity due to different levels of E/A. We assume that the cost of debt remains constant for E/A ratios at or above a certain level of industry-standard E/A ratio, referred to here as an *Industry* E/A. For example, guided by regulation over time, many analysts and regulators view 8% as an "acceptable" level of capital and thus this value can be used as an estimate of the Industry E/A. So, when the bank's E/A is at or above the Industry E/A ratio, the cost of debt is simply equal to the bank's *initial* value of rD (denoted below as rD_0). However, if the bank's E/A dips *below* the Industry E/A threshold, then we expect creditors to react to this *lower* capital buffer by *increasing* their required return on their deposits and other debt. This capital-related "threshold effect" can be modeled as follows[19]:

$$rD = rD_0 + \left[\left((\text{CapDum} \cdot (rD_0 - rD^*)) \right) \cdot \left(\frac{\text{Industry E/A}}{\text{E/A}} \right) \right] \quad (10.3)$$

where

rD = final cost of debt (*after* adjusting for the bank's E/A choice),

rD_0 = initial cost of debt (*before* adjusting for the bank's E/A choice),

rD^* = "base" deposit rate (e.g., a money market rate independent of the bank's specific risk such as the **Federal Funds Rate**, the **Secured Overnight Financing Rate**, "SOFR," or a short-term **U.S. T-bill rate**),

CapDum = equals 1 if the bank's E/A is *less than* the Industry E/A and zero, otherwise,

Industry E/A = an industry-standard acceptable equity capital ratio (usually at or around 8%), and

E/A = the bank's specific Tangible Common Equity-to-Total Assets ratio.

---

[19] As E/A decreases, the bank's financial leverage, or "Equity Multiplier" (as measured by the inverse of this E/A ratio), increases. Thus, the above equation shows that the cost of debt remains stable at first but then rises as the bank's leverage is raised above some "threshold," as defined as the industry average level of financial leverage. This positive relationship between the cost of debt and financial leverage is supported by the "trade-off theory" of capital structure that is commonly described in finance textbooks (e.g., see Brigham and Ehrhardt, 2020).

Equation (10.3) describes how lower capital ratios can cause creditors to *raise* their required returns on their investments which, in turn, will *decrease* the bank's Net Interest Income (NII) because the bank's returns on its loans and other earning assets are assumed to remain unchanged as the E/A ratio is varied. Thus, the bank's NII will *not* decrease if it maintains an E/A ratio at or above the Industry E/A. As mentioned earlier, this is one way to model this effect on the bank's financing costs but other capital adequacy benchmarks beyond Tangible Common Equity can be used.

In addition to the above effect on the bank's cost of debt, we assume that E/A affects the bank's long-term growth rate (*g*) as follows:

$$g = (1-d) \cdot \text{ROE} \cdot \left(\frac{\text{Industry E/A}}{\text{E/A}} \right) \quad (10.4)$$

where

g = long-term growth rate,

d = Dividend Payout Ratio = (Total Dividends / Net Income) and so $(1-d)$ = the Retention Ratio,

ROE = Return on Equity = NI / *E*,

Industry E/A = an industry-standard acceptable equity capital ratio (usually at or around 8%), and

E/A = the bank's specific Tangible Common Equity-to-Total Assets ratio.

Equation (10.4) shows our original relationship for the long-term growth rate based on Chapter 3's discussion of the IVM but makes one important modification by including a ratio of the two capital ratios: $\left(\frac{\text{Industry E/A}}{\text{E/A}} \right)$. This ratio in parentheses captures the *inverse* relationship between growth and equity capital. As Hempel and Simonson (1999) and others have noted, the "sustainable" growth rate of a bank is negatively related to the bank's E/A ratio. This inverse relationship could occur because as the E/A ratio increases, the cost of equity plays a bigger role in the firm's **Weighted Average Cost of Capital** (or "WACC") and thus the overall cost of capital is increased. In turn, a larger WACC leads to an increased "hurdle rate" for which the bank's investments need to earn to maximize shareholder value. This will then lead to a *drop* in the dollar amount of investments that are profitable for the bank and will discourage future investment and *reduce* the bank's growth rate.[20]

The choice of E/A also affects our estimate of the bank's expected equity return (R_E) because the above effect on the cost of debt shown by Equation (10.3) can also have an impact on the firm's expected Return on Equity (ROE$_{t+1}$) due to changes in Net Interest Income. This can be seen by the following model of R_E, which was first presented in Chapter 3 related to the IVM method:

$$R_E = DY_t + \{[(1-d) + DY_t - (d \cdot DY_t)] \cdot ROE_t + 1\} \quad (10.5)$$

where

R_E = the bank's expected equity return,

DY_t = current dividend yield = Total Dividends / Market Value of Equity,

d = dividend payout ratio = Total Dividends / Net Income, and

ROE_{t+1} = expected return on equity = NI / E.

Equation (10.5) shows that a bank investor's expected equity return (R_E) is positively related to the bank's expected return on equity (ROE$_{t+1}$) and so any factor that affects the bank's NI (such as a change in the cost of debt due to higher financial leverage) can also affect R_E. Further, recall from Chapter 3 that when we use a constant growth dividend discount model (DDM), the difference between the firm's expected equity return (R_E) and its long-term growth rate (g) is equal to its future dividend yield as follows:

$$\text{Expected Dividend Yield} = DY_{t+1} = R_E - g \quad (10.6)$$

Overall, Equations (10.3)–(10.6) show the linkages between a bank's E/A choice and its impact on the "MRT" **factors of the IVM**. That is, the cost of debt relationship in (10.3) captures the E/A choice's impact on the Magnitude of cash flows while (10.4) describes the impact on the Timing

---

[20] See Brigham and Ehrhardt (2020) for a more detailed explanation of the linkage between the weight of equity in a firm's capital structure, WACC, and its impact on future investments and growth.

of cash flows and (10.5) illustrates the effect on the bank's Riskiness of cash flows.

We can now develop an estimate of the bank's capital adequacy choice using the following form of the IVM that explicitly quantifies the change in market value (denoted by the "delta" sign, Δ):

$$\Delta V_E = \left[\frac{\Delta(d \cdot \text{NI})}{(R_E - g)} \right] = \left[\frac{d \cdot [(-\Delta rD \cdot \text{Debt}) \cdot (1-t)]}{(\Delta R_E - \Delta g)} \right] :$$

$$= \left[\frac{d \cdot [(-\Delta rD \cdot \text{Debt}) \cdot (1-t)]}{\Delta \text{Expected Dividend Yield}} \right] \quad (10.7)$$

where

- d = expected dividend payout ratio for next year ($\text{DIV}_1 / \text{NI}_1$),
- Impact on Net Interest Income = $(-\Delta rD \cdot \text{Debt})$,
- Impact on Expected Dividend Yield = $\Delta \text{Expected Dividend Yield}$ = $(\Delta R_E - \Delta g)$,
- t = marginal corporate tax rate,
- R_E = expected return on the bank's equity,
- g = constant growth rate of the bank's dividends, and
- **Expected Dividend Yield** = $(\text{DIV}_1 / V_{E,0})$ and this term equals $(R_E - g)$ for the Constant Growth version of the IVM.

We can use the above variant of the IVM described by Equation (10.7) in a numerical example for our hypothetical bank, ABC, based on some of the data we have been using in previous chapters related to ABC's Stylized Balance Sheet and Stylized Income Statement. These data can also be found in the "Capital Adequacy – Ch 10" tab of the **Integrated Valuation Model.xlsx** file.

Note that in this example ABC has an initial E/A ratio of 11.4% and an overall deposit rate, or total cost of debt (rD_0), of 2.12% while the base borrowing rate (rD^*) is 1.61%.[21] As noted in boldface from Table 10.1, the Industry Average E/A ratio is assumed to be 8.0% and ABC's bank

---

[21] As noted earlier in the discussion of Equation (10.3), the base borrowing rate could be a short-term money market rate that a bank with minimal default risk could borrow at (e.g., the Federal Funds rate or SOFR or a T-bill rate).

Table 10.1. Numerical Example of Capital Adequacy Choice.

Tot. Deposits & Other Debt ($ million)	1,400.0
Common Equity ($ million)	180.0
Net Interest Income (NII) ($ million)	35.0
Projected NI ($ million)	18.0
Initial Stock Price ($/ sh.)	20.17
Initial ROA (ROA_0)	1.14%
Initial Equity/TA ratio $(E/A)_0$	11.4%
Initial Dividend Yield (DY_t)	3.37%
Loan rate (rL)	5.25%
Base Borrowing Rate (rD^*)	1.61%
Initial Deposit rate (rD_0)	2.12%
Minimum E/A ratio	**6.0%**
Maximum E/A ratio	**12.0%**
Industry Average E/A ratio	**8.0%**
Dividend Payout (in decimals)	0.40
Tax Rate (in decimals)	0.20
Shares Outstanding (million)	10.00

Figure 10.3. Impact of Capital Adequacy Choices on ABC's Stock Price.

managers must decide how much capital to hold within their chosen range of 6.0–12.0%. That is, ABC must decide where within this E/A range the firm's market value can be maximized based on Equation (10.7). To do so, the FIs staff can analyze the impact of various levels of the E/A ratio on the bank's financing costs (rD), expected equity return (R_E), and long-term growth rate (g). Figure 10.3 displays the results of this type of "what-if" simulation on the expected *change* in ABC's stock price.

Figure 10.4. Costs and Benefits of ABC's Equity Capital Choices.

As we can see from Figure 10.3 and the data in Table 10.1, ABC's stock price is boosted around $2.48 per share (+12.3%) if it chooses an **optimal E/A ratio (E/A)*** of around 9.6% of total assets.[22] This specific OC* ratio equates the marginal benefit to the marginal cost of this capital ratio and thus maximizes the bank's stock price.[23] Any E/A ratio above or below 9.6% results in a lower change in ABC's stock price. Interestingly, this analysis suggests that ABC is currently holding too much capital because its current E/A ratio of 11.4% is much higher than the optimal value of 9.6%. Thus, the bank could maximize its market value by freeing up some capital and returning it to shareholders in the form of a stock buyback or special dividend.

The trade-off between the total costs and benefits of the bank's capital adequacy strategy can be seen below in Figure 10.4. As this graph shows, the benefits outweigh the costs in two places: when ABC's E/A ratio is around 7.8% and 9.6%. At around 7.8%, the less-negative effect on interest expense, expressed in millions of dollars based on the left-hand scale (compared to a 6.0% E/A ratio), and a lower dividend yield (based on the right-hand side scale) leads to a positive change in ABC's stock price of around $0.68 / share. However, the $2.48 gain in market value is greater at the optimal 9.55% E/A ratio because the negative effect of interest expense is now fully removed since this capital ratio is above the industry average

---

[22] More precisely, our Excel™ model suggests that an E/A ratio of 9.55% of total assets is expected to increase the stock price by $2.478 per share, or +12.29%.

[23] Technically, this optimal capital ratio can be obtained by numerical iterative methods like those found in typical spreadsheet software if a mathematical / analytical approach is not feasible. In our spreadsheet, we use Excel's *Solver* function with a "GRG Nonlinear" optimization technique to find the optimal E/A ratio reported here.

threshold. In this latter case, the E/A ratio also helps lower the expected dividend yield (DY_{t+1}), which further boosts ABC's stock price. So, when there are two or more E/A ratios that increase a bank's stock price, we always prefer the specific capital ratio that increases market value the most (in this case, at 9.55%).

As noted above, Figure 10.4 shows that the negative impact of higher interest expense due to lower levels of equity capital (via the left axis) is reduced as ABC increases its E/A ratio. Further, Equation (10.3) showed that this effect jumps to a zero value (i.e., no negative impact on interest expense) when ABC's E/A is above the industry average threshold. Thus, *higher* levels of capital help *lower* the cost of ABC's debt. However, the right axis of Figure 10.4 shows that the impact of E/A on the bank's expected dividend yield (i.e., $DY_{t+1} = R_E - g$) is nonlinear in nature as it first declines and then increases when the E/A ratio crosses the industry average threshold. It then repeats this oscillating pattern for higher levels of E/A because R_E and g decline at different rates while equity capital continues to increase. Although it is informative to conduct this type of quantitative analysis, it is also important to consider the qualitative aspects of capital adequacy management which are considered in the following.

10.7 Managerial Implications

Sam and Nina are considering the acceptable level of equity capital for ABC. They are aware that the regulatory minimum ratio of equity-to-assets for their bank is 8%, and currently the bank's optimal equity-to-assets ratio sits at around 9.6%. Recall that there are multiple regulatory capital ratios that banks must adhere to, and some of these ratios calculate equity against risk-weighted assets. Sam and Nina are also aware of growing concerns in the macroeconomy, and they understand ABC's own exposure to the changing macroeconomic environment via its portfolio of loans (although it is diversified, recall that a bank remains exposed to systematic, market-wide credit risk).

Although the bank is in regulatory compliance, what should Nina and Sam consider as it relates to the bank's current capital position? **If the bank suffers large losses to its loan portfolio, is a 9.6% *E/A* ratio a large enough capital buffer?** Do risk-adjusted capital ratios add enough additional support to remove any concerns Sam and Nina might have?

Or instead, should Sam and Nina increase the bank's capital position to improve their safety buffer? If they do this, what implications are there for the bank's cost of funding, earnings growth rate, and the range of profitable loans it can make? In the end, Nina and Sam must address these issues in a report to senior management that also considers the impact of their recommendation on the market value of ABC's equity.

10.8 Summary

Bank regulation is largely aimed at establishing and maintaining trust in the financial system. This trust is earned via safety, soundness, and integrity within the system. At times, however, regulation can be too burdensome in some areas, while at other times regulation can be too loose. Regulators and bankers constantly seek to find the right balance between the two. As noted at the beginning of the chapter, this process creates somewhat of a "regulatory pendulum," where the banking system swings between higher profits/looser regulation eras (e.g., the 1920s and early 2000s) and lower profits/tighter regulation periods (e.g., the 1930s and 2010s).

Following the 2008–2009 GFC, many regulations began to focus on the safety of banks deemed to be "too big to fail." Regulation can fail to achieve its purpose, and bad actors can sometimes skirt regulation (or violate the spirit of regulation). In some cases, this can create large-scale disasters in the financial system. The worst-case scenario is a systemic risk event, like what occurred during the Great Depression of the 1930s, in which many banks failed simultaneously. Chapter 11 focuses on this possibility, the risks that lead to a systemic event, and the effects of a systemic event, should it happen. As we can see from the above application of the IVM and Managerial Implications discussion, there is a strong case to be made from both a valuation perspective and a risk management perspective for banks to hold more capital than the regulatory minimums when it comes to capital adequacy and other regulations. Banks that are better prepared might not only increase their market value but also be in a better position to weather a future economic storm.

Chapter-End Questions

Answers to odd-numbered questions can be found at the end of this book.

1. **True or False:** The FDIC simply writes a check to make all the depositors whole when a bank fails.
2. **True or False:** Stress testing is a simulation exercise in which bankers and regulators test how the bank would perform under severely adverse conditions.
3. **Multiple Choice:** What is the potential impact of bank consolidation on access to credit for smaller borrowers?

    (A) Increased access to credit for smaller borrowers
    (B) Decreased access to credit for smaller borrowers
    (C) No impact on access to credit for smaller borrowers
    (D) The impacts are uncertain

4. **Multiple Choice:** What is the aim of capital requirements?

    (A) To increase the bank's profits
    (B) To create a buffer to protect the bank's depositors and other liabilities holders from a large decrease in the value of the bank's assets
    (C) To create a monopoly for the bank
    (D) None of the above

5. **Multiple Choice:** What is the primary role of the Financial Stability Oversight Council (FSOC)?

    (A) To monitor threats to financial stability
    (B) To facilitate coordination and information sharing among regulatory agencies
    (C) To designate nonbank institutions for regulatory oversight from the Federal Reserve
    (D) All of the above

6. **Short Answer:** How does deposit insurance impact bank runs and bank risk-taking?
7. **Short Answer:** What is the difference between Tier 1 and Tier 2 capital?

8. **Short Answer:** Identify some of the significant changes to the banking regulatory landscape brought about by the Dodd–Frank Act.

9. **Excel-based Question:** Here, we consider the impact of the E/A ratio on ABC's valuation. To answer these questions, use the "Capital Adequacy – Ch 10" tab of the **Integrated Valuation Model.xlsx** file. Start from the base case provided, in which the minimum E/A ratio is 6%, the maximum E/A ratio is 12%, and the industry average E/A is 8%.

    (A) What is ABC's new optimal E/A ratio given an industry-wide change in expectations to an average E/A of 9%?
    (B) What is the impact on ABC's stock price as a result of this change?
    (C) Given the industry average change, what is the change in ABC's deposit rate?

10. **Comprehensive Question:** Sam and Nina are considering ABC Bank's position relative to regulatory requirements. While the bank follows regulatory capital minimums, the two are considering whether the bank should increase its equity beyond those minimum levels. Advise Sam and Nina of the benefits and drawbacks of increasing bank capital to levels higher than those mandated by regulation.

References

Berger, A.N. and Bouwman, C.H.S. (2017). Bank liquidity creation, monetary policy, and financial crises. *Journal of Financial Stability*, 30, 139–155.

Berger, A.N., Karakaplan, M.U. and Roman, R.A. (2023). *The Economic and Financial Impacts of the COVID-19 Crisis Around the World: Expect the Unexpected*. Elsevier, Academic Press.

Berger, A.N., Miller, N.H. Petersen, M.A. Rajan, R.G. and Stein, J.C. (2005). Does function follow organizational form? Evidence from the lending practices of large and small banks. *Journal of Financial Economics*, 76(2), 237–269.

Berger, A.N. and Roman, R.A. (2020). *TARP and Other Bank Bailouts and Bail-Ins Around the World: Connecting Wall Street, Main Street, and the Financial System*. Elsevier, Academic Press.

Berger, A.N., Roman, R.A. and Sedunov, J. (2020). Do bank bailouts reduce or increase systemic risk? The effects of TARP on financial system stability. *Journal of Financial Intermediation*, 43, 100810.

Brigham, E.F. and Ehrhardt, M. (2020). *Financial Management: Theory and Practice*, 16th edition, pp. 821–822, Cengage.

Demirgüç-Kunt, A. and Huizinga, H. (2010). Bank activity and funding strategies: The impact on risk and returns. *Journal of Financial Economics*, 98(3), 626–650.

Demirgüç-Kunt, A., Kane, E. and Laeven, L. (2015). Deposit insurance around the world: A comprehensive analysis and database. *Journal of Financial Stability*, 20, 155–183.

Garcia, G. (2013). *Garn-St Germain Depository Institutions Act of 1982*. https://www.federalreservehistory.org/essays/garn-st-germain-act. Accessed June 19, 2023.

Hempel, G.H. and Simonson, D.G. (1999). *Bank Management: Text and Cases*, 5th edition. John Wiley & Sons.

Saunders, A., Cornett, M.M. and Erhemjamts, O. (2024). *Financial Institutions Management: A Risk Management Approach*, McGraw-Hill, New York.

Chapter 11

Systemic Risk

11.1 Introduction

In this chapter, we discuss the concept of systemic risk.[1] One seminal definition of systemic risk is that a financial crisis is "systemic" if many banks fail together, or if one bank's failure propagates as a contagion that causes the failure of many other banks (Acharya, 2009). Thus, systemic risk is important as it has the potential to impact all banks in the banking system simultaneously and can be created by most, if not all, of the sources of bank-level risk that we have discussed so far.

Since systemic risk impacts all financial institutions together, and because a bank can be affected by a systemic crisis sparked by another institution, it is a challenge for us to incorporate systemic risk into this book's Integrated Valuation Model (IVM). However, we can see from the IVM's concept of key value drivers: Magnitude, Riskiness, and Timing of cash flows ("MRT") that increased risk in the entire financial system can negatively impact a bank's market value. That is, as systemic risk rises, the magnitude and timing (i.e., growth) of a bank's cash flows can drop

---

[1] The academic literature has a growing and robust literature on systemic risk. Several surveys of this literature exist and can be informative. These surveys include the following: De Bandt *et al.*, 2012; Freixas *et al.*, 2015; Silva *et al.*, 2017; Benoit *et al.*, 2017; De Bandt and Hartmann, 2019; Berger and Sedunov, 2024; and Berger *et al.*, 2024. Some of the content in this chapter is closely related to Berger and Sedunov, 2024; and Berger *et al.*, 2024.

420 *Managing Financial Institutions: An Integrated Valuation Approach*

sharply while the riskiness and cost of equity spikes. In this case, all three of these value drivers are negatively impacted and so it is not surprising that bank stock prices plummeted during periods like 2008–2009 when systemic risk rose precipitously during the Global Financial Crisis (GFC).

Nevertheless, systemic risk remains worthy of discussion as there are wide-ranging implications of systemic crises, and large-scale efforts from regulators to prevent them. Accordingly, in this chapter, we provide a brief discussion of measuring systemic risk and sources of systemic risk for banks and financial institutions.

11.2 Measuring Systemic Risk

Numerous methods have been proposed for estimating systemic risk.[2] These methods range from measuring system-wide crisis probabilities to estimating bank-level contributions to systemic risk. Although there are many methods for estimating systemic risk, there is no consensus on which one specific measure stands above the rest. However, some have gained traction for use with policymakers and in the relevant academic literature. Here, we briefly highlight two of these measures: "ΔCoVaR" (Adrian and Brunnermeier, 2016) and "SRISK" (Brownlees and Engle, 2017).

First, **ΔCoVaR** is a method that estimates a *Conditional Value-at-Risk* metric (i.e., like VaR, which we had discussed as Value-at-Risk in Chapter 5). ΔCoVaR is a measure of systemic risk that estimates the *contribution* of a single institution to the total losses suffered by all institutions in the financial system, *conditional on* the occurrence of a financial crisis. The CoVaR methodology also allows for the estimation of an exposure metric, which calculates the impact of a financial crisis on a given institution. However, for the sake of brevity, we focus here on the contribution measure. CoVaR relies on quantile regression, which is a statistical method that allows the user to focus on different percentiles of a statistical distribution (in the case of the CoVaR measures, it makes the most sense to concentrate on far left-tail outcomes, like what we do with VaR).

Formally, an institution j's contribution to the financial system is given by the *difference* between the VaR of the financial system in its

---

[2]Another academic survey (Bisias *et al.*, 2012) provides a detailed overview of systemic risk measurement.

"normal" state (in this case, the median value) and the VaR of the financial system should institution j experience distress:

$$\Delta\text{CoVaR}_q^{s|j} = \Delta\text{CoVaR}_q^{s|X^j=\text{VaR}_q^j} - \Delta\text{CoVaR}_q^{s|Xj=\text{Median}^j} \quad (11.1)$$

where s represents the financial system, j represents the institution, q represents a probability level corresponding to a specific percentile in the far-left tail of the distribution of the institution's asset or equity returns, and X_j denotes the growth rate of the institution's market value of total assets. It is likely that our example bank, ABC, will not have a high value for ΔCoVaR, as it is a relatively small institution with $1.580 billion in assets. A shift from ABC's median state to its left-tail state, while devastating for ABC itself, may not lead to contagious or spillover effects on other financial institutions or the entire financial system. A larger bank, though, may have a much larger impact on the Value-at-Risk of the financial system. Using some simple numbers, let's assume that a very large financial institution, DEF bank, has $1 trillion in assets. Let us further assume that the VaR of the *entire financial system* conditional on DEF being in its *median* state is 5% of the system's total assets and that the VaR of the financial system conditional on DEF being in its 1% left-tail state (in other words, in severe distress) is 15% of total assets. DEF's ΔCoVaR would then be 10%, meaning that it is contributing an additional 10% of downside to the *financial system's* VaR, should it find itself in distress (i.e., ΔCoVaR = 15% tail value minus 5% median value = 10%). This is a large contribution, and it would mean that DEF is an institution that regulators should be mindful of in terms of preventing a systemic crisis. A possible failure of DEF could lead to widespread distress in the financial system, based on this ΔCoVaR measure.

Alternatively, **SRISK** is another widely used measure, that can also provide an estimate of a bank's contribution to systemic risk. SRISK estimates the potential capital shortfall a bank would face if a systemic crisis were to occur. Specifically, SRISK measures the amount of capital a bank would need to maintain a given capital ratio during a crisis (recall that we discussed capital adequacy in Chapter 10).

SRISK is calculated using the bank's stock returns along with the book value of the bank's liabilities (*Debt*). Specifically, from Brownlees and Engle (2017),

$$\text{SRISK} = k \cdot \text{Debt}_{i,t-1} - (1-k) \cdot (1 - \text{LRMES}_{i,t}) \cdot \text{Equity}_{i,i} \quad (11.2)$$

where k is a regulatory minimum level of equity to total assets. A reasonable choice for k is 8%, which is like the minimum required level of the total capital ratio described in Chapter 10. However, it is possible to set k to other values should the need arise. Importantly, "LRMES" is the Long-Run Marginal Expected Shortfall (or the "Long-Run MES" for short). This represents the decline in the bank's stock value conditional on a financial crisis. So, the SRISK measure is a combination of financial leverage (from the first term in 11.2) and co-movement (from the second term in 11.2). When an individual bank has a high level of leverage, its probability of failure may be higher (hence our discussion of capital adequacy rules in Chapter 10).

When a bank's stock co-moves more with that of other banks, it is more likely to suffer from a negative event concurrently with other institutions — in other words, *more* co-movement can lead to a *higher* potential for contagion of catastrophic events in the banking system. Separately, these issues can be problematic for banks. Together, high leverage *and* co-movement can take a dramatic event at one financial institution and spread it to many others.[3] In this case, we can return to our usual bank, ABC, to make a simple calculation of its SRISK. In Chapter 3, we see that ABC has $1.580 billion (or $1,580 million) in assets, funded by $1,400 million in liabilities and $180 million in equity. Let's assume that ABC's LRMES is 5%, meaning that then the rest of the financial system is experiencing a tail event, ABC's equity will decline by 5%. Its SRISK is then

$$\text{SRISK} = 8\% \cdot (\$1,400) - (92\%) \cdot (1 - 5\%) \cdot \$180 = -\$45.32 \text{ million} \quad (11.3)$$

The result of Equation (11.3) shows that *conditional on a financial crisis*, ABC would have a shortfall of $45.32 million relative to regulatory minimums. For any bank, the greater this shortfall, the greater exposure it has to a financial crisis, and the greater its potential contribution to a crisis, should it be the next to fail.

Finally, it is important to note that different measures of systemic risk may not be highly correlated, and at times they may disagree.

---

[3] See NYU's V-Lab (vlab.stern.nyu.edu) for up-to-date estimates of SRISK for banks in the U.S. and around the world.

Disagreements among established measures of systemic risk tend to occur more during good times than bad. During times of crisis, most measures of systemic risk will spike, as correlations across many bank-related risk variables will rise in tandem. However, it is potentially most important to understand which banks are the biggest contributors to systemic risk *before* a crisis unfolds, so that preemptive action can be taken (see, for example, by using the "first lines of defense" we discuss in the following). So, one course of action is to look at multiple measures of systemic risk to gain a consensus view about which banks may be riskiest if a crisis were to occur. The two measures presented here, as well as other available measures, can capture different aspects of systemic risk and rely on differing methodologies. For example, ΔCoVaR relies on a regression framework while SRISK does not, and SRISK more explicitly captures leverage risk relative to ΔCoVaR. It is quite possible (and even likely) to calculate different systemic risk measures for a given bank and arrive at somewhat different conclusions.

11.3 Sources of Systemic Risk

We turn our attention now to understanding from where systemic risk arises. In other words, we look to the academic literature to understand what can contribute to a bank's systemic importance. In some cases, sources of systemic risk are related to the structure of a bank (e.g., its size or interconnectedness). In other cases, systemic risk contributions can arise from the bank's business model and choices (e.g., leverage, credit allocation). We provide in this section a brief summary and description of places in which systemic risks can build up.

11.4 Systemic Risk Arising from Bank Structure

11.4.1 *Too-big-to-fail banks*

An institution is considered "too-big-to-fail" ("TBTF") if it is large enough that its distress or failure can spill over to other institutions, causing them distress or even their own failure. The failure of a TBTF institution can significantly amplify a financial crisis. Institutions grow large by acquiring other institutions and aggressively expanding their services. Due to their large footprint, their failure can also spill into the real economy, as a reduction in credit supply and other services can impact households and businesses alike. TBTF is also related to policy choices. Policymakers may prioritize bailouts to TBTF institutions to protect the financial system, or to shelter their own reputations. Thus, because of the possibility of implied bailouts, institutions might be incentivized to become TBTF (see, e.g., Kane, 1990; Stern and Feldman, 2004; Mishkin, 2006). Due to the increased likelihood of a bailout, TBTF banks often also enjoy reduced costs of capital due to market participants' perception of lower risk for these banks. As a result, it is possible for TBTF firms to then have **moral hazard** incentives, meaning that they are likely to take on more risks, and, by extension, increase their probability of failure (e.g., Cetorelli and Traina, 2021). In the United States, due to the Dodd–Frank Act's switch to a "bail-in" system, some of these distortions should no longer be persistent, however, regulators have not yet been faced with handling the failure of a large and interconnected institution. To this point, the closest example is Silicon Valley Bank in 2023, in which uninsured depositors were protected, but the bank itself was ultimately closed.

11.4.2 *Too-interconnected-to-fail banks*

In addition to size, **interconnections** also play an important role in the build-up of systemic risk and the propagation of a financial crisis. In this case, we are concerned about banks that are connected to other institutions and financial markets through interbank lending, derivatives, or other linkages (for example, Lehman Brothers in 2008). Banks that are connected to an important, "central" institution can experience distress when the highly interconnected institution experiences distress, as it may not be able to fulfill its responsibilities as a counterparty. Banks connected to this institution would miss out on expected payments or the delivery of securities, and thus fail to meet their own obligations to other counterparties. This type of interconnectedness can lead to the realization of several risks in a cascading effect through the financial system, causing widespread bank failures. To date, a large literature on interconnectedness has developed.[4] The concern for the interconnection of financial institutions plays a clear role in the SRISK measure we discussed above, via the LRMES component.

---

[4] Culp *et al.* (2018) survey the literature on interconnectedness, paying particular attention to credit default swaps and sovereign debt.

11.4.3 *Too-many-to-fail*

A final concern for the structure of the financial system is the risk of "too-many-to-fail" (or "TMTF" for short). Rather than the case of one large bank failing and causing a ripple effect throughout the financial system, the concern here is that many (potentially smaller) banks fail simultaneously, possibly due to correlated risk exposures. As small- and medium-sized banks are far less likely to receive bailout protection from regulators, they may be incentivized to correlate their risk-taking and risk-exposures to potentially fail simultaneously in the event of a financial calamity (e.g., Acharya and Yorulmazer, 2007; Acharya, 2009). This practice can also be referred to as "herding." This correlated risk-taking can lead to a higher degree of correlation between bank stock prices, which in turn would have important implications for a bank's equity capital buffer (as discussed in Chapter 10). Relaxed enforcement of regulations ("regulatory forbearance") can exacerbate the TMTF problem (Brown and Dinc, 2011). It may also be the case that regulations by themselves can induce bank herding behavior.

11.5 Sources of Systemic Risk Arising from the Bank's Decision-Making

Due to the ever-changing marginal benefits and marginal costs of a bank's managerial decisions, we present in the following the main sources of banking risk-taking which can lead to increased systemic risk. As we can see from this section, many of the sources of heightened systemic risk relate to the numerous bank risks we examined earlier in Chapters 4–10. While these risks are important on their own, when they lead to the failure of a bank that is either too-big-, too-interconnected-, or too-many-to-fail, they can lead to cascading effects on other institutions and the overall economy. The potential systemic component to many types of risk-taking further highlights the importance of risk management, not only for individual banks but also for the entire banking system.

11.5.1 *Lowered credit standards*

As the economy is experiencing good times, banks may raise their credit risks both by having riskier loans in their portfolios and by increasing the amount of credit available. As we saw in Chapter 6, lending is usually the biggest source of a bank's revenues and profits, thus creating large incentives to expand its loan portfolio and take on more risk, especially during strong economic conditions. Moreover, this is why regulators implement the countercyclical capital buffer that we discussed in Chapter 10. There are also potentially important interactions between reduced bank credit standards, real estate market outcomes, financial market stability, and the real economy that can create or exacerbate a systemic event. Moreover, a bank's willingness to increase exposure to credit risk can be influenced by incentives created from capital charges, FDIC premiums, stress tests, and other regulatory actions.

11.5.2 *Leverage risk*

For banks, capital ratios are very important and are a focus of regulators as we discussed in Chapter 10 and throughout this book – these ratios are the inverse of financial leverage. As leverage increases, a bank's margin for error decreases, and in an extreme case, even a small loss can lead to insolvency, which can quickly spill over to counterparties in the financial system. A higher capital ratio (and by extension lower leverage) can make a bank safer and less susceptible to unforeseen shocks. Moreover, lower leverage reduces moral hazard incentives for banks to take on other risks that might be encouraged by the likelihood of a bailout or from mispriced deposit insurance. Higher capital ratios may also reduce systemic risks by enhancing the public perception of safety in the banking system, which reduces the likelihood of bank runs.

11.5.3 *Liquidity risk*

Bank liquidity risk (discussed in Chapter 8) can also contribute to systemic risk, especially as it relates to bank runs (e.g., driven by depositors) and liquidity shortages. Acharya *et al.* (2011) show that bank liquidity tends to be counter-cyclical, that is, too low during good times and too high during times of crisis. Moreover, problems in interbank funding markets (e.g., the repurchase, or "repo," markets) can also create liquidity risk, as it might become difficult for institutions to fund short-term liquidity needs. In all, distress stemming from a lack of liquidity can lead to an institution (or set of institutions) to experience cash shortfalls with its counterparties. In turn, this can lead to simultaneous distress across multiple institutions that may be interconnected.

11.5.4 *Operational risk*

Operational risk (discussed in Chapter 9) is the risk of loss resulting from inadequate or failed internal processes, people, and systems, or from external events (Jarrow, 2008). As discussed in Chapter 9, operational risk can lead to very large losses (in some cases billions of dollars) for a bank. Due to a large-scale operational risk event, a financial institution may encounter difficulties meeting obligations to counterparties or insolvency risk if the loss from the operational risk event results in the loss of the bank's equity in its entirety. If the bank facing this large operational risk loss is highly leveraged or interconnected, the once-idiosyncratic operational risk can even become one that is systemic in nature. Berger *et al.* (2022) indeed find that operational losses (especially large ones) contribute to increased systemic risk.

11.5.5 *Executive behavior*

The compensation packages of CEOs and other bank executives may incentivize risk-taking behavior. For example, the value of stock options is positively related to the volatility of the underlying asset. If a bank management is compensated with many options, then they may be incentivized to increase the volatility of the bank to increase the value of their own pay package. Thus, the bank's board of directors might want to alter these packages to reduce these incentives (e.g., via "claw back" rules or linking pay to interest rates).

Managerial behavior is also important and has been well-studied in academic literature. Evidence suggests, for example, that banks with overconfident CEOs have higher contributions to systemic risk (Lee *et al.*, 2020). In all, executive incentives, compensation, and behavior can lead a bank down a path of increased risk-taking that is not in the best interests of the shareholders but instead benefits management themselves. In keeping with other sources of risk, if these banks are highly leveraged or highly interconnected, then risk-taking stemming from these incentives can quickly become a systemic event as the risks are realized.

11.5.6 *Financial innovations*

Financial innovation can be highly beneficial to financial institutions and the banking system. For example, structured finance (that is, securitization activity) can provide a way for banks to manage exposure to credit and interest rate risks while derivatives can allow banks to hedge against various risk exposures. Alternatively, there might also be downsides when users do not understand these instruments well or use them to speculate rather than to hedge. In related academic literature, Thakor (2012) shows how such innovations can lead to financial institution failures. When the misuse of financial innovation becomes widespread (as in, for example, the GFC with subprime securitization) or concentrated in large institutions (for example, with AIG writing a large amount of CDS insurance on subprime assets) the associated risks can lead to bank failures, which can become widespread in nature.

11.5.7 *Competition*

To date, the academic literature is not in agreement on the impact of bank competition on risk-taking. On one hand, increased bank competition can result in lower loan interest rates, which can reduce credit risk by lowering moral hazard and adverse selection risk-taking incentives for borrowers.[5] However, increased bank competition can also lead to reduced market power and lower profit margins. In turn, these effects can encourage more risk-taking at the bank level. Depending on where this increased risk-taking is concentrated (and especially when a given banking market is highly concentrated to begin with), the realized risks can lead to spillover to other institutions, creating a systemic event.

11.5.8 *Regulation*

Regulation can impact both systemic risk and the risk appetite of a financial institution. Above, we discuss issues related to leverage and capital adequacy, upon which regulators keep a watchful eye. However,

---

[5] As first described in Chapter 1, adverse selection refers to the process by which banks try to identify and screen out risky borrowers. In some situations, banks are incentivized to relax their screening process and lend to higher risk borrowers without concern for how these loans may impact the overall riskiness of the loan portfolio.

regulators may also act in the form of imposing sanctions to limit risk-taking at financial institutions. Berger *et al.* (2022) find that these sanctions (called enforcement actions) can lower systemic risk. On the other hand, regulators might instead have incentives (for their own self-interest) to delay acting until conditions become exceptionally bad (e.g., Boot and Thakor, 1993). This regulatory forbearance was an important issue during the Savings & Loan Crisis of the 1980s, in which regulators did not immediately close distressed thrifts (many of which had negative net interest margins), which led to these institutions gambling for resurrection and ultimately worsened into a more wide-spread crisis.

11.5.9 *Monetary policy*

Monetary policy — that is, the central bank's control over the country's money supply — can impact the stability of the financial system through its effects on both banks and financial markets, as monetary policy influences the level of interest rates in the market (for one discussion, among many in the academic literature, see Kashyap and Siegert, 2020). One stark example of monetary policy influencing the financial system was the 2023 U.S. Regional Banking Crisis, in which several financial institutions suffered losses in the market value of their Treasury bond portfolios as the Federal Reserve increased interest rates at a rapid pace to fight inflation in the aftermath of the COVID-19 crisis.

11.5.10 *Sovereign risk*

Sovereign risk (the risk that an individual country can default on its obligations) can be problematic for the financial systems in multiple countries. Acharya *et al.* (2014) model the feedback loop that can emerge between sovereign risk and the credit risk undertaken by financial institutions in each country. This cyclical view can relate to bank holdings of sovereign debt: as governments become riskier, the yield-to-maturity on their debt rises, which reduces its value. Banks holding this debt (in some cases in large quantities) suffer losses on their portfolios, which endangers these firms. If these banks are larger institutions, the implication of a potential bailout means that their government might need to borrow more, which in turn makes its sovereign debt even more risky. The result is a negative feedback loop in which governments and banks become continually riskier. Furthermore, Pagano and Sedunov (2016) show that spillovers and feedback loops can happen not only within countries but also across borders between both governments and financial systems.

11.5.11 *Shadow banking*

Shadow banks are financial institutions that perform functions like those of banks. However, these institutions do not rely on deposits for funding. Examples of shadow banks include hedge funds, private credit funds, finance companies, or money market mutual funds. Instead of deposits, these institutions fund themselves with other types of short-term debt that are usually purchased by money market funds, and that are potentially even more prone to runs. As the shadow banking system has developed, the traditional financial intermediation functions described in Chapter 1 have become increasingly fragmented.[6] To this end, the largest institutions in the U.S. financial system are shadow banks. For example, in the second quarter of 2021, Blackrock had nearly $9.5 trillion in assets under management. Connections between shadow banks and traditional banks have emerged over time, and these connections have important implications for systemic risk, as the distress or failure of a shadow institution can spread to the traditional financial system (Boot and Thakor, 2014). Two stark examples of this interconnection include the failure of LTCM in 1998 and the failure of Archegos Capital in 2021. Both were hedge funds that failed and created difficulties for financial institutions linked to these funds.

11.6 Mitigating or Preventing Systemic Risk and Crises

As we mentioned above, it is difficult for institutions themselves to manage a systemic crisis. Institutions can help reduce the likelihood of a systemic crisis by mitigating risk-taking behaviors that can lead to their own failure or a correlated failure of financial institutions. But an individual institution cannot necessarily control the behavior of other institutions whose failure can create a contagious systemic event. Thus, it is important for regulators to attempt to take action to prevent systemic crises from

---

[6] See Pozsar *et al.* (2013) for a thorough mapping and description of the shadow banking system.

occurring, as these events can lead to devastating losses for institutions, markets, and the real economy, in addition to requiring large-scale intervention from regulators.

As noted above, systemic risk is difficult for an individual institution to manage because it is generally a macroeconomic problem (though it can have roots at the bank level), thus regulators will normally stick to policies that mandate bank-level actions, but with a view on preserving the stability of the entire financial system. Although actions at the bank level can contribute to systemic risk, a bank cannot control the actions of other institutions to which it is interconnected. As noted earlier, this makes it a challenge to incorporate systemic risk directly into the Integrated Valuation Model (IVM) we have developed throughout the book.

However, as noted earlier in this chapter, a bank's market value can be affected by systemic risk if, say, a market-wide disruption creates liquidity risk shocks that, in turn, affect the FIs Net Income (NI), as well as its Required Equity Return (R_E) and Sustainable Growth rate (g). Since all three of these factors are key value drivers related to the Magnitude, Riskiness, and Timing of a bank's cash flows (referred to as "MRT" in Chapter 3), we can see that a systemic liquidity shock is likely to have a negative effect on the FIs market value. For example, this negative impact on bank value can occur if a sudden shock to the firm's liquidity lowers the magnitude and timing of cash flow while raising the riskiness of these future flows. Such a system-wide shock could also lead to tighter regulation and increased monitoring of bank activities which would, in effect, impose a greater "regulatory tax" on the bank, further reducing "M" and "T" while raising "R" in the context of the IVM.

One potential consideration for regulators is policies that are "first lines of defense." The idea for these policies is to reduce the probability of a future crisis, or should one occur, reduce its severity. Generally, these policies are meant to help proactively keep systemically important financial institutions safer than they otherwise would be during good times. In turn, when systemically important institutions are safer before a crisis starts, they may be less likely to experience distress that would worsen the crisis. These preemptive policies help regulators avoid scrambling for a resolution after a crisis has started and aim to be preventative in nature. Such policies include items like minimum capital and liquidity requirements that we discussed earlier and can also act as substitutes or complements to one another in reducing risks (e.g., Walther, 2016).

Berger and Roman (2020) discuss three ways that "first lines of defense" can mitigate risk in the banking system. They are (1) the *Prudential Mechanism*, in which regulators cover choices made at the bank level, such as leverage risk, liquidity risk, or credit risk, (2) the *Certification Mechanism* which is aimed at keeping public trust in financial institutions high, thus limiting the likelihood of bank runs, and (3) the *Subsidy Mechanism* in which governments can directly support financial institutions.

More specifically, "first lines of defense" cover most of the **financial regulations** that we have discussed in Chapters 8, 9, and 10. First, **bank capital requirements** work through the prudential and certification mechanisms — these regulations are aimed at keeping banks safe via building up sufficiently large capital buffers (linked to various sources of risk), while also conveying to the public that banks are in compliance with the guidelines, thus strengthening public perception of the safety of the financial system. As noted earlier, some banks regarded as systemically important face additional capital surcharges, which are included to further reduce the likelihood of a failure from a bank that may be very large or very interconnected.[7]

A second type of "first line of defense" is **liquidity requirements** (like the Liquidity Coverage Ratio and Net Stable Funding Ratio that we cover in Chapter 8). As discussed in Chapter 8, liquidity risk is the risk of a sudden surge in demand for liquid funds by customers and may require a bank to engage in "fire sales," liquidating assets in short order at less than fair market prices or foregoing profitable investments such as positive net present value loans. Liquidity requirements are thus meant to lessen the probability of a shock to a bank's liquidity, which can then lead to reduced distress or failure. Importantly, for large and/or connected institutions, these requirements help ensure that they can meet their obligations to counterparties and avoid distress that can fuel a bank run or

---

[7]To this end, the Financial Stability Board (FSB) regularly publishes a list of "Global Systemically Important Banks" (G-SIBs). The 2023 list can be found at https://www.fsb.org/2023/11/2023-list-of-global-systemically-important-banks-g-sibs/. Here, we can see that JP Morgan Chase faced an additional 2.5% capital surcharge due to its level of systemic importance, as gauged by the FSB. Other banks like Bank of America, Citigroup, Goldman Sachs, and BNY Mellon also make the list but are in lower buckets, and thus face lower capital surcharges.

bank panic. Like capital requirements, liquidity requirements are effective via both the *Prudential* and *Certification Mechanisms*.

A third type of "first line of defense" is **bank stress testing**. As discussed in Chapter 10, these tests simulate severe scenarios in, say, the macroeconomy or banking system, and evaluate the ability of banks to continue to operate through these scenarios. Banks that are not able to pass the stress tests are subject to actions that are aimed at remediating any shortcomings that are discovered during the testing process. Overall, we can think of stress tests as forward-looking tests that force banks to evaluate their positions relative to potential future risks. This stands in contrast to other capital requirements that we have discussed above, which are backward-looking. Stress tests are also effective via the *Prudential* and *Certification Mechanisms*, like capital and liquidity requirements described above.

A fourth type of "first line of defense" is **prudential supervision**, in which government regulators monitor bank behavior. These evaluations can happen both through on-site exams and submitted reports. An end-product of this evaluation process can be a rating system, in which banks are scored along the lines of their ability to manage or mitigate risk. Shortcomings along these lines can lead to recommendations to management or more formal enforcement actions (EAs) against banks or their managers. These formal enforcement actions include prescribed actions that must be followed. Like the first lines of defense discussed above, prudential supervision is again meant to be effective through both the *Prudential* and *Certification Mechanisms*.

A fifth and final type of "first line of defense" that we consider here is **deposit insurance**. As we had discussed in Chapter 10, deposit insurance can create moral hazard incentives that increase the riskiness of banks. Thus, deposit insurance schemes typically require regulations to offset these issues. However, deposit insurance allows for the continuation of bank functions even during times of distress, as it helps insulate banks against runs. This can mitigate the likelihood or severity of a systemic crisis by preventing the failure of banks due to rumor-based bank runs or other contagious events. Deposit insurance thus affects the financial system via the *Certification Mechanism* (as it helps prevent bank runs) and the *Subsidy Mechanism* (as it allows banks to borrow at low rates, due to the public perception of increased safety).

11.7 Managerial Implications

Sam and Nina are considering ABC's level of risk exposure relative to both its own portfolio and to other banks in the financial system. ABC is a relatively small institution, as it has $1.580 billion in assets. Likely, it will not be a concern to regulators as a bank that is considered too-big-to-fail or too-interconnected-to-fail.

Potentially, though, Sam and Nina realize that ABC's risk-taking and allocation might be highly correlated with other banks in the financial system that are similar in size. Moreover, ABC may have exposure to other, larger banks via interconnections from derivative contracts used for hedging interest rate risk or via interbank borrowing the firm uses to handle daily liquidity needs.

As we discussed in Chapter 10, ABC is a bank that complies with all regulations. However, **how should Sam and Nina view their bank's position relative to other institutions?** Although their risk management process has done well to preserve the bank's equity in an isolated risk event, **what would happen to ABC if other institutions experienced financial distress, or if there was a broader macroeconomic shock that led to a contagious, system-wide credit event?** How should Sam and Nina consider evaluating the bank's risk position as it relates to *other* institutions – **are ABC's risks too correlated with others or is ABC too reliant on other institutions for sources of liquidity? If so, what actions, if any, could Sam and Nina take to mitigate the potential for risk spillover, should a systemic event occur?**

11.8 Summary

In this chapter, we discussed the concept of systemic risk. As we can see, systemic risk impacts all banks together, and even though it is a challenge for us to incorporate systemic risk into this book's IVM, it is apparent that a bank's market value can be greatly affected by a systemic crisis sparked by another financial institution, and that systemic crises can be wide-ranging in their implications. Moreover, we can see that systemic risk can be created through many channels of risk, which emphasizes the importance of proper risk management for all financial institutions.

Chapter-End Questions

Answers to odd-numbered questions can be found at the end of this book.

1. **True or False:** One definition of systemic risk is that it is the risk that a single bank's failure will cause the failure of many other banks.
2. **True or False:** Bank liquidity risk can contribute to systemic risk concerns.
3. **Multiple Choice:** What does ΔCoVaR estimate?
   (A) The contribution of a single institution to the total losses suffered by all institutions in the financial system, conditional on the occurrence of a financial crisis
   (B) The potential capital shortfall a bank would face if a systemic crisis were to occur
   (C) The amount of capital a bank would need to maintain a given capital ratio during a crisis
   (D) The decline in the bank's stock value conditional on a financial crisis
4. **Multiple Choice:** What does SRISK estimate?
   (A) The contribution of a single institution to the total losses suffered by all institutions in the financial system, conditional on the occurrence of a financial crisis
   (B) The potential capital shortfall a bank would face if a systemic crisis were to occur
   (C) The amount of capital a bank would need to maintain a given capital ratio during a crisis
   (D) The decline in the bank's stock value, conditional on a financial crisis
5. **Multiple Choice:** Which of the following sources of risk can impact financial system stability?
   (A) Lowered Credit Standards
   (B) Leverage Risk
   (C) Competition
   (D) Sovereign Risk
   (E) All of the above

6. **Short Answer:** How can operational risk become systemic in nature?
7. **Short Answer:** What are Too-Big-to-Fail, Too-Interconnected-to-Fail, and Too-Many-to-Fail banks?
8. **Short Answer:** What are the potential downsides of financial innovation as it relates to systemic risk?
9. **Short Answer:** Though we do not model systemic risk in the IVM, provide a short discussion of how systemic risk can impact the valuation of a bank through the lens of the IVM.
10. **Comprehensive Question:** As Sam and Nina continue to manage their institution, they consider how their bank could contribute to or be exposed to systemic risk. Provide them with a brief discussion on how some of the decisions they make in their day-to-day management of the bank can impact financial system stability.

References

Acharya, V. V. (2009). A theory of systemic risk and design of prudential bank regulation, *Journal of Financial Stability*, 5(3), 224–255.

Acharya, V. V., Drechsler, I. and Schnabl, P. (2014). A pyrrhic victory? Bank bailouts and sovereign credit risk, *The Journal of Finance*, 69(6), 2689–2739.

Acharya, V. V. and Yorulmazer, T. (2007). Too many to fail—An analysis of time-inconsistency in bank closure policies, *Journal of Financial Intermediation*, 16(1), 1–31.

Acharya, V. V., Shin, H. S. and Yorulmazer, T. (2011). Crisis resolution and bank liquidity, *Review of Financial Studies*, 24(6), 2166–2205.

Adrian, T. and Brunnermeier, M. K. (2016). CoVaR, *American Economic Review*, 106(7), 1705–1741.

Benoit, S., Colliard, J.-E., Hurlin, C. and Pérignon, C. (2017). Where the risks lie: A survey on systemic risk, *Review of Finance*, 21(1), 109–152.

Berger, A. N., Cai, J., Roman, R. A. and Sedunov, J. (2022). Supervisory enforcement actions against banks and systemic risk, *Journal of Banking & Finance*, 140, 106222.

Berger, A. N., Curti, F., Mihov, A. and Sedunov, J. (2022). Operational risk is more systemic than you think: Evidence from U.S. bank holding companies, *Journal of Banking and Finance*, 143, Article 106619.

Berger, A. N. and Roman, R. A. (2020). *TARP and Other Bank Bailouts and Bail-Ins Around the World: Connecting Wall Street, Main Street, and the Financial System* (1st ed.). Elsevier.

Berger, A,N. and Sedunov, J. (2024). The Life Cycle of Systemic Risk and Crises *Journal of Money, Credit, and Banking*, 56(8).

Berger, A.N., Peydró, J., Sedunov, J. and Taboada, A.G. (2024). Systemic risks, crises, and connections of the real economy, banking sector, and financial markets. In A.N. Berger, P. Molyneux, and J.O.S. Wilson (eds.), *Oxford Handbook of Banking Fourth Edition*. Oxford University Press.

Bisias, D., Flood, M., Lo, A. W. and Valavanis, S. (2012). A survey of systemic risk analytics. *Annual Review of Financial Economics*, 4(1), 255–296.

Boot, A. W. A. and Thakor, A. V. (1993). Self-interested bank regulation, *American Economic Review*, 83(2), 206–212.

Boot, A. W. A. and Thakor, A. V. (2014). *Commercial Banking and Shadow Banking* A. N. Berger, P. Molyneux, & J. O. S. Wilson (eds.). Oxford University Press.

Brown, C. O. and Dinç, I. S. (2011). Too many to fail? Evidence of regulatory forbearance when the banking sector is weak, *Review of Financial Studies*, 24(4), 1378–1405.

Brownlees, C. and Engle, R. F. (2017). SRISK: A conditional capital shortfall measure of systemic risk, *Review of Financial Studies*, 30(1), 48–79.

Cetorelli, N. and Traina, J. (2021). Resolving "Too Big to Fail," *Journal of Financial Services Research*, 60(1), 1–23. https://doi.org/10.1007/s10693-021-00352-1.

Culp, C. L., van der Merwe, A. and Stärkle, B. J. (2018). Interconnectedness and Systemic Risk. In C. L. Culp, A. van der Merwe, and B. J. Stärkle (eds.), *Credit Default Swaps* (pp. 249–270).

De Bandt, O. and Hartmann, P. (2019). Systemic risk in banking after the great financial crisis. In A. N. Berger, P. Molyneux, & J. O. S. Wilson (eds.), *The Oxford Handbook of Banking* (pp. 846–884). Oxford University Press.

De Bandt, O., Hartmann, P. and Peydró, J. L. (2012). *Systemic Risk in Banking*. Oxford University Press.

Freixas, X., Laeven, L. and Peydró, J.L. (2015). *Systemic Risk, Crises and Macroprudential Policy*. MIT Press, Cambridge, MA.

Jarrow, R. A. (2008). Operational risk, *Journal of Banking & Finance*, 32(5), 870–879.

Kane, E. J. (1990). Principal-agent problems in S&L salvage, *The Journal of Finance*, 45(3), 755–764.

Kashyap, A. K. and Siegert, C. (2020). Financial stability considerations and monetary policy, *International Journal of Central Banking*, 16(1), 231–266.

Lee, J.-P., Lin, E. M. H., Lin, J. J. and Zhao, Y. (2020). Bank systemic risk and CEO overconfidence, *The North American Journal of Economics and Finance*, 54, 100946.

Mishkin, F. (2006). How big a problem is too big to fail? *Journal of Economic Literature*, XLIV, 988–1004.

Pagano, M. S. and Sedunov, J. (2016). A comprehensive approach to measuring the relation between systemic risk exposure and sovereign debt, *Journal of Financial Stability*, 23, 62–78.

Pozsar, Z., Adrian, T., Ashcraft, A. and Boesky, H. (2013). *Shadow Banking Economic Policy Review*, 19(2).

Silva, W., Kimura, H. and Sobreiro, V. A. (2017). An analysis of the literature on systemic financial risk: A survey, *Journal of Financial Stability*, 28, 91–114.

Stern, G. H. Feldman, R. J. (2004). *Too Big to Fail: The Hazards of Bank Bailouts*. Brookings Institution Press.

Thakor, A. V. (2012). Incentives to innovate and financial crises, *Journal of Financial Economics*, 103(1), 130–148.

Walther, A. (2016). Jointly Optimal Regulation of Bank Capital and Liquidity, *Journal of Money, Credit and Banking*, 48(2–3), 415–448.

Chapter 12

Integrated Risk Management: Putting It All Together

12.1 Introduction

Bank risk management continues to evolve over time. As we have discussed in prior chapters, the ever-changing nature of competition between commercial banks and other financial institutions has encouraged new ways to manage risk that maximize firm value. This final chapter describes a potentially powerful way to control these risks in a comprehensive manner, which we call "Integrated Risk Management" (or "IRM"). Chapters 3–10 introduced several risks that banks face and ways to manage items like market risk and liquidity risk on an *individual, stand-alone basis*.

In this chapter, we show how a bank can increase firm value even further by solving for the optimal amounts of exposure over *multiple* risks *simultaneously*.[1] As we illustrate in the following, we briefly review the concepts from Chapters 5 and 8 that show, via the use of an Excel™ spreadsheet first mentioned in the *Preface* of this book, how to maximize

---

[1] Most textbooks such as Hempel and Simonson (1999) and Saunders *et al.* (2024) primarily focus on the stand-alone risks that banks face. We examine these bank risks in this manner in Chapters 3–10 but also include here in Chapter 12 an integrated approach to solve several risks simultaneously. This method presents the reader with an alternative way to view a bank's risk management problem. See Pagano (2001, 2004) and Schrand and Unal (1998) for examples of integrated risk management and their applications to commercial banks and non-financial firms, respectively.

the value of a bank's equity by managing **market-related** and **liquidity risks** on a stand-alone basis. We then present an *Integrated Risk Management* version of the IVM technique we first introduced in Chapter 3. This IRM version of our valuation model enables us to solve simultaneously for the optimal levels of risk across all the risks described in Chapters 3 through 10 and listed in the following[2]:

1. Credit Allocation via C* (Chapter 3)
2. Interest Rate Risk via RGAP* and MDGAP* (Chapter 4)
3. Market Risk via VaR* (Chapter 5)
4. Credit Risk via CVaR* (Chapter 6)
5. Off-Balance Sheet Risk via Contingent Assets minus Contingent Liabilities (Chapter 7)
6. Liquidity Risk via LCR* (Chapter 8)
7. Operational Risk via OFC* (Chapter 9)
8. Capital Adequacy/Insolvency Risk via (E/A)* (Chapter 10).

To help explain the IRM approach, we use our Excel™ spreadsheet to demonstrate how *all eight* optimal levels of risk can be managed simultaneously. In this way, we can take full advantage of the spreadsheet tool to apply this book's concepts to a hypothetical firm like ABC and, if we wish, to real-world banks. To begin, review the first tab of the spreadsheet labeled "Introduction." This tab summarizes a *four-step process* for the key risks described in our book and provides links to jump between each of these risks, including a final link labeled "Integrated Risks – Ch 12" that allows for all risks to be managed simultaneously. The four steps are organized into multiple tabs within the spreadsheet:

1. **Introduction** (first tab of the spreadsheet that provides links to all risk-related tabs of the file),

---

[2] The asterisks following the risks noted in the following represent the optimal levels of risk that can maximize the bank's market value. In prior chapters, these optimal levels were found by focusing on each risk individually. In this chapter, the optimal levels are chosen by allowing all risks (and hedge ratios) to vary simultaneously. Note that this integrated approach applies to all the risks listed here except for Off-Balance Sheet (OBS) risk, which does not lend itself to be easily integrated into a simultaneous risk management framework due to the optionality and inter-dependencies of these OBS items. So, OBS risk is still solved for on an individual basis in this chapter.

Integrated Risk Management: Putting It All Together 441

2. **IVM Inputs** (second tab that includes the key financial statement data mentioned in the following),
3. **Individual Risks tabs** that focus on all the risks described in Chapters 3 to 10, and
4. "Integrated Risks – Chapter 12" tab that solves simultaneously for the optimal levels of risk that maximize the bank's market value of equity (V_E).

The Introduction page is displayed in Figure 12.1 and can be used to easily move from one section of the spreadsheet to another using the relevant links. It is the file's "home base" which enables you to easily return to this tab via links labeled "Introduction" in the upper right corner of all the subsequent tabs in the spreadsheet.

After reviewing the Introduction tab, we must enter some basic financial information about the bank which can be primarily obtained from the firm's balance sheet and income statements. As you can see in Figure 12.2, this basic information, as well as some additional estimates that you must make, are already provided for the hypothetical bank, ABC, in the "IVM Inputs" tab. Keep in mind that throughout the entire spreadsheet, any cell highlighted in **blue** is a changeable value. As mentioned earlier, note that in the **upper right-hand corner** of this tab (and all subsequent tabs in the spreadsheet), there is a link labeled "Introduction" which allows you to quickly return to the introductory page.

If you wish to use this spreadsheet with a real-world bank's data, we recommend that you make a copy of the spreadsheet file and give it another

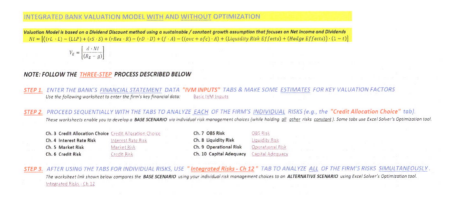

Figure 12.1. The Integrated Valuation Model's (IVM) Introductory Page.

INPUTS FOR INTEGRATED BANK VALUATION MODEL *Use the following link to Return to Introduction tab:* Introduction

Valuation Model is based on a Dividend Discount method using a sustainable / constant growth assumption that focuses on Net Income and Dividends

$$NI = [((rL \cdot L) - (LLP) + (rS \cdot S) + (rRes \cdot R) - (rD \cdot D) + (f \cdot A) - ((ovc + ofc) \cdot A) + (Liquidity\ Risk\ Effects) + (Hedge\ Effects)) \cdot (1 - t)]$$

$$V_E = \left[\frac{d \cdot NI}{(R_E - g)}\right]$$

NOTE: FOLLOW THE THREE-STEP PROCESS DESCRIBED BELOW

STEP 1. ENTER THE BANK'S FINANCIAL STATEMENT DATA BELOW & ALSO MAKE SOME ESTIMATES FOR KEY VALUATION FACTORS

FINANCIAL STATEMENT DATA, PRO FORMA FINANCIALS, & ADDITIONAL UNDERLYING ASSUMPTIONS THAT DRIVE THE FIRM'S MICRO FACTORS:
NOTE: To estimate the effect of all Risk Management choices in the additional tabs, please enter values in Blue cells below and elsewhere in this file.
Also, please be sure to keep units consistent (e.g., if using millions of dollars, then shares outstanding should be in millions of shares.

Enter Company Name and USD units of financials to the right: ABC ("A Banking Company") in $ Millions

	Definition / Sources		Historical
ABC ("A Banking Company") BALANCE SHEET Inputs:	Fiscal Year-end (FYE)		2022
Total Assets (TA)	Total Assets: Includes all asset items		1580.0
Cash, Cash Equivalents & Federal Funds Sold (R)	Includes: Cash+Reserves+Deposits with Banks+Fed Funds Sold		25.0
Securities & Investments (S)	Includes: Investments+Trading Account Assets+Brokerage Rec.		700.0
Gross Loans (GL)	From Balance Sheet		830
Allowance for Loan Losses (ALL)	From Balance Sheet		30
Net Loans (NL)	From Balance Sheet		800.00
Goodwill & Intangible Assets (GW)	From Balance Sheet		10.0
Other Non-Earning Assets & Intangibles (OA)	Includes: Net Fixed Assets & Other Assets		45.0
Total Assets (TA)			1580.0
Deposits (DEPO)	From Balance Sheet		1400.0
Other Borrowed Money (OBM)	All other Liabilites (Items from Balance Sheet not in Deposits)		0.0
Total Liabilities (D)	Includes all liabilities (Deposits, short-term and L-T OBM, Pref. Stc		1400.0
Common Stock Equity (BVE)	From Balance Sheet (book value of common equity)		180.0
Tot. Liabilities & Equity			1580.0
Market Value of Equity (MVE)	MVE: Stock price x shares outstanding	$	152.00
Stock Price per Share	Actual from a market data source at FYE	$	15.20

Figure 12.2. The IVM's Financial Data Input Page.

name so that you can then enter your bank's financial information in the "IVM Inputs" tab of this new file. Once you have reviewed the first two tabs of the spreadsheet, you can then explore all the remaining 12 tabs if you wish. To demonstrate the spreadsheet's capabilities while also conserving space in this chapter, we describe here only two of the stand-alone risk tabs related to **Market Risk** (Chapter 5) and **Liquidity Risk** (Chapter 8).

These two risks are chosen because the market risk tab of the spreadsheet demonstrates how we can solve for the optimal Value-at-Risk (or **VaR***) using a mathematically derived "analytical" approach. In addition, this example of market risk shows how our optimal choice *directly* affects the bank's market value of equity. That is, our choice of VaR* immediately affects the bank's stock price.

In contrast, the liquidity risk tab uses an iterative, constrained "optimization" method to find the optimal "Liquidity Coverage Ratio," denoted as **LCR***. This latter optimization method is useful when it is not easy to solve for the optimal risk levels directly via calculus-based analytical techniques. In addition, rather than directly affecting ABC's market value of equity, the optimal choice of LCR affects the bank's equity in an *indirect* way via changes in the firm's Net Income (NI), cost of equity (R_E), and growth rate (g). As we see later in this chapter, the constrained optimization method is especially useful for computing the optimal solution when we are handling multiple risks simultaneously.

12.2 Market Risk Example of Stand-alone Risk Management (from Chapter 5)

Presented in the following is a brief recap of the costs and benefits of using the RiskMetrics/Variance–Covariance method to estimate the market-related risk of a bank's securities holdings in bonds, currencies, stocks, etc. Refer to Chapter 5 for a more extensive discussion of this method, if necessary. As you recall, we approach this problem by identifying the total benefits and total costs of hedging the bank's market risk using the volatility of the returns on the bank's investment portfolio. In this way, we can see the change in the bank's market value of equity due to the hedging decision by comparing the value of the bank with hedging ($V_{E,\text{Hedged}}$) versus its value without hedging ($V_{E,\text{Unhedged}}$) as follows:

$$\Delta V_E = V_{E,\text{Hedged}} - V_{E,\text{Unhedged}} = \text{Total Benefit of Hedge} - \text{Total Cost of Hedge}$$

$$\Delta V_E = \$\text{Reduction in Portfolio VaR} - (\text{fixed headging cost} + \text{variable hedging cost})$$

$$\Delta V_E = [2.33 \cdot (\sigma_{UH} - \text{Hedged } \sigma_P) \cdot \text{Invested Assets}] - [C + ((v \cdot h) \cdot (h \cdot \text{Invested Assets}))]$$

$$= [2.33 \cdot (h \cdot \sigma_{UH}) \cdot \text{Invested Assets}] - [(c + (v \cdot h^2)) \cdot \text{Invested Assets}] \quad (12.1)$$

where

ΔV_E = change in market value due to hedging some portion of the Invested Assets = $V_{E,\text{Hedged}} - V_{E,\text{Unedged}}$,

h = hedge ratio = Dollar Amount Hedged / Investment Portfolio Value = \$Hedged / Invested Assets,

C = fixed cost of hedging (paid upfront, in dollars; and can also be expressed as a percentage of the bank's Invested Assets, where $C = c \cdot$ Invested Assets),

v = variable cost of hedging as a percentage of \$Hedged, where \$Hedged = $h \cdot$ Invested Assets,

σ_{UH} = unhedged portfolio's standard deviation,

Hedged $\sigma_p = (1 - h) \cdot \sigma_{UH}$ = hedged portfolio's standard deviation (can also be referred to as σ_H),

$Reduction in Portfolio VaR = $ value of extreme volatility that is reduced by hedging = $2.33 \cdot (\sigma_{UH} - \textbf{Hedged } \sigma_P) \cdot$ Invested Assets = $2.33 \cdot (\boldsymbol{h} \cdot \sigma_{UH}) \cdot$ Invested Assets, and

Critical value = 2.33 (1% tail based on the normal distribution assumption).

The first term in square brackets of Equation (12.1) identifies the incremental benefits of hedging all or a portion (h) of the bank's market risk while the second term in square brackets shows the costs of this hedge when a worst-case 1% tail event ($2.33 \cdot \sigma_P$) occurs. We define these hedging benefits as the dollar amount of losses *avoided* due to hedging a portion of the potential price shock to the portfolio from market risk. Using the notation from above, we show that this "Total Benefit of Hedge" equals $2.33 \cdot (\boldsymbol{h} \cdot \sigma_{UH}) \cdot$ Invested Assets. So, as the hedge ratio (h) rises, this benefit also increases. However, the second term in (12.1) illustrates the exponentially rising "Total Cost of Hedge" due to its variable cost component: $(v \cdot h^2) \cdot$ Invested Assets. Thus, there is a classic trade-off between the costs and benefits of hedging.

Based on the above discussion of Equation (12.1), we can see how this market risk management decision can impact the bank's equity value using the principles of the IVM by varying the **hedge ratio**, h, between values ranging from 0 (no hedging) to 1.0 (hedging the entire risk exposure). Presented in Figure 12.3 is a view of the IVM spreadsheet tab labeled "Market Risk – Ch 5" which shows in blue shading the key cells that need to be estimated to compute the portfolio's risk and how much of

Using the Variance-Covariance Method of Value at Risk (VaR) to manage Impact of Market Portfolio Risk on a Bank's Equity Value (V_E)

IVM Valuation effects for Market VaR hedging							
Initial NI ($)		18.000	*from Credit Allocation tab*	*uses: Change In MVE = Change In VaR - Hedging Cost*			
Initial Dividend / sh.	$	0.72		Unhedged VaR		**4.078**	
Initial Stock Price / sh.	$	**20.17**		Unhedged VaR (%)		0.0058	
				Indicator (I)=		-1	
Sec. & Trading Portfolio ($)		700		Hedged VaR		1.702	
Expected Annual Average Return		2.50%		Initial h estimate		-0.5825	
Expected Daily Average Return		0.01%		Fixed Cost > Benefit?		No	
Unhedged Portfolio std. dev. in % (s.d.)		0.25%					
Extreme Shock (s.d.)		2.33					
Hedged Portfolio std.dev. in %		0.104%		**Optimal h***		**-0.5825**	*Note: h* is zero if Fixed Costs > Max. Ben.*
Hedge Fixed Cost as % of Port. (c)		0.000%		**Target VaR***		**1.702**	
Hedge Var. Cost as % of Port. (v)		0.500%		**Stock Price***	$	**20.28**	
Dividend Payout		0.40	in decimals	**% Chg. In Price**		**0.6%**	
Tax Rate		0.20	in decimals	Fixed Cost ($ mil.)		0.0	
Div. Yield (Re - g)		0.0357	*from Credit Allocation tab*	Price Effect/sh		0.00	
Shares Outstanding		10.0000					

Figure 12.3. Key Values for IVM's Market Risk Tab.

this portfolio should be hedged via *h* to maximize the bank's market value of equity.[3]

Figure 12.3 shows that ABC has $700 million in its investment portfolio and its expected *daily* return and standard deviation are 1 basis point and 25 bps, respectively. These values are based on the blue shaded cells corresponding to the rows labeled "Expected Annual Average Return" (2.50%) and "Unhedged Portfolio std. dev. in %." Also, we can see in the upper left portion of the figure that ABC's current stock price is $20.17 *prior* to its choice of how to hedge the portfolio's market risk. In this example, ABC is vulnerable to *increases* in volatility that might emanate from various markets in which it invests (i.e., bonds, stocks, currencies, and commodities). ABC's bank managers must decide whether this market risk exposure on its $700 million investment portfolio has a material effect and then choose the "optimal hedge ratio" that maximizes the bank's stock price.

To explore the impact of different hedge ratios, we must also enter in the blue shaded cells of the "Market Risk – Ch 5" tab our estimates of what constitutes an "Extreme Shock," as measured in standard deviations, as well as our estimates of ABC's fixed and variable costs related to hedging. Typically, we use 2.33 standard deviations to measure an extreme shock because it represents the 1% chance of a large drop in the bank's portfolio value when returns are normally distributed. In this example, we assume ABC's fixed costs for hedging are zero while its variable hedging expenses are 0.50% of the bank's $700 million portfolio. To estimate these numbers, a bank's internal risk management analysts need to work with the bank's management and accounting teams to obtain the fixed and variable costs of running an effective market risk management operation. Although this can be a time-consuming effort, it is worthwhile for senior management to invest resources in this effort so that ABC knows when the costs of hedging might outweigh the benefits (and vice versa).

The rest of the values in Figure 12.3 that are shown in white cells represent estimates or historical financial data obtained from the spreadsheet's earlier tabs labeled "IVM Inputs" and "Credit Allocation Choice –

---

[3] Note that starting on row 80 of this tab of the spreadsheet, we also present some examples of how to use Market Risk VaR concepts for a 3-asset portfolio using the Variance–Covariance and Historic Simulation methods. However, these examples are separate and independent of the VaR application described in Figure 12.3 and rows 1–79 of this tab.

Ch 3." This latter tab is used as the starting point for valuing ABC's stock price ($20.17) and is considered our "Base" case. This value serves as a benchmark to compare with the stock price obtained for each of our subsequent risk management's hedging choices (selected on a stand-alone basis).

Using an analytical approach based on Equation (12.1) above, the Market Risk tab shows in yellow shading and boldface on the right-hand side of Figure 12.3 that the optimal hedge ratio for ABC's portfolio is –0.5825, which indicates that the firm should hedge 58.25% of its portfolio by *shorting* this percentage via one or more financial derivatives such as forwards, futures, options, and/or swaps. By doing so, the bank will reduce its unhedged VaR from $4.078 million to a less-risky VaR of $1.702 million (shown in yellow shading immediately below the optimal hedge ratio). Right below the hedged VaR value is the estimated stock price if ABC implements the optimal hedge ratio ($20.28) and its percentage change (+0.6%) from the base stock price of $20.17. This numerical exercise suggests that, given the bank's hedging costs and the portfolio's underlying volatility, hedging ABC's investment portfolio does not materially increase ABC's stock price. Thus, ABC's managers must decide whether a 0.6% increase in stock value is worth the effort of implementing a market risk management program.

12.3 Liquidity Example of Stand-alone Risk Management (from Chapter 8)

This section illustrates an example from Chapter 8 of how we can use the "Solver" **optimization tool** within Excel™ to model trade-offs between the costs and benefits of managing ABC's liquidity risk. First, we can approach this problem by spelling out the total benefits and total costs of managing the bank's liquidity risk. In this way, we can see the change in the bank's market value of equity by comparing the value of the bank using stored "excess" liquidity with the value associated with purchased liquidity by using the bank's net income (NI) formula and shown as follows:

$$NI = (rL \cdot L) + (rS \cdot S) - (rD \cdot D) - (rP \cdot E[\max(0, W - S^*)]) \quad (12.2)$$

Based on the above drivers of a bank's net profit, we see how liquidity risk management decisions can impact the bank's market value using the principles of the IVM. In fact, we can estimate the valuation effect of the bank's risk management choice by using the following extension of the IVM from Chapter 3 that explicitly quantifies the change in market value (denoted by the "delta" sign, Δ):

$$\Delta V_E = \left[\frac{\Delta(d \cdot NI)}{(R_E - g)}\right] = \left[\frac{d \cdot [(\text{Liquidity Risk Benefit} - \text{Liquidity Risk Cost}) \cdot (1-t)]}{(R_E - g)}\right]$$

$$= \left[\frac{d \cdot [(\text{Liquidity Risk Benefit} - \text{Liquidity Risk Cost}) \cdot (1-t)]}{\text{Expected Dividend Yield}}\right]$$

(12.3)

where

d = expected dividend payout ratio for next year (DIV$_1$ / NI$_1$),

Liquidity risk benefit = the total cost of *purchased* liquidity that can be *avoided* by holding excess cash on hand = $rP \cdot (1 - \text{Prob}(W > S^*)) \cdot \max[0, W - S^*]$,

rP = a "penalty" interest rate that the bank must pay if the bank has a sudden cash shortfall and must find new funds very quickly,

Probability of avoiding a cash shortfall = $(1 - \text{Prob}(W > S^*))$, and where Prob($W > S^*$) is the probability of a cash shortfall whenever the demand for liquidity (W) is greater than the supply of liquid assets available to meet this demand (S^*),[4]

Simulated excess liquid assets = S^* = Excess Liquid Assets as a % of Total Securities $\cdot$ LCR $\cdot$ E[Net Cash Outflow], so that S^* can vary with the bank's choice of LCR,[5]

---

[4] This component and the simulated excess liquid assets (S^*) defined right below this term are key drivers of the potential Liquidity Risk Benefit described in Equation (12.3).

[5] Recall from Chapter 8 that LCR can be defined as High Quality Liquid Assets / E(Net Cash Outflows). Re-arranging this equation algebraically shows that HQLA = LCR $\cdot$ E(Net Cash Outflows) and this can be used as a proxy for S (if we assume all securities, S, are considered High Quality Liquid Assets). Thus, S^* can be estimated by multiplying S by the percentage of securities that are not needed for daily operations (i.e., S^* = Excess Liquid Assets as % of Total Securities x Total Securities). We can then use this relationship, along with S = LCR $\cdot$ E(Net Cash Outflows), to allow S^* to vary as the bank changes its LCR via S^* = Excess Liquid Assets as % of Total Securities $\cdot$ LCR $\cdot$ E(Net Cash Outflows).

Liquidity Risk Cost = the opportunity cost of *stored* liquidity *incurred* by holding excess cash on the balance sheet = $(rL - rS) \cdot S^*$, and where S^* is defined as shown above and in the following footnote (i.e., S^* = Excess Liquid Assets as % of Total Securities $\cdot$ LCR $\cdot$ E[Net Cash Outflow]) so that it can vary with the bank's choice of LCR,

rL = return on the bank's total dollar amount of loans (L),

rS = return on the bank's total dollar investment in securities (S),

rD = interest paid on the bank's dollar amount of liabilities like deposits and other borrowed money (D),

t = marginal corporate tax rate,

R_E = expected return on the bank's equity,

g = constant growth rate of the bank's dividends, and

Expected Dividend Yield = $(DIV_1 / V_{E,0})$ and, as shown earlier in Chapter 3, equals $(R_E - g)$ from the Constant Growth version of the IVM.

We can now use the above variant of the IVM described in Equation (12.3) with a numerical example for our hypothetical bank, ABC, by using our Excel™ spreadsheet, as shown in Figure 12.4.

As Figure 12.4 shows via the blue shaded cells in the second column, we need to estimate five key variables that will affect the optimal Liquidity Coverage Ratio (LCR*):

1. the percentage of assets held in cash and securities that is above and beyond the level of liquid assets needed for normal bank operations ("Excess Cash & Sec.");
2. the penalty interest rate that the bank must pay if they need to borrow quickly for emergency funding purposes;
3. the expected cash outflows if there is a sudden, abnormally high level of liquidity demands on the bank (e.g., from rapid withdrawals and/or unexpectedly high loan demand);
4. the bank's average LCR; and
5. the standard deviation of annual changes in the bank's LCR.

By combining the information from Figure 12.4 with the net profit equation of (12.2), we can find the optimal Liquidity Coverage Ratio (LCR*) and its impact on ABC's stock price by using iterative, constrained optimization

INTEGRATED VALUATION MODEL (IVM): MANAGING LIQUIDITY RISK

$$NI = [((rL \cdot L) - (LLP) + (rS \cdot S) + (rRes \cdot R) - (rD \cdot D) + (f \cdot A) - ((ovc + ofc) \cdot A) + (Liquidity\ Risk\ Effects)$$

$$V_E = \left[\frac{d \cdot NI}{(R_E - g)}\right]$$

NOTE: To estimate the effect of this Risk Management choice, enter values in Blue cells below and see the imp

Based on Financial Institution's Data along with Random LCR & "Excess" Securities

Integrated Valuation effects for LIQUIDITY RISK via LCR adjustments

Total Assets	$	1,580.0	Note: User can enter choices in the Blue cells
Cash & Sec.	$	725.0	
Net Loans	$	800.0	
Total Deposits	$	1,400.0	
Projected NI	$	18.0	
Initial Stock Price / sh.	$	20.17	from Credit Allocation tab
Excess Cash & Sec. (%)		50%	
Excess Cash & Sec.	$	362.5	
Loan rate (rL)		5.24%	
Securities Ret. (rS)		2.50%	
Deposit rate (rD)		2.11%	
Penalty rate (rP)		6.00%	this could be based on the Fed's discount rate
E(Outflows)	$	700.0	
Initial LCR		1.036	
LCR Average		1.10	
LCR Std. Dev.		0.05	Prob. (Avoid Outflow)	0.95943
			Optimal LCR*	1.187
Dividend Payout		0.40	in decimal	Stock Price*	$ 24.63
Tax Rate		0.20	in decimal	% Chg. In Price	22.2%
Div. Yield (Re - g)		0.0357	from Credit Allocation tab	
Shares Outstanding		10.00		

Figure 12.4. Key Values for IVM's Liquidity Risk Tab.

techniques. For liquidity risk and some of the other stand-alone risks contained in our spreadsheet file, we cannot find a "closed form" analytical solution to this optimization problem and thus we need to use the Excel™ *Solver* function. Figure 12.5 shows the dialog box that appears within the "Liquidity Risk – Chapter 8" tab when we use the following steps within the spreadsheet to access and run the Solver command[6]:

---

[6]Note that the commands described here, and related screenshots of the spreadsheet and dialog boxes, are based on Microsoft® Excel™ for Microsoft 365 MSO (Version 2311 Build 16.0.17029.20028; 64-bit version). If you are using a different version of this software, the specific commands as well as the "look and feel" of the spreadsheet might be different. The main point is that, regardless of the version you are using, one can search

450 *Managing Financial Institutions: An Integrated Valuation Approach*

Figure 12.5. Dialog Box for Using the Solver Optimization Function to Find LCR*.

1. Choose **Data** from the spreadsheet's main menu;
2. Click on the **Solver icon** (typically found on the far right side of the "ribbon" bar of the spreadsheet);
3. Select the "GRG Nonlinear" choice from the drop-down menu related to the "Select a Solving Method" feature within the Solver dialog box; and
4. Press the "Solve" button and wait for the spreadsheet to use constrained optimization techniques to find an optimal LCR (which will then be displayed in cell F32 of the spreadsheet tab).

---

for the *Solver* function and then select the "GRG Nonlinear" method for performing stand-alone risk optimization. As we show later, we use the "Evolutionary" method when performing optimization across multiple risks (i.e., via integrated risk management rather than stand-alone risk management). As Excel's capabilities continue to evolve, we can also modify this spreadsheet in the future to take advantage of any new and relevant features.

Note that the top of the dialog box indicates the "objective function" of the optimization problem is to maximize the cell called "Stock_Price" (cell F33) by changing "Optimal_LCR" (cell F32) while being subject to "Constraints" that limit the range of possible LCR values to between 0.01 and 3.00. You can use the "Change" button in this dialog box to modify these constraints if you wish. If not, then simply pressing the "Solve" button will generate the optimal LCR solution. Depending on the complexity of the problem, it might take anywhere from a few seconds to over 1 minute to find the optimal value. This optimization process varies the bank's LCR in an iterative manner to find the ratio that maximizes ABC's stock price by comparing the opportunity costs of stored liquidity to the benefits of avoiding the penalty rate for any funds that need to be purchased on an emergency basis. In this numerical example, the *net* benefit of holding stored liquidity is maximized when the LCR is around 1.187 and results in a stock price of $24.63 (which is a +22.2% increase from the baseline stock price of $20.17). In contrast to our market risk management example, managing ABC's LCR appears to have a much larger impact on the firm's market value. So, the analysis of market risk and liquidity risk suggests that ABC's managers might want to focus more on optimizing its bank's LCR rather than the VaR of its investment portfolio. Indeed, just knowing where to focus senior management's attention is a valuable outcome of this type of analysis.

12.4 Example of Integrated Risk Management across All Bank Risks

Now that we have considered two examples of how to manage bank risk on a stand-alone basis, we can see how to perform "Integrated Risk Management" (or "IRM") by finding the optimal level for all the risks noted at the beginning of this chapter. This cannot be done via an analytical/mathematical method and so we rely on the *Solver* optimization function once again to now compute several optimal hedge ratios simultaneously based on the main risks covered in this book. To do so, we can build upon Equations (12.2) and (12.3) to include additional variables that form a more generalized and comprehensive set of factors that affect a bank's profitability:

$$NI = ((rL \cdot L) - (LLP) + (rS \cdot S) + (rRes \cdot R) - (rD \cdot D) + (f \cdot A) \\ - ((ovc + ofc) \cdot A) + \text{(Liquidity Risk Effects)} \\ + \text{(Hedge Effects)}) \cdot (1 - t) \qquad (12.4)$$

where

LLP = loan loss provision for the current period,

rRes = return on total dollar amount invested in bank reserves (R),

f = fee income received by the bank and expressed as a percentage of total assets (A),

ovc and ofc = operating costs that are variable (ovc) and fixed (ofc), shown as a percentage of assets (A),

Liquidity Risk Effects = includes all the factors noted earlier in this chapter related to the costs and benefits of adjusting the bank's Liquidity Coverage Ratio (LCR),

Hedge Effects = includes all costs and benefits of hedging the other risk factors described in this book (e.g., credit allocation, interest rates, market, credit, OBS, operational, and capital adequacy), and

t = the bank's corporate tax rate.

Using the above drivers of a bank's net profit, we can see how all risk management decisions can influence the bank's market value using the principles of the IVM. Like we have done earlier in this chapter, we can estimate the valuation effect of the bank's risk management choices by using the following extension of the IVM from Chapter 3 that explicitly quantifies the change in market value (denoted by the Greek letter, delta, Δ):

$$\Delta V_E = \left[\frac{\Delta(d \cdot NI)}{\Delta(R_E - g)}\right] = \Delta\left[\frac{d \cdot \left[\begin{array}{c}(rL \cdot L) - (LLP) + (rS \cdot S) + (rRes \cdot R) - (rD \cdot D) + (f \cdot A) \\ -((ovc + ofc) \cdot A) + (Liquidity\ Risk\ Effects) + (Hedge\ Effects)\end{array}\right] \cdot (1-t)}{(R_E - g)}\right]$$

$$= \Delta\left[\frac{d \cdot [(Bank\ Operating\ Profit + Liquidity\ Risk\ Effects + Hedge\ Effects) \cdot (1-t)]}{Expected\ Dividend\ Yield}\right]$$

(12.5)

where

Bank Operating Profit = a summary variable for all pretax operating profit items *not* directly included in the bank's risk management decisions = (($rL \cdot L$) − (LLP) + ($rS \cdot S$) + ($rRes \cdot R$) − ($rD \cdot D$) + ($f \cdot A$) − ((ovc + ofc) · A)),

Liquidity Risk Effects = {Liquidity Risk Benefit} − {Liquidity Risk Cost}
$$= \{rP \cdot (1 - Prob(W > S^*)) \cdot \max[0, W - S^*]\}$$
$$- \{(rL - rS) \cdot S^*\},$$

Hedge Effects = Overall Sum of the Net Benefits (Total Benefits minus Total Costs) for *all* Hedging choices described in this book, and

$$\text{Expected Dividend Yield} = (R_E - g).$$

Equation (12.5) distills the three key drivers of a bank's profitability: (1) "traditional" pretax operating profit, (2) the effects of liquidity risk management, and (3) the net impact of all other hedging decisions. However, Equation (12.5) is still a rather daunting formula for managers to deal with. Thankfully, computerized optimization tools such as Excel's *Solver* function enable us to find a solution across a bank's numerous hedging choices that maximize the firm's market value of equity.

Our spreadsheet contains a tab labeled "Integrated Risks – Chapter 12" that can help solve this multi-faceted risk management problem. As Figure 12.6 shows, the top portion of the tab shows a summary of ABC's estimated stock price using a "Base Scenario" where the bank makes all its risk management choices on a *stand-alone* basis as well as an "Alternative Scenario" which allows for a *simultaneous* solution to the risk management problem. The figure also provides some other information like key financial ratios as well as ABC's expected market capitalization and stock return relative to the bank's prior values (the latter are

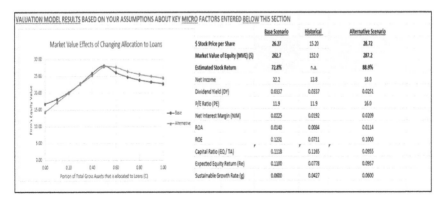

Figure 12.6. Summary Results of Stand-Alone and Integrated Risk Management Choices for ABC.

displayed under the column labeled "Historical"). Both scenarios report substantial increases in stock price by actively managing the firm's risks although using the simultaneous, integrated approach increases firm value the most ($28.72 vs. $26.27).

In this numerical example, explicitly considering the inter-relationships between the various risks can lead to a 9.3% improvement in ABC's stock price ($28.72) over stand-alone risk management ($26.27). However, the Alternative Scenario outperforms the Base Scenario only when ABC's credit allocation, C, is above 50% of total assets (i.e., above 0.5 on the graph in Figure 12.6). This result shows the importance of choosing the amount invested in loans in an optimal way. As we show later in this section, ABC's optimal level of loans should be around 53% when managing all risks simultaneously. So, Figure 12.6 tells us that the integrated risk management approach *outperforms* the stand-alone method when ABC is at or *above* 52% but *underperforms* when the bank chooses to allocate *less* than this amount to loans (e.g., below the 50% level). For example, if ABC chooses to invest a sub-optimally low level of 40% of its assets in higher-earning loans, then the bank's stock price is $0.61 higher (or +2.4%) when using a *stand-alone* approach ($25.90 vs. $25.29).

The reason for this underperformance when ABC chooses a sub-optimal level of C is due to the integrated method's explicit consideration of each of the bank's risks in relation to each other. An integrated approach necessarily assumes *all* the bank's risks are chosen optimally. Thus, if one risk (in this case, the credit allocation choice) is chosen sub-optimally on a stand-alone basis, it can cause the other hedging decisions to be 'out of sync' with this sub-optimal credit decision. Consequently, it is important to use an integrated risk management approach in a holistic, comprehensive manner to maximize a bank's potential market value.

Figures 12.7, 12.8, and 12.9 provide snapshots of the individual risks we have discussed in a summary format with the Base Scenario (stand-alone) optimal hedging choices displayed in the first column of data and the Alternative Scenario hedge ratios (obtained via integrated risk management) in the third column (while the second column presents Historical data, where available or relevant). The values highlighted in yellow shading represent the optimal hedging decisions and their impact on ABC's stock price. For the Base Scenario, these values will not change unless you go back to the spreadsheet tab for a specific individual risk and make changes there on a stand-alone basis. In contrast, the values highlighted in blue shading under the Alternative Scenario column heading can be

Ch. 3 Credit Allocation Choice				
Credit Allocation Decision	Base Scenario	Historical		Alternative Scenario
Base Lending Rate	0.0330	in decimals		0.0330
Lending Rate	0.0524	0.0507		0.0507
Base Borrowing Rate	0.0161	in decimals		0.0161
Borrowing Rate	0.0211	0.0203		0.0203
Optimal $C^* = L/(A+ALL)$	0.5883	0.5371		0.5361
Target Gross Loans* ($)	$ 947.2	830.0	$	863.2
Change in Net Interest Income ($)	$ 6.35		$	1.68
Change in Dividends per sh. (ΔDPS)	$ 0.20		$	0.05
Change in Stock Price / sh.	$ 4.06		$	1.50

Ch. 4 Interest Rate Risk				
Repricing Gap Hedging Choice	Base	Historical		Alternative Scenario
Rate Sensitive Assets (RSA)	$ 728.3	728.3	$	728.3
Rate Sensitive Liabilities (RSL)	$ 900.0	900.0	$	900.0
Repricing Gap: RGAP = RSA-RSL	$ (171.7)	-171.7	$	(171.7)
Interest Rate Shock	1.000%			1.000%
Hedge Fixed Cost (c)	0.000%	as % of RGAP		0.00%
Hedge Var. Cost (v)	2.000%	as % of RGAP		2.00%
Initial absolute value of hedge ratio h*	0.2500			0.3679
Optimal RGAP hedge ratio h*	-0.2500			-0.3679
Target RGAP* ($)	$ (128.8)		$	(108.5)
RGAP hedging Total Benefit	$ 0.43		$	0.63
RGAP hedging Total Cost	$ 0.21		$	0.46
Change in Net Interest Income	$ 0.21		$	0.17
Change in Dividends / sh. (ΔDPS)	$ 0.01		$	0.01
Change in Stock Price / sh.	$ 0.19		$	0.15

Mod. Duration Gap Hedging Choice	Base	Historical		Alternative Scenario
Mod. Duration of Assets (MDA) in yrs	5.00			5.00
Mod. Duration of Liabilities (MDL) in yrs	2.00			2.00
Leverage Adjusted MDGAP (yrs)	3.23			3.23
Interest Rate Shock	1.000%			1.000%
Hedge Fixed Cost (c)	0.000%	as % of TA		0.00%
Hedge Var. Cost (v)	2.000%	as % of TA		2.00%
Initial absolute value of hedge ratio h*	0.8070			0.7884
Optimal MDGAP hedge ratio h*	-0.8070			-0.7884
Target MDGAP* (yrs)	0.623			0.683
MDGAP hedging Total Benefit	$ 41.16		$	40.21
MDGAP hedging Total Cost	$ 20.58		$	19.64
Change in Market Value of Equity	$ 20.58		$	20.57
Change in Stock Price / sh.	$ 2.06		$	2.06

Figure 12.7. Summary of Bank Risks from Chapters 3–6.

Ch. 5 Market Risk

Value-at-Risk (VaR) Hedging Choice	Base		Alternative Scenario	
Sec. & Trading Portfolio ($)	$	700.0	$	700.0
Expected Annual Average Return		2.50%		2.50%
Expected Daily Average Return		0.010%		0.01%
Unhedged Portfolio std. dev. in % (s.d.)		0.250%		0.25%
Extreme Shock (s.d.)		2.33		2.33
Hedged Portfolio std.dev. in %		0.104%		0.104%
Hedge Fixed Cost as % of Port. (c)		0.000%		0.00%
Hedge Var. Cost as % of Port. (v)		0.500%		0.50%
Initial absolute value of hedge ratio h*		0.5825		0.5838
Optimal VaR hedge ratio h*		-0.5825		-0.5838
Target VaR*	$	1.70	$	1.70
VaR hedging Total Benefit	$	2.38	$	2.38
VaR hedging Total Cost	$	1.19	$	1.19
Change in Market Value of Equity	$	1.19	$	1.19
Change in Stock Price / sh.	$	0.12	$	0.12

Ch. 6 Credit Risk

Credit VaR (CVaR) Hedging Choice	Base		Alternative Scenario	
Securities Portfolio	$	700.0	$	700.0
Gross Loan Portfolio	$	830.0	$	830.0
Total Credit Portfolio	$	1,530.0	$	1,530.0
Unhedged Sec. Port. std. dev. (ann.)		3.50%		3.50%
Unhedged Loan Port. std. dev. (ann.)		3.50%		3.50%
Correlation between Sec. & Loans		100.00%		100.00%
Annual std. dev. of Tot. Credit Port.		3.50%		3.50%
Unhedged Portfolio std. dev. ($)	$	53.6	$	53.6
Extreme Shock (s.d.)		2.33		2.33
Hedged Portfolio std.dev. ($)	$	24.4	$	24.1
Hedge Fixed Cost as % of Invest. (c)		0.973%		0.97%
Hedge Var. Cost as % of Invest. (v)		7.500%		7.50%
Initial absolute value of hedge ratio h*		0.5437		0.5492
Optimal CVaR hedge ratio h*		-0.5437		-0.5492
Target CVaR*	$	56.94	$	56.24
CVaR hedging Total Benefit	$	67.83	$	68.53
CVaR hedging Total Cost	$	48.80	$	49.50
Change in Market Value of Equity	$	19.03	$	19.03
Change in Stock Price / sh.	$	1.90	$	1.90

Figure 12.7. Summary of Bank Risks from Chapters 3–6 (*Continued*).

Integrated Risk Management: Putting It All Together   457

Ch. 7 Off-Balance Sheet (OBS) Risk

OBS Effects	Base Scenario	Historical	Alternative Scenario
Initial Total Assets	$ 1,580.0		$ 1,580.00
Initial Equity	$ 180.0		180.0
Contingent Assets	$ 1,000.0		$ 1,000.0
Delta Cont. A (dCA)	0.10		0.10
ON-Balance Sheet Impact of CA	$ 100.00		$ 100.0
Contingent Liabilities	$ 400.0		$ 400.0
Delta Cont. L (dCL)	0.20		0.20
ON-Balance Sheet Impact of CL	$ 80.00		$ 80.0
Tot. Assets + CA - CL	$ 1,600.00		$ 1,600.00
Equity = EQ + CA - CL	$ 200.00		$ 200.00
Change in Market Value of Equity	$ 20.00		$ 20.00
Change in Stock Price / sh.	$ 2.00		$ 2.00

Ch. 8 Liquidity Risk

Liquidity Risk Choice	Base Scenario	Historical	Alternative Scenario
Total Assets	$ 1,580.0		$ 1,580.0
Cash & Sec.	$ 725.0		$ 691.8
Net Loans	$ 800.0		$ 863.2
Total Deposits	$ 1,400.0		$ 1,400.0
Excess Cash & Sec. (%)	50%		50%
Excess Cash & Sec.	$ 362.5		345.9
Loan rate (rL)	5.24%		5.07%
Securities Ret. (rS)	2.50%		2.50%
Deposit rate (rD)	2.11%		2.03%
Penalty rate (rP)	6.00%		6.00%
E(Outflows)	$ 700.0		$ 700.0
Initial LCR	1.036		1.04
LCR Average	1.10		1.10
LCR Std. Dev.	0.05		0.05
Dividend Payout	0.40		0.40
Tax Rate	0.20		0.20
Div. Yield (Re - g)	0.0357		0.0357
Shares Outstanding	10.0		10.00
Opt. Liquidity Coverage Ratio LCR*	1.187		1.365
Prob. (Avoid Extreme Cash Outflow)	0.95943		1.00000
LCR management Total Benefit	$ 16.38		$ 13.34
LCR management Total Cost	$ 11.39		$ 12.27
Change in Pretax Income	$ 4.98		$ 1.07
Change in Dividends / sh. (ΔDPS)	$ 0.16		$ 0.03
Change in Market Value of Equity	$ 44.68		$ 9.55
Change in Stock Price / sh.	$ 4.47		$ 0.96

Figure 12.8. Summary of Bank Risks from Chapters 7–8.

458 *Managing Financial Institutions: An Integrated Valuation Approach*

Ch. 9 Operational Risk

Operational Risk Choice	Base Scenario	Historical	Alternative Scenario
Total Revenue	$ 86.092		$ 86.092
Average Oper. Losses / year (% of Tot. Re	1.85%		2.00%
Sensitivity of Spending on Oper. Risk (k)	0.00001		0.00001
Distribution's Power Law parameter (a)	2.0		2.0
Prob. of Projected Losses exceeding: 1.85	2.9%		2.5%
Minimum Operating Cost (% of Tot. Rev.)	0.05%		0.10%
NOTE: The maximum OC* is set to the following:			3.00%
*Initial Optimal Operating Risk Cost: OC**	0.72%		1.90%
Optimal Operating Risk Cost: OC*	**0.72%**		**1.90%**
Prob. Of Operating Loss at ofc* > Avg. Loss	19.4%		2.8%
Oper. Risk management Total Benefit	$ 1.28		1.67
Oper. Risk management Total Cost	$ 0.62		1.63
Change in Pretax Income	$ 0.67		0.04
Change in Dividends / sh. (ΔDPS)	$ 0.02		0.00
Change in Stock Price / sh.	$ 0.60	$	0.04

Ch. 10 Capital Adequacy

Capital Ratio Choice	Base Scenario	Historical	Alternative Scenario
Loan rate (rL)	5.24%		5.24%
Base Borrowing Rate (rD*)	1.61%		1.61%
Initial Deposit rate (rD$_0$)	2.11%		2.11%
Minimum E/A ratio	6.0%		6.0%
Maximum E/A ratio	12.0%		12.0%
Industry Average E/A	8.0%		8.0%
New Deposit Rate (rD)	2.11%		2.11%
Dividend Payout (in decimal)	0.40		0.40
Initial Dividend Yield (DY$_i$)	3.37%		3.37%
Total Assets	$ 1,580.00	$	1,580.00
Total Deposits	$ 1,400.00	$	1,400.00
New Net Income (NI)	$ 18.00	$	18.00
New Equity	150.84	$	150.83
ROE with New Equity	11.93%		11.93%
Eq. Ret. (Re): min = rL	10.77%		10.77%
Growth Rate (g)	6.00%		6.00%
(Re - g): minimum = .01	4.77%		4.77%
Initial E/A ratio	9.55%		9.55%
Optimal E/A ratio (E/A)*	**9.55%**		**9.55%**
Capital Adequacy Total Benefit	$ -	$	-
Capital Adequacy Total Cost	4.77%		4.77%
Change in Market Value of Equity	$ 24.78	$	24.78
Change in Stock Price / sh.	$ 2.48	$	2.48

Figure 12.9. Summary of Bank Risks from Chapters 9–10.

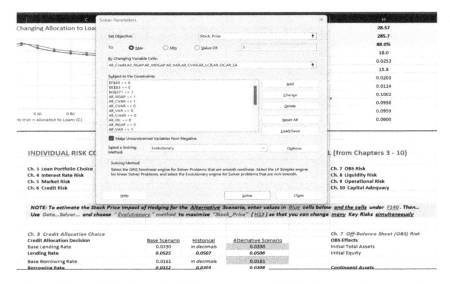

Figure 12.10. Dialog Box for Using the Solver Optimization Function to Find an Integrated Risk Management Solution across ABC's Main Risks.

changed directly in the "Integrated Risks – Chapter 12" tab. You can make these changes manually or, as we show later, you can use the *Solver* function to solve all optimal hedging choices in an integrated, simultaneous manner.

Now, that we are acquainted with the main components of the "Integrated Risks – Ch 12" tab, we can create an integrated risk management solution by following similar steps that were first outlined earlier in Figure 12.5 when we examined the ":Liquidity Risk – Ch 8" tab. As shown in Figure 12.10, we can use a dialog box within Excel™ to access and run the *Solver* command within the "Integrated Risks – Chapter 12" tab, as follows:

1. Choose **Data** from the spreadsheet's main menu;
2. Click on the **Solver icon** (usually located on the far-right side of the "ribbon" bar of the spreadsheet);
3. Select the "Evolutionary" choice from the drop-down menu related to the "Select a Solving Method" feature within the Solver dialog box[7]; and

---

[7]Note that, in contrast to using Solver for stand-alone risks like the LCR* choice described earlier, we use the "Evolutionary" **solution method** rather than the "GRG Nonlinear" approach. The Evolutionary technique is best suited for solving across numerous risks and

4. Press the "Solve" button and wait for the spreadsheet to use constrained optimization techniques to find an optimal LCR (which will then be displayed in cell F32 of the spreadsheet tab).

As we had seen when discussing Liquidity Risk, note that the top of the dialog box in Figure 12.10 indicates the "objective function" of the optimization problem is to maximize the cell called "Stock_Price" (cell H13). However, in this example, the bank's stock price is maximized by changing multiple cells such as "All_Credit" (for the C* term in cell F46), "All_RGAP" (for the Repricing Gap related to short-term interest rate risk in cell F60), and so forth for a total of 8 risk management decisions. In addition, we now have many more variables and values within the "Constraints"

---

is more likely to find a "global maximum" stock price in this case. This approach can take a bit longer to find a solution (e.g., more than 1 minute rather than a few seconds), so be patient as it searches iteratively for an optimal set of hedge ratios.

Note that this approach focuses on the total costs and total benefits of managing multiple risks and applies basic principles of microeconomics to find the optimal level of overall risk to maximize the bank's stock price. What this approach does *not* require are correlations between the various bank risks. For example, to find this optimal risk level, we do not need to estimate the correlation between, say, interest rate and credit risk, as the cost-benefit analysis, combined with its impact on the bank's cost of equity (R_E) and growth rate (g) are necessary and sufficient conditions. In theory, we could try and model how changes in the optimal hedge ratios (h^*) for each bank risk are affected by the correlations between all the risks noted in this chapter. However, this would make our model much more complex as it would require an additional set of assumptions about correlations across all risks, as well as how different hedge ratios could affect those correlations. This more-involved approach is beyond our book's scope and is difficult to apply in practice due to the addition of many new assumptions, some of which might be unknowable on an a priori basis.

Also, keep in mind that this optimization approach does not include the bank's OBS risk management choice. This is due to the inherently complicated interactions between many of the contingent asset and liability choices related to loan takedowns, credit default spreads, bond defaults, lawsuits, etc., that are not under the direct control of the bank. As explained in Chapter 8 related to OBS risk, the amount of contingent assets and liabilities that "hop on" the bank's balance sheet is primarily driven by bank customers and thus the bank's managers do not have much direct control over OBS risk. We therefore report the OBS risk values in the "Integrated Risks – Ch 12" tab and allow you to *manually* alter these numbers in the blue OBS-related cells rather than attempt to construct a very complex model of how customers might behave with these contingent assets and liabilities while simultaneously changing all the other bank risks. Such a model would take us well beyond the scope of our book's main goals.

portion of the dialog box to limit the range of possible values for each of these 8 risk-related variables. You can use the "Change" button in this dialog box to modify any of these constraints if you wish. If not, then simply pressing the "Solve" button will generate the optimal integrated risk management solution that maximizes ABC's stock price.

Depending on the complexity of the problem, it might take anywhere from a few seconds to over 1 minute to find the optimal value. This optimization process varies all 8 of the bank's risk-related variables in an iterative manner to find the ratios that maximize ABC's stock price by comparing the explicit and implicit costs of each risk to the benefits of managing these risks. As noted earlier in the discussion of Figure 12.6, the integrated risk management improves upon the stand-alone approach by choosing optimal hedge ratios and other optimal values that lead to a higher stock price for ABC ($28.72 vs. $26.27, or +9.3%).

In this example, the reason for the improvement in stock price is mainly driven by differences between the Base and Alternative scenarios related to the credit allocation choice ($C^* = 0.5883$ vs. 0.5336) and the liquidity coverage ratio ($LCR^* = 1.187$ vs. 1.365). Thus, integrated risk management helps increase ABC's stock price by taking on less credit risk (C^* is lower at 0.5361 of total assets) and raising more liquidity (LCR^* is higher at 1.365 times expected cash outflows) than the stand-alone approach. In addition, the equity-to-assets capital ratio is much higher for the stand-alone versus integrated method (11.18% vs. 9.55% of total assets). Thus, ABC can free up a substantial amount of costly capital by managing its risks in an integrated manner. Overall, we have shown that although the integrated risk management method can be a bit more complicated, it can also be value-enhancing for many banks by judiciously deviating from the stand-alone method's optimal hedge ratios for one or more key risks.[8]

---

[8] Note that, in contrast to conventional portfolio optimization, we do not need to explicitly estimate correlations between the various bank risks because each risk's impact on market value is computed directly with the IVM's three key variables, DIV_1, R_E, and g. Thus, the optimization program finds the optimal hedge ratios by considering each risk's impact on DIV_1, R_E, and g in a simultaneous fashion and thus implicitly infers correlations between the various risks without having to explicitly identify them ahead of time. Our approach of not requiring correlation estimates can be very useful because correlations between 8 of the bank's key risks can be quite volatile over time and across the business cycle. By avoiding these correlation estimates, we might be able to find a more stable solution to the integrated risk management problem.

12.4.1 *Managerial implications*

Nina and Sam are considering how best to manage ABC's numerous risks. Their initial analysis shows that actively managing these risks on a stand-alone basis to find optimal hedging decisions can increase the bank's stock price substantially. Compared to the prior year's stock price of $15.20, hedging eight of the bank's main risks in a stand-alone manner can raise the stock price to $26.27 for a +73% gain. Sam and Nina also noticed that the stock price was most affected by risk management choices related to credit (loan allocation levels and Credit VaR), interest rate risk (Modified Duration Gap), liquidity risk (Liquidity Coverage Ratio), and capital adequacy (Tangible Common Equity-to-Assets ratio). In addition, they saw that an integrated risk management approach can increase ABC's stock price even further to $28.72 for a +89% gain, although this approach would require more coordination and information sharing across the bank's different business units.

Although the bank is profitable and has been successful in the past, there appears to be a great deal of "money left on the table" by following a "Do Nothing" risk management policy. Given the sizable potential gains from taking a more active approach to managing the bank's risks, both Nina and Sam decide that they need to propose a major change in ABC's risk management policies but are faced with several questions that they and senior management must consider. **What resources are required to implement an effective, active risk management strategy (e.g., personnel skills, external and internal data requirements, software tools, accounting systems, and compliance supervision, to name just a few)?**

Should ABC start by focusing solely on one or two main risks on a stand-alone basis? **Or instead, is it better to implement a fully integrated risk management approach across all of ABC's main risks to achieve more economies of scale and operational efficiency?** Whichever approach they take, what are ABC's primary competitors doing in terms of risk management? For example, if ABC hedges all its interest rate risk but competitors do not, then ABC might suffer in comparison if interest rates move in a favorable direction for the competition. **Related to this point, what is senior management's tolerance for risk (or "risk appetite"), as well as their attitude to investing in capital and staff when competitors might be following a hands-off** "Do Nothing" **risk management policy?** This is an important behavioral/corporate culture question that must be addressed upfront to obtain senior management "buy-in" for a more active hedging strategy. In the end, Sam and Nina must address all these issues in a report to senior management.

Given the strategic importance of this recommendation to ABC's senior management and board of directors, Nina and Sam enlist their trusted lieutenants, Mitchell and Cecilia, to develop a more formal governance structure that can help senior managers and directors oversee the bank's risk management program. Such a risk management governance structure is normally organized as a never-ending cycle between four main responsibilities of senior management and board members:

1. Establish a **risk management philosophy** and **key goals** that are communicated to relevant staff.
2. Ensure the creation of **risk management metrics** that are consistent with the firm's philosophy and goals.
3. Be **informed** about the bank's key risks via the generation of **risk management reports** that are timely and relevant based on the chosen metrics.
4. **Adjust the bank's risk management philosophy, goals, and metrics** based on what is learned from the periodic risk management reports.

The four responsibilities can be shown in graphical form in Figure 12.11.

The four-person team also thinks that a graphic that summarizes their qualitative assessment of each of the bank's main risks might be a good way to convey their detailed quantitative work in a more easily

Figure 12.11. The Cycle of Risk Management Oversight by Senior Management/Board of Directors.

Risk	+ / 0 / −	Comments
Interest Rate	+	Stable NIM despite falling rates
Market	+	Acceptable VaR violations
Credit	−	Growing NPL and LLP
OBS	0	Adequate Contingent Assets
Liquidity	+	LCR>100% & Stable Pyramid
Capital Adequacy	0	(Equity / Assets) > 8%
Overall Assessment	++	**Good Risk Mgmt despite uptick in Credit Risk**

Figure 12.12. A Qualitative Risk Assessment of ABC.

understood format. To this end, Figure 12.12 provides such a framework with a simple "+/0/−" rubric, where a plus sign (+) means the ABC is doing better than its peers within this risk area and a negative sign (−) indicates they are lagging their peers. As Figure 12.12 shows, the team thinks ABC is doing well in terms of managing its interest rate, market, and liquidity risks while performing worse (or neutral) in terms of credit and OBS risks, as well as capital adequacy. Overall, the team thinks ABC's risks are being managed fairly well but more work needs to be done to improve the bank's credit risk management.

Sam, Nina, Cecilia, and Mitchell also realize that the bank's senior decision-makers will need to make **significant upfront (and ongoing) investments in people, systems, and processes** for the risk management initiative to be as successful as possible in enhancing shareholder value. With all this in mind, they set to work on further quantifying the costs and benefits of their risk management recommendation.

12.5 Summary

Bank risk management, on either a stand-alone or integrated basis, can have a significant effect on the firm's market value of equity. In this chapter, we first presented some examples of managing a bank's market- and liquidity-related risks in a stand-alone way. Given the numerical examples based on our hypothetical bank, ABC, we saw that, for this bank, liquidity risk management had a much larger (and positive) impact on firm value than hedging the bank's investment portfolio. We then observed that an integrated risk management policy increased ABC's stock price even further than a stand-alone approach but required a greater level of information and coordination across the various risks and business units. This trade-off between potentially higher gains from integrated risk management (IRM) versus higher information/coordination costs is an important factor that senior managers must consider when deciding to embark on a more active, integrated strategy. In addition, the bank's corporate culture in terms of risk tolerance and "risk appetite," as well as the hedging policies of its key competitors, are important behavioral/qualitative factors that warrant serious discussion before a final decision is made.

In sum, this book has tried to explain the key drivers of firm value via the **Magnitude, Riskiness, and Timing** of cash flows ("MRT") and how the "ART" of risk management (**Accept, Remove, or Transfer** risks) can affect these cash flows. To do so, we developed our "North Star" as a guide to understanding the trade-offs between various risk management choices and summarized these effects in the **Integrated Valuation Model** (or "IVM"). We hope that our efforts to convey these ideas can provide you with the concepts and tools to help make sense of the continually evolving competitive landscape for modern financial institutions.

Chapter-End Questions

Answers to odd-numbered questions can be found at the end of this book.

1. **True or False:** Integrated Risk Management (IRM) is a way to control risks in a comprehensive manner by solving for the optimal amounts of exposure over multiple risks simultaneously.
2. **True or False:** The integrated risk management approach always outperforms the stand-alone method.
3. **Multiple Choice:** What is the main purpose of the "Introduction" tab in the Excel™ spreadsheet used for IRM?

    (A) It provides links to all risk-related tabs of the file
    (B) It contains the key financial statement data
    (C) It focuses on all the risks described in Chapters 3–10
    (D) It solves simultaneously for the optimal levels of risk

4. **Multiple Choice:** What is the impact of the optimal choice of a liquidity risk management variable like the Liquidity Coverage Ratio (LCR) on the bank's market value equity?
   (A) It directly affects the bank's market value of equity
   (B) It affects the bank's equity in an indirect way via changes in the firm's Net Income (NI), cost of equity (R_E), and growth rate (g)
   (C) It has no impact on the bank's equity
   (D) It always reduces the bank's equity

5. **Multiple Choice:** What is the primary role of Excel's *Solver* function in the Integrated Valuation Model's spreadsheet?
   (A) To minimize the bank's risk
   (B) To maximize the bank's net profit
   (C) To find the optimal levels of risk that maximize a bank's stock price
   (D) To display financial data and graphs in a spreadsheet

6. **Excel-based Question for Interest Rate Risk (MDGAP*):** Answer the following questions about the leverage-adjusted modified duration gap (MDGAP) using the data presented in the following and shown in more detail within the "Interest Rate Risk – Ch 4" tab of the **Integrated Valuation Model.xlsx** file. How much interest rate risk exposure, as measured by its MDGAP, should ABC hedge (h^*) to maximize its stock price? For parts A–C of this question, you can assume the bank's managers are concerned about a 100-basis point increase in all interest rates, as shown in the "Interest Rate Risk – Ch 4" tab of the **Integrated Valuation Model.xlsx** file. Try this by starting with the MDGAP data in this tab where the variable costs (v) are 2% of the hedged exposure and then change the values in the blue cells related to the *Modified Duration of Assets* (MD_A) and *Modified Duration of Liabilities* (MD_L) based on the following questions. For part D of the question, use the "Integrated Risks – Ch 12" tab of the **Integrated Valuation Model.xlsx** file to perform an *integrated risk management* analysis.

Total Assets ($ million)	1,580
Total Liabilities ($ million)	1,400
Mod. Duration of Assets (MD_A)	5.00
Mod. Duration of Liabilities (MD_L)	2.00
Leverage-adjusted MDGAP (years)	3.228
Interest Rate shock	1.00%
Hedge Fixed Cost, c, (% of Tot. Assets)	0.00%
Hedge Variable Cost, v, (% of Tot. Assets)	2.00%
Shares Outstanding (million)	10.00

(A) On a *stand-alone basis*, calculate the optimal hedge ratio (h^*) to adjust the bank's modified durations of assets and liabilities to maximize the bank's value (*Hint*: review Equation (4.13) and footnote 16 in this chapter)

(B) How does h^* change if the variable hedging cost (v) rises to 4.0% of the interest rate risk exposure due to decreased liquidity and heightened volatility in the derivatives markets?

(C) As a second simulation, what happens to h^* if the increased variable cost for hedging also coincides with a decrease in the modified duration of assets (MD_A) to 4 years while the modified duration of liabilities (MD_L) increases to 3 years? Briefly explain how this h^* compares to the one calculated in part B.

(D) Repeat part C but use the "Modified Duration Gap Hedging Choice" under the "Ch 4 Interest Rate Risk" section of the spreadsheet's "Integrated Risks – Ch 12" tab *and* the **Solver** function to find an h^* for interest rate risk by optimizing on an *integrated basis* across *all* the bank's risks described in this tab. Compare the optimal hedge ratio for MDGAP in the "Alternative Scenario" column of this tab to the one computed in part C (which is also displayed under "Base" column within the Ch. 12 tab for ease of comparison). Also, compare any differences in the impact on ABC's stock price, as shown in row 13 at the top of the Ch. 12 tab. *Note: follow the instructions in this spreadsheet tab to learn how to perform the integrated risk management analysis using the* **Solver** *function.*

7. **Excel-based Question for Market Risk (VaR*):** Answer parts A–C about market risk, as measured by its RiskMetrics' Value-at-Risk (VaR), using the "Market Risk – Ch 5" tab of the **Integrated Valuation Model.xlsx** file. Then, use the "Integrated Risks – Ch 12" tab in this spreadsheet to answer part D via an integrated risk management approach. To begin, let's answer the question of how much market risk exposure on its $700 million securities portfolio should ABC hedge (h^*) to maximize its stock price on a *stand-alone* basis? Assume the bank's managers are concerned about an increase in the "Unhedged Portfolio's" **standard deviation** from the "base" scenario of 0.25% to 0.40%. Try this by starting with the base scenario in the Ch 5 tab where the variable costs (v) are 0.5% of the hedged exposure and then changing the values in the blue cell related to the *Unhedged Portfolio std. dev. in %* from 0.25% to 0.40%.

   (A) On a *stand-alone* basis, what is the optimal hedge ratio (h^*) for the above volatility shock and how does it compare to the base scenario's h^*?

   (B) Related to your answer in part A, what is the expected percentage change in ABC's stock price if management implemented this optimal hedge ratio?

   (C) What is the "target" VaR* based on Equation (5.12) and your answer to part A of this question?

   (D) How do your answers to parts A–B change if the bank uses an integrated risk management approach to solve all risks, including market risk, *simultaneously*? Use the "Ch 5 Market Risk" section within the "Integrated Risks – Chapter 12" tab to answer this question. Briefly explain the results you observe from this method.

8. **Excel-based Question for Credit Risk (CVaR*):** Answer parts A-C about credit risk, as measured by the RiskMetrics' Credit Value-at-Risk (CVaR) method, using the "Credit Risk – Chapter 6" tab of the **Integrated Valuation Model.xlsx** file. Then, use the "Integrated Risks – Chapter 12" tab in this spreadsheet to answer part D via an integrated risk management approach. To begin, let's answer the question of how much

market risk exposure on ABC's $1,530 million total credit portfolio (which includes total loans and securities), should the bank hedge (h^*) to maximize its stock price on a *stand-alone* basis? Assume the bank's managers are concerned with an increase in credit risk due to weakening macroeconomic conditions. Try this by starting with the "base" scenario in the "Credit Risk – Ch 6" tab of the **Integrated Valuation Model.xlsx** file where the variable costs (v) are 7.5% of the hedged exposure. Then, try changing the values in the blue cells related to *both* the *Unhedged Sec. Port. std. dev.* and *Unhedged Loan Port. std. dev.* from 3.50% to 5.00%.

(A) On a *stand-alone* basis, what is the optimal hedge ratio (h^*) for the above credit shock and how does it compare to the base scenario's h^*?

(B) Related to your answer in part A, what is the expected percentage change in ABC's stock price if management implemented this optimal hedge ratio?

(C) What is the "target" CVaR* based on Equation (6.19) and your answer to part A of this question?

(D) How do your answers to parts A and B change if the bank uses an integrated risk management approach to solve all risks, including credit risk, *simultaneously*? Use the "Ch 6 Credit Risk" section within the "Integrated Risks – Chapter 12" tab to answer this question. Briefly explain the results you observe from this method.

9. **Excel-based Question for Liquidity Risk (LCR*):** Answer part A about liquidity risk, as measured by its Liquidity Coverage Ratio (LCR), using the "Liquidity Risk – Chapter 8" tab of the **Integrated Valuation Model.xlsx** file. Then, use the "Integrated Risks – Chapter 12" tab in this spreadsheet to answer part B via an integrated risk management approach. To begin, let's answer the question of how much the bank's liquidity risk exposure on its $1,580 million in total assets affects ABC's *market value of equity* (i.e., its market capitalization or "market cap"). Assume ABC's managers are focused on how changes in the sudden demand for cash from borrowers and/or

creditors can affect the bank's market value due to concerns about the bank's ability to meet this demand. To do so, change the levels of expected cash outflows based on the following parts A and B. For example, examine these liquidity risk effects by starting with the current values in the blue cell related to the *Expected Outflows*.

(A) On a *stand-alone* basis, what happens to the bank's stock price and optimal Liquidity Coverage Ratio (LCR*) if the bank's expected "emergency" cash outflows (i.e., the E(Outflows) variable) rise from $700 million to $900 million? Note that you will need to use the spreadsheet's *Solver* function in the "Liquidity Risk – Chapter 8" tab to find this optimal solution because the model does not have a closed-form, analytical solution.

(B) How does your answer to part A change if the bank uses an integrated risk management approach to solve all risks, including liquidity risk, *simultaneously*? Use the "Ch. 8 Liquidity Risk" section within the "Integrated Risks – Chapter 12" tab to answer this question. Briefly explain the results you observe from this method.

10. **Comprehensive Question:** Given the potential benefits of integrated risk management (IRM) and the costs associated with it, should Nina and Sam recommend to ABC's management a *stand-alone* or *integrated* approach for its risk management strategy? Consider the relative costs and benefits of each approach given the bank's current risk management resources, information systems, corporate culture, risk tolerance, market conditions, and the hedging policies of its key competitors in your answer.

References

Hempel, G. H. and Simonson, D. G. (1999). *Bank Management: Text and Cases*, 5th edition. John Wiley & Sons.

Pagano, M. S. (2001). How theories of financial intermediation and corporate risk-management influence bank risk-taking, *Financial Markets, Institutions, and Instruments*, 10, 277–323.

Pagano, M.S. (2004) Using an alternative estimation method to perform comprehensive empirical tests: An application to interest rate risk-management, *Review of Quantitative Finance and Accounting*, 23, 377–406.

Saunders, A., Cornett, M.M. and Erhemjamts, O. (2024). *Financial Institutions Management: A Risk Management Approach*, McGraw-Hill, New York.

Schrand, C. M. and Unal, H. (1998). Hedging and coordinated risk management: Evidence from thrift conversions, *Journal of Finance*, 53, 979–1014.

Solutions to Odd-Numbered Chapter-End Questions

Chapter 1

1. **True.**
3. **A.** Channeling funds from savers to borrowers is the primary task of banks and other financial institutions.
5. **B.** The primary purpose of QAT is to convert low-liquidity instruments into high-liquidity instruments such as long-term bank loans into short-term deposits.
7. For financial institutions, the concept that "Form Follows Function" means that items that show up on the bank's financial statements (their "form") reflect the firm's primary activities (e.g., lending, investing, and brokerage). Thus, the financial statements effectively capture the actions taken by the institution (the "function").
9. Using the DuPont equation, we see that

$$\text{ROE} = \text{ROA} \cdot \text{EM} = \frac{\text{Net Income}}{\text{Total Assets}} \cdot \frac{\text{Total Assets}}{\text{Total Equity}} = \frac{\$10 \text{ million}}{\$2 \text{ billion}} \cdot \frac{\$2 \text{ billion}}{\$150 \text{ million}} = 0.5\% \cdot 13.33 = \mathbf{0.0667} \quad \text{or} \quad \mathbf{6.67\%}$$

We can say this financial institution is most likely a commercial bank or securities firm because of the low contribution of ROA to the institution's ROE and the much higher contribution of the EM to the institution's ROE.

Chapter 2

1. **False.** Some of the models we discuss, like the dividend discount model, provide a valuation estimate for *only* the bank's equity. A more general discounted cash flow (DCF) model uses the firm's cash flows to estimate a value for the entire firm.
3. **D.** Free cash flows are not calculated with explicit estimates of dividends.
5. **B.** The horizon value represents the discounted value of all future cash flows a firm will generate beyond a certain point in time. When projecting cash flows for a firm, at some point it makes sense to stop making specific projections and instead assume that cash flows will grow at a constant rate in perpetuity.
7. We can estimate the value of DEF's stock using the equation for a growing perpetuity:

$$P_0 = \frac{D_0(1+g)}{r-g} = \frac{\$1.50(1+3\%)}{10\%-3\%} = \$22.07$$

9. **Bank JKL does not currently pay a dividend. In three years (that is, at $t = 3$), the bank will begin paying a dividend of \$0.50/share, which it projects will grow by 5% per year in perpetuity. Bank JKL's investors require a 12% rate of return. What is the appropriate price for Bank JKL's stock today?**

Answer: We first need to find the horizon value of Bank JKL's dividends. It will begin paying the perpetuity at $t = 3$, so we are able to find the horizon value of the stream of dividends at $t = 2$:

$$HV_2 = \frac{D_3}{r-g} = \frac{\$0.50}{12\%-5\%} = \$7.14$$

We then must discount the horizon value back to its time zero value:

$$P_0 = \frac{HV_2}{(1+r)^2} = \frac{\$7.14}{(1.10)^2} = \$5.90$$

Chapter 3

1. **True.** FIs are usually unstable due to the high (and short-term) financial leverage they use. Thus, any concerns about bank profitability can trigger a "bank run" by creditors.
3. **B.** Derivatives (e.g., forwards, futures, swaps, and options) are used because they are usually highly liquid and have low transaction costs.
5. **C.** Heavy use of financial leverage creates a much greater likelihood of default and insolvency. The other choices are not concerns but instead are potential benefits of *lower* leverage.
7. **Answers are shown as follows:**
   (A) The expected total dividend is **$48 million** = ($80 million · 60%).
   (B) The sustainable growth rate (g) is **4.8%** = (12% · (1 − 0.60)).
   (C) Expected Return on Equity (R_E) is **8%** = (4% + (0.8 · 5)).
   (D) We can estimate the **market value of equity** for ABC using the Constant Growth Dividend Discount Model (DDM) with the provided data:
   1. **Total Dividends Available to Common Stockholders (DIV_1):** $48.0 million (from the first part of the question, shown above).
   2. **Expected Return on Equity (R_E):** 8% (calculated via the third part).
   3. **Dividend Payout Ratio (d):** 60% (given).

   The DDM formula of ABC's total market value based on the constant growth case is

   $$V_{E,0} = \frac{DIV_1}{(R_E - g)} = \frac{\$48 \text{ million}}{(0.080 - 0.048)} = \$1,500 \text{ million or } \$1.5 \text{ billion}$$

   To find ABC's stock price per share (SP_0), you can divide the market value by the number of shares outstanding (remember to use the same size of the units in the numerator and denominator; in this case, millions of dollars and millions of shares):

   $$SP_0 = \frac{\$1,500 \text{ million}}{20 \text{ million shares}} = \$75 \text{ per share}$$

476 Managing Financial Institutions: An Integrated Valuation Approach

9. As you can see from the following table, **the level of C^* first increases from 0.5883 to 0.6348** as the Interest Rate Spread ($rL - rD$) widens by 33 bps (+3.46% vs. +3.13%) but then actually *drops* to 0.4714 in the final scenario even though the Rate Spread continues to increase to +4.67%. This pattern occurs because we have imposed a 6% cap on the model's Sustainable Growth Rate (g). So, as the rate spread increases slightly to +3.46% in the middle column because the greater profitability of lending is not offset by a commensurately higher discount rate and so ABC's market value is maximized by raising its credit allocation to .6348. However, as the spread increases further to +4.67% in the last column, the spreadsheet shows in a table right below the Optimal Credit Allocation (C^*) cell that the 6% growth cap occurs at a *lower* level of C^* of 0.4714. So, any lending *above* this point will lead to a much *higher* discount rate relative to the growth rate (i.e., ($R_E - g$) rises significantly because R_E increases while g is capped at 6% when C^* exceeds 0.4714). Keep in mind that this occurs because we are holding *all* other variables *constant* in the valuation model based on the "IVM Inputs" tab. *Note*: If you are very experienced with Excel and wish to explore this growth cap further, see the formula in cell D162 of the spreadsheet and, if you wish, you can change this 6% to another amount and see how that affects your C^* estimate.

	Base Scenario	ΔBase Rates by +1%	Δonly rL^* by +1% more
Base Lending Rate (rL^*)	3.30%	4.30%	5.30%
Base Borrowing Rate (rD^*)	1.61	2.61	2.61
Lending Rate (rL)	5.24	7.03	7.80
Borrowing Rate (rD)	2.11	3.57	3.13
Rate Spread ($rL - rD$)	+3.13%	+3.46%	+4.67%
Optimal Credit Alloc. (C^*)	0.5883	0.6348	0.4714

Chapter 4

1. **False.** The "ARM" represents choices related to assets (A), rates (R), and mix (M) within a bank's balance sheet, allowing managers to navigate interest rate risk. Thus, bank managers should modify the "ARM" of their assets and liabilities to help mitigate the bank's interest rate risk.

3. **C.** This is the primary concern because refinancing risk exists when RSA < RSL and thus *rising* rates will squeeze the bank's interest rate spread. Conversely, reinvestment risk exists when RSA > RSL and thus *falling* rates will squeeze the bank's interest rate spread in this case.
5. **B.** Using financial derivatives like interest-rate forward contracts allows the bank to transfer risk to someone else.
7. Answers are shown in the following:

Modified Duration of ABC's Assets

Assets	Value ($ mil.)	Modified Duration (yrs)	Contribution to MD_A
Cash & Reserves	$5	0.00	$(4 / 100) \cdot 0.0 = 0.0$ yrs.
Investments	30	2.0	$(30 / 100) \cdot 2.0 = 0.6$ yrs.
Net Loans	60	5.00	$(60 / 100) \cdot 5.0 = 3.0$ yrs.
Other Assets	5	N.A.	N.A.
Total Assets	$100		$MD_A = 0.0 + 0.6 + 3.0 = \mathbf{3.6}$ **years**

Modified Duration of Liabilities

Liabilities	Value ($ mil.)	Modified Dur. (yrs)	Contribution to MD_L
Deposits	$60	1.50	$(60 / 90) \cdot 1.5 = 1.0$ yrs.
Other Borrowed Money	30	4.50	$(30 / 90) \cdot 4.5 = 1.5$ yrs.
Total Liabilities	$90		$MD_L = 1.0 + 1.5 = \mathbf{2.5}$ **years**

(A) See the above calculations in the boxes on the right: $MD_A = \mathbf{3.6}$ **years** and $MD_L = \mathbf{2.5}$ **years**

(B) $MDGAP = MD_A - \alpha \cdot MD_L = 3.6 - [(90/100) \cdot (2.5)] = 3.60 + 2.25 = \mathbf{+1.35}$ **years**

(C) $\Delta E = -MDGAP \cdot \Delta R \cdot TA = -(+1.35) \cdot (+0.02) \cdot (\$100 \text{ million}) = -0.0270 \cdot \$100 \text{ million} = \mathbf{-\$2.70}$ **million**

(D) The bank's managers can reduce this interest rate risk by going "short" interest rates via fixed income derivatives like futures, forwards, or put options. These derivatives would then provide a positive payout when rates rise and this gain could offset the decline in the bank's net asset exposure. Alternatively, the firm could do "on-balance sheet" hedging where it tries to use the "ARM" approach to shorten the duration of its assets and/or lengthen the duration of its liabilities

9. Answers are shown in the following:
   (A) By entering the relevant information provided above into the spreadsheet file, the **optimal hedge ratio (h^*) = –0.50 or –50%**. This is based on the cost–benefit relationship described by Equation (4.10) related to hedging RGAP: $h^* = (I \cdot (\Delta R)) / (2 \cdot v)$, where I is an indicator variable that equals –1 when (RGAP · ΔR) < 0 (and 0 when (RGAP · ΔR) > 0). In this case, $h^* = -1 \cdot (+0.02) / (2 \cdot 0.02) = -(0.02 / 0.04) = -\mathbf{0.50} = -\mathbf{50\%}$. Thus, $h = -0.50$ means the bank **should sell short 50% of its Repricing Gap exposure** to maximize its stock price.
   (B) Compared to the "Base" scenario's stock price of $20.17 shown in the spreadsheet, the above changes and hedge ratio of –0.50 can **increase the price by +4.4% to $21.06**.
   (C) Equation (4.12) shows that RGAP* = $(1 - | h^*|) \cdot$ unhedged RGAP = $(1 - |-0.50|) \cdot$ ($800 million – $1,000 million) = (0.50 · –$200 million) = **–$100 million**. So, after the hedge ratio of –50% has been implemented, the bank's target (or effective) RGAP will be –$100 million, which is much less than the unhedged RGAP. Thus, the bank's interest rate risk exposure has been reduced dramatically and will, in turn, help maximize its market value of equity.
   (D) With a 300-basis point rate increase, $h^* = -1 \cdot (+0.03) / (2 \cdot 0.02) = -(0.03 / 0.04) = -\mathbf{0.75} = -\mathbf{75\%}$. And, with 100 bps increase, $-1 \cdot (+0.01) / (2 \cdot 0.02) = -(0.01 / 0.04) = -\mathbf{0.25} = -\mathbf{25\%}$. So, we can see a clear pattern where the hedge ratio steadily increases as the interest rate shock becomes larger. This is somewhat intuitive because the *bigger* the potential rate shock leads to *greater* risk to the bank's Net Interest Income and so there is a larger incentive to hedge *more* of the exposure.

Chapter 5

1. **False.** The ES estimate is typically larger because it quantifies a potentially very large loss when it crosses over the 1% VaR threshold.
3. **D.** The text mentions that changes in interest rates, exchange rates, commodity prices, and stock prices can all adversely affect the market value of a bank's assets.

Solutions to Odd-Numbered Chapter-End Questions   479

5. **D.** The 1% daily VaR is approximately **$7.456 million**. Explanation: Using the formula from the passage, 1% daily VaR = Critical Value · Daily Standard Deviation of Returns · Invested Assets = 2.33 · 0.004 · $800 million = 0.00932 · $800 million = **$7.456 million**.

7. The **diversification benefit** of the portfolio is **$0.843 million**. This is calculated by subtracting the total portfolio VaR from the sum of the VaRs of the various sub-components ($6.018 million − $5.175 million). This benefit arises because the daily movements in bonds, stocks, currencies, and commodities are not perfectly (and positively) correlated with each other.

The **percentage reduction in VaR** due to the diversification benefit is **14.0%**. This is calculated by dividing the diversification benefit by the sum of the VaRs of the various sub-components and multiplying by 100 ($0.843 million/$6.018 million = **0.14 or 14.0%**).

9. Answers are shown in the following:
   (A) By entering the relevant information provided above into the spreadsheet file, the **optimal hedge ratio (h^*) = −0.9320 or −93.20%**. This is based on the cost–benefit relationship described by Equation (5.12) related to hedging the portfolio's VaR: −1 · (2.33 · σ_{UH}) / (2 · v)) = −(2.33 · 0.0040) / (2 · 0.005)) = −(0.00932 / 0.01000) = −0.9320 = −93.2%) where an indicator variable equals −1 when the bank owns (or is "long") some amount of marketable securities, S, which is the norm for FIs (i.e., S > 0). Thus, h^* = −0.932 means the bank **should sell short 93.2% of its market risk exposure** to maximize its stock price. Due to the increase in daily market volatility from 25 to 40 bps, there is now an incentive to hedge more of the securities portfolio.
   (B) Compared to the "Base" scenario's stock price of $20.17 shown in the spreadsheet, the above changes and hedge ratio of −0.932 can **increase the stock price by a relatively small +1.5% to $20.47**.
   (C) Equation (5.13) shows that **Target VaR* = (1 − | h^*|) · unhedged VaR = (1 − |−.932|) · ($6.524 million) = (0.068 · $6.524 million) = $0.444 million**. So, after the hedge ratio of −93.2% has been implemented, the bank's target (or effective) VaR will drop from the original $1.702 million estimate to $0.444 million, which is

much less than the base case's unhedged VaR of $4.078 million. Thus, the bank's market risk exposure has been reduced dramatically and will, in turn, help maximize its market value of equity.
(D) With a 2% variable cost factor, v, **the optimal hedge ratio drops sharply to −0.2330 or −23.30%**. This can be seen in the following calculation: $h^* = -1 \cdot (2.33 \cdot .0040) / (2 \cdot 0.02) = -(0.00932 / 0.0400) = -0.2330 = -23.3\%$. And the **change in stock price is very small (+0.4% or +$0.07 per share)** when compared to the answer to part B. In terms of a new target VaR, this figure rises dramatically to **$5.004 million** because a much smaller percentage of the exposure is now being hedged (23.3% vs. 93.2%). This can be calculated as follows: $= (1 - |h^*|) \cdot$ unhedged VaR $= (1 - |-.932|) \cdot (\$6.524) = (0.767 \cdot \$6.524 \text{ million}) = \$5.004$ **million**. The reason for the lower hedge ratio and higher target VaR* is due to the increased variable cost of hedging the bank's securities portfolio. So, higher risk management costs make it more expensive to reduce VaR and thus decrease the net benefits of hedging market risk. This is somewhat intuitive because *bigger* costs to hedge market risk will lead to a *smaller* incentive to hedge this exposure (and thus a *lower* hedge ratio).

Chapter 6

1. **False.** The text states that a bank's credit risk is indeed affected by the mix of investments and loans it grants to its customers. For example, credit card loans are usually much riskier than residential mortgages.
3. **D.** The text mentions that Character is the most qualitative aspect of the 5 Cs and represents the lender's overall assessment of the borrower's trustworthiness and willingness to repay the loan. According to John Pierpont Morgan, the famed financier, character is the first thing in credit, even before money or anything else. He believed that money cannot buy character and that a man he does not trust could not get money from him regardless of what collateral was provided. He considered character to be the fundamental basis of business.
5. **C.** Banks can "ration" credit by restricting loans to only high-quality borrowers to reduce the impact of adverse selection on loan pricing.

Solutions to Odd-Numbered Chapter-End Questions   481

7. **Answer:** The probability of repayment would be calculated as follows:

$$p_1 = \frac{\{1+RF_{0,1}\}}{\{1+RC_{0,1}\}} = \frac{\{1+0.02\}}{\{1+0.03\}} = 0.99029 \approx 99.0\%$$

$$PD_1 = 1 - p_1 = 1 - 0.99029 = 0.00971 \approx 1.0\%$$

Explanation: The probability of repayment is calculated based on the spot rates for the risk-free government security and the corporate bond. A lower probability of repayment indicates a higher risk of default. In this case, there is a 99% chance of getting repaid and thus there is only a 1% chance of default.

9. Answers are shown in the following:
   (A) By entering the relevant information provided above into the spreadsheet file, the **optimal hedge ratio (h^*) = −0.7767 or −77.67%** of the FIs total credit portfolio. This is based on the cost–benefit relationship described by Equation (6.18) related to hedging the portfolio's CVaR: $-1 \cdot (2.33 \cdot \sigma_{UH}) / (2 \cdot v)) = -(2.33 \cdot 0.050) / (2 \cdot 0.075)) = -(0.1165 / 0.1500) = -0.7767 = -77.67\%$ where we use an indicator variable that always equals −1 because the bank normally owns (or is "long") some amount of loans, L, and fixed income securities, S (i.e., $L > 0$ and $S > 0$). Thus, $h^* = -0.7767$ means the bank **should sell short 77.67% of its credit risk exposure** to maximize its stock price. This h^* is substantially larger in absolute magnitude when compared to the "base" optimal hedge ratio of −0.5437 (i.e., base $h^* = -(2.33 \cdot 0.035)/(2 \cdot 0.075)) = -(0.08155 / 0.1500) = -0.5437 = -54.37\%$). Thus, the bank has the incentive to hedge *more* when credit risk *increases*.
   (B) Compared to the "Base" scenario's stock price of $20.17 shown in the spreadsheet, the above changes and hedge ratio of −0.7767 can **increase the stock price by a relatively large +26.9% to $25.60.** The reason for the large jump in ABC's stock price is due to the relatively high credit risk of the portfolio, as measured by the annual standard deviation of 5.0%. This translates into a 1% chance of losing 11.7% (or more) of the bank's total credit portfolio. So, *greater* credit risk leads to a *larger* need to hedge. Thus, using

hedging to reduce the severity of the left tail of the bank's credit portfolio can greatly increase the stock price in this scenario.

(C) Equation (6.19) shows that **Target VaR*** = $(1 - |h^*|)$ · unhedged CVaR = $(1 - |-.7767|)$ · ($178.245 million) = $(0.2233 \cdot \$178.245$ million) = **$39.808 million**. So, after the hedge ratio of −77.67% has been implemented, the bank's target (or effective) CVaR* will drop from the original $56.937 million estimate to $39.808 million, which is much less than the base case's unhedged VaR of $124.772 million. Thus, the bank's credit risk exposure has been reduced dramatically and will, in turn, help maximize its market value of equity.

(D) With a higher 3% fixed cost factor, c, **the optimal hedge ratio drops to 0.00 or 0.0%**. Thus, the optimal decision is **to *not* hedge at all** because the fixed cost of $45.9 million outweighs the bank's maximum total benefit. One can see this from the graph labeled "Net Impact of Hedging Credit VaR" right below the spreadsheet's scenario analysis (highlighted in yellow). In that graph, we can see the "Change in Stock Price" is always *negative* for *any* value of h. This graph tells us that the fixed hedging costs outweigh the hedging benefits for all possible levels of the hedge ratio. Thus, the optimal thing to do is not incur this fixed cost and ***not* hedge at all**. By doing so, the bank can re-deploy the $45.9 million for other purposes and not "waste" it by trying to hedge the firm's credit risk. Indeed, for many smaller FIs, this situation is fairly common — the start-up and ongoing fixed costs of running a risk management program might not justify the benefits of such a program. These savings in fixed costs, in turn, **help boost ABC's stock price by +10.9% to $22.36** (vs. the $20.17 base price).

Lastly, the new target CVAR* can be calculated as follows: = $(1 - |h^*|)$ · unhedged CVaR = $(1 - |0.00|)$ · ($6.524) = $(1.00 \cdot \$124.772$ million) = **$124.772 million**. The reason for the lower hedge ratio and higher target CVaR* is due to the increased fixed cost of hedging the bank's credit portfolio. So, higher risk management costs make it more expensive to reduce CVaR and thus decrease the net benefits of hedging credit risk. This is somewhat intuitive because *larger* costs to hedge credit risk will lead to a *smaller* need to hedge this exposure (and thus a *lower, or zero*, hedge ratio).

Chapter 7

1. **True.** These are indeed the main types of asset-based contingent financing needs that a bank can provide to help insure borrowers against the frequency and severity of both expected and unexpected cash shortfalls.

3. **D.** Selling corporate credit risk protection via Credit Default Swap (CDS) contracts is a liability-based OBS activity that can lead to contingent liabilities because the bank owes a CDS buyer a financial payout if an underlying credit instrument goes into default.

5. **D.** The impact of OBS risk on a bank's market value of equity depends on several factors, including the dollar amounts of Contingent Assets (CA) and Contingent Liabilities (CL), and their respective deltas.

7. Using the formula in Equation (7.3), EQ = A − L + (CA − CL), we find that EQ = $300 million − $250 million + ($80 million − $90 million) = **$40 million** when we include OBS risk. This estimate of EQ is *$10 million less* than the simpler measure of *on-balance sheet common equity*: EQ = A − L = $300 million − $250 million = $50 million. The bank's common equity *decreases* when the contingent liabilities ($90 million) are *greater* than the contingent assets ($80 million).

9. Answers are shown in the following:

    (A) We define the SLR to be equal to [EQ + (CA − CL)] / [A + (CA − CL)], where CA = ($\delta_{CA} \cdot N_{CA}$) and CL = ($\delta_{CL} \cdot N_{CL}$). Using the values given in part A, we obtain

    SLR = [$180 million + [0.10 · {($500 million · 1.10)
    + ($300 million · 1.10) + $150 million + $50 million)}
    − 0.20 · ($400 million · 1.25)] / [$1,580 million
    + ($108 million − $100 million) = [$180 million
    + $8 million] / [$1,580 million + $8 million]
    = ($188 million / $1,588 million) = **0.1184 or 11.84%**.

    (B) By definition, the E/A ratio = [EQ / A]. Using the values in part A and the Excel™ file, we obtain

    $$E/A = \left[\frac{\$180 \text{ million}}{\$1,580 \text{ million}} \right] = 0.1139 \quad \text{or} \quad 11.39\%$$

    This result occurs because changes in CA and CL do *not* affect the on-balance sheet E/A ratio and so only the original values for common equity (EQ) and total assets (A) are needed for this calculation. Compared to the SLR in part A, we can see that ABC's E/A ratio is *lower* (11.39% vs. 11.84%) because it does not take into account the boost in equity when we add *more* CA than CL to the overall, comprehensive balance sheet that includes OBS risk. That is, common equity is increased by the *net difference* in (CA − CL) which, in this case, is +**$8 million** (i.e., $108 million − $100 million).

(C) We can use new OBS Delta sensitivities and the numerator portion of Equation (7.5) to answer this question:

New Market Cap = EQ = $180 million + [0.05 · ($500 million · 1.10)
+ ($300 million · 1.10) + $150 million
+ $50 million)} − 0.25 · ($400 million · 1.25)]
= $180 million + (0.05 · $1,080 million)
− (0.25 · $500 million)] = $180 million
+ $54 million − $125 million = **$109 million.**

In terms of stock price, we can divide EQ by the number of shares outstanding (i.e., 10 million in this case to show that **ABC's new stock price is $10.90 per share** ($109 million/10 million shares).

Compared to the original base scenario's market cap and stock price ($180 million and $18.00 per share), the new results show that the **change in ABC's market cap is −$71 million** (i.e., ΔEQ = CA − CL = $54 million − $125 million = −**$71 million**).

Accordingly, the **dollar change in stock price** equals the change in market cap divided by the number of shares outstanding: Δ**EQ / sh.** = **(CA − CL) / Number of Shares Outstanding** = −$71 million / 10 million shares = −**$7.10 per share**. In *percentage terms*, we can see that **ABC's stock price drops −39.4%** due to these changes in OBS risk items.

(D) With δ_{CA} rising back to 0.10 while δ_{CL} declines to 0.10, we can re-calculate ABC's market value and stock price as follows:

New Market Cap = EQ = $180 million
+ [0.10 · {($500 million · 1.10)
+ ($300 million · 1.10) + $150 million
+ $50 million)} − 0.10 · ($400 million · 1.25)]
= $180 million + (0.10 · $1,080 million)

$- (0.10 \cdot \$500 \text{ million})] = \$180 \text{ million} + \$108 \text{ million} - \$50 \text{ million} = \textbf{\$238 million}$.

In terms of stock price, we can divide EQ by the number of shares outstanding (i.e., 10 million in this case to show that **ABC's new stock price is $23.80 per share** ($238 million/ 10 million shares).

Compared to the original base scenario's market cap and stock price ($180 million and $18.00 per share), the new results show that the **change in ABC's market cap is +$58 million** (i.e., ΔEQ = CA − CL = $108 million − $50 million = **+$58 million**).

Accordingly, the **dollar change in stock price** equals the change in market cap divided by the number of shares outstanding: $\Delta EQ / \text{sh.} = (CA - CL) / $ **Number of Shares Outstanding** = +$58 million / 10 million shares = **+$5.80 per share**. In *percentage terms*, we can see that **ABC's stock price now rises +32.2%** due to these changes in OBS risk items.

Chapter 8

1. **True.** The base of the Financing Pyramid is larger than the other rows within the diagram shown in Figure 1 of this chapter, indicating that the largest percentage of financing should come from stable, low-cost insured deposits.
3. **B.** The text explains that asset-based liquidity risk typically refers to sudden customer demands for bank funds to finance items such as pre-approved lines of credit, loan commitments, and letters of credit. When these items "hop on" the balance sheet, they become assets for the bank.
5. **C.** Other Borrowed (OBM) is viewed as less desirable because it is "hot money" which typically leads to higher financing costs and less funding reliability because uninsured creditors are more likely to lose money if the bank encounters financial difficulties. Thus, they are most likely to pull their money from the bank because they face a large "downside" risk relative to a limited "upside" gain.
7. The **stock price** can be calculated using the Integrated Valuation Model's formula that was first introduced in Chapter 3:

$$\text{Stock Price} = \frac{(\text{Dividend Payout} \cdot \text{Projected Net Income})}{(\text{Dividend Yield} \cdot \text{Shares Outstanding})}$$

Substituting the given values, we obtain

$$\text{Stock Price} = \frac{(0.40 \cdot \$2.288 \text{ million})}{(0.0357 \cdot 1.00 \text{ million shares})} = \$25.64 \text{ per share}$$

The bank's **LN/Depo ratio** can be calculated as follows:

$$\frac{\text{LN}}{\text{Depo}} = \frac{\$58 \text{ million}}{\$90 \text{ million}} = \textbf{0.644 or 64.4\% of Deposits}$$

The bank's ROE can be calculated as follows:

$$\text{ROE} = \frac{\text{Net Income}}{\text{Common Equity}} = \frac{\$2.288 \text{ million}}{\$100 \text{ million} - \$90 \text{ million}}$$
$$= \textbf{0.2288} \quad \text{or} \quad \textbf{22.88\%}$$

9. Answers are shown in the following:
   (A) According to Equation (8.13) and the spreadsheet, an increase in expected outflows from $700 million to $900 million can have a *positive* effect on ABC's stock price because an optimal LCR* allows the bank to avoid a larger drain on liquidity. However, the increase in "excess" liquid assets from 50% to 60% of the bank's marketable securities imposes an opportunity cost because the return on these safer, more liquid assets will typically be much lower than what ABC can earn from alternative investments, such as loans. This opportunity cost has an offsetting *negative* impact on stock price. **The *net effect* of these two changes on ABC's stock price is *negative*, as it drops from a base level of $20.17 to $17.90 per share (i.e., a −11.2% change). In addition, the optimal LCR* decreases slightly from 1.187 to 1.172**.

   > In this scenario, the costs outweigh the benefits regardless of which LCR is chosen, but, overall, an LCR* of 1.172 minimizes the overall decline in market value. That is, an LCR* of 1.172 does the best in terms of handling the negative effects of an increase in liquidity risk. Ideally, we would like to see LCR* lead to an increase in ABC stock price, but this is not always possible when the demands on the bank's liquidity are very large.

(B) In this case, there is a larger *positive* effect from avoiding a sudden surge in demand for liquidity by ABC's borrowers and/or creditors. Thus, the Liquidity Risk Benefit is *larger* when rP is *higher* and *fully offsets* the negative effects described earlier in part A's response. **The *net effect* leads to a +10.8% gain in ABC's stock price (i.e., $22.34 vs. $20.17) while the LCR* changes only slightly to 1.175.** In this scenario, the spreadsheet shows there is a 93.33% chance of avoiding a large cash outflow. The expected benefits of avoiding paying the higher 8% penalty rate of "hot money" therefore offset the opportunity cost of holding more funds in safe, liquid assets. This is a good example of how **stored liquidity** can be beneficial (in comparison to **purchased liquidity**) when system-wide liquidity risk rises significantly.

Chapter 9

1. **True.** Operational risk covers risks related to employees, customers, processes, and other potentially non-financial risks that a financial institution may face.
3. **A.** The process starts with identifying areas of potential operational risk and collecting relevant data. These data include internal and external operational risk loss data that can be used to develop key risk indicators (KRIs). KRIs can help monitor risk factors within the bank and provide early warning signals for areas of increasing risk to help avoid incurring future losses, as the bank can set baseline levels for KRIs that are used as thresholds to indicate emerging problems.
5. **C.** Equity capital can create a buffer to protect the bank from a large and unexpected loss. A larger buffer means that the bank has a greater distance to a default, thus protecting the liability holders (in many cases, these are the depositors) from a catastrophic operational event.
7. The power law is

$$\Pr(L > x) = kx^{-\alpha}$$

Given the information from the problem we can plug in

$$\Pr(L > \$10) = 0.4(\$10)^{-1.5} = 1.26\%$$

9. Answers are shown in the following:
   (A) In this case, we can see that ABC will increase its optimal operational risk-related hedging from 0.72% of total revenue (in the base case) to **0.905%** of total revenue. The added sensitivity to operational risk means that the bank will devote more attention and resources to managing it.
   (B) Moving from $k = 0.00001$ to $k = 0.00002$ means that the bank can increase its stock price by finding its optimal risk management practices but at a reduced level. In our base case, optimal hedging leads to an increase in the stock price of +3.0%, whereas in the increased-sensitivity scenario, the bank's optimal hedging level leads to a **+1.9%** increase in the stock price.
   (C) Due to the higher level of sensitivity, the power law estimates that the probability of operational losses exceeding 1.85% of revenues increases from 2.9% to **5.8%**.
   (D) In this case, the bank will optimally devote slightly more resources to managing operational risk (**0.74%** of revenue relative to 0.72% in the base case). The resulting net benefit from hedging this risk is a bit higher than in the base case, leading to a **+3.4%** increase in ABC's stock price.

Chapter 10

1. **False.** The FDIC, to resolve a failing or failed bank, will transfer healthy assets and deposits to another financial institution. The FDIC's cash payout is limited to funding the difference between the deposits of the failing bank and any healthy assets it can transfer.
3. **B.** Smaller banks tend to be "soft information" lenders who lend to "soft information" borrowers like small businesses and borrowers. "Soft information" borrowers tend to be more informationally opaque, and smaller banks have a relative strength in assessing their creditworthiness. As fewer small banks exist via consolidation, the amount of credit available to informationally opaque borrowers may decline.
5. **D.** FSOC's primary roles include monitoring threats to financial stability, facilitating coordination and information sharing among regulatory agencies, designating non-bank institutions for regulatory oversight

from the Federal Reserve, and recommending heightened standards for large financial institutions with the goal of mitigating threats to financial stability.

7. Tier 1 capital is related to the bank as a "going concern" and absorbs losses on an ongoing basis. Tier 2 capital is related to the bank as a "gone concern" and generally absorbs the bank's losses before depositors and other creditors when a bank fails.

9. Answers are shown in the following:
   (A) Here, we need to change the spreadsheet's industry average E/A from 8% to 9% and then re-run the *Solver* function as noted in the file. In doing so, we find that ABC's new optimal E/A ratio is now **10.13%** relative to our base case of 9.55%.
   (B) The stock price for ABC will increase by **+23.23%** if it changes to the new optimal E/A ratio, given the changes in industry expectations.
   (C) You can refer to Chapter 10 tab's range of cells from C40 to C50 to locate the new deposit rate corresponding to the various values of the E/A ratio found in cells A40 to A50. Since the bank's optimal E/A ratio remains *above* the industry average, investors do *not* view its capital structure as risky relative to peer institutions, so its deposit rate remains unchanged at **2.11%**, as the leverage dummy is "turned off" in this case. That is, depositors are not concerned about greater default risk because the E/A ratio is above the industry average. In contrast, if ABC's E/A ratio fell below the industry average, we would expect depositors to become more nervous and therefore demand a higher rate on their deposits.

Chapter 11

1. **True.** Systemic risk is the concern that a large or very interconnected financial institution will experience distress or failure, causing others to experience distress or fail at the same time.

3. **A.** The CoVaR family of measures uses a quantile regression methodology to estimate the impact of the distress of one financial institution on other institutions in the financial system. The terms in the estimation procedure can be rearranged to instead calculate the impact of the distress of the system as a whole on a single bank or institution.

490   *Managing Financial Institutions: An Integrated Valuation Approach*

5. **E.** As we outline in the chapter, all of these risks can impact the financial system, by altering a bank's contribution to or exposure to systemic risk.
7. "Too-Big-to-Fail" banks are large institutions whose failure can significantly amplify a financial crisis. "Too-Interconnected-to-Fail" banks are banks that are connected to other institutions and financial markets through interbank lending, derivatives, or other linkages. Their failure can lead to the realization of several risks in a cascading effect through the financial system, causing widespread bank failures. "Too-Many-to-Fail" banks are banks that fail simultaneously with many other (potentially smaller) banks, possibly due to correlated risk exposures.
9. According to the IVM, as systemic risk rises, the magnitude and timing (i.e., growth) of a bank's cash flows can drop sharply, while the riskiness of cash flows and the cost of equity spikes. This negatively impacts all three key value drivers (Magnitude, Riskiness, and Timing of cash flows), leading to a decrease in the bank's market value.

Chapter 12

1. **True.** The text mentions that IRM is a potentially powerful way to control risks in a comprehensive manner by solving for the optimal amounts of exposure over multiple risks simultaneously.
3. **A.** The text mentions that the "Introduction" tab summarizes a three-step process for managing the key risks described in the book and provides links to jump easily between each of these risks.
5. **C.** The *Solver* function is used to find the optimal levels of risk based on explicit cost–benefit analyses and any relevant constraints on this optimization process. By doing so, the spreadsheet can help us find the proper levels of risk that maximize ABC's stock price by using iterative, constrained optimization techniques.
7. Answers are shown in the following:

    By entering the relevant information provided above into the spreadsheet file, the **optimal hedge ratio (h^*) = –0.9320 or –93.20%.** This is based on the cost–benefit relationship described by Equation (5.12) related to hedging the portfolio's VaR: $-1 \cdot (2.33 \cdot \sigma_{UH}) / (2 \cdot v)) = -(2.33 \cdot 0.0040) / (2 \cdot 0.005)) = -(0.00932 / 0.01000) = -0.9320 = -93.2\%$.) where an indicator variable equals –1 when the bank owns (or is "long") some amount of marketable securities, S, which is the norm for FIs (i.e., $S > 0$). Thus, $h^* = -0.932$ means the bank **should sell short 93.2% of its market risk exposure** to maximize its stock price. Due to the increase in daily market volatility from 25 to 40 bps, there is now an incentive to hedge more of the securities portfolio.

Compared to the "Base" scenario's stock price of $20.17 shown in the spreadsheet, the above changes and hedge ratio of −0.932 can **increase the stock price by a relatively small +1.5% to $20.47**. Equation (5.13) shows that **Target VaR* = $(1 - |h^*|)$ · unhedged VaR = $(1 - |-.932|)$ · ($6.524 million) = $(0.068 \cdot \$6.524$ million) = $0.444 million**. So, after the hedge ratio of −93.2% has been implemented, the bank's target (or effective) VaR will drop from the original $1.702 million estimate to $0.444 million, which is much less than the base case's unhedged VaR of $4.078 million. Thus, the bank's market risk exposure has been reduced dramatically and will, in turn, help maximize its market value of equity.

By using the "Alternative Scenario" column in the "Integrated Risks – Chapter 12" tab for Market Risk and the **Solver** function, **the optimal hedge ratio of −0.9129 (or −91.29%) does *not* change very much from its stand-alone h^* estimate of −0.9320. However, the stock price improved by $2.45 per share, from $26.46 to $28.91, which is a +9.3% increase** over the original estimate of ABC's stock price under the "Base Scenario" column. This result suggests that hedging market risk on an integrated, simultaneous basis *does* improve a bank's stock price that much.

9. Answers are shown in the following:

(A) According to Equation (8.13) and the spreadsheet, an increase in expected outflows from $700 million to $900 million can have a *positive* effect on ABC's stock price because an optimal LCR* allows the bank to *avoid* a larger drain on liquidity. In addition, **the optimal LCR*, at 1.187, remains the same as before the increased expected outflows**. However, the *net effect* of this LCR on ABC's cash flow to *investors* is a *positive* one because there is now a *greater* benefit of avoiding this larger liquidity demand. **Thus, the change in ABC's stock price is *positive*, as it rises from the prior level of $24.63 to $25.91 per share (i.e., a +5.2% improvement)**. In this scenario, the costs outweigh the benefits regardless of which LCR is chosen, but, overall, an LCR* of

1.187 minimizes the overall decline in market value. That is, an LCR* of 1.187 does the best in terms of handling the negative effects of this increase in expected outflows to $900 million.

(B) By using the "Alternative Scenario" column in the "Integrated Risks – Ch 12" tab for Liquidity Risk and the **Solver** function, **the optimal LCR* of around 1.37 is 15% higher than the stand-alone's LCR* 1.187**. The **Solver** function found that this LCR* based on the integrated risk management approach can improve upon the stand-alone's LCR* in terms of stock price. For example, **the stock price *increases* by a relatively large $2.89 per share, which is an +11.2% gain when compared to the "Base Scenario" price estimate (from $25.83 to $28.72)**. The result suggests that hedging credit risk with an integrated, simultaneous approach can improve a bank's stock price. Thus, this exercise shows that ABC's managers can benefit from controlling some of its liquidity risks via an *integrated* approach. Clearly, this finding is specific to the assumptions used here and an integrated approach could lead to a different stock price estimate if we use alternative choices in terms of the key drivers of liquidity risk outlined in Chapter 8.

Glossary

Chapter 1

Adverse Selection: Lender may not be able to effectively screen out low-quality borrowers or may charge too little (or too much) interest relative to the true risk of a loan.

Asymmetric Information: The problem that lenders do not have a complete set of information about potential borrowers.

Borrowers: Those who face a shortfall of funds.

Brokerage: Do not hold securities issued by borrowers (unlike what a DI might do with loans) but rather pass these securities directly on to savers to hold.

Commercial Banks: Institutions that are primarily focused on lending while funding the pool of loans with deposits.

Commodity Futures Trading Commission (CFTC): Government agency that regulates U.S. derivatives markets (primarily futures and swaps contracts).

Credit Unions: Provide the same services as a traditional commercial bank, but it is structured as a nonprofit institution that is owned by its members (depositors).

Dealer: Work to make markets in certain securities (for example, in over-the-counter bond markets, or, importantly during the GFC, the mortgage-backed security markets), where they serve to bring together buyers and sellers, but act as a principal intermediary between the two, buying from the seller and selling to the buyer.

Delegated Monitors: DI acts on behalf of the depositors to screen out bad borrowers and to monitor the actions and behavior of borrowers to whom funds were allocated.

Economies of Scale: The ability of intermediaries to more efficiently gather and process information about potential borrowers.

Federal Deposit Insurance Corporation (FDIC): Provides deposit insurance to commercial banks and savings banks in the United States.

Federal Reserve: Central bank of the U.S. that controls monetary policy through its open-market operations.

Fee: Amount earned to manage process (typically based on a percentage of the dollar value of the assets under management).

Financial Industry Regulatory Authority (FINRA): Self-regulatory organization that oversees brokers, securities exchanges, and over-the-counter markets operating in the U.S.

Financial Institution (FI): Helps facilitate economic growth and channel funds from savers to borrowers.

Financial Intermediation: The main economic functions of financial institutions.

Free Rider: Issue where the high cost of monitoring creates a collective action problem, in which most (or all) lenders do not monitor but rather wait for another lender to do so.

Insurance Companies: FI that allows individuals to share risk by pooling funds.

Glossary   495

Investment Banks: Help those with funding shortfalls raise capital via underwriting new issuances of debt or equity, advise companies on mergers and acquisitions, and provide other services like asset management and securities research.

Liquidity Insurance: Financial institutions' assurance of availability of funds due to their ability to create liquidity cheaply and efficiently through economies of scales.

Maturity Mismatches: Liquidity problem where individuals who lend on their own would be faced with the challenge of aligning the maturities of their loans (or assets) with their need for repeated (e.g., utility bills and groceries) or unexpected (e.g., home or car repair) cash outflows.

Monitoring: Strong oversight, without which risk-averse lenders may be less likely to lend, or they may charge higher interest rates, which can impact economic growth.

Moral Hazard: When without oversight, a borrower could misappropriate these funds by taking on excessively risky projects or investments.

Office of the Comptroller of the Currency (OCC): Is a national regulator in the United States that charters, regulates, and supervises all national banks and thrift institutions and also maintains safety and soundness by monitoring bank asset quality, liquidity, and compliance, among other aspects of bank quality and management.

Positive Externality: Factors that positively affect all participants in the secondary market and can make for a more efficient allocation of scarce financial resources.

Price Risk: Risk associated with an individual who holds their own portfolio of loans and is subject to price fluctuations caused not only by liquidity (and asymmetric information) but also by market value fluctuations that can be related to interest rate shocks or to the credit quality of the borrowers.

Qualitative Asset Transformation (QAT): Process of obtaining financing via one type of financial instrument (e.g., a short-term bank deposit) and then "transforming" it by investing the proceeds in a different type of financial instrument (e.g., a long-term loan such as a mortgage).

Savers: Those with a surplus of funds.

Savings and Loan (Thrift): Focuses its lending portfolio on mortgages (by law, these institutions are restricted in what proportion of their loan portfolio is held in commercial loans and must meet a minimum threshold for how much of their loan portfolio is allocated to mortgage lending) but otherwise behaves in the same way as a traditional commercial bank.

Securities and Exchange Commission (SEC): Operates to regulate financial markets, in which financial institutions providing brokerage functions operate.

Securities Brokers: Perform a brokerage function, by bringing together buyers and sellers of securities for direct ownership and typically earn a commission for doing so.

Search and Transaction Costs: Costs associated with the fact that without access to a financial institution with a large source of funds available to lend, borrowers would need to source their funding from many lenders.

Signals: Indicators of a borrower's quality that a bank must identify in order to solve the asymmetric information problem.

Spread: Difference between loan rate at which it lends and the financing rate it must pay to depositors and/or other creditors.

State Regulatory Authorities: Each U.S. State has its own banking regulatory authority that oversees banks within the state, regulating them under the state's own set of banking rules and regulations.

Stored Liquidity: Pool of liquid assets (cash and treasuries) bank maintains to help with liquidity needs such as deposit withdrawals or loan drawdowns.

Systemic Risk: Risk of system-wide breakdown of the economy.

Chapter 2

Depreciation and Amortization: Expenses that have been paid in cash upfront by the firm but are expensed over the purchased asset's useful life.

Discounted Cash Flow (DCF): Model based on idea that the market value of the company's assets is equal to the present value of the future cash flows it is expected to generate over time.

Dividend Discount Model (DDM): Special case of DCF based on dividend payments.

Free Cash Flow (FCF): The cash a company generates after it accounts for the cash needed to run its operations and maintain its fixed assets.

Free Cash Flow to Equity (FCFE): The amount of cash that the firm has available to pay dividends or conduct stock buybacks.

Ohlson Valuation Model: Model based on idea that the value of equity is equal to the sum of the current book value of equity and the present value of the excess profits the firm generates.

Residual Income: The profit the firm generates beyond what it needs to pay back its shareholders (or after subtracting out the opportunity cost of retaining a portion of current earnings).

Weighted Average Cost of Capital (WACC): Accounts for the cost of each of a firm's capital sources (e.g., typically debt, preferred stock, and common stock) and is a proxy for the average rate of return required from all the firm's investors.

Chapter 3

Allowance for Loan Losses: Estimate of future credit losses.

Bank Operating Profit: Profit generated by the firm when management does not choose to hedge any of its risks (generated from a "No Hedge" or "Do Nothing" risk management policy).

Capital Gain: Equals the projected percentage change in the firm's stock price.

Cost of the Bank's Debt Funding: Represents the average interest rate the bank pays on all debt (including deposit and other borrowed money, or OBM) multiplied by the total amount of debt.

Credit Allocation: A bank's allocation of assets to its loan portfolio (gross loans divided by total gross assets).

Dividend Payout Ratio (d): The ratio of Dividends divided by Net Income (DIV/NI) so that d represents the portion of a bank's profit that is distributed to shareholders each year.

Expected Equity Return (R_E): Term in IVM that captures the analyst's best guess of what shareholders anticipate in terms of a satisfactory return on its stock investment.

Hedge Effects: Term within IVM that captures the effect of a bank's decision to hedge risk, assuming that there are explicit marginal costs related to managing this risk relative to its implicit marginal benefits.

Integrated Valuation Model (IVM): More detailed valuation model based on DDM that integrates both the FIs risk-taking and risk-management choices in an explicit way so that we can identify the primary positive and negative effects of management's decisions on firm value in a more direct manner.

Liquidity Risk Effects: Term within IVM that deals with liquidity constraints.

Loan Loss Provisions (LLP): Represent a non-cash expense that takes account of the bank's best estimate about what are the expected future incremental credit losses that are not already accounted for on the Balance Sheet via the Allowance for Loan Losses (ALL).

Market Risk Premium: Measures how much extra return is required for a risk-averse investor to invest in the market portfolio rather than hold a risk-free security such as a 10-year Treasury note.

Glossary 499

MRT (aka Value Drivers): The three key drivers of firm value are magnitude, riskiness, and timing of cash flows where timing relates to when dividends will occur in the future and is captured by the growth in dividends.

Negative Dividend: Capital infusion to meet target capital ratio.

Net Interest Income (NII): Difference between the Interest Income banks earn and the Interest Expense they pay.

Other Borrowed Money (OBM): Represents all other liabilities that are not defined as traditional bank deposits and includes "hot money" items that can be relatively quickly withdrawn from the balance sheet such as Fed Funds Purchased, Repurchase Agreements (repos), and Commercial Paper, as well as longer-term liabilities like Medium Term Notes and Long-Term Bonds.

Return on Equity (ROE): Net income divided by common equity.

Retention Ration: One minus the Dividend Payout ratio.

Sustainable Growth Rate (g): Provides an estimate of how fast the firm's earnings and dividends can grow without issuing new equity or changing the bank's profitability and capital structure.

Chapter 4

Asset Liability Management (ALM): Managing refinancing and reinvestment risk through methods including interest rate hedging.

ARM: A manager's choices in terms of the dollar Amount (A), Rates (R), and Mix (M) of assets and liabilities on its balance sheet.

Cost–Benefit Analysis: Economic concept that a bank should choose an optimal level of hedging (h^*) where the marginal benefits and costs of hedging are equal.

Duration: The weighted average time-to-maturity of financial instruments.

Fixed Costs: Include all explicit, direct costs to start up and maintain a risk management team even if they do not hedge any exposures (usually include compensation for risk management personnel, as well as expenses for data, software, and any general overhead for the team).

Hedge Ratio: Way to measure how much to reduce a bank's interest rate risk exposure; shows what percentage of the bank's total exposure is hedged by some type of interest rate derivative.

Hedging Rule of Thumb: Estimates the upfront fixed costs of a risk management program and compares this cost to the program's potential benefits.

Macro Hedging: Looks holistically at the bank's specific risks (such as interest rate risk) across the entire balance sheet rather than focusing on sub-components of assets and liabilities (enables us to consider the trade-off between risk and return in terms of its overall effect on the bank's market value).

Micro Hedging: Specific sub-component of a bank's interest rate risk such as long-term bonds within its securities portfolio.

Minimum Variance Hedge Ratio: Estimated by performing a regression analysis of historical changes in the bank's risk exposure relative to past changes in a derivative security's value.

M-M Irrelevance Proposition: Implication that anything investors can do themselves; there is no benefit for the firm to do.

Modified Duration Gap (MDGAP): Takes a longer-term view by considering all future inflows and outflows from the bank's assets and liabilities to quantify the impact of interest rate shocks on the bank's market value of equity.

Off-Balance Sheet Hedging: Bank's choice to manage interest rate risk via derivative instruments, such as interest rate forwards, futures, options, and swaps.

On-Balance Sheet Hedging: Refers to the bank's choice to manage this interest rate risk by adjusting the maturity/duration of its assets relative to its liabilities.

Optimal Hedge Ratio (h^*): Enables the marginal benefit of hedging to equal the marginal cost of this risk management strategy and thus maximizes the bank's stock price.

Rate Sensitive Assets (RSA): Assets that will be affected by changes in interest rates over the next 12 months.

Rate Sensitive Liabilities (RSL): The dollar amount of deposits and Other Borrowed Money (OBM) that will mature within the 1-year period or which have a variable interest rate.

Refinancing Risk (Reinvestment Risk): A firm's exposure to uncertainty about rates when a longer period security is exchanged for shorter-term securities spread over that time period.

Repricing Gap (RGAP): Difference between RSA and RSL and a measure of short-term interest rate risk.

Runoffs: Caused when there is a sudden withdrawal of longer-term deposits and/or the early repayment of long-term loans; results in duration of assets and liabilities to shorten.

Variable Costs: Pertain to the actual expenses related to initiating and monitoring the bank's hedging positions, such as brokerage fees, bid-ask spreads, and margin/collateral requirements.

Chapter 5

Autocorrelation: Interrelationships between variable today and previous versions of itself.

Daily Earnings at Risk (DEAR): 1-day Value at Risk.

Diversification Benefit (Covariance Adjustment): By not putting the bank's money all in one "basket" of securities, the total portfolio's risk is substantially reduced because declines in, say, bonds could be offset by gains in stocks and currencies.

Expected Shortfall (ES): Represents the expected change in the bank's investment portfolio when it experiences an "extreme event" such as when the portfolio's loss exceeds its 1-day VaR.

Explicit Direct Hedging Costs: Costs associated with things such as bid-ask spreads, commissions, computer equipment, data services, and risk management personnel expenses.

Extreme Value Theory (EVT): Attempts to address the issue of sensitive outliers when using information far below the 1% threshold by borrowing from existing statistical techniques used in the physical sciences to help quantify rare events that represent large outliers.

Fat-Tailed (Leptokurtic) Distribution: When the average return and the two extreme tails of the distribution are more likely to occur when compared to a normally distributed set of investment returns (and this is especially true when considering assets that are less liquid, for example).

Implicit Indirect Hedging Costs: Include costs such as time spent by senior management supervising the risk managers and the opportunity cost of using the direct hedging costs for other potentially more valuable purposes within the bank.

Market Risk: Represents the possibility that the prices of a bank's main assets (e.g., loans, investments, and, for larger FI's, trading operations) can quickly decline in value due to changes in financial market conditions.

Monte Carlo Simulation (MC): Approach to calculating VaR that enables the analyst to use historical return data, along with summary statistics of the components of the portfolio's time series (e.g., the means, standard deviations, and correlations of the bond, stock, currency, and commodity investments) to create hypothetical returns for the portfolio that might occur in the future.

Net Exposure: Amount of risk the bank is exposed to (measured by subtracting the amount the bank has sold (short) from the amount the bank currently owns (long)).

Optimal (Target) VaR: Metric derived from the optimal hedge ratio that can help maximize the bank's stock value.

Portfolio Allocation Caps: Used to reduce a bank's incentive to invest a large portion of its portfolio in the riskiest types of securities.

RiskMetrics Approach (or Variance–Covariance VaR method): Approach to calculate VaR assumes that returns to an investment portfolio are normally distributed.

Value-at-Risk (VaR): Shows how much exposure to "tail risk" a bank's investment portfolio and/or trading operation possesses (assuming that a "high impact" but "low frequency" event is most concerning in terms of a bank's market risk).

What-If Simulation: Quantifies the Total Costs and Benefits of hedging the bank's market risk.

Zero-Risk Cash Account: Part of portfolio that behaves as a perfect hedge.

Chapter 6

Black Box: Difficulty of understanding why a machine learning model generated a specific decision.

Capacity: Represents the borrower's ability to repay the bank from internal sources, such as their cash flow and cash (or "near-cash") balances.

Capital: Refers to how much equity is invested in the business (or, for an individual, how much net worth they possess).

Character: Lender's overall assessment of the borrower's trustworthiness and willingness to repay the loan.

Collateral: Borrower pledges some asset (such as a fixed income instrument or a house/building) that can be taken by the bank if principal and interest are not fully repaid (protection for lender).

Concentration Limits: Limits that ensure that the bank's assets are well-diversified and not highly concentrated within a specific asset type (or within an industry sector or individual borrower).

Condition: (1) the loan-specific conditions (e.g., purpose of the loan and any restrictions/covenants related to the loan) and (2) the local economic and/or industry-specific conditions in which the borrower operates.

Credit: To believe or trust.

Credit Default Swap (CDS): A credit insurance product where a bank can pay an upfront fee as well as annual premiums to another FI to insure against a default by the bank's borrower(s).

Credit Portfolio: A bank's portfolio of loans and bonds.

Credit Risk: Represents the possibility that the bank's borrowers do not fully repay the principal and interest they owe on their loans to the financial institution.

Credit RiskMetrics: Concept with basic underlying assumption that the returns to a credit portfolio are normally distributed (which can be a questionable assumption for a fixed income investment); method allows managers to decide whether the tail risk associated with the bank's credit portfolio represents an acceptable amount of risk in relation to its equity capital.

Credit Value-at-Risk (CvaR): Shows how much exposure an FI has to "tail risk" within a bank's loans and risky bond investments.

Distance to Default (DD): Represents the percentage difference between a firm's assets and its default "trigger" relative to the volatility of its assets.

Expected Default Frequency (EDF): Measures the probability that loans that possess certain characteristics could default.

Loan Covenants: Restrictions on borrowers such as maximum debt-to-asset ratio.

Loss Given Default (LGD): Percentage of principal lost due to the default.

Margin Accounts: Make sure that counterparties have sufficient cash on hand to cope with daily fluctuations in their trading positions.

Merton/KMV credit model: Provides an objective estimate of a firm's PD based on the collective judgment and trading of stock market participants (provides the stock market's forward-looking opinion of what the firm's PD could be over a loan's life).

Macro Hedge: Hedge of total portfolio.

Micro Hedge: Occurs because the fixed costs and exponentially rising variable hedging costs limit the benefits of hedging bond investment.

Mortality Model: Approach developed by Altman that used historical data and principles from actuarial science to estimate a corporate bond's probability of default.

On-Balance Sheet Risk Management: A direct way to manage a bank's credit risk by controlling its impact on financial statements through making careful and conscious decisions to hold a well-diversified portfolio of bonds and loans.

Perfect Hedge: Equivalent to converting h-percentage portion of the bank's investments into an interest-free (and risk-free) cash account.

Probability of Default (PD): Likelihood of not getting repaid and ranges between 0% and 100%.

Ration: Restricting loans to only high-quality borrowers with, for example, relatively strong credit scores or who can put down relatively large down payments/deposits for the purchase of an asset.

Recovery Rate: Percentage of loan that is repaid.

Risk-Adjusted Return on Capital (RAROC): Helps decide whether a loan, bond, or entire credit portfolio is delivering an acceptable return for the level of risk the bank is facing.

Tail Risk: A very low probability of a large loss.

Term Structure model: Approach uses the current yield to maturity of government and corporate bonds for varying maturities (e.g., 1- and 2-year yields) to infer the likelihood of default for a company that has a similar bond rating.

Trading Limits: Ensure the total dollar exposure to counterparties does not exceed acceptable debt levels.

Yield Curve: A graph of bond yields for different maturities that all have the same credit risk.

Chapter 7

Asset-Backed Securities: Packaged collections of relatively homogeneous assets such as auto loans, credit card receivables, and mortgages created to sell to other investors.

Asset Securitization: Activities like selling off some of its mortgages or other loans such as credit cards and/or auto loans.

Call Options: Gives a corporate borrower the right (but not obligation) to "call away" funds from the bank.

Cleaned Up: When borrowings must be fully repaid for at least one month during the period after a commercial line of credit is extended for one year.

Contingent Assets (CA): Allow banks to provide liquidity to their clients while boosting the bank's fee and interest income (include lines of credit, loan commitments, and letters of credit).

Glossary

Contingent Financing Needs: Demands for cash that must be financed by FI (i.e., lines of credit, loan commitments, letters of credit, loan guarantees, and derivative securities transactions).

Delta: The dollar change in contingent assets *relative to* the dollar change in the firm's financing needs.

Derivatives Transactions: Use of derivative securities such as forward and futures contracts, as well as options and swaps, to manage risk and/or speculate on price movements in financial markets.

Exercise: In reference to the option-like nature of OBS risk, it pertains to the situation where a bank is therefore obligated to provide funds whenever the corporate borrower needs them because the borrower has cash needs that *exceed* the firm's internal liquidity resources.

In-the-Money (ITM): If the firms' financing needs are *greater than* its excess cash.

Letters of Credit (L/C): A "backstop" form of credit support for a commercial client, often used to facilitate international trade between buyers and sellers who do not know much about the counterparty's creditworthiness.

Liability-Based Contingencies: Contingency-based services that, when exercised, lead to a *liability* being added to the bank's balance sheet.

Lines of Credit: Bank pre-approves a dollar amount limit based on how much the bank is willing to lend to a customer on an "on-demand" basis.

Loan Commitments: Used by commercial borrowers that are planning to need a relatively large amount of financing sometime in the next 1–2 years.

Loan Guarantees: Act as a credit backstop to facilitate business and consumer transactions (the bank normally charges an annual fee of 2% or less to compensate for the possibility that the bank's client does not make its promised payment(s) to another creditor).

Matrix Approach: Analysis method where a bank analyst can vary both delta estimates to create a range of possible effects on the bank's common equity and capital ratio.

Moneyness: Dynamic between in-the-money and out-of-the-money options (with *greater* moneyness existing when the option is *more* ITM).

Notional Value: Bank's total dollar amount of lines, commitments, L/Cs, and derivative positions it has offered to its customers.

Off-Balance Sheet Risk (OBS): Pertains to the impact on the FI's performance when a bank's future obligations quickly turn into actual outflows to its customers or other counterparties.

Reinsurance: For insurance firms, a way of offsetting risk where firm can *buy* a CDS to offset some or all risk associated with a CDS contract it has sold and is worried may default.

Strike Price: Price at which option can be exercised.

Supplementary Leverage Ratio (SLR): Broader definition of the equity capital ratio.

Takedowns: Depending on the client's relationship with the bank, a small annual fee of 0.1% to 2.0% of the maximum limit of the line of credit might be charged to compensate the FI for having to hold in reserve enough liquidity to finance future drawdowns on the line.

Chapter 8

Asset-Based Liquidity Risk: Refers to sudden customer demands for bank funds to finance items, such as pre-approved lines of credit, loan commitments, and letters of credit.

Bank Run: Occurs when many depositors and other creditors "run" to withdraw their funds simultaneously from a bank (caused by news or uncertainty).

Banking Panic: Occurs when the run on one bank causes creditors of other banks to suddenly withdraw their funds from these other FIs, causing stress across the entire banking system.

Financing Diamond: Alternative financing choice when core deposits are minimal or non-existent.

Financing Needs: Bank's total needs to cover incremental expenses, withdrawals, and investments.

Financing Pyramid: Basic logic that the bank should rely first and foremost on low-cost and stable sources of financing such as insured deposits and then, if that is not sufficient to meet all financing needs, to then rely on higher-cost and more volatile financing, such as OBM and, ultimately, Common Equity.

High-Quality Liquid Assets (HQLA): Level 1 assets + Level 2A assets + Level 2B assets.

Liability-Based Liquidity Risk: Refers to sudden demands for bank funds to finance deposit withdrawals or make payments to other parties such as creditors, Credit Default Swap (CDS) owners, regulators (for fines), and plaintiffs (for lawsuits).

Liquidity: The ability to quickly convert a financial instrument into cash at, or close to, its fair market value.

Liquidity Coverage Ratio (LCR): Ratio of high-quality liquid assets to expected 30-day net cash outflows.

Liquidity Index (LI): Attempts to quantify the potential losses on a bank's assets if some of them must be sold quickly at "fire sale" prices to meet a rapid surge in liquidity needs.

Liquidity Risk: FI's exposure to sudden demands for cash from its customers that need to borrow and/or withdraw funds (frequency and severity of cash demands can vary widely and unexpectedly).

Loan-to-Deposit Ratio (LN/Depo): Simple ratio of the average levels of Total Gross Loans to Total Deposits (liquidity risk higher when LN / Depo is higher because it means more deposits are needed to fund the bank's lending activity).

Maturity Mismatch: Mismatch in duration that occurs when depository FIs make longer-term, illiquid loans that are typically financed by highly liquid shorter-term deposits because they can be withdrawn (i.e., converted into cash) at a moment's notice.

Purchased Liquidity: When a bank can raise cash for financing by obtaining additional borrowing.

Stored Liquidity: When a bank can raise cash for financing by selling other assets or holding cash outright.

Chapter 9

Business Indicator Component (BIC): A measure of income that grows with the bank's size.

Governance, Risk, and Control (GRC) Methods: Tools that can reduce both the frequency and severity of fraud, administrative errors, etc.

Internal Loss Multiplier (ILM): Related to the bank's operational risk losses over the previous ten years.

Key Risk Indicators (KRIs): Indicators that can help monitor risk factors within the bank and provide early warning signals for areas of increasing risk to help avoid incurring future losses (banks can set baseline levels for KRIs that are used as thresholds to indicate emerging problems).

Lines of Defense: Business line level, enterprise level, and internal audit help provide security.

Operational Risk: The risk related to people and processes at financial institutions.

Operational Risk Management: Spending related to dealing with operational risks.

Optimal Cost Ratio (OC*): Ratio that equates the marginal benefit to the marginal cost of the operational risk management strategy and thus maximizes the bank's stock price.

Risk Control Self-Assessments (RCSA): A systematic process by which the firm reviews its operational risk controls and can prioritize remediation efforts for shortfalls (can always choose to simply accept the risk as well).

Risk-Based Capital (RBC): Regulation of capital requirements to insulate the bank's debtholders against a large, unexpected loss (considers bank size and track record of operational risk losses).

Chapter 10

2010 Dodd–Frank Wall Street Reform and Consumer Protection Act: Legislation passed after the GFC that brought a focus on systemic risk, the risk of financial system failure, to the forefront.

Additional Tier 1 (AT1): Items that are not part of the bank's common equity but can behave like equity and absorb losses when needed, like hybrid securities such as preferred stock.

Bank Term Funding Program: Created by the Federal Reserve during the 2023 regional bank crisis, allowing banks to borrow against their U.S. Treasury and agency debt/MBS holdings at par value.

Capital Adequacy: Acceptable level for the E/A ratio.

Capital Conservation Buffer: Meant to make sure that banks have an additional layer of capital that can be used to absorb losses.

Capital Requirements: Set rules for the portion of a bank's funding that must come from equity. The aim is to create a buffer to protect the bank's depositors and other liabilities holders from a large decrease in the value of the bank's assets.

Common Equity Tier 1 (CET1): Regarded as the highest-quality capital the bank has; it can absorb losses the instant they occur.

Community Reinvestment Act (CRA): Regulation enacted in 1977 that requires the Federal Reserve and other regulators (namely, the FDIC and the Office of the Comptroller of the Currency, OCC) to ensure that commercial banks are meeting the credit needs of the communities within which they operate.

Comprehensive Capital Analysis and Review (CCAR): 2011 qualitative and quantitative assessment, of which the results were publicly reported, that checked whether institutions had enough capital to withstand times of economic and financial stress.

Consumer Financial Protection Bureau (CFPB): An independent bureau that exists within the Federal Reserve to protect "consumers from unfair, deceptive, or abusive practices and take action against companies that break the law."

Contractionary Monetary Policy: Employed by the central bank to restrict the amount of cash in the financial system, thus making it scarcer, and raising its price (that is, interest rates); could include increasing reserve requirements.

Countercyclical Capital Buffer (CCyB): Meant to "protect the banking sector from periods of excess aggregate credit growth."

Deposit Insurance: Run by a governmental entity and protects deposits (although not all deposits, as some can be uninsured) against the failure of a depository institution.

Dodd–Frank Act Stress Tests (DFAST): A stress test in which banks simulate the impact of worst-case scenarios on their business; each year, the Federal Reserve presents at least two different stress scenarios for banks to consider.

Equity Capital Ratio (E/A) or Capital Adequacy Ratio: Key factor that can affect a bank's market value of equity; can be viewed as a safety buffer to protect the bank from becoming insolvent if the bank experiences large, unexpected losses.

Expansionary Monetary Policy: Employed by the central bank to increase the supply of available money and thus lower interest rates; could include reducing reserve requirements so that banks can lend more.

Financial Stability Oversight Council (FSOC): Created by Dodd–Frank; primary roles include monitoring threats to financial stability, facilitating coordination and information sharing among regulatory agencies, designating nonbank institutions for regulatory oversight from the Federal Reserve, and recommending heightened standards for large financial institutions with the goal of mitigating threats to financial stability.

Liquidity Coverage Ratio: Ensures that banks have enough stored liquidity to withstand 30 days of typical cash outflows.

Net Stable Funding Ratio: Designed to ensure that banks have stable sources of funding to guide them through a difficult period, as shorter-term funding (also referred to as "hot money") can be a source of instability.

Office of Financial Research (OFR): Created by Dodd–Frank; supports FSOC's mission through research and data/information collection.

Orderly Liquidation Authority (OLA): Created by Dodd–Frank to organize the process by which the liquidation of large financial institutions can occur and expand these rules to cover nonbank financial institutions and insurance companies.

Orderly Liquidation Fund: Created by Dodd–Frank and overseen by the FDIC to unwind an institution that is not insured by the FDIC or the Securities Investor Protection Corporation (SIPC).

Quantitative Easing (QE): When central bank purchases a large amount of Treasuries (and in recent years mortgage-backed securities) to stimulate economic activity.

Redlining: Practice of discriminating against low-income neighborhoods.

Regulatory Forbearance: When regulators make a choice to not intervene with a troubled bank or set of banks.

Risk-Weighted Assets (RWA): Is the sum of all the bank's risk-weighted assets (allows the bank and regulators to properly view the bank's size in the context of the riskiness of its assets).

Stress Capital Buffer: For stress-tested banking, this is an additional capital buffer (minimum of 2.5%) that replaces the capital conservation buffer.

Stress Testing: A simulation exercise in which bankers and regulators test how the bank would perform under severely adverse conditions.

Supervisory Capital Assessment Program (SCAP): First iteration of stress tests in 2009.

Threshold Effect: The cost of debt remains stable at first but then rises as the bank's leverage is raised above some "threshold," as defined as the industry average level of financial leverage.

Tier 1 Capital: Bank's capital that absorbs losses on an ongoing basis, and within this category, banks must also differentiate between *Common Equity Tier 1* **(CET1)** and *Additional Tier 1* **(AT1)**.

Tier 2 Capital: Generally items that absorb the bank's losses before depositors and other creditors (e.g., loan loss provisions) when a bank fails.

Too Big to Fail (TBTF): As regulators show their willingness (or the necessity) to rescue or bail out the largest financial institutions in the event of a potential bank failure, the incentive for a bank to grow in size (to access government bailouts) increases.

Troubled Asset Relief Program (TARP): Noteworthy action during the GFC where the U.S. Treasury bought troubled mortgage-backed securities to help recapitalize the financial system and increase its liquidity.

Volcker Rule: Created by Dodd–Frank to limit the ability for commercial banks to engage in proprietary trading, a practice in which a bank would use depositors' funds to trade (or make potentially speculative investments) on behalf of the bank itself.

Chapter 11

Bank Capital Requirements: Regulations aimed at keeping banks safe via building up capital buffers (linked to various sources of risk), while also conveying to the public that banks are in compliance with the guidelines, thus strengthening public perception of the safety of the financial system.

Certification Mechanism: Aimed at keeping public trust in financial institutions high, thus limiting the likelihood of bank runs.

Conditional Value-at-Risk (ΔCoVaR): A measure of systemic risk that estimates the contribution of a single institution to the total losses suffered by all institutions in the financial system, conditional on the occurrence of a financial crisis.

First Lines of Defense: Policies to reduce the probability of a future crisis, or should one occur, reduce its severity.

Herding: As small and medium-sized banks are far less likely to receive bailout protection from regulators, they may be incentivized to correlate their risk-taking and risk-exposures to potentially fail simultaneously in the event of a financial calamity.

Interconnections: Banks that are connected to other institutions and financial markets through interbank lending, derivatives, or other linkages.

Liquidity Requirements: Meant to lessen the probability of a shock to a bank's liquidity, which can then lead to reduced distress or failure.

Long-Run Marginal Expected Shortfall (Long-Run MES): Represents the decline in the bank's stock value conditional on a financial crisis.

Monetary Policy: The central bank's control over the country's money supply.

Prudential Mechanism: Regulators cover choices made at the bank level, such as leverage risk, liquidity risk, or credit risk.

Prudential Supervision: Government regulators monitor bank behavior through on-site exams and submitted reports.

Regulatory Forbearance: Relaxed enforcement of regulations.

Shadow banks: Financial institutions that perform functions like those of banks but do not rely on deposits for funding (i.e., hedge funds, private equity, money market mutual funds).

Sovereign risk: The risk that an individual country can default on its obligations.

SRISK: Estimates the potential capital shortfall a bank would face if a systemic crisis were to occur; measures the amount of capital a bank would need to maintain a given capital ratio during a crisis.

Subsidy Mechanism: Governments can directly support financial institutions.

Too-Big-to-Fail (TBTF): An institution considered this if it is large enough that its distress or failure can spill over to other institutions, causing them distress or even their own failure.

Too-Many-to-Fail (TMTF): Concern that many (potentially smaller) banks fail simultaneously, possibly due to correlated risk exposures.

Chapter 12

Bank Operating Profit: A summary variable for all pretax operating profit items not directly included in the bank's risk management decisions.

Hedge Ratio: Between 0 (no hedging) and 1.0 (hedging the entire risk exposure).

Integrated Risk Management (IRM): Model that shows how a bank can increase firm value by solving for the optimal amounts of exposure over multiple risks simultaneously.

Liquidity Risk Cost: The opportunity cost of stored liquidity incurred by holding excess cash on the balance sheet.

Index

A

Additional Tier 1 Capital, 395
adverse selection, 6–8, 14, 220–221, 428
Asset-based Liquidity Risk, 312
Asset Liability Management, 108, 126, 146, 332
asymmetric information, 3–4, 6, 8, 11, 15, 77, 127, 220

B

banking panic, x, 310–312, 331, 390–391, 404
Bank Operating Profit, 65, 67, 452
bank run, x, 15, 250, 310–311, 331, 349, 390–391, 426, 432–433
Bank Term Funding Program, 403
borrowers, 1–3, 5–9, 11–12, 14, 20, 24, 76–79, 151, 157, 211, 214, 221–222, 224, 232–233, 251, 275–276, 278, 287, 303, 387, 394, 403, 428
brokerage, 2–4, 18–19, 22, 24, 66, 132, 165
Business Indicator Component, 367

C

Capacity, 213
Capital, 18, 29, 39, 73, 75, 86, 89, 91, 93, 175, 213, 356, 360, 366, 393–394, 396–398, 400, 405–406, 411–412, 430
capital conservation buffer, 397–398, 400
capital requirements, 52, 90, 181, 366, 384, 389, 394–395, 398, 400, 432–433
Certification Mechanism, 432–433
Character, 214
Collateral, 213
commercial banks, 1–2, 17, 19, 21, 76–77, 168, 247, 278, 321, 335, 399, 402, 405, 439
Commodity Futures Trading Commission, 19
Common Equity Tier 1, 395–396, 514
Community Reinvestment Act, 405
Comprehensive Capital Analysis and Review, 400
concentration limits, 212, 249, 263, 295–296

Conditional Value at Risk (ΔCoVaR), 420
Consumer Financial Protection Bureau, 405
contingent assets, 274–275, 285–290, 292–294, 297–298, 304, 460
contingent financing needs, 273–274
contractionary monetary policy, 399
countercyclical capital buffer, 397–398, 426
credit default swaps, x, 15, 250, 263, 274, 280, 290, 304
Credit Risk, 14, 66, 76, 80–82, 88, 173, 211, 221, 243, 246, 248, 251, 256–258, 260–261, 263, 280, 283, 295
credit unions, 20, 405
Credit Value at Risk (CVaR), 232–235, 237–245, 251–253, 255–260

D
dealer, 19, 22, 331, 403
delegated monitors, 3, 8–9, 337
delta, 266, 287–290, 292, 294, 298, 300–302, 323–326, 344, 350, 378, 410, 447, 452
deposit insurance, 17, 20, 76, 312, 389–391, 393–394, 398, 426, 433
Depreciation & Amortization, 29
Discounted Cash Flow, 28, 62, 87
diversification effect, 177
Dividend Discount Model, x, 28, 36–37, 52, 62–63, 75, 84, 87, 89–91
Dodd-Frank, 297, 400–402, 405, 424
Dodd-Frank Act Stress Tests, 400
duration, 14, 100, 114–124, 126, 146, 151–158, 162, 174, 176, 236, 245–246

E
equity capital ratio, 55, 294, 299, 302, 405, 407–408
expansionary monetary policy, 399
Expected Equity Return, 71, 73–75, 80
Expected Shortfall, 168, 171–172, 189–190, 207, 422

F
Federal Deposit Insurance Corporation, 17, 391
Federal Reserve, 8, 17–18, 66, 114, 123, 150, 193, 318, 339, 356, 359, 388, 399–405, 429
fee, 3–4, 20–21, 275–277, 280, 282, 304, 312, 367, 452
fixed costs, 136, 138, 143
Financial Industry Regulatory Authority, 18
Financial Stability Oversight Council, 401
Financing Diamond, 317, 320, 326
financing needs, 23, 285–287, 290, 318–319, 321–325
Financing Pyramid, 317, 319, 326
first lines of defense, 423, 431–433
fixed costs, 58, 67, 132, 206, 254, 256–257, 261, 376, 445, 505
free cash flow, 29, 31–33, 35–36, 85
Free Cash Flow to Equity, 35, 52, 60, 62, 85

H
Hedge Effects, 56, 65, 68, 103, 248, 452–453
hedge ratio, 129, 134–144, 195, 197–206, 253–255, 257–258, 260–261, 443–444, 446
herding, 425
High Quality Liquid Assets, 328, 340, 343, 345, 447

Index 519

I
Insurance companies, 8, 21–24, 215, 365
Integrated Risk Management, x, 72, 144, 439, 451, 453–454, 459, 461, 465
Integrated Valuation Model, viii, x, 10, 13, 28, 51–52, 68, 73, 84, 88, 104, 255, 419, 431, 441, 465
interconnections, 17, 424, 434
Internal Loss Multiplier, 367
in-the-money, 287, 325
investment banks, 1, 20, 278

K
key risk indicators, 361

L
Letters of Credit, 212, 276–277
Liability-based Contingencies, 280
Liability-based Liquidity Risk, 310, 314
Lines of credit, 274
liquidity, 67–68, 84, 89, 99, 145, 147, 149, 151, 202, 315–322, 341–349, 389–390
Liquidity Coverage Ratio, 324, 327–328, 340–343, 345, 348, 399, 432, 442, 448, 452, 462
liquidity requirements, 398, 431–433
liquidity risk, viii, x, 7, 9, 13, 15, 22, 59, 68, 84, 151, 273–274, 283, 309–311, 313, 315–322, 324–327, 329–335, 337–344, 346–349, 399, 426, 431–432, 439, 442, 446, 449, 451, 453, 462, 464
Liquidity Risk Cost, 89, 345, 448
Liquidity Risk Effects, 56, 58, 65, 67, 69–70, 89, 103, 452–453
Loan Commitments, x, 15, 276, 285, 303–304, 312, 397
loan covenants, 214, 221, 249, 263

loan guarantees, 115, 123, 277
Loan Loss Provision, 56, 66, 96, 103, 247–248, 283, 395
Long-Run MES, 422
Loss Given Default, 216–220

M
macro hedging, 130, 261
Market Risk, 13–14, 125, 165, 168, 192–194, 196, 203, 205, 232, 234, 251–252, 403, 442–446
Merton / KMV credit model, 230, 268
micro hedging, 130, 257–258, 261
minimum variance hedge ratio, 130, 198
M-M Irrelevance Proposition, 126
Modified Duration Gap, 115, 118, 122, 146, 462
Monetary policy, 429
monitoring, 2–4, 7–9, 13, 18–19, 24, 132, 165, 280, 362–363, 390, 401, 431
Monte Carlo simulation, 183, 185, 207, 241–242
moral hazard, 7–9, 15, 213, 220–221, 319, 390–391, 393–394, 398, 424, 426, 428, 433
mortality model, 223

N
net exposure, 167
net interest income, x, 56–57, 99–101

O
Off Balance Sheet Risk, 249–250, 273
Office of Financial Research, 401
Office of the Comptroller of the Currency, 18, 405
Ohlson Valuation, 43
On-balance sheet hedging, 126

Operational Risk, 16, 67, 169, 355–356, 360–361, 364, 366, 374, 377, 381–383, 427
optimal cost ratio, 381
optimal hedge ratio, 135–138, 141–143, 198, 202–205, 255–258, 261, 445–446
Orderly Liquidation Authority, 402
Orderly Liquidation Fund, 402
Other Borrowed Money, 53, 101, 103, 118, 161, 247, 282–284, 313–317, 348, 477

P

probability of default, 215, 217, 220, 223, 228–229, 231–232, 265
prudential mechanism, 432
prudential supervision, 433
purchased liquidity, 10, 283, 312, 315–317, 322, 335–338, 340, 343–344, 346–347, 390, 446

Q

qualitative asset transformation, 2, 165, 211
quantitative easing, 404

R

Rate Sensitive Assets, 101, 136, 145
Rate Sensitive Liabilities, 101, 136. 145
redlining, 405
regulatory forbearance, 388, 425, 429
Repricing Gap, 100–101, 104–105, 107–108, 113, 145, 460
residual income, 43
Risk Adjusted Return on Capital (RAROC), 173, 235, 242–246, 263
risk-based capital, 16, 356, 363, 366, 394
risk control self-assessments, 362

RiskMetrics Approach, 171, 235, 239
risk-weighted assets, 395, 397, 413

S

savers, 1–5, 7, 9, 24, 279, 388, 403
savings and loan, 20, 388
Securities and Exchange Commission, 18
securities brokers, 22
Shadow banks, 430
Sovereign risk, 429
spread, 3–4, 8, 20, 22–23, 88, 110–111, 150, 167, 231, 245–246, 264–266, 422
SRISK, 420–424
State Regulatory Authorities, 18
stored liquidity, 9–10, 283, 312–313, 317, 321–322, 324, 337–338, 340, 343, 345–347, 390, 399, 448, 451
stress capital buffer, 400
Stress Testing, 400
Subsidy Mechanism, 432–433
Sustainable Growth Rate, 70, 73, 81, 89
systemic risk, 5, 16, 54, 397, 401, 404, 414, 419–428, 430–431, 434

T

takedowns, 115, 123, 275, 285, 290, 296, 303, 312, 322, 324, 334, 338, 460
threshold effect, 407
Tier 1 capital, 55, 395–396
Tier 2 capital, 395
too-big-to-fail, 388, 396, 423, 434
Too-Many-to-Fail, 425
Troubled Asset Relief Program, 404

V

Value-at-Risk, 168, 232, 420–421, 442
variable costs, 58, 68, 132, 136, 143, 204, 207, 256–257, 261–262, 445
Volcker Rule, 402

W

Weighted Average Cost of Capital, 30, 408

www.ingramcontent.com/pod-product-compliance
Lightning Source LLC
Chambersburg PA
CBHW072348100725
29074CB00038B/40